NEW YORK STATE

CRIMINAL PROCEDURE

2019 EDITION

Revised May 19, 2019
By Evgenia Naumchenko

NEW YORK LEGISLATURE

13

Part THREE Special Proceedings and Miscellaneous Procedures 332

Title U Special Proceedings Which Replace, Suspend or Abate Criminal Actions 384

§ 1.00. Short title

This chapter shall be known as the criminal procedure law, and may be cited as "CPL".

§ 1.10. Applicability of chapter to actions and matter occurring before and after effective date

1. The provisions of this chapter apply exclusively to:

(a) All criminal actions and proceedings commenced upon or after the effective date thereof and all appeals and other post-judgment proceedings relating or attaching thereto; and

(b) All matters of criminal procedure prescribed in this chapter which do not constitute a part of any particular action or case, occurring upon or after such effective date.

2. The provisions of this chapter apply to (a) all criminal actions and proceedings commenced prior to the effective date thereof but still pending on such date, and (b) all appeals and other post-judgment proceedings commenced upon or after such effective date which relate or attach to criminal actions and proceedings commenced or concluded prior to such effective date; provided that, if application of such provisions in any particular case would not be feasible or would work injustice, the provisions of the code of criminal procedure apply thereto.

3. The provisions of this chapter do not impair or render ineffectual any proceedings or procedural matters which occurred prior to the effective date thereof.

§ 1.20. Definitions of terms of general use in this chapter

Except where different meanings are expressly specified in subsequent provisions of this chapter, the term definitions contained in section 10.00 of the penal law are applicable to this chapter, and, in addition, the following terms have the following meanings:

1. "Accusatory instrument" means an indictment, an indictment ordered reduced pursuant to subdivision one-a of section 210.20 of this chapter, an information, a simplified information, a prosecutor's information, a superior court information, a misdemeanor complaint or a felony complaint. Every accusatory instrument, regardless of the person designated therein as accuser, constitutes an accusation on behalf of the state as plaintiff and must be entitled "the people of the state of New York" against a designated person, known as the defendant.

2. "Local criminal court accusatory instrument" means any accusatory instrument other than an indictment or a superior court information.

3. "Indictment" means a written accusation by a grand jury, more fully defined and described in article two hundred, filed with a superior court, which charges one or more defendants with the commission of one or more offenses, at least one of which is a crime, and which serves as a basis for prosecution thereof.

3-a. "Superior court information" means a written accusation by a district attorney more fully defined and described in articles one hundred ninety-five and two hundred, filed with a superior court pursuant to article one hundred ninety-five, which charges one or more defendants with the commission of one or more offenses, at least one of which is a crime, and which serves as a basis for prosecution thereof.

4. "Information" means a verified written accusation by a person, more fully defined and described in article one hundred, filed with a local criminal court, which charges one or more defendants with the commission of one or more offenses, none of which is a felony, and which may serve both to commence a criminal action and as a basis for prosecution thereof.

5. [There are two subdivisions 5] "Simplified traffic information" means a written accusation, more fully defined and described in article one hundred, by a police officer or other public servant authorized by law to issue same, filed with a local criminal court, which, being in a brief or simplified form prescribed by the commissioner of motor vehicles, charges a person with one or more traffic infractions or misdemeanors relating to traffic, and which may serve both to commence a criminal action for such offense and as a basis for prosecution thereof.

5. [There are two subdivisions 5]

(a) "Simplified information" means a simplified traffic information, a simplified parks information, or a simplified environmental conservation information.

(b) "Simplified traffic information" means a written accusation by a police officer, or other public servant authorized by law to issue same, more fully defined and described in article one hundred, filed with a local criminal court, which, being in a brief or simplified form prescribed by the commissioner of motor vehicles, charges a person with one or more traffic infractions or misdemeanors relating to traffic, and which may serve both to commence a criminal action for such offense and as a basis for prosecution thereof.

(c) "Simplified parks information" means a written accusation by a police officer, or other public servant authorized by law to issue same, filed with a local criminal court, which, being in a brief or simplified form prescribed by the commissioner of parks and recreation, charges a person with one or more offenses, other than a felony, for which a uniform simplified parks information may be issued pursuant to the parks and recreation law and the navigation law, and which may serve both to commence a criminal action for such offense and as a basis for prosecution thereof.

(d) "Simplified environmental conservation information" means a written accusation by a police officer, or other public servant authorized by law to issue same, filed with a local criminal court, which being in a brief or simplified form prescribed by the commissioner of environmental conservation, charges a person with one or more offenses, other than a felony, for which a uniform simplified environmental conservation simplified* information may be issued pursuant to the environmental conservation law, and which may serve both to commence a criminal action for such offense and as a basis for prosecution thereof.

6. "Prosecutor's information" means a written accusation by a district attorney, more fully defined and described in article one hundred, filed with a local criminal court, which charges one or more defendants with the commission of one or more offenses, none of which is a felony, and which serves as a basis for prosecution thereof.

7. "Misdemeanor complaint" means a verified written accusation by a person, more fully defined and described in article one hundred, filed with a local criminal court, which charges one or more defendants with the commission of one or more offenses, at least one of which is a misdemeanor and none of which is a felony, and which serves to commence a criminal action but which may not, except upon the defendant's consent, serve as a basis for prosecution of the offenses charged therein.

8. "Felony complaint" means a verified written accusation by a person, more fully defined and described in article one hundred, filed with a local criminal court, which charges one or more defendants with the commission of one or more felonies and which serves to commence a criminal action but not as a basis for prosecution thereof.

9. "Arraignment" means the occasion upon which a defendant against whom an accusatory instrument has been filed appears before the court in which the criminal action is pending for the purpose of having such court acquire and exercise control over his person with respect to such accusatory instrument and of setting the course of further proceedings in the action.

10. "Plea," in addition to its ordinary meaning as prescribed in sections 220.10 and 340.20, means, where appropriate, the occasion upon which a defendant enters such a plea to an accusatory instrument.

11. "Trial." A jury trial commences with the selection of the jury and includes all further proceedings through the rendition of a verdict. A non-jury trial commences with the first opening address, if there be any, and, if not, when the first witness is sworn, and includes all further proceedings through the rendition of a verdict.

12. "Verdict" means the announcement by a jury in the case of a jury trial, or by the court in the case of a non-jury trial, of its decision upon the defendant's guilt or innocence of the charges submitted to or considered by it.

13. "Conviction" means the entry of a plea of guilty to, or a verdict of guilty upon, an accusatory instrument other than a felony complaint, or to one or more counts of such instrument.

14. "Sentence" means the imposition and entry of sentence upon a conviction.

15. "Judgment." A judgment is comprised of a conviction and the sentence imposed thereon and is completed by imposition and entry of the sentence.

16. "Criminal action." A criminal action (a) commences with the filing of an accusatory instrument against a defendant in a criminal court, as specified in subdivision seventeen; (b) includes the filing of all further accusatory instruments directly derived from the initial one, and all proceedings, orders and motions conducted or made by a criminal court in the course of disposing of any such accusatory instrument, or which, regardless of the court in which they occurred or were made, could properly be considered as a part of the record of the case by an appellate court upon an appeal from a judgment of conviction; and (c) terminates with the imposition of sentence or some other final disposition in a criminal court of the last accusatory instrument filed in the case.

17. "Commencement of criminal action." A criminal action is commenced by the filing of an accusatory instrument against a defendant in a criminal court, and, if more than one

accusatory instrument is filed in the course of the action, it commences when the first of such instruments is filed.

18. "Criminal proceeding" means any proceeding which (a) constitutes a part of a criminal action or (b) occurs in a criminal court and is related to a prospective, pending or completed criminal action, either of this state or of any other jurisdiction, or involves a criminal investigation.

19. "Criminal court" means any court defined as such by section 10.10.

20. "Superior court" means any court defined as such by subdivision two of section 10.10.

21. "Local criminal court" means any court defined as such by subdivision three of section 10.10.

22. "Intermediate appellate court" means any court possessing appellate jurisdiction, other than the court of appeals.

23. "Judge" means any judicial officer who is a member of or constitutes a court, whether referred to in another provision of law as a justice or by any other title.

24. "Trial jurisdiction." A criminal court has "trial jurisdiction" of an offense when an indictment or an information charging such offense may properly be filed with such court, and when such court has authority to accept a plea to, try or otherwise finally dispose of such accusatory instrument.

25. "Preliminary jurisdiction." A criminal court has "preliminary jurisdiction" of an offense when, regardless of whether it has trial jurisdiction thereof, a criminal action for such offense may be commenced therein, and when such court may conduct proceedings with respect thereto which lead or may lead to prosecution and final disposition of the action in a court having trial jurisdiction thereof.

26. "Appearance ticket" means a written notice issued by a public servant, more fully defined in section 150.10, requiring a person to appear before a local criminal court in connection with an accusatory instrument to be filed against him therein.

27. "Summons" means a process of a local criminal court or superior court, more fully defined in section 130.10, requiring a defendant to appear before such court for the purpose of arraignment upon an accusatory instrument filed therewith by which a criminal action against him has been commenced.

28. "Warrant of arrest" means a process of a local criminal court, more fully defined in section 120.10, directing a police officer to arrest a defendant and to bring him before such court for the purpose of arraignment upon an accusatory instrument filed therewith by which a criminal action against him has been commenced.

29. "Superior court warrant of arrest" means a process of a superior court directing a police officer to arrest a defendant and to bring him before such court for the purpose of arraignment upon an indictment filed therewith by which a criminal action against him has been commenced.

30. "Bench warrant" means a process of a criminal court in which a criminal action is pending, directing a police officer, or a uniformed court officer, pursuant to paragraph b of subdivision two of section 530.70 of this chapter, to take into custody a defendant in such action who has previously been arraigned upon the accusatory instrument by which the action was commenced, and to bring him before such court. The function of a

bench warrant is to achieve the court appearance of a defendant in a pending criminal action for some purpose other than his initial arraignment in the action.

31. "Prosecutor" means a district attorney or any other public servant who represents the people in a criminal action.

32. "District attorney" means a district attorney, an assistant district attorney or a special district attorney, and, where appropriate, the attorney general, an assistant attorney general, a deputy attorney general, a special deputy attorney general, or the special prosecutor and inspector general for the protection of people with special needs or his or her assistants when acting pursuant to their duties in matters arising under article twenty of the executive law, or the inspector general of New York for transportation or his or her deputies when acting pursuant to article four-B of the executive law.

33. "Peace officer" means a person listed in section 2.10 of this chapter.

34. "Police officer." The following persons are police officers:

(a) A sworn member of the division of state police;

(b) Sheriffs, under-sheriffs and deputy sheriffs of counties outside of New York City;

(c) A sworn officer of an authorized county or county parkway police department;

(d) A sworn officer of an authorized police department or force of a city, town, village or police district;

(e) A sworn officer of an authorized police department of an authority or a sworn officer of the state regional park police in the office of parks and recreation;

(f) A sworn officer of the capital police force of the office of general services;

(g) An investigator employed in the office of a district attorney;

(h) An investigator employed by a commission created by an interstate compact who is, to a substantial extent, engaged in the enforcement of the criminal laws of this state;

(i) The chief and deputy fire marshals, the supervising fire marshals and the fire marshals of the bureau of fire investigation of the New York City fire department;

(j) A sworn officer of the division of law enforcement in the department of environmental conservation;

(k) A sworn officer of a police force of a public authority created by an interstate compact;

(l) Long Island railroad police.

(m) A special investigator employed in the statewide organized crime task force, while performing his assigned duties pursuant to section seventy-a of the executive law.

(n) A sworn officer of the Westchester county department of public safety services who, on or prior to June thirtieth, nineteen hundred seventy-nine was appointed as a sworn officer of the division of Westchester county parkway police or who was appointed on or after July first, nineteen hundred seventy-nine to the title of police officer, sergeant, lieutenant, captain or inspector or who, on or prior to January thirty-first, nineteen hundred eighty-three, was appointed as a Westchester county deputy sheriff.

(o) A sworn officer of the water-supply police employed by the city of New York, appointed to protect the sources, works, and transmission of water supplied to the city of New York, and to protect persons on or in the vicinity of such water sources, works, and transmission.

(p) Persons appointed as railroad police officers pursuant to section eighty-eight of the railroad law.

(q) An employee of the department of taxation and finance (i) assigned to enforcement of the taxes imposed under or pursuant to the authority of article twelve-A of the tax law and administered by the commissioner of taxation and finance, taxes imposed under or pursuant to the authority of article eighteen of the tax law and administered by the commissioner, taxes imposed under article twenty of the tax law, or sales or compensating use taxes relating to petroleum products or cigarettes imposed under article twenty-eight or pursuant to the authority of article twenty-nine of the tax law and administered by the commissioner or (ii) designated as a revenue crimes specialist and assigned to the enforcement of the taxes described in paragraph (c) of subdivision four of section 2.10 of this title, for the purpose of applying for and executing search warrants under article six hundred ninety of this chapter, for the purpose of acting as a claiming agent under article thirteen-A of the civil practice law and rules in connection with the enforcement of the taxes referred to above and for the purpose of executing warrants of arrest relating to the respective crimes specified in subdivision four of section 2.10 of this title.

(r) Any employee of the Suffolk county department of parks who is appointed as a Suffolk county park police officer.

(s) A university police officer appointed by the state university pursuant to paragraph 1 of subdivision two of section three hundred fifty-five of the education law.

(t) A sworn officer of the department of public safety of the Buffalo municipal housing authority who has achieved or been granted the status of sworn police officer and has been certified by the division of criminal justice services as successfully completing an approved basic course for police officers.

(u) Persons appointed as Indian police officers pursuant to section one hundred fourteen of the Indian law.

(v) Supervisor of forest ranger services; assistant supervisor of forest ranger services; forest ranger 3; forest ranger 2; forest ranger 1 employed by the state department of environmental conservation or sworn officer of the division of forest protection and fire management in the department of environmental conservation responsible for wild land search and rescue, wild land fire management in the state as prescribed in subdivision eighteen of section 9-0105 and title eleven of article nine of the environmental conservation law, exercising care, custody and control of state lands administered by the department of environmental conservation.

34-a. "Geographical area of employment." The "geographical area of employment" of certain police officers is as follows:

(a) [Expires Sept 1, 2019] Except as provided in paragraph (d) of this subdivision, New York state constitutes the "geographical area of employment" of any police officer employed as such by an agency of the state or by an authority which functions throughout the state, or a police officer designated by the superintendent of state police pursuant to section two hundred twenty-three of the executive law;

(a) [Eff Sept 1, 2019] Except as provided in paragraph (d), New York state constitutes the "geographical area of employment" of any police officer employed as such by an agency of the state or by an authority which functions throughout the state;

(b) A county, city, town or village, as the case may be, constitutes the "geographical area of employment" of any police officer employed as such by an agency of such political subdivision or by an authority which functions only in such political subdivision; and

(c) Where an authority functions in more than one county, the "geographical area of employment" of a police officer employed thereby extends through all of such counties.

(d) The geographical area of employment of a police officer appointed by the state university is the campuses and other property of the state university, including any portion of a public highway which crosses or abuts such property.

(e) The geographical area of employment of a police officer appointed pursuant to section one hundred fourteen of the Indian law is within the county of Franklin, and within that county, only within the boundary of the St. Regis reservation, except that if the superintendent of state police has certified such officer with expanded jurisdiction within the county of Franklin, pursuant to subdivision eight-a of such section, the geographical area of employment of such police officer shall also include the area of expanded jurisdiction set forth in that subdivision.

35. "Commitment to the custody of the sheriff," when referring to an order of a court located in a county or city which has established a department of correction, means commitment to the commissioner of correction of such county or city.

36. "County" ordinarily means (a) any county outside of New York City or (b) New York City in its entirety. Unless the context requires a different construction, New York City, despite its five counties, is deemed a single county within the meaning of the provisions of this chapter in which that term appears.

37. "Lesser included offense." When it is impossible to commit a particular crime without concomitantly committing, by the same conduct, another offense of lesser grade or degree, the latter is, with respect to the former, a "lesser included offense." In any case in which it is legally possible to attempt to commit a crime, an attempt to commit such crime constitutes a lesser included offense with respect thereto.

38. "Oath" includes an affirmation and every other mode authorized by law of attesting to the truth of that which is stated.

39. "Petty offense" means a violation or a traffic infraction.

40. "Evidence in chief" means evidence, received at a trial or other criminal proceeding in which a defendant's guilt or innocence of an offense is in issue, which may be considered as a part of the quantum of substantive proof establishing or tending to establish the commission of such offense or an element thereof or the defendant's connection therewith.

41. "Armed felony" means any violent felony offense defined in section 70.02 of the penal law that includes as an element either:

(a) possession, being armed with or causing serious physical injury by means of a deadly weapon, if the weapon is a loaded weapon from which a shot, readily capable of producing death or other serious physical injury may be discharged; or

(b) display of what appears to be a pistol, revolver, rifle, shotgun, machine gun or other firearm.

42. "Juvenile offender" means (1) a person, thirteen years old who is criminally responsible for acts constituting murder in the second degree as defined in subdivisions one and two of section 125.25 of the penal law, or such conduct as a sexually motivated felony, where authorized pursuant to section 130.91 of the penal law; and (2) a person fourteen or fifteen years old who is criminally responsible for acts constituting the crimes defined in subdivisions one and two of section 125.25 (murder in the second degree) and in subdivision three of such section provided that the underlying crime for the murder charge is one for which such person is criminally responsible; section 135.25 (kidnapping in the first degree); 150.20 (arson in the first degree); subdivisions one and two of section 120.10 (assault in the first degree); 125.20 (manslaughter in the first degree); subdivisions one and two of section 130.35 (rape in the first degree); subdivisions one and two of section 130.50 (criminal sexual act in the first degree); 130.70 (aggravated sexual abuse in the first degree); 140.30 (burglary in the first degree); subdivision one of section 140.25 (burglary in the second degree); 150.15 (arson in the second degree); 160.15 (robbery in the first degree); subdivision two of section 160.10 (robbery in the second degree) of the penal law; or section 265.03 of the penal law, where such machine gun or such firearm is possessed on school grounds, as that phrase is defined in subdivision fourteen of section 220.00 of the penal law; or defined in the penal law as an attempt to commit murder in the second degree or kidnapping in the first degree, or such conduct as a sexually motivated felony, where authorized pursuant to section 130.91 of the penal law.

43. "Judicial hearing officer" means a person so designated pursuant to provisions of article twenty-two of the judiciary law.

44. "Adolescent offender" means a person charged with a felony committed on or after October first, two thousand eighteen when he or she was sixteen years of age or on or after October first, two thousand nineteen, when he or she was seventeen years of age.

Article 2 Peace Officers

§ 2.10. Persons designated as peace officers

Notwithstanding the provisions of any general, special or local law or charter to the contrary, only the following persons shall have the powers of, and shall be peace officers:

1. Constables or police constables of a town or village, provided such designation is not inconsistent with local law.

2. The sheriff, undersheriff and deputy sheriffs of New York city and sworn officers of the Westchester county department of public safety services appointed after January thirty-first, nineteen hundred eighty-three to the title of public safety officer and who perform the functions previously performed by a Westchester county deputy sheriff on or prior to such date.

3. Investigators of the office of the state commission of investigation.

4. Employees of the department of taxation and finance designated by the commissioner of taxation and finance as peace officers and assigned by the commissioner of taxation and finance

(a) to the enforcement of any of the criminal or seizure and forfeiture provisions of the tax law relating to (i) taxes imposed under or pursuant to the authority of article twelve-A of the tax law and administered by the commissioner, (ii) taxes imposed under or pursuant to the authority of article eighteen of the tax law and administered by the commissioner, (iii) taxes imposed under article twenty of the tax law, or (iv) sales or compensating use taxes relating to petroleum products or cigarettes imposed under article twenty-eight or pursuant to the authority of article twenty-nine of the tax law and administered by the commissioner or

(b) to the enforcement of any provision of the penal law relating to any of the taxes described in paragraph (a) of this subdivision and relating to crimes effected through the use of a statement or document filed with the department in connection with the administration of such taxes or

(c) as revenue crimes specialist and assigned to the enforcement of any of the criminal provisions of the tax law relating to taxes administered by the commissioner of taxation and finance other than those taxes set forth in paragraph (a) of this subdivision or any provision of the penal law relating to such taxes, and those provisions of the penal law (i) relating to any of the foregoing taxes and (ii) relating to crimes effected through the use of a statement or document filed with the department in connection with the administration of such foregoing taxes or

(d) to the enforcement of any provision of law which is subject to enforcement by criminal penalties and which relates to the performance by persons employed by the department of taxation and finance of the duties of their employment.

Provided, however, that nothing in this subdivision shall be deemed to authorize any such employee designated as a peace officer after November first, nineteen hundred eighty-five to carry, possess, repair or dispose of a firearm unless the appropriate license therefor has been issued pursuant to section 400.00 of the penal law, and further provided that, prior to such designation by the commissioner each such employee shall have successfully completed the training requirements specified in section 2.30 of this article. Provided, further, that any license issued to such employee pursuant to such peace officer designation by the commissioner shall relate only to the firearm issued to such employee by the department of taxation and finance and such permit shall not cover any other firearms. The foregoing sentence shall not be deemed to prohibit such peace officer from applying for a separate permit relating to non-departmental firearms.

5. Employees of the New York city department of finance assigned to enforcement of the tax on cigarettes imposed by title D of chapter forty-six of the administrative code of the city of New York by the commissioner of finance.

6. Confidential investigators and inspectors, as designated by the commissioner, of the department of agriculture and markets, pursuant to rules of the department.

7. Officers or agents of a duly incorporated society for the prevention of cruelty to animals.

7-a. [Expires and repealed Aug 11, 2019] Officers or agents of a duly incorporated society for the prevention of cruelty to children in Rockland county; provided, however, that nothing in this subdivision shall be deemed to authorize such officer or agent to carry, possess, repair, or dispose of a firearm unless the appropriate license therefor has been issued pursuant to section 400.00 of the penal law; and provided further that such officer or agent shall exercise the powers of a peace officer only when he is acting pursuant to his special duties.

8. Inspectors and officers of the New York city department of health when acting pursuant to their special duties as set forth in section 564-11.0 of the administrative code of the city of New York; provided, however, that nothing in this subdivision shall be deemed to authorize such officer to carry, possess, repair or dispose of a firearm unless the appropriate license therefor has been issued pursuant to section 400.00 of the penal law.

9. Park rangers in Suffolk county, who shall be authorized to issue appearance tickets, simplified traffic informations, simplified parks informations and simplified environmental conservation informations.

10. Broome county park rangers who shall be authorized to issue appearance tickets, simplified traffic informations, simplified parks informations, and simplified environmental conservation informations; provided, however, that nothing in this subdivision shall be deemed to authorize such officer to carry, possess, repair or dispose of a firearm unless the appropriate license therefor has been issued pursuant to section 400.00 of the penal law.

11. Park rangers in Onondaga and Cayuga counties, who shall be authorized to issue appearance tickets, simplified traffic informations, simplified parks informations and simplified environmental conservation informations, within the respective counties of Onondaga and Cayuga.

12. Special police officers designated by the commissioner and the directors of in-patient facilities in the office of mental health pursuant to section 7.25 of the mental hygiene law, and special police officers designated by the commissioner and the directors of facilities under his or her jurisdiction in the office for people with developmental disabilities pursuant to section 13.25 of the mental hygiene law; provided, however, that nothing in this subdivision shall be deemed to authorize such officers to carry, possess, repair or dispose of a firearm unless the appropriate license therefor has been issued pursuant to section 400.00 of the penal law.

13. Persons designated as special police officers by the director of a hospital in the department of health pursuant to section four hundred fifty-five of the public health law; provided, however, that nothing in this subdivision shall be deemed to authorize such officer to carry, possess, repair or dispose of a firearm unless the appropriate license therefor has been issued pursuant to section 400.00 of the penal law.

14. [Repealed]

15. Uniformed enforcement forces of the New York state thruway authority, when acting pursuant to subdivision two of section three hundred sixty-one of the public authorities law; provided, however, that nothing in this subdivision shall be deemed to authorize such officer to carry, possess, repair or dispose of a firearm unless the appropriate license therefor has been issued pursuant to section 400.00 of the penal law.

16. Employees of the department of health designated pursuant to section thirty-three hundred eighty-five of the public health law; provided, however, that nothing in this subdivision shall be deemed to authorize such officer to carry, possess, repair or dispose of a firearm unless the appropriate license therefor has been issued pursuant to section 400.00 of the penal law.

17. Uniformed housing guards of the Buffalo municipal housing authority.

18. Bay constable of the city of Rye, the villages of Mamaroneck, South Nyack and bay constables of the towns of East Hampton, Hempstead, Oyster Bay, Riverhead, Southampton, Southold, Islip, Shelter Island, Brookhaven, Babylon, Smithtown, Huntington and North Hempstead; provided, however, that nothing in this subdivision shall be deemed to authorize the bay constables in the city of Rye, the village of South Nyack or the towns of Brookhaven, Babylon, Southold, East Hampton, Riverhead, Islip, other than a bay constable of the town of Islip who prior to April third, nineteen hundred ninety-eight served as harbormaster for such town and whose position was reclassified as bay constable for such town prior to such date, Smithtown, Huntington and Shelter Island to carry, possess, repair or dispose of a firearm unless the appropriate license therefor has been issued pursuant to section 400.00 of the penal law.

19. Harbor masters appointed by a county, city, town or village.

20. Bridge and tunnel officers, sergeants and lieutenants of the Triborough bridge and tunnel authority.

21.

a. Uniformed court officers of the unified court system.

b. Court clerks of the unified court system in the first and second departments.

c. Marshall, deputy marshall, clerk or uniformed court officer of a district court.

(d)** So in original. Marshalls or deputy marshalls of a city court, provided, however, that nothing in this subdivision shall be deemed to authorize such officer to carry, possess, repair or dispose of a firearm unless the appropriate license therefor has been issued pursuant to section 400.00 of the penal law.

e. Uniformed court officers of the city of Mount Vernon.

f. Uniformed court officers of the city of Jamestown.

22. Patrolmen appointed by the Lake George park commission; provided however that nothing in this subdivision shall be deemed to authorize such officer to carry, possess, repair or dispose of a firearm unless the appropriate license therefor has been issued pursuant to section 400.00 of the penal law.

23. Parole officers or warrant officers in the department of corrections and community supervision.

23-a. Parole revocation specialists in the department of corrections and community supervision; provided, however, that nothing in this subdivision shall be deemed to authorize such employee to carry, possess, repair or dispose of a firearm unless the appropriate license therefor has been issued pursuant to section 400.00 of the penal law.

24. Probation officers.

25. Officials, as designated by the commissioner of the department of corrections and community supervision pursuant to rules of the department, and correction officers of any state correctional facility or of any penal correctional institution.

26. Peace officers designated pursuant to the provisions of the New York state defense emergency act, as set forth in chapter seven hundred eighty-four of the laws of nineteen hundred fifty-one, as amended, when acting pursuant to their special duties during a period of attack or imminent attack by enemy forces, or during official drills called to combat natural or man-made disasters, or during official drills in preparation for an attack by enemy forces or in preparation for a natural or man-made disaster; provided, however, that nothing in this subdivision shall be deemed to authorize such officer to carry, possess, repair or dispose of a firearm unless the appropriate license therefor has been issued pursuant to section 400.00 of the penal law; and provided further, that such officer shall have the powers set forth in section 2.20 of this article only during a period of imminent or actual attack by enemy forces and during drills authorized under section twenty-nine-b of article two-B of the executive law, providing for the use of civil defense forces in disasters. Notwithstanding any other provision of law, such officers shall have the power to direct and control traffic during official drills in preparation for an attack by enemy forces or in preparation for combating natural or man-made disasters; however, this grant does not include any of the other powers set forth in section 2.20 of this article.

27. New York city special patrolmen appointed by the police commissioner pursuant to subdivision c or e of section 434a-7.0 or subdivision c or e of section 14-106 of the administrative code of the city of New York; provided, however, that nothing in this subdivision shall be deemed to authorize such officer to carry, possess, repair or dispose of a firearm unless the appropriate license therefor has been issued pursuant to section 400.00 of the penal law and the employer has authorized such officer to possess a firearm during any phase of the officers on-duty employment. Special patrolmen shall have the powers set forth in section 2.20 of this article only when they are acting pursuant to their special duties; provided, however, that the following categories of New York city special patrolmen shall have such powers whether or not they are acting pursuant to their special duties: school safety officers employed by the board of education of the city of New York; parking control specialists, taxi and limousine inspectors, urban park rangers and evidence and property control specialists employed by the city of New York; and further provided that, with respect to the aforementioned categories of New York city special patrolmen, where such a special patrolman has been appointed by the police commissioner and, upon the expiration of such appointment the police commissioner has neither renewed such appointment nor explicitly determined that such appointment shall not be renewed, such appointment shall remain in full force and effect indefinitely, until such time as the police commissioner expressly determines to either renew or terminate such appointment.

28. All officers and members of the uniformed force of the New York city fire department as set forth and subject to the limitations contained in section 487a-15.0 of the administrative code of the city of New York; provided, however, that nothing in this subdivision shall be deemed to authorize such officer to carry, possess, repair or

dispose of a firearm unless the appropriate license therefor has been issued pursuant to section 400.00 of the penal law.

29. Special police officers for horse racing, appointed pursuant to the provisions of the pari-mutuel revenue law as set forth in chapter two hundred fifty-four of the laws of nineteen hundred forty, as amended; provided, however, that nothing in this subdivision shall be deemed to authorize such officer to carry, possess, repair or dispose of a firearm unless the appropriate license therefor has been issued pursuant to section 400.00 of the penal law.

30. Supervising fire inspectors, fire inspectors, the fire marshal and assistant fire marshals, all of whom are full-time employees of the county of Nassau fire marshal's office.

31. [Repealed]

32. Investigators of the department of motor vehicles, pursuant to section three hundred ninety-two-b of the vehicle and traffic law; provided, however, that nothing in this subdivision shall be deemed to authorize such officer to carry, possess, repair or dispose of a firearm unless the appropriate license therefor has been issued pursuant to section 400.00 of the penal law.

33. A city marshall of the city of New York who has received training in firearms handling from the federal bureau of investigation or in the New York city police academy, or in the absence of the available training programs from the federal bureau of investigation and the New York city police academy, from another law enforcement agency located in the state of New York, and who has received a firearms permit from the license division of the New York city police department.

34. Waterfront and airport investigators, pursuant to subdivision four of section ninety-nine hundred six of the unconsolidated laws; provided, however, that nothing in this subdivision shall be deemed to authorize such officer to carry, possess, repair or dispose of a firearm unless the appropriate license therefor has been issued pursuant to section 400.00 of the penal law.

35. Special investigators appointed by the state board of elections, pursuant to section 3-107 of the election law.

36. Investigators appointed by the state liquor authority, pursuant to section fifteen of the alcoholic beverage control law; provided, however, that nothing in this subdivision shall be deemed to authorize such officer to carry, possess, repair or dispose of a firearm unless the appropriate license therefor has been issued pursuant to section 400.00 of the penal law.

37. Special patrolmen of a political subdivision, appointed pursuant to section two hundred nine-v of the general municipal law; provided, however, that nothing in this subdivision shall be deemed to authorize such officer to carry, possess, repair or dispose of a firearm unless the appropriate license therefor has been issued pursuant to section 400.00 of the penal law.

38. A special investigator of the New York city department of investigation who has received training in firearms handling in the New York police academy and has received a firearms permit from the license division of the New York city police department.

39. Broome county special patrolman, appointed by the Broome county attorney; provided, however, that nothing in this subdivision shall be deemed to authorize such officer to carry, possess, repair or dispose of a firearm unless the appropriate license therefor has been issued pursuant to section 400.00 of the penal law.

40. Special officers employed by the city of New York or by the New York city health and hospitals corporation; provided, however, that nothing in this subdivision shall be deemed to authorize such officer to carry, possess, repair or dispose of a firearm unless the appropriate license therefor has been issued pursuant to section 400.00 of the penal law. The New York city health and hospitals corporation shall employ peace officers appointed pursuant to this subdivision to perform the patrol, investigation, and maintenance of the peace duties of special officer, senior special officer and hospital security officer, provided however that nothing in this subdivision shall prohibit managerial, supervisory, or state licensed or certified professional employees of the corporation from performing such duties where they are incidental to their usual duties, or shall prohibit police officers employed by the city of New York from performing these duties.

41. Fire police squads organized pursuant to section two hundred nine-c of the general municipal law, at such times as the fire department, fire company or an emergency rescue and first aid squad of the fire department or fire company are on duty, or when, on orders of the chief of the fire department or fire company of which they are members, they are separately engaged in response to a call for assistance pursuant to the provisions of section two hundred nine of the general municipal law; provided, however, that nothing in this subdivision shall be deemed to authorize such officer to carry, possess, repair or dispose of a firearm unless the appropriate license therefor has been issued pursuant to section 400.00 of the penal law.

42. Special deputy sheriffs appointed by the sheriff of a county within which any part of the grounds of Cornell university or the grounds of any state institution constituting a part of the educational and research plants owned or under the supervision, administration or control of said university are located pursuant to section fifty-seven hundred nine of the education law; provided, however, that nothing in this subdivision shall be deemed to authorize such officer to carry, possess, repair or dispose of a firearm unless the appropriate license therefor has been issued pursuant to section 400.00 of the penal law.

43. Housing patrolmen of the Mount Vernon housing authority, acting pursuant to rules of the Mount Vernon housing authority; provided, however, that nothing in this subdivision shall be deemed to authorize such officer to carry, possess, repair or dispose of a firearm unless the appropriate license therefor has been issued pursuant to section 400.00 of the penal law.

44. The officers, employees and members of the New York city division of fire prevention, in the bureau of fire, as set forth and subject to the limitations contained in subdivision one of section 487a-1.0 of the administrative code of the city of New York; provided, however, that nothing in this subdivision shall be deemed to authorize such officer to carry, possess, repair or dispose of a firearm unless the appropriate license therefor has been issued pursuant to section 400.00 of the penal law.

45. Persons appointed and designated as peace officers by the Niagara frontier transportation authority, pursuant to subdivision thirteen of section twelve hundred ninety-nine-e of the public authorities law.

46. Persons appointed as peace officers by the Sea Gate Association pursuant to the provisions of chapter three hundred ninety-one of the laws of nineteen hundred forty, provided, however, that nothing in this subdivision shall be deemed to authorize such officer to carry, possess, repair or dispose of a firearm unless the appropriate license therefor has been issued pursuant to section 400.00 of the penal law.

47. Employees of the department of financial services when designated as peace officers by the superintendent of financial services and acting pursuant to their special duties as set forth in article four of the financial services law; provided, however, that nothing in this subdivision shall be deemed to authorize such officer to carry, possess, repair or dispose of a firearm unless the appropriate license therefor has been issued pursuant to section 400.00 of the penal law.

48. New York state air base security guards when they are designated as peace officers under military regulations promulgated by the chief of staff to the governor and when performing their duties as air base security guards pursuant to orders issued by appropriate military authority; provided, however, that nothing in this subdivision shall be deemed to authorize such guards to carry, possess, repair or dispose of a firearm unless the appropriate license therefor has been issued pursuant to section 400.00 of the penal law.

49. Members of the army national guard military police and air national guard security personnel belonging to the organized militia of the state of New York when they are designated as peace officers under military regulations promulgated by the adjutant general and when performing their duties as military police officers or air security personnel pursuant to orders issued by appropriate military authority; provided, however, that nothing in this subdivision shall be deemed to authorize such military police or air security personnel to carry, possess, repair or dispose of a firearm unless the appropriate license therefor has been issued pursuant to section 400.00 of the penal law.

50. Transportation supervisors in the city of White Plains appointed by the commissioner of public safety in the city of White Plains; provided, however, that nothing in this subdivision shall be deemed to authorize such officer to carry, possess, repair or dispose of a firearm unless the appropriate license therefor has been issued pursuant to section 400.00 of the penal law.

51. Officers and members of the fire investigation division of the fire department of the city of Rochester, the city of Binghamton and the city of Utica, when acting pursuant to their special duties in matters arising under the laws relating to fires, the extinguishment thereof and fire perils; provided, however, that nothing in this subdivision shall be deemed to authorize such officer to carry, possess, repair or dispose of a firearm unless the appropriate license therefor has been issued pursuant to section 400.00 of the penal law.

52. Security hospital treatment assistants, as so designated by the commissioner of the office of mental health while performing duties in or arising out of the course of their

employment; provided, however, that nothing in this subdivision shall be deemed to authorize such employee to carry, possess, repair or dispose of a firearm unless the appropriate license therefor has been issued pursuant to section 400.00 of the penal law.

53. Authorized agents of the municipal directors of weights and measures in the counties of Suffolk, Nassau and Westchester when acting pursuant to their special duties as set forth in section one hundred eighty-one of the agriculture and markets law; provided, however, that nothing in this subdivision shall be deemed to authorize such officer to carry, possess, repair or dispose of a firearm unless the appropriate license therefor has been issued pursuant to section 400.00 of the penal law.

54. Special police officers appointed pursuant to section one hundred fifty-eight of the town law; provided, however, that nothing in this subdivision shall be deemed to authorize such officer to carry, possess, repair or dispose of a firearm unless the appropriate license therefor has been issued pursuant to section 400.00 of the penal law.

55. [Expired July 1, 1993]

56. Dog control officers of the town of Brookhaven, who at the discretion of the town board may be designated as constables for the purpose of enforcing article twenty-six of the agriculture and markets law and for the purpose of issuing appearance tickets permitted under article seven of such law; provided, however, that nothing in this subdivision shall be deemed to authorize such officer to carry, possess, repair or dispose of a firearm unless the appropriate license therefor has been issued pursuant to section 400.00 of the penal law.

57. Harbor Park rangers employed by the Snug Harbor cultural center in Richmond county and appointed as New York city special patrolmen by the police commissioner pursuant to subdivision c of section 14-106 of the administrative code of the city of New York. Notwithstanding any provision of law, rule or regulation, such officers shall be authorized to issue appearance tickets pursuant to section 150.20 of this chapter, and shall have such other powers as are specified in section 2.20 of this article only when acting pursuant to their special duties. Nothing in this subdivision shall be deemed to authorize such officers to carry, possess, repair or dispose of a firearm unless the appropriate license therefor has been issued pursuant to section 400.00 of the penal law and the employer has authorized such officer to possess a firearm during any phase of the officer's on-duty employment.

57-a. [There are two subdivisions 57-a] Seasonal park rangers of the Westchester county department of public safety while employed as authorized by the commissioner of public safety/sheriff of the county of Westchester; provided, however, that nothing in this subdivision shall be deemed to authorize such officer to carry, possess, repair or dispose of a firearm unless the appropriate license therefor has been issued pursuant to section 400.00 of the penal law.

57-a. [There are two subdivisions 57-a] Officers of the Westchester county public safety emergency force, when activated by the commissioner of public safety/sheriff of the county of Westchester; provided, however that nothing in this subdivision shall be deemed to authorize such officer to carry, possess, repair or dispose of a firearm unless the appropriate license therefor has been issued pursuant to section 400.00 of the penal law.

58. Uniformed members of the security force of the Troy housing authority provided, however, that nothing in this subdivision shall be deemed to authorize such officer to carry, possess, repair or dispose of a firearm unless the appropriate license therefor has been issued pursuant to section 400.00 of the penal law.

59. Officers and members of the sanitation police of the department of sanitation of the city of New York, duly appointed and designated as peace officers by such department; provided, however, that nothing in this subdivision shall be deemed to authorize such officer to carry, possess, repair or dispose of a firearm unless the appropriate license therefor has been issued pursuant to section 400.00 of the penal law. Provided, further, that nothing in this subdivision shall be deemed to apply to officers and members of the sanitation police regularly and exclusively assigned to enforcement of such city's residential recycling laws.

60. [Repealed]

61. Chief fire marshall, assistant chief fire marshall, fire marshall II and fire marshall I, all of whom are full-time employees of the Suffolk county department of fire, rescue and emergency services, when acting pursuant to their special duties in matters arising under the laws relating to fires, the extinguishment thereof and fire perils; provided, however, that nothing in this subdivision shall be deemed to authorize such officer to carry, possess, repair or dispose of a firearm unless the appropriate license therefor has been issued pursuant to section 400.00 of the penal law.

62. [There are two subdivisions 62] Chief fire marshall, assistant chief fire marshall, fire marshall II and fire marshall I, all of whom are full-time employees of the town of Babylon, when acting pursuant to their special duties in matters arising under the laws relating to fires, the extinguishment thereof and fire perils; provided, however, that nothing in this subdivision shall be deemed to authorize such officer to carry, possess, repair or dispose of a firearm unless the appropriate license therefor has been issued pursuant to section 400.00 of the penal law.

62. [There are two subdivisions 62] Employees of the division for youth assigned to transport and warrants units who are specifically designated by the director in accordance with section five hundred four-b of the executive law, provided, however, that nothing in this subdivision shall be deemed to authorize such employees to carry, possess, repair or dispose of a firearm unless the appropriate license therefor has been issued pursuant to section 400.00 of the penal law.

63. [There are two subdivisions 63] Uniformed members of the fire marshal's office in the town of Southampton and the town of Riverhead, when acting pursuant to their special duties in matters arising under the laws relating to fires, the extinguishment thereof and fire perils; provided, however that nothing in this subdivision shall be deemed to authorize such officer to carry, possess, repair or dispose of a firearm unless the appropriate license therefor has been issued pursuant to section 400.00 of the penal law.

63. [There are two subdivisions 63] Employees of the town court of the town of Greenburgh serving as a security officer; provided, however, that nothing in this

subdivision will be deemed to authorize such officer to carry, possess, repair or dispose of a firearm unless the appropriate license therefor has been issued pursuant to section 400.00 of the penal law or to authorize such officer to carry or possess a firearm except while on duty.

64. Cell block attendants employed by the city of Buffalo police department; provided, however, that nothing in this subdivision shall be deemed to authorize such officer to carry, possess, repair or dispose of a firearm unless the appropriate license therefor has been issued pursuant to section 400.00 of the penal law.

65. Chief fire marshall, assistant chief fire marshall, fire marshall II and fire marshall I, all of whom are full-time employees of the town of Brookhaven, when acting pursuant to their special duties in matters arising under the laws relating to fires, the extinguishment thereof and fire perils; provided, however, that nothing in this subdivision shall be deemed to authorize such officer to carry, possess, repair or dispose of a firearm unless the appropriate license thereof has been issued pursuant to section 400.00 of the penal law.

66. Employees of the village court of the village of Spring Valley serving as security officers at such village court; provided, however, that nothing in this subdivision shall be deemed to authorize such officer to carry, possess, repair or dispose of a firearm unless the appropriate license therefor has been issued pursuant to section 400.00 of the penal law.

67. Employees of the town court of the town of Putnam Valley serving as a security officer; provided, however, that nothing in this subdivision will be deemed to authorize such officer to carry, possess, repair or dispose of a firearm unless the appropriate license therefor has been issued pursuant to section 400.00 of the penal law or to authorize such officer to carry or possess a firearm except while on duty.

68. [There are five subdivisions 68] Employees of the town court of the town of Southampton serving as uniformed court officers at such town court; provided, however, that nothing in this subdivision shall be deemed to authorize such officer to carry, possess, repair or dispose of a firearm unless the appropriate license therefor has been issued pursuant to section 400.00 of the penal law.

68. [There are five subdivisions 68] The state inspector general and investigators designated by the state inspector general; provided, however, that nothing in this subdivision shall be deemed to authorize the state inspector general or such investigators to carry, possess, repair or dispose of a firearm unless the appropriate license therefor has been issued pursuant to section 400.00 of the penal law.

68. [There are five subdivisions 68] Dog control officers of the town of Arcadia, who at the discretion of the town board may be designated as constables for the purpose of enforcing article twenty-six of the agriculture and markets law and for the purpose of issuing appearance tickets permitted under article seven of such law; provided, however, that nothing in this subdivision shall be deemed to authorize such officer to carry, possess, repair or dispose of a firearm unless the appropriate license therefor has been issued pursuant to section 400.00 of the penal law.

68. [There are five subdivisions 68] Employees appointed by the sheriff of Livingston county, when acting pursuant to their special duties serving as uniformed marine patrol

officers; provided, however, that nothing in this subdivision shall be deemed to authorize such officer to carry, possess, repair or dispose of a firearm unless the appropriate license has been issued pursuant to section 400.00 of the penal law or to authorize such officer to carry or possess a firearm except while on duty.

68. [There are five subdivisions 68] Persons employed by the Chautauqua county sheriff's office serving as court security officers; provided, however, that nothing in this subdivision shall be deemed to authorize such officer to carry, possess, repair or dispose of a firearm unless the appropriate license therefor has been issued pursuant to section 400.00 of the penal law.

69. Employees of the village court of the village of Amityville serving as uniformed court officers at such village court; provided, however, that nothing in this subdivision shall be deemed to authorize such officer to carry, possess, repair or dispose of a firearm unless the appropriate license therefor has been issued pursuant to section 400.00 of the penal law.

70. Employees appointed by the sheriff of Yates county, pursuant to their special duties serving as uniformed marine patrol officers; provided, however, that nothing in this subdivision shall be deemed to authorize such officer to carry, possess, repair or dispose of a firearm unless the appropriate license has been issued pursuant to section 400.00 of the penal law or to authorize such officer to carry or possess a firearm except while on duty.

71. Town of Smithtown fire marshalls when acting pursuant to their special duties in matters arising under the laws relating to fires, the extinguishment thereof and fire perils; provided, however, that nothing in this subdivision shall be deemed to authorize such officers to carry, possess, repair or dispose of a firearm unless the appropriate license therefor has been issued pursuant to section 400.00 of the penal law.

72. Persons employed by Canisius college as members of the security force of such college; provided, however, that nothing in this subdivision shall be deemed to authorize such officer to carry, possess, repair or dispose of a firearm unless the appropriate license therefor has been issued pursuant to section 400.00 of the penal law.

73. Employees of the town court of the town of Newburgh serving as uniformed court officers at such town court; provided, however, that nothing in this subdivision shall be deemed to authorize such officer to carry, possess, repair or dispose of a firearm unless the appropriate license therefor has been issued pursuant to section 400.00 of the penal law.

74. [There are four subdivisions 74]

a. Special deputy sheriffs appointed by the sheriff of Tompkins county pursuant to paragraphs b and c of this subdivision; provided, however, that nothing in this subdivision shall be deemed to authorize such officer to carry, possess, repair or dispose of a firearm unless the appropriate license therefor has been issued pursuant to section 400.00 of the penal law.

b. For the protection of the grounds, buildings and property of Ithaca college the prevention of crime and the enforcement of law and order, and for the enforcement of such rules and regulations as the board of trustees of Ithaca college shall from time to time make, the sheriff of Tompkins county may appoint and remove following consultation with Ithaca college such number of special deputy sheriffs as is determined by the sheriff to be necessary for the maintenance of public order at Ithaca college, such appointments to be made from persons nominated by the president of Ithaca college. Such special deputy sheriffs shall comply with requirements as established by the sheriff and shall act only within Tompkins county. Such special deputy sheriffs so appointed shall be employees of the college and subject to its supervision and control as outlined in the terms and conditions to be mutually agreed upon between the sheriff and Ithaca college. Such special deputy sheriffs shall have the powers of peace officers and shall act solely within the said grounds or premises owned or administered by Ithaca college, except in those rare and special situations when requested by the sheriff to provide assistance on any public highway which crosses or adjoins such property. Ithaca college will provide legal defense and indemnification, and hold harmless the county of Tompkins, its officers and employees and the Tompkins county sheriff, its officers and employees, from all claims arising out of conduct by or injury to, such personnel while carrying out their law enforcement functions except in those situations when they are acting under the direct supervision and control of the county or sheriff's department.

c. Every special deputy sheriff so appointed shall, before entering upon the duties of his or her office, take and subscribe the oath of office prescribed by article thirteen of the constitution of the state of New York which oath shall be filed in the office of the county clerk of Tompkins county. Every special deputy sheriff appointed under this subdivision when on regular duty shall wear conspicuously a metallic shield with a designating number and the words "Special Deputy Sheriff Ithaca College" thereon.

74. [There are four subdivisions 74] Parks and recreation forest rangers employed by the office of parks, recreation and historic preservation; provided, however, that nothing in this subdivision shall be deemed to authorize such individuals to carry, possess, repair or dispose of a firearm unless the appropriate license therefor has been issued pursuant to section 400.00 of the penal law.

74. [There are four subdivisions 74] Employees of the village court of the village of Quogue, town of Southampton serving as uniformed court officers at such village court; provided, however, that nothing in this subdivision shall be deemed to authorize such officer to carry, possess, repair or dispose of a firearm unless the appropriate license therefor has been issued pursuant to section 400.00 of the penal law.

74. [There are four subdivisions 74] Employees of the town court of the town of East Hampton serving as uniformed court officers at such town court; provided, however, that nothing in this subdivision shall be deemed to authorize such officer to carry, possess, repair or dispose of a firearm unless the appropriate license therefor has been issued pursuant to section 400.00 of the penal law.

75. [There are three subdivisions 75] Dog control officers of the town of Clarence, who at the discretion of the town board may be designated as constables for the purpose of enforcing article twenty-six of the agriculture and markets law and for the purpose of issuing appearance tickets permitted under article seven of the agriculture and markets law; provided, however, that nothing in this subdivision shall be deemed to authorize

such officers to carry, possess, repair or dispose of a firearm unless the appropriate license therefor has been issued pursuant to section 400.00 of the penal law.

75. [There are three subdivisions 75] Airport security guards, senior airport security guards, airport security supervisors, retired police officers, and supervisors of same, who are designated by resolution of the town board of the town of Islip to provide security at Long Island MacArthur Airport when acting pursuant to their duties as such, and such authority being specifically limited to the grounds of the said airport. However, nothing in this subdivision shall be deemed to authorize such officer to carry, possess, repair or dispose of a firearm unless the appropriate license therefor has been issued pursuant to section 400.00 of the penal law.

75. [There are three subdivisions 75] Officers and members of the fire investigation unit of the fire department of the city of Buffalo when acting pursuant to their special duties in matters arising under the laws relating to fires, the extinguishment thereof and fire perils; provided, however, that nothing in this subdivision shall be deemed to authorize such officer to carry, possess, repair or dispose of a firearm unless the appropriate license therefor has been issued pursuant to section 400.00 of the penal law.

76. [There are two subdivisions 76] Employees of the village court of the village of Southampton, town of Southampton serving as uniformed court officers at such village court; provided, however, that nothing in this subdivision shall be deemed to authorize such officer to carry, possess, repair or dispose of a firearm unless the appropriate license therefor has been issued pursuant to section 400.00 of the penal law.

76. [There are two subdivisions 76] Animal control officers employed by the city of Peekskill; provided, however, that nothing in this subdivision shall be deemed to authorize such individuals to carry, possess, repair or dispose of a firearm unless the appropriate license therefor has been issued pursuant to section 400.00 of the penal law.

77. [There are two subdivisions 77]

(a) Syracuse University peace officers appointed by the chief law enforcement officer of the city of Syracuse pursuant to paragraphs (b), (c) and (d) of this subdivision, who shall be authorized to issue appearance tickets and simplified traffic informations; provided, however, that nothing in this subdivision shall be deemed to authorize any such officer to carry, possess, repair or dispose of a firearm unless the appropriate license therefor has been issued pursuant to section 400.00 of the penal law.

(b) For the protection of the grounds, buildings and property of Syracuse University, the prevention of crime and the enforcement of law and order, and for the enforcement of such rules and regulations as Syracuse University shall from time to time establish, the chief law enforcement officer of the city of Syracuse may appoint and remove, following consultations with Syracuse University; such number of Syracuse University peace officers as is determined by the chief law enforcement officer of the city of Syracuse to be necessary for the maintenance of public order at such university, such appointments to be made from persons nominated by the chancellor of Syracuse University. Such peace officers shall comply with such requirements as shall be established by the chief law enforcement officer of the city of Syracuse. Such Syracuse University peace officers so appointed shall be employees of such university, and subject to its supervision and control and the terms and conditions to be mutually agreed upon between the chief law enforcement officer of the city of Syracuse and Syracuse University. Nothing in this paragraph shall limit the authority of Syracuse University to remove such peace officers. Such Syracuse University peace officers shall have the powers of peace officers within the geographical area of employment of the grounds or premises owned, controlled or administered by Syracuse University within the county of Onondaga, except in those situations when requested by the chief law enforcement officer of the city of Syracuse or his or her designee, including by means of written protocols agreed to by the chief law enforcement officer of the city of Syracuse and Syracuse University, to provide assistance on any public highway which crosses or adjoins such grounds or premises. Syracuse University shall provide legal defense and indemnification, and hold harmless the city of Syracuse, and its officers and employees from all claims arising out of conduct by or injury to, such peace officers while carrying out their law enforcement functions, except in those situations when they are acting under the direct supervision and control of the chief law enforcement officer of the city of Syracuse, or his or her designee.

(c) Every Syracuse University peace officer so appointed shall, before entering upon the duties of his or her office, take and subscribe the oath of office prescribed by article thirteen of the state constitution, which oath shall be filed in the office of the county clerk of the county of Onondaga. Every such peace officer appointed pursuant to this subdivision when on regular duty shall conspicuously wear a metallic shield with a designating number and the words "Syracuse University Peace Officer" engraved thereon.

(d) To become eligible for appointment as a Syracuse University peace officer a candidate shall, in addition to the training requirements as set forth in section 2.30 of this article, complete the course of instruction in public and private law enforcement established pursuant to paragraph (c) of subdivision five of section sixty-four hundred fifty of the education law.

77. [There are two subdivisions 77] Chief fire marshal, assistant chief fire marshal, and fire marshals, all of whom are full-time employees of the town of East Hampton, when acting pursuant to their special duties in matters arising under the laws relating to fires, the extinguishment thereof and fire perils; provided, however, that nothing in this subdivision shall be deemed to authorize such officer to carry, possess, repair or dispose of a firearm unless the appropriate license therefor has been issued pursuant to section 400.00 of the penal law.

78. A security officer employed by a community college who is specifically designated as a peace officer by the board of trustees of a community college pursuant to subdivision five-a of section sixty-three hundred six of the education law, or by a community college regional board of trustees pursuant to subdivision four-a of section sixty-three hundred ten of the education law; provided, however, that nothing in this subdivision shall be deemed to authorize such officer to carry, possess, repair or dispose of a firearm unless the appropriate license therefor has been issued pursuant to section 400.00 of the penal law.

79. [There are four subdivisions 79] Court security officers employed by the Wayne county sheriff's office; provided however, that nothing in this subdivision shall be deemed to authorize such officer to carry, possess, repair or dispose of a firearm unless the appropriate license therefor has been issued pursuant to section 400.00 of the penal law.

79. [There are four subdivisions 79] Supervisors and members of the arson investigation bureau and fire inspection bureau of the office of fire prevention and control when acting pursuant to their special duties in matters arising under the laws relating to fires, their prevention, extinguishment, investigation thereof, and fire perils; provided, however, that nothing in this subdivision shall be deemed to authorize such employees to carry, possess, repair, or dispose of a firearm unless the appropriate license therefor has been issued pursuant to section 400.00 of the penal law.

79. [There are four subdivisions 79] Peace officers appointed by the city university of New York pursuant to subdivision sixteen of section sixty-two hundred six of the education law, who shall have the powers set forth in section 2.20 of this article whether or not they are acting pursuant to their special duties; provided, however, that nothing in this subdivision shall be deemed to authorize such officer to carry, possess, repair or dispose of a firearm unless the appropriate license therefor has been issued pursuant to section 400.00 of the penal law.

79. [There are four subdivisions 79] Animal control officers of the city of Elmira, who at the discretion of the city council of the city of Elmira may be designated as constables for the purpose of enforcing article twenty-six of the agriculture and markets law, and for the purpose of issuing appearance tickets permitted under article seven of such law; provided, however, that nothing in this subdivision shall be deemed to authorize such officer to carry, possess, repair or dispose of a firearm unless the appropriate license therefor has been issued pursuant to section 400.00 of the penal law.

80. Employees of the Onondaga county sheriff's department serving as uniformed court security officers at Onondaga county court facilities; provided, however, that nothing in this subdivision shall be deemed to authorize such officers to carry, possess, repair or dispose of a firearm unless the appropriate license therefor has been issued pursuant to section 400.00 of the penal law.

81. [There are six subdivisions 81] Members of the security force employed by Erie County Medical Center; provided however, that nothing in this subdivision shall be deemed to authorize such officer to carry, possess, repair or dispose of a firearm unless the appropriate license therefor has been issued pursuant to section 400.00 of the penal law.

81. [There are six subdivisions 81] Employees of the town of Riverhead serving as court officers at town of Riverhead court facilities; provided, however, that nothing in this subdivision shall be deemed to authorize such officers to carry, possess, repair or dispose of a firearm unless the appropriate license therefor has been issued pursuant to section 400.00 of the penal law.

81. [There are six subdivisions 81] Employees of the town court of the town of Southold serving as uniformed court officers at such town court; provided, however, that nothing in this subdivision shall be deemed to authorize such officer to carry, possess, repair or

dispose of a firearm unless the appropriate license therefor has been issued pursuant to section 400.00 of the penal law.

81. [There are six subdivisions 81] Commissioners of and court officers in the department of public safety for the town of Rye when acting pursuant to their special duties in matters arising under the laws relating to maintaining the safety and security of citizens, judges and court personnel in the town court, and effecting the safe and secure transport of persons under the custody of said department; provided, however, that nothing in this subdivision shall be deemed to authorize such employees to carry, possess, repair, or dispose of a firearm unless the appropriate license therefor has been issued pursuant to section 400.00 of the penal law.

81. [There are six subdivisions 81] Employees of the town of Yorktown serving as court attendants at town of Yorktown court facilities; provided, however, that nothing in this subdivision shall be deemed to authorize such employees to carry, possess, repair or dispose of a firearm unless the appropriate license therefor has been issued pursuant to section 400.00 of the penal law.

81. [There are six subdivisions 81] Employees of the Lewis county sheriff's department serving as uniformed court security officers at Lewis county court facilities; provided, however, that nothing in this subdivision shall be deemed to authorize such officers to carry, possess, repair or dispose of a firearm unless the appropriate license therefor has been issued pursuant to section 400.00 of the penal law.

82. Employees of the New York city business integrity commission designated as peace officers by the chairperson of such commission; provided, however, that nothing in this subdivision shall be deemed to authorize such officer to carry, possess, repair or dispose of a firearm unless the appropriate license therefor has been issued pursuant to section 400.00 of the penal law.

83. Members of the security force employed by Kaleida Health within and directly adjacent to the hospital buildings on the medical campus located between East North Street, Goodell Street, Main Street and Michigan Avenue. These officers shall only have the powers listed in paragraph (c) of subdivision one of section 2.20 of this article, as well as the power to detain an individual for a reasonable period of time while awaiting the arrival of law enforcement, provided that the officer has actual knowledge, or probable cause to believe, that such individual has committed an offense; provided however, that nothing in this subdivision shall be deemed to authorize such officer to carry, possess, repair or dispose of a firearm unless the appropriate license therefor has been issued pursuant to section 400.00 of the penal law.

84.

(a) Public safety officers employed by the University of Rochester who are designated as peace officers by the board of trustees of the University of Rochester pursuant to paragraphs (b), (c), and (d) of this subdivision; provided, however, that nothing in this subdivision shall be deemed to authorize any such officer to carry, possess, repair or dispose of a firearm unless the appropriate license therefor has been issued pursuant to section 400.00 of the penal law.

(b) For the protection of the grounds, buildings and property of the University of Rochester, the prevention of crime and the enforcement of law and order, the board of trustees of the University of Rochester may appoint and remove such number of public safety officers designated as peace officers as is determined by the board of trustees to be necessary for the maintenance of public order consistent with this subdivision. Such peace officers shall comply with such requirements as shall be mutually agreed upon between the chief law enforcement officers of the applicable local law enforcement jurisdictions and the University of Rochester. Such University of Rochester peace officers so appointed shall be employees of the University of Rochester and subject to its supervision and control. Such University of Rochester peace officers shall have the powers of peace officers within the geographic area of employment of the grounds or premises owned, controlled or administered by the University of Rochester within the county of Monroe , on any public street and sidewalk that abuts the grounds, buildings or property of such university, and beyond such geographic area upon the request of the chief law enforcement officer of the local law enforcement jurisdiction or his or her designee, for the purpose of transporting an individual who has been arrested in accordance with section 140.27 of this chapter and when no local law enforcement officer is available for transporting such individual in a timely manner.

(c) The University of Rochester shall provide legal defense and indemnification to applicable municipality and its officers and employees, and hold them harmless, against all claims arising out of conduct by or injury to such peace officers while carrying out their special duties, except in those situations when they are acting as agents of the chief law enforcement officer of the applicable local law enforcement jurisdiction or his or her designee.

(d) To become eligible for designation as a University of Rochester peace officer, a candidate shall, in addition to the training requirements as set forth in section 2.30 of this article, complete the course of instruction in public and private law enforcement established pursuant to subdivision three of section sixty-four hundred thirty-five of the education law.

§ 2.15. Federal law enforcement officers; powers

The following federal law enforcement officers shall have the powers set forth in paragraphs (a) (with the exception of the powers provided by paragraph (b) of subdivision one and paragraph (b) of subdivision three of section 140.25 of this chapter), (b), (c) and (h) of subdivision one of section 2.20 of this article:

1. Federal Bureau of Investigation special agents.
2. United States Secret Service special agents.
3. Immigration and Customs Enforcement special agents, deportation officers, and detention and deportation officers.
4. United States Marshals and Marshals Service deputies.
5. Drug Enforcement Administration special agents.
6. Federal Protective Officers, including law enforcement security officers, criminal investigators and police officers of the Federal Protective Service.
7. United States Customs and Border Protection Officers and United States Customs and Border Protection Border Patrol agents.
8. United States Postal Service police officers and inspectors.

9. United States park police; provided, however that, notwithstanding any provision of this section to the contrary, such park police shall also have the powers set forth in paragraph (b) of subdivision one of section 140.25 of this chapter and the powers set forth in paragraphs (d), (e) and (g) of subdivision one of section 2.20 of this article.

10. United States probation officers.

11. United States General Services Administration special agents.

12. United States Department of Agriculture special agents.

13. Bureau of Alcohol, Tobacco and Firearms special agents.

14. Internal Revenue Service special agents and inspectors.

15. Officers of the United States bureau of prisons.

16. United States Fish and Wildlife special agents.

17. United States Naval Investigative Service special agents.

18. United States Department of State special agents.

19. Special agents of the defense criminal investigative service of the United States department of defense.

20. United States Department of Commerce, Office of Export Enforcement, special agents.

21. United States Department of Veterans Administration police officers employed at the Veterans Administration Medical Center in Batavia.

22. Federal Reserve law enforcement officers.

23. Federal air marshal program special agents.

24. [There are two subdivisions 24] United States department of transportation federal police officers and police supervisors assigned to the United States Merchant Marine Academy in Kings Point, New York; provided, however that, notwithstanding any provision of this section to the contrary, such police shall also have the powers set forth in paragraph (b) of subdivision one of section 140.25 of this chapter and the powers set forth in paragraphs (d), (e) and (g) of subdivision one of section 2.20 of this article when acting pursuant to their special duties within the geographical area of their employment or within one hundred yards of such geographical area.

24. [There are two subdivisions 24] United States Coast Guard Investigative Service special agents.

25. United States Department of Commerce, special agents and enforcement officers of the National Oceanic and Atmospheric Administration's Fisheries Office for Law Enforcement.

26. Department of the Army special agents, detectives and police officers.

27. United States Department of Interior, park rangers with law enforcement authority.

28. United States Environmental Protection Agency special agents with law enforcement authority.

29. United States mint police.

§ 2.16. Watershed protection and enforcement officers; powers, duties, jurisdiction for arrests

1. Watershed protection and enforcement officers appointed by the city of Peekskill shall have the powers set forth in paragraphs (a), (b), (c), (f), (g), and (h) of subdivision one of section 2.20 of this article; provided, however, that nothing in this section shall be deemed to authorize such officer to carry, possess, repair, or dispose of a firearm

unless the appropriate license therefor has been issued pursuant to section 400.00 of the penal law. Watershed protection and enforcement officers shall complete the training requirements set forth in section 2.30 of this article.

2. The city of Peekskill may appoint the following persons as watershed protection and enforcement officers:

(a) the water superintendent;

(b) the deputy assistant to the water superintendent; and

(c) the watershed inspector or inspectors.

3. The duties of the watershed protection and enforcement officers shall be to enforce those provisions of the environmental conservation law and the penal law which relate to the contamination of water in those areas of the Hollow Brook watershed located within the city of Peekskill, including its reservoirs, shoreline, and tributaries, and those areas of the Hollow Brook watershed and Wiccopee reservoir located outside of the city of Peekskill in the counties of Putnam and Westchester, including its reservoirs, shoreline, and tributaries.

4. Notwithstanding paragraph (b) of subdivision thirty-four-a of section 1.20 of this title and paragraph (b) of subdivision five of section 140.25 of this chapter, watershed protection and enforcement officers are authorized to make arrests and issue appearance tickets in those areas of the Hollow Brook watershed and Wiccopee reservoir located outside of the city of Peekskill in the counties of Putnam and Westchester, including along its reservoirs, shoreline, and tributaries.

§ 2.20. Powers of peace officers

1. The persons designated in section 2.10 of this article shall have the following powers:

(a) The power to make warrantless arrests pursuant to section 140.25 of this chapter.

(b) The power to use physical force and deadly physical force in making an arrest or preventing an escape pursuant to section 35.30 of the penal law.

(c) The power to carry out warrantless searches whenever such searches are constitutionally permissible and acting pursuant to their special duties.

(d) The power to issue appearance tickets pursuant to subdivision three of section 150.20 of this chapter, when acting pursuant to their special duties. New York city special patrolmen shall have the power to issue an appearance ticket only when it is pursuant to rules and regulations of the police commissioner of the city of New York.

(e) The power to issue uniform appearance tickets pursuant to article twenty-seven of the parks, recreation and historic preservation law and to issue simplified traffic informations pursuant to section 100.25 of this chapter and section two hundred seven of the vehicle and traffic law whenever acting pursuant to their special duties.

(f) The power to issue a uniform navigation summons and/or complaint pursuant to section nineteen of the navigation law whenever acting pursuant to their special duties.

(g) The power to issue uniform appearance tickets pursuant to article seventy-one of the environmental conservation law, whenever acting pursuant to their special duties.

(h) The power to possess and take custody of firearms not owned by the peace officer, for the purpose of disposing, guarding, or any other lawful purpose, consistent with his duties as a peace officer.

(i) Any other power which a particular peace officer is otherwise authorized to exercise by any general, special or local law or charter whenever acting pursuant to his special duties, provided such power is not inconsistent with the provisions of the penal law or this chapter.

(j) Uniformed court officers shall have the power to issue traffic summonses and complaints for parking, standing, or stopping violations pursuant to the vehicle and traffic law whenever acting pursuant to their special duties.

2. For the purposes of this section a peace officer acts pursuant to his special duties when he performs the duties of his office, pursuant to the specialized nature of his particular employment, whereby he is required or authorized to enforce any general, special or local law or charter, rule, regulation, judgment or order.

3. A peace officer, whether or not acting pursuant to his special duties, who lawfully exercises any of the powers conferred upon him pursuant to this section, shall be deemed to be acting within the scope of his public employment for purposes of defense and indemnification rights and benefits that he may be otherwise entitled to under the provisions of section fifty-k of the general municipal law, section seventeen or eighteen of the public officers law, or any other applicable section of law.

§ 2.30. Training requirements for peace officers

1. Every peace officer in the state of New York must successfully complete a training program, a portion of which shall be prescribed by the municipal police training council and a portion of which shall be prescribed by his or her employer. The portion prescribed by the municipal police training council shall be comprised of subjects, and the hours each is to be taught, that shall be required of all types or classes of peace officers. The hours of instruction required by the municipal police training council shall not exceed one hundred eighty, unless a greater amount is either required by law or regulation, or is requested by the employer.

The segment prescribed by the employer for its employees shall be comprised of subjects, and the hours each is to be taught, relating to the special nature of the duties of the peace officers employed by it provided, however, that when the subjects prescribed by the employer are identical to the subjects in the training program required by the municipal police training council, the employer shall not be required to provide duplicate training for those subjects.

2. Each state or local agency, unit of local government, state or local commission, or public authority, or public or private organization which employs peace officers shall provide the training mandated by this section, the cost of which will be borne by the employer. Each peace officer satisfactorily completing the course prescribed by the municipal police training council shall be awarded a certificate by the division of criminal justice services attesting to that effect, and no person appointed as a peace officer shall exercise the powers of a peace officer, unless he or she has received such certification within twelve months of appointment.

3. No employer shall allow any peace officer it employs to carry or use a weapon during any phase of the officer's official duties, which constitutes on-duty employment, unless the officer has satisfactorily completed a course of training approved by the municipal police training council in the use of deadly physical force and firearms and other

weapons, and annually receives instruction in deadly physical force and the use of firearms and other weapons as approved by the municipal police training council.

4. Upon the failure or refusal to comply with the requirements of this section, the commissioner of the division of criminal justice services shall apply to the supreme court for an order directed to the person responsible requiring compliance. Upon such application, the court may issue such order as may be just, and a failure to comply with the order of the court shall be a contempt of court and punishable as such.

5. Every employer of peace officers shall report to the division of criminal justice services, in such form and at such time as the division may by regulation require, the names of all peace officers who have satisfactorily completed any of the training requirements prescribed by this section.

6. A certificate attesting to satisfactory completion of the training requirements imposed under this section awarded to any peace officer by the executive director of the municipal police training council pursuant to this section shall remain valid:

(a) during the holder's continuous service as a peace officer; and

(b) for two years after the date of the commencement of an interruption in such service where the holder had, immediately prior to such interruption, served as a peace officer for less than two consecutive years; or

(c) for four years after the date of the commencement of an interruption in such service where the holder had, immediately prior to such interruption, served as a peace officer for two consecutive years or longer.

As used in this subdivision, the term "interruption" shall mean a period of separation from employment as a peace officer by reason of such officer's leave of absence, resignation or removal, other than removal for cause.

Title B The Criminal Courts

Article 10 The Criminal Courts

§ 10.10. The criminal courts; enumeration and definitions

1. The "criminal courts" of this state are comprised of the superior courts and the local criminal courts.

2. "Superior court" means:

(a) The supreme court; or

(b) A county court.

3. "Local criminal court" means:

(a) A district court; or

(b) The New York City criminal court; or

(c) A city court; or

(d) A town court; or

(e) A village court; or

(f) A supreme court justice sitting as a local criminal court; or

(g) A county judge sitting as a local criminal court.

4. "City court" means any court for a city, other than New York City, having trial jurisdiction of offenses of less than felony grade only committed within such city, whether such court is entitled a city court, a municipal court, a police court, a recorder's court or is known by any other name or title.

5. "Town court." A "town court" is comprised of all the town justices of a town.

6. "Village court." A "village court" is comprised of the justice of a village, or all the justices thereof if there be more than one, or, at a time when he or they are absent, an associate justice of a village who is authorized to perform the functions of a village justice during his absence.

7. Notwithstanding any other provision of this section, a court specified herein which possesses civil as well as criminal jurisdiction does not act as a criminal court when acting solely in the exercise of its civil jurisdiction, and an order or determination made by such a court in its civil capacity is not an order or determination of a criminal court even though it may terminate or otherwise control or affect a criminal action or proceeding.

§ 10.20. Superior courts; jurisdiction

1. Superior courts have trial jurisdiction of all offenses. They have:

(a) Exclusive trial jurisdiction of felonies; and

(b) Trial jurisdiction of misdemeanors concurrent with that of the local criminal courts; and

(c) Trial jurisdiction of petty offenses, but only when such an offense is charged in an indictment which also charges a crime.

2. Superior courts have preliminary jurisdiction of all offenses, but they exercise such jurisdiction only by reason of and through the agency of their grand juries.

3. Superior court judges may, in their discretion, sit as local criminal courts for the following purposes:

(a) conducting arraignments, as provided in subdivision two of section 170.15 and subdivision two of section 180.20 of this chapter;

(b) issuing warrants of arrests, as provided in subdivision one of section 120.70 of this chapter; and

(c) issuing search warrants, as provided in article six hundred ninety of this chapter.

§ 10.30. Local criminal courts; jurisdiction

1. Local criminal courts have trial jurisdiction of all offenses other than felonies. They have:

(a) Exclusive trial jurisdiction of petty offenses except for the superior court jurisdiction thereof prescribed in paragraph (c) of subdivision one of section 10.20; and

(b) Trial jurisdiction of misdemeanors concurrent with that of the superior courts but subject to divestiture thereof by the latter in any particular case.

2. Local criminal courts have preliminary jurisdiction of all offenses subject to divestiture thereof in any particular case by the superior courts and their grand juries.

3. Notwithstanding the provisions of subdivision one, a superior court judge sitting as a local criminal court does not have trial jurisdiction of any offense, but has preliminary jurisdiction only, as provided in subdivision two.

Notice

/ This section has more than one version with varying effective dates.

§ 10.40. [Eff until Sept 1, 2019] Chief administrator to prescribe forms and to authorize use of electronic filing

1. The chief administrator of the courts shall have the power to adopt, amend and rescind forms for the efficient and just administration of this chapter. A failure by any party to submit papers in compliance with forms authorized by this section shall not be grounds for that reason alone for denial or granting of any motion.

2.

(a) Notwithstanding any other provision of law, the chief administrator, with the approval of the administrative board of the courts, may promulgate rules authorizing a program in the use of electronic means ("e-filing") in the supreme court and in the county court for (i) the filing with a court of an accusatory instrument for the purpose of commencement of a criminal action or proceeding in a superior court, as provided by articles one hundred ninety-five and two hundred of this chapter, and (ii) the filing and service of papers in pending criminal actions and proceedings. Provided, however, the chief administrator shall consult with the county clerk of a county outside the city of New York before the use of electronic means is to be authorized in the supreme court or county court of such county, afford him or her the opportunity to submit comments with respect thereto, consider any such comments and obtain the agreement thereto of such county clerk.

(b)

(i) Except as otherwise provided in this paragraph, participation in this program shall be strictly voluntary and will take place only upon consent of all parties in the criminal action or proceeding; except that a party's failure to consent to participation shall not bar any other party to the action from filing and serving papers by electronic means upon the court or any other party to such action or proceeding who has consented to participation. Filing an accusatory instrument by electronic means with the court for the purpose of commencement of a criminal action or proceeding shall not require the consent of any other party; provided, however, that upon such filing any person who is the subject of such accusatory instrument and any attorney for such person shall be permitted to immediately review and obtain copies of such instrument if such person or attorney would have been authorized by law to review or copy such instrument if it had been filed with the court in paper form.

No party shall be compelled, directly or indirectly, to participate in e-filing. All parties shall be notified clearly, in plain language, about their options to participate in e-filing. Where a party is not represented by counsel, the clerk shall explain such party's options for electronic filing in plain language, including the option for expedited processing, and shall inquire whether he or she wishes to participate, provided however the unrepresented litigant may participate in the program only upon his or her request, which shall be documented in the case file, after said party has been presented with sufficient information in plain language concerning the program.

(ii) The chief administrator may eliminate the requirement of consent to participation in this program in supreme and county courts of not more than six counties provided he or she may not eliminate such requirement for a court without the consent of the district attorney, the consent of the criminal defense bar as defined in subdivision three of this section and the consent of the county clerk of the county in which such court presides. Notwithstanding the foregoing provisions of this subparagraph, the chief administrator shall not eliminate the requirement of consent to participation in a county hereunder until he or she shall have provided all persons and organizations, or their representative or representatives, who regularly appear in criminal actions or proceedings in the superior court of such county with reasonable notice and opportunity to submit comments with respect thereto and shall have given due consideration to all such comments, nor until he or she shall have consulted with the members of the advisory committee specified in subparagraph (v) of paragraph (u) of subdivision two of section two hundred twelve of the judiciary law.

(c) Where the chief administrator eliminates the requirement of consent as provided in subparagraph (ii) of paragraph (b) of this subdivision, he or she shall afford counsel the opportunity to opt out of the program, via presentation of a prescribed form to be filed with the court where the criminal action is pending. Said form shall permit an attorney to opt out of participation in the program under any of the following circumstances, in which event, he or she will not be compelled to participate:

(i) Where the attorney certifies in good faith that he or she lacks appropriate computer hardware and/or connection to the internet and/or scanner or other device by which documents may be converted to an electronic format; or

(ii) Where the attorney certifies in good faith that he or she lacks the requisite knowledge in the operation of such computers and/or scanners necessary to participate. For the purposes of this subparagraph, the knowledge of any employee of an attorney, or any employee of the attorney's law firm, office or business who is subject to such attorney's direction, shall be imputed to the attorney.

Notwithstanding the foregoing provisions of this paragraph: (A) where a party is not represented by counsel, the clerk shall explain such party's options for electronic filing in plain language, including the option for expedited processing, and shall inquire whether he or she wishes to participate, provided however the unrepresented litigant may participate in the program only upon his or her request, which shall be documented in the case file, after said party has been presented with sufficient information in plain language concerning the program; (B) a party not represented by counsel who has chosen to participate in the program shall be afforded the opportunity to opt out of the program for any reason via presentation of a prescribed form to be filed with the clerk of the court where the proceeding is pending; and (C) a court may exempt any attorney from being required to participate in the program upon application for such exemption, showing good cause therefor.

(d)

(i) Nothing in this section shall affect or change any existing laws governing the sealing and confidentiality of court records in criminal proceedings or access to court records by the parties to such proceedings, nor shall this section be construed to compel a party to file a sealed document by electronic means.

(ii) Notwithstanding any other provision of this section, no paper or document that is filed by electronic means in a criminal proceeding in supreme court or county court shall be available for public inspection on-line. Subject to the provisions of existing laws governing the sealing and confidentiality of court records, nothing herein shall prevent the unified court system from sharing statistical information that does not include any papers or documents filed with the action; and, provided further, that this paragraph shall not prohibit the chief administrator, in the exercise of his or her discretion, from posting papers or documents that have not been sealed pursuant to law on a public website maintained by the unified court system where: (A) the website is not the website established by the rules promulgated pursuant to paragraph (a) of this subdivision, and (B) to do so would be in the public interest. For purposes of this subparagraph, the chief administrator, in determining whether posting papers or documents on a public website is in the public interest, shall, at a minimum, take into account for each posting the following factors: (A) the type of case involved; (B) whether such posting would cause harm to any person, including especially a minor or crime victim; (C) whether such posting would include lewd or scandalous matters; and (D) the possibility that such papers or documents may ultimately be sealed.

(iii) Nothing in this section shall affect or change existing laws governing service of process, nor shall this section be construed to abrogate existing personal service requirements as set forth in the criminal procedure law.

3. For purposes of this section, the following terms shall have the following meanings:

(a) "Consent of the criminal defense bar" shall mean that consent has been obtained from all provider offices and/or organizations in the county that represented twenty-five percent or more of the persons represented by public defense providers pursuant to section seven hundred twenty-two of the county law, as shown in the most recent annual reports filed pursuant to subdivision one of section seven hundred twenty-two-f of the county law. Such consent, when given, must be expressed in a written document that is provided by a person who is authorized to consent on behalf of the relevant public defender organization, agency or office; and

(b) "Electronic means" shall be as defined in subdivision (f) of rule twenty-one hundred three of the civil practice law and rules; and

(c) The "filing and service of papers in pending criminal actions and proceedings" shall include the filing and service of a notice of appeal pursuant to section 460.10 of this chapter.

Title C General Principles Relating to Requirements For and Exemptions From Criminal Prosecution

Article 20 Geographical Jurisdiction of Offenses

§ 20.10. Geographical jurisdiction of offenses; definitions of terms

The following definitions are applicable to this article:

1. "This state" means New York State as its boundaries are prescribed in the state law, and the space over it.

2. "County" means any of the sixty-two counties of this state as its boundaries are prescribed by law, and the space over it.

3. "Result of an offense." When a specific consequence, such as the death of the victim in a homicide case, is an element of an offense, the occurrence of such consequence

constitutes the "result" of such offense. An offense of which a result is an element is a "result offense."

4. "Particular effect of an offense." When conduct constituting an offense produces consequences which, though not necessarily amounting to a result or element of such offense, have a materially harmful impact upon the governmental processes or community welfare of a particular jurisdiction, or result in the defrauding of persons in such jurisdiction, such conduct and offense have a "particular effect" upon such jurisdiction.

§ 20.20. Geographical jurisdiction of offenses; jurisdiction of state

Except as otherwise provided in this section and section 20.30, a person may be convicted in the criminal courts of this state of an offense defined by the laws of this state, committed either by his own conduct or by the conduct of another for which he is legally accountable pursuant to section 20.00 of the penal law, when:

1. Conduct occurred within this state sufficient to establish:

(a) An element of such offense; or

(b) An attempt to commit such offense; or

(c) A conspiracy or criminal solicitation to commit such offense, or otherwise to establish the complicity of at least one of the persons liable therefor; provided that the jurisdiction accorded by this paragraph extends only to conviction of those persons whose conspiratorial or other conduct of complicity occurred within this state; or

2. Even though none of the conduct constituting such offense may have occurred within this state:

(a) The offense committed was a result offense and the result occurred within this state. If the offense was one of homicide, it is presumed that the result, namely the death of the victim, occurred within this state if the victim's body or a part thereof was found herein; or

(b) The statute defining the offense is designed to prevent the occurrence of a particular effect in this state and the conduct constituting the offense committed was performed with intent that it would have such effect herein; or

(c) The offense committed was an attempt to commit a crime within this state; or

(d) The offense committed was conspiracy to commit a crime within this state and an overt act in furtherance of such conspiracy occurred within this state; or

3. The offense committed was one of omission to perform within this state a duty imposed by the laws of this state. In such case, it is immaterial whether such person was within or outside this state at the time of the omission.

§ 20.30. Geographical jurisdiction of offenses; effect of laws of other jurisdictions upon this state's jurisdiction

1. Notwithstanding the provisions of section 20.20, the courts of this state do not have jurisdiction to convict a person of an alleged offense partly committed within this state but consummated in another jurisdiction, or an offense of criminal solicitation, conspiracy or attempt in this state to commit a crime in another jurisdiction, or an offense of criminal facilitation in this state of a felony committed in another jurisdiction, unless the conduct constituting the consummated offense or, as the case may be, the conduct constituting the crime solicited, conspiratorially contemplated or facilitated,

constitutes an offense under the laws of such other jurisdiction as well as under the laws of this state.

2. The courts of this state are not deprived of the jurisdiction accorded them by section 20.20 to convict a person of an offense defined by the laws of this state, partly committed in another jurisdiction but consummated in this state, or an offense of attempt or conspiracy in another jurisdiction to commit in this state a crime defined by the laws of this state, by the circumstance that the conduct constituting the consummated offense or, as the case may be, the crime attempted or conspiratorially contemplated, does not constitute an offense under the laws of such other jurisdiction.

§ 20.40. Geographical jurisdiction of offenses; jurisdiction of counties

A person may be convicted in an appropriate criminal court of a particular county, of an offense of which the criminal courts of this state have jurisdiction pursuant to section 20.20, committed either by his or her own conduct or by the conduct of another for which he or she is legally accountable pursuant to section 20.00 of the penal law, when:

1. Conduct occurred within such county sufficient to establish:

(a) An element of such offense; or

(b) An attempt or a conspiracy to commit such offense; or

2. Even though none of the conduct constituting such offense may have occurred within such county:

(a) The offense committed was a result offense and the result occurred in such county; or

(b) The offense committed was one of homicide and the victim's body or a part thereof was found in such county; or

(c) Such conduct had, or was likely to have, a particular effect upon such county or a political subdivision or part thereof, and was performed with intent that it would, or with knowledge that it was likely to, have such particular effect therein; or

(d) The offense committed was attempt, conspiracy or criminal solicitation to commit a crime in such county; or

(e) The offense committed was criminal facilitation of a felony committed in such county; or

3. The offense committed was one of omission to perform a duty imposed by law, which duty either was required to be or could properly have been performed in such county. In such case, it is immaterial whether such person was within or outside such county at the time of the omission; or

4. Jurisdiction of such offense is accorded to the courts of such county pursuant to any of the following rules:

(a) An offense of abandonment of a child or non-support of a child may be prosecuted in (i) any county in which such child resided during the period of abandonment or non-support, or (ii) any county in which such person resided during such period, or (iii) any county in which such person was present during such period, provided that he was arrested for such offense in such county or the criminal action therefor was commenced while he was present therein.

(b) An offense of bigamy may be prosecuted either in the county in which such offense was committed or in (i) any county in which bigamous cohabitation subsequently occurred, or (ii) any county in which such person was present after the commission of the offense, provided that he was arrested for such offense in such county or the criminal action therefor was commenced while he was present therein.

(c) An offense committed within five hundred yards of the boundary of a particular county, and in an adjoining county of this state, may be prosecuted in either such county.

(d) An offense committed anywhere on the Hudson river southward of the northern boundary of New York City, or anywhere on New York bay between Staten Island and Long Island, may be prosecuted in any of the five counties of New York City.

(e) An offense committed upon any bridge or in any tunnel having terminals in different counties may be prosecuted in any terminal county.

(f) An offense committed on board a railroad train, aircraft or omnibus operating as a common carrier may be prosecuted in any county through or over which such common carrier passed during the particular trip, or in any county in which such trip terminated or was scheduled to terminate.

(g) An offense committed in a private vehicle during a trip thereof extending through more than one county may be prosecuted in any county through which such vehicle passed in the course of such trip.

(h) An offense committed on board a vessel navigating or lying in any river, canal or lake flowing through or situated within this state, may be prosecuted in any county bordering upon such body of water, or in which it is located, or through which it passes; and if such offense was committed upon a vessel operating as a common carrier, it may be prosecuted in any county bordering upon any body of water upon which such vessel navigated or passed during the particular trip.

(i) An offense committed in the Atlantic Ocean within two nautical miles from the shore at high water mark may be prosecuted in an appropriate court of the county the shore line of which is closest to the point where the offense was committed. A crime committed more than two nautical miles from the shore but within the boundary of this state may be prosecuted in the supreme court of the county the shore line of which is closest to the point where the crime was committed.

(j) An offense of forgery may be prosecuted in any county in which the defendant, or another for whose conduct the defendant is legally accountable pursuant to section 20.00 of the penal law, possessed the instrument.

(k) An offense of offering of a false instrument for filing, or of larceny by means of a false pretense therein, may be prosecuted (i) in any county in which such instrument was executed, in whole or in part, or (ii) in any county in which any of the goods or services for which payment or reimbursement is sought by means of such instrument were purported to have been provided.

(l) An offense of identity theft or unlawful possession of personal identifying information and all criminal acts committed as part of the same criminal transaction as defined in subdivision two of section 40.10 of this chapter may be prosecuted (i) in any county in which part of the offense took place regardless of whether the defendant was actually present in such county, or (ii) in the county in which the person who suffers financial loss resided at the time of the commission of the offense, or (iii) in the county where the person whose personal identifying information was used in the commission of the offense resided at the time of the commission of the offense. The law enforcement agency of any such county shall take a police report of the matter and provide the complainant with a copy of such report at no charge.

(m) An offense under the tax law or the penal law of filing a false or fraudulent return, report, document, declaration, statement, or filing, or of tax evasion, fraud, or larceny resulting from the filing of a false or fraudulent return, report, document, declaration, or filing in connection with the payment of taxes to the state or a political subdivision of the state, may be prosecuted in any county in which an underlying transaction reflected, reported or required to be reflected or reported, in whole or part, on such return, report, document, declaration, statement, or filing occurred.

(n)

(i) An organized retail theft crime, where the defendant knows that such crime is a part of a coordinated plan, scheme or venture of organized retail theft crimes committed by two or more persons, may be prosecuted in any county in which such defendant committed at least one such organized retail theft crime; provided, however, that the county of prosecution is contiguous to another county in which one or more of such other organized retail theft crimes was committed. Multiple organized retail theft crimes committed by the same defendant may be joined in one indictment if authorized and appropriate in accordance with the provisions of section 200.20 of this chapter, provided, however, that notwithstanding section 200.40 of this chapter, no more than one defendant may be charged in the same indictment or prosecuted as part of the same trial under this paragraph. For purposes of this paragraph, the five counties that comprise New York city shall be deemed contiguous with each other.

(ii) For purposes of this paragraph, "organized retail theft crime" shall mean the crime of larceny, including by trick, fraud, embezzlement, stealing or false pretenses, of retail merchandise in quantities that would not normally be purchased for personal use or consumption, for the purposes of reselling, trading, or otherwise reentering such retail merchandise in commerce.

§ 20.50. Geographical jurisdiction of offenses; jurisdiction of cities, towns and villages

1. The principles prescribed in section 20.40, governing geographical jurisdiction over offenses as between counties of this state, are, where appropriate, applicable to the determination of geographical jurisdiction over offenses as between cities, towns and villages within a particular county unless a different determination is required by the provisions of some other express provision of statute.

2. Where an offense prosecutable in a local criminal court is committed in a city other than New York City, or in a town or village, but within one hundred yards of any other such political subdivision, it may be prosecuted in either such political subdivision.

§ 20.60. Geographical jurisdiction of offenses; communications and transportation of property between jurisdictions

For purposes of this article:

1. An oral or written statement made by a person in one jurisdiction to a person in another jurisdiction by means of telecommunication, mail or any other method of communication is deemed to be made in each such jurisdiction.

2. A person who causes property to be transported from one jurisdiction to another by means of mail, common carrier or any other method is deemed to have personally transported it in each jurisdiction, and if delivery is made in the second jurisdiction he is deemed to have personally made such delivery therein.

3. A person who causes by any means the use of a computer or computer service in one jurisdiction from another jurisdiction is deemed to have personally used the computer or computer service in each jurisdiction.

Article 30 Timeliness of Prosecutions and Speedy Trial

§ 30.10. Timeliness of prosecutions; periods of limitation

1. A criminal action must be commenced within the period of limitation prescribed in the ensuing subdivisions of this section.

2. Except as otherwise provided in subdivision three:

(a) A prosecution for a class A felony, or rape in the first degree as defined in section 130.35 of the penal law, or a crime defined or formerly defined in section 130.50 of the penal law, or aggravated sexual abuse in the first degree as defined in section 130.70 of the penal law, or course of sexual conduct against a child in the first degree as defined in section 130.75 of the penal law may be commenced at any time;

(b) A prosecution for any other felony must be commenced within five years after the commission thereof;

(c) A prosecution for a misdemeanor must be commenced within two years after the commission thereof;

(d) A prosecution for a petty offense must be commenced within one year after the commission thereof.

3. Notwithstanding the provisions of subdivision two, the periods of limitation for the commencement of criminal actions are extended as follows in the indicated circumstances:

(a) A prosecution for larceny committed by a person in violation of a fiduciary duty may be commenced within one year after the facts constituting such offense are discovered or, in the exercise of reasonable diligence, should have been discovered by the aggrieved party or by a person under a legal duty to represent him who is not himself implicated in the commission of the offense.

(b) A prosecution for any offense involving misconduct in public office by a public servant including, without limitation, an offense defined in article four hundred ninety-six of the penal law, may be commenced against a public servant, or any other person acting in concert with such public servant at any time during such public servant's service in such office or within five years after the termination of such service; provided however, that in no event shall the period of limitation be extended by more than five years beyond the period otherwise applicable under subdivision two of this section.

(c) A prosecution for any crime set forth in title twenty-seven or article seventy-one of the environmental conservation law may be commenced within four years after the facts constituting such crime are discovered or, in the exercise of reasonable diligence, should have been discovered by a public servant who has the responsibility to enforce the provisions of said title and article.

(d) A prosecution for any misdemeanor set forth in the tax law or chapter forty-six of the administrative code of the city of New York must be commenced within three years after the commission thereof.

(e) A prosecution for course of sexual conduct against a child in the second degree as defined in section 130.80 of the penal law may be commenced within five years of the commission of the most recent act of sexual conduct.

(f) For purposes of a prosecution involving a sexual offense as defined in article one hundred thirty of the penal law, other than a sexual offense delineated in paragraph (a) of subdivision two of this section, committed against a child less than eighteen years of age, incest in the first, second or third degree as defined in sections 255.27, 255.26 and 255.25 of the penal law committed against a child less than eighteen years of age, or use of a child in a sexual performance as defined in section 263.05 of the penal law, the period of limitation shall not begin to run until the child has reached the age of twenty-three or the offense is reported to a law enforcement agency or statewide central register of child abuse and maltreatment, whichever occurs earlier.

(g) A prosecution for any felony defined in article four hundred ninety of the penal law must be commenced within eight years after the commission thereof provided, however, that in a prosecution for a felony defined in article four hundred ninety of the penal law, if the commission of such felony offense resulted in, or created a foreseeable risk of, death or serious physical injury to another person, the prosecution may be commenced at any time; provided, however, that nothing in this paragraph shall be deemed to shorten or otherwise lessen the period, defined in any other applicable law, in which a prosecution for a felony designated in this paragraph may be commenced.

4. In calculating the time limitation applicable to commencement of a criminal action, the following periods shall not be included:

(a) Any period following the commission of the offense during which (i) the defendant was continuously outside this state or (ii) the whereabouts of the defendant were continuously unknown and continuously unascertainable by the exercise of reasonable diligence. However, in no event shall the period of limitation be extended by more than five years beyond the period otherwise applicable under subdivision two.

(b) When a prosecution for an offense is lawfully commenced within the prescribed period of limitation therefor, and when an accusatory instrument upon which such prosecution is based is subsequently dismissed by an authorized court under directions or circumstances permitting the lodging of another charge for the same offense or an offense based on the same conduct, the period extending from the commencement of the thus defeated prosecution to the dismissal of the accusatory instrument does not constitute a part of the period of limitation applicable to commencement of prosecution by a new charge.

§ 30.20. Speedy trial; in general

1. After a criminal action is commenced, the defendant is entitled to a speedy trial.

2. Insofar as is practicable, the trial of a criminal action must be given preference over civil cases; and the trial of a criminal action where the defendant has been committed to the custody of the sheriff during the pendency of the criminal action must be given preference over other criminal actions.

§ 30.30. Speedy trial; time limitations

1. Except as otherwise provided in subdivision three, a motion made pursuant to paragraph (e) of subdivision one of section 170.30 or paragraph (g) of subdivision one of section 210.20 must be granted where the people are not ready for trial within:

(a) six months of the commencement of a criminal action wherein a defendant is accused of one or more offenses, at least one of which is a felony;

(b) ninety days of the commencement of a criminal action wherein a defendant is accused of one or more offenses, at least one of which is a misdemeanor punishable by a sentence of imprisonment of more than three months and none of which is a felony;

(c) sixty days of the commencement of a criminal action wherein the defendant is accused of one or more offenses, at least one of which is a misdemeanor punishable by a sentence of imprisonment of not more than three months and none of which is a crime punishable by a sentence of imprisonment of more than three months;

(d) thirty days of the commencement of a criminal action wherein the defendant is accused of one or more offenses, at least one of which is a violation and none of which is a crime.

2. Except as provided in subdivision three, where a defendant has been committed to the custody of the sheriff in a criminal action he must be released on bail or on his own recognizance, upon such conditions as may be just and reasonable, if the people are not ready for trial in that criminal action within:

(a) ninety days from the commencement of his commitment to the custody of the sheriff in a criminal action wherein the defendant is accused of one or more offenses, at least one of which is a felony;

(b) thirty days from the commencement of his commitment to the custody of the sheriff in a criminal action wherein the defendant is accused of one or more offenses, at least one of which is a misdemeanor punishable by a sentence of imprisonment of more than three months and none of which is a felony;

(c) fifteen days from the commencement of his commitment to the custody of the sheriff in a criminal action wherein the defendant is accused of one or more offenses, at least one of which is a misdemeanor punishable by a sentence of imprisonment of not more than three months and none of which is a crime punishable by a sentence of imprisonment of more than three months;

(d) five days from the commencement of his commitment to the custody of the sheriff in a criminal action wherein the defendant is accused of one or more offenses, at least one of which is a violation and none of which is a crime.

3.

(a) Subdivisions one and two do not apply to a criminal action wherein the defendant is accused of an offense defined in sections 125.10, 125.15, 125.20, 125.25, 125.26 and 125.27 of the penal law.

(b) A motion made pursuant to subdivisions one or two upon expiration of the specified period may be denied where the people are not ready for trial if the people were ready for trial prior to the expiration of the specified period and their present unreadiness is due to some exceptional fact or circumstance, including, but not limited to, the sudden unavailability of evidence material to the people's case, when the district attorney has exercised due diligence to obtain such evidence and there are reasonable grounds to believe that such evidence will become available in a reasonable period.

(c) A motion made pursuant to subdivision two shall not:

(i) apply to any defendant who is serving a term of imprisonment for another offense;

(ii) require the release from custody of any defendant who is also being held in custody pending trial of another criminal charge as to which the applicable period has not yet elapsed;

(iii) prevent the redetention of or otherwise apply to any defendant who, after being released from custody pursuant to this section or otherwise, is charged with another crime or violates the conditions on which he has been released, by failing to appear at a judicial proceeding at which his presence is required or otherwise.

4. In computing the time within which the people must be ready for trial pursuant to subdivisions one and two, the following periods must be excluded:

(a) a reasonable period of delay resulting from other proceedings concerning the defendant, including but not limited to: proceedings for the determination of competency and the period during which defendant is incompetent to stand trial; demand to produce; request for a bill of particulars; pre-trial motions; appeals; trial of other charges; and the period during which such matters are under consideration by the court; or

(b) the period of delay resulting from a continuance granted by the court at the request of, or with the consent of, the defendant or his counsel. The court must grant such a continuance only if it is satisfied that postponement is in the interest of justice, taking into account the public interest in the prompt dispositions of criminal charges. A defendant without counsel must not be deemed to have consented to a continuance unless he has been advised by the court of his rights under these rules and the effect of his consent; or

(c)

(i) the period of delay resulting from the absence or unavailability of the defendant. A defendant must be considered absent whenever his location is unknown and he is attempting to avoid apprehension or prosecution, or his location cannot be determined by due diligence. A defendant must be considered unavailable whenever his location is known but his presence for trial cannot be obtained by due diligence; or

(ii) where the defendant has either escaped from custody or has failed to appear when required after having previously been released on bail or on his own recognizance, and provided the defendant is not in custody on another matter, the period extending from the day the court issues a bench warrant pursuant to section 530.70 because of the defendant's failure to appear in court when required, to the day the defendant subsequently appears in the court pursuant to a bench warrant or voluntarily or otherwise; or

(d) a reasonable period of delay when the defendant is joined for trial with a co-defendant as to whom the time for trial pursuant to this section has not run and good cause is not shown for granting a severance; or

(e) the period of delay resulting from detention of the defendant in another jurisdiction provided the district attorney is aware of such detention and has been diligent and has made reasonable efforts to obtain the presence of the defendant for trial; or

(f) the period during which the defendant is without counsel through no fault of the court; except when the defendant is proceeding as his own attorney with the permission of the court; or

(g) other periods of delay occasioned by exceptional circumstances, including but not limited to, the period of delay resulting from a continuance granted at the request of a district attorney if (i) the continuance is granted because of the unavailability of evidence material to the people's case, when the district attorney has exercised due diligence to obtain such evidence and there are reasonable grounds to believe that such evidence will become available in a reasonable period; or (ii) the continuance is granted to allow the district attorney additional time to prepare the people's case and additional time is justified by the exceptional circumstances of the case.

(h) the period during which an action has been adjourned in contemplation of dismissal pursuant to sections 170.55, 170.56 and 215.10 of this chapter.

(i) The period prior to the defendant's actual appearance for arraignment in a situation in which the defendant has been directed to appear by the district attorney pursuant to subdivision three of section 120.20 or subdivision three of section 210.10.

(j) the period during which a family offense is before a family court until such time as an accusatory instrument or indictment is filed against the defendant alleging a crime constituting a family offense, as such term is defined in section 530.11 of this chapter.

5. For purposes of this section,

(a) where the defendant is to be tried following the withdrawal of the plea of guilty or is to be retried following a mistrial, an order for a new trial or an appeal or collateral attack, the criminal action and the commitment to the custody of the sheriff, if any, must be deemed to have commenced on the date the withdrawal of the plea of guilty or the date the order occasioning a retrial becomes final;

(b) where a defendant has been served with an appearance ticket, the criminal action must be deemed to have commenced on the date the defendant first appears in a local criminal court in response to the ticket;

(c) where a criminal action is commenced by the filing of a felony complaint, and thereafter, in the course of the same criminal action either the felony complaint is replaced with or converted to an information, prosecutor's information or misdemeanor complaint pursuant to article 180 or a prosecutor's information is filed pursuant to section 190.70, the period applicable for the purposes of subdivision one must be the period applicable to the charges in the new accusatory instrument, calculated from the date of the filing of such new accusatory instrument; provided, however, that when the aggregate of such period and the period of time, excluding the periods provided in subdivision four, already elapsed from the date of the filing of the felony complaint to the date of the filing of the new accusatory instrument exceeds six months, the period applicable to the charges in the felony complaint must remain applicable and continue as if the new accusatory instrument had not been filed;

(d) where a criminal action is commenced by the filing of a felony complaint, and thereafter, in the course of the same criminal action either the felony complaint is replaced with or converted to an information, prosecutor's information or misdemeanor complaint pursuant to article 180 or a prosecutor's information is filed pursuant to section 190.70, the period applicable for the purposes of subdivision two must be the period applicable to the charges in the new accusatory instrument, calculated from the date of the filing of such new accusatory instrument; provided, however, that when the aggregate of such period and the period of time, excluding the periods provided in subdivision four, already elapsed from the date of the filing of the felony complaint to the date of the filing of the new accusatory instrument exceeds ninety days, the period applicable to the charges in the felony complaint must remain applicable and continue as if the new accusatory instrument had not been filed.

(e) where a count of an indictment is reduced to charge only a misdemeanor or petty offense and a reduced indictment or a prosecutor's information is filed pursuant to subdivisions one-a and six of section 210.20, the period applicable for the purposes of subdivision one of this section must be the period applicable to the charges in the new accusatory instrument, calculated from the date of the filing of such new accusatory instrument; provided, however, that when the aggregate of such period and the period of time, excluding the periods provided in subdivision four of this section, already elapsed from the date of the filing of the indictment to the date of the filing of the new accusatory instrument exceeds six months, the period applicable to the charges in the indictment must remain applicable and continue as if the new accusatory instrument had not been filed;

(f) where a count of an indictment is reduced to charge only a misdemeanor or petty offense and a reduced indictment or a prosecutor's information is filed pursuant to subdivisions one-a and six of section 210.20, the period applicable for the purposes of subdivision two of this section must be the period applicable to the charges in the new accusatory instrument, calculated from the date of the filing of such new accusatory instrument; provided, however, that when the aggregate of such period and the period of time, excluding the periods provided in subdivision four of this section, already elapsed from the date of the filing of the indictment to the date of the filing of the new accusatory instrument exceeds ninety days, the period applicable to the charges in the indictment must remain applicable and continue as if the new accusatory instrument had not been filed.

6. The procedural rules prescribed in subdivisions one through seven of section 210.45 with respect to a motion to dismiss an indictment are also applicable to a motion made pursuant to subdivision two.

Article 40 Exemption From Prosecution by Reason of Previous Prosecution

§ 40.10. Previous prosecution; definitions of terms

The following definitions are applicable to this article:

1. "Offense." An "offense" is committed whenever any conduct is performed which violates a statutory provision defining an offense; and when the same conduct or criminal transaction violates two or more such statutory provisions each such violation constitutes a separate and distinct offense. The same conduct or criminal transaction also establishes separate and distinct offenses when, though violating only one statutory provision, it results in death, injury, loss or other consequences to two or more victims, and such result is an element of the offense as defined. In such case, as many offenses are committed as there are victims.

2. "Criminal transaction" means conduct which establishes at least one offense, and which is comprised of two or more or a group of acts either (a) so closely related and connected in point of time and circumstance of commission as to constitute a single criminal incident, or (b) so closely related in criminal purpose or objective as to constitute elements or integral parts of a single criminal venture.

§ 40.20. Previous prosecution; when a bar to second prosecution

1. A person may not be twice prosecuted for the same offense.

2. A person may not be separately prosecuted for two offenses based upon the same act or criminal transaction unless:

(a) The offenses as defined have substantially different elements and the acts establishing one offense are in the main clearly distinguishable from those establishing the other; or

(b) Each of the offenses as defined contains an element which is not an element of the other, and the statutory provisions defining such offenses are designed to prevent very different kinds of harm or evil; or

(c) One of such offenses consists of criminal possession of contraband matter and the other offense is one involving the use of such contraband matter, other than a sale thereof; or

(d) One of the offenses is assault or some other offense resulting in physical injury to a person, and the other offense is one of homicide based upon the death of such person from the same physical injury, and such death occurs after a prosecution for the assault or other non-homicide offense; or

(e) Each offense involves death, injury, loss or other consequence to a different victim; or

(f) One of the offenses consists of a violation of a statutory provision of another jurisdiction, which offense has been prosecuted in such other jurisdiction and has there been terminated by a court order expressly founded upon insufficiency of evidence to establish some element of such offense which is not an element of the other offense, defined by the laws of this state; or

(g) The present prosecution is for a consummated result offense, as defined in subdivision three of section 20.10, which occurred in this state and the offense was the result of a conspiracy, facilitation or solicitation prosecuted in another state.

(h) One of such offenses is enterprise corruption in violation of section 460.20 of the penal law, racketeering in violation of federal law or any comparable offense pursuant to the law of another state and a separate or subsequent prosecution is not barred by section 40.50 of this article.

(i) One of the offenses consists of a violation of 18 U.S.C. 371, where the object of the conspiracy is to attempt in any manner to evade or defeat any federal income tax or the payment thereof, or a violation of 26 U.S.C. 7201, 26 U.S.C. 7202, 26 U.S.C. 7203, 26 U.S.C. 7204, 26 U.S.C. 7205, 26 U.S.C. 7206 or 26 U.S.C. 7212(A), where the purpose is to evade or defeat any federal income tax or the payment thereof, and the other offense is committed for the purpose of evading or defeating any New York state or New York city income taxes and is defined in article one hundred fifty-five of the penal law, article one hundred seventy of the penal law, article one hundred seventy-five of the penal law, article thirty-seven of the tax law or chapter forty of title eleven of the administrative code of the city of New York.

§ 40.30. Previous prosecution; what constitutes

1. Except as otherwise provided in this section, a person "is prosecuted" for an offense, within the meaning of section 40.20, when he is charged therewith by an accusatory instrument filed in a court of this state or of any jurisdiction within the United States, and when the action either:

(a) Terminates in a conviction upon a plea of guilty; or

(b) Proceeds to the trial stage and a jury has been impaneled and sworn or, in the case of a trial by the court without a jury, a witness is sworn.

2. Despite the occurrence of proceedings specified in subdivision one, a person is not deemed to have been prosecuted for an offense, within the meaning of section 40.20, when:

(a) Such prosecution occurred in a court which lacked jurisdiction over the defendant or the offense; or

(b) Such prosecution was for a lesser offense than could have been charged under the facts of the case, and the prosecution was procured by the defendant, without the knowledge of the appropriate prosecutor, for the purpose of avoiding prosecution for a greater offense.

3. Despite the occurrence of proceedings specified in subdivision one, if such proceedings are subsequently nullified by a court order which restores the action to its pre-pleading status or which directs a new trial of the same accusatory instrument, the nullified proceedings do not bar further prosecution of such offense under the same accusatory instrument.

4. Despite the occurrence of proceedings specified in subdivision one, if such proceedings are subsequently nullified by a court order which dismisses the accusatory instrument but authorizes the people to obtain a new accusatory instrument charging the same offense or an offense based upon the same conduct, the nullified proceedings do not bar further prosecution of such offense under any new accusatory instrument obtained pursuant to such court order or authorization.

§ 40.40. Separate prosecution of jointly prosecutable offenses; when barred

1. Where two or more offenses are joinable in a single accusatory instrument against a person by reason of being based upon the same criminal transaction, pursuant to paragraph (a) of subdivision two of section 200.20, such person may not, under circumstances prescribed in this section, be separately prosecuted for such offenses even though such separate prosecutions are not otherwise barred by any other section of this article.

2. When (a) one of two or more joinable offenses of the kind specified in subdivision one is charged in an accusatory instrument, and (b) another is not charged therein, or in any other accusatory instrument filed in the same court, despite possession by the people of evidence legally sufficient to support a conviction of the defendant for such uncharged offense, and (c) either a trial of the existing accusatory instrument is commenced or the action thereon is disposed of by a plea of guilty, any subsequent prosecution for the uncharged offense is thereby barred.

3. When (a) two or more of such offenses are charged in separate accusatory instruments filed in the same court, and (b) an application by the defendant for consolidation thereof for trial purposes, pursuant to subdivision five of section 200.20 or section 100.45, is improperly denied, the commencement of a trial of one such accusatory instrument bars any subsequent prosecution upon any of the other accusatory instruments with respect to any such offense.

§ 40.50. Previous prosecution; enterprise corruption

1. The following definitions are applicable to this section:

(a) A criminal act or offense is "specifically included" when a count of an accusatory instrument charging a person with enterprise corruption alleges a pattern of criminal activity and the act or offense is alleged to be a criminal act within such pattern.

(b) A criminal act is "a part of" a pattern of criminal activity alleged in a count of enterprise corruption when it is committed prior to commencement of the criminal action in which enterprise corruption is charged and was committed in furtherance of the same common scheme or plan or with intent to participate in or further the affairs of the same criminal enterprise to which the crimes specifically included in the pattern are connected.

(c) A person "is prosecuted" for an offense when he is prosecuted for it within the meaning of section 40.30 of this article or when an indictment or a count of an indictment charging that offense is dismissed pursuant to section 210.20 of this chapter without authorization to submit the charge to the same or another grand jury, or the indictment or the count of the indictment charging that offense is dismissed following the granting of a motion to suppress pursuant to article 710 of this chapter, unless an appeal from the order granting the motion to dismiss or suppress is pending.

(d) An offense was "not prosecutable" in an accusatory instrument in which a person was charged with enterprise corruption when there was no geographical jurisdiction of that offense in the county where the accusatory instrument was filed, or when the offense was prosecutable in the county and was not barred from prosecution by section 40.20 or 40.40 of this article or by any other provision of law but the prosecutor filing the accusatory instrument was not empowered by law to prosecute the offense.

2. A person who has been previously prosecuted for an offense may not be subsequently prosecuted for enterprise corruption based upon a pattern of criminal activity in which that prior offense, or another offense based upon the same act or criminal transaction, is specifically included unless:

(a) he was convicted of that prior offense; and

(b) the subsequent pattern of criminal activity in which he participated includes at least one criminal act for which he was not previously prosecuted, which was a felony, and which occurred after that prior conviction.

3. A person who has been previously prosecuted for enterprise corruption may not be subsequently prosecuted for an offense specifically included in the pattern of criminal activity upon which it was based, or another offense based upon the same act or criminal transaction, unless the offense is a class A felony and was not prosecutable in the accusatory instrument in which the person was charged with enterprise corruption.

4. A person may not be separately prosecuted for enterprise corruption and for an offense specifically included in the pattern of criminal activity upon which it is based or another offense based upon the same act or transaction, unless the offense is a class A felony and is not prosecutable in the accusatory instrument in which the person is charged with enterprise corruption.

5. A person who has been previously prosecuted for enterprise corruption may not be subsequently prosecuted for an offense which, while not specifically included in the pattern of criminal activity on which the prior charge of enterprise corruption was based, was nonetheless a part of that pattern, unless the offense was a class A or B felony and either the offense was not prosecutable in the accusatory instrument in which the person was charged with enterprise corruption or the people show, by clear and convincing evidence, that the prosecutor did not possess evidence legally sufficient to support a conviction of that offense at the time of the earlier prosecution and evidence of that offense was not presented as part of the case in chief in the earlier prosecution.

6. A person who has been previously prosecuted for enterprise corruption may not be subsequently prosecuted for enterprise corruption based upon a pattern of criminal activity that specifically includes a criminal act that was also specifically included in the pattern upon which the prior charge of enterprise corruption was based.

7. A person may not be separately prosecuted for enterprise corruption in two accusatory instruments based upon a pattern of criminal activity, alleged in either instrument, that specifically includes a criminal act that is also specifically included in the pattern upon which the other charge of enterprise corruption is based.

8. When a person is charged in an accusatory instrument with both one or more counts of enterprise corruption and with another offense or offenses specifically included in or otherwise a part of the pattern or patterns of criminal activity upon which the charge or charges of enterprise corruption is or are based, and the court orders that any of the counts be tried separately pursuant to subdivision one of section 200.40 of this chapter, this section shall not apply and subsequent prosecution of the remaining counts or offenses shall not be barred.

9. A person who has been previously prosecuted for racketeering pursuant to federal law, or any comparable offense pursuant to the law of another state may not be subsequently prosecuted for enterprise corruption based upon a pattern of criminal activity that specifically includes a criminal act that was also specifically included in the pattern of racketeering activity upon which the prior charge of racketeering was based provided, however, that this section shall not be construed to prohibit the subsequent prosecution of any other offense specifically included in or otherwise a part of a pattern of racketeering activity alleged in any such prior prosecution for racketeering or other comparable offense.

Article 50 Compulsion of Evidence by Offer of Immunity

§ 50.10. Compulsion of evidence by offer of immunity; definitions of terms

The following definitions are applicable to this article:

1. "Immunity." A person who has been a witness in a legal proceeding, and who cannot, except as otherwise provided in this subdivision, be convicted of any offense or subjected to any penalty or forfeiture for or on account of any transaction, matter or

thing concerning which he gave evidence therein, possesses "immunity" from any such conviction, penalty or forfeiture. A person who possesses such immunity may nevertheless be convicted of perjury as a result of having given false testimony in such legal proceeding, and may be convicted of or adjudged in contempt as a result of having contumaciously refused to give evidence therein.

2. "Legal proceeding" means a proceeding in or before any court or grand jury, or before any body, agency or person authorized by law to conduct the same and to administer the oath or to cause it to be administered.

3. "Give evidence" means to testify or produce physical evidence.

§ 50.20. Compulsion of evidence by offer of immunity

1. Any witness in a legal proceeding, other than a grand jury proceeding, may refuse to give evidence requested of him on the ground that it may tend to incriminate him and he may not, except as provided in subdivision two, be compelled to give such evidence.

2. Such a witness may be compelled to give evidence in such a proceeding notwithstanding an assertion of his privilege against self-incrimination if:

(a) The proceeding is one in which, by express provision of statute, a person conducting or connected therewith is declared a competent authority to confer immunity upon witnesses therein; and

(b) Such competent authority (i) orders such witness to give the requested evidence notwithstanding his assertion of his privilege against self-incrimination, and (ii) advises him that upon so doing he will receive immunity.

3. A witness who is ordered to give evidence pursuant to subdivision two and who complies with such order receives immunity. Such witness is not deprived of such immunity because such competent authority did not comply with statutory provisions requiring notice to a specified public servant of intention to confer immunity.

4. A witness who, without asserting his privilege against self-incrimination, gives evidence in a legal proceeding other than a grand jury proceeding does not receive immunity.

5. The rules governing the circumstances in which witnesses may be compelled to give evidence and in which they receive immunity therefor in a grand jury proceeding are prescribed in section 190.40.

§ 50.30. Authority to confer immunity in criminal proceedings; court a competent authority

In any criminal proceeding, other than a grand jury proceeding, the court is a competent authority to confer immunity in accordance with the provisions of section 50.20, but only when expressly requested by the district attorney to do so.

Title D Rules of Evidence, Standards of Proof and Related Matters

Article 60 Rules of Evidence and Related Matters

§ 60.10. Rules of evidence; in general

Unless otherwise provided by statute or by judicially established rules of evidence applicable to criminal cases, the rules of evidence applicable to civil cases are, where appropriate, also applicable to criminal proceedings.

§ 60.15. Rules of evidence; what witnesses may be called

1. Unless otherwise expressly provided, in any criminal proceeding involving a defendant in which evidence is or may be received, both the people and the defendant may as a matter of right call and examine witnesses, and each party may cross-examine every witness called by the other party.

2. A defendant may testify in his own behalf, but his failure to do so is not a factor from which any inference unfavorable to him may be drawn.

§ 60.20. Rules of evidence; testimonial capacity; evidence given by children

1. Any person may be a witness in a criminal proceeding unless the court finds that, by reason of infancy or mental disease or defect, he does not possess sufficient intelligence or capacity to justify the reception of his evidence.

2. Every witness more than nine years old may testify only under oath unless the court is satisfied that such witness cannot, as a result of mental disease or defect, understand the nature of an oath. A witness less than nine years old may not testify under oath unless the court is satisfied that he or she understands the nature of an oath. If under either of the above provisions, a witness is deemed to be ineligible to testify under oath, the witness may nevertheless be permitted to give unsworn evidence if the court is satisfied that the witness possesses sufficient intelligence and capacity to justify the reception thereof. A witness understands the nature of an oath if he or she appreciates the difference between truth and falsehood, the necessity for telling the truth, and the fact that a witness who testifies falsely may be punished.

3. A defendant may not be convicted of an offense solely upon unsworn evidence given pursuant to subdivision two.

§ 60.22. Rules of evidence; corroboration of accomplice testimony

1. A defendant may not be convicted of any offense upon the testimony of an accomplice unsupported by corroborative evidence tending to connect the defendant with the commission of such offense.

2. An "accomplice" means a witness in a criminal action who, according to evidence adduced in such action, may reasonably be considered to have participated in:

(a) The offense charged; or

(b) An offense based upon the same or some of the same facts or conduct which constitute the offense charged.

3. A witness who is an accomplice as defined in subdivision two is no less such because a prosecution or conviction of himself would be barred or precluded by some defense or exemption, such as infancy, immunity or previous prosecution, amounting to a collateral impediment to such a prosecution or conviction, not affecting the conclusion that such witness engaged in the conduct constituting the offense with the mental state required for the commission thereof.

§ 60.25. Rules of evidence; identification by means of previous recognition, in absence of present identification

1. In any criminal proceeding in which the defendant's commission of an offense is in issue, testimony as provided in subdivision two may be given by a witness when:

(a) Such witness testifies that:

(i) He or she observed the person claimed by the people to be the defendant either at the time and place of the commission of the offense or upon some other occasion relevant to the case; and

(ii) On a subsequent occasion he or she observed, under circumstances consistent with such rights as an accused person may derive under the constitution of this state or of the United States, a person or, where the observation is made pursuant to a blind or blinded procedure as defined in paragraph (c) of this subdivision, a pictorial, photographic, electronic, filmed or video recorded reproduction of a person whom he or she recognized as the same person whom he or she had observed on the first or incriminating occasion; and

(iii) He or she is unable at the proceeding to state, on the basis of present recollection, whether or not the defendant is the person in question; and

(b) It is established that the defendant is in fact the person whom the witness observed and recognized or whose pictorial, photographic, electronic, filmed or video recorded reproduction the witness observed and recognized on the second occasion. Such fact may be established by testimony of another person or persons to whom the witness promptly declared his or her recognition on such occasion and by such pictorial, photographic, electronic, filmed or video recorded reproduction.

(c) For purposes of this section, a "blind or blinded procedure" is one in which the witness identifies a person in an array of pictorial, photographic, electronic, filmed or video recorded reproductions under circumstances where, at the time the identification is made, the public servant administering such procedure: (i) does not know which person in the array is the suspect, or (ii) does not know where the suspect is in the array viewed by the witness. The failure of a public servant to follow such a procedure shall be assessed solely for purposes of this article and shall result in the preclusion of testimony regarding the identification procedure as evidence in chief, but shall not constitute a legal basis to suppress evidence made pursuant to subdivision six of section 710.20 of this chapter. This article neither limits nor expands subdivision six of section 710.20 of this chapter.

2. Under circumstances prescribed in subdivision one of this section, such witness may testify at the criminal proceeding that the person whom he or she observed and recognized or whose pictorial, photographic, electronic, filmed or video recorded reproduction he or she observed and recognized on the second occasion is the same person whom he or she observed on the first or incriminating occasion. Such testimony, together with the evidence that the defendant is in fact the person whom the witness observed and recognized or whose pictorial, photographic, electronic, filmed or video recorded reproduction he or she observed and recognized on the second occasion, constitutes evidence in chief.

§ 60.30. Rules of evidence; identification by means of previous recognition, in addition to present identification

In any criminal proceeding in which the defendant's commission of an offense is in issue, a witness who testifies that (a) he or she observed the person claimed by the people to be the defendant either at the time and place of the commission of the offense or upon some other occasion relevant to the case, and (b) on the basis of present recollection, the defendant is the person in question and (c) on a subsequent occasion he or she observed the defendant, or where the observation is made pursuant to a blind or blinded procedure, as defined in paragraph (c) of subdivision one of section 60.25 of this article, a pictorial, photographic, electronic, filmed or video recorded reproduction of the defendant, under circumstances consistent with such rights as an accused person may derive under the constitution of this state or of the United States, and then also recognized him or her or the pictorial, photographic, electronic, filmed or video recorded reproduction of him or her as the same person whom he or she had observed on the first or incriminating occasion, may, in addition to making an identification of the defendant at the criminal proceeding on the basis of present recollection as the person whom he or she observed on the first or incriminating occasion, also describe his or her previous recognition of the defendant and testify that the person whom he or she observed or whose pictorial, photographic, electronic, filmed or video recorded reproduction he or she observed on such second occasion is the same person whom he or she had observed on the first or incriminating occasion. Such testimony and such pictorial, photographic, electronic, filmed or video recorded reproduction constitutes evidence in chief.

§ 60.35. Rules of evidence; impeachment of own witness by proof of prior contradictory statement

1. When, upon examination by the party who called him, a witness in a criminal proceeding gives testimony upon a material issue of the case which tends to disprove the position of such party, such party may introduce evidence that such witness has previously made either a written statement signed by him or an oral statement under oath contradictory to such testimony.

2. Evidence concerning a prior contradictory statement introduced pursuant to subdivision one may be received only for the purpose of impeaching the credibility of the witness with respect to his testimony upon the subject, and does not constitute evidence in chief. Upon receiving such evidence at a jury trial, the court must so instruct the jury.

3. When a witness has made a prior signed or sworn statement contradictory to his testimony in a criminal proceeding upon a material issue of the case, but his testimony does not tend to disprove the position of the party who called him and elicited such testimony, evidence that the witness made such prior statement is not admissible, and such party may not use such prior statement for the purpose of refreshing the recollection of the witness in a manner that discloses its contents to the trier of the facts.

§ 60.40. Rules of evidence; proof of previous conviction; when allowed

1. If in the course of a criminal proceeding, any witness, including a defendant, is properly asked whether he was previously convicted of a specified offense and answers in the negative or in an equivocal manner, the party adverse to the one who called him may independently prove such conviction. If in response to proper inquiry whether he has ever been convicted of any offense the witness answers in the negative or in an equivocal manner, the adverse party may independently prove any previous conviction of the witness.

2. If a defendant in a criminal proceeding, through the testimony of a witness called by him, offers evidence of his good character, the people may independently prove any previous conviction of the defendant for an offense the commission of which would tend to negate any character trait or quality attributed to the defendant in such witness' testimony.

3. Subject to the limitations prescribed in section 200.60, the people may prove that a defendant has been previously convicted of an offense when the fact of such previous conviction constitutes an element of the offense charged, or proof thereof is otherwise essential to the establishment of a legally sufficient case.

§ 60.42. Rules of evidence; admissibility of evidence of victim's sexual conduct in sex offense cases

Evidence of a victim's sexual conduct shall not be admissible in a prosecution for an offense or an attempt to commit an offense defined in article one hundred thirty of the penal law unless such evidence:

1. proves or tends to prove specific instances of the victim's prior sexual conduct with the accused; or

2. proves or tends to prove that the victim has been convicted of an offense under section 230.00 of the penal law within three years prior to the sex offense which is the subject of the prosecution; or

3. rebuts evidence introduced by the people of the victim's failure to engage in sexual intercourse, oral sexual conduct, anal sexual conduct or sexual contact during a given period of time; or

4. rebuts evidence introduced by the people which proves or tends to prove that the accused is the cause of pregnancy or disease of the victim, or the source of semen found in the victim; or

5. is determined by the court after an offer of proof by the accused outside the hearing of the jury, or such hearing as the court may require, and a statement by the court of its findings of fact essential to its determination, to be relevant and admissible in the interests of justice.

§ 60.43. Rules of evidence; admissibility of evidence of victim's sexual conduct in non-sex offense cases

Evidence of the victim's sexual conduct, including the past sexual conduct of a deceased victim, may not be admitted in a prosecution for any offense, attempt to commit an offense or conspiracy to commit an offense defined in the penal law unless such evidence is determined by the court to be relevant and admissible in the interests of justice, after an offer of proof by the proponent of such evidence outside the hearing of the jury, or such hearing as the court may require, and a statement by the court of its findings of fact essential to its determination.

§ 60.44. Use of anatomically correct dolls

Any person who is less than sixteen years old may in the discretion of the court and where helpful and appropriate, use an anatomically correct doll in testifying in a criminal proceeding based upon conduct prohibited by article one hundred thirty, article two hundred sixty or section 255.25, 255.26 or 255.27 of the penal law.

§ 60.45. Rules of evidence; admissibility of statements of defendants

1. Evidence of a written or oral confession, admission, or other statement made by a defendant with respect to his participation or lack of participation in the offense charged, may not be received in evidence against him in a criminal proceeding if such statement was involuntarily made.

2. A confession, admission or other statement is "involuntarily made" by a defendant when it is obtained from him:

(a) By any person by the use or threatened use of physical force upon the defendant or another person, or by means of any other improper conduct or undue pressure which impaired the defendant's physical or mental condition to the extent of undermining his ability to make a choice whether or not to make a statement; or

(b) By a public servant engaged in law enforcement activity or by a person then acting under his direction or in cooperation with him:

(i) by means of any promise or statement of fact, which promise or statement creates a substantial risk that the defendant might falsely incriminate himself; or

(ii) in violation of such rights as the defendant may derive from the constitution of this state or of the United States.

3.

(a) Where a person is subject to custodial interrogation by a public servant at a detention facility, the entire custodial interrogation, including the giving of any required advice of the rights of the individual being questioned, and the waiver of any rights by the individual, shall be recorded by an appropriate video recording device if the interrogation involves a class A-1 felony, except one defined in article two hundred twenty of the penal law; felony offenses defined in section 130.95 and 130.96 of the penal law; or a felony offense defined in article one hundred twenty-five or one hundred thirty of such law that is defined as a class B violent felony offense in section 70.02 of the penal law. For purposes of this paragraph, the term "detention facility" shall mean a police station, correctional facility, holding facility for prisoners, prosecutor's office or other facility where persons are held in detention in connection with criminal charges that have been or may be filed against them.

(b) No confession, admission or other statement shall be subject to a motion to suppress pursuant to subdivision three of section 710.20 of this chapter based solely upon the failure to video record such interrogation in a detention facility as defined in paragraph (a) of this subdivision. However, where the people offer into evidence a confession, admission or other statement made by a person in custody with respect to his or her participation or lack of participation in an offense specified in paragraph (a) of this subdivision, that has not been video recorded, the court shall consider the failure to record as a factor, but not as the sole factor, in accordance with paragraph (c) of this subdivision in determining whether such confession, admission or other statement shall be admissible.

(c) Notwithstanding the requirement of paragraph (a) of this subdivision, upon a showing of good cause by the prosecutor, the custodial interrogation need not be recorded. Good cause shall include, but not be limited to:

(i) If electronic recording equipment malfunctions.

(ii) If electronic recording equipment is not available because it was otherwise being used.

(iii) If statements are made in response to questions that are routinely asked during arrest processing.

(iv) If the statement is spontaneously made by the suspect and not in response to police questioning.

(v) If the statement is made during an interrogation that is conducted when the interviewer is unaware that a qualifying offense has occurred.

(vi) If the statement is made at a location other than the "interview room" because the suspect cannot be brought to such room, e.g., the suspect is in a hospital or the suspect is out of state and that state is not governed by a law requiring the recordation of an interrogation.

(vii) If the statement is made after a suspect has refused to participate in the interrogation if it is recorded, and appropriate effort to document such refusal is made.

(viii) If such statement is not recorded as a result of an inadvertent error or oversight, not the result of any intentional conduct by law enforcement personnel.

(ix) If it is law enforcement's reasonable belief that such recording would jeopardize the safety of any person or reveal the identity of a confidential informant.

(x) If such statement is made at a location not equipped with a video recording device and the reason for using that location is not to subvert the intent of the law. For purposes of this section, the term "location" shall include those locations specified in paragraph (b) of subdivision four of section 305.2 of the family court act.

(d) In the event the court finds that the people have not shown good cause for the non-recording of the confession, admission, or other statement, but determines that a non-recorded confession, admission or other statement is nevertheless admissible because it was voluntarily made then, upon request of the defendant, the court must instruct the jury that the people's failure to record the defendant's confession, admission or other statement as required by this section may be weighed as a factor, but not as the sole factor, in determining whether such confession, admission or other statement was voluntarily made, or was made at all.

(e) Video recording as required by this section shall be conducted in accordance with standards established by rule of the division of criminal justice services.

§ 60.46. Rules of evidence, family offense proceedings in family court

Evidence of a written or oral admission or any testimony given by either party, or evidence derived therefrom, in a proceeding under article eight of the family court act without the benefit of counsel in such proceeding may not be received into evidence in a criminal proceeding except for the purposes of impeachment unless such party waives the right to counsel on the record. Nothing herein shall be deemed to prohibit any testimony or exhibits received into evidence in a criminal proceeding, or any orders, decisions or judgments arising from such proceeding from being received into evidence in any proceeding under article eight of the family court act.

§ 60.47 Possession of condoms; receipt into evidence

Evidence that a person was in possession of one or more condoms may not be admitted at any trial, hearing, or other proceeding in a prosecution for section 230.00 or section 240.37 of the penal law for the purpose of establishing probable cause for an arrest or proving any person's commission or attempted commission of such offense.

§ 60.48. Rules of evidence; admissibility of evidence of victim's manner of dress in sex offense cases

Evidence of the manner in which the victim was dressed at the time of the commission of an offense may not be admitted in a prosecution for any offense, or an attempt to commit an offense, defined in article one hundred thirty of the penal law, unless such evidence is determined by the court to be relevant and admissible in the interests of justice, after an offer of proof by the proponent of such evidence outside the hearing of the jury, or such hearing as the court may require, and a statement by the court of its findings of fact essential to its determination.

§ 60.50. Rules of evidence; statements of defendants; corroboration

A person may not be convicted of any offense solely upon evidence of a confession or admission made by him without additional proof that the offense charged has been committed.

§ 60.55. Rules of evidence; psychiatric testimony in certain cases

1. When, in connection with the affirmative defense of lack of criminal responsibility by reason of mental disease or defect, a psychiatrist or licensed psychologist testifies at a trial concerning the defendant's mental condition at the time of the conduct charged to constitute a crime, he must be permitted to make a statement as to the nature of any examination of the defendant, the diagnosis of the mental condition of the defendant and his opinion as to the extent, if any, to which the capacity of the defendant to know or appreciate the nature and consequence of such conduct, or its wrongfulness, was impaired as a result of mental disease or defect at that time.

The psychiatrist or licensed psychologist must be permitted to make any explanation reasonably serving to clarify his diagnosis and opinion, and may be cross-examined as to any matter bearing on his competency or credibility or the validity of his diagnosis or opinion.

2. Any statement made by the defendant to a psychiatrist or licensed psychologist during his examination of the defendant shall be inadmissible in evidence on any issue other than that of the affirmative defense of lack of criminal responsibility, by reason of mental disease or defect. The statement shall, however, be admissible upon the issue of the affirmative defense of lack of criminal responsibility by reason of mental disease or defect, whether or not it would otherwise be deemed a privileged communication. Upon receiving the statement in evidence, the court must instruct the jury that the statement is to be considered only on the issue of such affirmative defense and may not be considered by it in its determination of whether the defendant committed the act constituting the crime charged.

§ 60.60. Rules of evidence; certificates concerning judgments of conviction and fingerprints

1. A certificate issued by a criminal court, or the clerk thereof, certifying that a judgment of conviction against a designated defendant has been entered in such court, constitutes presumptive evidence of the facts stated in such certificate.

2. A report of a public servant charged with the custody of official fingerprint records which contains a certification that the fingerprints of a designated person who has

previously been convicted of an offense are identical with those of a defendant in a criminal action, constitutes presumptive evidence of the fact that such defendant has previously been convicted of such offense.

§ 60.70. Rules of evidence; dangerous drugs destroyed pursuant to court order

The destruction of dangerous drugs pursuant to the provisions of article seven hundred fifteen hereof shall not preclude the admission on trial or in a proceeding in connection therewith of testimony or evidence where such testimony or evidence would otherwise have been admissible if such drugs had not been destroyed.

§ 60.75. Rules of evidence; chemical test evidence

In any prosecution where two or more offenses against the same defendant are properly joined in one indictment or charged in two accusatory instruments properly consolidated for trial purposes and where one such offense charges a violation of any subdivision of section eleven hundred ninety-two of the vehicle and traffic law, chemical test evidence properly admissible as evidence of intoxication under subdivision one of section eleven hundred ninety-five of such law shall also, if relevant, be received in evidence with regard to the remaining charges in the indictments.

§ 60.76. Rules of evidence; rape crisis counselor evidence in certain cases

Where disclosure of a communication which would have been privileged pursuant to section forty-five hundred ten of the civil practice law and rules is sought on the grounds that the privilege has been waived or that disclosure is required pursuant to the constitution of this state or the United States, the party seeking disclosure must file a written motion supported by an affidavit containing specific factual allegations providing grounds that disclosure is required. Upon the filing of such motion and affidavit, the court shall conduct an in camera review of the communication outside the presence of the jury and of counsel for all parties in order to determine whether disclosure of any portion of the communication is required.

Article 65 [Expires and Repealed Sept 1, 2019] Use of Closed-Circuit Television for Certain Child Witnesses

§ 65.00. [Expires and repealed Sept 1, 2019] Definitions

As used in this article:

1. "Child witness" means a person fourteen years old or less who is or will be called to testify in a criminal proceeding, other than a grand jury proceeding, concerning an offense defined in article one hundred thirty of the penal law or section 255.25, 255.26 or 255.27 of such law which is the subject of such criminal proceeding.

2. "Vulnerable child witness" means a child witness whom a court has declared to be vulnerable.

3. "Testimonial room" means any room, separate and apart from the courtroom, which is furnished comfortably and less formally than a courtroom and from which the testimony of a vulnerable child witness can be transmitted to the courtroom by means of live, two-way closed-circuit television.

4. "Live, two-way closed-circuit television" means a simultaneous transmission, by closed-circuit television, or other electronic means, between the courtroom and the testimonial room in accordance with the provisions of section 65.30.

5. "Operator" means the individual authorized by the court to operate the closed-circuit television equipment used in accordance with the provisions of this article.

6. A person occupies "a position of authority with respect to a child" when he or she is a parent, guardian or other person responsible for the custody or care of the child at the relevant time or is any other person who maintains an ongoing personal relationship with such parent, guardian or other person responsible for custody or care, which relationship involves his or her living, or his or her frequent and repeated presence, in the same household or premises as the child.

§ 65.10. [Expires and repealed Sept 1, 2019] Closed-circuit television; general rule; declaration of vulnerability

1. A child witness shall be declared vulnerable when the court, in accordance with the provisions of section 65.20, determines by clear and convincing evidence that it is likely that such child witness will suffer serious mental or emotional harm if required to testify at a criminal proceeding without the use of live, two-way closed-circuit television and that the use of such live, two-way closed-circuit television will diminish the likelihood or extent of, such harm.

2. When the court declares a child witness to be vulnerable, it shall, except as provided in subdivision four of section 65.30, authorize the taking of the testimony of the vulnerable child witness from the testimonial room by means of live, two-way closed-circuit television. Under no circumstances shall the provisions of this article be construed to authorize a closed-circuit television system by which events in the courtroom are not transmitted to the testimonial room during the testimony of the vulnerable child witness.

3. Nothing herein shall be contrued [construed]* to preclude the court from exercising its power to close the courtroom or from exercising any authority it otherwise may have to protect the well-being of a witness and the rights of the defendant.

§ 65.20. [Expires and repealed Sept 1, 2019] Closed-circuit television; procedure for application and grounds for determination

1. Prior to the commencement of a criminal proceeding; other than a grand jury proceeding, either party may apply to the court for an order declaring that a child witness is vulnerable.

2. A child witness should be declared vulnerable when the court, in accordance with the provisions of this section, determines by clear and convincing evidence that the child witness would suffer serious mental or emotional harm that would substantially impair the child witness' ability to communicate with the finder of fact without the use of live, two-way closed-circuit television.

3. A motion pursuant to subdivision one of this section must be made in writing at least eight days before the commencement of trial or other criminal proceeding upon reasonable notice to the other party and with an opportunity to be heard.

4. The motion papers must state the basis for the motion and must contain sworn allegations of fact which, if true, would support a determination by the court that the child witness is vulnerable. Such allegations may be based upon the personal knowledge of the deponent or upon information and belief, provided that, in the latter event, the sources of such information and the grounds for such belief are stated.

5. The answering papers may admit or deny any of the alleged facts and may, in addition, contain sworn allegations of fact relevant to the motion, including the rights of the defendant, the need to protect the child witness and the integrity of the truth-finding function of the trier of fact.

6. Unless all material facts alleged in support of the motion made pursuant to subdivision one of this section are conceded, the court shall, in addition to examining the papers and hearing oral argument, conduct an appropriate hearing for the purpose of making findings of fact essential to the determination of the motion. Except as provided in subdivision six of this section, it may subpoena or call and examine witnesses, who must either testify under oath or be permitted to give unsworn testimony pursuant to subdivision two of section 60.20 and must authorize the attorneys for the parties to do the same.

7. Notwithstanding any other provision of law, the child witness who is alleged to be vulnerable may not be compelled to testify at such hearing or to submit to any psychological or psychiatric examination. The failure of the child witness to testify at such hearing shall not be a ground for denying a motion made pursuant to subdivision one of this section. Prior statements made by the child witness relating to any allegations of conduct constituting an offense defined in article one hundred thirty of the penal law or incest as defined in section 255.25, 255.26 or 255.27 of such law or to any allegation of words or conduct constituting an attempt to prevent, impede or deter the child witness from cooperating in the investigation or prosecution of the offense shall be admissible at such hearing, provided, however, that a declaration that a child witness is vulnerable may not be based solely upon such prior statements.

8.

(a) Notwithstanding any of the provisions of article forty-five of the civil practice law and rules, any physician, psychologist, nurse or social worker who has treated a child witness may testify at a hearing conducted pursuant to subdivision five of this section concerning the treatment of such child witness as such treatment relates to the issue presented at the hearing, provided that any otherwise applicable statutory privileges concerning communications between the child witness and such physician, psychologist, nurse or social worker in connection with such treatment shall not be deemed waived by such testimony alone, except to the limited extent of permitting the court alone to examine in camera reports, records or documents, if any, prepared by such physician, psychologist, nurse or social worker. If upon such examination the court determines that such reports, records or documents, or any one or portion thereof, contain information material and relevant to the issue of whether the child witness is a vulnerable child witness, the court shall disclose such information to both the attorney for the defendant and the district attorney.

(b) At any time after a motion has been made pursuant to subdivision one of this section, upon the demand of the other party the moving party must furnish the demanding party with a copy of any and all of such records, reports or other documents in the possession of such other party and must, in addition, supply the court with a copy of all such reports, records or other documents which are the subject of the demand. At any time after a demand has been made pursuant to this paragraph, the moving party may demand that property of the same kind or character in possession of the party that originally made such demand be furnished to the moving party and, if so furnished, be supplied, in addition, to the court.

9.

(a) Prior to the commencement of the hearing conducted pursuant to subdivision five of this section, the district attorney shall, subject to a protective order, comply with the provisions of subdivision one of section 240.45 of this chapter as they concern any witness whom the district attorney intends to call at the hearing and the child witness.

(b) Before a defendant calls a witness at such hearing, he or she must, subject to a protective order, comply with the provisions of subdivision two of section 240.45 of this chapter as they concern all the witnesses the defendant intends to call at such hearing.

10. The court may consider, in determining whether there are factors which would cause the child witness to suffer serious mental or emotional harm, a finding that any one or more of the following circumstances have been established by clear and convincing evidence:

(a) The manner of the commission of the offense of which the defendant is accused was particularly heinous or was characterized by aggravating circumstances.

(b) The child witness is particularly young or otherwise particularly subject to psychological harm on account of a physical or mental condition which existed before the alleged commission of the offense.

(c) At the time of the alleged offense, the defendant occupied a position of authority with respect to the child witness.

(d) The offense or offenses charged were part of an ongoing course of conduct committed by the defendant against the child witness over an extended period of time.

(e) A deadly weapon or dangerous instrument was allegedly used during the commission of the crime.

(f) The defendant has inflicted serious physical injury upon the child witness.

(g) A threat, express or implied, of physical violence to the child witness or a third person if the child witness were to report the incident to any person or communicate information to or cooperate with a court, grand jury, prosecutor, police officer or peace officer concerning the incident has been made by or on behalf of the defendant.

(h) A threat, express or implied, of the incarceration of a parent or guardian of the child witness, the removal of the child witness from the family or the dissolution of the family of the child witness if the child witness were to report the incident to any person or communicate information to or cooperate with a court, grand jury, prosecutor, police officer or peace officer concerning the incident has been made by or on behalf of the defendant.

(i) A witness other than the child witness has received a threat of physical violence directed at such witness or to a third person by or on behalf of the defendant.

(j) The defendant, at the time of the inquiry, (i) is living in the same household with the child witness, (ii) has ready access to the child witness or (iii) is providing substantial financial support for the child witness.

(k) The child witness has previously been the victim of an offense defined in article one hundred thirty of the penal law or incest as defined in section 255.25, 255.26 or 255.27 of such law.

(l) According to expert testimony, the child witness would be particularly suceptible [susceptible]* to psychological harm if required to testify in open court or in the physical presence of the defendant.

11. Irrespective of whether a motion was made pursuant to subdivision one of this section, the court, at the request of either party or on its own motion, may decide that a child witness may be vulnerable based on its own observations that a child witness who has been called to testify at a criminal proceeding is suffering severe mental or emotional harm and therefore is physically or mentally unable to testify or to continue to testify in open court or in the physical presence of the defendant and that the use of live, two-way closed-circuit television is necessary to enable the child witness to testify. If the court so decides, it must conduct the same hearing that subdivision five of this section requires when a motion is made pursuant to subdivision one of this section, and it must make findings of fact pursuant to subdivisions nine and eleven of this section, before determining that the child witness is vulnerable.

12. In deciding whether a child witness is vulnerable, the court shall make findings of fact which reflect the causal relationship between the existence of any one or more of the factors set forth in subdivision nine of this section or other relevant factors which the court finds are established and the determination that the child witness is vulnerable. If the court is satisfied that the child witness is vulnerable and that, under the facts and circumstances of the particular case, the defendant's constitutional rights to an impartial jury or of confrontation will not be impaired, it may enter an order granting the application for the use of live, two-way closed-circuit television.

13. When the court has determined that a child witness is a vulnerable child witness, it shall make a specific finding as to whether placing the defendant and the child witness in the same room during the testimony of the child witness will contribute to the likelihood that the child witness will suffer severe mental or emotional harm. If the court finds that placing the defendant and the child witness in the same room during the testimony of the child witness will contribute to the likelihood that the child witness will suffer severe mental or emotional harm, the order entered pursuant to subdivision eleven of this section shall direct that the defendant remain in the courtroom during the testimony of the vulnerable child witness.

§ 65.30. [Expires and repealed Sept 1, 2019] Closed-circuit television; special testimonial procedures

1. When the court has entered an order pursuant to section 65.20, the testimony of the vulnerable child witness shall be taken in the testimonial room and the image and voice of the vulnerable child witness, as well as the image of all other persons other than the operator present in the testimonial room, shall be transmitted live by means of closed-circuit television to the courtroom. The courtroom shall be equipped with monitors sufficient to permit the judge, jury, defendant and attorneys to observe the demeanor of the vulnerable child witness during his or her testimony. Unless the courtroom has been

closed pursuant to court order, the public shall also be permitted to hear the testimony and view the image of the vulnerable child witness.

2. In all instances, the image of the jury shall be simultaneously transmitted to the vulnerable child witness in the testimonial room. If the court order issued pursuant to section 65.20 specifies that the vulnerable child witness shall testify outside the physical presence of the defendant, the image of the defendant and the image and voice of the person examining the vulnerable child witness shall also be simultaneously transmitted to the vulnerable child witness in the testimonial room.

3. The operator shall place herself or himself and the closed-circuit television equipment in a position that permits the entire testimony of the vulnerable child witness to be transmitted to the courtroom but limits the ability of the vulnerable child witness to see or hear the operator or the equipment.

4. Notwithstanding any provision of this article, if the court in a particular case involving a vulnerable child witness determines that there is no live, two-way closed-circuit television equipment available in the court or another court in the county or which can be transported to the court from another county or that such equipment, if available, is technologically inadequate to protect the constitutional rights of the defendant, it shall not permit the use of the closed-circuit television procedures authorized by this article.

5. If the order of the court entered pursuant to section 65.20 requires that the defendant remain in the courtroom, the attorney for the defendant and the district attorney shall also remain in the courtroom unless the court is satisfied that their presence in the testimonial room will not impede full and private communication between the defendant and his or her attorney and will not encourage the jury to draw an inference adverse to the interest of the defendant.

6. Upon request of the defendant, the court shall instruct the jury that they are to draw no inference from the use of live, two-way closed-circuit television in the examination of the vulnerable child witness.

7. The vulnerable child witness shall testify under oath except as specified in subdivision two of section 60.20. The examination and cross-examination of the vulnerable child witness shall, in all other respects, be conducted in the same manner as if the vulnerable child witness had testified in the courtroom.

8. When the testimony of the vulnerable child witness is transmitted from the testimonial room into the courtroom, the court stenographer shall record the textimony [testimony]* in the same manner as if the vulnerable child witness had testified in the courtroom.

Article 70 Standards of Proof

§ 70.10. Standards of proof; definitions of terms

The following definitions are applicable to this chapter:

1. "Legally sufficient evidence" means competent evidence which, if accepted as true, would establish every element of an offense charged and the defendant's commission thereof; except that such evidence is not legally sufficient when corroboration required by law is absent.

2. "Reasonable cause to believe that a person has committed an offense" exists when evidence or information which appears reliable discloses facts or circumstances which

are collectively of such weight and persuasiveness as to convince a person of ordinary intelligence, judgment and experience that it is reasonably likely that such offense was committed and that such person committed it. Except as otherwise provided in this chapter, such apparently reliable evidence may include or consist of hearsay.

§ 70.20. Standards of proof for conviction

No conviction of an offense by verdict is valid unless based upon trial evidence which is legally sufficient and which establishes beyond a reasonable doubt every element of such offense and the defendant's commission thereof.

Part TWO The Principal Proceedings

Title H Preliminary Proceedings in Local Criminal Court

Article 95 Pre-Criminal Proceeding Settlements

§ 95.00. Pre-criminal proceeding settlement. [Expires and repealed March 31, 2019]

When a county district attorney of a county located in a city of one million or more recovers monies before the filing of an accusatory instrument as defined in subdivision one of section 1.20 of this chapter, after injured parties have been appropriately compensated, the district attorney's office shall retain a percentage of the remaining such monies in recognition that such monies were recovered as a result of investigations undertaken by such office. For each recovery the total amount of such monies to be retained by the county district attorney's office shall equal ten percent of the first twenty-five million dollars received by such office, plus seven and one-half percent of such monies received by such office in excess of twenty-five million dollars but less than fifty million dollars, plus five percent of any such monies received by such office in excess of fifty million dollars but less than one hundred million dollars, plus one percent of such monies received by such office in excess of one hundred million dollars. The remainder of such monies shall be paid by the district attorney's office to the state and to the county in equal amounts within thirty days of receipt, where disposition of such monies is not otherwise prescribed by law. Monies distributed to a county district attorney's office pursuant to this section shall be used to enhance law enforcement efforts within the state of New York. On December first of each year, every district attorney shall provide the governor, temporary president of the senate and speaker of the assembly with an annual report detailing the total amount of monies received as described herein by his or her office and a description of how and where such funds were distributed by his or her office but shall not include a description of the distribution of monies where the disclosure of such information would interfere with a law enforcement investigation or a judicial proceeding. The report shall include a detailed description of any entity to which funds are distributed, including but not limited to, whether it is a profit or not-for-profit entity, where it is located, and the intended use of the monies distributed, and shall state the law enforcement purpose.

§ 100.05. Commencement of action; in general

A criminal action is commenced by the filing of an accusatory instrument with a criminal court, or, in the case of a juvenile offender or adolescent offender, other than an adolescent offender charged with only a violation or traffic infraction, the youth part of the superior court, and if more than one such instrument is filed in the course of the same criminal action, such action commences when the first of such instruments is filed. The only way in which a criminal action can be commenced in a superior court, other than a criminal action against a juvenile offender or adolescent offender is by the filing therewith by a grand jury of an indictment against a defendant who has never been held by a local criminal court for the action of such grand jury with respect to any charge contained in such indictment. Otherwise, a criminal action can be commenced only in a local criminal court, by the filing therewith of a local criminal court accusatory instrument, namely:

1. An information; or
2. A simplified information; or
3. A prosecutor's information; or
4. A misdemeanor complaint; or
5. A felony complaint.

§ 100.07. Commencement of action; effect of family court proceeding

A criminal court shall have concurrent jurisdiction over cognizable family offenses, as defined in subdivision one of section 530.11 of this chapter and in subdivision one of section eight hundred twelve of the family court act, notwithstanding the fact that a family court has or may be exercising jurisdiction over a petition under article eight of the family court act containing substantially the same allegations as are set forth in the accusatory instrument or indictment.

§ 100.10. Local criminal court and youth part of the superior court accusatory instruments; definitions thereof

1. An "information" is a verified written accusation by a person, filed with a local criminal court, charging one or more other persons with the commission of one or more offenses, none of which is a felony. It may serve as a basis both for the commencement of a criminal action and for the prosecution thereof in a local criminal court.

2.

(a) A "simplified traffic information" is a written accusation by a police officer, or other public servant authorized by law to issue same, filed with a local criminal court, which charges a person with the commission of one or more traffic infractions and/or misdemeanors relating to traffic, and which, being in a brief or simplified form prescribed by the commissioner of motor vehicles, designates the offense or offenses charged but contains no factual allegations of an evidentiary nature supporting such charge or charges. It serves as a basis for commencement of a criminal action for such traffic offenses, alternative to the charging thereof by a regular information, and, under circumstances prescribed in section 100.25, it may serve, either in whole or in part, as a basis for prosecution of such charges.

(b) A "simplified parks information" is a written accusation by a police officer or other public servant authorized by law to issue same, filed with a local criminal court, which charges a person with the commission of one or more offenses, other than a felony, for which a uniform simplified parks information may be issued pursuant to the parks and recreation law and navigation law, and which being in a brief or simplified form prescribed by the commissioner of parks and recreation, designates the offense or offenses charged but contains no factual allegations of an evidentiary nature supporting such charge or charges. It serves as a basis for commencement of a criminal action for such offenses, alternative to the charging thereof by a regular information, and, under circumstances parescribed [prescribed]* in section 100.25, it may serve, either in whole or in part, as a basis for prosecution of such charges.

(c) A "simplified environmental conservation information" is a written accusation by a police officer or other public servant authorized by law to issue same, filed with a local criminal court, which charges a person with the commission of one or more offenses, other than a felony, for which a uniform simplified environmental conservation information may be issued pursuant to the environmental conservation law, and which being in a brief or simplified form prescribed by the commissioner of environmental conservation, designates the offense or offenses charged but contains no factual allegations of an evidentiary nature supporting such charge or charges. It serves as a basis for commencement of a criminal action for such offenses, alternative to the charging thereof by a regular information, and, under circumstances prescribed in section 100.25, it may serve, either in whole or in part, as a basis for prosecution of such charges.

3. A "prosecutor's information" is a written accusation by a district attorney, filed with a local criminal court, either (a) at the direction of a grand jury pursuant to section 190.70, or (b) at the direction of a local criminal court pursuant to section 180.50 or 180.70, or (c) at the district attorney's own instance pursuant to subdivision two of section 100.50, or (d) at the direction of a superior court pursuant to subdivision one-a of section 210.20, charging one or more persons with the commission of one or more offenses, none of which is a felony. It serves as a basis for the prosecution of a criminal action, but it commences a criminal action only where it results from a grand jury direction issued in a case not previously commenced in a local criminal court.

4. A "misdemeanor complaint" is a verified written accusation by a person, filed with a local criminal court, charging one or more other persons with the commission of one or more offenses, at least one of which is a misdemeanor and none of which is a felony. It serves as a basis for the commencement of a criminal action, but it may serve as a basis for prosecution thereof only where a defendant has waived prosecution by information pursuant to subdivision three of section 170.65.

5. A "felony complaint" is a verified written accusation by a person, filed with a local criminal court, or youth part of the superior court, charging one or more other persons with the commission of one or more felonies. It serves as a basis for the commencement of a criminal action, but not as a basis for prosecution thereof.

§ 100.15. Information, misdemeanor complaint and felony complaint; form and content

1. An information, a misdemeanor complaint and a felony complaint must each specify the name of the court with which it is filed and the title of the action, and must be subscribed and verified by a person known as the "complainant." The complainant may be any person having knowledge, whether personal or upon information and belief, of the commission of the offense or offenses charged. Each instrument must contain an accusatory part and a factual part. The complainant's verification of the instrument is deemed to apply only to the factual part thereof and not to the accusatory part.

2. The accusatory part of each such instrument must designate the offense or offenses charged. As in the case of an indictment, and subject to the rules of joinder applicable to indictments, two or more offenses may be charged in separate counts. Also as in the case of an indictment, such instrument may charge two or more defendants provided that all such defendants are jointly charged with every offense alleged therein.

3. The factual part of such instrument must contain a statement of the complainant alleging facts of an evidentiary character supporting or tending to support the charges. Where more than one offense is charged, the factual part should consist of a single factual account applicable to all the counts of the accusatory part. The factual allegations may be based either upon personal knowledge of the complainant or upon information and belief. Nothing contained in this section, however, limits or affects the requirement, prescribed in subdivision one of section 100.40, that in order for an information or a count thereof to be sufficient on its face, every element of the offense charged and the defendant's commission thereof must be supported by non-hearsay allegations of such information and/or any supporting depositions.

4. Where a felony complaint charges a violent felony offense defined in section 70.02 of the penal law and such offense is an armed felony as defined in subdivision forty-one of section 1.20,

(a) the accusatory part of the instrument must designate the offense as an armed felony, and (b) the factual part of the instrument must allege facts of an evidentiary character supporting or tending to support such designation.

§ 100.20. Supporting deposition; definition, form and content

A supporting deposition is a written instrument accompanying or filed in connection with an information, a simplified information, a misdemeanor complaint or a felony complaint, subscribed and verified by a person other than the complainant of such accusatory instrument, and containing factual allegations of an evidentiary character, based either upon personal knowledge or upon information and belief, which supplement those of the accusatory instrument and support or tend to support the charge or charges contained therein.

§ 100.25. Simplified information; form and content; defendant's right to supporting deposition; notice requirement

1. A simplified information must be substantially in the form prescribed by the commissioner of motor vehicles, the commissioner of parks and recreation, or the commissioner of environmental conservation, as the case may be.

2. A defendant charged by a simplified information is, upon a timely request, entitled as a matter of right to have filed with the court and served upon him, or if he is

represented by an attorney, upon his attorney, a supporting deposition of the complainant police officer or public servant, containing allegations of fact, based either upon personal knowledge or upon information and belief, providing reasonable cause to believe that the defendant committed the offense or offenses charged. To be timely, such a request must, except as otherwise provided herein and in subdivision three of this section, be made before entry of a plea of guilty to the charge specified and before commencement of a trial thereon, but not later than thirty days after the date the defendant is directed to appear in court as such date appears upon the simplified information and upon the appearance ticket issued pursuant thereto. If the defendant's request is mailed to the court, the request must be mailed within such thirty day period. Upon such a request, the court must order the complainant police officer or public servant to serve a copy of such supporting deposition upon the defendant or his attorney, within thirty days of the date such request is received by the court, or at least five days before trial, whichever is earlier, and to file such supporting deposition with the court together with proof of service thereof. Notwithstanding any provision to the contrary, where a defendant is issued an appearance ticket in conjunction with the offense charged in the simplified information and the appearance ticket fails to conform with the requirements of subdivision two of section 150.10, a request is timely when made not later than thirty days after (a) entry of the defendant's plea of not guilty when he or she has been arraigned in person, or (b) written notice to the defendant of his or her right to receive a supporting deposition when a plea of not guilty has been submitted by mail.

3. When at least one of the offenses charged in a simplified information is a misdemeanor, the court may, upon motion of the defendant, for good cause shown and consistent with the interest of justice, permit the defendant to request a supporting deposition beyond the thirty day request period set forth in subdivision two of this section provided, however, that no motion may be brought under this subdivision after ninety days has elapsed from the date the defendant is directed to appear in court as such date appears upon the simplified information and upon the appearance ticket issued pursuant thereto.

4. Notwithstanding any provision of law to the contrary, where a person is charged by a simplified information and is served with an appearance ticket as defined in section 150.10, such appearance ticket shall contain the following language: "NOTICE: YOU ARE ENTITLED TO RECEIVE A SUPPORTING DEPOSITION FURTHER EXPLAINING THE CHARGES PROVIDED YOU REQUEST SUCH SUPPORTING DEPOSITION WITHIN THIRTY DAYS FROM THE DATE YOU ARE DIRECTED TO APPEAR IN COURT AS SET FORTH ON THIS APPEARANCE TICKET. DO YOU REQUEST A SUPPORTING DEPOSITION? [ ]YES [ ]NO"

§ 100.30. Information, misdemeanor complaint, felony complaint, supporting deposition and proof of service of supporting deposition; verification

1. An information, a misdemeanor complaint, a felony complaint, a supporting deposition, and proof of service of a supporting deposition may be verified in any of the following manners:

(a) Such instrument may be sworn to before the court with which it is filed.

(b) Such instrument may be sworn to before a desk officer in charge at a police station or police headquarters or any of his superior officers.

(c) Where such instrument is filed by any public servant following the issuance and service of an appearance ticket, and where by express provision of law another designated public servant is authorized to administer the oath with respect to such instrument, it may be sworn to before such public servant.

(d) Such instrument may bear a form notice that false statements made therein are punishable as a class A misdemeanor pursuant to section 210.45 of the penal law, and such form notice together with the subscription of the deponent constitute a verification of the instrument.

(e) Such instrument may be sworn to before a notary public.

2. An instrument specified in subdivision one may be verified in any manner prescribed therein unless in a particular case the court expressly directs verification in a particular manner prescribed in said subdivision one.

§ 100.35. Prosecutor's information; form and content

A prosecutor's information must contain the name of the local criminal court with which it is filed and the title of the action, and must be subscribed by the district attorney by whom it is filed. Otherwise it should be in the form prescribed for an indictment, pursuant to section 200.50, and must, in one or more counts, allege the offense or offenses charged and a plain and concise statement of the conduct constituting each such offense. The rules prescribed in sections 200.20 and 200.40 governing joinder of different offenses and defendants in a single indictment are also applicable to a prosecutor's information.

§ 100.40. Local criminal court and youth part of the superior court accusatory instruments; sufficiency on face

1. An information, or a count thereof, is sufficient on its face when:

(a) It substantially conforms to the requirements prescribed in section 100.15; and

(b) The allegations of the factual part of the information, together with those of any supporting depositions which may accompany it, provide reasonable cause to believe that the defendant committed the offense charged in the accusatory part of the information; and

(c) Non-hearsay allegations of the factual part of the information and/or of any supporting depositions establish, if true, every element of the offense charged and the defendant's commission thereof.

2. A simplified information is sufficient on its face when, as provided by subdivision one of section 100.25, it substantially conforms to the requirement therefor prescribed by or pursuant to law; provided that when the filing of a supporting deposition is ordered by the court pursuant to subdivision two of said section 100.25, a failure of the complainant police officer or public servant to comply with such order within the time provided by subdivision two of said section 100.25 renders the simplified information insufficient on its face.

3. A prosecutor's information, or a count thereof, is sufficient on its face when it substantially conforms to the requirements prescribed in section 100.35.

4. A misdemeanor complaint or a felony complaint, or a count thereof, is sufficient on its face when:

(a) It substantially conforms to the requirements prescribed in section 100.15; and

(b) The allegations of the factual part of such accusatory instrument and/or any supporting depositions which may accompany it, provide reasonable cause to believe that the defendant committed the offense charged in the accusatory part of such instrument.

§ 100.45. Information, prosecutor's information, misdemeanor complaint; severance, consolidation, amendment, bill of particulars

1. Where appropriate, the provisions of sections 200.20 and 200.40 and paragraph (n) of subdivision four of section 20.40 of this chapter, governing severance of counts of an indictment and severance of defendants for trial purposes, and governing consolidation of indictments for trial purposes, apply to informations, to prosecutor's informations and to misdemeanor complaints.

2. The provisions of section 200.70 governing amendment of indictments apply to prosecutor's informations.

3. At any time before the entry of a plea of guilty to or the commencement of a trial of an information, the court may, upon application of the people and with notice to the defendant and opportunity to be heard, order the amendment of the accusatory part of such information by addition of a count charging an offense supported by the allegations of the factual part of such information and/or any supporting depositions which may accompany it. In such case, the defendant must be accorded any reasonable adjournment necessitated by the amendment.

4. The provisions of section 200.95, governing bills of particulars with respect to indictments, apply to informations, to misdemeanor complaints and to prosecutor's informations.

§ 100.50. Superseding informations and prosecutor's informations

1. If at any time before entry of a plea of guilty to or commencement of a trial of an information or a prosecutor's information, another information or, as the case may be, another prosecutor's information is filed with the same local criminal court charging the defendant with an offense charged in the first instrument, the first such instrument is, with respect to such offense, superseded by the second and, upon the defendant's arraignment upon the latter, the count of the first instrument charging such offense must be dismissed by the court. The first instrument is not, however, superseded with respect to any count contained therein which charges an offense not charged in the second instrument.

2. At any time before entry of a plea of guilty to or commencement of a trial of an information, the district attorney may file with the local criminal court a prosecutor's information charging any offenses supported, pursuant to the standards prescribed in subdivision one of section 100.40, by the allegations of the factual part of the original information and/or any supporting depositions which may accompany it. In such case, the original information is superseded by the prosecutor's information and, upon the defendant's arraignment upon the latter, is deemed dismissed.

3. A misdemeanor complaint must or may be replaced and superseded by an information pursuant to the provisions of section 170.65.

§ 100.55. Local criminal court accusatory instruments; in what courts filed

1. Any local criminal court accusatory instrument may be filed with a district court of a particular county when an offense charged therein was allegedly committed in such county or that part thereof over which such court has jurisdiction.

2. Any local criminal court accusatory instrument may be filed with the New York City criminal court when an offense charged therein was allegedly committed in New York City.

3. Any local criminal court accusatory instrument may be filed with a city court of a particular city when an offense charged therein was allegedly committed in such city.

4. An information, a simplified information, a prosecutor's information or a misdemeanor complaint may be filed with a town court of a particular town when an offense charged therein was allegedly committed anywhere in such town other than in a village thereof having a village court.

5. An information, a simplified information, a prosecutor's information or a misdemeanor complaint may be filed with a village court of a particular village when an offense charged therein was allegedly committed in such village.

6. A felony complaint may be filed with any town court or village court of a particular county when a felony charged therein was allegedly committed in some town of such county. Such court need not be that of the town or village in which such felony was allegedly committed.

7. An information, a simplified information, a misdemeanor complaint or a felony complaint may be filed with a judge of a superior court sitting as a local criminal court when an offense charged therein was allegedly committed in a county in which such judge is then present and in which he either resides or is currently holding, or has been assigned to hold, a term of a superior court.

8. Where it is otherwise expressly provided by law that a particular kind of accusatory instrument may under given circumstances be filed with a local criminal court other than one authorized by this section, nothing contained in this section precludes the filing of such accusatory instrument accordingly.

9. In any case where each of two or more local criminal courts is authorized as a proper court with which to file an accusatory instrument, such an instrument may, in the absence of an express provision of law to the contrary, be filed with any one of such courts but not with more than one.

10. For purposes of this section, an offense is "committed in" a particular county, city, town, village or other specified political subdivision or area, not only when it is in fact committed therein but also when it is, for other reasons specified in sections 20.40 and 20.50, prosecutable in the criminal courts having geographical jurisdiction over such political subdivision or area.

11. Notwithstanding any provision of law to the contrary, a local criminal court accusatory instrument may be filed with a local criminal court while it is operating an off-hours arraignment part designated in accordance with paragraph (w) of subdivision one of section two hundred twelve of the judiciary law provided that an offense charged

therein was allegedly committed in the county in which the local criminal court is located.

§ 100.60. Youth part of the superior court accusatory instruments; in what courts filed

Any youth part of the superior court accusatory instrument may be filed with the youth part of the superior court of a particular county when an offense charged therein was allegedly committed in such county or that part thereof over which such court has jurisdiction.

Article 110 Requiring Defendant's Appearance in Local Criminal Court or Youth Part of Superior Court for Arraignment

§ 110.10. Methods of requiring defendant's appearance in local criminal court or youth part of the superior court for arraignment; in general

1. After a criminal action has been commenced in a local criminal court or youth part of the superior court by the filing of an accusatory instrument therewith, a defendant who has not been arraigned in the action and has not come under the control of the court may under certain circumstances be compelled or required to appear for arraignment upon such accusatory instrument by:

(a) The issuance and execution of a warrant of arrest, as provided in article one hundred twenty; or

(b) The issuance and service upon him of a summons, as provided in article one hundred thirty; or

(c) Procedures provided in articles five hundred sixty, five hundred seventy, five hundred eighty, five hundred ninety and six hundred for securing attendance of defendants in criminal actions who are not at liberty within the state.

2. Although no criminal action against a person has been commenced in any court, he may under certain circumstances be compelled or required to appear in a local criminal court or youth part of a superior court for arraignment upon an accusatory instrument to be filed therewith at or before the time of his appearance by:

(a) An arrest made without a warrant, as provided in article one hundred forty; or

(b) The issuance and service upon him of an appearance ticket, as provided in article one hundred fifty.

§ 110.20. Local criminal court or youth part of the superior court accusatory instruments; notice thereof to district attorney

When a criminal action in which a crime is charged is commenced in a local criminal court, or youth part of the superior court other than the criminal court of the city of New York, a copy of the accusatory instrument shall be promptly transmitted to the appropriate district attorney upon or prior to the arraignment of the defendant on the accusatory instrument. If a police officer or a peace officer is the complainant or the filer of a simplified information, or has arrested the defendant or brought him before the local criminal court or youth part of the superior court on behalf of an arresting person pursuant to subdivision one of section 140.20, such officer or his agency shall transmit the copy of the accusatory instrument to the appropriate district attorney. In all other cases, the clerk of the court in which the defendant is arraigned shall so transmit it.

§ 120.10. Warrant of arrest; definition, function, form and content

1. A warrant of arrest is a process issued by a local criminal court directing a police officer to arrest a defendant designated in an accusatory instrument filed with such court and to bring him before such court in connection with such instrument. The sole function of a warrant of arrest is to achieve a defendant's court appearance in a criminal action for the purpose of arraignment upon the accusatory instrument by which such action was commenced.

2. A warrant of arrest must be subscribed by the issuing judge and must state or contain (a) the name of the issuing court, and (b) the date of issuance of the warrant, and (c) the name or title of an offense charged in the underlying accusatory instrument, and (d) the name of the defendant to be arrested or, if such be unknown, any name or description by which he can be identified with reasonable certainty, and (e) the police officer or officers to whom the warrant is addressed, and (f) a direction that such officer arrest the defendant and bring him before the issuing court.

3. A warrant of arrest may be addressed to a classification of police officers, or to two or more classifications thereof, as well as to a designated individual police officer or officers. Multiple copies of such a warrant may be issued.

§ 120.20. Warrant of arrest; when issuable

1. When a criminal action has been commenced in a local criminal court or youth part of the superior court by the filing therewith of an accusatory instrument, other than a simplified traffic information, against a defendant who has not been arraigned upon such accusatory instrument and has not come under the control of the court with respect thereto:

(a) such court may, if such accusatory instrument is sufficient on its face, issue a warrant for such defendant's arrest; or

(b) if such accusatory instrument is not sufficient on its face as prescribed in section 100.40, and if the court is satisfied that on the basis of the available facts or evidence it would be impossible to draw and file an accusatory instrument that is sufficient on its face, the court must dismiss the accusatory instrument.

2. Even though such accusatory instrument is sufficient on its face, the court may refuse to issue a warrant of arrest based thereon until it has further satisfied itself, by inquiry or examination of witnesses, that there is reasonable cause to believe that the defendant committed an offense charged. Upon such inquiry or examination, the court may examine, under oath or otherwise, any available person whom it believes may possess knowledge concerning the subject matter of the charge.

3. Notwithstanding the provisions of subdivision one, if a summons may be issued in lieu of a warrant of arrest pursuant to section 130.20, and if the court is satisfied that the defendant will respond thereto, it may not issue a warrant of arrest. Upon the request of the district attorney, in lieu of a warrant of arrest or summons, the court may instead authorize the district attorney to direct the defendant to appear for arraignment on a designated date if it is satisfied that the defendant will so appear.

§ 120.30. Warrant of arrest; by what courts issuable and in what courts returnable

1. A warrant of arrest may be issued only by the local criminal court or youth part of the superior court with which the underlying accusatory instrument has been filed, and it may be made returnable in such issuing court only.

2. The particular local criminal court or courts or youth part of the superior court with which any particular local criminal court or youth part of the superior court accusatory instrument may be filed for the purpose of obtaining a warrant of arrest are determined, generally, by the provisions of section 100.55 or 100.60 of this title. If, however, a particular accusatory instrument may pursuant to said section 100.55 be filed with a particular town court and such town court is not available at the time such instrument is sought to be filed and a warrant obtained, such accusatory instrument may be filed with the town court of any adjoining town of the same county. If such instrument may be filed pursuant to said section 100.55 with a particular village court and such village court is not available at the time, it may be filed with the town court of the town embracing such village, or if such town court is not available either, with the town court of any adjoining town of the same county.

§ 120.40. Warrant of arrest; attaching accusatory instrument to warrant of town court, village court or city court

A town court, village court or city court which issues a warrant of arrest may attach thereto a duplicate copy of the underlying accusatory instrument. If one or more duplicate copies of the warrant are issued, such court may attach as many copies of such accusatory instrument to copies of such warrant as it chooses. In any case where, pursuant to subdivision five of section 120.90, a defendant arrested upon such a warrant of arrest is brought before a local criminal court other than the town court, village court or city court in which the warrant is returnable, a copy of the accusatory instrument constitutes a valid basis for arraignment, as provided in subdivision one of section 170.15.

§ 120.50. Warrant of arrest; to what police officers addressed

A warrant of arrest may be addressed to any police officer or classification of police officers whose geographical area of employment embraces either the place where the offense charged was allegedly committed or the locality of the court by which the warrant is issued.

§ 120.55. Warrant of arrest; defendant under parole or probation supervision

If the defendant named within a warrant of arrest issued by a local criminal court or youth part of the superior court pursuant to the provisions of this article, or by a superior court issued pursuant to subdivision three of section 210.10 of this chapter, is under the supervision of the state department of corrections and community supervision or a local or state probation department, then a warrant for his or her arrest may be executed by a parole officer or probation officer, when authorized by his or her probation director, within his or her geographical area of employment. The execution of the warrant by a parole officer or probation officer shall be upon the same conditions and conducted in the same manner as provided for execution of a warrant by a police officer.

§ 120.60. Warrant of arrest; what police officers may execute

1. A warrant of arrest may be executed by (a) any police officer to whom it is addressed, or (b) any other police officer delegated to execute it under circumstances prescribed in subdivisions two and three.

2. A police officer to whom a warrant of arrest is addressed may delegate another officer to whom it is not addressed to execute such warrant as his agent when:

(a) He has reasonable cause to believe that the defendant is in a particular county other than the one in which the warrant is returnable; and

(b) The warrant is, pursuant to section 120.70, executable in such other county without endorsement by a local criminal court thereof; and

(c) The geographical area of employment of the delegated police officer embraces the locality where the arrest is to be made.

3. Under circumstances specified in subdivision two, the police officer to whom the warrant is addressed may inform the delegated officer, by telecommunication, mail or any other means, of the issuance of the warrant, of the offense charged in the underlying accusatory instrument and of all other pertinent details, and may request him to act as his agent in arresting the defendant pursuant to such warrant. Upon such request, the delegated police officer is to the same extent as the delegating officer, authorized to make such arrest pursuant to the warrant within the geographical area of such delegated officer's employment. Upon so arresting the defendant, he must proceed as provided in subdivisions two and four of section 120.90.

§ 120.70. Warrant of arrest; where executable

1. A warrant of arrest issued by a district court, by the New York City criminal court, the youth part of a superior court or by a superior court judge sitting as a local criminal court may be executed anywhere in the state.

2. A warrant of arrest issued by a city court, a town court or a village court may be executed:

(a) In the county of issuance or in any adjoining county; or

(b) Anywhere else in the state upon the written endorsement thereon of a local criminal court of the county in which the arrest is to be made. When so endorsed, the warrant is deemed the process of the endorsing court as well as that of the issuing court.

§ 120.80. Warrant of arrest; when and how executed

1. A warrant of arrest may be executed on any day of the week and at any hour of the day or night.

2. Unless encountering physical resistance, flight or other factors rendering normal procedure impractical, the arresting police officer must inform the defendant that a warrant for his arrest for the offense designated therein has been issued. Upon request of the defendant, the officer must show him the warrant if he has it in his possession. The officer need not have the warrant in his possession, and, if he has not, he must show it to the defendant upon request as soon after the arrest as possible.

3. In order to effect the arrest, the police officer may use such physical force as is justifiable pursuant to section 35.30 of the penal law.

4. In order to effect the arrest, the police officer may, under circumstances and in the manner prescribed in this subdivision, enter any premises in which he reasonably

believes the defendant to be present; provided, however, that where the premises in which the officer reasonably believes the defendant to be present is the dwelling of a third party who is not the subject of the arrest warrant, the officer shall proceed in the manner specified in article 690 of this chapter. Before such entry, he must give, or make reasonable effort to give, notice of his authority and purpose to an occupant thereof, unless there is reasonable cause to believe that the giving of such notice will:

(a) Result in the defendant escaping or attempting to escape; or

(b) Endanger the life or safety of the officer or another person; or

(c) Result in the destruction, damaging or secretion of material evidence.

5. If the officer is authorized to enter premises without giving notice of his authority and purpose, or if after giving such notice he is not admitted, he may enter such premises, and by a breaking if necessary.

§ 120.90. Warrant of arrest; procedure after arrest

1. Upon arresting a defendant for any offense pursuant to a warrant of arrest in the county in which the warrant is returnable or in any adjoining county, or upon so arresting him or her for a felony in any other county, a police officer, if he or she be one to whom the warrant is addressed, must without unnecessary delay bring the defendant before the local criminal court or youth part of the superior court in which such warrant is returnable, provided that, where a local criminal court or youth part of the superior court in the county in which the warrant is returnable hereunder is operating an off-hours arraignment part designated in accordance with paragraph (w) of subdivision one of section two hundred twelve of the judiciary law at the time of defendant's return, such police officer may bring the defendant before such local criminal court or youth part of the superior court.

2. Upon arresting a defendant for any offense pursuant to a warrant of arrest in a county adjoining the county in which the warrant is returnable, or upon so arresting him for a felony in any other county, a police officer, if he be one delegated to execute the warrant pursuant to section 120.60, must without unnecessary delay deliver the defendant or cause him to be delivered to the custody of the officer by whom he was so delegated, and the latter must then proceed as provided in subdivision one.

3. Upon arresting a defendant for an offense other than a felony pursuant to a warrant of arrest in a county other than the one in which the warrant is returnable or one adjoining it, a police officer, if he be one to whom the warrant is addressed, must inform the defendant that he has a right to appear before a local criminal court of the county of arrest for the purpose of being released on his own recognizance or having bail fixed. If the defendant does not desire to avail himself of such right, the officer must request him to endorse such fact upon the warrant, and upon such endorsement the officer must without unnecessary delay bring him before the court in which the warrant is returnable. If the defendant does desire to avail himself of such right, or if he refuses to make the aforementioned endorsement, the officer must without unnecessary delay bring him before a local criminal court of the county of arrest. Such court must release the defendant on his own recognizance or fix bail for his appearance on a specified date in the court in which the warrant is returnable. If the defendant is in default of bail, the

officer must without unnecessary delay bring him before the court in which the warrant is returnable.

4. Upon arresting a defendant for an offense other than a felony pursuant to a warrant of arrest in a county other than the one in which the warrant is returnable or one adjoining it, a police officer, if he be one delegated to execute the warrant pursuant to section 120.60, may hold the defendant in custody in the county of arrest for a period not exceeding two hours for the purpose of delivering him to the custody of the officer by whom he was delegated to execute such warrant. If the delegating officer receives custody of the defendant during such period, he must proceed as provided in subdivision three. Otherwise, the delegated officer must inform the defendant that he has a right to appear before a local criminal court for the purpose of being released on his own recognizance or having bail fixed. If the defendant does not desire to avail himself of such right, the officer must request him to make, sign and deliver to him a written statement of such fact, and if the defendant does so, the officer must retain custody of him but must without unnecessary delay deliver him or cause him to be delivered to the custody of the delegating police officer. If the defendant does desire to avail himself of such right, or if he refuses to make and deliver the aforementioned statement, the delegated or arresting officer must without unnecessary delay bring him before a local criminal court of the county of arrest and must submit to such court a written statement reciting the material facts concerning the issuance of the warrant, the offense involved, and all other essential matters relating thereto. Upon the submission of such statement, such court must release the defendant on his own recognizance or fix bail for his appearance on a specified date in the court in which the warrant is returnable. If the defendant is in default of bail, the officer must retain custody of him but must without unnecessary delay deliver him or cause him to be delivered to the custody of the delegating officer. Upon receiving such custody, the latter must without unnecessary delay bring the defendant before the court in which the warrant is returnable.

5. Whenever a police officer is required pursuant to this section to bring an arrested defendant before a town court in which a warrant of arrest is returnable, and if such town court is not available at the time, such officer must, if a copy of the underlying accusatory instrument has been attached to the warrant pursuant to section 120.40, instead bring such defendant before any village court embraced, in whole or in part, by such town, or any local criminal court of an adjoining town or city of the same county or any village court embraced, in whole or in part, by such adjoining town. When the court in which the warrant is returnable is a village court which is not available at the time, the officer must in such circumstances bring the defendant before the town court of the town embracing such village or any other village court within such town or, if such town court or village court is not available either, before the local criminal court of any town or city of the same county which adjoins such embracing town or, before the local criminal court of any village embraced in whole or in part by such adjoining town. When the court in which the warrant is returnable is a city court which is not available at the time, the officer must in such circumstances bring the defendant before the local criminal court of

any adjoining town or village embraced in whole or in part by such adjoining town of the same county.

5-a. Whenever a police officer is required, pursuant to this section, to bring an arrested defendant before a youth part of a superior court in which a warrant of arrest is returnable, and if such court is not in session, such officer must bring such defendant before the most accessible magistrate designated by the appellate division of the supreme court in the applicable department to act as a youth part.

6. Before bringing a defendant arrested pursuant to a warrant before the local criminal court or youth part of a superior court in which such warrant is returnable, a police officer must without unnecessary delay perform all fingerprinting and other preliminary police duties required in the particular case. In any case in which the defendant is not brought by a police officer before such court but, following his arrest in another county for an offense specified in subdivision one of section 160.10, is released by a local criminal court of such other county on his own recognizance or on bail for his appearance on a specified date before the local criminal court before which the warrant is returnable, the latter court must, upon arraignment of the defendant before it, direct that he be fingerprinted by the appropriate officer or agency, and that he appear at an appropriate designated time and place for such purpose.

7. Upon arresting a juvenile offender or adolescent offender, the police officer shall immediately notify the parent or other person legally responsible for his care or the person with whom he is domiciled, that the juvenile offender or adolescent offender has been arrested, and the location of the facility where he is being detained.

8. Upon arresting a defendant, other than a juvenile offender, for any offense pursuant to a warrant of arrest, a police officer shall, upon the defendant's request, permit the defendant to communicate by telephone provided by the law enforcement facility where the defendant is held to a phone number located anywhere in the United States or Puerto Rico, for the purposes of obtaining counsel and informing a relative or friend that he or she has been arrested, unless granting the call will compromise an ongoing investigation or the prosecution of the defendant.

Article 130 The Summons

§ 130.10. Summons; definition, function, form and content

1. A summons is a process issued by a local criminal court directing a defendant designated in an information, a prosecutor's information, a felony complaint or a misdemeanor complaint filed with such court, or a youth part of a superior court directing a defendant designated in a felony complaint, or by a superior court directing a defendant designated in an indictment filed with such court, to appear before it at a designated future time in connection with such accusatory instrument. The sole function of a summons is to achieve a defendant's court appearance in a criminal action for the purpose of arraignment upon the accusatory instrument by which such action was commenced.

2. A summons must be subscribed by the issuing judge and must state or contain (a) the name of the issuing court, and (b) the name of the defendant to whom it is addressed, and (c) the name or title of an offense charged in the underlying accusatory instrument, and (d) the date of issuance of the summons, and (e) the date and time

when it is returnable, and (f) a direction that the defendant appear before the issuing court at such time.

§ 130.20. Summons; by what courts issuable and in what courts returnable

A summons may be issued only by the local criminal court or superior court with which the accusatory instrument underlying it has been filed, and it may be made returnable in such issuing court only.

§ 130.30. Summons; when issuable

A local criminal court or youth part of the superior court may issue a summons in any case in which, pursuant to section 120.20, it is authorized to issue a warrant of arrest based upon an information, a prosecutor's information, a felony complaint or a misdemeanor complaint. If such information, prosecutor's information, felony complaint or misdemeanor complaint is not sufficient on its face as prescribed in section 100.40, and if the court is satisfied that on the basis of the available facts or evidence it would be impossible to draw and file an authorized accusatory instrument that is sufficient on its face, the court must dismiss the accusatory instrument. A superior court may issue a summons in any case in which, pursuant to section 210.10, it is authorized to issue a warrant of arrest based upon an indictment.

§ 130.40. Summons; service

1. A summons may be served by a police officer, or by a complainant at least eighteen years old or by any other person at least eighteen years old designated by the court.
2. A summons may be served anywhere in the county of issuance or anywhere in an adjoining county.

§ 130.50. Summons; defendant's failure to appear

If after the service of a summons the defendant does not appear in the designated local criminal court or superior court at the time such summons is returnable, the court may issue a warrant of arrest.

§ 130.60. Summons; fingerprinting of defendant

1. Upon the arraignment of a defendant whose court attendance has been secured by the issuance and service of a summons, based upon an indictment, a prosecutor's information or upon an information, felony complaint or misdemeanor complaint filed by a complainant who is a police officer, the court must, if an offense charged in the accusatory instrument is one specified in subdivision one of section 160.10, direct that the defendant be fingerprinted by the appropriate police officer or agency, and that he or she appear at an appropriate designated time and place for such purpose.
2. Upon the arraignment of a defendant whose court attendance has been secured by the issuance and service of a summons based upon an information or misdemeanor complaint filed by a complainant who is not a police officer, and who has not previously been fingerprinted, the court may, if it finds reasonable cause to believe that the defendant has committed an offense specified in subdivision one of section 160.10, direct that the defendant be fingerprinted by the appropriate police officer or agency and that he appear at an appropriate designated time and place for such purpose. A defendant whose court appearance has been secured by the issuance and service of a criminal summons based upon a misdemeanor complaint or information filed by a complainant who is not a police officer, must be directed by the court, upon conviction of

the defendant, to be fingerprinted by the appropriate police officer or agency and the court must also direct that the defendant appear at an appropriate designated time and place for such purpose, if the defendant is convicted of any offense specified in subdivision one of section 160.10.

Article 140 Arrest Without a Warrant

§ 140.05. Arrest without a warrant; in general

A person who has committed or is believed to have committed an offense and who is at liberty within the state may, under circumstances prescribed in this article, be arrested for such offense although no warrant of arrest therefor has been issued and although no criminal action therefor has yet been commenced in any criminal court.

§ 140.10. Arrest without a warrant; by police officer; when and where authorized

1. Subject to the provisions of subdivision two, a police officer may arrest a person for:

(a) Any offense when he or she has reasonable cause to believe that such person has committed such offense in his or her presence; and

(b) A crime when he or she has reasonable cause to believe that such person has committed such crime, whether in his or her presence or otherwise.

2. A police officer may arrest a person for a petty offense, pursuant to subdivision one, only when:

(a) Such offense was committed or believed by him or her to have been committed within the geographical area of such police officer's employment or within one hundred yards of such geographical area; and

(b) Such arrest is made in the county in which such offense was committed or believed to have been committed or in an adjoining county; except that the police officer may follow such person in continuous close pursuit, commencing either in the county in which the offense was or is believed to have been committed or in an adjoining county, in and through any county of the state, and may arrest him or her in any county in which he or she apprehends him or her.

3. A police officer may arrest a person for a crime, pursuant to subdivision one, whether or not such crime was committed within the geographical area of such police officer's employment, and he or she may make such arrest within the state, regardless of the situs of the commission of the crime. In addition, he or she may, if necessary, pursue such person outside the state and may arrest him or her in any state the laws of which contain provisions equivalent to those of section 140.55.

4. [Expires and repealed Sept 1, 2019] Notwithstanding any other provisions of this section, a police officer shall arrest a person, and shall not attempt to reconcile the parties or mediate, where such officer has reasonable cause to believe that:

(a) a felony, other than subdivision three, four, nine or ten of section 155.30 of the penal law, has been committed by such person against a member of the same family or household, as member of the same family or household is defined in subdivision one of section 530.11 of this chapter; or

(b) a duly served order of protection or special order of conditions issued pursuant to subparagraph (i) or (ii) of paragraph (o) of subdivision one of section 330.20 of this chapter is in effect, or an order of which the respondent or defendant has actual knowledge because he or she was present in court when such order was issued, where the order appears to have been issued by a court of competent jurisdiction of this or another state, territorial or tribal jurisdiction; and

(i) Such order directs that the respondent or defendant stay away from persons on whose behalf the order of protection or special order of conditions has been issued and the respondent or defendant committed an act or acts in violation of such "stay away" provision of such order; or

(ii) The respondent or defendant commits a family offense as defined in subdivision one of section eight hundred twelve of the family court act or subdivision one of section 530.11 of this chapter in violation of such order of protection or special order of conditions.

The provisions of this subdivision shall apply only to orders of protection issued pursuant to sections two hundred forty and two hundred fifty-two of the domestic relations law, articles four, five, six and eight of the family court act and section 530.12 of this chapter, special orders of conditions issued pursuant to subparagraph (i) or (ii) of paragraph (o) of subdivision one of section 330.20 of this chapter insofar as they involve a victim or victims of domestic violence as defined by subdivision one of section four hundred fifty-nine-a of the social services law or a designated witness or witnesses to such domestic violence, and to orders of protection issued by courts of competent jurisdiction in another state, territorial or tribal jurisdiction. In determining whether reasonable cause exists to make an arrest for a violation of an order issued by a court of another state, territorial or tribal jurisdiction, the officer shall consider, among other factors, whether the order, if available, appears to be valid on its face or whether a record of the order exists on the statewide registry of orders of protection and warrants established pursuant to section two hundred twenty-one-a of the executive law or the protection order file maintained by the national crime information center; provided, however, that entry of the order of protection or special order of conditions into the statewide registry or the national protection order file shall not be required for enforcement of the order. When a special order of conditions is in effect and a defendant or respondent has been taken into custody pursuant to this paragraph, nothing contained in this paragraph shall restrict or impair a police officer from acting pursuant to section 9.41 of the mental hygiene law; or

(c) a misdemeanor constituting a family offense, as described in subdivision one of section 530.11 of this chapter and section eight hundred twelve of the family court act, has been committed by such person against such family or household member, unless the victim requests otherwise. The officer shall neither inquire as to whether the victim seeks an arrest of such person nor threaten the arrest of any person for the purpose of discouraging requests for police intervention. Notwithstanding the foregoing, when an officer has reasonable cause to believe that more than one family or household member has committed such a misdemeanor, the officer is not required to arrest each such person. In such circumstances, the officer shall attempt to identify and arrest the primary physical aggressor after considering: (i) the comparative extent of any injuries inflicted by and between the parties; (ii) whether any such person is threatening or has threatened future harm against another party or another family or household member; (iii) whether any such person has a prior history of domestic violence that the officer can reasonably ascertain; and (iv) whether any such person acted defensively to protect himself or herself from injury. The officer shall evaluate each complaint separately to determine who is the primary physical aggressor and shall not base the decision to arrest or not to arrest on the willingness of a person to testify or otherwise participate in a judicial proceeding.

The protected party in whose favor the order of protection or temporary order of protection is issued may not be held to violate an order issued in his or her favor nor may such protected party be arrested for violating such order.

Nothing contained in this subdivision shall be deemed to (a) require the arrest of any person when the officer reasonably believes the person's conduct is justifiable under article thirty-five of title C of the penal law; or (b) restrict or impair the authority of any municipality, political subdivision, or the division of state police from promulgating rules, regulations and policies requiring the arrest of persons in additional circumstances where domestic violence has allegedly occurred.

No cause of action for damages shall arise in favor of any person by reason of any arrest made by a police officer pursuant to this subdivision, except as provided in sections seventeen and eighteen of the public officers law and sections fifty-k, fifty-l, fifty-m and fifty-n of the general municipal law, as appropriate.

5. Upon investigating a report of a crime or offense between members of the same family or household as such terms are defined in section 530.11 of this chapter and section eight hundred twelve of the family court act, a law enforcement officer shall prepare, file, and translate, in accordance with section two hundred fourteen-b or eight hundred forty of the executive law, a written report of the incident, on a form promulgated pursuant to section eight hundred thirty-seven of the executive law, including statements made by the victim and by any witnesses, and make any additional reports required by local law enforcement policy or regulations. Such report shall be prepared and filed, whether or not an arrest is made as a result of the officers' investigation, and shall be retained by the law enforcement agency for a period of not less than four years. Where the reported incident involved an offense committed against a person who is sixty-five years of age or older a copy of the report required by this subdivision shall be sent to the New York state committee for the coordination of police services to elderly persons established pursuant to section eight hundred forty-four-b of the executive law. Where the reported incident involved an offense committed by an individual known by the law enforcement officer to be under probation or parole supervision, he or she shall transmit a copy of the report as soon as practicable to the supervising probation department or the department of corrections and community supervision.

§ 140.15. Arrest without a warrant; when and how made by police officer

1. A police officer may arrest a person for an offense, pursuant to section 140.10, at any hour of any day or night.

2. The arresting police officer must inform such person of his authority and purpose and of the reason for such arrest unless he encounters physical resistance, flight or other factors rendering such procedure impractical.

3. In order to effect such an arrest, such police officer may use such physical force as is justifiable pursuant to section 35.30 of the penal law.

4. In order to effect such an arrest, a police officer may enter premises in which he reasonably believes such person to be present, under the same circumstances and in the same manner as would be authorized, by the provisions of subdivisions four and five of section 120.80, if he were attempting to make such arrest pursuant to a warrant of arrest.

§ 140.20. Arrest without a warrant; procedure after arrest by police officer

1. Upon arresting a person without a warrant, a police officer, after performing without unnecessary delay all recording, fingerprinting and other preliminary police duties required in the particular case, must except as otherwise provided in this section, without unnecessary delay bring the arrested person or cause him to be brought before a local criminal court and file therewith an appropriate accusatory instrument charging him with the offense or offenses in question. The arrested person must be brought to the particular local criminal court, or to one of them if there be more than one, designated in section 100.55 as an appropriate court for commencement of the particular action; except that:

(a) If the arrest is for an offense other than a class A, B, C or D felony or a violation of section 130.25, 130.40, 205.10, 205.17, 205.19 or 215.56 of the penal law committed in a town, but not in a village thereof having a village court, and the town court of such town is not available at the time, the arrested person may be brought before the local criminal court of any village within such town or, any adjoining town, village embraced in whole or in part by such adjoining town, or city of the same county; and

(b) If the arrest is for an offense other than a class A, B, C or D felony or a violation of section 130.25, 130.40, 205.10, 205.17, 205.19 or 215.56 of the penal law committed in a village having a village court and such court is not available at the time, the arrested person may be brought before the town court of the town embracing such village or any other village court within such town, or, if such town or village court is not available either, before the local criminal court of any adjoining town, village embraced in whole or in part by such adjoining town, or city of the same county; and

(c) If the arrest is for an offense committed in a city, and the city court thereof is not available at the time, the arrested person may be brought before the local criminal court of any adjoining town or village, or village court embraced by an adjoining town, within the same county as such city; and

(d) If the arrest is for a traffic infraction or for a misdemeanor relating to traffic, the police officer may, instead of bringing the arrested person before the local criminal court of the political subdivision or locality in which the offense was allegedly committed, bring him or her before the local criminal court of the same county nearest available by highway travel to the point of arrest; and

(e) Notwithstanding any other provision of this section, where a local criminal court in the county in which the defendant is arrested is operating an off-hours arraignment part designated in accordance with paragraph (w) of subdivision one of section two hundred twelve of the judiciary law at the time of defendant's arrest, the arrested person may be brought before such local criminal court.

2. If the arrest is for an offense other than a class A, B, C or D felony or a violation of section 130.25, 130.40, 205.10, 205.17, 205.19 or 215.56 of the penal law, the arrested person need not be brought before a local criminal court as provided in subdivision one, and the procedure may instead be as follows:

(a) A police officer may issue and serve an appearance ticket upon the arrested person and release him from custody, as prescribed in subdivision two of section 150.20; or

(b) The desk officer in charge at a police station, county jail or police headquarters, or any of his superior officers, may, in such place fix pre-arraignment bail and, upon deposit thereof, issue and serve an appearance ticket upon the arrested person and release him from custody, as prescribed in section 150.30.

3. If (a) the arrest is for an offense other than a class A, B, C or D felony or a violation of section 130.25, 130.40, 205.10, 205.17, 205.19 or 215.56 of the penal law, and (b) owing to unavailability of a local criminal court the arresting police officer is unable to bring the arrested person before such a court with reasonable promptness, either an appearance ticket must be served unconditionally upon the arrested person or pre-arraignment bail must be fixed, as prescribed in subdivision two. If pre-arraignment bail is fixed but not posted, such arrested person may be temporarily held in custody but must be brought before a local criminal court without unnecessary delay. Nothing contained in this subdivision requires a police officer to serve an appearance ticket upon an arrested person or release him from custody at a time when such person appears to be under the influence of alcohol, narcotics or other drug to the degree that he may endanger himself or other persons.

4. If after arresting a person, for any offense, a police officer upon further investigation or inquiry determines or is satisfied that there is not reasonable cause to believe that the arrested person committed such offense or any other offense based upon the conduct in question, he need not follow any of the procedures prescribed in subdivisions one, two and three, but must immediately release such person from custody.

5. Before service of an appearance ticket upon an arrested person pursuant to subdivision two or three, the issuing police officer must, if the offense designated in such appearance ticket is one of those specified in subdivision one of section 160.10, cause such person to be fingerprinted in the same manner as would be required were no appearance ticket to be issued or served.

6. Upon arresting a juvenile offender or a person sixteen or commencing October first, two thousand nineteen, seventeen years of age without a warrant, the police officer shall immediately notify the parent or other person legally responsible for his or her care or the person with whom he or she is domiciled, that such offender or person has been arrested, and the location of the facility where he or she is being detained. If the officer determines that it is necessary to question a juvenile offender or such person, the officer must take him or her to a facility designated by the chief administrator of the courts as a suitable place for the questioning of children or, upon the consent of a parent or other person legally responsible for the care of the juvenile or such person, to his or her residence and there question him or her for a reasonable period of time. A juvenile or such person shall not be questioned pursuant to this section unless he or she and a

person required to be notified pursuant to this subdivision, if present, have been advised:

(a) of the juvenile offender's or such person's right to remain silent;

(b) that the statements made by him or her may be used in a court of law;

(c) of his or her right to have an attorney present at such questioning; and

(d) of his or her right to have an attorney provided for him or her without charge if he or she is unable to afford counsel.

In determining the suitability of questioning and determining the reasonable period of time for questioning such a juvenile offender or person, his or her age, the presence or absence of his or her parents or other persons legally responsible for his or her care and notification pursuant to this subdivision shall be included among relevant considerations.

7. Upon arresting a person, other than a juvenile offender, for any offense without a warrant, a police officer shall, upon the arrested person's request, permit him or her to communicate by telephone provided by the law enforcement facility where the defendant is held to a phone number located in the United States or Puerto Rico, for the purposes of obtaining counsel and informing a relative or friend that he or she has been arrested, unless granting the call will compromise an ongoing investigation or the prosecution of the defendant.

8. If the arrest is for a juvenile offender or adolescent offender other than an arrest for a violation or a traffic infraction, such offender shall be brought before the youth part of the superior court. If the youth part is not in session, such offender shall be brought before the most accessible magistrate designated by the appellate division of the supreme court in the applicable department to act as a youth part.

§ 140.25. Arrest without a warrant; by peace officer

1. A peace officer, acting pursuant to his special duties, may arrest a person for:

(a) Any offense when he has reasonable cause to believe that such person has committed such offense in his presence; and

(b) A crime when he has reasonable cause to believe that such person has committed such crime, whether in his presence or otherwise.

2. A peace officer acts "pursuant to his special duties" in making an arrest only when the arrest is for:

(a) An offense defined by a statute which such peace officer, by reason of the specialized nature of his particular employment or by express provision of law, is required or authorized to enforce; or

(b) An offense committed or reasonably believed by him to have been committed in such manner or place as to render arrest of the offender by such peace officer under the particular circumstances an integral part of his specialized duties.

3. A peace officer, whether or not he is acting pursuant to his special duties, may arrest a person for an offense committed or believed by him to have been committed within the geographical area of such peace officer's employment, as follows:

(a) He may arrest such person for any offense when such person has in fact committed such offense in his presence; and

(b) He may arrest such person for a felony when he has reasonable cause to believe that such person has committed such felony, whether in his presence or otherwise.

4. A peace officer, when outside the geographical area of his employment, may, anywhere in the state, arrest a person for a felony when he has reasonable cause to believe that such person has there committed such felony in his presence, provided that such arrest is made during or immediately after the allegedly criminal conduct or during the alleged perpetrator's immediate flight therefrom.

5. For the purposes of this section, the "geographical area of employment" of a peace officer is as follows:

(a) The "geographical area of employment" of any peace officer employed as such by any agency of the state consists of the entire state;

(b) The "geographical area of employment" of any peace officer employed as such by an agency of a county, city, town or village consists of (i) such county, city, town or village, as the case may be, and (ii) any other place where he is, at a particular time, acting in the course of his particular duties or employment;

(c) The "geographical area of employment" of any peace officer employed as such by any private organization consists of any place in the state where he is, at a particular time, acting in the course of his particular duties or employment.

§ 140.27. Arrest without a warrant; when and how made; procedure after arrest by peace officer

1. The rules governing the manner in which a peace officer may make an arrest, pursuant to section 140.25, are the same as those governing arrests by police officers, as prescribed in section 140.15.

2. Upon arresting a person without a warrant, a peace officer, except as otherwise provided in subdivision three or three-a, must without unnecessary delay bring him or cause him to be brought before a local criminal court, as provided in section 100.55 and subdivision one of section 140.20, and must without unnecessary delay file or cause to be filed therewith an appropriate accusatory instrument. If the offense which is the subject of the arrest is one of those specified in subdivision one of section 160.10, the arrested person must be fingerprinted and photographed as therein provided. In order to execute the required post-arrest functions, such arresting peace officer may perform such functions himself or he may enlist the aid of a police officer for the performance thereof in the manner provided in subdivision one of section 140.20.

3. If (a) the arrest is for an offense other than a class A, B, C or D felony or a violation of section 130.25, 130.40, 205.10, 205.17, 205.19 or 215.56 of the penal law and (b) owing to unavailability of a local criminal court such peace officer is unable to bring or cause the arrested person to be brought before such a court with reasonable promptness, the arrested person must be brought to an appropriate police station, county jail or police headquarters where he must be dealt with in the manner prescribed in subdivision three of section 140.20, as if he had been arrested by a police officer.

3-a. If the arrest is for a juvenile offender or adolescent offender other than an arrest for violations or traffic infractions, such offender shall be brought before the youth part of the superior court. If the youth part is not in session, such offender shall be brought before the most accessible magistrate designated by the appellate division of the supreme court in the applicable department to act as a youth part.

4. If the arrest is for an offense other than a class A, B, C or D felony or a violation of section 130.25, 130.40, 205.10, 205.17, 205.19 or 215.56 of the penal law, the arrested person need not be brought before a local criminal court as provided in subdivision two, and the procedure may instead be as follows:

(a) The arresting peace officer, where he is specially authorized by law to issue and serve an appearance ticket, may issue and serve an appearance ticket upon the arrested person and release him from custody; or

(b) The arresting peace officer, where he is not specially authorized by law to issue and serve an appearance ticket, may enlist the aid of a police officer and request that such officer issue and serve an appearance ticket upon the arrested person, and upon such issuance and service the latter must be released from custody.

5. Upon arresting a juvenile offender or a person sixteen or commencing October first, two thousand nineteen, seventeen years of age without a warrant, the peace officer shall immediately notify the parent or other person legally responsible for his or her care or the person with whom he or she is domiciled, that such offender or person has been arrested, and the location of the facility where he or she is being detained. If the officer determines that it is necessary to question a juvenile offender or such person, the officer must take him or her to a facility designated by the chief administrator of the courts as a suitable place for the questioning of children or, upon the consent of a parent or other person legally responsible for the care of a juvenile offender or such person, to his or her residence and there question him or her for a reasonable period of time. A juvenile offender or such person shall not be questioned pursuant to this section unless the juvenile offender or such person and a person required to be notified pursuant to this subdivision, if present, have been advised:

(a) of his or her right to remain silent;

(b) that the statements made by the juvenile offender or such person may be used in a court of law;

(c) of his or her right to have an attorney present at such questioning; and

(d) of his or her right to have an attorney provided for him or her without charge if he or she is unable to afford counsel.

In determining the suitability of questioning and determining the reasonable period of time for questioning such a juvenile offender or such person, his or her age, the presence or absence of his or her parents or other persons legally responsible for his or her care and notification pursuant to this subdivision shall be included among relevant considerations.

§ 140.30. Arrest without a warrant; by any person; when and where authorized

1. Subject to the provisions of subdivision two, any person may arrest another person (a) for a felony when the latter has in fact committed such felony, and (b) for any offense when the latter has in fact committed such offense in his presence.

2. Such an arrest, if for a felony, may be made anywhere in the state. If the arrest is for an offense other than a felony, it may be made only in the county in which such offense was committed.

§ 140.35. Arrest without a warrant; by person acting other than as a police officer or a peace officer; when and how made

1. A person may arrest another person for an offense pursuant to section 140.30 at any hour of any day or night.

2. Such person must inform the person whom he is arresting of the reason for such arrest unless he encounters physical resistance, flight or other factors rendering such procedure impractical.

3. In order to effect such an arrest, such person may use such physical force as is justifiable pursuant to subdivision four of section 35.30 of the penal law.

§ 140.40. Arrest without a warrant; by person acting other than as a police officer or a peace officer; procedure after arrest

1. A person making an arrest pursuant to section 140.30 must without unnecessary delay deliver or attempt to deliver the person arrested to the custody of an appropriate police officer, as defined in subdivision five. For such purpose, he may solicit the aid of any police officer and the latter, if he is not himself an appropriate police officer, must assist in delivering the arrested person to an appropriate officer. If the arrest is for a felony, the appropriate police officer must, upon receiving custody of the arrested person, perform all recording, fingerprinting and other preliminary police duties required in the particular case. In any case, the appropriate police officer, upon receiving custody of the arrested person, except as otherwise provided in subdivisions two and three, must bring him, on behalf of the arresting person, before an appropriate local criminal court, as defined in subdivision five, and the arresting person must without unnecessary delay file an appropriate accusatory instrument with such court.

2. If (a) the arrest is for an offense other than a class A, B, C or D felony or a violation of section 130.25, 130.40, 205.10, 205.17, 205.19 or 215.56 of the penal law and (b) owing to unavailability of a local criminal court the appropriate police officer having custody of the arrested person is unable to bring him before such a court with reasonable promptness, the arrested person must be dealt with in the manner prescribed in subdivision three of section 140.20, as if he had been arrested by a police officer.

3. If the arrest is for an offense other than a class A, B, C or D felony or a violation of section 130.25, 130.40, 205.10, 205.17, 205.19 or 215.56 of the penal law, the arrested person need not be brought before a local criminal court, as provided in subdivision one, and the procedure may instead be as follows:

(a) An appropriate police officer may issue and serve an appearance ticket upon the arrested person and release him from custody, as prescribed in subdivision two of section 150.20; or

(b) The desk officer in charge at the appropriate police officer's station, county jail or police headquarters, or any of his superior officers, may, in such place, fix pre-arraignment bail and, upon deposit thereof, issue and serve an appearance ticket upon the arrested person and release him from custody, as prescribed in section 150.30.

4. Notwithstanding any other provision of this section, a police officer is not required to take an arrested person into custody or to take any other action prescribed in this section on behalf of the arresting person if he has reasonable cause to believe that the

arrested person did not commit the alleged offense or that the arrest was otherwise unauthorized.

5. If a police officer takes an arrested juvenile offender or a person sixteen or commencing October first, two thosuand nineteen, seventeen years of age into custody, the police officer shall immediately notify the parent or other person legally responsible for his or her care or the person with whom he or she is domiciled, that such offender or person has been arrested, and the location of the facility where he or she is being detained. If the officer determines that it is necessary to question a juvenile offender or such person the officer must take him or her to a facility designated by the chief administrator of the courts as a suitable place for the questioning of children or, upon the consent of a parent or other person legally responsible for the care of the juvenile offender or such person, to his or her residence and there question him or her for a reasonable period of time. A juvenile offender or such person shall not be questioned pursuant to this section unless he or she and a person required to be notified pursuant to this subdivision, if present, have been advised:

(a) of his or her right to remain silent;

(b) that the statements made by the juvenile offender or such person may be used in a court of law;

(c) of his or her right to have an attorney present at such questioning; and

(d) of his or her right to have an attorney provided for him or her without charge if he or she is unable to afford counsel.

In determining the suitability of questioning and determining the reasonable period of time for questioning such a juvenile offender or such person, his or her age, the presence or absence of his or her parents or other persons legally responsible for his or her care and notification pursuant to this subdivision shall be included among relevant considerations.

6. As used in this section:

(a) An "appropriate police officer" means one who would himself be authorized to make the arrest in question as a police officer pursuant to section 140.10;

(b) An "appropriate local criminal court" means one with which an accusatory instrument charging the offense in question may properly be filed pursuant to the provisions of section 100.55.

§ 140.45. Arrest without a warrant; dismissal of insufficient local criminal court accusatory instrument

If a local criminal court accusatory instrument filed with a local criminal court pursuant to section 140.20, 140.25 or 140.40 is not sufficient on its face, as prescribed in section 100.40, and if the court is satisfied that on the basis of the available facts or evidence it would be impossible to draw and file an accusatory instrument which is sufficient on its face, it must dismiss such accusatory instrument and discharge the defendant.

§ 140.50. Temporary questioning of persons in public places; search for weapons

1. In addition to the authority provided by this article for making an arrest without a warrant, a police officer may stop a person in a public place located within the geographical area of such officer's employment when he reasonably suspects that such person is committing, has committed or is about to commit either (a) a felony or (b) a

misdemeanor defined in the penal law, and may demand of him his name, address and an explanation of his conduct.

2. Any person who is a peace officer and who provides security services for any court of the unified court system may stop a person in or about the courthouse to which he is assigned when he reasonably suspects that such person is committing, has committed or is about to commit either (a) a felony or (b) a misdemeanor defined in the penal law, and may demand of him his name, address and an explanation of his conduct.

3. When upon stopping a person under circumstances prescribed in subdivisions one and two a police officer or court officer, as the case may be, reasonably suspects that he is in danger of physical injury, he may search such person for a deadly weapon or any instrument, article or substance readily capable of causing serious physical injury and of a sort not ordinarily carried in public places by law-abiding persons. If he finds such a weapon or instrument, or any other property possession of which he reasonably believes may constitute the commission of a crime, he may take it and keep it until the completion of the questioning, at which time he shall either return it, if lawfully possessed, or arrest such person.

4. In cities with a population of one million or more, information that establishes the personal identity of an individual who has been stopped, questioned and/or frisked by a police officer or peace officer, such as the name, address or social security number of such person, shall not be recorded in a computerized or electronic database if that individual is released without further legal action; provided, however, that this subdivision shall not prohibit police officers or peace officers from including in a computerized or electronic database generic characteristics of an individual, such as race and gender, who has been stopped, questioned and/or frisked by a police officer or peace officer.

§ 140.55. Arrest without a warrant; by peace officers of other states for offense committed outside state; uniform close pursuit act

1. As used in this section, the word "state" shall include the District of Columbia.

2. Any peace officer of another state of the United States, who enters this state in close pursuit and continues within this state in such close pursuit of a person in order to arrest him, shall have the same authority to arrest and hold in custody such person on the ground that he has committed a crime in another state which is a crime under the laws of the state of New York, as police officers of this state have to arrest and hold in custody a person on the ground that he has committed a crime in this state.

3. If an arrest is made in this state by an officer of another state in accordance with the provisions of subdivision two, he shall without unnecessary delay take the person arrested before a local criminal court which shall conduct a hearing for the sole purpose of determining if the arrest was in accordance with the provisions of subdivision two, and not of determining the guilt or innocence of the arrested person. If such court determines that the arrest was in accordance with such subdivision, it shall commit the person arrested to the custody of the officer making the arrest, who shall without unnecessary delay take him to the state from which he fled. If such court determines that the arrest was unlawful, it shall discharge the person arrested.

4. This section shall not be construed so as to make unlawful any arrest in this state which would otherwise be lawful.

5. Upon the taking effect of this section it shall be the duty of the secretary of state to certify a copy of this section to the executive department of each of the states of the United States.

6. This section shall apply only to peace officers of a state which by its laws has made similar provision for the arrest and custody of persons closely pursued within the territory thereof.

7. If any part of this section is for any reason declared void, it is declared to be the intent of this section that such invalidity shall not affect the validity of the remaining portions of this section.

8. This section may be cited as the uniform act on close pursuit.

Article 150 The Appearance Ticket

§ 150.10. Appearance ticket; definition, form and content

1. An appearance ticket is a written notice issued and subscribed by a police officer or other public servant authorized by state law or local law enacted pursuant to the provisions of the municipal home rule law to issue the same, directing a designated person to appear in a designated local criminal court at a designated future time in connection with his alleged commission of a designated offense. A notice conforming to such definition constitutes an appearance ticket regardless of whether it is referred to in some other provision of law as a summons or by any other name or title.

2. When an appearance ticket as defined in subdivision one of this section is issued to a person in conjunction with an offense charged in a simplified information, said appearance ticket shall contain the language, set forth in subdivision four of section 100.25, notifying the defendant of his right to receive a supporting deposition.

§ 150.20. Appearance ticket; when and by whom issuable

1. Whenever a police officer is authorized pursuant to section 140.10 to arrest a person without a warrant for an offense other than a class A, B, C or D felony or a violation of section 130.25, 130.40, 205.10, 205.17, 205.19 or 215.56 of the penal law, he may, subject to the provisions of subdivisions three and four of section 150.40, instead issue to and serve upon such person an appearance ticket.

2.

(a) Whenever a police officer has arrested a person without a warrant for an offense other than a class A, B, C or D felony or a violation of section 130.25, 130.40, 205.10, 205.17, 205.19 or 215.56 of the penal law pursuant to section 140.10, or (b) whenever a peace officer, who is not authorized by law to issue an appearance ticket, has arrested a person for an offense other than a class A, B, C or D felony or a violation of section 130.25, 130.40, 205.10, 205.17, 205.19 or 215.56 of the penal law pursuant to section 140.25, and has requested a police officer to issue and serve upon such arrested person an appearance ticket pursuant to subdivision four of section 140.27, or (c) whenever a person has been arrested for an offense other than a class A, B, C or D felony or a violation of section 130.25, 130.40, 205.10, 205.17, 205.19 or 215.56 of the penal law and has been delivered to the custody of an appropriate police officer pursuant to section 140.40, such police officer may, instead of bringing such person before a local criminal court and promptly filing or causing the arresting peace officer or arresting person to file a local criminal court accusatory instrument therewith, issue to and serve upon such person an appearance ticket. The issuance and service of an appearance ticket under such circumstances may be conditioned upon a deposit of pre-arraignment bail, as provided in section 150.30.

3. A public servant other than a police officer, who is specially authorized by state law or local law enacted pursuant to the provisions of the municipal home rule law to issue and serve appearance tickets with respect to designated offenses other than class A, B, C or D felonies or violations of section 130.25, 130.40, 205.10, 205.17, 205.19 or 215.56 of the penal law, may in such cases issue and serve upon a person an appearance ticket when he has reasonable cause to believe that such person has committed a crime, or has committed a petty offense in his presence.

§ 150.30. Appearance ticket; issuance and service thereof after arrest upon posting of pre-arraignment bail

1. Issuance and service of an appearance ticket by a police officer following an arrest without a warrant, as prescribed in subdivision two of section 150.20, may be made conditional upon the posting of a sum of money, known as pre-arraignment bail. In such case, the bail becomes forfeit upon failure of such person to comply with the directions of the appearance ticket. The person posting such bail must complete and sign a form which states (a) the name, residential address and occupation of each person posting cash bail; and (b) the title of the criminal action or proceeding involved; and (c) the offense or offenses which are the subjects of the action or proceeding involved, and the status of such action or proceeding; and (d) the name of the principal and the nature of his involvement in or connection with such action or proceeding; and (e) the date of the principal's next appearance in court; and (f) an acknowledgement that the cash bail will be forfeited if the principal does not comply with the directions of the appearance ticket; and (g) the amount of money posted as cash bail. Such pre-arraignment bail may be posted as provided in subdivision two or three.

2. A desk officer in charge at a police station, county jail, or police headquarters, or any of his superior officers, may in such place, fix pre-arraignment bail, in an amount prescribed in this subdivision, and upon the posting thereof must issue and serve an appearance ticket upon the arrested person, give a receipt for the bail, and release such person from custody. Such pre-arraignment bail may be fixed in the following amounts:

(a) If the arrest was for a class E felony, any amount not exceeding seven hundred fifty dollars.

(b) If the arrest was for a class A misdemeanor, any amount not exceeding five hundred dollars.

(c) If the arrest was for a class B misdemeanor or an unclassified misdemeanor, any amount not exceeding two hundred fifty dollars.

(d) If the arrest was for a petty offense, any amount not exceeding one hundred dollars.

3. A police officer, who has arrested a person without a warrant pursuant to subdivision two of section 150.20 of this chapter for a traffic infraction, may, where he reasonably believes that such arrested person is not licensed to operate a motor vehicle by this state or any state covered by a reciprocal compact guaranteeing appearance as is

provided in section five hundred seventeen of the vehicle and traffic law, fix pre-arraignment bail in the amount of fifty dollars; provided, however, such bail shall be posted by means of a credit card or similar device. Upon the posting thereof, said officer must issue and serve an appearance ticket upon the arrested person, give a receipt for the bail, and release such person from custody.

4. The chief administrator of the courts shall establish a system for the posting of pre-arraignment bail by means of credit card or similar device, as is provided by section two hundred twelve of the judiciary law. The head of each police department or police force and of any state department, agency, board, commission or public authority having police officers who fix pre-arraignment bail as provided herein may elect to use the system established by the chief administrator or may establish such other system for the posting of pre-arraignment bail by means of credit card or similar device as he or she may deem appropriate.

§ 150.40. Appearance ticket; where returnable; how and where served

1. An appearance ticket must be made returnable in a local criminal court designated in section 100.55 as one with which an information for the offense in question may be filed.

2. An appearance ticket, other than one issued for a traffic infraction relating to parking, must be served personally, except that an appearance ticket issued for the violation of a local zoning ordinance or local zoning law, or of a building or sanitation code may be served in any manner authorized for service under section three hundred eight of the civil practice law and rules.

3. An appearance ticket may be served anywhere in the county in which the designated offense was allegedly committed or in any adjoining county, and may be served elsewhere as prescribed in subdivision four.

4. A police officer may, for the purpose of serving an appearance ticket upon a person, follow him in continuous close pursuit, commencing either in the county in which the alleged offense was committed or in an adjoining county, in and through any county of the state, and may serve such appearance ticket upon him in any county in which he overtakes him.

§ 150.50. Appearance ticket; filing a local criminal court accusatory instrument; dismissal of insufficient instrument

1. A police officer or other public servant who has issued and served an appearance ticket must, at or before the time such appearance ticket is returnable, file or cause to be filed with the local criminal court in which it is returnable a local criminal court accusatory instrument charging the person named in such appearance ticket with the offense specified therein. Nothing herein contained shall authorize the use of a simplified information when not authorized by law.

2. If such accusatory instrument is not sufficient on its face, as prescribed in section 100.40, and if the court is satisfied that on the basis of the available facts or evidence it would be impossible to draw and file an accusatory instrument which is sufficient on its face, it must dismiss such accusatory instrument.

§ 150.60. Appearance ticket; defendant's failure to appear

If after the service of an appearance ticket and the filing of a local criminal court accusatory instrument charging the offense designated therein, the defendant does not appear in the designated local criminal court at the time such appearance ticket is returnable, the court may issue a summons or a warrant of arrest based upon the local criminal court accusatory instrument filed.

§ 150.70. Appearance ticket; fingerprinting of defendant

Upon the arraignment of a defendant who has not been arrested and whose court attendance has been secured by the issuance and service of an appearance ticket pursuant to subdivision one of section 150.20, the court must, if an offense charged in the accusatory instrument is one specified in subdivision one of section 160.10, direct that the defendant be fingerprinted by the appropriate police officer or agency, and that he appear at an appropriate designated time and place for such purpose.

§ 150.75. Appearance ticket; certain cases

1. The provisions of this section shall apply in any case wherein the defendant is alleged to have committed an offense defined in section 221.05 of the penal law, and no other offense is alleged, notwithstanding any provision of this chapter or any other law to the contrary.

2. Whenever the defendant is arrested without a warrant, an appearance ticket shall promptly be issued and served upon him, as provided in this article. The issuance and service of the appearance ticket may be made conditional upon the posting of pre-arraignment bail as provided in section 150.30 of this chapter but only if the appropriate police officer (a) is unable to ascertain the defendant's identity or residence address; or (b) reasonably suspects that the identification or residence address given by the defendant is not accurate; or (c) reasonably suspects that the defendant does not reside within the state. No warrant of arrest shall be issued unless the defendant has failed to appear in court as required by the terms of the appearance ticket or by the court.

Article 160 Fingerprinting and Photographing of Defendant After Arrest—criminal Identification Records and Statistics

§ 160.10. Fingerprinting; duties of police with respect thereto

1. Following an arrest, or following the arraignment upon a local criminal court accusatory instrument of a defendant whose court attendance has been secured by a summons or an appearance ticket under circumstances described in sections 130.60 and 150.70, the arresting or other appropriate police officer or agency must take or cause to be taken fingerprints of the arrested person or defendant if an offense which is the subject of the arrest or which is charged in the accusatory instrument filed is:

(a) A felony; or

(b) A misdemeanor defined in the penal law; or

(c) A misdemeanor defined outside the penal law which would constitute a felony if such person had a previous judgment of conviction for a crime; or

(d) Loitering for the purpose of engaging in a prostitution offense as defined in subdivision two of section 240.37 of the penal law.

(e) [Redesignated]

2. In addition, a police officer who makes an arrest for any offense, either with or without a warrant, may take or cause to be taken the fingerprints of the arrested person if such police officer:

(a) Is unable to ascertain such person's identity; or

(b) Reasonably suspects that the identification given by such person is not accurate; or

(c) Reasonably suspects that such person is being sought by law enforcement officials for the commission of some other offense.

3. Whenever fingerprints are required to be taken pursuant to subdivision one or permitted to be taken pursuant to subdivision two, the photograph and palmprints of the arrested person or the defendant, as the case may be, may also be taken.

4. The taking of fingerprints as prescribed in this section and the submission of available information concerning the arrested person or the defendant and the facts and circumstances of the crime charged must be in accordance with the standards established by the commissioner of the division of criminal justice services.

§ 160.20. Fingerprinting; forwarding of fingerprints

Upon the taking of fingerprints of an arrested person or defendant as prescribed in section 160.10, the appropriate police officer or agency must without unnecessary delay forward two copies of such fingerprints to the division of criminal justice services.

§ 160.30. Fingerprinting; duties of division of criminal justice services

1. Upon receiving fingerprints from a police officer or agency pursuant to section 160.20 of this chapter, the division of criminal justice services must, except as provided in subdivision two of this section, classify them and search its records for information concerning a previous record of the defendant, including any adjudication as a juvenile delinquent pursuant to article three of the family court act, or as a youthful offender pursuant to article seven hundred twenty of this chapter, and promptly transmit to such forwarding police officer or agency a report containing all information on file with respect to such defendant's previous record, if any, or stating that the defendant has no previous record according to its files. Such a report, if certified, constitutes presumptive evidence of the facts so certified.

2. If the fingerprints so received are not sufficiently legible to permit accurate and complete classification, they must be returned to the forwarding police officer or agency with an explanation of the defects and a request that the defendant's fingerprints be retaken if possible.

§ 160.40. Fingerprinting; transmission of report received by police

1. Upon receipt of a report of the division of criminal justice services as provided in section 160.30, the recipient police officer or agency must promptly transmit such report or a copy thereof to the district attorney of the county and two copies thereof to the court in which the action is pending.

2. Upon receipt of such report the court shall furnish a copy thereof to counsel for the defendant or, if the defendant is not represented by counsel, to the defendant.

§ 160.45. Polygraph tests; prohibition against

1. No district attorney, police officer or employee of any law enforcement agency shall request or require any victim of a sexual assault crime to submit to any polygraph test or psychological stress evaluator examination.

110

2. As used in this section, "victim of a sexual assault crime" means any person alleged to have sustained an offense under article one hundred thirty or section 255.25, 255.26 or 255.27 of the penal law.

§ 160.50. Order upon termination of criminal action in favor of the accused

1. Upon the termination of a criminal action or proceeding against a person in favor of such person, as defined in subdivision three of this section, unless the district attorney upon motion with not less than five days notice to such person or his or her attorney demonstrates to the satisfaction of the court that the interests of justice require otherwise, or the court on its own motion with not less than five days notice to such person or his or her attorney determines that the interests of justice require otherwise and states the reasons for such determination on the record, the record of such action or proceeding shall be sealed and the clerk of the court wherein such criminal action or proceeding was terminated shall immediately notify the commissioner of the division of criminal justice services and the heads of all appropriate police departments and other law enforcement agencies that the action has been terminated in favor of the accused, and unless the court has directed otherwise, that the record of such action or proceeding shall be sealed. Upon receipt of notification of such termination and sealing:

(a) every photograph of such person and photographic plate or proof, and all palmprints and fingerprints taken or made of such person pursuant to the provisions of this article in regard to the action or proceeding terminated, except a dismissal pursuant to section 170.56 or 210.46 of this chapter, and all duplicates and copies thereof, except a digital fingerprint image where authorized pursuant to paragraph (e) of this subdivision, shall forthwith be, at the discretion of the recipient agency, either destroyed or returned to such person, or to the attorney who represented such person at the time of the termination of the action or proceeding, at the address given by such person or attorney during the action or proceeding, by the division of criminal justice services and by any police department or law enforcement agency having any such photograph, photographic plate or proof, palmprint or fingerprints in its possession or under its control;

(b) any police department or law enforcement agency, including the division of criminal justice services, which transmitted or otherwise forwarded to any agency of the United States or of any other state or of any other jurisdiction outside the state of New York copies of any such photographs, photographic plates or proofs, palmprints and fingerprints, including those relating to actions or proceedings which were dismissed pursuant to section 170.56 or 210.46 of this chapter, shall forthwith formally request in writing that all such copies be destroyed or returned to the police department or law enforcement agency which transmitted or forwarded them, and, if returned, such department or agency shall, at its discretion, either destroy or return them as provided herein, except that those relating to dismissals pursuant to section 170.56 or 210.46 of this chapter shall not be destroyed or returned by such department or agency;

(c) all official records and papers, including judgments and orders of a court but not including published court decisions or opinions or records and briefs on appeal, relating to the arrest or prosecution, including all duplicates and copies thereof, on file with the division of criminal justice services, any court, police agency, or prosecutor's office shall be sealed and not made available to any person or public or private agency;

(d) such records shall be made available to the person accused or to such person's designated agent, and shall be made available to (i) a prosecutor in any proceeding in which the accused has moved for an order pursuant to section 170.56 or 210.46 of this chapter, or (ii) a law enforcement agency upon ex parte motion in any superior court, or in any district court, city court or the criminal court of the city of New York provided that such court sealed the record, if such agency demonstrates to the satisfaction of the court that justice requires that such records be made available to it, or (iii) any state or local officer or agency with responsibility for the issuance of licenses to possess guns, when the accused has made application for such a license, or (iv) the New York state department of corrections and community supervision when the accused is on parole supervision as a result of conditional release or a parole release granted by the New York state board of parole, and the arrest which is the subject of the inquiry is one which occurred while the accused was under such supervision, or (v) any prospective employer of a police officer or peace officer as those terms are defined in subdivisions thirty-three and thirty-four of section 1.20 of this chapter, in relation to an application for employment as a police officer or peace officer; provided, however, that every person who is an applicant for the position of police officer or peace officer shall be furnished with a copy of all records obtained under this paragraph and afforded an opportunity to make an explanation thereto, or (vi) the probation department responsible for supervision of the accused when the arrest which is the subject of the inquiry is one which occurred while the accused was under such supervision; and

(e) where fingerprints subject to the provisions of this section have been received by the division of criminal justice services and have been filed by the division as digital images, such images may be retained, provided that a fingerprint card of the individual is on file with the division which was not sealed pursuant to this section or section 160.55 of this article.

2. A report of the termination of the action or proceeding in favor of the accused shall be sufficient notice of sealing to the commissioner of the division of criminal justice services unless the report also indicates that the court directed that the record not be sealed in the interests of justice. Where the court has determined pursuant to subdivision one of this section that sealing is not in the interest of justice, the clerk of the court shall include notification of that determination in any report to such division of the disposition of the action or proceeding.

3. For the purposes of subdivision one of this section, a criminal action or proceeding against a person shall be considered terminated in favor of such person where:

(a) an order dismissing the entire accusatory instrument against such person pursuant to article four hundred seventy was entered; or

(b) an order to dismiss the entire accusatory instrument against such person pursuant to section 170.30, 170.50, 170.55, 170.56, 180.70, 210.20, 210.46 or 210.47 of this chapter was entered or deemed entered, or an order terminating the prosecution against such person was entered pursuant to section 180.85 of this chapter, and the people have not appealed from such order or the determination of an appeal or appeals by the people from such order has been against the people; or

(c) a verdict of complete acquittal was made pursuant to section 330.10 of this chapter; or

(d) a trial order of dismissal of the entire accusatory instrument against such person pursuant to section 290.10 or 360.40 of this chapter was entered and the people have not appealed from such order or the determination of an appeal or appeals by the people from such order has been against the people; or

(e) an order setting aside a verdict pursuant to section 330.30 or 370.10 of this chapter was entered and the people have not appealed from such order or the determination of an appeal or appeals by the people from such order has been against the people and no new trial has been ordered; or

(f) an order vacating a judgment pursuant to section 440.10 of this chapter was entered and the people have not appealed from such order or the determination of an appeal or appeals by the people from such order has been against the people, and no new trial has been ordered; or

(g) an order of discharge pursuant to article seventy of the civil practice law and rules was entered on a ground which invalidates the conviction and the people have not appealed from such order or the determination of an appeal or appeals by the people from such order has been against the people; or

(h) where all charges against such person are dismissed pursuant to section 190.75 of this chapter. In such event, the clerk of the court which empaneled the grand jury shall serve a certification of such disposition upon the division of criminal justice services and upon the appropriate police department or law enforcement agency which upon receipt thereof, shall comply with the provisions of paragraphs (a), (b), (c) and (d) of subdivision one of this section in the same manner as is required thereunder with respect to an order of a court entered pursuant to said subdivision one; or

(i) prior to the filing of an accusatory instrument in a local criminal court against such person, the prosecutor elects not to prosecute such person. In such event, the prosecutor shall serve a certification of such disposition upon the division of criminal justice services and upon the appropriate police department or law enforcement agency which, upon receipt thereof, shall comply with the provisions of paragraphs (a), (b), (c) and (d) of subdivision one of this section in the same manner as is required thereunder with respect to an order of a court entered pursuant to said subdivision one.

(j) following the arrest of such person, the arresting police agency, prior to the filing of an accusatory instrument in a local criminal court but subsequent to the forwarding of a copy of the fingerprints of such person to the division of criminal justice services, elects not to proceed further. In such event, the head of the arresting police agency shall serve a certification of such disposition upon the division of criminal justice services which, upon receipt thereof, shall comply with the provisions of paragraphs (a), (b), (c) and (d) of subdivision one of this section in the same manner as is required thereunder with respect to an order of a court entered pursuant to said subdivision one.

(k) (i) The accusatory instrument alleged a violation of article two hundred twenty or section 240.36 of the penal law, prior to the taking effect of article two hundred twenty-one of the penal law, or a violation of article two hundred twenty-one of the penal law; (ii) the sole controlled substance involved is marijuana; (iii) the conviction was only for a violation or violations; and (iv) at least three years have passed since the offense occurred.

(l) An order dismissing an action pursuant to section 215.40 of this chapter was entered.

4. A person in whose favor a criminal action or proceeding was terminated, as defined in paragraph (a) through (h) of subdivision two of this section, prior to the effective date of this section, may upon motion apply to the court in which such termination occurred, upon not less than twenty days notice to the district attorney, for an order granting to such person the relief set forth in subdivision one of this section, and such order shall be granted unless the district attorney demonstrates to the satisfaction of the court that the interests of justice require otherwise. A person in whose favor a criminal action or proceeding was terminated, as defined in paragraph (i) or (j) of subdivision two of this section, prior to the effective date of this section, may apply to the appropriate prosecutor or police agency for a certification as described in said paragraph (i) or (j) granting to such person the relief set forth therein, and such certification shall be granted by such prosecutor or police agency.

§ 160.55. Order upon termination of criminal action by conviction for noncriminal offense; entry of waiver; administrative findings

1. Upon the termination of a criminal action or proceeding against a person by the conviction of such person of a traffic infraction or a violation, other than a violation of loitering as described in paragraph (d) or (e) of subdivision one of section 160.10 of this chapter or the violation of operating a motor vehicle while ability impaired as described in subdivision one of section eleven hundred ninety-two of the vehicle and traffic law, unless the district attorney upon motion with not less than five days notice to such person or his or her attorney demonstrates to the satisfaction of the court that the interests of justice require otherwise, or the court on its own motion with not less than five days notice to such person or his or her attorney determines that the interests of justice require otherwise and states the reasons for such determination on the record, the clerk of the court wherein such criminal action or proceeding was terminated shall immediately notify the commissioner of the division of criminal justice services and the heads of all appropriate police departments and other law enforcement agencies that the action has been terminated by such conviction. Upon receipt of notification of such termination:

(a) every photograph of such person and photographic plate or proof, and all palmprints and fingerprints taken or made of such person pursuant to the provisions of this article in regard to the action or proceeding terminated, and all duplicates and copies thereof, except a digital fingerprint image where authorized pursuant to paragraph (e) of this subdivision, except for the palmprints and fingerprints concerning a disposition of harassment in the second degree as defined in section 240.26 of the penal law, committed against a member of the same family or household as the defendant, as defined in subdivision one of section 530.11 of this chapter, and determined pursuant to subdivision eight-a of section 170.10 of this title, shall forthwith be, at the discretion of the recipient agency, either destroyed or returned to such person, or to the attorney who represented such person at the time of the termination of the action or proceeding, at the address given by such person or attorney during the action or proceeding, by the division of criminal justice services and by any police department or law enforcement agency having any such photograph, photographic plate or proof, palmprints or fingerprints in its possession or under its control;

(b) any police department or law enforcement agency, including the division of criminal justice services, which transmitted or otherwise forwarded to any agency of the United States or of any other state or of any other jurisdiction outside the state of New York copies of any such photographs, photographic plates or proofs, palmprints and fingerprints, shall forthwith formally request in writing that all such copies be destroyed or returned to the police department or law enforcement agency which transmitted or forwarded them, and upon such return such department or agency shall, at its discretion, either destroy or return them as provided herein;

(c) all official records and papers relating to the arrest or prosecution, including all duplicates and copies thereof, on file with the division of criminal justice services, police agency, or prosecutor's office shall be sealed and not made available to any person or public or private agency;

(d) the records referred to in paragraph (c) of this subdivision shall be made available to the person accused or to such person's designated agent, and shall be made available to (i) a prosecutor in any proceeding in which the accused has moved for an order pursuant to section 170.56 or 210.46 of this chapter, or (ii) a law enforcement agency upon ex parte motion in any superior court, or in any district court, city court or the criminal court of the city of New York provided that such court sealed the record, if such agency demonstrates to the satisfaction of the court that justice requires that such records be made available to it, or (iii) any state or local officer or agency with responsibility for the issuance of licenses to possess guns, when the accused has made application for such a license, or (iv) the New York state department of corrections and community supervision when the accused is under parole supervision as a result of conditional release or parole release granted by the New York state board of parole and the arrest which is the subject of the inquiry is one which occurred while the accused was under such supervision, or (v) the probation department responsible for supervision of the accused when the arrest which is the subject of the inquiry is one which occurred while the accused was under such supervision, or (vi) a police agency, probation department, sheriff's office, district attorney's office, department of correction of any municipality and parole department, for law enforcement purposes, upon arrest in instances in which the individual stands convicted of harassment in the second degree, as defined in section 240.26 of the penal law, committed against a member of the same family or household as the defendant, as defined in subdivision one of section 530.11 of this chapter, and determined pursuant to subdivision eight-a of section 170.10 of this title; and

(e) where fingerprints subject to the provisions of this section have been received by the division of criminal justice services and have been filed by the division as digital images, such images may be retained, provided that a fingerprint card of the individual is on file with the division which was not sealed pursuant to this section or section 160.50 of this article.

2. A report of the termination of the action or proceeding by conviction of a traffic violation or a violation other than a violation of loitering as described in paragraph (d) or (e) of subdivision one of section 160.10 of this title or the violation of operating a motor vehicle while ability impaired as described in subdivision one of section eleven hundred ninety-two of the vehicle and traffic law, shall be sufficient notice of sealing to the commissioner of the division of criminal justice services unless the report also indicates that the court directed that the record not be sealed in the interests of justice. Where the court has determined pursuant to subdivision one of this section that sealing is not in the interests of justice, the clerk of the court shall include notification of that determination in any report to such division of the disposition of the action or proceeding. When the defendant has been found guilty of a violation of harassment in the second degree and it was determined pursuant to subdivision eight-a of section 170.10 of this title that such violation was committed against a member of the same family or household as the defendant, the clerk of the court shall include notification of that determination in any report to such division of the disposition of the action or proceeding for purposes of paragraph (a) and subparagraph (vi) of paragraph (d) of subdivision one of this section.

3. A person against whom a criminal action or proceeding was terminated by such person's conviction of a traffic infraction or violation other than a violation of loitering as described in paragraph (d) or (e) of subdivision one of section 160.10 of this chapter or the violation of operating a motor vehicle while ability impaired as described in subdivision one of section eleven hundred ninety-two of the vehicle and traffic law, prior to the effective date of this section, may upon motion apply to the court in which such termination occurred, upon not less than twenty days notice to the district attorney, for an order granting to such person the relief set forth in subdivision one of this section, and such order shall be granted unless the district attorney demonstrates to the satisfaction of the court that the interests of justice require otherwise.

4. This section shall not apply to an action terminated in a manner described in paragraph (k) of subdivision two of section 160.50 of this chapter.

5.

(a) When a criminal action or proceeding is terminated against a person by the entry of a waiver of a hearing pursuant to paragraph (c) of subdivision ten of section eleven hundred ninety-two of the vehicle and traffic law or section forty-nine-b of the navigation law, the record of the criminal action shall be sealed in accordance with this subdivision. Upon the entry of such waiver, the court or the clerk of the court shall immediately notify the commissioner of the division of criminal justice services and the heads of all appropriate police departments and other law enforcement agencies that a waiver has been entered and that the record of the action shall be sealed when the person reaches the age of twenty-one or three years from the date of commission of the offense, whichever is the greater period of time. At the expiration of such period, the commissioner of the division of criminal justice services and the heads of all appropriate police departments and other law enforcement agencies shall take the actions required by paragraphs (a), (b) and (c) of subdivision one of section 160.50 of this article.

(b) Where a person under the age of twenty-one is referred by the police to the department of motor vehicles for action pursuant to section eleven hundred ninety-two-a or eleven hundred ninety-four-a of the vehicle and traffic law, or section forty-nine-b of the navigation law and a finding in favor of the motorist or operator is rendered, the commissioner of the department of motor vehicles shall, as soon as practicable, but not later than three years from the date of commission of the offense or when such person reaches the age of twenty-one, whichever is the greater period of time, notify the commissioner of the division of criminal justice services and the heads of all appropriate police departments and other law enforcement agencies that such finding in favor of the motorist or operator was rendered. Upon receipt of such notification, the commissioner of the division of criminal justice services and the heads of such police departments and other law enforcement agencies shall take the actions required by paragraphs (a), (b) and (c) of subdivision one of section 160.50 of this article.

(c) Where a person under the age of twenty-one is referred by the police to the department of motor vehicles for action pursuant to section eleven hundred ninety-two-a or eleven hundred ninety-four-a of the vehicle and traffic law, or section forty-nine-b of the navigation law, and no notification is received by the commissioner of the division of criminal justice services and the heads of all appropriate police departments and other law enforcement agencies pursuant to paragraph (b) of this subdivision, such commissioner of the division of criminal justice services and such heads of police departments and other law enforcement agencies shall, after three years from the date of commission of the offense or when the person reaches the age of twenty-one, whichever is the greater period of time, take the actions required by paragraphs (a), (b) and (c) of subdivision one of section 160.50 of this article.

§ 160.58. Conditional sealing of certain controlled substance, marihuana or specified offense convictions

1. A defendant convicted of any offense defined in article two hundred twenty or two hundred twenty-one of the penal law or a specified offense defined in subdivision five of section 410.91 of this chapter who has successfully completed a judicial diversion program under article two hundred sixteen of this chapter, or one of the programs heretofore known as drug treatment alternative to prison or another judicially sanctioned drug treatment program of similar duration, requirements and level of supervision, and has completed the sentence imposed for the offense or offenses, is eligible to have such offense or offenses sealed pursuant to this section.

2. The court that sentenced the defendant to a judicially sanctioned drug treatment program may on its own motion, or on the defendant's motion, order that all official records and papers relating to the arrest, prosecution and conviction which resulted in the defendant's participation in the judicially sanctioned drug treatment program be conditionally sealed. In such case, the court may also conditionally seal the arrest, prosecution and conviction records for no more than three of the defendant's prior eligible misdemeanors, which for purposes of this subdivision shall be limited to misdemeanor offenses defined in article two hundred twenty or two hundred twenty-one

of the penal law. The court may only seal the records of the defendant's arrests, prosecutions and convictions when:

(a) the sentencing court has requested and received from the division of criminal justice services or the Federal Bureau of Investigation a fingerprint based criminal history record of the defendant, including any sealed or suppressed information. The division of criminal justice services shall also include a criminal history report, if any, from the Federal Bureau of Investigation regarding any criminal history information that occurred in other jurisdictions. The division is hereby authorized to receive such information from the Federal Bureau of Investigation for this purpose. The parties shall be permitted to examine these records;

(b) the defendant or court has identified the misdemeanor conviction or convictions for which relief may be granted;

(c) the court has received documentation that the sentences imposed on the eligible misdemeanor convictions have been completed, or if no such documentation is reasonably available, a sworn affidavit that the sentences imposed on the prior misdemeanors have been completed; and

(d) the court has notified the district attorney of each jurisdiction in which the defendant has been convicted of an offense with respect to which sealing is sought, and the court or courts of record for such offenses, that the court is considering sealing the records of the defendant's eligible misdemeanor convictions. Both the district attorney and the court shall be given a reasonable opportunity, which shall not be less than thirty days, in which to comment and submit materials to aid the court in making such a determination.

3. At the request of the defendant or the district attorney of a county in which the defendant committed a crime that is the subject of the sealing application, the court may conduct a hearing to consider and review any relevant evidence offered by either party that would aid the court in its decision whether to seal the records of the defendant's arrests, prosecutions and convictions. In making such a determination, the court shall consider any relevant factors, including but not limited to: (i) the circumstances and seriousness of the offense or offenses that resulted in the conviction or convictions; (ii) the character of the defendant, including his or her completion of the judicially sanctioned treatment program as described in subdivision one of this section; (iii) the defendant's criminal history; and (iv) the impact of sealing the defendant's records upon his or her rehabilitation and his or her successful and productive reentry and reintegration into society, and on public safety.

4. When a court orders sealing pursuant to this section, all official records and papers relating to the arrests, prosecutions, and convictions, including all duplicates and copies thereof, on file with the division of criminal justice services or any court shall be sealed and not made available to any person or public or private agency; provided, however, the division shall retain any fingerprints, palmprints and photographs, or digital images of the same.

5. When the court orders sealing pursuant to this section, the clerk of such court shall immediately notify the commissioner of the division of criminal justice services, and any court that sentenced the defendant for an offense which has been conditionally sealed, regarding the records that shall be sealed pursuant to this section.

6. Records sealed pursuant to this subdivision shall be made available to:

(a) the defendant or the defendant's designated agent;

(b) qualified agencies, as defined in subdivision nine of section eight hundred thirty-five of the executive law, and federal and state law enforcement agencies, when acting within the scope of their law enforcement duties; or

(c) any state or local officer or agency with responsibility for the issuance of licenses to possess guns, when the person has made application for such a license; or

(d) any prospective employer of a police officer or peace officer as those terms are defined in subdivisions thirty-three and thirty-four of section 1.20 of this chapter, in relation to an application for employment as a police officer or peace officer; provided, however, that every person who is an applicant for the position of police officer or peace officer shall be furnished with a copy of all records obtained under this paragraph and afforded an opportunity to make an explanation thereto.

7. The court shall not seal the defendant's record pursuant to this section while any charged offense is pending.

8. If, subsequent to the sealing of records pursuant to this subdivision, the person who is the subject of such records is arrested for or formally charged with any misdemeanor or felony offense, such records shall be unsealed immediately and remain unsealed; provided, however, that if such new misdemeanor or felony arrest results in a termination in favor of the accused as defined in subdivision three of section 160.50 of this article or by conviction for a non criminal offense as described in section 160.55 of this article, such unsealed records shall be conditionally sealed pursuant to this section.

§ 160.59. Sealing of certain convictions

1. Definitions: As used in this section, the following terms shall have the following meanings:

(a) "Eligible offense" shall mean any crime defined in the laws of this state other than a sex offense defined in article one hundred thirty of the penal law, an offense defined in article two hundred sixty-three of the penal law, a felony offense defined in article one hundred twenty-five of the penal law, a violent felony offense defined in section 70.02 of the penal law, a class A felony offense defined in the penal law, a felony offense defined in article one hundred five of the penal law where the underlying offense is not an eligible offense, an attempt to commit an offense that is not an eligible offense if the attempt is a felony, or an offense for which registration as a sex offender is required pursuant to article six-C of the correction law. For the purposes of this section, where the defendant is convicted of more than one eligible offense, committed as part of the same criminal transaction as defined in subdivision two of section 40.10 of this chapter, those offenses shall be considered one eligible offense.

(b) "Sentencing judge" shall mean the judge who pronounced sentence upon the conviction under consideration, or if that judge is no longer sitting in a court in the jurisdiction in which the conviction was obtained, any other judge who is sitting in the criminal court where the judgment of conviction was entered.

1-a. The chief administrator of the courts shall, pursuant to section 10.40 of this chapter, prescribe a form application which may be used by a defendant to apply for sealing pursuant to this section. Such form application shall include all the essential elements required by this section to be included in an application for sealing. Nothing in this subdivision shall be read to require a defendant to use such form application to apply for sealing.

2.

(a) A defendant who has been convicted of up to two eligible offenses but not more than one felony offense may apply to the court in which he or she was convicted of the most serious offense to have such conviction or convictions sealed. If all offenses are offenses with the same classification, the application shall be made to the court in which the defendant was last convicted.

(b) An application shall contain (i) a copy of a certificate of disposition or other similar documentation for any offense for which the defendant has been convicted, or an explanation of why such certificate or other documentation is not available; (ii) a sworn statement of the defendant as to whether he or she has filed, or then intends to file, any application for sealing of any other eligible offense; (iii) a copy of any other such application that has been filed; (iv) a sworn statement as to the conviction or convictions for which relief is being sought; and (v) a sworn statement of the reason or reasons why the court should, in its discretion, grant such sealing, along with any supporting documentation.

(c) A copy of any application for such sealing shall be served upon the district attorney of the county in which the conviction, or, if more than one, the convictions, was or were obtained. The district attorney shall notify the court within forty-five days if he or she objects to the application for sealing.

(d) When such application is filed with the court, it shall be assigned to the sentencing judge unless more than one application is filed in which case the application shall be assigned to the county court or the supreme court of the county in which the criminal court is located, who shall request and receive from the division of criminal justice services a fingerprint based criminal history record of the defendant, including any sealed or suppressed records. The division of criminal justice services also shall include a criminal history report, if any, from the federal bureau of investigation regarding any criminal history information that occurred in other jurisdictions. The division is hereby authorized to receive such information from the federal bureau of investigation for this purpose, and to make such information available to the court, which may make this information available to the district attorney and the defendant.

3. The sentencing judge, or county or supreme court shall summarily deny the defendant's application when:

(a) the defendant is required to register as a sex offender pursuant to article six-C of the correction law; or

(b) the defendant has previously obtained sealing of the maximum number of convictions allowable under section 160.58 of the criminal procedure law; or

(c) the defendant has previously obtained sealing of the maximum number of convictions allowable under subdivision four of this section; or

(d) the time period specified in subdivision five of this section has not yet been satisfied; or

(e) the defendant has an undisposed arrest or charge pending; or

(f) the defendant was convicted of any crime after the date of the entry of judgement of the last conviction for which sealing is sought; or

(g) the defendant has failed to provide the court with the required sworn statement of the reasons why the court should grant the relief requested; or

(h) the defendant has been convicted of two or more felonies or more than two crimes.

4. Provided that the application is not summarily denied for the reasons set forth in subdivision three of this section, a defendant who stands convicted of up to two eligible offenses, may obtain sealing of no more than two eligible offenses but not more than one felony offense.

5. Any eligible offense may be sealed only after at least ten years have passed since the imposition of the sentence on the defendant's latest conviction or, if the defendant was sentenced to a period of incarceration, including a period of incarceration imposed in conjunction with a sentence of probation, the defendant's latest release from incarceration. In calculating the ten year period under this subdivision, any period of time the defendant spent incarcerated after the conviction for which the application for sealing is sought, shall be excluded and such ten year period shall be extended by a period or periods equal to the time served under such incarceration.

6. Upon determining that the application is not subject to mandatory denial pursuant to subdivision three of this section and that the application is opposed by the district attorney, the sentencing judge or county or supreme court shall conduct a hearing on the application in order to consider any evidence offered by either party that would aid the sentencing judge in his or her decision whether to seal the records of the defendant's convictions. No hearing is required if the district attorney does not oppose the application.

7. In considering any such application, the sentencing judge or county or supreme court shall consider any relevant factors, including but not limited to:

(a) the amount of time that has elapsed since the defendant's last conviction;

(b) the circumstances and seriousness of the offense for which the defendant is seeking relief, including whether the arrest charge was not an eligible offense;

(c) the circumstances and seriousness of any other offenses for which the defendant stands convicted;

(d) the character of the defendant, including any measures that the defendant has taken toward rehabilitation, such as participating in treatment programs, work, or schooling, and participating in community service or other volunteer programs;

(e) any statements made by the victim of the offense for which the defendant is seeking relief;

(f) the impact of sealing the defendant's record upon his or her rehabilitation and upon his or her successful and productive reentry and reintegration into society; and

(g) the impact of sealing the defendant's record on public safety and upon the public's confidence in and respect for the law.

8. When a sentencing judge or county or supreme court orders sealing pursuant to this section, all official records and papers relating to the arrests, prosecutions, and convictions, including all duplicates and copies thereof, on file with the division of criminal justice services or any court shall be sealed and not made available to any

person or public or private agency except as provided for in subdivision nine of this section; provided, however, the division shall retain any fingerprints, palmprints and photographs, or digital images of the same. The clerk of such court shall immediately notify the commissioner of the division of criminal justice services regarding the records that shall be sealed pursuant to this section. The clerk also shall notify any court in which the defendant has stated, pursuant to paragraph (b) of subdivision two of this section, that he or she has filed or intends to file an application for sealing of any other eligible offense.

9. Records sealed pursuant to this section shall be made available to:

(a) the defendant or the defendant's designated agent;

(b) qualified agencies, as defined in subdivision nine of section eight hundred thirty-five of the executive law, and federal and state law enforcement agencies, when acting within the scope of their law enforcement duties; or

(c) any state or local officer or agency with responsibility for the issuance of licenses to possess guns, when the person has made application for such a license; or

(d) any prospective employer of a police officer or peace officer as those terms are defined in subdivisions thirty-three and thirty-four of section 1.20 of this chapter, in relation to an application for employment as a police officer or peace officer; provided, however, that every person who is an applicant for the position of police officer or peace officer shall be furnished with a copy of all records obtained under this paragraph and afforded an opportunity to make an explanation thereto; or

(e) the criminal justice information services division of the federal bureau of investigation, for the purposes of responding to queries to the national instant criminal background check system regarding attempts to purchase or otherwise take possession of firearms, as defined in 18 USC 921 (a) (3).

10. A conviction which is sealed pursuant to this section is included within the definition of a conviction for the purposes of any criminal proceeding in which the fact of a prior conviction would enhance a penalty or is an element of the offense charged.

11. No defendant shall be required or permitted to waive eligibility for sealing pursuant to this section as part of a plea of guilty, sentence or any agreement related to a conviction for an eligible offense and any such waiver shall be deemed void and wholly unenforceable.

§ 160.60. Effect of termination of criminal actions in favor of the accused

Upon the termination of a criminal action or proceeding against a person in favor of such person, as defined in subdivision two of section 160.50 of this chapter, the arrest and prosecution shall be deemed a nullity and the accused shall be restored, in contemplation of law, to the status he occupied before the arrest and prosecution. The arrest or prosecution shall not operate as a disqualification of any person so accused to pursue or engage in any lawful activity, occupation, profession, or calling. Except where specifically required or permitted by statute or upon specific authorization of a superior court, no such person shall be required to divulge information pertaining to the arrest or prosecution.

§ 170.10. Arraignment upon information, simplified traffic information, prosecutor's information or misdemeanor complaint; defendant's presence, defendant's rights, court's instructions and bail matters

1. Following the filing with a local criminal court of an information, a simplified information, a prosecutor's information or a misdemeanor complaint, the defendant must be arraigned thereon. The defendant must appear personally at such arraignment except under the following circumstances:

(a) In any case where a simplified information is filed and a procedure is provided by law which is applicable to all offenses charged in such simplified information and, if followed, would dispense with an arraignment or personal appearance of the defendant, nothing contained in this section affects the validity of such procedure or requires such personal appearance;

(b) In any case in which the defendant's appearance is required by a summons or an appearance ticket, the court in its discretion may, for good cause shown, permit the defendant to appear by counsel instead of in person.

2. Upon any arraignment at which the defendant is personally present, the court must immediately inform him, or cause him to be informed in its presence, of the charge or charges against him and must furnish him with a copy of the accusatory instrument.

3. The defendant has the right to the aid of counsel at the arraignment and at every subsequent stage of the action. If he appears upon such arraignment without counsel, he has the following rights:

(a) To an adjournment for the purpose of obtaining counsel; and

(b) To communicate, free of charge, by letter or by telephone provided by the law enforcement facility where the defendant is held to a phone number located in the United States, or Puerto Rico, for the purposes of obtaining counsel and informing a relative or friend that he or she has been charged with an offense; and

(c) To have counsel assigned by the court if he is financially unable to obtain the same; except that this paragraph does not apply where the accusatory instrument charges a traffic infraction or infractions only.

4. Except as provided in subdivision five, the court must inform the defendant:

(a) Of his rights as prescribed in subdivision three; and the court must not only accord him opportunity to exercise such rights but must itself take such affirmative action as is necessary to effectuate them; and

(b) Where a traffic infraction or a misdemeanor relating to traffic is charged, that a judgment of conviction for such offense would in addition to subjecting the defendant to the sentence provided therefor render his license to drive a motor vehicle and his certificate of registration subject to suspension and revocation as prescribed by law and that a plea of guilty to such offense constitutes a conviction thereof to the same extent as a verdict of guilty after trial; and

(c) Where the accusatory instrument is a simplified traffic information, that the defendant has a right to have a supporting deposition filed, as provided in section 100.25; and

(d) Where the accusatory instrument is a misdemeanor complaint, that the defendant may not be prosecuted thereon or required to enter a plea thereto unless he consents to the same, and that in the absence of such consent such misdemeanor complaint will for prosecution purposes have to be replaced and superseded by an information; and

(e) Where an information, a simplified information, a prosecutor's information, a misdemeanor complaint, a felony complaint or an indictment charges harassment in the second degree, as defined in section 240.26 of the penal law, if there is a judgment of conviction for such offense and such offense is determined to have been committed against a member of the same family or household as the defendant, as defined in subdivision one of section 530.11 of this chapter, the record of such conviction shall be accessible for law enforcement purposes and not sealed, as specified in paragraph (a) and subparagraph (vi) of paragraph (d) of subdivision one of section 160.55 of this title; and

5. In any case in which a defendant has appeared for arraignment in response to a summons or an appearance ticket, a printed statement upon such process of any court instruction required by the provisions of subdivision four, other than those specified in paragraphs (d) and (e) thereof, constitutes compliance with such provisions with respect to the instruction so printed.

6. If a defendant charged with a traffic infraction or infractions only desires to proceed without the aid of counsel, the court must permit him to do so. In all other cases, the court must permit the defendant to proceed without the aid of counsel if it is satisfied that he made such decision with knowledge of the significance thereof, but if it is not so satisfied it may not proceed until the defendant is provided with counsel, either of his own choosing or by assignment. Regardless of the kind or nature of the charges, a defendant who proceeds at the arraignment without counsel does not waive his right to counsel, and the court must inform him that he continues to have such right as well as all the rights specified in subdivision three which are necessary to effectuate it, and that he may exercise such rights at any stage of the action.

7. Upon the arraignment, the court, unless it intends to make a final disposition of the action immediately thereafter, must, as provided in subdivision one of section 530.20, issue a securing order either releasing the defendant on his own recognizance or fixing bail for his future appearance in the action; except that where a defendant appears by counsel pursuant to paragraph (b) of subdivision one of this section, the court must release the defendant on his own recognizance.

8. Notwithstanding any other provision of law to the contrary, a local criminal court may not, at arraignment or within thirty days of arraignment on a simplified traffic information charging a violation of subdivision two, two-a, three, four or four-a of section eleven hundred ninety-two of the vehicle and traffic law and upon which a notation has been made pursuant to subdivision twelve of section eleven hundred ninety-two of the vehicle and traffic law, accept a plea of guilty to a violation of any subdivision of section eleven hundred ninety-two of the vehicle and traffic law, nor to any other traffic infraction arising out of the same incident, nor to any other traffic infraction, violation or misdemeanor where the court is aware that such offense was charged pursuant to an accident

involving death or serious physical injury, except upon written consent of the district attorney.

8-a.

(a) Where an information, a simplified information, a prosecutor's information, a misdemeanor complaint, a felony complaint or an indictment charges harassment in the second degree as defined in section 240.26 of the penal law, the people may serve upon the defendant and file with the court a notice alleging that such offense was committed against a member of the same family or household as the defendant, as defined in subdivision one of section 530.11 of this chapter. Such notice must be served within fifteen days after arraignment on an information, a simplified information, a prosecutor's information, a misdemeanor complaint, a felony complaint or an indictment for such charge and before trial. Such notice must include the name of the person alleged to be a member of the same family or household as the defendant and specify the specific family or household relationship as defined in subdivision one of section 530.11 of this chapter.

(b) If a defendant, charged with harassment in the second degree as defined in section 240.26 of the penal law stipulates, or admits in the course of a plea disposition, that the person against whom the charged offense is alleged to have been committed is a member of the same family or household as the defendant, as defined in subdivision one of section 530.11 of this chapter, such allegation shall be deemed established for purposes of paragraph (a) and subparagraph (vi) of paragraph (d) of subdivision one of section 160.55 of this title. If the defendant denies such allegation, the people may, by proof beyond a reasonable doubt, prove as part of their case that the alleged victim of such offense was a member of the same family or household as the defendant. In such circumstances, the trier of fact shall make its determination with respect to such allegation orally on the record or in writing.

9. Nothing contained in this section applies to the arraignment of corporate defendants, which is governed generally by the provisions of article six hundred.

10. Notwithstanding any contrary provision of this section, when an off-hours arraignment part designated in accordance with paragraph (w) of subdivision one of section two hundred twelve of the judiciary law is in operation in the county in which the court is located, the court must adjourn the proceedings before it, and direct that the proceedings be continued in such off-hours part when the defendant has appeared before the court without counsel and no counsel is otherwise available at the time of such appearance to aid the defendant, unless the defendant desires to proceed without the aid of counsel and the court is satisfied, pursuant to subdivision six of this section, that the defendant made such decision with knowledge of the significance thereof.

§ 170.15. Removal of action from one local criminal court to another

Under circumstances prescribed in this section, a criminal action based upon an information, a simplified information, a prosecutor's information or a misdemeanor complaint may be removed from one local criminal court to another:

1. When a defendant arrested by a police officer for an offense other than a felony, allegedly committed in a city or town, has, owing to special circumstances and pursuant to law, not been brought before the particular local criminal court which by reason of the

situs of such offense has trial jurisdiction thereof, but, instead, before a local criminal court which does not have trial jurisdiction thereof, and therein stands charged with such offense by information, simplified information or misdemeanor complaint, such local criminal court must arraign him upon such accusatory instrument. If the defendant desires to enter a plea of guilty thereto immediately following such arraignment, such local criminal court must permit him to do so and must thereafter conduct the action to judgment. Otherwise, it must remit the action, together with all pertinent papers and documents, to the local criminal court which has trial jurisdiction of the action, and the latter court must then conduct such action to judgment or other final disposition.

2. When a defendant arrested by a police officer for an offense other than a felony has been brought before a superior court judge sitting as a local criminal court for arraignment upon an information, simplified information or misdemeanor complaint charging such offense, such judge must, as a local criminal court, arraign the defendant upon such accusatory instrument. Such judge must then remit the action, together with all pertinent papers and documents, to a local criminal court having trial jurisdiction thereof. The latter court must then conduct such action to judgment or other final disposition.

3. At any time within the period provided by section 255.20, where a defendant is arraigned upon an information, a simplified information, a prosecutor's information or a misdemeanor complaint pending in a city court, town court or a village court having trial jurisdiction thereof, a judge of the county court of the county in which such city court, town court or village court is located may, upon motion of the defendant or the people, order that the action be transferred for disposition from the court in which the matter is pending to another designated local criminal court of the county, upon the ground that disposition thereof within a reasonable time in the court from which removal is sought is unlikely owing to:

(a) Death, disability or other incapacity or disqualification of all of the judges of such court; or

(b) Inability of such court to form a jury in a case, in which the defendant is entitled to and has requested a jury trial.

4. Notwithstanding any provision of this section to the contrary, in any county outside a city having a population of one million or more, upon or after arraignment of a defendant on an information, a simplified information, a prosecutor's information or a misdemeanor complaint pending in a local criminal court, such court may, upon motion of the defendant and with the consent of the district attorney, order that the action be removed from the court in which the matter is pending to another local criminal court in the same county which has been designated a drug court by the chief administrator of the courts, and such drug court may then conduct such action to judgement or other final disposition; provided, however, that an order of removal issued under this subdivision shall not take effect until five days after the date the order is issued unless, prior to such effective date, the drug court notifies the court that issued the order that:

(a) it will not accept the action, in which event the order shall not take effect, or

(b) it will accept the action on a date prior to such effective date, in which event the order shall take effect upon such prior date.

Upon providing notification pursuant to paragraph (a) or (b) of this subdivision, the drug court shall promptly give notice to the defendant, his or her counsel and the district attorney.

5.

(a) Notwithstanding any provision of this section to the contrary, in any county outside a city having a population of one million or more, upon or after arraignment of a defendant on an information, a simplified information, a prosecutor's information or a misdemeanor complaint pending in a local criminal court, such court may, upon motion of the defendant and after giving the district attorney an opportunity to be heard, order that the action be removed from the court in which the matter is pending to another local criminal court in the same county, or with consent of the district attorney to another court in an adjoining county, that has been designated as a human trafficking court by the chief administrator of the courts, and such human trafficking court may then conduct such action to judgement or other final deposition; provided, however, that an order of removal issued under this subdivision shall not take effect until five days after the date the order is issued unless, prior to such effective date, the human trafficking court notifies the court that issued the order that:

i. it will not accept the action, in which event the order shall not take effect; or

ii. it will accept the action on a date prior to such effective date, in which event the order shall take effect upon such prior date.

(b) Upon providing notification pursuant to subparagraph i or ii of paragraph (a) of this subdivision, the human trafficking court shall promptly give notice to the defendant, his or her counsel, and the district attorney.

§ 170.20. Divestiture of jurisdiction by indictment; removal of case to superior court at district attorney's instance

1. If at any time before entry of a plea of guilty to or commencement of a trial of a local criminal court accusatory instrument containing a charge of misdemeanor, an indictment charging the defendant with such misdemeanor is filed in a superior court, the local criminal court is thereby divested of jurisdiction of such misdemeanor charge and all proceedings therein with respect thereto are terminated.

2. At any time before entry of a plea of guilty to or commencement of a trial of an accusatory instrument specified in subdivision one, the district attorney may apply for an adjournment of the proceedings in the local criminal court upon the ground that he intends to present the misdemeanor charge in question to a grand jury with a view to prosecuting it by indictment in a superior court. In such case, the local criminal court must adjourn the proceedings to a date which affords the district attorney reasonable opportunity to pursue such action, and may subsequently grant such further adjournments for that purpose as are reasonable under the circumstances. Following the granting of such adjournment or adjournments, the proceedings must be as follows:

(a) If such charge is presented to a grand jury within the designated period and either an indictment or a dismissal of such charge results, the local criminal court is thereby divested of jurisdiction of such charge, and all proceedings in the local criminal court with respect thereto are terminated.

(b) If the misdemeanor charge is not presented to a grand jury within the designated period, the proceedings in the local criminal court must continue.

§ 170.25. Divestiture of jurisdiction by indictment; removal of case to superior court at defendant's instance

1. At any time before entry of a plea of guilty to or commencement of a trial of a local criminal court accusatory instrument containing a charge of misdemeanor, a superior court having jurisdiction to prosecute such misdemeanor charge by indictment may, upon motion of the defendant made upon notice to the district attorney, showing good cause to believe that the interests of justice so require, order that such charge be prosecuted by indictment and that the district attorney present it to the grand jury for such purpose.

2. Such order stays the proceedings in the local criminal court pending submission of the charge to the grand jury. Upon the subsequent filing of an indictment in the superior court, the proceedings in the local criminal court terminate and the defendant must be required to appear for arraignment upon the indictment in the manner prescribed in subdivisions one and two of section 210.10. Upon the subsequent filing of a grand jury dismissal of the charge, the proceedings in the local criminal court terminate and the superior court must, if the defendant is not at liberty on his own recognizance, discharge him from custody or exonerate his bail, as the case may be.

3. At any time before entry of a plea of guilty to or commencement of a trial of or within thirty days of arraignment on an accusatory instrument specified in subdivision one, whichever occurs first, the defendant may apply to the local criminal court for an adjournment of the proceedings therein upon the ground that he intends to make a motion in a superior court, pursuant to subdivision one, for an order that the misdemeanor charge be prosecuted by indictment. In such case, the local criminal court must adjourn the proceedings to a date which affords the defendant reasonable opportunity to pursue such action, and may subsequently grant such further adjournments for that purpose as are reasonable under the circumstances. Following the granting of such adjournment or adjournments, the proceedings must be as follows:

(a) If a motion in a superior court is not made by the defendant within the designated period, the proceedings in the local criminal court must continue.

(b) If a motion in a superior court is made by the defendant within the designated period, such motion stays the proceedings in the local criminal court until the entry of an order determining such motion.

(c) If the superior court enters an order granting the motion, such order stays the proceedings in the local criminal court as provided in subdivision two; and upon a subsequent indictment or dismissal of such charge by the grand jury, the proceedings in the local criminal court terminate as provided in subdivision two.

(d) If the superior court enters an order denying the motion, the proceedings in the local criminal court must continue.

4. Upon application of a defendant who on the basis of an order issued by a superior court pursuant to subdivision one is awaiting grand jury action, and who, at the time of such order or subsequent thereto, has been committed to the custody of the sheriff pending grand jury action, and who has been confined in such custody for a period of

more than forty-five days without the occurrence of any grand jury action or disposition, the superior court which issued such order must release him on his own recognizance unless:

(a) The lack of a grand jury disposition during such period of confinement was due to the defendant's request, action or condition, or occurred with his consent; or

(b) The people have shown good cause why such order of release should not be issued. Such good cause must consist of some compelling fact or circumstance which precluded grand jury action within the prescribed period or rendered the same against the interest of justice.

§ 170.30. Motion to dismiss information, simplified information, prosecutor's information or misdemeanor complaint

1. After arraignment upon an information, a simplified information, a prosecutor's information or a misdemeanor complaint, the local criminal court may, upon motion of the defendant, dismiss such instrument or any count thereof upon the ground that:

(a) It is defective, within the meaning of section 170.35; or

(b) The defendant has received immunity from prosecution for the offense charged, pursuant to sections 50.20 or 190.40; or

(c) The prosecution is barred by reason of a previous prosecution, pursuant to section 40.20; or

(d) The prosecution is untimely, pursuant to section 30.10; or

(e) The defendant has been denied the right to a speedy trial; or

(f) There exists some other jurisdictional or legal impediment to conviction of the defendant for the offense charged; or

(g) Dismissal is required in furtherance of justice, within the meaning of section 170.40.

2. A motion pursuant to this section, except a motion pursuant to paragraph (e) of subdivision one, should be made within the period provided by section 255.20. A motion made pursuant to paragraph (e) of subdivision one should be made prior to the commencement of trial or entry of a plea of guilty.

3. Upon the motion, a defendant who is in a position adequately to raise more than one ground in support thereof should raise every such ground upon which he intends to challenge the accusatory instrument. A subsequent motion based upon such a ground not so raised may be summarily denied, although the court, in the interest of justice and for good cause shown, may in its discretion entertain and dispose of such a motion on the merits notwithstanding.

4. After arraignment upon an information, a simplified information, a prosecutor's information or misdemeanor complaint on a charge of prostitution pursuant to section 230.00 of the penal law or loitering for the purposes of prostitution pursuant to subdivision two of section 240.37 of the penal law, provided that the person does not stand charged with loitering for the purpose of patronizing a prostitute, where such offense allegedly occurred when the person was sixteen or seventeen years of age, the local criminal court may dismiss such charge in its discretion in the interest of justice on the ground that a defendant participated in services provided to him or her.

§ 170.35. Motion to dismiss information, simplified information, prosecutor's information or misdemeanor complaint; as defective

1. An information, a simplified information, a prosecutor's information or a misdemeanor complaint, or a count thereof, is defective within the meaning of paragraph (a) of subdivision one of section 170.30 when:

(a) It is not sufficient on its face pursuant to the requirements of section 100.40; provided that such an instrument or count may not be dismissed as defective, but must instead be amended, where the defect or irregularity is of a kind that may be cured by amendment and where the people move to so amend; or

(b) The allegations demonstrate that the court does not have jurisdiction of the offense charged; or

(c) The statute defining the offense charged is unconstitutional or otherwise invalid.

2. An information is also defective when it is filed in replacement of a misdemeanor complaint pursuant to section 170.65 but without satisfying the requirements stated therein.

3. A prosecutor's information is also defective when:

(a) It is filed at the direction of a grand jury, pursuant to section 190.70, and the offense or offenses charged are not among those authorized by such grand jury direction; or

(b) It is filed by the district attorney at his own instance, pursuant to subdivision two of section 100.50, and the factual allegations of the original information underlying it and any supporting depositions are not legally sufficient to support the charge in the prosecutor's information.

§ 170.40. Motion to dismiss information, simplified traffic information, prosecutor's information or misdemeanor complaint; in furtherance of justice

1. An information, a simplified traffic information, a prosecutor's information or a misdemeanor complaint, or any count thereof, may be dismissed in the interest of justice, as provided in paragraph (g) of subdivision one of section 170.30 when, even though there may be no basis for dismissal as a matter of law upon any ground specified in paragraphs (a) through (f) of said subdivision one of section 170.30, such dismissal is required as a matter of judicial discretion by the existence of some compelling factor, consideration or circumstance clearly demonstrating that conviction or prosecution of the defendant upon such accusatory instrument or count would constitute or result in injustice. In determining whether such compelling factor, consideration, or circumstance exists, the court must, to the extent applicable, examine and consider, individually and collectively, the following:

(a) the seriousness and circumstances of the offense;

(b) the extent of harm caused by the offense;

(c) the evidence of guilt, whether admissible or inadmissible at trial;

(d) the history, character and condition of the defendant;

(e) any exceptionally serious misconduct of law enforcement personnel in the investigation, arrest and prosecution of the defendant;

(f) the purpose and effect of imposing upon the defendant a sentence authorized for the offense;

(g) the impact of a dismissal on the safety or welfare of the community;

(h) the impact of a dismissal upon the confidence of the public in the criminal justice system;

(i) where the court deems it appropriate, the attitude of the complainant or victim with respect to the motion;

(j) any other relevant fact indicating that a judgment of conviction would serve no useful purpose.

2. An order dismissing an accusatory instrument specified in subdivision one in the interest of justice may be issued upon motion of the people or of the court itself as well as upon that of the defendant. Upon issuing such an order, the court must set forth its reasons therefor upon the record.

§ 170.45. Motion to dismiss information, simplified traffic information, prosecutor's information or misdemeanor complaint; procedure

The procedural rules prescribed in section 210.45 with respect to the making, consideration and disposition of a motion to dismiss an indictment are also applicable to a motion to dismiss an information, a simplified traffic information, a prosecutor's information or a misdemeanor complaint.

§ 170.50. Motion in superior court to dismiss prosecutor's information

1. At any time after arraignment in a local criminal court upon a prosecutor's information filed at the direction of a grand jury and before entry of a plea of guilty thereto or commencement of a trial thereof, the local criminal court wherein the prosecutor's information is filed may, upon motion of the defendant, dismiss such prosecutor's information or a count thereof upon the ground that:

(a) The evidence before the grand jury was not legally sufficient to support the charge; or

(b) The grand jury proceeding resulting in the filing of such prosecutor's information was defective.

2. The criteria and procedures for consideration and disposition of such motion are the same as those prescribed in sections 210.30 and 210.35, governing consideration and disposition of a motion to dismiss an indictment on the ground of insufficiency of grand jury evidence or of a defective grand jury proceeding; and, where appropriate, the general procedural rules prescribed in section 210.45 for consideration and disposition of a motion to dismiss an indictment are also applicable.

3. Upon dismissing a prosecutor's information or a count thereof pursuant to this section, the court may, upon application of the people, in its discretion authorize the people to resubmit the charge or charges to the same or another grand jury. In the absence of such authorization, such charge or charges may not be resubmitted to a grand jury. The rules prescribed in subdivisions eight and nine of section 210.45 concerning the discharge of a defendant from custody or exoneration of bail in the absence of an authorization to resubmit an indictment to a grand jury, and concerning the issuance of a securing order and the effective period thereof where such an authorization is issued, apply equally where a prosecutor's information is dismissed pursuant to this section.

§ 170.55. Adjournment in contemplation of dismissal

1. Upon or after arraignment in a local criminal court upon an information, a simplified information, a prosecutor's information or a misdemeanor complaint, and before entry of a plea of guilty thereto or commencement of a trial thereof, the court may, upon motion of the people or the defendant and with the consent of the other party, or upon the court's own motion with the consent of both the people and the defendant, order that the action be "adjourned in contemplation of dismissal," as prescribed in subdivision two.

2. An adjournment in contemplation of dismissal is an adjournment of the action without date ordered with a view to ultimate dismissal of the accusatory instrument in furtherance of justice. Upon issuing such an order, the court must release the defendant on his own recognizance. Upon application of the people, made at any time not more than six months, or in the case of a family offense as defined in subdivision one of section 530.11 of this chapter, one year, after the issuance of such order, the court may restore the case to the calendar upon a determination that dismissal of the accusatory instrument would not be in furtherance of justice, and the action must thereupon proceed. If the case is not so restored within such six months or one year period, the accusatory instrument is, at the expiration of such period, deemed to have been dismissed by the court in furtherance of justice.

3. In conjunction with an adjournment in contemplation of dismissal the court may issue a temporary order of protection pursuant to section 530.12 or 530.13 of this chapter, requiring the defendant to observe certain specified conditions of conduct.

4. Where the local criminal court information, simplified information, prosecutor's information, or misdemeanor complaint charges a crime or violation between spouses or between parent and child, or between members of the same family or household, as the term "members of the same family or household" is defined in subdivision one of section 530.11 of this chapter, the court may as a condition of an adjournment in contemplation of dismissal order, require that the defendant participate in an educational program addressing the issues of spousal abuse and family violence.

5. The court may grant an adjournment in contemplation of dismissal on condition that the defendant participate in dispute resolution and comply with any award or settlement resulting therefrom.

6. The court may as a condition of an adjournment in contemplation of dismissal order, require the defendant to perform services for a public or not-for-profit corporation, association, institution or agency. Such condition may only be imposed where the defendant has consented to the amount and conditions of such service. The court may not impose such conditions in excess of the length of the adjournment.

6-a. The court may, as a condition of an authorized adjournment in contemplation of dismissal, where the defendant has been charged with an offense and the elements of such offense meet the criteria of an "eligible offense" and such person qualified as an "eligible person" as such terms are defined in section four hundred fifty-eight-l of the social services law, require the defendant to participate in an education reform program in accordance with section four hundred fifty-eight-l of the social services law.

7. The court may, as a condition of an adjournment in contemplation of dismissal order, where a defendant is under twenty-one years of age and is charged with (a) a

misdemeanor or misdemeanors other than section eleven hundred ninety-two of the vehicle and traffic law, in which the record indicates the consumption of alcohol by the defendant may have been a contributing factor, or (b) a violation of paragraph (a) of subdivision one of section sixty-five-b of the alcoholic beverage control law, require the defendant to attend an alcohol awareness program established pursuant to subdivision (a) of section 19.07 of the mental hygiene law.

8. The granting of an adjournment in contemplation of dismissal shall not be deemed to be a conviction or an admission of guilt. No person shall suffer any disability or forfeiture as a result of such an order. Upon the dismissal of the accusatory instrument pursuant to this section, the arrest and prosecution shall be deemed a nullity and the defendant shall be restored, in contemplation of law, to the status he occupied before his arrest and prosecution.

9. Notwithstanding any other provision of this section, a court may not issue an order adjourning an action in contemplation of dismissal if the offense is for a violation of the vehicle and traffic law related to the operation of a motor vehicle (except one related to parking, stopping or standing), or a violation of a local law, rule or ordinance related to the operation of a motor vehicle (except one related to parking, stopping or standing), if such offense was committed by the holder of a commercial learner's permit or a commercial driver's license or was committed in a commercial motor vehicle, as defined in subdivision four of section five hundred one-a of the vehicle and traffic law.

§ 170.56. Adjournment in contemplation of dismissal in cases involving marihuana

1. Upon or after arraignment in a local criminal court upon an information, a prosecutor's information or a misdemeanor complaint, where the sole remaining count or counts charge a violation or violations of section 221.05, 221.10, 221.15, 221.35 or 221.40 of the penal law and before the entry of a plea of guilty thereto or commencement of a trial thereof, the court, upon motion of a defendant, may order that all proceedings be suspended and the action adjourned in contemplation of dismissal, or upon a finding that adjournment would not be necessary or appropriate and the setting forth in the record of the reasons for such findings, may dismiss in furtherance of justice the accusatory instrument; provided, however, that the court may not order such adjournment in contemplation of dismissal or dismiss the accusatory instrument if: (a) the defendant has previously been granted such adjournment in contemplation of dismissal, or (b) the defendant has previously been granted a dismissal under this section, or (c) the defendant has previously been convicted of any offense involving controlled substances, or (d) the defendant has previously been convicted of a crime and the district attorney does not consent or (e) the defendant has previously been adjudicated a youthful offender on the basis of any act or acts involving controlled substances and the district attorney does not consent.

2. Upon ordering the action adjourned in contemplation of dismissal, the court must set and specify such conditions for the adjournment as may be appropriate, and such conditions may include placing the defendant under the supervision of any public or private agency. At any time prior to dismissal the court may modify the conditions or extend or reduce the term of the adjournment, except that the total period of adjournment shall not exceed twelve months. Upon violation of any condition fixed by

the court, the court may revoke its order and restore the case to the calendar and the prosecution thereupon must proceed. If the case is not so restored to the calendar during the period fixed by the court, the accusatory instrument is, at the expiration of such period, deemed to have been dismissed in the furtherance of justice.

3. Upon or after dismissal of such charges against a defendant not previously convicted of a crime, the court shall order that all official records and papers, relating to the defendant's arrest and prosecution, whether on file with the court, a police agency, or the New York state division of criminal justice services, be sealed and, except as otherwise provided in paragraph (d) of subdivision one of section 160.50 of this chapter, not made available to any person or public or private agency; except, such records shall be made available under order of a court for the purpose of determining whether, in subsequent proceedings, such person qualifies under this section for a dismissal or adjournment in contemplation of dismissal of the accusatory instrument.

4. Upon the granting of an order pursuant to subdivision three, the arrest and prosecution shall be deemed a nullity and the defendant shall be restored, in contemplation of law, to the status he occupied before his arrest and prosecution.

§ 170.60. Requirement of plea to information, simplified information or prosecutor's information

Unless an information, a simplified information or a prosecutor's information is dismissed or the criminal action thereon terminated or abated pursuant to a provision of this article or some other provision of law, the defendant must be required to enter a plea thereto.

§ 170.65. Replacement of misdemeanor complaint by information and waiver thereof

1. A defendant against whom a misdemeanor complaint is pending is not required to enter a plea thereto. For purposes of prosecution, such instrument must, except as provided in subdivision three, be replaced by an information, and the defendant must be arraigned thereon. If the misdemeanor complaint is supplemented by a supporting deposition and such instruments taken together satisfy the requirements for a valid information, such misdemeanor complaint is deemed to have been converted to and to constitute a replacing information.

2. An information which replaces a misdemeanor complaint need not charge the same offense or offenses, but at least one count thereof must charge the commission by the defendant of an offense based upon conduct which was the subject of the misdemeanor complaint. In addition, the information may, subject to the rules of joinder, charge any other offense which the factual allegations thereof or of any supporting depositions accompanying it are legally sufficient to support, even though such offense is not based upon conduct which was the subject of the misdemeanor complaint.

3. A defendant who has been arraigned upon a misdemeanor complaint may waive prosecution by information and consent to be prosecuted upon the misdemeanor complaint. In such case, the defendant must be required, either upon the date of the waiver or subsequent thereto, to enter a plea to the misdemeanor complaint.

§ 170.70. Release of defendant upon failure to replace misdemeanor complaint by information

Upon application of a defendant against whom a misdemeanor complaint is pending in a local criminal court, and who, either at the time of his arraignment thereon or subsequent thereto, has been committed to the custody of the sheriff pending disposition of the action, and who has been confined in such custody for a period of more than five days, not including Sunday, without any information having been filed in replacement of such misdemeanor complaint, the criminal court must release the defendant on his own recognizance unless:

1. The defendant has waived prosecution by information and consented to be prosecuted upon the misdemeanor complaint, pursuant to subdivision three of section 170.65; or

2. The court is satisfied that there is good cause why such order of release should not be issued. Such good cause must consist of some compelling fact or circumstance which precluded replacement of the misdemeanor complaint by an information or a prosecutor's information within the prescribed period.

§ 170.75. [Repealed]

§ 170.80. Proceedings regarding certain prostitution charges; certain persons aged sixteen or seventeen

1. Notwithstanding any other provision of law, at any time at or after arraignment on a charge of prostitution pursuant to section 230.00 of the penal law or loitering for the purposes of prostitution pursuant to subdivision two of section 240.37 of the penal law, provided that the person does not stand charged with loitering for the purpose of patronizing a prostitute, where such offense allegedly occurred when the person was sixteen or seventeen years of age except where, after consultation with counsel, a knowing and voluntary plea of guilty has been entered to such charge, any judge or justice hearing any stage of such case may, upon consent of the defendant after consultation with counsel:

(a) conditionally convert such charge in accordance with subdivision three of this section and retain it as a person in need of supervision proceeding for all purposes, and shall make such proceeding fully subject to the provisions and grant any relief available under article seven of the family court act; and/or

(b) order the provision of any of the specialized services enumerated in title eight-A of article six of the social services law, as may be reasonably available.

2. In the event of a conviction by plea or verdict to such charge or charges of prostitution or loitering for the purposes of prostitution as described in subdivision one of this section, the court must find that the person is a youthful offender for the purpose of such charge and proceed in accordance with article seven hundred twenty of this chapter, provided, however, that the available sentence shall be the sentence that may be imposed for a violation as defined in subdivision three of section 10.00 of the penal law. In such case, the records of the investigation and proceedings relating to such charge shall be sealed in accordance with section 720.35 of this chapter.

3.

(a) When a charge of prostitution or loitering for the purposes of prostitution has been conditionally converted to a person in need of supervision proceeding pursuant to subdivision one of this section, the defendant shall be deemed a "sexually exploited child" as defined in subdivision one of section four hundred forty-seven-a of the social services law and therefore shall not be considered an adult for purposes related to the charges in the person in need of supervision proceeding. Sections seven hundred eighty-one, seven hundred eighty-two, seven hundred eighty-two-a, seven hundred eighty-three and seven hundred eighty-four of the family court act shall apply to any proceeding conditionally converted under this section.

(b) The court after hearing from the parties shall state the condition or conditions of such conversion, which may include the individual's participation in specialized services provided pursuant to title eight-A of article six of the social services law and other appropriate services available to persons in need of supervision in accordance with article seven of the family court act.

(c)

(i) The court may, upon written application by the people at any time during the pendency of the person in need of supervision proceeding or during any disposition thereof, but in no event later than the individual's eighteenth birthday, restore the accusatory instrument if the court is satisfied by competent proof that the individual, without just cause, is not in substantial compliance with the condition or conditions of the conversion.

(ii) Notice of such an application to restore an accusatory instrument shall be served on the person and his or her counsel by the court. The notice shall include a statement setting forth a reasonable description of why the person is not in substantial compliance with the condition or conditions of the conversion and a date upon which such person shall appear before the court. The court shall afford the person the right to counsel and the right to be heard. Upon such appearance, the court must advise the person of the contents of the notice and the consequences of a finding of failure to substantially comply with the conditions of conversion. At the time of such appearance the court must ask the person whether he or she wishes to make any statement with respect to such alleged failure to substantially comply. In determining whether such person has failed to substantially comply with the terms of the conversion, the court shall conduct a hearing at which time such person may cross-examine witnesses and present evidence on his or her own behalf. Any findings the court shall make, shall be made on the court record. If the court finds that such person did not substantially comply, it may restore the accusatory instrument pursuant to subparagraph (i) of this paragraph, modify the terms of conversion in accordance with this section or otherwise continue such terms as in its discretion it deems just and proper.

(iii) If such accusatory instrument is restored pursuant to subparagraph (i) of this paragraph, the proceeding shall continue in accordance with subdivision two of this section. If the individual does not comply with services or does not return to court, the individual shall be returned in accordance with the provisions of article seven of the family court act.

4. At the conclusion of a person in need of supervision proceeding pursuant to this section, all records of the investigation and proceedings relating to such proceedings, including records created before the charge was conditionally converted, shall be sealed in accordance with section 720.35 of this chapter.

§ 180.10. Proceedings upon felony complaint; arraignment; defendant's rights, court's instructions and bail matters

1. Upon the defendant's arraignment before a local criminal court upon a felony complaint, the court must immediately inform him, or cause him to be informed in its presence, of the charge or charges against him and that the primary purpose of the proceedings upon such felony complaint is to determine whether the defendant is to be held for the action of a grand jury with respect to the charges contained therein. The court must furnish the defendant with a copy of the felony complaint.

2. The defendant has a right to a prompt hearing upon the issue of whether there is sufficient evidence to warrant the court in holding him for the action of a grand jury, but he may waive such right.

3. The defendant has a right to the aid of counsel at the arraignment and at every subsequent stage of the action, and, if he appears upon such arraignment without counsel, has the following rights:

(a) To an adjournment for the purpose of obtaining counsel; and

(b) To communicate, free of charge, by letter or by telephone provided by the law enforcement facility where the defendant is held to a phone number located in the United States or Puerto Rico, for the purpose of obtaining counsel and informing a relative or friend that he or she has been charged with an offense; and

(c) To have counsel assigned by the court in any case where he is financially unable to obtain the same.

4. The court must inform the defendant of all rights specified in subdivisions two and three. The court must accord the defendant opportunity to exercise such rights and must itself take such affirmative action as is necessary to effectuate them.

5. If the defendant desires to proceed without the aid of counsel, the court must permit him to do so if it is satisfied that he made such decision with knowledge of the significance thereof, but if it is not so satisfied it may not proceed until the defendant is provided with counsel, either of his own choosing or by assignment. A defendant who proceeds at the arraignment without counsel does not waive his right to counsel, and the court must inform him that he continues to have such right as well as all the rights specified in subdivision three which are necessary to effectuate it, and that he may exercise such rights at any stage of the action.

6. Upon the arraignment, the court, unless it intends immediately thereafter to dismiss the felony complaint and terminate the action, must issue a securing order which, as provided in subdivision two of section 530.20, either releases the defendant on his own recognizance or fixes bail or commits him to the custody of the sheriff for his future appearance in such action.

7. Notwithstanding any contrary provision of this section, when an off-hours arraignment part designated in accordance with paragraph (w) of subdivision one of section two hundred twelve of the judiciary law is in operation in the county in which the court is located, the court must adjourn the proceedings before it, and direct that the proceedings be continued in such off-hours part when the defendant has appeared

before the court without counsel and no counsel is otherwise available at the time of such appearance to aid the defendant.

§ 180.20. Proceedings upon felony complaint; removal of action from one local criminal court to another

Under circumstances prescribed in this section, a criminal action based upon a pending felony complaint may be removed from one local criminal court to another:

1. When a defendant arrested by a police officer for a felony allegedly committed in a town has not been brought before the town court of the town, or as the case may be before the village court of the village, in which the felony charged was allegedly committed, but, instead, to another local criminal court of the county and there stands charged with such offense by felony complaint, such latter court must arraign him upon such felony complaint. Such court must then either:

(a) Dispose of the felony complaint pursuant to this article. If such disposition results in a reduction of the felony charge and the filing of an information or prosecutor's information charging a misdemeanor or a petty offense pursuant to section 180.50 or subdivision two or three of section 180.70, such court must conduct the action to judgment or other final disposition; or

(b) Remit the action upon the felony complaint, together with all pertinent papers and documents, to the town court of the town, or as the case may be to the village court of the village, in which the felony charged was allegedly committed. In such case, the latter court must dispose of the felony complaint pursuant to this article.

1-a. When a defendant arrested by a police officer for a felony allegedly committed in a city has not been brought before the city court of such city but, instead, to the local criminal court of an adjoining town or village of the same county and there stands charged with such offense by felony complaint, such latter court must arraign him upon such felony complaint. Such court must then either:

(a) Dispose of the felony complaint pursuant to this article. If such disposition results in a reduction of the felony charge and the filing of an information or prosecutor's information charging a misdemeanor or a petty offense pursuant to section 180.50 or subdivision two or three of section 180.70 of this article, such court must conduct the action to judgment or other final disposition; or

(b) Remit the action upon the felony complaint, together with all pertinent papers and documents, to the city court of the city in which the felony charged was allegedly committed. In such case, the latter court must dispose of the felony complaint pursuant to this article.

2. When a defendant arrested by a police officer for a felony has been brought before a superior court judge sitting as a local criminal court for arraignment upon a felony complaint charging such felony, such judge must, as a local criminal court, arraign the defendant upon such felony complaint. Such court must then either:

(a) Dispose of the felony complaint pursuant to this article. If however, such disposition results in a reduction of the charge and the filing of an information or prosecutor's information charging a misdemeanor or a petty offense, such judge, after arraigning the defendant upon such accusatory instrument, must remit the action, together with all pertinent papers and documents, to a local criminal court having trial jurisdiction of the offense charged, and the latter court must then conduct the action to judgment or other final disposition; or

(b) Remit the action upon the felony complaint, together with all pertinent papers and documents, to a local criminal court having geographical jurisdiction over the area in which the felony charged was allegedly committed. In such case, such latter court must dispose of the felony complaint pursuant to this article.

3. Notwithstanding any provision of this section to the contrary, in any county outside a city having a population of one million or more, upon or after arraignment of a defendant on a felony complaint pending in a local criminal court having preliminary jurisdiction thereof, such court may, upon motion of the defendant and with the consent of the district attorney, order that the action be removed from the court in which the matter is pending to another local criminal court in the same county which has been designated a drug court by the chief administrator of the courts, and such drug court may then dispose of such felony complaint pursuant to this article; provided, however, that an order of removal issued under this subdivision shall not take effect until five days after the date the order is issued unless, prior to such effective date, the drug court notifies the court that issued the order that:

(a) it will not accept the action, in which event the order shall not take effect, or

(b) it will accept the action on a date prior to such effective date, in which event the order shall take effect upon such prior date.

Upon providing notification pursuant to paragraph (a) or (b) of this subdivision, the drug court shall promptly give notice to the defendant, his or her counsel and the district attorney.

4.

(a) Notwithstanding any provision of this section to the contrary, in any county outside a city having a population of one million or more, upon or after arraignment of a defendant on a felony complaint pending in a local criminal court having preliminary jurisdiction thereof, such court may, upon motion of the defendant and after giving the district attorney an opportunity to be heard, order that the action be removed from the court in which the matter is pending to another local criminal court in the same county, or with consent of the district attorney to another court in an adjoining county, that has been designated as a human trafficking court by the chief administrator of the courts, and such human trafficking court may then conduct such action to judgment or other final disposition; provided, however, that an order of removal issued under this subdivision shall not take effect until five days after the date the order is issued unless, prior to such effective date, the human trafficking court notifies the court that issued the order that:

i. it will not accept the action, in which event the order shall not take effect; or

ii. it will accept the action on a date prior to such effective date, in which event the order shall take effect upon such prior date.

(b) Upon providing notification pursuant to subparagraph i or ii of paragraph (a) of this subdivision, the human trafficking court shall promptly give notice to the defendant, his or her counsel and the district attorney.

§ 180.30. Proceedings upon felony complaint; waiver of hearing; action to be taken

If the defendant waives a hearing upon the felony complaint, the court must either:

1. Order that the defendant be held for the action of a grand jury of the appropriate superior court with respect to the charge or charges contained in the felony complaint. In such case, the court must promptly transmit to such superior court the order, the felony complaint, the supporting depositions and all other pertinent documents. Until such papers are received by the superior court, the action is deemed to be still pending in the local criminal court; or

2. Make inquiry, pursuant to section 180.50, for the purpose of determining whether the felony complaint should be dismissed and an information, a prosecutor's information or a misdemeanor complaint filed with the court in lieu thereof.

§ 180.40. Proceedings upon felony complaint; application in superior court following hearing or waiver of hearing

Where the local criminal court has held a defendant for the action of a grand jury, the district attorney may, at any time before such matter is submitted to the grand jury, apply, ex parte, to the appropriate superior court for an order directing that the felony complaint and other papers transmitted to such court pursuant to subdivision one of section 180.30 be returned to the local criminal court for reconsideration of the action to be taken. The superior court may issue such an order if it is satisfied that the felony complaint is defective or that such action is required in the interest of justice.

§ 180.50. Proceedings upon felony complaint; reduction of charge

1. Whether or not the defendant waives a hearing upon the felony complaint, the local criminal court may, upon consent of the district attorney, make inquiry for the purpose of determining whether (a) the available facts and evidence relating to the conduct underlying the felony complaint provide a basis for charging the defendant with an offense other than a felony, and (b) if so, whether the charge should, in the manner prescribed in subdivision three, be reduced from one for a felony to one for a non-felony offense. Upon such inquiry, the court may question any person who it believes may possess information relevant to the matter, including the defendant if he wishes to be questioned.

2. If after such inquiry the court is satisfied that there is reasonable cause to believe that the defendant committed an offense other than a felony, it may order the indicated reduction as follows:

(a) If there is not reasonable cause to believe that the defendant committed a felony in addition to the non-felony offense in question, the court may as a matter of right order a reduction of the charge to one for the non-felony offense;

(b) If there is reasonable cause to believe that the defendant committed a felony in addition to the non-felony offense, the court may order a reduction of the charge to one for the non-felony offense only if (i) it is satisfied that such reduction is in the interest of justice, and (ii) the district attorney consents thereto; provided, however, that the court may not order such reduction where there is reasonable cause to believe that the defendant committed a class A felony, other than those defined in article two hundred twenty of the penal law, or any armed felony as defined in subdivision forty-one of section 1.20.

3. A charge is "reduced" from a felony to a non-felony offense, within the meaning of this section, by replacing the felony complaint with, or converting it to, another local criminal court accusatory instrument, as follows:

(a) If the factual allegations of the felony complaint and/or any supporting depositions are legally sufficient to support the charge that the defendant committed the non-felony offense in question, the court may:

(i) Direct the district attorney to file with the court a prosecutor's information charging the defendant with such non-felony offense; or

(ii) Request the complainant of the felony complaint to file with the court an information charging the defendant with such non-felony offense. If such an information is filed, any supporting deposition supporting or accompanying the felony complaint is deemed also to support or accompanying [accompany]* the replacing information; or

(iii) Convert the felony complaint, or a copy thereof, into an information by notations upon or attached thereto which make the necessary and appropriate changes in the title of the instrument and in the names of the offense or offenses charged. In case of such conversion, any supporting deposition supporting or accompanying the felony complaint is deemed also to support or accompany the information to which it has been converted;

(b) If the non-felony offense in question is a misdemeanor, and if the factual allegations of the felony complaint together with those of any supporting depositions, though providing reasonable cause to believe that the defendant committed such misdemeanor are not legally sufficient to support such misdemeanor charge, the court may cause such felony complaint to be replaced by or converted to a misdemeanor complaint charging the misdemeanor in question, in the manner prescribed in subparagraphs two and three of paragraph (a) of this subdivision.

(c) An information, a prosecutor's information or a misdemeanor complaint filed pursuant to this section may, pursuant to the ordinary rules of joinder, charge two or more offenses, and it may jointly charge with each offense any two or more defendants originally so charged in the felony complaint;

(d) Upon the filing of an information, a prosecutor's information or a misdemeanor complaint pursuant to this section, the court must dismiss the felony complaint from which such accusatory instrument is derived. It must then arraign the defendant upon the new accusatory instrument and inform him of his rights in connection therewith in the manner provided in section 170.10.

4. Upon making any finding other than that specified in subdivision two, the court must conduct a hearing upon the felony complaint, unless the defendant has waived the same. In the case of such waiver the court must order that the defendant be held for the action of a grand jury.

§ 180.60. Proceedings upon felony complaint; the hearing; conduct thereof

A hearing upon a felony complaint must be conducted as follows:

1. The district attorney must conduct such hearing on behalf of the people.

2. The defendant may as a matter of right be present at such hearing.

3. The court must read to the defendant the felony complaint and any supporting depositions unless the defendant waives such reading.

141

4. Each witness, whether called by the people or by the defendant, must, unless he would be authorized to give unsworn evidence at a trial, testify under oath. Each witness, including any defendant testifying in his own behalf, may be cross-examined.

5. The people must call and examine witnesses and offer evidence in support of the charge.

6. The defendant may, as a matter of right, testify in his own behalf.

7. Upon request of the defendant, the court may, as a matter of discretion, permit him to call and examine other witnesses or to produce other evidence in his behalf.

8. Upon such a hearing, only non-hearsay evidence is admissible to demonstrate reasonable cause to believe that the defendant committed a felony; except that reports of experts and technicians in professional and scientific fields and sworn statements of the kinds specified in subdivisions two and three of section 190.30 are admissible to the same extent as in a grand jury proceeding, unless the court determines, upon application of the defendant, that such hearsay evidence is, under the particular circumstances of the case, not sufficiently reliable, in which case the court shall require that the witness testify in person and be subject to cross-examination.

9. The court may, upon application of the defendant, exclude the public from the hearing and direct that no disclosure be made of the proceedings.

10. Such hearing should be completed at one session. In the interest of justice, however, it may be adjourned by the court but, in the absence of a showing of good cause therefor, no such adjournment may be for more than one day.

§ 180.70. Proceedings upon felony complaint; disposition of felony complaint after hearing

At the conclusion of a hearing, the court must dispose of the felony complaint as follows:

1. If there is reasonable cause to believe that the defendant committed a felony, the court must, except as provided in subdivision three, order that the defendant be held for the action of a grand jury of the appropriate superior court, and it must promptly transmit to such superior court the order, the felony complaint, the supporting depositions and all other pertinent documents. Until such papers are received by the superior court, the action is deemed to be still pending in the local criminal court.

2. If there is not reasonable cause to believe that the defendant committed a felony but there is reasonable cause to believe that he committed an offense other than a felony, the court may, by means of procedures prescribed in subdivision three of section 180.50, reduce the charge to one for such non-felony offense.

3. If there is reasonable cause to believe that the defendant committed a felony in addition to a non-felony offense, the court may, instead of ordering the defendant held for the action of a grand jury as provided in subdivision one, reduce the charge to one for such non-felony offense as provided in subdivision two, if (a) it is satisfied that such reduction is in the interest of justice, and (b) the district attorney consents thereto; provided, however, that the court may not order such reduction where there is reasonable cause to believe the defendant committed a class A felony, other than those defined in article two hundred twenty of the penal law, or any armed felony as defined in subdivision forty-one of section 1.20.

4. If there is not reasonable cause to believe that the defendant committed any offense, the court must dismiss the felony complaint and discharge the defendant from custody if he is in custody, or, if he is at liberty on bail, it must exonerate the bail.

§ 180.75. Proceedings upon felony complaint; juvenile offender

1. When a juvenile offender or adolescent offender is arraigned before the youth part of a superior court or the most accessible magistrate designated by the appellate division of the supreme court in the applicable department to act as a youth part, the provisions of article seven hundred twenty-two of this chapter shall apply in lieu of the provisions of sections 180.30, 180.50 and 180.70 of this article.

2. [Repealed]

3. [Repealed]

4. [Repealed]

5. [Repealed]

6. [Repealed]

§ 180.80. Proceedings upon felony complaint; release of defendant from custody upon failure of timely disposition

Upon application of a defendant against whom a felony complaint has been filed with a local criminal court or the youth part of a superior court, and who, since the time of his arrest or subsequent thereto, has been held in custody pending disposition of such felony complaint, and who has been confined in such custody for a period of more than one hundred twenty hours or, in the event that a Saturday, Sunday or legal holiday occurs during such custody, one hundred forty-four hours, without either a disposition of the felony complaint or commencement of a hearing thereon, the court must release him on his own recognizance unless:

1. The failure to dispose of the felony complaint or to commence a hearing thereon during such period of confinement was due to the defendant's request, action or condition, or occurred with his consent; or

2. Prior to the application:

(a) The district attorney files with the court a written certification that an indictment has been voted; or

(b) An indictment or a direction to file a prosecutor's information charging an offense based upon conduct alleged in the felony complaint was filed by a grand jury; or

3. The court is satisfied that the people have shown good cause why such order of release should not be issued. Such good cause must consist of some compelling fact or circumstance which precluded disposition of the felony complaint within the prescribed period or rendered such action against the interest of justice.

§ 180.85. Termination of prosecution

1. After arraignment of a defendant upon a felony complaint, other than a felony complaint charging an offense defined in section 125.10, 125.15, 125.20, 125.25, 125.26 or 125.27 of the penal law, either party or the local criminal court or superior court before which the action is pending, on its own motion, may move in accordance with the provisions of this section for an order terminating prosecution of the charges contained in such felony complaint on consent of the parties.

2. A motion to terminate a prosecution pursuant to this section may only be made where the count or counts of the felony complaint have not been presented to a grand jury or otherwise disposed of in accordance with this chapter. Such motion shall be filed in writing with the local criminal court or superior court in which the felony complaint is pending not earlier than twelve months following the date of arraignment on such felony complaint. Upon the filing of such motion, the court shall fix a return date and provide the parties with at least thirty days' written notice of the motion and return date.

3. Where, upon motion to terminate a prosecution pursuant to this section, both parties consent to such termination, the court, on the return date of such motion, shall enter an order terminating such prosecution. For purposes of this subdivision, a party that is given written notice of a motion to terminate a prosecution shall be deemed to consent to such termination unless, prior to the return date of such motion, such party files a notice of opposition thereto with the court. Except as otherwise provided in subdivision four, where such a notice of opposition is filed, the court, on the return date of the motion, shall enter an order denying the motion to terminate the prosecution.

4. Notwithstanding any other provision of this section, where the people file a notice of opposition pursuant to subdivision three, the court, on the return date of the motion, may defer disposition of such motion for a period of forty-five days. In such event, if the count or counts of such felony complaint are presented to a grand jury or otherwise disposed of within such period, the court, upon the expiration thereof, shall enter an order denying the motion to terminate the prosecution. If such count or counts are not presented to a grand jury or otherwise disposed of within such period, the court, upon the expiration thereof, shall enter an order terminating the prosecution unless, within the forty-five day period, the people, on at least five days' written notice to the defendant, show good cause for their failure to present or otherwise dispose of such count or counts. If such good cause is shown, the court, upon expiration of the forty-five day period, shall enter an order denying the motion to terminate the prosecution.

5. Notwithstanding any other provision of law, the defendant's appearance in court on the return date of the motion or on any other date shall not be required as a prerequisite to entry of an order under this section.

6. The period from the filing of a motion pursuant to this section until entry of an order disposing of such motion shall not, by reason of such motion, be considered a period of delay for purposes of subdivision four of section 30.30, nor shall such period, by reason of such motion, be excluded in computing the time within which the people must be ready for trial pursuant to such section 30.30.

7. Where a prosecution is terminated pursuant to this section, nothing contained herein shall preclude the people from subsequently filing an indictment charging the same count or counts provided such filing is in accordance with the provisions of this section, article thirty and any other relevant provisions of this chapter. Where the people indicate their intention to seek an indictment following the entry of an order terminating a prosecution pursuant to this section, the court shall, notwithstanding any provision of section 160.50 to the contrary, stay sealing under that section for a reasonable period not to exceed thirty days to permit the people an opportunity to pursue such indictment.

8. Where an order denying a party's motion to terminate a prosecution is entered pursuant to this section, such party may not file a subsequent motion to terminate the prosecution pursuant to this section for at least six months from the date on which such order is entered.

9. Notwithstanding any other provision of this section, where a motion to terminate a prosecution is filed with a local criminal court pursuant to subdivision two, and, prior to the determination thereof, such court is divested of jurisdiction by the filing of an indictment charging the offense or offenses contained in the felony complaint, such motion shall be deemed to have been denied as of the date of such divestiture.

10. The chief administrator of the courts, in consultation with the director of the division of criminal justice services and representatives of appropriate prosecutorial and criminal defense organizations in the state, shall adopt forms for the motion to terminate a prosecution authorized by subdivision one and for the notice of opposition specified in subdivision three.

Article 182 [Expires and Repealed Sept 1, 2019] Alternate Method of Court Appearance

§ 182.10. [Expires and repealed Sept 1, 2019] Definition of terms

As used in this article:

1. "Independent audio-visual system" means an electronic system for the transmission and receiving of audio and visual signals, encompassing encoded signals, frequency domain multiplexing or other suitable means to preclude the unauthorized reception and decoding of the signals by commercially available television receivers, channel converters, or other available receiving devices.

2. "Electronic appearance" means an appearance in which various participants, including the defendant, are not present in the court, but in which, by means of an independent audio-visual system, (a) all of the participants are simultaneously able to see and hear reproductions of the voices and images of the judge, counsel, defendant, police officer, and any other appropriate participant, and (b) counsel is present with the defendant, or if the defendant waives the presence of counsel on the record, the defendant and his or her counsel are able to see and hear each other and engage in private conversation.

§ 182.20. [Expires and repealed Sept 1, 2019] Electronic appearance; general rule

1. Notwithstanding any other provision of law and except as provided in section 182.30 of this article, the court, in its discretion, may dispense with the personal appearance of the defendant, except an appearance at a hearing or trial, and conduct an electronic appearance in connection with a criminal action pending in Albany, Bronx, Broome, Erie, Kings, New York, Niagara, Oneida, Onondaga, Ontario, Orange, Putnam, Queens, Richmond, St. Lawrence, Tompkins, Chautauqua, Cattaraugus, Clinton, Essex, Montgomery, Rensselaer, Warren, Westchester, Suffolk, Herkimer or Franklin county, provided that the chief administrator of the courts has authorized the use of electronic appearance and the defendant, after consultation with counsel, consents on the record. Such consent shall be required at the commencement of each electronic appearance to such electronic appearance.

2. If, for any reason, the court determines on its own motion or on the motion of any party that the conduct of an electronic appearance may impair the legal rights of the

defendant, it shall not permit the electronic appearance to proceed. If, for any other articulated reason, either party requests at any time during the electronic appearance that such appearance be terminated, the court shall grant such request and adjourn the proceeding to a date certain. Upon the adjourned date the proceeding shall be recommenced from the point at which the request for termination of the electronic appearance had been granted.

3. The electronic appearance shall be conducted in accordance with rules issued by the chief administrator of the courts.

4. When the defendant makes an electronic appearance, the court stenographer shall record any statements in the same manner as if the defendant had made a personal appearance. No electronic recording of any electronic appearance may be made, viewed or inspected except as may be authorized by the rules issued by the chief administrator of the courts.

§ 182.30. [Expires and repealed Sept 1, 2019] Electronic appearance; conditions and limitations

The following conditions and limitations apply to all electronic appearances:

1. The defendant may not enter a plea of guilty to, or be sentenced upon a conviction of, a felony.

2. The defendant may not enter a plea of not responsible by reason of mental disease or defect.

3. The defendant may not be committed to the state department of mental hygiene pursuant to article seven hundred thirty of this chapter.

4. The defendant may not enter a plea of guilty to a misdemeanor conditioned upon a promise of incarceration unless such incarceration will be imposed only in the event that the defendant fails to comply with a term or condition imposed under the original sentence.

5. A defendant who has been convicted of a misdemeanor may not be sentenced to a period of incarceration which exceeds the time the defendant has already served when sentence is imposed.

§ 182.40. [Expires and repealed Sept 1, 2019] Approval by the chief administrator of the courts

1. The appropriate administrative judge shall submit to the chief administrator of the courts a written proposal for the use of electronic appearance in his or her jurisdiction. If the chief administrator of the courts approves the proposal, installation of an independent audio-visual system may begin.

2. Upon completion of the installation of an independent audio-visual system, the commission on cable television shall inspect, test, and examine the independent audio-visual system and certify to the chief administrator of the courts whether the system complies with the definition of an independent audio-visual system and is technically suitable for the conducting of electronic appearances as intended.

3. The chief administrator of the courts shall issue rules governing the use of electronic appearances.

Article 185 [Expired]

§§ 185.10–185.40. [Expired]

Title I Preliminary Proceedings in Superior Court

Article 190 The Grand Jury and Its Proceedings

§ 190.05. Grand jury; definition and general functions

A grand jury is a body consisting of not less than sixteen nor more than twenty-three persons, impaneled by a superior court and constituting a part of such court, the functions of which are to hear and examine evidence concerning offenses and concerning misconduct, nonfeasance and neglect in public office, whether criminal or otherwise, and to take action with respect to such evidence as provided in section 190.60.

§ 190.10. Grand jury; for what courts drawn

The appellate division of each judicial department shall adopt rules governing the number and the terms for which grand juries shall be drawn and impaneled by the superior courts within its department; provided, however, that a grand jury may be drawn and impaneled for any extraordinary term of the supreme court upon the order of a justice assigned to hold such term.

§ 190.15. Grand jury; duration of term and discharge

1. A term of a superior court for which a grand jury has been impaneled remains in existence at least until and including the opening date of the next term of such court for which a grand jury has been designated. Upon such date, or within five days preceding it, the court may, upon declaration of both the grand jury and the district attorney that such grand jury has not yet completed or will be unable to complete certain business before it, extend the term of court and the existence of such grand jury to a specified future date, and may subsequently order further extensions for such purpose.

2. At any time when a grand jury is in recess and no other appropriate grand jury is in existence in the county, the court may, upon application of the district attorney or of a defendant held by a local criminal court for the action of a grand jury, order such grand jury reconvened for the purpose of dealing with a matter requiring grand jury action.

§ 190.20. Grand jury; formation, organization and other matters preliminary to assumption of duties

1. The mode of selecting grand jurors and of drawing and impaneling grand juries is governed by the judiciary law.

2. Neither the grand jury panel nor any individual grand juror may be challenged, but the court may:

(a) At any time before a grand jury is sworn, discharge the panel and summon another panel if it finds that the original panel does not substantially conform to the requirements of the judiciary law; or

(b) At any time after a grand juror is drawn, refuse to swear him, or discharge him after he has been sworn, upon a finding that he is disqualified from service pursuant to the judiciary law, or incapable of performing his duties because of bias or prejudice, or guilty of misconduct in the performance of his duties such as to impair the proper functioning of the grand jury.

3. After a grand jury has been impaneled, the court must appoint one of the grand jurors as foreman and another to act as foreman during any absence or disability of the foreman. At some time before commencement of their duties, the grand jurors must appoint one of their number as secretary to keep records material to the conduct of the grand jury's business.

4. The grand jurors must be sworn by the court. The oath may be in any form or language which requires the grand jurors to perform their duties faithfully.

5. After a grand jury has been sworn, the court must deliver or cause to be delivered to each grand juror a printed copy of all the provisions of this article, and the court may, in addition, give the grand jurors any oral and written instructions relating to the proper performance of their duties as it deems necessary or appropriate.

6. If two or more grand juries are impaneled at the same court term, the court may thereafter, for good cause, transfer grand jurors from one panel to another, and any grand juror so transferred is deemed to have been sworn as a member of the panel to which he has been transferred.

§ 190.25. Grand jury; proceedings and operation in general

1. Proceedings of a grand jury are not valid unless at least sixteen of its members are present. The finding of an indictment, a direction to file a prosecutor's information, a decision to submit a grand jury report and every other affirmative official action or decision requires the concurrence of at least twelve members thereof.

2. The foreman or any other grand juror may administer an oath to any witness appearing before the grand jury.

3. Except as provided in subdivision three-a of this section, during the deliberations and voting of a grand jury, only the grand jurors may be present in the grand jury room. During its other proceedings, the following persons, in addition to witnesses, may, as the occasion requires, also be present:

(a) The district attorney;

(b) A clerk or other public servant authorized to assist the grand jury in the administrative conduct of its proceedings;

(c) A stenographer authorized to record the proceedings of the grand jury;

(d) An interpreter. Upon request of the grand jury, the prosecutor must provide an interpreter to interpret the testimony of any witness who does not speak the English language well enough to be readily understood. Such interpreter must, if he has not previously taken the constitutional oath of office, first take an oath before the grand jury that he will faithfully interpret the testimony of the witness and that he will keep secret all matters before such grand jury within his knowledge;

(e) A public servant holding a witness in custody. When a person held in official custody is a witness before a grand jury, a public servant assigned to guard him during his grand jury appearance may accompany him in the grand jury room. Such public servant must, if he has not previously taken the constitutional oath of office, first take an oath before the grand jury that he will keep secret all matters before it within his knowledge.

(f) An attorney representing a witness pursuant to section 190.52 of this chapter while that witness is present.

(g) An operator, as that term is defined in section 190.32 of this chapter, while the videotaped examination of either a special witness or a child witness is being played.

(h) A social worker, rape crisis counselor, psychologist or other professional providing emotional support to a child witness twelve years old or younger, or a social worker or informal caregiver, as provided in subdivision two of section two hundred six of the elder law, for a vulnerable elderly person as provided in subdivision three of section 260.31 of the penal law, who is called to give evidence in a grand jury proceeding concerning a crime defined in article one hundred twenty-one, article one hundred thirty, article two hundred sixty, section 120.10, 125.10, 125.15, 125.20, 125.25, 125.26, 125.27, 255.25, 255.26 or 255.27 of the penal law provided that the district attorney consents. Such support person shall not provide the witness with an answer to any question or otherwise participate in such proceeding and shall first take an oath before the grand jury that he or she will keep secret all matters before such grand jury within his or her knowledge.

3-a. Upon the request of a deaf or hearing-impaired grand juror, the prosecutor shall provide a sign language interpreter for such juror. Such interpreter shall be present during all proceedings of the grand jury which the deaf or hearing-impaired grand juror attends, including deliberation and voting. The interpreter shall, if he or she has not previously taken the constitutional oath of office, first take an oath before the grand jury that he or she will faithfully interpret the testimony of the witnesses and the statements of the prosecutor, judge and grand jurors; keep secret all matters before such grand jury within his or her knowledge; and not seek to influence the deliberations and voting of such grand jury.

4.

(a) Grand jury proceedings are secret, and no grand juror, or other person specified in subdivision three of this section or section 215.70 of the penal law, may, except in the lawful discharge of his duties or upon written order of the court, disclose the nature or substance of any grand jury testimony, evidence, or any decision, result or other matter attending a grand jury proceeding. For the purpose of assisting the grand jury in conducting its investigation, evidence obtained by a grand jury may be independently examined by the district attorney, members of his staff, police officers specifically assigned to the investigation, and such other persons as the court may specifically authorize. Such evidence may not be disclosed to other persons without a court order. Nothing contained herein shall prohibit a witness from disclosing his own testimony.

(b) When a district attorney obtains evidence during a grand jury proceeding which provides reasonable cause to suspect that a child has been abused or maltreated, as those terms are defined by section ten hundred twelve of the family court act, he must apply to the court supervising the grand jury for an order permitting disclosure of such evidence to the state central register of child abuse and maltreatment. A district attorney need not apply to the court for such order if he has previously made or caused a report to be made to the state central register of child abuse and maltreatment pursuant to section four hundred thirteen of the social services law and the evidence obtained during the grand jury proceeding, or substantially similar information, was included in such report. The district attorney's application to the court shall be made ex parte and in camera. The court must grant the application and permit the district attorney to disclose the evidence to the state central register of child abuse and maltreatment unless the court finds that such disclosure would jeopardize the life or safety of any person or interfere with a continuing grand jury proceeding.

5. The grand jury is the exclusive judge of the facts with respect to any matter before it.

6. The legal advisors of the grand jury are the court and the district attorney, and the grand jury may not seek or receive legal advice from any other source. Where necessary or appropriate, the court or the district attorney, or both, must instruct the grand jury concerning the law with respect to its duties or any matter before it, and such instructions must be recorded in the minutes.

§ 190.30. Grand jury; rules of evidence

1. Except as otherwise provided in this section, the provisions of article sixty, governing rules of evidence and related matters with respect to criminal proceedings in general, are, where appropriate, applicable to grand jury proceedings.

2. A report or a copy of a report made by a public servant or by a person employed by a public servant or agency who is a physicist, chemist, coroner or medical examiner, firearms identification expert, examiner of questioned documents, fingerprint technician, or an expert or technician in some comparable scientific or professional field, concerning the results of an examination, comparison or test performed by him in connection with a case which is the subject of a grand jury proceeding, may, when certified by such person as a report made by him or as a true copy thereof, be received in such grand jury proceeding as evidence of the facts stated therein.

2-a. When the electronic transmission of a certified report, or certified copy thereof, of the kind described in subdivision two or three-a of this section or a sworn statement or copy thereof, of the kind described in subdivision three of this section results in a written document, such written document may be received in such grand jury proceeding provided that: (a) a transmittal memorandum completed by the person sending the report contains a certification that the report has not been altered and a description of the report specifying the number of pages; and (b) the person who receives the electronically transmitted document certifies that such document and transmittal memorandum were so received; and (c) a certified report or a certified copy or sworn statement or sworn copy thereof is filed with the court within twenty days following arraignment upon the indictment; and (d) where such written document is a sworn statement or sworn copy thereof of the kind described in subdivision three of this section, such sworn statement or sworn copy thereof is also provided to the defendant or his counsel within twenty days following arraignment upon the indictment.

3. A written or oral statement, under oath, by a person attesting to one or more of the following matters may be received in such grand jury proceeding as evidence of the facts stated therein:

(a) that person's ownership or lawful custody of, or license to occupy, premises, as defined in section 140.00 of the penal law, and of the defendant's lack of license or privilege to enter or remain thereupon;

(b) that person's ownership of, or possessory right in, property, the nature and monetary amount of any damage thereto and the defendant's lack of right to damage or tamper with the property;

(c) that person's ownership or lawful custody of, or license to possess property, as defined in section 155.00 of the penal law, including an automobile or other vehicle, its value and the defendant's lack of superior or equal right to possession thereof;

(d) that person's ownership of a vehicle and the absence of his consent to the defendant's taking, operating, exercising control over or using it;

(e) that person's qualifications as a dealer or other expert in appraising or evaluating a particular type of property, his expert opinion as to the value of a certain item or items of property of that type, and the basis for his opinion;

(f) that person's identity as an ostensible maker, drafter, drawer, endorser or other signator of a written instrument and its falsity within the meaning of section 170.00 of the penal law;

(g) that person's ownership of, or possessory right in, a credit card account number or debit card account number, and the defendant's lack of superior or equal right to use or possession thereof.

Provided, however, that no such statement shall be admitted when an adversarial examination of such person has been previously ordered pursuant to subdivision 8 of section 180.60, unless a transcript of such examination is admitted.

3-a. A sex offender registration form, sex offender registration continuation/supplemental form, sex offender registry address verification form, sex offender change of address form or a copy of such form maintained by the division of criminal justice services concerning an individual who is the subject of a grand jury proceeding, may, when certified by a person designated by the commissioner of the division of criminal justice services as the person to certify such records, as a true copy thereof, be received in such grand jury proceeding as evidence of the facts stated therein.

4. An examination of a child witness or a special witness by the district attorney videotaped pursuant to section 190.32 of this chapter may be received in evidence in such grand jury proceeding as the testimony of such witness.

5. Nothing in subdivisions two, three or four of this section shall be construed to limit the power of the grand jury to cause any person to be called as a witness pursuant to subdivision three of section 190.50.

6. Wherever it is provided in article sixty that the court in a criminal proceeding must rule upon the competency of a witness to testify or upon the admissibility of evidence, such ruling may in an equivalent situation in a grand jury proceeding, be made by the district attorney.

7. Wherever it is provided in article sixty that a court presiding at a jury trial must instruct the jury with respect to the significance, legal effect or evaluation of evidence, the district attorney, in an equivalent situation in a grand jury proceeding, may so instruct the grand jury.

8.

(a) A business record may be received in such grand jury proceedings as evidence of the following facts and similar facts stated therein:

(i) a person's use of, subscription to and charges and payments for communication equipment and services including but not limited to equipment or services provided by telephone companies and internet service providers, but not including recorded conversations or images communicated thereby; and

(ii) financial transactions, and a person's ownership or possessory interest in any account, at a bank, insurance company, brokerage, exchange or banking organization as defined in section two of the banking law.

(b) Any business record offered for consideration by a grand jury pursuant to paragraph (a) of this subdivision must be accompanied by a written statement, under oath, that (i) contains a list or description of the records it accompanies, (ii) attests in substance that the person making the statement is a duly authorized custodian of the records or other employee or agent of the business who is familiar with such records, and (iii) attests in substance that such records were made in the regular course of business and that it was the regular course of such business to make such records at the time of the recorded act, transaction, occurrence or event, or within a reasonable time thereafter. Such written statement may also include a statement identifying the name and job description of the person making the statement, specifying the matters set forth in subparagraph (ii) of this paragraph and attesting that the business has made a diligent search and does not possess a particular record or records addressing a matter set forth in paragraph (a) of this subdivision, and such statement may be received at grand jury proceedings as evidence of the fact that the business does not possess such record or records. When records of a business are accompanied by more than one sworn written statement of its employees or agents, such statements may be considered together in determining the admissibility of the records under this subdivision. For the purpose of this subdivision, the term "business records" does not include any records prepared by law enforcement agencies or prepared by any entity in anticipation of litigation.

(c) Any business record offered to a grand jury pursuant to paragraph (a) of this subdivision that includes material beyond that described in such paragraph (a) shall be redacted to exclude such additional material, or received subject to a limiting instruction that the grand jury shall not consider such additional material in support of any criminal charge.

(d) No such records shall be admitted when an adversarial examination of such a records custodian or other employee of such business who was familiar with such records has been previously ordered pursuant to subdivision eight of section 180.60 of this chapter, unless a transcript of such examination is admitted.

(e) Nothing in this subdivision shall affect the admissibility of business records in the grand jury on any basis other than that set forth in this subdivision.

§ 190.32. Videotaped examination; definitions, application, order and procedure

(1) Definitions. As used in this section:

(a) "Child witness" means a person twelve years old or less whom the people intend to call as witness in a grand jury proceeding to give evidence concerning any crime defined in article one hundred thirty or two hundred sixty or section 255.25, 255.26 or 255.27 of the penal law of which the person was a victim.

(b) "Special witness" means a person whom the people intend to call as a witness in a grand jury proceeding and who is either:

(i) Unable to attend and testify in person in the grand jury proceeding because the person is either physically ill or incapacitated; or

(ii) More than twelve years old and who is likely to suffer very severe emotional or mental stress if required to testify in person concerning any crime defined in article one hundred thirty or two hundred sixty or section 255.25, 255.26 or 255.27 of the penal law to which the person was a witness or of which the person was a victim.

(c) "Operator" means a person employed by the district attorney who operates the video camera to record the examination of a child witness or a special witness.

2. In lieu of requiring a witness who is a child witness to appear in person and give evidence in a grand jury proceeding, the district attorney may cause the examination of such witness to be videotaped in accordance with the provisions of subdivision five of this section.

3. Whenever the district attorney has reason to believe that a witness is a special witness, he may make an ex parte application to the court for an order authorizing the videotaping of an examination of such special witness and the subsequent introduction in evidence in a grand jury proceeding of that videotape in lieu of the live testimony of such special witness. The application must be in writing, must state the grounds of the application and must contain sworn allegations of fact, whether of the district attorney or another person or persons, supporting such grounds. Such allegations may be based upon personal knowledge of the deponent or upon information and belief, provided, that in the latter event, the sources of such information and the grounds for such belief are stated.

4. If the court is satisfied that a witness is a special witness, it shall issue an order authorizing the videotaping of such special witness in accordance with the provisions of subdivision five of this section. The court order and the application and all supporting papers shall not be disclosed to any person except upon further court order.

5. The videotaping of an examination either of a child witness or a special witness shall proceed as follows:

(a) An examination of a child witness or a special witness which is to be videotaped pursuant to this section may be conducted anywhere and at any time provided that the operator begins the videotape by recording a statement by the district attorney of the date, time and place of the examination. In addition, the district attorney shall identify himself, the operator and all other persons present.

(b) An accurate clock with a sweep second hand shall be placed next to or behind the witness in such position as to enable the operator to videotape the clock and the witness together during the entire examination. In the alternative, a date and time generator shall be used to superimpose the day, hour, minute and second over the video portion of the recording during the entire examination.

(c) A social worker, rape crisis counselor, psychologist or other professional providing emotional support to a child witness or to a special witness, as defined in subparagraph

(ii) of paragraph (b) of subdivision one of this section, or any of those persons enumerated in paragraphs (a), (b), (c), (d), (e), (f) and (g) of subdivision three of section 190.25 may be present during the videotaping except that a doctor, nurse or other medical assistant also may be present if required by the attendant circumstances. Each person present, except the witness, must, if he has not previously taken a constitutional oath of office or an oath that he will keep secret all matters before a grand jury, must take an oath on the record that he will keep secret the videotaped examination.

(d) The district attorney shall state for the record the name of the witness, and the caption and the grand jury number, if any, of the case. If the witness to be examined is a child witness, the date of the witness' birth must be recorded. If the witness to be examined is a special witness, the date of the order authorizing the videotaped examination and the name of the justice who issued the order shall be recorded.

(e) If the witness will give sworn testimony, the administration of the oath must be recorded. If the witness will give unsworn testimony, a statement that the testimony is not under oath must be recorded.

(f) If the examination requires the use of more than one tape, the operator shall record a statement of the district attorney at the end of each tape declaring that such tape has ended and referring to the succeeding tape. At the beginning of such succeeding tape, the operator shall record a statement of the district attorney identifying himself, the witness being examined and the number of tapes which have been used to record the examination of such witness. At the conclusion of the examination the operator shall record a statement of the district attorney certifying that the recording has been completed, the number of tapes on which the recording has been made and that such tapes constitute a complete and accurate record of the examination of the witness.

(g) A videotape of an examination conducted pursuant to this section shall not be edited unless upon further order of the court.

6. When the videotape is introduced in evidence and played in the grand jury, the grand jury stenographer shall record the examination in the same manner as if the witness had testified in person.

7. Custody of the videotape shall be maintained in the same manner as custody of the grand jury minutes.

§ 190.35. Grand jury; definitions of terms

The term definitions contained in section 50.10 are applicable to sections 190.40, 190.45 and 190.50.

§ 190.40. Grand jury; witnesses, compulsion of evidence and immunity

1. Every witness in a grand jury proceeding must give any evidence legally requested of him regardless of any protest or belief on his part that it may tend to incriminate him.

2. A witness who gives evidence in a grand jury proceeding receives immunity unless:

(a) He has effectively waived such immunity pursuant to section 190.45; or

(b) Such evidence is not responsive to any inquiry and is gratuitously given or volunteered by the witness with knowledge that it is not responsive.

(c) The evidence given by the witness consists only of books, papers, records or other physical evidence of an enterprise, as defined in subdivision one of section 175.00 of the penal law, the production of which is required by a subpoena duces tecum, and the witness does not possess a privilege against self-incrimination with respect to the production of such evidence. Any further evidence given by the witness entitles the witness to immunity except as provided in subparagraph [paragraphs]* (a) and (b) of this subdivision.

§ 190.45. Grand jury; waiver of immunity

1. A waiver of immunity is a written instrument subscribed by a person who is or is about to become a witness in a grand jury proceeding, stipulating that he waives his privilege against self-incrimination and any possible or prospective immunity to which he would otherwise become entitled, pursuant to section 190.40, as a result of giving evidence in such proceeding.

2. A waiver of immunity is not effective unless and until it is sworn to before the grand jury conducting the proceeding in which the subscriber has been called as a witness.

3. A person who is called by the people as a witness in a grand jury proceeding and requested by the district attorney to subscribe and swear to a waiver of immunity before giving evidence has a right to confer with counsel before deciding whether he will comply with such request, and, if he desires to avail himself of such right, he must be accorded a reasonable time in which to obtain and confer with counsel for such purpose. The district attorney must inform the witness of all such rights before obtaining his execution of such a waiver of immunity. Any waiver obtained, subscribed or sworn to in violation of the provisions of this subdivision is invalid and ineffective.

4. If a grand jury witness subscribes and swears to a waiver of immunity upon a written agreement with the district attorney that the interrogation will be limited to certain specified subjects, matters or areas of conduct, and if after the commencement of his testimony he is interrogated and testifies concerning another subject, matter or area of conduct not included in such written agreement, he receives immunity with respect to any further testimony which he may give concerning such other subject, matter or area of conduct and the waiver of immunity is to that extent ineffective.

§ 190.50. Grand jury; who may call witnesses; defendant as witness

1. Except as provided in this section, no person has a right to call a witness or appear as a witness in a grand jury proceeding.

2. The people may call as a witness in a grand jury proceeding any person believed by the district attorney to possess relevant information or knowledge.

3. The grand jury may cause to be called as a witness any person believed by it to possess relevant information or knowledge. If the grand jury desires to hear any such witness who was not called by the people, it may direct the district attorney to issue and serve a subpoena upon such witness, and the district attorney must comply with such direction. At any time after such a direction, however, or at any time after the service of a subpoena pursuant to such a direction and before the return date thereof, the people may apply to the court which impaneled the grand jury for an order vacating or modifying such direction or subpoena on the ground that such is in the public interest. Upon such application, the court may in its discretion vacate the direction or subpoena, attach reasonable conditions thereto, or make other appropriate qualification thereof.

4. Notwithstanding the provisions of subdivision three, the district attorney may demand that any witness thus called at the instance of the grand jury sign a waiver of immunity

pursuant to section 190.45 before being sworn, and upon such demand no oath may be administered to such witness unless and until he complies therewith.

5. Although not called as a witness by the people or at the instance of the grand jury, a person has a right to be a witness in a grand jury proceeding under circumstances prescribed in this subdivision:

(a) When a criminal charge against a person is being or is about to be or has been submitted to a grand jury, such person has a right to appear before such grand jury as a witness in his own behalf if, prior to the filing of any indictment or any direction to file a prosecutor's information in the matter, he serves upon the district attorney of the county a written notice making such request and stating an address to which communications may be sent. The district attorney is not obliged to inform such a person that such a grand jury proceeding against him is pending, in progress or about to occur unless such person is a defendant who has been arraigned in a local criminal court upon a currently undisposed of felony complaint charging an offense which is a subject of the prospective or pending grand jury proceeding. In such case, the district attorney must notify the defendant or his attorney of the prospective or pending grand jury proceeding and accord the defendant a reasonable time to exercise his right to appear as a witness therein;

(b) Upon service upon the district attorney of a notice requesting appearance before a grand jury pursuant to paragraph (a), the district attorney must notify the foreman of the grand jury of such request, and must subsequently serve upon the applicant, at the address specified by him, a notice that he will be heard by the grand jury at a given time and place. Upon appearing at such time and place, and upon signing and submitting to the grand jury a waiver of immunity pursuant to section 190.45, such person must be permitted to testify before the grand jury and to give any relevant and competent evidence concerning the case under consideration. Upon giving such evidence, he is subject to examination by the people.

(c) Any indictment or direction to file a prosecutor's information obtained or filed in violation of the provisions of paragraph (a) or (b) is invalid and, upon a motion made pursuant to section 170.50 or section 210.20, must be dismissed; provided that a motion based upon such ground must be made not more than five days after the defendant has been arraigned upon the indictment or, as the case may be, upon the prosecutor's information resulting from the grand jury's direction to file the same. If the contention is not so asserted in timely fashion, it is waived and the indictment or prosecutor's information may not thereafter be challenged on such ground.

6. A defendant or person against whom a criminal charge is being or is about to be brought in a grand jury proceeding may request the grand jury, either orally or in writing, to cause a person designated by him to be called as a witness in such proceeding. The grand jury may as a matter of discretion grant such request and cause such witness to be called pursuant to subdivision three.

7. Where a subpoena is made pursuant to this section, all papers and proceedings relating to the subpoena and any motion to quash, fix conditions, modify or compel compliance shall be kept secret and not disclosed to the public by any public officer or public employee or any other individual described in section 215.70 of the penal law.

This subdivision shall not apply where the person subpoenaed and the prosecutor waive the provisions of this subdivision.

This subdivision shall not prevent the publication of decisions and orders made in connection with such proceedings or motions, provided the caption and content of the decision are written or altered by the court to reasonably preclude identification of the person subpoenaed.

§ 190.52. Grand jury; attorney for witness

1. Any person who appears as a witness and has signed a waiver of immunity in a grand jury proceeding, has a right to an attorney as provided in this section. Such a witness may appear with a retained attorney, or if he is financially unable to obtain counsel, an attorney who shall be assigned by the superior court which impaneled the grand jury. Such assigned attorney shall be assigned pursuant to the same plan and in the same manner as counsel are provided to persons charged with crime pursuant to section seven hundred twenty-two of the county law.

2. The attorney for such witness may be present with the witness in the grand jury room. The attorney may advise the witness, but may not otherwise take any part in the proceeding.

3. The superior court which impaneled the grand jury shall have the same power to remove an attorney from the grand jury room as such court has with respect to an attorney in a courtroom.

§ 190.55. Grand jury; matters to be heard and examined; duties and authority of district attorney

1. A grand jury may hear and examine evidence concerning the alleged commission of any offense prosecutable in the courts of the county, and concerning any misconduct, nonfeasance or neglect in public office by a public servant, whether criminal or otherwise.

2. District attorneys are required or authorized to submit evidence to grand juries under the following circumstances:

(a) A district attorney must submit to a grand jury evidence concerning a felony allegedly committed by a defendant who, on the basis of a felony complaint filed with a local criminal court of the county, has been held for the action of a grand jury of such county, except where indictment has been waived by the defendant pursuant to article one hundred ninety-five.

(b) A district attorney must submit to a grand jury evidence concerning a misdemeanor allegedly committed by a defendant who has been charged therewith by a local criminal court accusatory instrument, in any case where a superior court of the county has, pursuant to subdivision one of section 170.25, ordered that such misdemeanor charge be prosecuted by indictment in a superior court.

(c) A district attorney may submit to a grand jury any available evidence concerning an offense prosecutable in the courts of the county, or concerning misconduct, nonfeasance or neglect in public office by a public servant, whether criminal or otherwise.

§ 190.60. Grand jury; action to be taken

After hearing and examining evidence as prescribed in section 190.55, a grand jury may:

1. Indict a person for an offense, as provided in section 190.65;
2. Direct the district attorney to file a prosecutor's information with a local criminal court, as provided in section 190.70;
3. Direct the district attorney to file a request for removal to the family court, as provided in section 190.71 of this article.
4. Dismiss the charge before it, as provided in section 190.75;
5. Submit a grand jury report, as provided in section 190.85.

§ 190.65. Grand jury; when indictment is authorized

1. Subject to the rules prescribing the kinds of offenses which may be charged in an indictment, a grand jury may indict a person for an offense when (a) the evidence before it is legally sufficient to establish that such person committed such offense provided, however, such evidence is not legally sufficient when corroboration that would be required, as a matter of law, to sustain a conviction for such offense is absent, and (b) competent and admissible evidence before it provides reasonable cause to believe that such person committed such offense.
2. The offense or offenses for which a grand jury may indict a person in any particular case are not limited to that or those which may have been designated, at the commencement of the grand jury proceeding, to be the subject of the inquiry; and even in a case submitted to it upon a court order, pursuant to the provisions of section 170.25, directing that a misdemeanor charge pending in a local criminal court be prosecuted by indictment, the grand jury may indict the defendant for a felony if the evidence so warrants.
3. Upon voting to indict a person, a grand jury must, through its foreman or acting foreman, file an indictment with the court by which it was impaneled.

§ 190.70. Grand jury; direction to file prosecutor's information and related matters

1. Except in a case submitted to it pursuant to the provisions of section 170.25, a grand jury may direct the district attorney to file in a local criminal court a prosecutor's information charging a person with an offense other than a felony when (a) the evidence before it is legally sufficient to establish that such person committed such offense, and (b) competent and admissible evidence before it provides reasonable cause to believe that such person committed such offense. In such case, the grand jury must, through its foreman or acting foreman, file such direction with the court by which it was impaneled.
2. Such direction must be signed by the foreman or acting foreman. It must contain a plain and concise statement of the conduct constituting the offense to be charged, equivalent in content and precision to the factual statement required to be contained in an indictment pursuant to subdivision seven of section 200.50. Subject to the rules prescribed in sections 200.20 and 200.40 governing joinder in a single indictment of multiple offenses and multiple defendants, such grand jury direction may, where appropriate, specify multiple offenses of less than felony grade and multiple defendants, and may direct that the prospective prosecutor's information charge a single defendant

with multiple offenses, or multiple defendants jointly with either a single offense or multiple offenses.

3. Upon the filing of such grand jury direction, the court must, unless such direction is insufficient on its face, issue an order approving such direction and ordering the district attorney to file such a prosecutor's information in a designated local criminal court having trial jurisdiction of the offense or offenses in question.

§ 190.71. Grand jury; direction to file request for removal to family court

(a) Except as provided in subdivision six of section 200.20 of this chapter, a grand jury may not indict (i) a person thirteen years of age for any conduct or crime other than conduct constituting a crime defined in subdivisions one and two of section 125.25 (murder in the second degree) or such conduct as a sexually motivated felony, where authorized pursuant to section 130.91 of the penal law; (ii) a person fourteen or fifteen years of age for any conduct or crime other than conduct constituting a crime defined in subdivisions one and two of section 125.25 (murder in the second degree) and in subdivision three of such section provided that the underlying crime for the murder charge is one for which such person is criminally responsible; 135.25 (kidnapping in the first degree); 150.20 (arson in the first degree); subdivisions one and two of section 120.10 (assault in the first degree); 125.20 (manslaughter in the first degree); subdivisions one and two of section 130.35 (rape in the first degree); subdivisions one and two of section 130.50 (criminal sexual act in the first degree); 130.70 (aggravated sexual abuse in the first degree); 140.30 (burglary in the first degree); subdivision one of section 140.25 (burglary in the second degree); 150.15 (arson in the second degree); 160.15 (robbery in the first degree); subdivision two of section 160.10 (robbery in the second degree) of the penal law; subdivision four of section 265.02 of the penal law, where such firearm is possessed on school grounds, as that phrase is defined in subdivision fourteen of section 220.00 of the penal law; or section 265.03 of the penal law, where such machine gun or such firearm is possessed on school grounds, as that phrase is defined in subdivision fourteen of section 220.00 of the penal law; or defined in the penal law as an attempt to commit murder in the second degree or kidnapping in the first degree, or such conduct as a sexually motivated felony, where authorized pursuant to section 130.91 of the penal law.

(b) A grand jury may vote to file a request to remove a charge to the family court if it finds that a person sixteen, or commencing October first, two thousand nineteen, seventeen years of age or younger did an act which, if done by a person over the age of sixteen, or commencing October first, two thousand nineteen, seventeen, would constitute a crime provided (1) such act is one for which it may not indict; (2) it does not indict such person for a crime; and (3) the evidence before it is legally sufficient to establish that such person did such act and competent and admissible evidence before it provides reasonable cause to believe that such person did such act.

(c) Upon voting to remove a charge to the family court pursuant to subdivision (b) of this section, the grand jury must, through its foreman or acting foreman, file a request to transfer such charge to the family court. Such request shall be filed with the court by which it was impaneled. It must (1) allege that a person named therein did any act which, if done by a person over the age of sixteen, would constitute a crime; (2) specify the act and the time and place of its commission; and (3) be signed by the foreman or the acting foreman.

(d) Upon the filing of such grand jury request, the court must, unless such request is improper or insufficient on its face, issue an order approving such request and direct that the charge be removed to the family court in accordance with the provisions of article seven hundred twenty-five of this chapter.

§ 190.75. Grand jury; dismissal of charge

1. If upon a charge that a designated person committed a crime, either (a) the evidence before the grand jury is not legally sufficient to establish that such person committed such crime or any other offense, or (b) the grand jury is not satisfied that there is reasonable cause to believe that such person committed such crime or any other offense, it must dismiss the charge. In such case, the grand jury must, through its foreman or acting foreman, file its finding of dismissal with the court by which it was impaneled.

2. If the defendant was previously held for the action of the grand jury by a local criminal court, the superior court to which such dismissal is presented must order the defendant released from custody if he is in the custody of the sheriff, or, if he is at liberty on bail, it must exonerate the bail.

3. When a charge has been so dismissed, it may not again be submitted to a grand jury unless the court in its discretion authorizes or directs the people to resubmit such charge to the same or another grand jury. If in such case the charge is again dismissed, it may not again be submitted to a grand jury.

4. Whenever all charges against a designated person have been so dismissed, the district attorney must within ninety days of the filing of the finding of such dismissal, notify that person of the dismissal by regular mail to his last known address unless resubmission has been permitted pursuant to subdivision three of this section or an order of postponement of such service is obtained upon a showing of good cause and exigent circumstances.

§ 190.80. Grand jury; release of defendant upon failure of timely grand jury action

Upon application of a defendant who on the basis of a felony complaint has been held by a local criminal court for the action of a grand jury, and who, at the time of such order or subsequent thereto, has been committed to the custody of the sheriff pending such grand jury action, and who has been confined in such custody for a period of more than forty-five days, or, in the case of a juvenile offender or adolescent offender, thirty days, without the occurrence of any grand jury action or disposition pursuant to subdivision one, two or three of section 190.60, the superior court by which such grand jury was or is to be impaneled must release him on his own recognizance unless:

(a) The lack of a grand jury disposition during such period of confinement was due to the defendant's request, action or condition, or occurred with his consent; or

(b) The people have shown good cause why such order of release should not be issued. Such good cause must consist of some compelling fact or circumstance which precluded grand jury action within the prescribed period or rendered the same against the interest of justice.

§ 190.85. Grand jury; grand jury reports

1. The grand jury may submit to the court by which it was impaneled, a report:

(a) Concerning misconduct, non-feasance or neglect in public office by a public servant as the basis for a recommendation of removal or disciplinary action; or

(b) Stating that after investigation of a public servant it finds no misconduct, non-feasance or neglect in office by him provided that such public servant has requested the submission of such report; or

(c) Proposing recommendations for legislative, executive or administrative action in the public interest based upon stated findings.

2. The court to which such report is submitted shall examine it and the minutes of the grand jury and, except as otherwise provided in subdivision four, shall make an order accepting and filing such report as a public record only if the court is satisfied that it complies with the provisions of subdivision one and that:

(a) The report is based upon facts revealed in the course of an investigation authorized by section 190.55 and is supported by the preponderance of the credible and legally admissible evidence; and

(b) When the report is submitted pursuant to paragraph (a) of subdivision one, that each person named therein was afforded an opportunity to testify before the grand jury prior to the filing of such report, and when the report is submitted pursuant to paragraph (b) or (c) of subdivision one, it is not critical of an identified or identifiable person.

3. The order accepting a report pursuant to paragraph (a) of subdivision one, and the report itself, must be sealed by the court and may not be filed as a public record, or be subject to subpoena or otherwise be made public until at least thirty-one days after a copy of the order and the report are served upon each public servant named therein, or if an appeal is taken pursuant to section 190.90, until the affirmance of the order accepting the report, or until reversal of the order sealing the report, or until dismissal of the appeal of the named public servant by the appellate division, whichever occurs later. Such public servant may file with the clerk of the court an answer to such report, not later than twenty days after service of the order and report upon him. Such an answer shall plainly and concisely state the facts and law constituting the defense of the public servant to the charges in said report, and, except for those parts of the answer which the court may determine to be scandalously or prejudicially and unnecessarily inserted therein, shall become an appendix to the report. Upon the expiration of the time set forth in this subdivision, the district attorney shall deliver a true copy of such report, and the appendix if any, for appropriate action, to each public servant or body having removal or disciplinary authority over each public servant named therein.

4. Upon the submission of a report pursuant to subdivision one, if the court finds that the filing of such report as a public record, may prejudice fair consideration of a pending criminal matter, it must order such report sealed and such report may not be subject to subpoena or public inspection during the pendency of such criminal matter, except upon order of the court.

5. Whenever the court to which a report is submitted pursuant to paragraph (a) of subdivision one is not satisfied that the report complies with the provisions of subdivision two, it may direct that additional testimony be taken before the same grand

jury, or it must make an order sealing such report, and the report may not be filed as a public record, or be subject to subpoena or otherwise be made public.

§ 190.90. Grand jury; appeal from order concerning grand jury reports

1. When a court makes an order accepting a report of a grand jury pursuant to paragraph (a) of subdivision one of section 190.85, any public servant named therein may appeal the order; and when a court makes an order sealing a report of a grand jury pursuant to subdivision five of section 190.85, the district attorney or other attorney designated by the grand jury may appeal the order.

2. When a court makes an order sealing a report of a grand jury pursuant to subdivision five of section 190.85, the district attorney or other attorney designated by the grand jury may, within ten days after service of a copy of the order and report upon each public servant named in the report, appeal the order to the appellate division of the department in which the order was made, by filing in duplicate a notice of appeal from the order with the clerk of the court in which the order was made and by serving a copy of such notice of appeal upon each such public servant. Notwithstanding any contrary provision of section 190.85, a true copy of the report of the grand jury shall be served, together with such notice of appeal, upon each such public servant.

3. The mode of and time for perfecting an appeal pursuant to this section, and the mode of and procedure for the argument thereof, are determined by the rules of the appellate division of the department in which the appeal is brought. Such rules shall prescribe the matters referred to in subdivision one of section 460.70 and in section 460.80, except that such appeal is a preferred cause and the appellate division of each department shall promulgate rules to effectuate such preference.

4. The record and all other presentations on appeal shall remain sealed, except that upon reversal of the order sealing the report or dismissal of the appeal of the named public servant by the appellate division, the report of the grand jury, with the appendix, if any, shall be filed as a public record as provided in subdivision three of section 190.85.

5. The procedure provided for in this section shall be the exclusive manner of reviewing an order made pursuant to section 190.85 and the appellate division of the supreme court shall be the sole court having jurisdiction of such an appeal. The order of the appellate division finally determining such appeal shall not be subject to review in any other court or proceeding.

6. The grand jury in an appeal pursuant to this section shall be represented by the district attorney unless the report relates to him or his office, in which event the grand jury may designate another attorney.

Article 195 Waiver of Indictment

§ 195.10. Waiver of indictment; in general

1. A defendant may waive indictment and consent to be prosecuted by superior court information when:
(a) a local criminal court has held the defendant for the action of a grand jury; and
(b) the defendant is not charged with a class A felony punishable by death or life imprisonment; and
(c) the district attorney consents to the waiver.

2. A defendant may waive indictment pursuant to subdivision one in either:

(a) the local criminal court in which the order was issued holding the defendant for action of a grand jury, at the time such order is issued; or

(b) the appropriate superior court, at any time prior to the filing of an indictment by the grand jury.

§ 195.20. Waiver of indictment; written instrument

A waiver of indictment shall be evidenced by a written instrument, which shall contain the name of the court in which it is executed, the title of the action, and the name, date and approximate time and place of each offense to be charged in the superior court information to be filed by the district attorney pursuant to section 195.40. The offenses named may include any offense for which the defendant was held for action of a grand jury and any offense or offenses properly joinable therewith pursuant to sections 200.20 and 200.40. The written waiver shall also contain a statement by the defendant that he is aware that:

(a) under the constitution of the state of New York he has the right to be prosecuted by indictment filed by a grand jury;

(b) he waives such right and consents to be prosecuted by superior court information to be filed by the district attorney;

(c) the superior court information to be filed by the district attorney will charge the offenses named in the written waiver; and

(d) the superior court information to be filed by the district attorney will have the same force and effect as an indictment filed by a grand jury.

The written waiver shall be signed by the defendant in open court in the presence of his attorney. The consent of the district attorney shall be endorsed thereon.

§ 195.30. Waiver of indictment; approval of waiver by the court

The court shall determine whether the waiver of indictment complies with the provisions of sections 195.10 and 195.20. If satisfied that the waiver complies with such provisions, the court shall approve the waiver and execute a written order to that effect. When the waiver is approved by a local criminal court, the local criminal court shall promptly transmit to the appropriate superior court the written waiver and order approving the waiver, along with all other documents pertinent to the action. Until such papers are received by the superior court, the action is deemed to be pending in the local criminal court.

§ 195.40. Waiver of indictment; filing of superior court information

When indictment is waived in a superior court the district attorney shall file a superior court information in such court at the time the waiver is executed. When indictment is waived in a local criminal court the district attorney shall file a superior court information in the appropriate superior court within ten days of the execution of the court order approving the waiver. Upon application of a defendant whose waiver of indictment has been approved by the court, and who, at the time of such approval or subsequent thereto, has been committed to the custody of the sheriff pending disposition of the action, and who has been confined in such custody for a period of more than ten days from the date of approval without the filing by the district attorney of a superior court information, the superior court must release him on his own recognizance unless:

(a) The failure of the district attorney to file a superior court information during such period of confinement was due to defendant's request, action or condition or occurred with his consent; or

(b) The people have shown good cause why such order of release should not be issued. Such good cause must consist of some compelling fact or circumstance which precluded the filing of the superior court information within the prescribed period.

Article 200 Indictment and Related Instruments

§ 200.10. Indictment; definition

An indictment is a written accusation by a grand jury, filed with a superior court, charging a person, or two or more persons jointly, with the commission of a crime, or with the commission of two or more offenses at least one of which is a crime. Except as used in Article 190, the term indictment shall include a superior court information.

§ 200.15. Superior court information; definition

A superior court information is a written accusation by a district attorney filed in a superior court pursuant to article one hundred ninety-five, charging a person, or two or more persons jointly, with the commission of a crime, or with the commission of two or more offenses, at least one of which is a crime. A superior court information may include any offense for which the defendant was held for action of a grand jury and any offense or offenses properly joinable therewith pursuant to sections 200.20 and 200.40, but shall not include an offense not named in the written waiver of indictment executed pursuant to section 195.20. A superior court information has the same force and effect as an indictment and all procedures and provisions of law applicable to indictments are also applicable to superior court informations, except where otherwise expressly provided.

§ 200.20. Indictment; what offenses may be charged; joinder of offenses and consolidation of indictments

1. An indictment must charge at least one crime and may, in addition, charge in separate counts one or more other offenses, including petty offenses, provided that all such offenses are joinable pursuant to the principles prescribed in subdivision two.

2. Two offenses are "joinable" when:

(a) They are based upon the same act or upon the same criminal transaction, as that term is defined in subdivision two of section 40.10; or

(b) Even though based upon different criminal transactions, such offenses, or the criminal transactions underlying them, are of such nature that either proof of the first offense would be material and admissible as evidence in chief upon a trial of the second, or proof of the second would be material and admissible as evidence in chief upon a trial of the first; or

(c) Even though based upon different criminal transactions, and even though not joinable pursuant to paragraph (b), such offenses are defined by the same or similar statutory provisions and consequently are the same or similar in law; or

(d) Though not directly joinable with each other pursuant to paragraph (a), (b) or (c), each is so joinable with a third offense contained in the indictment. In such case, each of the three offenses may properly be joined not only with each of the other two but also with any further offense joinable with either of the other two, and the chain of joinder may be further extended accordingly.

3. In any case where two or more offenses or groups of offenses charged in an indictment are based upon different criminal transactions, and where their joinability rests solely upon the fact that such offenses, or as the case may be at least one offense of each group, are the same or similar in law, as prescribed in paragraph (c) of subdivision two, the court, in the interest of justice and for good cause shown, may, upon application of either a defendant or the people, in its discretion, order that any such offenses be tried separately from the other or others thereof. Good cause shall include but not be limited to situations where there is:

(a) Substantially more proof on one or more such joinable offenses than on others and there is a substantial likelihood that the jury would be unable to consider separately the proof as it relates to each offense.

(b) A convincing showing that a defendant has both important testimony to give concerning one count and a genuine need to refrain from testifying on the other, which satisfies the court that the risk of prejudice is substantial.

(i) Good cause, under this paragraph (b), may be established in writing or upon oral representation of counsel on the record. Any written or oral representation may be based upon information and belief, provided the sources of such information and the grounds of such belief are set forth.

(ii) Upon the request of counsel, any written or recorded showing concerning the defendant's genuine need to refrain from testifying shall be ex parte and in camera. The in camera showing shall be sealed but a court for good cause may order unsealing. Any statements made by counsel in the course of an application under this paragraph (b) may not be offered against the defendant in any criminal action for impeachment purposes or otherwise.

4. When two or more indictments against the same defendant or defendants charge different offenses of a kind that are joinable in a single indictment pursuant to subdivision two, the court may, upon application of either the people or a defendant, order that such indictments be consolidated and treated as a single indictment for trial purposes. If such indictments, in addition to charging offenses which are so joinable charge other offenses which are not so joinable, they may nevertheless be consolidated for the limited purpose of jointly trying the joinable offenses. In such case, such indictments remain in existence with respect to any nonjoinable offenses and may be prosecuted accordingly. Nothing herein precludes the consolidation of an indictment with a superior court information.

5. A court's determination of an application for consolidation pursuant to subdivision four is discretionary; except that where an application by the defendant seeks consolidation with respect to offenses which are, pursuant to paragraph (a) of subdivision two, of a kind that are joinable in a single indictment by reason of being based upon the same act or criminal transaction, the court must order such consolidation unless good cause to the contrary be shown.

6. Where an indictment charges at least one offense against a defendant who was under the age of seventeen, or commencing October first, two thousand nineteen,

eighteen at the time of the commission of the crime and who did not lack criminal responsibility for such crime by reason of infancy, the indictment may, in addition, charge in separate counts one or more other offenses for which such person would not have been criminally responsible by reason of infancy, if:

(a) the offense for which the defendant is criminally responsible and the one or more other offenses for which he or she would not have been criminally responsible by reason of infancy are based upon the same act or upon the same criminal transaction, as that term is defined in subdivision two of section 40.10 of this chapter; or

(b) the offenses are of such nature that either proof of the first offense would be material and admissible as evidence in chief upon a trial of the second, or proof of the second would be material and admissible as evidence in chief upon a trial of the first.

§ 200.30. Indictment; duplicitous counts prohibited

1. Each count of an indictment may charge one offense only.

2. For purpose of this section, a statutory provision which defines the offense named in the title thereof by providing, in different subdivisions or paragraphs, different ways in which such named offense may be committed, defines a separate offense in each such subdivision or paragraph, and a count of an indictment charging such named offense which, without specifying or clearly indicating the particular subdivision or paragraph of the statutory provision, alleges facts which would support a conviction under more than one such subdivision or paragraph, charges more than one offense.

§ 200.40. Indictment; joinder of defendants and consolidation of indictments against different defendants

1. Two or more defendants may be jointly charged in a single indictment provided that:

(a) all such defendants are jointly charged with every offense alleged therein; or

(b) all the offenses charged are based upon a common scheme or plan; or

(c) all the offenses charged are based upon the same criminal transaction as that term is defined in subdivision two of section 40.10; or

(d) if the indictment includes a count charging enterprise corruption:

(i) all the defendants are jointly charged with every count of enterprise corruption alleged therein; and

(ii) every offense, other than a count alleging enterprise corruption, is a criminal act specifically included in the pattern of criminal activity on which the charge or charges of enterprise corruption is or are based; and

(iii) each such defendant could have been jointly charged with at least one of the other defendants, absent an enterprise corruption count, under the provisions of paragraph (a), (b) or (c) of this subdivision, in an accusatory instrument charging at least one such specifically included criminal act. For purposes of this subparagraph, joinder shall not be precluded on the ground that a specifically included criminal act which is necessary to permit joinder is not currently prosecutable, when standing alone, by reason of previous prosecution or lack of geographical jurisdiction.

Even in such case, the court, upon motion of a defendant or the people made within the period provided by section 255.20, may for good cause shown order in its discretion that any defendant be tried separately from the other or from one or more or all of the others. Good cause shall include, but not be limited to, a finding that a defendant or the people will be unduly prejudiced by a joint trial or, in the case of a prosecution involving a charge of enterprise corruption, a finding that proof of one or more criminal acts alleged to have been committed by one defendant but not one or more of the others creates a likelihood that the jury may not be able to consider separately the proof as it relates to each defendant, or in such a case, given the scope of the pattern of criminal activity charged against all the defendants, a particular defendant's comparatively minor role in it creates a likelihood of prejudice to him. Upon such a finding of prejudice, the court may order counts to be tried separately, grant a severance of defendants or provide whatever other relief justice requires.

2. When two or more defendants are charged in separate indictments with an offense or offenses but could have been so charged in a single indictment under subdivision one above, the court may, upon application of the people, order that such indictments be consolidated and the charges be heard in a single trial. If such indictments also charge offenses not properly the subject of a single indictment under subdivision one above, those offenses shall not be consolidated, but shall remain in existence and may be separately prosecuted. Nothing herein precludes the consolidation of an indictment with a superior court information.

Notice

/ This section has more than one version with varying effective dates.

§ 200.50. Indictment; form and content [Effective until November 1, 2019]

An indictment must contain:

1. The name of the superior court in which it is filed; and

2. The title of the action and, where the defendant is a juvenile offender, a statement in the title that the defendant is charged as a juvenile offender; and

3. A separate accusation or count addressed to each offense charged, if there be more than one; and

4. A statement in each count that the grand jury, or, where the accusatory instrument is a superior court information, the district attorney, accuses the defendant or defendants of a designated offense, provided that in any prosecution under article four hundred eighty-five of the penal law, the designated offense shall be the specified offense, as defined in subdivision three of section 485.05 of the penal law, followed by the phrase "as a hate crime", and provided further that in any prosecution under section 490.25 of the penal law, the designated offense shall be the specified offense, as defined in subdivision three of section 490.05 of the penal law, followed by the phrase "as a crime of terrorism"; and provided further that in any prosecution under section 130.91 of the penal law, the designated offense shall be the specified offense, as defined in subdivision two of section 130.91 of the penal law, followed by the phrase "as a sexually motivated felony"; and provided further that in any prosecution under section 496.06 of the penal law, the designated offense shall be the specified offense, as defined in subdivision two of such section, followed by the phrase "as a public corruption crime"; and

5. A statement in each count that the offense charged therein was committed in a designated county; and

6. A statement in each count that the offense charged therein was committed on, or on or about, a designated date, or during a designated period of time; and

7. A plain and concise factual statement in each count which, without allegations of an evidentiary nature,

(a) asserts facts supporting every element of the offense charged and the defendant's or defendants' commission thereof with sufficient precision to clearly apprise the defendant or defendants of the conduct which is the subject of the accusation; and

(b) in the case of any armed felony, as defined in subdivision forty-one of section 1.20, states that such offense is an armed felony and specifies the particular implement the defendant or defendants possessed, were armed with, used or displayed or, in the case of an implement displayed, specifies what the implement appeared to be; and

(c) in the case of any hate crime, as defined in section 485.05 of the penal law, specifies, as applicable, that the defendant or defendants intentionally selected the person against whom the offense was committed or intended to be committed; or intentionally committed the act or acts constituting the offense, in whole or in substantial part because of a belief or perception regarding the race, color, national origin, ancestry, gender, religion, religious practice, age, disability or sexual orientation of a person; and

(d) in the case of a crime of terrorism, as defined in section 490.25 of the penal law, specifies, as applicable, that the defendant or defendants acted with intent to intimidate or coerce a civilian population, influence the policy of a unit of government by intimidation or coercion, or affect the conduct of a unit of government by murder, assassination or kidnapping; and

(e) in the case of a sexually motivated felony, as defined in section 130.91 of the penal law, asserts facts supporting the allegation that the offense was sexually motivated; and

8. The signature of the foreman or acting foreman of the grand jury, except where the indictment has been ordered reduced pursuant to subdivision one-a of section 210.20 of this chapter or the accusatory instrument is a superior court information; and

9. The signature of the district attorney.

§ 200.60. Indictment; allegations of previous convictions prohibited

1. When the fact that the defendant has been previously convicted of an offense raises an offense of lower grade to one of higher grade and thereby becomes an element of the latter, an indictment for such higher offense may not allege such previous conviction. If a reference to previous conviction is contained in the statutory name or title of such an offense, such name or title may not be used in the indictment, but an improvised name or title must be used which, by means of the phrase "as a felony" or in some other manner, labels and distinguishes the offense without reference to a previous conviction. This subdivision does not apply to an indictment or a count thereof that charges escape in the second degree pursuant to subdivision two of section 205.10 of the penal law, or escape in the first degree pursuant to section 205.15 thereof.

2. An indictment for such an offense must be accompanied by a special information, filed by the district attorney with the court, charging that the defendant was previously convicted of a specified offense. Except as provided in subdivision three, the people

may not refer to such special information during the trial nor adduce any evidence concerning the previous conviction alleged therein.

3. After commencement of the trial and before the close of the people's case, the court, in the absence of the jury, must arraign the defendant upon such special information, and must advise him that he may admit the previous conviction alleged, deny it or remain mute. Depending upon the defendant's response, the trial of the indictment must then proceed as follows:

(a) If the defendant admits the previous conviction, that element of the offense charged in the indictment is deemed established, no evidence in support thereof may be adduced by the people, and the court must submit the case to the jury without reference thereto and as if the fact of such previous conviction were not an element of the offense. The court may not submit to the jury any lesser included offense which is distinguished from the offense charged solely by the fact that a previous conviction is not an element thereof.

(b) If the defendant denies the previous conviction or remains mute, the people may prove that element of the offense charged before the jury as a part of their case. In any prosecution under subparagraph (ix) of paragraph (a) of subdivision one of section 125.27 of the penal law, if the defendant denies the previous murder conviction or remains mute, the people may prove that element of the offense only after the jury has first found the defendant guilty of intentionally causing the death of a person as charged in the indictment, in which case the court shall then permit the people and the defendant to offer evidence and argument consistent with the relevant provisions of section 260.30 of this chapter with respect to the previous murder conviction.

4. Nothing contained in this section precludes the people from proving a prior conviction before a grand jury or relieves them from the obligation or necessity of so doing in order to submit a legally sufficient case.

§ 200.61. Indictment; special information for operators of for-hire vehicles

1. The provisions of this section shall govern the procedures for determining whether a defendant is eligible to receive the sentence set forth in subdivision one of section 60.07 of the penal law upon conviction of a specified offense as defined in subdivision two of such section 60.07.

2. To receive the sentence set forth in subdivision one of section 60.07 of the penal law, an indictment for such specified offense must be accompanied by a special information, filed by the district attorney with the court, alleging that the victim of such offense was operating a for-hire vehicle in the course of providing for-hire vehicle services at the time of the commission of such offense.

3. Prior to the commencement of the trial, the court, in the absence of the jury, must arraign the defendant upon such special information, and must advise him that he may admit that the alleged victim of such offense was operating a for-hire vehicle in the course of providing for-hire vehicle services at the time of the alleged commission of such offense, deny such allegation or remain mute. Depending upon the defendant's response, the trial of the indictment must proceed as follows:

(a) If the defendant admits that the alleged victim of such specified offense charged was operating a for-hire vehicle in the course of providing for-hire vehicle services at the time of the commission of such alleged offense, such allegation, and only such allegation, shall be deemed established for purposes of eligibility, if the defendant is convicted of the underlying specified offense, for a sentence pursuant to subdivision one of section 60.07 of the penal law.

(b) If the defendant denies such allegation or remains mute, the people may, by proof beyond a reasonable doubt, prove as part of their case before the jury or, where the defendant has waived a jury trial, the court, that the alleged victim of such offense was operating a for-hire vehicle in the course of providing for-hire vehicle services at the time of the commission of the offense.

4. Where a jury, pursuant to paragraph (b) of subdivision three of this section, is charged with determining whether the alleged victim of such specified offense was operating a for-hire vehicle in the course of providing for-hire vehicle services, such jury shall consider and render its verdict on such matter only if it convicts the defendant of such specified offense or specified offenses charged.

5. For purposes of this section, the terms "for-hire vehicle", "for-hire vehicle services" and "specified offense" shall have the meanings set forth in section 60.07 of the penal law.

§ 200.62. Indictment; special information for child sexual assault offender

1. Whenever a person is charged with the commission or attempted commission of an offense defined in article one hundred thirty of the penal law which constitutes a felony and it appears that the victim of such offense was less than fifteen years old, an indictment for such offense may be accompanied by a special information, filed by the district attorney with the court, alleging that the victim was less than fifteen years old at the time of the commission of the offense; provided, however, that such an information need not be filed when the age of the victim is an element of the offense.

2. Prior to trial, or after the commencement of the trial but before the close of the people's case, the court, in the absence of the jury, must arraign the defendant upon such information and advise him or her that he or she may admit such allegation, deny it or remain mute. Depending upon the defendant's response, the trial of the indictment must proceed as follows:

(a) If the defendant admits that the alleged victim was less than fifteen years old at the time of the commission or attempted commission of the offense, that allegation shall be deemed established for all subsequent purposes, including sentencing pursuant to section 70.07 of the penal law.

(b) If the defendant denies such allegation or remains mute, the people may, by proof beyond a reasonable doubt, prove before the jury or, where the defendant has waived a jury trial, the court, that the alleged victim was less than fifteen years old at the time of the commission or attempted commission of the offense.

(c) Nothing in this subdivision shall prevent the people, in a trial before the court or a jury, from making reference to and introducing evidence of the victim's age.

3. Where a jury, pursuant to paragraph (b) of subdivision two of this section, makes the determination of whether the alleged victim of the offense was less than fifteen years old, such jury shall consider and render its verdict on such issue only after rendering its verdict with regard to the offense.

170

4. A determination pursuant to this section that the victim was less than fifteen years old at the time of the commission of the offense shall be binding in any future proceeding in which the issue may arise unless the underlying conviction or determination is vacated or reversed.

§ 200.63. Indictment; special information for aggravated family offense

1. Whenever a person is charged with the commission or attempted commission of an aggravated family offense as defined in section 240.75 of the penal law, an indictment or information for such offense shall be accompanied by a special information, filed by the district attorney with the court, alleging that the defendant was previously convicted of a specified offense as defined in subdivision two of section 240.75 of the penal law, that at the time of the previous offense the defendant and the person against whom the offense was committed were members of the same family or household as defined in subdivision one of section 530.11 of this chapter, and that such previous conviction took place within the time period specified in subdivision one of section 240.75 of the penal law. Except as provided herein, the people may not refer to such special information during trial nor adduce any evidence concerning the allegations therein.

2. Prior to the commencement of the trial, the court, in the absence of the jury, must arraign the defendant upon such information and advise him or her that he or she may admit each such allegation, deny any such allegation or remain mute with respect to any such allegation. Depending upon the defendant's response, the trial of the indictment or information must then proceed as follows:

(a)

(i) If the previous conviction is for an aggravated family offense as defined in section 240.75 of the penal law, and the defendant admits the previous conviction or that it took place within the time period specified in subdivision one of section 240.75 of the penal law, such admitted allegation or allegations shall be deemed established for the purposes of the present prosecution, including sentencing pursuant to section 70.00 of the penal law. The court must submit the case to the jury as if such admitted allegation or allegations were not elements of the offense.

(ii) If the defendant denies the previous conviction or remains mute with respect to it, the people may prove, beyond a reasonable doubt, that element of the offense before the jury as a part of their case.

(iii) If the defendant denies that the previous conviction took place within the time period specified in subdivision one of section 240.75 of the penal law, or remains mute with respect to that matter, the people may prove, beyond a reasonable doubt, before the jury as part of their case, that the previous conviction took place within the time period specified.

(b)

(i) If the previous conviction is for a specified offense as defined in subdivision two of section 240.75 of the penal law, other than an aggravated family offense, and the defendant admits such previous conviction, that it took place within the time period specified in subdivision one of section 240.75 of the penal law, or that the defendant and the person against whom the offense was committed were members of the same family or household as defined in subdivision one of section 530.11 of this chapter, such admitted allegation or allegations shall be deemed established for the purposes of the present prosecution, including sentencing pursuant to section 70.00 of the penal law. The court must submit the case to the jury as if the admitted allegation or allegations were not elements of the offense.

(ii) If the defendant denies the previous conviction or remains mute with respect to it, the people may prove, beyond a reasonable doubt, that element of the offense before the jury as a part of their case.

(iii) If the defendant denies that the previous conviction took place within the time period specified in subdivision one of section 240.75 of the penal law, or remains mute with respect to that matter, the people may prove, beyond a reasonable doubt, before the jury as part of their case, that the previous conviction took place within the time period specified.

(iv) If the defendant denies that the defendant and the person against whom the previous offense was committed were members of the same family or household as defined in subdivision one of section 530.11 of this chapter, or remains mute with respect to that matter, the people may prove, beyond a reasonable doubt, that element of the offense before the jury as a part of their case.

§ 200.65. Indictment; special information for enterprise corruption and criminal possession or use of a biological weapon or chemical weapon

When filing an indictment which charges enterprise corruption in violation of article four hundred sixty of the penal law, criminal possession of a chemical weapon or biological weapon in violation of section 490.37, 490.40, or 490.45 of the penal law, or criminal use of a chemical weapon or biological weapon in violation of section 490.47, 490.50, or 490.55 of the penal law, the district attorney must submit a statement to the court attesting that he or she has reviewed the substance of the evidence presented to the grand jury and concurs in the judgment that the charge is consistent with legislative findings in article four hundred sixty or four hundred ninety of the penal law, as applicable. For purposes of this section only, "district attorney" means the district attorney of the county, the attorney general, or the deputy attorney general in charge of the organized crime task force, or where such person is actually absent or disabled, the person authorized to act in his or her stead.

§ 200.70. Indictment; amendment of

1. At any time before or during trial, the court may, upon application of the people and with notice to the defendant and opportunity to be heard, order the amendment of an indictment with respect to defects, errors or variances from the proof relating to matters of form, time, place, names of persons and the like, when such an amendment does not change the theory or theories of the prosecution as reflected in the evidence before the grand jury which filed such indictment, or otherwise tend to prejudice the defendant on the merits. Where the accusatory instrument is a superior court information, such an amendment may be made when it does not tend to prejudice the defendant on the merits. Upon permitting such an amendment, the court must, upon application of the defendant, order any adjournment of the proceedings which may, by reason of such amendment, be necessary to accord the defendant adequate opportunity to prepare his defense.

2. An indictment may not be amended in any respect which changes the theory or theories of the prosecution as reflected in the evidence before the grand jury which filed it; nor may an indictment or superior court information be amended for the purpose of curing:

(a) A failure thereof to charge or state an offense; or

(b) Legal insufficiency of the factual allegations; or

(c) A misjoinder of offenses; or

(d) A misjoinder of defendants.

§ 200.80. Indictment; superseding indictments

If at any time before entry of a plea of guilty to an indictment or commencement of a trial thereof another indictment is filed in the same court charging the defendant with an offense charged in the first indictment, the first indictment is, with respect to such offense, superseded by the second and, upon the defendant's arraignment upon the second indictment, the count of the first indictment charging such offense must be dismissed by the court. The first indictment is not, however, superseded with respect to any count contained therein which charges an offense not charged in the second indictment. Nothing herein precludes the filing of a superseding indictment when the first accusatory instrument is a superior court information.

§ 200.90. [Repealed]

§ 200.95. Indictment; bill of particulars

1. Definitions.

(a) "Bill of particulars" is a written statement by the prosecutor specifying, as required by this section, items of factual information which are not recited in the indictment and which pertain to the offense charged and including the substance of each defendant's conduct encompassed by the charge which the people intend to prove at trial on their direct case, and whether the people intend to prove that the defendant acted as principal or accomplice or both, and items of factual information which are not recited in a special forfeiture information or prosecutor's forfeiture information containing one or more forfeiture counts and which pertain to the substance of each defendant's conduct giving rise to the forfeiture claim, the approximate value of property for which forfeiture is sought, the nature and extent of the defendant's interest in such property, and the extent of the defendant's gain, if any, from the offense charged. However, the prosecutor shall not be required to include in the bill of particulars matters of evidence relating to how the people intend to prove the elements of the offense charged or how the people intend to prove any item of factual information included in the bill of particulars.

(b) "Request for a bill of particulars" is a written request served by defendant upon the people, without leave of the court, requesting a bill of particulars, specifying the items of factual information desired, and alleging that defendant cannot adequately prepare or conduct his defense without the information requested.

2. Bill of particulars upon request. Upon a timely request for a bill of particulars by a defendant against whom an indictment is pending, the prosecutor shall within fifteen days of the service of the request or as soon thereafter as is practicable, serve upon the defendant or his attorney, and file with the court, the bill of particulars, except to the

extent the prosecutor shall have refused to comply with the request pursuant to subdivision four of this section.

3. Timeliness of request. A request for a bill of particulars shall be timely if made within thirty days after arraignment and before the commencement of trial. If the defendant is not represented by counsel, and has requested an adjournment to obtain counsel or to have counsel assigned, the thirty day period shall commence, for the purposes of a request for a bill of particulars by the defendant, on the date counsel initially appears on his behalf. However, the court may direct compliance with a request for a bill of particulars that, for good cause shown, could not have been made within the time specified.

4. Request refused. The prosecutor may refuse to comply with the request for a bill of particulars or any portion of the request for a bill of particulars to the extent he reasonably believes that the item of factual information requested is not authorized to be included in a bill of particulars, or that such information is not necessary to enable the defendant adequately to prepare or conduct his defense, or that a protective order would be warranted or that the demand is untimely. Such refusal shall be made in a writing, which shall set forth the grounds of such belief as fully as possible, consistent with the reason for the refusal. Within fifteen days of the request or as soon thereafter as practicable, the refusal shall be served upon the defendant and a copy shall be filed with the court.

5. Court ordered bill of particulars. Where a prosecutor has timely served a written refusal pursuant to subdivision four of this section and upon motion, made in writing, of a defendant, who has made a request for a bill of particulars and whose request has not been complied with in whole or in part, the court must, to the extent a protective order is not warranted, order the prosecutor to comply with the request if it is satisfied that the items of factual information requested are authorized to be included in a bill of particulars, and that such information is necessary to enable the defendant adequately to prepare or conduct his defense and, if the request was untimely, a finding of good cause for the delay. Where a prosecutor has not timely served a written refusal pursuant to subdivision four of this section the court must, unless it is satisfied that the people have shown good cause why such an order should not be issued, issue an order requiring the prosecutor to comply or providing for any other order authorized by subdivision one of section 240.70.

6. Motion procedure. A motion for a bill of particulars shall be made as prescribed in section 255.20. Upon an order granting a motion pursuant to this section, the prosecutor must file with the court a bill of particulars, reciting every item of information designated in the order, and serve a copy thereof upon the defendant. Pending such filing and service, the proceedings are stayed.

7. Protective order.

(a) The court in which the criminal action is pending may, upon motion of the prosecutor, or of any affected person, or upon determination of a motion of defendant for a court ordered bill of particulars, or upon its own initiative, issue a protective order denying, limiting, conditioning, delaying or regulating the bill of particulars for good cause, including constitutional limitations, danger to the integrity of physical evidence or a substantial risk of physical harm, intimidation, economic reprisal, bribery or unjustified annoyance or embarrassment to any person or an adverse effect upon the legitimate needs of law enforcement, including the protection of the confidentiality of informants, or any other factor or set of factors which outweighs the need for the bill of particulars.

(b) An order limiting, conditioning, delaying or regulating the bill of particulars may, among other things, require that any material copied or derived therefrom be maintained in the exclusive possession of the attorney for the defendant and be used for the exclusive purpose of preparing for the defense of the criminal action.

8. Amendment. At any time before commencement of trial, the prosecutor may, without leave of the court, serve upon defendant and file with the court an amended bill of particulars. At any time during trial, upon application of the prosecutor and with notice to the defendant and an opportunity for him to be heard, the court must, upon finding that no undue prejudice will accrue to defendant and that the prosecutor has acted in good faith, permit the prosecutor to amend the bill of particulars. Upon any amendment of the bill of particulars, the court must, upon application of defendant, order an adjournment of the proceedings or any other action it deems appropriate which may, by reason of the amendment, be necessary to accord the defendant an adequate opportunity to defend.

Article 210 Proceedings in Superior Court From Filing of Indictment to Plea

§ 210.05. Indictment and superior court information exclusive methods of prosecution

The only methods of prosecuting an offense in a superior court are by an indictment filed therewith by a grand jury or by a superior court information filed therewith by a district attorney.

§ 210.10. Requirement of and methods of securing defendant's appearance for arraignment upon indictment

After an indictment has been filed with a superior court, the defendant must be arraigned thereon. He must appear personally at such arraignment, and his appearance may be secured as follows:

1. If the defendant was previously held by a local criminal court for the action of the grand jury, and if he is confined in the custody of the sheriff pursuant to a previous court order issued in the same criminal action, the superior court must direct the sheriff to produce the defendant for arraignment on a specified date and the sheriff must comply with such direction. The court must give at least two days notice of the time and place of the arraignment to an attorney, if any, who has previously filed a notice of appearance in behalf of the defendant with such superior court, or if no such notice of appearance has been filed, to an attorney, if any, who filed a notice of appearance in behalf of the defendant with the local criminal court.

2. If a felony complaint against the defendant was pending in a local criminal court or if the defendant was previously held by a local criminal court for the action of the grand jury, and if the defendant is at liberty on his or her own recognizance or on bail pursuant to a previous court order issued in the same criminal action, the superior court must, upon at least two days notice to the defendant and his or her surety, to any person other than the defendant who posted cash bail and to any attorney who would be entitled to notice under circumstances prescribed in subdivision one, direct the defendant to appear before the superior court for arraignment on a specified date. If the defendant

fails to appear on such date, the court may issue a bench warrant and, in addition, may forfeit the bail, if any. Upon taking the defendant into custody pursuant to such bench warrant, the executing police officer must without unnecessary delay bring the defendant before such superior court for arraignment. If such superior court is not available, the executing police officer may bring the defendant to the local correctional facility of the county in which such superior court sits, to be detained there until not later than the commencement of the next session of such court occurring on the next business day.

3. If the defendant has not previously been held by a local criminal court for the action of the grand jury and the filing of the indictment constituted the commencement of the criminal action, the superior court must order the indictment to be filed as a sealed instrument until the defendant is produced or appears for arraignment, and must issue a superior court warrant of arrest. Upon the request of the district attorney, in lieu of a superior court warrant of arrest, the court may issue a summons if it is satisfied that the defendant will respond thereto. Upon the request of the district attorney, in lieu of a warrant of arrest or summons, the court may instead authorize the district attorney to direct the defendant to appear for arraignment on a designated date if it is satisfied that the defendant will so appear. A superior court warrant of arrest is executable anywhere in the state. Such warrant may be addressed to any police officer whose geographical area of employment embraces either the place where the offense charged was allegedly committed or the locality of the court by which the warrant is issued. It must be executed in the same manner as an ordinary warrant of arrest, as provided in section 120.80, and following the arrest the executing police officer must without unnecessary delay perform all recording, fingerprinting, photographing and other preliminary police duties required in the particular case, and bring the defendant before the superior court. If such superior court is not available, the executing police officer may bring the defendant to the local correctional facility of the county in which such superior court sits, to be detained there until not later than the commencement of the next session of such court occurring on the next business day.

4. A superior court warrant of arrest may be executed by (a) any police officer to whom it is addressed or (b) any other police officer delegated to execute it under circumstances prescribed in subdivisions five and six.

5. The issuing court may authorize the delegation of such warrant. Where the issuing court has so authorized, a police officer to whom a superior court warrant of arrest is addressed may delegate another police officer to whom it is not addressed to execute such warrant as his agent when:

(a) He has reasonable cause to believe that the defendant is in a particular county other than the one in which the warrant is returnable; and

(b) The geographical area of employment of the delegated police officer embraces the locality where the arrest is to be made.

6. Under circumstances specified in subdivision five, the police officer to whom the warrant is addressed may inform the delegated officer, by telecommunication, mail or any other means, of the issuance of the warrant, of the offense charged in the underlying accusatory instrument and of all other pertinent details, and may request

such officer to act as his or her agent in arresting the defendant pursuant to such warrant. Upon such request, the delegated police officer is to the same extent as the delegating officer, authorized to make such arrest pursuant to the warrant within the geographical area of such delegated officer's employment. Upon so arresting the defendant, he or she must without unnecessary delay deliver the defendant or cause the defendant to be delivered to the custody of the police officer by whom he or she was so delegated, and the latter must then without unnecessary delay bring the defendant before a court in which such warrant is returnable. If such court is not available, the delegating officer may bring the defendant to the local correctional facility of the county in which such court sits, to be detained there until not later than the commencement of the next session of such court occurring on the next business day.

§ 210.15. Arraignment upon indictment; defendant's rights, court's instructions and bail matters

1. Upon the defendant's arraignment before a superior court upon an indictment, the court must immediately inform him, or cause him to be informed in its presence, of the charge or charges against him, and the district attorney must cause him to be furnished with a copy of the indictment.

2. The defendant has a right to the aid of counsel at the arraignment and at every subsequent stage of the action, and, if he appears upon such arraignment without counsel, has the following rights:

(a) To an adjournment for the purpose of obtaining counsel; and

(b) To communicate, free of charge, by letter or by telephone provided by the law enforcement facility where the defendant is held to a phone number located in the United States or Puerto Rico, for the purposes of obtaining counsel and informing a relative or friend that he or she has been charged with an offense; and

(c) To have counsel assigned by the court in any case where he is financially unable to obtain the same.

3. The court must inform the defendant of all rights specified in subdivision two. The court must accord the defendant opportunity to exercise such rights and must itself take such affirmative action as is necessary to effectuate them.

4. [Repealed]

5. If the defendant desires to proceed without the aid of counsel, the court must permit him to do so if it is satisfied that he made such decision with knowledge of the significance thereof, but if it is not so satisfied it may not proceed until the defendant is provided with counsel, either of his own choosing or by assignment. A defendant who proceeds at the arraignment without counsel does not waive his right to counsel, and the court must inform him that he continues to have such right as well as all the rights specified in subdivision two which are necessary to effectuate it, and that he may exercise such rights at any stage of the action.

6. Upon the arraignment, the court, unless it intends to make a final disposition of the action immediately thereafter, must, as provided in section 530.40, issue a securing order, releasing the defendant on his own recognizance or fixing bail or committing him to the custody of the sheriff for his future appearance in such action.

§ 210.16. Requirement of HIV related testing in certain cases

1.

(a) In a case where an indictment or a superior court information has been filed with a superior court which charges the defendant with a felony offense enumerated in any section of article one hundred thirty of the penal law where an act of "sexual intercourse", "oral sexual conduct" or "anal sexual conduct," as those terms are defined in section 130.00 of the penal law, is required as an essential element for the commission thereof, the court shall, upon a request of the victim within six months of the date of the crimes charged, order that the defendant submit to human immunodeficiency virus (HIV) related testing. Testing of a defendant shall be ordered when the result would provide medical benefit to the victim or a psychological benefit to the victim. Medical benefit shall be found when the following elements are satisfied: (i) a decision is pending about beginning, continuing, or discontinuing a medical intervention for the victim; and (ii) the result of an HIV test of the accused could affect that decision, and could provide relevant information beyond that which would be provided by an HIV test of the victim. If testing the defendant would provide medical benefit to the victim or a psychological benefit to the victim, then the testing is to be conducted by a state, county, or local public health officer designated by the order. Test results, which shall not be disclosed to the court, shall be communicated to the defendant and the victim named in the order in accordance with the provisions of section twenty-seven hundred eighty-five-a of the public health law.

(b) For the purposes of this section, the terms "victim" and "applicant" mean the person with whom the defendant is charged to have engaged in an act of "sexual intercourse", "oral sexual conduct" or "anal sexual conduct", as those terms are defined in section 130.00 of the penal law, where such conduct with such victim was the basis for charging the defendant with an offense specified in paragraph (a) of this subdivision.

2. Any request made by the victim pursuant to this section must be in writing, filed with the court within six months of the date of the crimes charged, and provided by the court to the defendant or his or her counsel. The request must be filed with the court prior to or within forty-eight hours after the indictment or superior court information has been filed with the superior court; provided however that, for good cause shown, the court may permit such request to be filed at a later stage of the action within six months of the date of the crimes charged.

3. At any stage in the action within six months of the date of the crimes charged, prior to the final disposition of the indictment or superior court information and while the defendant is charged with an offense specified in paragraph (a) of subdivision one of this section, the victim may request that the defendant submit to a follow-up HIV related test. Such request must be in writing, filed with the court and provided by the court to the defendant or his or her counsel. Upon a finding that the follow-up HIV related test is medically appropriate the court must order that the defendant submit to such test. The court shall not make such finding of medical appropriateness unless the follow-up HIV related test is to be administered a sufficient time after the charged offense to be consistent with guidelines that may be issued by the commissioner of health. There shall be no more than one follow-up HIV related test absent a showing of extraordinary circumstances.

4. Any requests, related papers and orders made or filed pursuant to this section, together with any papers or proceedings related thereto, shall be sealed by the court and not made available for any purpose, except as may be necessary for the conduct of judicial proceedings directly related to the provisions of this section. All proceedings on such requests shall be held in camera.

5. The application for an order to compel a defendant to undergo an HIV related test may be made by the victim but, if the victim is an infant or incompetent person, the application may also be made by a representative as defined in section twelve hundred one of the civil practice law and rules. The application must state that: (a) the applicant was the victim of the offense enumerated in paragraph (a) of subdivision one of this section of which the defendant is charged; and (b) the applicant has been offered pre-HIV test counseling and post-HIV test counseling by a public health officer in accordance with article twenty-seven-F of the public health law and has been advised, in accordance with any guidelines that may be issued by the commissioner of health, of (i) the limitations on the information to be obtained through an HIV test on the proposed subject; (ii) current scientific assessments of the risk of transmission of HIV from the exposure he or she may have experienced; and (iii) the need for the applicant to undergo HIV related testing to definitively determine his or her HIV status.

6. The court shall conduct a hearing only if necessary to determine if the applicant is the victim of the offense of which the defendant is charged or to determine whether a follow-up test is medically appropriate. The court ordered test must be performed within forty-eight hours of the date on which the court ordered the test, provided, however, that whenever the defendant is not tested within the period prescribed by the court, the court must again order that the defendant undergo an HIV related test. The defendant shall be advised of information as to HIV testing and medical treatment in accordance with any guidelines that may be issued by the commissioner of health.

7.

(a) Test results shall be disclosed subject to the following limitations, which shall be specified in any order issued pursuant to this section:

(i) disclosure of confidential HIV related information shall be limited to that information which is necessary to fulfill the purpose for which the order is granted; and

(ii) disclosure of confidential HIV related information shall be made to the defendant upon his or her request, and disclosure to a person other than the defendant shall be limited to the person making the application; redisclosure shall be permitted only to the victim, the victim's immediate family, guardian, physicians, attorneys, medical or mental health providers and to his or her past and future contacts to whom there was or is a reasonable risk of HIV transmission and shall not be permitted to any other person or the court.

(b) Unless inconsistent with this section, the court's order shall direct compliance with and conform to the provisions of article twenty-seven-F of the public health law. Such order shall include measures to protect against disclosure to others of the identity and HIV status of the applicant and of the person tested and may include such other measures as the court deems necessary to protect confidential information.

8. Any failure to comply with the provisions of this section or section twenty-seven hundred eighty-five-a of the public health law shall not impair or affect the validity of any proceeding upon the indictment or superior court information.

9. No information obtained as a result of a consent, hearing or court order for testing issued pursuant to this section nor any information derived therefrom may be used as evidence in any criminal or civil proceeding against the defendant which relates to events that were the basis for charging the defendant with an offense enumerated in paragraph (a) of subdivision one of this section, provided however that nothing in this section shall prevent prosecution of a witness testifying in any court hearing held pursuant to this section for perjury pursuant to article two hundred ten of the penal law.

§ 210.20. Motion to dismiss or reduce indictment

1. After arraignment upon an indictment, the superior court may, upon motion of the defendant, dismiss such indictment or any count thereof upon the ground that:

(a) Such indictment or count is defective, within the meaning of section 210.25; or

(b) The evidence before the grand jury was not legally sufficient to establish the offense charged or any lesser included offense; or

(c) The grand jury proceeding was defective, within the meaning of section 210.35; or

(d) The defendant has immunity with respect to the offense charged, pursuant to section 50.20 or 190.40; or

(e) The prosecution is barred by reason of a previous prosecution, pursuant to section 40.20; or

(f) The prosecution is untimely, pursuant to section 30.10; or

(g) The defendant has been denied the right to a speedy trial; or

(h) There exists some other jurisdictional or legal impediment to conviction of the defendant for the offense charged; or

(i) Dismissal is required in the interest of justice, pursuant to section 210.40.

1-a. After arraignment upon an indictment, if the superior court, upon motion of the defendant pursuant to this subdivision or paragraph b of subdivision one of this section challenging the legal sufficiency of the evidence before the grand jury, finds that the evidence before the grand jury was not legally sufficient to establish the commission by the defendant of the offense charged in any count contained within the indictment, but was legally sufficient to establish the commission of a lesser included offense, it shall order the count or counts of the indictment with respect to which the finding is made reduced to allege the most serious lesser included offense with respect to which the evidence before the grand jury was sufficient, except that where the most serious lesser included offense thus found is a petty offense, and the court does not find evidence of the commission of any crime in any other count of the indictment, it shall order the indictment dismissed and a prosecutor's information charging the petty offense filed in the appropriate local criminal court. The motion to dismiss or reduce any count of an indictment based on legal insufficiency to establish the offense charged shall be made in accordance with the procedure set forth in subdivisions one through seven of section 210.45, provided however, the court shall state on the record the basis for its determination. Upon entering an order pursuant to this subdivision, the court shall consider the appropriateness of any securing order issued pursuant to article 510 of this chapter.

2. A motion pursuant to this section, except a motion pursuant to paragraph (g) of subdivision one, should be made within the period provided in section 255.20. A motion made pursuant to paragraph (g) of subdivision one must be made prior to the commencement of trial or entry of a plea of guilty.

3. Upon the motion, a defendant who is in a position adequately to raise more than one ground in support thereof should raise every such ground upon which he intends to challenge the indictment. A subsequent motion based upon any such ground not so raised may be summarily denied, although the court, in the interest of justice and for good cause shown, may in its discretion entertain and dispose of such a motion on the merits notwithstanding.

4. Upon dismissing an indictment or a count thereof upon any of the grounds specified in paragraphs (a), (b), (c) and (i) of subdivision one, or, upon dismissing a superior court information or a count thereof upon any of the grounds specified in paragraphs (a) or (i) of subdivision one, the court may, upon application of the people, in its discretion authorize the people to submit the charge or charges to the same or another grand jury. When the dismissal is based upon some other ground, such authorization may not be granted. In the absence of authorization to submit or resubmit, the order of dismissal constitutes a bar to any further prosecution of such charge or charges, by indictment or otherwise, in any criminal court within the county.

5. If the court dismisses one or more counts of an indictment, against a defendant who was under the age of sixteen at the time of the commission of the crime and who did not lack criminal responsibility for such crime by reason of infancy, and one or more other counts of the indictment having been joined in the indictment solely with the dismissed count pursuant to subdivision six of section 200.20 is not dismissed, the court must direct that such count be removed to the family court in accordance with article seven hundred twenty-five of this chapter.

6. The effectiveness of an order reducing a count or counts of an indictment or dismissing an indictment and directing the filing of a prosecutor's information or dismissing a count or counts of an indictment charging murder in the first degree shall be stayed for thirty days following the entry of such order unless such stay is otherwise waived by the people. On or before the conclusion of such thirty-day period, the people shall exercise one of the following options:

(a) Accept the court's order by filing a reduced indictment, by dismissing the indictment and filing a prosecutor's information, or by filing an indictment containing any count or counts remaining after dismissal of the count or counts charging murder in the first degree, as appropriate;

(b) Resubmit the subject count or counts to the same or a different grand jury within thirty days of the entry of the order or such additional time as the court may permit upon a showing of good cause; provided, however, that if in such case an order is again entered with respect to such count or counts pursuant to subdivision one-a of this section, such count or counts may not again be submitted to a grand jury. Where the people exercise this option, the effectiveness of the order further shall be stayed pending a determination by the grand jury and the filing of a new indictment, if voted, charging the resubmitted count or counts;

(c) Appeal the order pursuant to subdivision one or one-a of section 450.20. Where the people exercise this option, the effectiveness of the order further shall be stayed in accordance with the provisions of subdivision two of section 460.40.

If the people fail to exercise one of the foregoing options, the court's order shall take effect and the people shall comply with paragraph (a) of this subdivision.

§ 210.25. Motion to dismiss indictment; as defective

An indictment or a count thereof is defective within the meaning of paragraph (a) of subdivision one of section 210.20 when:

1. It does not substantially conform to the requirements stated in article two hundred; provided that an indictment may not be dismissed as defective, but must instead be amended, where the defect or irregularity is of a kind that may be cured by amendment, pursuant to section 200.70, and where the people move to so amend; or

2. The allegations demonstrate that the court does not have jurisdiction of the offense charged; or

3. The statute defining the offense charged is unconstitutional or otherwise invalid.

§ 210.30. Motion to dismiss or reduce indictment on ground of insufficiency of grand jury evidence; motion to inspect grand jury minutes

1. A motion to dismiss an indictment or a count thereof pursuant to paragraph (b) of subdivision one of section 210.20 or a motion to reduce a count or counts of an indictment pursuant to subdivision one-a of section 210.20 must be preceded or accompanied by a motion to inspect the grand jury minutes, as prescribed in subdivision two of this section.

2. A motion to inspect grand jury minutes is a motion by a defendant requesting an examination by the court and the defendant of the stenographic minutes of a grand jury proceeding resulting in an indictment for the purpose of determining whether the evidence before the grand jury was legally sufficient to support the charges or a charge contained in such indictment.

3. Unless good cause exists to deny the motion to inspect the grand jury minutes, the court must grant the motion. It must then proceed to examine the minutes and to determine the motion to dismiss or reduce the indictment. If the court, after examining the minutes, finds that release of the minutes, or certain portions thereof, to the parties is necessary to assist the court in making its determination on the motion, it may release the minutes or such portions thereof to the parties. Provided, however, such release shall be limited to that grand jury testimony which is relevant to a determination of whether the evidence before the grand jury was legally sufficient to support a charge or charges contained in such indictment. Prior to such release the district attorney shall be given an opportunity to present argument to the court that the release of the minutes, or any portion thereof, would not be in the public interest. For purposes of this section, the minutes shall include any materials submitted to the grand jury pursuant to subdivision eight of section 190.30 of this chapter.

4. If the court determines that there is not reasonable cause to believe that the evidence before the grand jury may have been legally insufficient, it may in its discretion

either (a) deny both the motion to inspect and the motion to dismiss or reduce, or (b) grant the motion to inspect notwithstanding and proceed to examine the minutes and to determine the motion to dismiss or reduce.

5. In any case, the court must place on the record its ruling upon the motion to inspect.

6. The validity of an order denying any motion made pursuant to this section is not reviewable upon an appeal from an ensuing judgment of conviction based upon legally sufficient trial evidence.

7. Notwithstanding any other provision of law, where the indictment is filed against a juvenile offender or adolescent offender, the court shall dismiss the indictment or count thereof where the evidence before the grand jury was not legally sufficient to establish the offense charged or any lesser included offense for which the defendant is criminally responsible. Upon such dismissal, unless the court shall authorize the people to resubmit the charge to a subsequent grand jury, and upon a finding that there was sufficient evidence to believe defendant is a juvenile delinquent as defined in subdivision (a) of section seven hundred twelve of the family court act and upon specifying the act or acts it found sufficient evidence to believe defendant committed, the court may direct that such matter be removed to family court in accordance with the provisions of article seven hundred twenty-five of this chapter.

§ 210.35. Motion to dismiss indictment; defective grand jury proceeding

A grand jury proceeding is defective within the meaning of paragraph (c) of subdivision one of section 210.20 when:

1. The grand jury was illegally constituted; or

2. The proceeding is conducted before fewer than sixteen grand jurors; or

3. Fewer than twelve grand jurors concur in the finding of the indictment; or

4. The defendant is not accorded an opportunity to appear and testify before the grand jury in accordance with the provisions of section 190.50; or

5. The proceeding otherwise fails to conform to the requirements of article one hundred ninety to such degree that the integrity thereof is impaired and prejudice to the defendant may result.

§ 210.40. Motion to dismiss indictment; in furtherance of justice

1. An indictment or any count thereof may be dismissed in furtherance of justice, as provided in paragraph (i) of subdivision one of section 210.20, when, even though there may be no basis for dismissal as a matter of law upon any ground specified in paragraphs (a) through (h) of said subdivision one of section 210.20, such dismissal is required as a matter of judicial discretion by the existence of some compelling factor, consideration or circumstance clearly demonstrating that conviction or prosecution of the defendant upon such indictment or count would constitute or result in injustice. In determining whether such compelling factor, consideration, or circumstance exists, the court must, to the extent applicable, examine and consider, individually and collectively, the following:

(a) the seriousness and circumstances of the offense;

(b) the extent of harm caused by the offense;

(c) the evidence of guilt, whether admissible or inadmissible at trial;

(d) the history, character and condition of the defendant;

(e) any exceptionally serious misconduct of law enforcement personnel in the investigation, arrest and prosecution of the defendant;

(f) the purpose and effect of imposing upon the defendant a sentence authorized for the offense;

(g) the impact of a dismissal upon the confidence of the public in the criminal justice system;

(h) the impact of a dismissal on the safety or welfare of the community;

(i) where the court deems it appropriate, the attitude of the complainant or victim with respect to the motion;

(j) any other relevant fact indicating that a judgment of conviction would serve no useful purpose.

2. In addition to the grounds specified in subdivision one of this section, a count alleging enterprise corruption in violation of article four hundred sixty of the penal law may be dismissed in the interest of justice where prosecution of that count is inconsistent with the stated legislative findings in said article. Upon a motion pursuant to this section, the court must inspect the evidence before the grand jury and such other evidence or information as it may deem proper.

3. An order dismissing an indictment in the interest of justice may be issued upon motion of the people or of the court itself as well as upon that of the defendant. Upon issuing such an order, the court must set forth its reasons therefor upon the record.

§ 210.43. Motion to remove juvenile offender to family court [Repealed]

§ 210.45. Motion to dismiss indictment; procedure

1. A motion to dismiss an indictment pursuant to section 210.20 must be made in writing and upon reasonable notice to the people. If the motion is based upon the existence or occurrence of facts, the motion papers must contain sworn allegations thereof, whether by the defendant or by another person or persons. Such sworn allegations may be based upon personal knowledge of the affiant or upon information and belief, provided that in the latter event the affiant must state the sources of such information and the grounds of such belief. The defendant may further submit documentary evidence supporting or tending to support the allegations of the moving papers.

2. The people may file with the court, and in such case must serve a copy thereof upon the defendant or his counsel, an answer denying or admitting any or all of the allegations of the moving papers, and may further submit documentary evidence refuting or tending to refute such allegations.

3. After all papers of both parties have been filed, and after all documentary evidence, if any, has been submitted, the court must consider the same for the purpose of determining whether the motion is determinable without a hearing to resolve questions of fact.

4. The court must grant the motion without conducting a hearing if:

(a) The moving papers allege a ground constituting legal basis for the motion pursuant to subdivision one of section 210.20; and

(b) Such ground, if based upon the existence or occurrence of facts, is supported by sworn allegations of all facts essential to support the motion; and

(c) The sworn allegations of fact essential to support the motion are either conceded by the people to be true or are conclusively substantiated by unquestionable documentary proof.

5. The court may deny the motion without conducting a hearing if:

(a) The moving papers do not allege any ground constituting legal basis for the motion pursuant to subdivision one of section 210.20; or

(b) The motion is based upon the existence or occurrence of facts, and the moving papers do not contain sworn allegations supporting all the essential facts; or

(c) An allegation of fact essential to support the motion is conclusively refuted by unquestionable documentary proof.

6. If the court does not determine the motion pursuant to subdivision four or five, it must conduct a hearing and make findings of fact essential to the determination thereof. The defendant has a right to be present in person at such hearing but may waive such right.

7. Upon such a hearing, the defendant has the burden of proving by a preponderance of the evidence every fact essential to support the motion.

8. When the court dismisses the entire indictment without authorizing resubmission of the charge or charges to a grand jury, it must order that the defendant be discharged from custody if he is in the custody of the sheriff, or if he is at liberty on bail it must exonerate the bail.

9. When the court dismisses the entire indictment but authorizes resubmission of the charge or charges to a grand jury, such authorization is, for purposes of this subdivision, deemed to constitute an order holding the defendant for the action of a grand jury with respect to such charge or charges. Such order must be accompanied by a securing order either releasing the defendant on his own recognizance or fixing bail or committing him to the custody of the sheriff pending resubmission of the case to the grand jury and the grand jury's disposition thereof. Such securing order remains in effect until the first to occur of any of the following:

(a) A statement to the court by the people that they do not intend to resubmit the case to a grand jury;

(b) Arraignment of the defendant upon an indictment or prosecutor's information filed as a result of resubmission of the case to a grand jury. Upon such arraignment, the arraigning court must issue a new securing order;

(c) The filing with the court of a grand jury dismissal of the case following resubmission thereof;

(d) The expiration of a period of forty-five days from the date of issuance of the order; provided that such period may, for good cause shown, be extended by the court to a designated subsequent date if such be necessary to accord the people reasonable opportunity to resubmit the case to a grand jury.

Upon the termination of the effectiveness of the securing order pursuant to paragraph (a), (c) or (d), the court must immediately order that the defendant be discharged from custody if he is in the custody of the sheriff, or if he is at liberty on bail it must exonerate the bail. Although expiration of the period of time specified in paragraph (d) without any resubmission or grand jury disposition of the case terminates the effectiveness of the securing order, it does not terminate the effectiveness of the order authorizing resubmission.

§ 210.46. Adjournment in contemplation of dismissal in marihuana cases in a superior court

Upon or after arraignment in a superior court upon an indictment where the sole remaining count or counts charge a violation or violations of section 221.05, 221.10, 221.15, 221.35 or 221.40 of the penal law and before the entry of a plea of guilty thereto or commencement of a trial thereof, the court, upon motion of a defendant, may order that all proceedings be suspended and the action adjourned in contemplation of dismissal or may dismiss the indictment in furtherance of justice, in accordance with the provisions of section 170.56 of this chapter.

§ 210.47. Adjournment in contemplation of dismissal in misdemeanor cases in superior court

Upon or after the arraignment in a superior court upon an indictment where the sole remaining count or counts charge a misdemeanor offense, and before the entry of a plea of guilty thereto or commencement of a trial thereof, the court, upon motion of the people or the defendant and with the consent of the other party, or upon the court's own motion with the consent of both the people and the defendant, may order that all proceedings be suspended and the action adjourned in contemplation of dismissal, in accordance with the provisions of section 170.55 of this chapter.

§ 210.50. Requirement of plea

Unless an indictment is dismissed or the criminal action thereon terminated or abated pursuant to the provisions of this article or some other provision of law, the defendant must be required to enter a plea thereto.

Article 215 Adjournment in Contemplation of Dismissal for Purposes of Referring Selected Felonies to Dispute Resolution

§ 215.10. Referral of selected felonies to dispute resolution

Upon or after arraignment in a local criminal court upon a felony complaint, or upon or after arraignment in a superior court upon an indictment or superior court information, and before final disposition thereof, the court, with the consent of the people and of the defendant, and with reasonable notice to the victim and an opportunity for the victim to be heard, may order that the action be adjourned in contemplation of dismissal, for the purpose of referring the action to a community dispute center established pursuant to article twenty-one-A of the judiciary law. Provided, however, that the court may not order any action adjourned in contemplation of dismissal if the defendant is charged therein with: (i) a class A felony, or (ii) a violent felony offense as defined in section 70.02 of the penal law, or (iii) any drug offense as defined in article two hundred twenty of the penal law, or (iv) a felony upon the conviction of which defendant must be sentenced as a second felony offender, a second violent felony offender, or a persistent violent felony offender pursuant to sections 70.06, 70.04 and 70.08 of the penal law, or a felony upon the conviction of which defendant may be sentenced as a persistent felony offender pursuant to section 70.10 of such law.

§ 215.20. Victim; definition

For purposes of section 215.10 of this article, "victim" means any person alleged to have sustained physical or financial injury to person or property as a direct result of the crime or crimes charged in a felony complaint, superior court information, or indictment.

§ 215.30. Adjournment in contemplation of dismissal; restoration to calendar; dismissal of action

Upon issuing an order adjourning an action in contemplation of dismissal pursuant to section 215.10 of this article, the court must release the defendant on his own recognizance and refer the action to a dispute resolution center established pursuant to article twenty-one-A of the judiciary law. No later than forty-five days after an action has been referred to a dispute resolution center, such center must advise the district attorney as to whether the charges against defendant have been resolved. Thereafter, if defendant has agreed to pay a fine, restitution or reparation, the district attorney must be advised every thirty days as to the status of such fine, restitution or reparation. Upon application of the people, made at any time not more than six months after the issuance of an order adjourning an action in contemplation of dismissal, the court may restore the action to the calendar upon a determination that dismissal of the accusatory instrument would not be in furtherance of justice, and the action must thereupon proceed. Notwithstanding the foregoing, where defendant has agreed to pay a fine, restitution, or reparation, but has not paid such fine, restitution or reparation, upon application of the people, made at any time not more than one year after the issuance of an order adjourning an action in contemplation of dismissal, the court may restore the action to the calendar upon a determination that defendant has failed to pay such fine, restitution, or reparation, and the action must thereupon proceed.

§ 215.40. Dismissal of action; effect thereof; records

If an action has not been restored to the calendar within six months, or where the defendant has agreed to pay a fine, restitution or reparation but has not paid such fine, restitution or reparation, within one year, of the issuance of an order adjourning the action in contemplation of dismissal, the accusatory instrument shall be deemed to have been dismissed by the court in furtherance of justice at the expiration of such six month or one year period, as the case may be. Upon dismissal of an action, the arrest and prosecution shall be deemed a nullity, and defendant shall be restored to the status he or she occupied before his or her arrest and prosecution. All papers and records relating to an action that has been dismissed pursuant to this section shall be subject to the sealing provisions of section 160.50 of this chapter.

Article 216 Judicial Diversion Program for Certain Felony Offenders

§ 216.00. Definitions

The following definitions are applicable to this article:

1. [Eff until July 5, 2021] "Eligible defendant" means any person who stands charged in an indictment or a superior court information with a class B, C, D or E felony offense defined in article one hundred seventy-nine, two hundred twenty or two hundred twenty-one of the penal law or any other specified offense as defined in subdivision four of section 410.91 of this chapter, provided, however, a defendant is not an "eligible defendant" if he or she:

(a) within the preceding ten years, excluding any time during which the offender was incarcerated for any reason between the time of commission of the previous felony and the time of commission of the present felony, has previously been convicted of: (i) a violent felony offense as defined in section 70.02 of the penal law or (ii) any other offense for which a merit time allowance is not available pursuant to subparagraph (ii) of paragraph (d) of subdivision one of section eight hundred three of the correction law, or (iii) a class A felony offense defined in article two hundred twenty of the penal law; or (b) has previously been adjudicated a second violent felony offender pursuant to section 70.04 of the penal law or a persistent violent felony offender pursuant to section 70.08 of the penal law.

A defendant who also stands charged with a violent felony offense as defined in section 70.02 of the penal law or an offense for which merit time allowance is not available pursuant to subparagraph (ii) of paragraph (d) of subdivision one of section eight hundred three of the correction law for which the court must, upon the defendant's conviction thereof, sentence the defendant to incarceration in state prison is not an eligible defendant while such charges are pending. A defendant who is excluded from the judicial diversion program pursuant to this paragraph or paragraph (a) or (b) of this subdivision may become an eligible defendant upon the prosecutor's consent.

1. [Eff July 5, 2021] "Eligible defendant" means any person who stands charged in an indictment or a superior court information with a class B, C, D or E felony offense defined in article two hundred twenty or two hundred twenty-one of the penal law or any other specified offense as defined in subdivision four of section 410.91 of this chapter, provided, however, a defendant is not an "eligible defendant" if he or she:

(a) within the preceding ten years, excluding any time during which the offender was incarcerated for any reason between the time of commission of the previous felony and the time of commission of the present felony, has previously been convicted of: (i) a violent felony offense as defined in section 70.02 of the penal law or (ii) any other offense for which a merit time allowance is not available pursuant to subparagraph (ii) of paragraph (d) of subdivision one of section eight hundred three of the correction law, or (iii) a class A felony offense defined in article two hundred twenty of the penal law; or

(b) has previously been adjudicated a second violent felony offender pursuant to section 70.04 of the penal law or a persistent violent felony offender pursuant to section 70.08 of the penal law.

A defendant who also stands charged with a violent felony offense as defined in section 70.02 of the penal law or an offense for which merit time allowance is not available pursuant to subparagraph (ii) of paragraph (d) of subdivision one of section eight hundred three of the correction law for which the court must, upon the defendant's conviction thereof, sentence the defendant to incarceration in state prison is not an eligible defendant while such charges are pending. A defendant who is excluded from the judicial diversion program pursuant to this paragraph or paragraph (a) or (b) of this subdivision may become an eligible defendant upon the prosecutor's consent.

2. "Alcohol and substance abuse evaluation" means a written assessment and report by a court-approved entity or licensed health care professional experienced in the treatment of alcohol and substance abuse, or by an addiction and substance abuse counselor credentialed by the office of alcoholism and substance abuse services pursuant to section 19.07 of the mental hygiene law, which shall include:

(a) an evaluation as to whether the defendant has a history of alcohol or substance abuse or alcohol or substance dependence, as such terms are defined in the diagnostic and statistical manual of mental disorders, fourth edition, and a co-occurring mental disorder or mental illness and the relationship between such abuse or dependence and mental disorder or mental illness, if any;

(b) a recommendation as to whether the defendant's alcohol or substance abuse or dependence, if any, could be effectively addressed by judicial diversion in accordance with this article;

(c) a recommendation as to the treatment modality, level of care and length of any proposed treatment to effectively address the defendant's alcohol or substance abuse or dependence and any co-occurring mental disorder or illness; and

(d) any other information, factor, circumstance, or recommendation deemed relevant by the assessing entity or specifically requested by the court.

§ 216.05. Judicial diversion program; court procedures

1. At any time after the arraignment of an eligible defendant, but prior to the entry of a plea of guilty or the commencement of trial, the court at the request of the eligible defendant, may order an alcohol and substance abuse evaluation. An eligible defendant may decline to participate in such an evaluation at any time. The defendant shall provide a written authorization, in compliance with the requirements of any applicable state or federal laws, rules or regulations authorizing disclosure of the results of the assessment to the defendant's attorney, the prosecutor, the local probation department, the court, authorized court personnel and other individuals specified in such authorization for the sole purpose of determining whether the defendant should be offered judicial diversion for treatment for substance abuse or dependence, alcohol abuse or dependence and any co-occurring mental disorder or mental illness.

2. Upon receipt of the completed alcohol and substance abuse evaluation report, the court shall provide a copy of the report to the eligible defendant and the prosecutor.

3.

(a) Upon receipt of the evaluation report either party may request a hearing on the issue of whether the eligible defendant should be offered alcohol or substance abuse treatment pursuant to this article. At such a proceeding, which shall be held as soon as practicable so as to facilitate early intervention in the event that the defendant is found to need alcohol or substance abuse treatment, the court may consider oral and written arguments, may take testimony from witnesses offered by either party, and may consider any relevant evidence including, but not limited to, evidence that:

(i) the defendant had within the preceding ten years (excluding any time during which the offender was incarcerated for any reason between the time of the acts that led to the youthful offender adjudication and the time of commission of the present offense) been adjudicated a youthful offender for: (A) a violent felony offense as defined in section 70.02 of the penal law; or (B) any offense for which a merit time allowance is not available pursuant to subparagraph (ii) of paragraph (d) of subdivision one of section eight hundred three of the correction law; and

(ii) in the case of a felony offense defined in subdivision four of section 410.91 of this chapter, any statement of or submitted by the victim, as defined in paragraph (a) of subdivision two of section 380.50 of this chapter.

(b) Upon completion of such a proceeding, the court shall consider and make findings of fact with respect to whether:

(i) the defendant is an eligible defendant as defined in subdivision one of section 216.00 of this article;

(ii) the defendant has a history of alcohol or substance abuse or dependence;

(iii) such alcohol or substance abuse or dependence is a contributing factor to the defendant's criminal behavior;

(iv) the defendant's participation in judicial diversion could effectively address such abuse or dependence; and

(v) institutional confinement of the defendant is or may not be necessary for the protection of the public.

4. When an authorized court determines, pursuant to paragraph (b) of subdivision three of this section, that an eligible defendant should be offered alcohol or substance abuse treatment, or when the parties and the court agree to an eligible defendant's participation in alcohol or substance abuse treatment, an eligible defendant may be allowed to participate in the judicial diversion program offered by this article. Prior to the court's issuing an order granting judicial diversion, the eligible defendant shall be required to enter a plea of guilty to the charge or charges; provided, however, that no such guilty plea shall be required when:

(a) the people and the court consent to the entry of such an order without a plea of guilty; or

(b) based on a finding of exceptional circumstances, the court determines that a plea of guilty shall not be required. For purposes of this subdivision, exceptional circumstances exist when, regardless of the ultimate disposition of the case, the entry of a plea of guilty is likely to result in severe collateral consequences.

5. The defendant shall agree on the record or in writing to abide by the release conditions set by the court, which, shall include: participation in a specified period of alcohol or substance abuse treatment at a specified program or programs identified by the court, which may include periods of detoxification, residential or outpatient treatment, or both, as determined after taking into account the views of the health care professional who conducted the alcohol and substance abuse evaluation and any health care professionals responsible for providing such treatment or monitoring the defendant's progress in such treatment; and may include: (i) periodic court appearances, which may include periodic urinalysis; (ii) a requirement that the defendant refrain from engaging in criminal behaviors; (iii) if the defendant needs treatment for opioid abuse or dependence, that he or she may participate in and receive medically prescribed drug treatments under the care of a health care professional licensed or certified under title eight of the education law, acting within his or her lawful scope of practice, provided that no court shall require the use of any specified type or brand of drug during the course of medically prescribed drug treatments.

6. Upon an eligible defendant's agreement to abide by the conditions set by the court, the court shall issue a securing order providing for bail or release on the defendant's own recognizance and conditioning any release upon the agreed upon conditions. The period of alcohol or substance abuse treatment shall begin as specified by the court and as soon as practicable after the defendant's release, taking into account the availability of treatment, so as to facilitate early intervention with respect to the defendant's abuse or condition and the effectiveness of the treatment program. In the event that a treatment program is not immediately available or becomes unavailable during the course of the defendant's participation in the judicial diversion program, the court may release the defendant pursuant to the securing order.

7. When participating in judicial diversion treatment pursuant to this article, any resident of this state who is covered under a private health insurance policy or contract issued for delivery in this state pursuant to article thirty-two, forty-three or forty-seven of the insurance law or article forty-four of the public health law, or who is covered by a self-funded plan which provides coverage for the diagnosis and treatment of chemical abuse and chemical dependence however defined in such policy; shall first seek reimbursement for such treatment in accordance with the provisions of such policy or contract.

8. During the period of a defendant's participation in the judicial diversion program, the court shall retain jurisdiction of the defendant, provided, however, that the court may allow such defendant to (i) reside in another jurisdiction, or (ii) participate in alcohol and substance abuse treatment and other programs in the jurisdiction where the defendant resides or in any other jurisdiction, while participating in a judicial diversion program under conditions set by the court and agreed to by the defendant pursuant to subdivisions five and six of this section. The court may require the defendant to appear in court at any time to enable the court to monitor the defendant's progress in alcohol or substance abuse treatment. The court shall provide notice, reasonable under the circumstances, to the people, the treatment provider, the defendant and the defendant's counsel whenever it orders or otherwise requires the appearance of the defendant in court. Failure to appear as required without reasonable cause therefor shall constitute a violation of the conditions of the court's agreement with the defendant.

9.

(a) If at any time during the defendant's participation in the judicial diversion program, the court has reasonable grounds to believe that the defendant has violated a release condition or has failed to appear before the court as requested, the court shall direct the defendant to appear or issue a bench warrant to a police officer or an appropriate peace officer directing him or her to take the defendant into custody and bring the defendant before the court without unnecessary delay; provided, however, that under no circumstances shall a defendant who requires treatment for opioid abuse or dependence be deemed to have violated a release condition on the basis of his or her participation in medically prescribed drug treatments under the care of a health care professional licensed or certified under title eight of the education law, acting within his or her lawful scope of practice. The provisions of subdivision one of section 530.60 of this chapter relating to revocation of recognizance or bail shall apply to such proceedings under this subdivision.

(b) In determining whether a defendant violated a condition of his or her release under the judicial diversion program, the court may conduct a summary hearing consistent with due process and sufficient to satisfy the court that the defendant has, in fact, violated the condition.

(c) If the court determines that the defendant has violated a condition of his or her release under the judicial diversion program, the court may modify the conditions thereof, reconsider the order of recognizance or bail pursuant to subdivision two of section 510.30 of this chapter, or terminate the defendant's participation in the judicial diversion program; and when applicable proceed with the defendant's sentencing in accordance with the agreement. Notwithstanding any provision of law to the contrary, the court may impose any sentence authorized for the crime of conviction in accordance with the plea agreement, or any lesser sentence authorized to be imposed on a felony drug offender pursuant to paragraph (b) or (c) of subdivision two of section 70.70 of the penal law taking into account the length of time the defendant spent in residential treatment and how best to continue treatment while the defendant is serving that sentence. In determining what action to take for a violation of a release condition, the court shall consider all relevant circumstances, including the views of the prosecutor, the defense and the alcohol or substance abuse treatment provider, and the extent to which persons who ultimately successfully complete a drug treatment regimen sometimes relapse by not abstaining from alcohol or substance abuse or by failing to comply fully with all requirements imposed by a treatment program. The court shall also consider using a system of graduated and appropriate responses or sanctions designed to address such inappropriate behaviors, protect public safety and facilitate, where possible, successful completion of the alcohol or substance abuse treatment program.

(d) Nothing in this subdivision shall be construed as preventing a court from terminating a defendant's participation in the judicial diversion program for violating a release condition when such a termination is necessary to preserve public safety. Nor shall anything in this subdivision be construed as precluding the prosecution of a defendant for the commission of a different offense while participating in the judicial diversion program.

(e) A defendant may at any time advise the court that he or she wishes to terminate participation in the judicial diversion program, at which time the court shall proceed with the case and, where applicable, shall impose sentence in accordance with the plea agreement. Notwithstanding any provision of law to the contrary, the court may impose any sentence authorized for the crime of conviction in accordance with the plea agreement, or any lesser sentence authorized to be imposed on a felony drug offender pursuant to paragraph (b) or (c) of subdivision two of section 70.70 of the penal law taking into account the length of time the defendant spent in residential treatment and how best to continue treatment while the defendant is serving that sentence.

10. Upon the court's determination that the defendant has successfully completed the required period of alcohol or substance abuse treatment and has otherwise satisfied the conditions required for successful completion of the judicial diversion program, the court

shall comply with the terms and conditions it set for final disposition when it accepted the defendant's agreement to participate in the judicial diversion program. Such disposition may include, but is not limited to: (a) requiring the defendant to undergo a period of interim probation supervision and, upon the defendant's successful completion of the interim probation supervision term, notwithstanding the provision of any other law, permitting the defendant to withdraw his or her guilty plea and dismissing the indictment; or (b) requiring the defendant to undergo a period of interim probation supervision and, upon successful completion of the interim probation supervision term, notwithstanding the provision of any other law, permitting the defendant to withdraw his or her guilty plea, enter a guilty plea to a misdemeanor offense and sentencing the defendant as promised in the plea agreement, which may include a period of probation supervision pursuant to section 65.00 of the penal law; or (c) allowing the defendant to withdraw his or her guilty plea and dismissing the indictment.

11. Nothing in this article shall be construed as restricting or prohibiting courts or district attorneys from using other lawful procedures or models for placing appropriate persons into alcohol or substance abuse treatment.

Title J Prosecution of Indictments in Superior Courts—Plea to Sentence

Article 220 The Plea

§ 220.10. Plea; kinds of pleas

The only kinds of pleas which may be entered to an indictment are those specified in this section:

1. The defendant may as a matter of right enter a plea of "not guilty" to the indictment.

2. Except as provided in subdivision five, the defendant may as a matter of right enter a plea of "guilty" to the entire indictment.

3. Except as provided in subdivision five, where the indictment charges but one crime, the defendant may, with both the permission of the court and the consent of the people, enter a plea of guilty of a lesser included offense.

4. Except as provided in subdivision five, where the indictment charges two or more offenses in separate counts, the defendant may, with both the permission of the court and the consent of the people, enter a plea of:

(a) Guilty of one or more but not all of the offenses charged; or

(b) Guilty of a lesser included offense with respect to any or all of the offenses charged; or

(c) Guilty of any combination of offenses charged and lesser offenses included within other offenses charged.

5.

(a)

(i) Where the indictment charges one of the class A felonies defined in article two hundred twenty of the penal law or the attempt to commit any such class A felony, then any plea of guilty entered pursuant to subdivision three or four of this section must be or must include at least a plea of guilty of a class B felony.

(ii) [Repealed]

(iii) Where the indictment charges one of the class B felonies defined in article two hundred twenty of the penal law then any plea of guilty entered pursuant to subdivision three or four must be or must include at least a plea of guilty of a class D felony.

(b) Where the indictment charges any class B felony, other than a class B felony defined in article two hundred twenty of the penal law or a class B violent felony offense as defined in subdivision one of section 70.02 of the penal law, then any plea of guilty entered pursuant to subdivision three or four must be or must include at least a plea of guilty of a felony.

(c) Where the indictment charges a felony, other than a class A felony or class B felony defined in article two hundred twenty of the penal law or class B or class C violent felony offense as defined in subdivision one of section 70.02 of the penal law, and it appears that the defendant has previously been subjected to a predicate felony conviction as defined in penal law section 70.06 then any plea of guilty entered pursuant to subdivision three or four must be or must include at least a plea of guilty of a felony.

(d) Where the indictment charges a class A felony, other than those defined in article two hundred twenty of the penal law, or charges a class B or class C violent felony offense as defined in subdivision one of section 70.02 of the penal law, then a plea of guilty entered pursuant to subdivision three or four must be as follows:

(i) Where the indictment charges a class A felony offense or a class B violent felony offense which is also an armed felony offense then a plea of guilty must include at least a plea of guilty to a class C violent felony offense;

(ii) Except as provided in subparagraph (i) of this paragraph, where the indictment charges a class B violent felony offense or a class C violent felony offense, then a plea of guilty must include at least a plea of guilty to a class D violent felony offense;

(iii) Where the indictment charges the class D violent felony offense of criminal possession of a weapon in the third degree as defined in subdivision four of section 265.02 of the penal law, and the defendant has not been previously convicted of a class A misdemeanor defined in the penal law in the five years preceding the commission of the offense, then a plea of guilty must be either to the class E violent felony offense of attempted criminal possession of a weapon in the third degree or to the class A misdemeanor of criminal possession of a weapon in the fourth degree as defined in subdivision one of section 265.01 of the penal law;

(iv) Where the indictment charges the class D violent felony offenses of criminal possession of a weapon in the third degree as defined in subdivision four of section 265.02 of the penal law and the provisions of subparagraph (iii) of this paragraph do not apply, or subdivision five, seven or eight of section 265.02 of the penal law, then a plea of guilty must include at least a plea of guilty to a class E violent felony offense.

(e) A defendant may not enter a plea of guilty to the crime of murder in the first degree as defined in section 125.27 of the penal law; provided, however, that a defendant may enter such a plea with both the permission of the court and the consent of the people when the agreed upon sentence is either life imprisonment without parole or a term of imprisonment for the class A-I felony of murder in the first degree other than a sentence of life imprisonment without parole.

(f) The provisions of this subdivision shall apply irrespective of whether the defendant is thereby precluded from entering a plea of guilty of any lesser included offense.

(g) Where the defendant is a juvenile offender, the provisions of paragraphs (a), (b), (c) and (d) of this subdivision shall not apply and any plea entered pursuant to subdivision three or four of this section, must be as follows:

(i) If the indictment charges a person fourteen or fifteen years old with the crime of murder in the second degree any plea of guilty entered pursuant to subdivision three or four must be a plea of guilty of a crime for which the defendant is criminally responsible;

(ii) If the indictment does not charge a crime specified in subparagraph (i) of this paragraph, then any plea of guilty entered pursuant to subdivision three or four of this section must be a plea of guilty of a crime for which the defendant is criminally responsible unless a plea of guilty is accepted pursuant to subparagraph (iii) of this paragraph;

(iii) Where the indictment does not charge a crime specified in subparagraph (i) of this paragraph, the district attorney may recommend removal of the action to the family court. Upon making such recommendation the district attorney shall submit a subscribed memorandum setting forth: (1) a recommendation that the interests of justice would best be served by removal of the action to the family court; and (2) if the indictment charges a thirteen year old with the crime of murder in the second degree, or a fourteen or fifteen year old with the crimes of rape in the first degree as defined in subdivision one of section 130.35 of the penal law, or criminal sexual act in the first degree as defined in subdivision one of section 130.50 of the penal law, or an armed felony as defined in paragraph (a) of subdivision forty-one of section 1.20 of this chapter specific factors, one or more of which reasonably supports the recommendation, showing, (i) mitigating circumstances that bear directly upon the manner in which the crime was committed, or (ii) where the defendant was not the sole participant in the crime, that the defendant's participation was relatively minor although not so minor as to constitute a defense to the prosecution, or (iii) possible deficiencies in proof of the crime, or (iv) where the juvenile offender has no previous adjudications of having committed a designated felony act, as defined in subdivision eight of section 301.2 of the family court act, regardless of the age of the offender at the time of commission of the act, that the criminal act was not part of a pattern of criminal behavior and, in view of the history of the offender, is not likely to be repeated.

If the court is of the opinion based on specific factors set forth in the district attorney's memorandum that the interests of justice would best be served by removal of the action to the family court, a plea of guilty of a crime or act for which the defendant is not criminally responsible may be entered pursuant to subdivision three or four of this section, except that a thirteen year old charged with the crime of murder in the second degree may only plead to a designated felony act, as defined in subdivision eight of section 301.2 of the family court act.

Upon accepting any such plea, the court must specify upon the record the portion or portions of the district attorney's statement the court is relying upon as the basis of its opinion and that it believes the interests of justice would best be served by removal of the proceeding to the family court. Such plea shall then be deemed to be a juvenile delinquency fact determination and the court upon entry thereof must direct that the action be removed to the family court in accordance with the provisions of article seven hundred twenty-five of this chapter.

(h) Where the indictment charges the class E felony offense of aggravated harassment of an employee by an inmate as defined in section 240.32 of the penal law, then a plea of guilty must include at least a plea of guilty to a class E felony.

6. The defendant may, with both the permission of the court and the consent of the people, enter a plea of not responsible by reason of mental disease or defect to the indictment in the manner prescribed in section 220.15 of this chapter.

§ 220.15. Plea; plea of not responsible by reason of mental disease or defect

1. The defendant may, with both the permission of the court and the consent of the people, enter a plea of not responsible by reason of mental disease or defect to the entire indictment. The district attorney must state to the court either orally on the record or in a writing filed with the court that the people consent to the entry of such plea and that the people are satisfied that the affirmative defense of lack of criminal responsibility by reason of mental disease or defect would be proven by the defendant at a trial by a preponderance of the evidence. The district attorney must further state to the court in detail the evidence available to the people with respect to the offense or offenses charged in the indictment, including all psychiatric evidence available or known to the people. If necessary, the court may conduct a hearing before accepting such plea. The district attorney must further state to the court the reasons for recommending such plea. The reasons shall be stated in detail and not in conclusory terms.

2. Counsel for the defendant must state that in his opinion defendant has the capacity to understand the proceedings and to assist in his own defense and that the defendant understands the consequences of a plea of not responsible by reason of mental disease or defect. Counsel for the defendant must further state whether in his opinion defendant has any viable defense to the offense or offenses charged in the indictment other than the affirmative defense of lack of criminal responsibility by reason of mental disease or defect. Counsel for the defendant must further state in detail the psychiatric evidence available to the defendant with respect to such latter affirmative defense.

3. Before accepting a plea of not responsible by reason of mental disease or defect, the court must address the defendant in open court and determine that he understands each of the following:

(a) The nature of the charge to which the plea is offered, and the consequences of such plea;

(b) That he has the right to plead not guilty or to persist in that plea if it has already been entered;

(c) That he has the right to be tried by a jury, the right to the assistance of counsel, the right to confront and cross-examine witnesses against him, and the right not to be compelled to incriminate himself;

(d) That if he pleads not responsible by reason of mental disease or defect there will be no trial with respect to the charges contained in the indictment, so that by offering such plea he waives the right to such trial;

(e) That if he pleads not responsible by reason of mental disease or defect the court will ask him questions about the offense or offenses charged in the indictment and that he will thereby waive his right not to be compelled to incriminate himself; and

(f) That the acceptance of a plea of not responsible by reason of mental disease or defect is the equivalent of a verdict of not responsible by reason of mental disease or defect after trial.

4. The court shall not accept a plea of not responsible by reason of mental disease or defect without first determining that there is a factual basis for such plea. The court must address the defendant personally in open court and determine that the plea is voluntary, knowingly made, and not the result of force, threats, or promises. The court must inquire whether the defendant's willingness to plead results from prior discussions between the district attorney and counsel for the defendant. The court must be satisfied that the defendant understands the proceedings against him, has sufficient capacity to assist in his own defense and understands the consequences of a plea of not responsible by reason of mental disease or defect. The court may make such inquiry as it deems necessary or appropriate for the purpose of making the determinations required by this section.

5. Before accepting a plea of not responsible by reason of mental disease or defect, the court must find and state each of the following on the record in detail and not in conclusory terms:

(a) That it is satisfied that each element of the offense or offenses charged in the indictment would be established beyond a reasonable doubt at a trial;

(b) That the affirmative defense of lack of criminal responsibility by reason of mental disease or defect would be proven by the defendant at a trial by a preponderance of the evidence;

(c) That the defendant has the capacity to understand the proceedings against him and to assist in his own defense;

(d) That such plea by the defendant is knowingly and voluntarily made and that there is a factual basis for the plea;

(e) That the acceptance of such plea is required in the interest of the public in the effective administration of justice.

6. When a plea of not responsible by reason of mental disease or defect is accepted by the court and recorded upon the minutes, the provisions of section 330.20 of this chapter shall govern all subsequent proceedings against the defendant.

§ 220.20. Plea; meaning of lesser included offense for plea purposes

1. A "lesser included offense," within the meaning of subdivisions four and five of section 220.10 relating to the entry of a plea of guilty to an offense of lesser grade than one charged in a count of an indictment, means not only a "lesser included offense" as that term is defined in subdivision thirty-seven of section 1.20, but also one which is deemed to be such pursuant to the following rules:

(a) Where the only culpable mental state required for the crime charged is that the proscribed conduct be performed intentionally, any lesser offense consisting of reckless or criminally negligent, instead of intentional, performance of the same conduct is deemed to constitute a lesser included offense;

(b) Where the only culpable mental state required for the crime charged is that the proscribed conduct be performed recklessly, any lesser offense consisting of criminally negligent, instead of reckless, performance of the same conduct is deemed to constitute a lesser included offense;

(c) Where according to the allegations of a count a defendant's participation in the crime charged consisted in whole or in part of solicitation of another person to engage in the proscribed conduct, the offense of criminal solicitation, in any appropriate degree, is, with respect to such defendant, deemed to constitute a lesser included offense;

(d) Where according to the allegations of a count a defendant's participation in the crime charged consisted in whole or in part of conspiratorial agreement or conduct with another person to engage in the proscribed conduct, the crime of conspiracy, in any appropriate degree, is, with respect to such defendant, deemed to constitute a lesser included offense;

(e) Where according to the allegations of a count charging a felony a defendant's participation in such felony consisted in whole or in part of providing another person with means or opportunity for engaging in the proscribed conduct, the crime of criminal facilitation, in any appropriate degree, is, with respect to such defendant, deemed to constitute a lesser included offense;

(f) Where the crime charged is assault or attempted assault, in any degree, allegedly committed by intentionally causing or attempting to cause physical injury to a person by the immediate use of physical force against him, or where the crime charged is menacing, as defined in section 120.15 of the penal law, the offense of harassment, as defined in subdivision one of section 240.25 of the penal law, is deemed to constitute a lesser included offense;

(g) Where the crime charged is murder in the second degree as defined in subdivision three of section 125.25 of the penal law, allegedly committed in the course of the commission or attempted commission of a designated one of the underlying felonies enumerated in said subdivision, or during immediate flight therefrom, such designated underlying felony or attempted felony is deemed to constitute a lesser included offense. If such designated underlying felony is alleged to be robbery, burglary, kidnapping, or arson, without specification of the degree thereof, or an attempt to commit the same, a plea of guilty may be entered to the lowest degree thereof only, or as the case may be to attempted commission of such felony in its lowest degree, unless the allegations of the count clearly indicate the existence of all the elements of a higher degree;

(h) Where the crime charged is criminal sale of a controlled substance, any offense of criminal sale or possession of a controlled substance, in any degree, is deemed to constitute a lesser included offense.

(i) Where the crime charged is criminal possession of a controlled substance, any offense of criminal possession of a controlled substance, in any degree, is deemed to constitute a lesser included offense.

(j) Where the offense charged is unlawful disposal of hazardous wastes in violation of section 27-0914 of the environmental conservation law, any offense of unlawful disposal or possession of hazardous wastes as set forth in sections 71-2707, 71-2709, 71-2711 and 71-2713 of such law, in any degree, is deemed to constitute a lesser included offense;

(k) Where the offense charged is unlawful possession of hazardous wastes in violation of section 27-0914 of the environmental conservation law, any offense of unlawful possession of hazardous wastes as set forth in sections 71-2707 and 71-2709 of such law, in any degree, is deemed to constitute a lesser included offense.

2. An offense is deemed to be a lesser included offense with respect to a crime charged in an indictment, pursuant to the provisions of subdivision one, only for purposes of conviction upon a plea of guilty and not for purposes of conviction by verdict. For the latter purpose, an offense constitutes a lesser included one only when it conforms to the definition of that term contained in subdivision thirty-seven of section 1.20.

§ 220.30. Plea; plea of guilty to part of indictment; plea covering other indictments

1. A plea of guilty not embracing the entire indictment, entered pursuant to the provisions of subdivision four or five of section 220.10, is a "plea of guilty to part of the indictment."

2. The entry and acceptance of a plea of guilty to part of the indictment constitutes a disposition of the entire indictment.

3.

(a)

(i) Except as provided in paragraph (b), or in paragraph (c) dealing with juvenile offenders, a plea of guilty, whether to the entire indictment or to part of the indictment, may, with both the permission of the court and the consent of the people, be entered and accepted upon the condition that it constitutes a complete disposition of one or more other indictments against the defendant then pending.

(ii) If the other indictment or indictments are pending in a different court or courts, they shall not be disposed of under this subdivision unless the other courts and the appropriate prosecutors also transmit their written permission and consent as provided in subdivision four of section 220.50 of this article; in such a case the court in which the plea is entered shall so notify the other courts which, upon such notice, shall dismiss the appropriate indictments pending therein.

(b)

(i) A plea of guilty, whether to the entire indictment or to part of the indictment for any crime other than a class A felony, may not be accepted on the condition that it constitutes a complete disposition of one or more other indictments against the defendant wherein is charged a class A-I felony as defined in article two hundred twenty of the penal law or the attempt to commit any such class A-I felony, except that an eligible youth, as defined in subdivision two of section 720.10, may plea to a class B felony, upon consent of the district attorney, for purposes of adjudication as a youthful offender.

(ii) Where it appears that the defendant has previously been subjected to a predicate felony conviction as defined in paragraph (b) of subdivision (1) of section 70.06 of the penal law, a plea of guilty, whether to the entire indictment or to part of the indictment, of any offense other than a felony may not be accepted on the condition that it constitutes a complete disposition of one or more other indictments against the defendant wherein is charged a felony, other than a class A felony or a class B or class C violent felony offense as defined in subdivision one of section 70.02 of the penal law.

(iii) A plea of guilty, whether to the entire indictment or part of the indictment for any crime other than a class A felony or a class B or class C violent felony offense as defined in subdivision one of section 70.02 of the penal law, may not be accepted on the condition that it constitutes a complete disposition of one or more other indictments against the defendant wherein is charged a class A felony, other than those defined in article two hundred twenty of the penal law, or a class B violent felony offense which is also an armed felony offense.

(iv) Except as provided in subparagraph (iii) of this paragraph, a plea of guilty, whether to the entire indictment or part of the indictment, for any crime other than a class A felony or a class B, C, or D violent felony offense as defined in subdivision one of section 70.02 of the penal law, may not be accepted on the condition that it constitutes a complete disposition of one or more other indictments against the defendant wherein is charged a class B or class C violent felony offense as defined in subdivision one of section 70.02 of the penal law,

(v) A plea of guilty, whether to the entire indictment or part of the indictment, for any crime other than a violent felony offense as defined in section 70.02 of the penal law, may not be accepted on the condition that it constitutes a complete disposition of one or more other indictments against the defendant wherein is charged the class D violent felony offenses of criminal possession of a weapon in the third degree as defined in subdivision four, five, seven or eight of section 265.02 of the penal law; provided, however, a plea of guilty, whether to the entire indictment or part of the indictment, for the class A misdemeanor of criminal possession of a weapon in the fourth degree as defined in subdivision one of section 265.01 of the penal law may be accepted on the condition that it constitutes a complete disposition of one or more other indictments against the defendant wherein is charged the class D violent felony offense of criminal possession of a weapon in the third degree as defined in subdivision four of section 265.02 of the penal law when the defendant has not been previously convicted of a class A misdemeanor defined in the penal law in the five years preceding the commission of the offense.

(vi) A plea of guilty, whether to the entire indictment or to part of the indictment for any crime other than a felony, may not be accepted on the condition that it constitutes a complete disposition of one or more other indictments against the defendant wherein is charged a class B felony other than a class B violent felony offense as defined in subdivision one of section 70.02 of the penal law.

(vii) A defendant may not enter a plea of guilty to the crime of murder in the first degree as defined in section 125.27 of the penal law; provided, however, that a defendant may enter such a plea with both the permission of the court and the consent of the people when the agreed upon sentence is either life imprisonment without parole or a term of imprisonment for the class A-I felony of murder in the first degree other than a sentence of life imprisonment without parole.

(viii) A plea of guilty, whether to the entire indictment or to part of the indictment for any crime other than a class A or class B felony may not be accepted on condition that it constitutes a complete disposition of one or more other indictments against the defendant wherein is charged a class A-II felony defined in article two hundred twenty of the penal law or the attempt to commit any such felony.

(ix) A plea of guilty, whether to the entire indictment or to part of the indictment for any crime other than a class B, a class C, or a class D felony, may not be accepted on condition that it constitutes a complete disposition of one or more other indictments against the defendant wherein is charged a class B felony defined in article two hundred twenty of the penal law.

(c) Where the defendant is a juvenile offender, a plea of guilty, whether to the entire indictment or to part of the indictment, of any offense other than one for which the defendant is criminally responsible may not be accepted on the condition that it constitutes a complete disposition of one or more other indictments against the defendant.

§ 220.35. Hearing on predicate felony conviction

In any case where the defendant offers to enter a plea of guilty of a misdemeanor to constitute a disposition of the entire indictment or to constitute a complete disposition of one or more other indictments, or both, and the permission of the court and the consent of the people must be withheld solely upon the ground that it appears the defendant has previously been subjected to a predicate felony conviction as defined in paragraph (b) of subdivision one of section 70.06 of the penal law the court, if the defendant does not admit such predicate felony conviction, may conduct the hearing required by section 400.21 for the purpose of determining whether the plea may be entered or must be rejected. The finding upon any such hearing shall also be binding upon the defendant for the purpose of sentence.

§ 220.40. Plea; plea of not guilty; meaning

A plea of not guilty constitutes a denial of every allegation of the indictment.

§ 220.50. Plea; entry of plea

1. A plea to an indictment, other than one against a corporation, must be entered orally by the defendant in person; except that a plea to an indictment which does not charge a felony may, with the permission of the court, be entered by counsel upon submission by him of written authorization of the defendant.

2. A plea to an indictment against a corporation must be entered by counsel.

3. If a defendant who is required to enter a plea to an indictment refuses to do so or remains mute, the court must enter a plea of not guilty to the indictment in his behalf.

4. Where the permission of the court and the consent of the people are a prerequisite to the entry of a plea of guilty, the court and the prosecutor must either orally on the record or in a writing filed with the indictment state their reason for granting permission or consenting, as the case may be, to entry of the plea of guilty.

5. When a sentence is agreed upon by the prosecutor and a defendant as a predicate to entry of a plea of guilty, the court or the prosecutor must orally on the record, or in writing filed with the court, state the sentence agreed upon as a condition of such plea.

6. Where the defendant consents to a plea of guilty to the indictment, or part of the indictment, or consents to be prosecuted by superior court information as set forth in section 195.20 of this chapter, and if the defendant and prosecutor agree that as a condition of the plea or the superior court information certain property shall be forfeited by the defendant, the description and present estimated monetary value of the property shall be stated in court by the prosecutor at the time of plea. Within thirty days of the acceptance of the plea or superior court information by the court, the prosecutor shall send to the commissioner of the division of criminal justice services a document containing the name of the defendant, the description and present estimated monetary value of the property, and the date the plea or superior court information was accepted. Any property forfeited by the defendant as a condition to a plea of guilty to an indictment, or a part thereof, or to a superior court information, shall be disposed of in accordance with the provisions of section thirteen hundred forty-nine of the civil practice law and rules.

7. [Repealed Sept 1, 2019] Prior to accepting a defendant's plea of guilty to a count or counts of an indictment or a superior court information charging a felony offense, the court must advise the defendant on the record, that if the defendant is not a citizen of the United States, the defendant's plea of guilty and the court's acceptance thereof may result in the defendant's deportation, exclusion from admission to the United States or denial of naturalization pursuant to the laws of the United States. Where the plea of guilty is to a count or counts of an indictment charging a felony offense other than a violent felony offense as defined in section 70.02 of the penal law or an A-I felony offense other than an A-I felony as defined in article two hundred twenty of the penal law, the court must also, prior to accepting such plea, advise the defendant that, if the defendant is not a citizen of the United States and is or becomes the subject of a final order of deportation issued by the United States Immigration and Naturalization Service, the defendant may be paroled to the custody of the Immigration and Naturalization Service for deportation purposes at any time subsequent to the commencement of any indeterminate or determinate prison sentence imposed as a result of the defendant's plea. The failure to advise the defendant pursuant to this subdivision shall not be deemed to affect the voluntariness of a plea of guilty or the validity of a conviction, nor shall it afford a defendant any rights in a subsequent proceeding relating to such defendant's deportation, exclusion or denial of naturalization.

§ 220.51. Notice before entry of plea or trial involving a public official

Prior to trial, and before accepting a defendant's plea to a count or counts of an indictment or a superior court information charging a felony offense, the court must individually advise the defendant, on the record, that if at the time of the alleged felony crime the defendant was a public official, as defined in subdivision six of section one hundred fifty-six of the retirement and social security law, the defendant's plea of guilty and the court's acceptance thereof or conviction after trial may result in proceedings for the reduction or revocation of such defendant's pension pursuant to article three-B of the retirement and social security law.

§ 220.60. Plea; change of plea

1. A defendant who has entered a plea of not guilty to an indictment may as a matter of right withdraw such plea at any time before rendition of a verdict and enter a plea of guilty to the entire indictment pursuant to subdivision two, but subject to the limitation in subdivision five of section 220.10.

2. A defendant who has entered a plea of not guilty to an indictment may, with both the permission of the court and the consent of the people, withdraw such plea at any time before the rendition of a verdict and enter: (a) a plea of guilty to part of the indictment pursuant to subdivision three or four but subject to the limitation in subdivision five of section 220.10, or (b) a plea of not responsible by reason of mental disease or defect to the indictment pursuant to section 220.15 of this chapter.

3. At any time before the imposition of sentence, the court in its discretion may permit a defendant who has entered a plea of guilty to the entire indictment or to part of the indictment, or a plea of not responsible by reason of mental disease or defect, to withdraw such plea, and in such event the entire indictment, as it existed at the time of such plea, is restored.

4. When a special information has been filed pursuant to section 200.61 or 200.62 of this chapter, a defendant may enter a plea of guilty to the count or counts of the indictment to which the special information applies without admitting the allegations of the special information. Whenever a defendant enters a plea of guilty to the count or counts of the indictment to which the special information applies without admitting the allegations of the special information, the court must, unless the people consent otherwise, conduct a hearing in accordance with paragraph (b) of subdivision two of section 200.62 or paragraph (b) of subdivision three of section 200.61 of this chapter, whichever is applicable.

Article 230 Removal of Action

§ 230.10. Removal of action; from supreme court to county court and from county court to supreme court; at instance of court

Upon order of an appropriate court or judge, made at its or his own instance pursuant to rules established by the appellate division of the appropriate department, (a) an indictment filed with the supreme court at a term held in a particular county outside of New York City may, prior to entry of a plea of guilty thereto or commencement of a trial thereof, be removed to the county court of such county, and (b) an indictment filed in a county court may similarly be removed to the supreme court at a term held or to be held in the same county. Each of the appellate divisions of the second, third and fourth departments may establish rules authorizing such removals with respect to the superior courts within its department, and prescribing the courts or judges who may order such removals and other procedural matters involved therein.

§ 230.20. Removal of action; removal from county court to supreme court and change of venue; upon motion of party

1. At any time within the period provided by section 255.20, the appellate division of the department embracing the county, upon motion of either the defendant or the people, may, for good cause shown, order that the indictment and action be removed from the county court to the supreme court at a term held or to be held in the same county.

2. At any time within the period provided by section 255.20, the appellate division of the department embracing the county in which the superior court is located may, upon motion of either the defendant or the people demonstrating reasonable cause to believe that a fair and impartial trial cannot be had in such county, order either:

(a) that the indictment and action be removed from such superior court to a designated superior court of or located in another county; or

(b) that the commissioner of jurors of such county, in consultation with the appropriate administrative judge of the judicial district in which the county is located, expand the pool of jurors to encompass prospective jurors from the jury lists of counties that are within the judicial district in which, and that are geographically contiguous with the county in which, such superior court is located.

In making such determination the appellate division shall consider, among other factors, the hardship on potential jurors and the potential depletion of a county's qualified juror list that may result from an order expanding the jury pool. An order of removal under paragraph (a) herein must, if the defendant is in custody at the time, include a provision for transfer of custody by the sheriff or other appropriate public servant of the county of confinement to the sheriff or other appropriate public servant of the county to which the action has been removed. If the order is issued upon motion of the people, the appellate division may impose such conditions as it deems equitable and appropriate to insure that the removal does not subject the defendant to an unreasonable burden in making his defense. Any additional cost to the people incurred in complying with the order must be borne by the county from which the action originated.

3. Any motion made pursuant to this section must be based upon papers stating the grounds therefor, and must be made within the period provided by section 255.20 and upon five days notice thereof together with service of the moving papers upon, as the case may be, (a) the district attorney or (b) either the defendant or his counsel. In any case, the motion must be made returnable either during the appellate division term during which such moving papers are served or during the next term thereof.

4. If the appellate division grants the motion and orders a removal of the action, a certified copy of such order must be filed with the clerk of the superior court in which the indictment is pending. Such clerk must thereupon transmit such instrument, together with the pertinent papers and proceedings of the action, including all undertakings for appearances of the defendant and of the witnesses, or a certified copy or copies of the same, to the term of the superior court to which the action has been removed. Such latter court must then proceed to conduct the action to judgment or other final disposition.

§ 230.30. Removal of action; stay of trial pending motion therefor

1. At any time when a timely motion for removal of an action from the county court to the supreme court or for a change of venue may be made pursuant to section 230.20, a justice holding a term of the supreme court in the district in which the indictment is pending, or a justice of the appellate division of the department in which the indictment is pending, upon application of either the defendant or the people, may, in his discretion and for good cause shown, order that the trial of such indictment be stayed for a designated period, not to exceed thirty days from the issuance of such order, to allow

the applicant party to make a motion in the appropriate court for removal of the action from a county court to the supreme court or for a change of venue.

2. Such an order may be issued only upon an application made in writing and after reasonable notice and opportunity to be heard has been accorded the other party.

3. Upon issuing the order, the supreme court justice or appellate division justice must cause the order to be filed with the clerk of the court in which the indictment is pending. Thereafter, no further proceedings may be had in such court until a motion for removal or change of venue, as the case may be, if made within the designated period, has been determined, or until such designated period has expired without any such motion having been made.

4. When such an application for a stay has been made to and denied by a justice of the supreme court or a justice of the appellate division, a second such application may not be made to any other such justice.

§ 230.40. Removal of action; determinations and rulings before and after removal; by which courts made

Upon any removal of an indictment and action from one superior court to another pursuant to the provisions of this article, determinations and rulings with respect to the action made before such removal are not thereby rendered invalid. All subsequent determinations and rulings must be made by the court to which the action is removed; and such latter court is deemed to have control of the grand jury minutes underlying the indictment for the purpose of determining post-removal motions addressed to the legal sufficiency of the grand jury evidence or the validity of the grand jury proceeding.

Article 240 Discovery

§ 240.10. Discovery; definition of terms

The following definitions are applicable to this article:

1. "Demand to produce" means a written notice served by and on a party to a criminal action, without leave of the court, demanding to inspect property pursuant to this article and giving reasonable notice of the time at which the demanding party wishes to inspect the property designated.

2. "Attorneys' work product" means property to the extent that it contains the opinions, theories or conclusions of the prosecutor, defense counsel or members of their legal staffs.

3. "Property" means any existing tangible personal or real property, including, but not limited to, books, records, reports, memoranda, papers, photographs, tapes or other electronic recordings, articles of clothing, fingerprints, blood samples, fingernail scrapings or handwriting specimens, but excluding attorneys' work product.

4. "At the trial" means as part of the people's or the defendant's direct case.

§ 240.20. Discovery; upon demand of defendant

1. Except to the extent protected by court order, upon a demand to produce by a defendant against whom an indictment, superior court information, prosecutor's information, information, or simplified information charging a misdemeanor is pending, the prosecutor shall disclose to the defendant and make available for inspection, photographing, copying or testing, the following property:

(a) Any written, recorded or oral statement of the defendant, and of a co-defendant to be tried jointly, made, other than in the course of the criminal transaction, to a public servant engaged in law enforcement activity or to a person then acting under his direction or in cooperation with him;

(b) Any transcript of testimony relating to the criminal action or proceeding pending against the defendant, given by the defendant, or by a co-defendant to be tried jointly, before any grand jury;

(c) Any written report or document, or portion thereof, concerning a physical or mental examination, or scientific test or experiment, relating to the criminal action or proceeding which was made by, or at the request or direction of a public servant engaged in law enforcement activity, or which was made by a person whom the prosecutor intends to call as a witness at trial, or which the people intend to introduce at trial;

(d) Any photograph or drawing relating to the criminal action or proceeding which was made or completed by a public servant engaged in law enforcement activity, or which was made by a person whom the prosecutor intends to call as a witness at trial, or which the people intend to introduce at trial;

(e) Any photograph, photocopy or other reproduction made by or at the direction of a police officer, peace officer or prosecutor of any property prior to its release pursuant to the provisions of section 450.10 of the penal law, irrespective of whether the people intend to introduce at trial the property or the photograph, photocopy or other reproduction.

(f) Any other property obtained from the defendant, or a co-defendant to be tried jointly;

(g) Any tapes or other electronic recordings which the prosecutor intends to introduce at trial, irrespective of whether such recording was made during the course of the criminal transaction;

(h) Anything required to be disclosed, prior to trial, to the defendant by the prosecutor, pursuant to the constitution of this state or of the United States.

(i) The approximate date, time and place of the offense charged and of defendant's arrest.

(j) In any prosecution under penal law section 156.05 or 156.10, the time, place and manner of notice given pursuant to subdivision six of section 156.00 of such law.

(k) in any prosecution commenced in a manner set forth in this subdivision alleging a violation of the vehicle and traffic law, in addition to any material required to be disclosed pursuant to this article, any other provision of law, or the constitution of this state or of the United States, any written report or document, or portion thereof, concerning a physical examination, a scientific test or experiment, including the most recent record of inspection, or calibration or repair of machines or instruments utilized to perform such scientific tests or experiments and the certification certificate, if any, held by the operator of the machine or instrument, which tests or examinations were made by or at the request or direction of a public servant engaged in law enforcement activity or which was made by a person whom the prosecutor intends to call as a witness at trial, or which the people intend to introduce at trial.

2. The prosecutor shall make a diligent, good faith effort to ascertain the existence of demanded property and to cause such property to be made available for discovery

where it exists but is not within the prosecutor's possession, custody or control; provided, that the prosecutor shall not be required to obtain by subpoena duces tecum demanded material which the defendant may thereby obtain.

§ 240.30. Discovery; upon demand of prosecutor

1. Except to the extent protected by court order, upon a demand to produce by the prosecutor, a defendant against whom an indictment, superior court information, prosecutor's information, information, or simplified information charging a misdemeanor is pending shall disclose and make available for inspection, photographing, copying or testing, subject to constitutional limitations:

(a) any written report or document, or portion thereof, concerning a physical or mental examination, or scientific test, experiment, or comparisons, made by or at the request or direction of, the defendant, if the defendant intends to introduce such report or document at trial, or if the defendant has filed a notice of intent to proffer psychiatric evidence and such report or document relates thereto, or if such report or document was made by a person, other than defendant, whom defendant intends to call as a witness at trial; and

(b) any photograph, drawing, tape or other electronic recording which the defendant intends to introduce at trial.

2. The defense shall make a diligent good faith effort to make such property available for discovery where it exists but the property is not within its possession, custody or control, provided, that the defendant shall not be required to obtain by subpoena duces tecum demanded material that the prosecutor may thereby obtain.

§ 240.35. Discovery; refusal of demand

Notwithstanding the provisions of sections 240.20 and 240.30, the prosecutor or the defendant, as the case may be, may refuse to disclose any information which he reasonably believes is not discoverable by a demand to produce, pursuant to section 240.20 or section 240.30 as the case may be, or for which he reasonably believes a protective order would be warranted. Such refusal shall be made in a writing, which shall set forth the grounds of such belief as fully as possible, consistent with the objective of the refusal. The writing shall be served upon the demanding party and a copy shall be filed with the court.

§ 240.40. Discovery; upon court order

1. Upon motion of a defendant against whom an indictment, superior court information, prosecutor's information, information, or simplified information charging a misdemeanor is pending, the court in which such accusatory instrument is pending:

(a) must order discovery as to any material not disclosed upon a demand pursuant to section 240.20, if it finds that the prosecutor's refusal to disclose such material is not justified; (b) must, unless it is satisfied that the people have shown good cause why such an order should not be issued, order discovery or any other order authorized by subdivision one of section 240.70 as to any material not disclosed upon demand pursuant to section 240.20 where the prosecutor has failed to serve a timely written refusal pursuant to section 240.35; (c) may order discovery with respect to any other property, which the people intend to introduce at the trial, upon a showing by the defendant that discovery with respect to such property is material to the preparation of his or her defense, and that the request is reasonable; and (d) where property in the people's possession, custody, or control that consists of a deoxyribonucleic acid ("DNA") profile obtained from probative biological material gathered in connection with the investigation or prosecution of the defendant and the defendant establishes that such profile complies with federal bureau of investigation or state requirements, whichever are applicable and as such requirements are applied to law enforcement agencies seeking a keyboard search or similar comparison, and that the data meets state DNA index system or national DNA index system criteria as such criteria are applied to law enforcement agencies seeking such a keyboard search or similar comparison, the court may order an entity that has access to the combined DNA index system or its successor system to compare such DNA profile against DNA databanks by keyboard searches, or a similar method that does not involve uploading, upon notice to both parties and the entity required to perform the search, upon a showing by the defendant that such a comparison is material to the presentation of his or her defense and that the request is reasonable. For purposes of this paragraph, a "keyboard search" shall mean a search of a DNA profile against the databank in which the profile that is searched is not uploaded to or maintained in the databank. Upon granting the motion pursuant to paragraph (c) of this subdivision, the court shall, upon motion of the people showing such to be material to the preparation of their case and that the request is reasonable, condition its order of discovery by further directing discovery by the people of property, of the same kind or character as that authorized to be inspected by the defendant, which he or she intends to introduce at the trial.

2. Upon motion of the prosecutor, and subject to constitutional limitation, the court in which an indictment, superior court information, prosecutor's information, information, or simplified information charging a misdemeanor is pending:

(a) must order discovery as to any property not disclosed upon a demand pursuant to section 240.30, if it finds that the defendant's refusal to disclose such material is not justified; and

(b) may order the defendant to provide non-testimonial evidence. Such order may, among other things, require the defendant to:

(i) Appear in a line-up;

(ii) Speak for identification by witness or potential witness;

(iii) Be fingerprinted;

(iv) Pose for photographs not involving reenactment of an event;

(v) Permit the taking of samples of blood, hair or other materials from his body in a manner not involving an unreasonable intrusion thereof or a risk of serious physical injury thereto;

(vi) Provide specimens of his handwriting;

(vii) Submit to a reasonable physical or medical inspection of his body.

This subdivision shall not be construed to limit, expand, or otherwise affect the issuance of a similar court order, as may be authorized by law, before the filing of an accusatory instrument consistent with such rights as the defendant may derive from the constitution of this state or of the United States. This section shall not be construed to limit or otherwise affect the administration of a chemical test where otherwise authorized pursuant to section one thousand one hundred ninety-four-a of the vehicle and traffic law.

3. An order pursuant to this section may be denied, limited or conditioned as provided in section 240.50.

§ 240.43. Discovery; disclosure of prior uncharged criminal, vicious or immoral acts

Upon a request by a defendant, the prosecutor shall notify the defendant of all specific instances of a defendant's prior uncharged criminal, vicious or immoral conduct of which the prosecutor has knowledge and which the prosecutor intends to use at trial for purposes of impeaching the credibility of the defendant. Such notification by the prosecutor shall be made immediately prior to the commencement of jury selection, except that the court may, in its discretion, order such notification and make its determination as to the admissibility for impeachment purposes of such conduct within a period of three days, excluding Saturdays, Sundays and holidays, prior to the commencement of jury selection.

§ 240.44. Discovery; upon pre-trial hearing

Subject to a protective order, at a pre-trial hearing held in a criminal court at which a witness is called to testify, each party, at the conclusion of the direct examination of each of its witnesses, shall, upon request of the other party, make available to that party to the extent not previously disclosed:

1. Any written or recorded statement, including any testimony before a grand jury, made by such witness other than the defendant which relates to the subject matter of the witness's testimony.

2. A record of a judgment of conviction of such witness other than the defendant if the record of conviction is known by the prosecutor or defendant, as the case may be, to exist.

3. The existence of any pending criminal action against such witness other than the defendant if the pending criminal action is known by the prosecutor or defendant, as the case may be, to exist.

§ 240.45. Discovery; upon trial, of prior statements and criminal history of witnesses

1. After the jury has been sworn and before the prosecutor's opening address, or in the case of a single judge trial after commencement and before submission of evidence, the prosecutor shall, subject to a protective order, make available to the defendant:

(a) Any written or recorded statement, including any testimony before a grand jury and an examination videotaped pursuant to section 190.32 of this chapter, made by a person whom the prosecutor intends to call as a witness at trial, and which relates to the subject matter of the witness's testimony;

(b) A record of judgment of conviction of a witness the people intend to call at trial if the record of conviction is known by the prosecutor to exist;

(c) The existence of any pending criminal action against a witness the people intend to call at trial, if the pending criminal action is known by the prosecutor to exist.

The provisions of paragraphs (b) and (c) of this subdivision shall not be construed to require the prosecutor to fingerprint a witness or otherwise cause the division of criminal justice services or other law enforcement agency or court to issue a report concerning a witness.

2. After presentation of the people's direct case and before the presentation of the defendant's direct case, the defendant shall, subject to a protective order, make available to the prosecutor:

(a) any written or recorded statement made by a person other than the defendant whom the defendant intends to call as a witness at the trial, and which relates to the subject matter of the witness's testimony;

(b) a record of judgment of conviction of a witness, other than the defendant, the defendant intends to call at trial if the record of conviction is known by the defendant to exist;

(c) the existence of any pending criminal action against a witness, other than the defendant, the defendant intends to call at trial, if the pending criminal action is known by the defendant to exist.

§ 240.50. Discovery; protective orders

1. The court in which the criminal action is pending may, upon motion of either party, or of any affected person, or upon determination of a motion of either party for an order of discovery, or upon its own initiative, issue a protective order denying, limiting, conditioning, delaying or regulating discovery pursuant to this article for good cause, including constitutional limitations, danger to the integrity of physical evidence or a substantial risk of physical harm, intimidation, economic reprisal, bribery or unjustified annoyance or embarrassment to any person or an adverse effect upon the legitimate needs of law enforcement, including the protection of the confidentiality of informants, or any other factor or set of factors which outweighs the usefulness of the discovery.

2. An order limiting, conditioning, delaying or regulating discovery may, among other things, require that any material copied or derived therefrom be maintained in the exclusive possession of the attorney for the discovering party and be used for the exclusive purpose of preparing for the defense or prosecution of the criminal action.

3. A motion for a protective order shall suspend discovery of the particular matter in dispute.

4. Notwithstanding any other provision of this article, the personal residence address of a police officer or correction officer shall not be required to be disclosed except pursuant to an order issued by a court following a finding of good cause.

§ 240.60. Discovery; continuing duty to disclose

If, after complying with the provisions of this article or an order pursuant thereto, a party finds, either before or during trial, additional material subject to discovery or covered by such order, he shall promptly comply with the demand or order, refuse to comply with the demand where refusal is authorized, or apply for a protective order.

§ 240.70. Discovery; sanctions; fees

1. If, during the course of discovery proceedings, the court finds that a party has failed to comply with any of the provisions of this article, the court may order such party to permit discovery of the property not previously disclosed, grant a continuance, issue a protective order, prohibit the introduction of certain evidence or the calling of certain witnesses or take any other appropriate action.

2. The failure of the prosecution to call as a witness a person specified in subdivision one of section 240.20 of this article or of any party to introduce disclosed material at the

trial shall not, by itself, constitute grounds for any sanction or for adverse comment thereupon by any party in summation to the jury or at any other point.

3. A fee for copies of records required to be disclosed may be charged. Such fee shall not exceed twenty-five cents per photocopy not in excess of nine inches by fourteen inches, or the actual cost of reproducing any other record, except when a different fee is otherwise prescribed by law.

§ 240.75. Discovery; certain violations

The failure of the prosecutor or any agent of the prosecutor to disclose statements that are required to be disclosed under subdivision one of section 240.44 or paragraph (a) of subdivision one of section 240.45 of this article shall not constitute grounds for any court to order a new pre-trial hearing or set aside a conviction, or reverse, modify or vacate a judgment of conviction in the absence of a showing by the defendant that there is a reasonable possibility that the non-disclosure materially contributed to the result of the trial or other proceeding; provided, however, that nothing in this section shall affect or limit any right the defendant may have to a re-opened pre-trial hearing when such statements were disclosed before the close of evidence at trial.

§ 240.80. Discovery; when demand, refusal and compliance made

1. A demand to produce shall be made within thirty days after arraignment and before the commencement of trial. If the defendant is not represented by counsel, and has requested an adjournment to obtain counsel or to have counsel assigned, the thirty-day period shall commence, for purposes of a demand by the defendant, on the date counsel initially appears on his behalf. However, the court may direct compliance with a demand to produce that, for good cause shown, could not have been made within the time specified.

2. A refusal to comply with a demand to produce shall be made within fifteen days of the service of the demand to produce, but for good cause may be made thereafter.

3. Absent a refusal to comply with a demand to produce, compliance with such demand shall be made within fifteen days of the service of the demand or as soon thereafter as practicable.

§ 240.90. Discovery; motion procedure

1. A motion by a prosecutor for discovery shall be made within forty-five days after arraignment, but for good cause shown may be made at any time before commencement of trial.

2. A motion by a defendant for discovery shall be made as prescribed in section 255.20 of this chapter.

3. Where the interests of justice so require, the court may permit a party to a motion for an order of discovery or a protective order, or other affected person, to submit papers or to testify ex parte or in camera. Any such papers and transcript of such testimony shall be sealed, but shall constitute a part of the record on appeal.

Article 250 Pre-Trial Notices of Defenses

§ 250.10. Notice of intent to proffer psychiatric evidence; examination of defendant upon application of prosecutor

1. As used in this section, the term "psychiatric evidence" means:

(a) Evidence of mental disease or defect to be offered by the defendant in connection with the affirmative defense of lack of criminal responsibility by reason of mental disease or defect.

(b) Evidence of mental disease or defect to be offered by the defendant in connection with the affirmative defense of extreme emotional disturbance as defined in paragraph (a) of subdivision one of section 125.25 of the penal law and paragraph (a) of subdivision two of section 125.27 of the penal law.

(c) Evidence of mental disease or defect to be offered by the defendant in connection with any other defense not specified in the preceding paragraphs.

2. Psychiatric evidence is not admissible upon a trial unless the defendant serves upon the people and files with the court a written notice of his intention to present psychiatric evidence. Such notice must be served and filed before trial and not more than thirty days after entry of the plea of not guilty to the indictment. In the interest of justice and for good cause shown, however, the court may permit such service and filing to be made at any later time prior to the close of the evidence.

3. When a defendant, pursuant to subdivision two of this section, serves notice of intent to present psychiatric evidence, the district attorney may apply to the court, upon notice to the defendant, for an order directing that the defendant submit to an examination by a psychiatrist or licensed psychologist as defined in article one hundred fifty-three of the education law designated by the district attorney. If the application is granted, the psychiatrist or psychologist designated to conduct the examination must notify the district attorney and counsel for the defendant of the time and place of the examination. Defendant has a right to have his counsel present at such examination. The district attorney may also be present. The role of each counsel at such examination is that of an observer, and neither counsel shall be permitted to take an active role at the examination.

4. After the conclusion of the examination, the psychiatrist or psychologist must promptly prepare a written report of his findings and evaluation. A copy of such report must be made available to the district attorney and to the counsel for the defendant. No transcript or recording of the examination is required, but if one is made, it shall be made available to both parties prior to the trial.

5. If the court finds that the defendant has willfully refused to cooperate fully in the examination ordered pursuant to subdivision three of this section it may preclude introduction of testimony by a psychiatrist or psychologist concerning mental disease or defect of the defendant at trial. Where, however, the defendant has other proof of his affirmative defense, and the court has found that the defendant did not submit to or cooperate fully in the examination ordered by the court, this other evidence, if otherwise competent, shall be admissible. In such case, the court must instruct the jury that the defendant did not submit to or cooperate fully in the pre-trial psychiatric examination ordered by the court pursuant to subdivison three of this section and that such failure may be considered in determining the merits of the affirmative defense.

§ 250.20. Notice of alibi

1. At any time, not more than twenty days after arraignment, the people may serve upon the defendant or his counsel, and file a copy thereof with the court, a demand that

if the defendant intends to offer a trial defense that at the time of the commission of the crime charged he was at some place or places other than the scene of the crime, and to call witnesses in support of such defense, he must, within eight days of service of such demand, serve upon the people, and file a copy thereof with the court, a "notice of alibi," reciting (a) the place or places where the defendant claims to have been at the time in question, and (b) the names, the residential addresses, the places of employment and the addresses thereof of every such alibi witness upon whom he intends to rely. For good cause shown, the court may extend the period for service of the notice.

2. Within a reasonable time after receipt of the defendant's witness list but not later than ten days before trial, the people must serve upon the defendant or his counsel, and file a copy thereof with the court, a list of the witnesses the people propose to offer in rebuttal to discredit the defendant's alibi at the trial together with the residential addresses, the places of employment and the addresses thereof of any such rebuttal witnesses. A witness who will testify that the defendant was at the scene of the crime is not such an alibi rebuttal witness. For good cause shown, the court may extend the period for service of the list of witnesses by the people.

3. If at the trial the defendant calls such an alibi witness without having served the demanded notice of alibi, or if having served such a notice he calls a witness not specified therein, the court may exclude any testimony of such witness relating to the alibi defense. The court may in its discretion receive such testimony, but before doing so, it must, upon application of the people, grant an adjournment not in excess of three days.

4. Similarly, if the people fail to serve and file a list of any rebuttal witnesses, the provisions of subdivision three, above, shall reciprocally apply.

5. Both the defendant and the people shall be under a continuing duty to promptly disclose the names and addresses of additional witnesses which come to the attention of either party subsequent to filing their witness lists as provided in this section.

§ 250.30. Notice of defenses in offenses involving computers

1. In any prosecution in which the defendant seeks to invoke any of the defenses specified in section 156.50 of the penal law, the defendant must within forty-five days after arraignment and not less than twenty days before the commencement of the trial serve upon the people and file with the court a written notice of his intention to present such defense. For good cause shown, the court may extend the period for service of the notice.

2. The notice served must specify the subdivision or subdivisions upon which the defendant relies and must also state the reasonable grounds that led the defendant to believe that he had the authorization required by the statute or the right required by the statute to engage in such conduct.

3. If at the trial the defendant seeks to invoke any of the defenses specified in section 156.50 of the penal law without having served the notice as required, or seeks to invoke a subdivision or a ground not specified in the notice, the court may exclude any testimony or evidence in regard to the defense, or any subdivision or ground, not noticed. The court may in its discretion, for good cause shown, receive such testimony

or evidence, but before doing so, it may, upon application of the people, grant an adjournment.

§ 250.40. Notice of intent to seek death penalty

1. A sentence of death may not be imposed upon a defendant convicted of murder in the first degree unless, pursuant to subdivision two of this section, the people file with the court and serve upon the defendant a notice of intent to seek the death penalty.

2. In any prosecution in which the people seek a sentence of death, the people shall, within one hundred twenty days of the defendant's arraignment upon an indictment charging the defendant with murder in the first degree, serve upon the defendant and file with the court in which the indictment is pending a written notice of intention to seek the death penalty. For good cause shown the court may extend the period for service and filing of the notice.

3. Notwithstanding any other provisions of law, where the people file a notice of intent to seek the death penalty pursuant to this section the defendant shall be entitled to an additional sixty days for the purpose of filing new motions or supplementing pending motions.

4. A notice of intent to seek the death penalty may be withdrawn at any time by a written notice of withdrawal filed with the court and served upon the defendant. Once withdrawn the notice of intent to seek the death penalty may not be refiled.

Article 255 Pre-Trial Motions

§ 255.10. Definitions

1. "Pre-trial motion" as used in this article means any motion by a defendant which seeks an order of the court:

(a) dismissing or reducing an indictment pursuant to article 210 or removing an action to the family court pursuant to article 722; or

(b) dismissing an information, prosecutor's information, simplified information or misdemeanor complaint pursuant to article 170; or

(c) granting discovery pursuant to article 240; or

(d) granting a bill of particulars pursuant to sections 100.45 or 200.90; or

(e) removing the action pursuant to sections 170.15, 230.20 or 230.30; or

(f) suppressing the use at trial of any evidence pursuant to article 710; or

(g) granting separate trials pursuant to article 100 or 200.

2. [None]

§ 255.20. Pre-trial motions; procedure

1. Except as otherwise expressly provided by law, whether the defendant is represented by counsel or elects to proceed pro se, all pre-trial motions shall be served or filed within forty-five days after arraignment and before commencement of trial, or within such additional time as the court may fix upon application of the defendant made prior to entry of judgment. In an action in which an eavesdropping warrant and application have been furnished pursuant to section 700.70 or a notice of intention to introduce evidence has been served pursuant to section 710.30, such period shall be extended until forty-five days after the last date of such service. If the defendant is not represented by counsel and has requested an adjournment to obtain counsel or to have

counsel assigned, such forty-five day period shall commence on the date counsel initially appears on defendant's behalf.

2. All pre-trial motions, with supporting affidavits, affirmations, exhibits and memoranda of law, whenever practicable, shall be included within the same set of motion papers, and shall be made returnable on the same date, unless the defendant shows that it would be prejudicial to the defense were a single judge to consider all the pre-trial motions. Where one motion seeks to provide the basis for making another motion, it shall be deemed impracticable to include both motions in the same set of motion papers pursuant to this subdivision.

3. Notwithstanding the provisions of subdivisions one and two hereof, the court must entertain and decide on its merits, at anytime [any time]* before the end of the trial, any appropriate pre-trial motion based upon grounds of which the defendant could not, with due diligence, have been previously aware, or which, for other good cause, could not reasonably have been raised within the period specified in subdivision one of this section or included within the single set of motion papers as required by subdivision two. Any other pre-trial motion made after the forty-five day period may be summarily denied, but the court, in the interest of justice, and for good cause shown, may, in its discretion, at any time before sentence, entertain and dispose of the motion on the merits.

4. Any pre-trial motion, whether made before or after expiration of the period specified in subdivision one of this section, may be referred by the court to a judicial hearing officer who shall entertain it in the same manner as a court. In the discharge of this responsibility, the judicial hearing officer shall have the same powers as a judge of the court making the assignment, except that the judicial hearing officer shall not determine the motion but shall file a report with the court setting forth findings of fact and conclusions of law. The rules of evidence shall be applicable at any hearing conducted hereunder by a judicial hearing officer. A transcript of any testimony taken, together with the exhibits or copies thereof, shall be filed with the report. The court shall determine the motion on the motion papers, affidavits and other documents submitted by the parties thereto, the record of the hearing before the judicial hearing officer, and the judicial hearing officer's report.

Article 260 Jury Trial—Generally

§ 260.10. Jury trial; requirement thereof

Except as otherwise provided in section 320.10, every trial of an indictment must be a jury trial.

§ 260.20. Jury trial; defendant's presence at trial

A defendant must be personally present during the trial of an indictment; provided, however, that a defendant who conducts himself in so disorderly and disruptive a manner that his trial cannot be carried on with him in the courtroom may be removed from the courtroom if, after he has been warned by the court that he will be removed if he continues such conduct, he continues to engage in such conduct.

§ 260.30. Jury trial; in what order to proceed

The order of a jury trial, in general, is as follows:

1. The jury must be selected and sworn.

2. The court must deliver preliminary instructions to the jury.

3. The people must deliver an opening address to the jury.

4. The defendant may deliver an opening address to the jury.

5. The people must offer evidence in support of the indictment.

6. The defendant may offer evidence in his defense.

7. The people may offer evidence in rebuttal of the defense evidence, and the defendant may then offer evidence in rebuttal of the people's rebuttal evidence. The court may in its discretion permit the parties to offer further rebuttal or surrebuttal evidence in this pattern. In the interest of justice, the court may permit either party to offer evidence upon rebuttal which is not technically of a rebuttal nature but more properly a part of the offering party's original case.

8. At the conclusion of the evidence, the defendant may deliver a summation to the jury.

9. The people may then deliver a summation to the jury.

10. The court must then deliver a charge to the jury.

11. The jury must then retire to deliberate and, if possible, render a verdict.

Article 270 Jury Trial—Formation and Conduct of Jury

§ 270.05. Trial jury; formation in general

1. A trial jury consists of twelve jurors, but "alternate jurors" may be selected and sworn pursuant to section 270.30.

2. The panel from which the jury is drawn is formed and selected as prescribed in the judiciary law. The first twelve members of the panel returned for the term who appear as their names are drawn and called, and who are not excluded as prescribed by this article, must be sworn and thereupon constitute the trial jury.

§ 270.10. Trial jury; challenge to the panel

1. A challenge to the panel is an objection made to the entire panel of prospective trial jurors returned for the term and may be taken to such panel or to any additional panel that may be ordered by the court. Such a challenge may be made only by the defendant and only on the ground that there has been such a departure from the requirements of the judiciary law in the drawing or return of the panel as to result in substantial prejudice to the defendant.

2. A challenge to the panel must be made before the selection of the jury commences, and, if it is not, such challenge is deemed to have been waived. Such challenge must be made in writing setting forth the facts constituting the ground of challenge. If such facts are denied by the people, witnesses may be called and examined by either party. All issues of fact and law arising on the challenge must be tried and determined by the court. If a challenge to the panel is allowed, the court must discharge that panel and order another panel of prospective trial jurors returned for the term.

§ 270.15. Trial jury; examination of prospective jurors; challenges generally

1.

(a) If no challenge to the panel is made as prescribed by section 270.10, or if such challenge is made and disallowed, the court shall direct that the names of not less than twelve members of the panel be drawn and called as prescribed by the judiciary law. Such persons shall take their places in the jury box and shall be immediately sworn to answer truthfully questions asked them relative to their qualifications to serve as jurors in the action. In its discretion, the court may require prospective jurors to complete a questionnaire concerning their ability to serve as fair and impartial jurors, including but not limited to place of birth, current address, education, occupation, prior jury service, knowledge of, relationship to, or contact with the court, any party, witness or attorney in the action and any other fact relevant to his or her service on the jury. An official form for such questionnaire shall be developed by the chief administrator of the courts in consultation with the administrative board of the courts. A copy of questionnaires completed by the members of the panel shall be given to the court and each attorney prior to examination of prospective jurors.

(b) The court shall initiate the examination of prospective jurors by identifying the parties and their respective counsel and briefly outlining the nature of case to all the prospective jurors. The court shall then put to the members of the panel who have been sworn pursuant to this subdivision and to any prospective jurors subsequently sworn, questions affecting their qualifications to serve as jurors in the action.

(c) The court shall permit both parties, commencing with the people, to examine the prospective jurors, individually or collectively, regarding their qualifications to serve as jurors. Each party shall be afforded a fair opportunity to question the prospective jurors as to any unexplored matter affecting their qualifications, but the court shall not permit questioning that is repetitious or irrelevant, or questions as to a juror's knowledge of rules of law. If necessary to prevent improper questioning as to any matter, the court shall personally examine the prospective jurors as to that matter. The scope of such examination shall be within the discretion of the court. After the parties have concluded their examinations of the prospective jurors, the court may ask such further questions as it deems proper regarding the qualifications of such prospective jurors.

1-a. The court may for good cause shown, upon motion of either party or any affected person or upon its own initiative, issue a protective order for a stated period regulating disclosure of the business or residential address of any prospective or sworn juror to any person or persons, other than to counsel for either party. Such good cause shall exist where the court determines that there is a likelihood of bribery, jury tampering or of physical injury or harassment of the juror.

2. Upon the completion of such examination by both parties, each, commencing with the people, may challenge a prospective juror for cause, as prescribed by section 270.20. If such challenge is allowed, the prospective juror must be excluded from service. After both parties have had an opportunity to challenge for cause, the court must permit them to peremptorily challenge any remaining prospective juror, as prescribed by section 270.25, and such juror must be excluded from service. The people must exercise their peremptory challenges first and may not, after the defendant has exercised his peremptory challenges, make such a challenge to any remaining prospective juror who is then in the jury box. If either party so requests, challenges for cause must be made and determined, and peremptory challenges must be made, within the courtroom but outside of the hearing of the prospective jurors in such manner as not to disclose which party made the challenge. The prospective jurors who are not excluded from service must retain their place in the jury box and must be immediately

sworn as trial jurors. They must be sworn to try the action in a just and impartial manner, to the best of their judgment, and to render a verdict according to the law and the evidence.

3. The court may thereupon direct that the persons excluded be replaced in the jury box by an equal number from the panel or, in its discretion, direct that all sworn jurors be removed from the jury box and that the jury box be occupied by such additional number of persons from the panel as the court shall direct. In the court's discretion, sworn jurors who are removed from the jury box as provided herein may be seated elsewhere in the courtroom separate and apart from the unsworn members of the panel or may be removed to the jury room or be allowed to leave the courthouse. The process of jury selection as prescribed herein shall continue until twelve persons are selected and sworn as trial jurors. The juror whose name was first drawn and called must be designated by the court as the foreperson, and no special oath need be administered to him or her. If before twelve jurors are sworn, a juror already sworn becomes unable to serve by reason of illness or other incapacity, the court must discharge him or her and the selection of the trial jury must be completed in the manner prescribed in this section.

4. A challenge for cause of a prospective juror which is not made before he is sworn as a trial juror shall be deemed to have been waived, except that such a challenge based upon a ground not known to the challenging party at that time may be made at any time before a witness is sworn at the trial. If such challenge is allowed by the court, the juror shall be discharged and the selection of the trial jury shall be completed in the manner prescribed in this section, except that if alternate jurors have been sworn, the alternate juror whose name was first drawn and called shall take the place of the juror so discharged.

§ 270.16. Capital cases; individual questioning for racial bias

1. In any case in which the crime charged may be punishable by death, the court shall, upon motion of either party, permit the parties, commencing with the people, to examine the prospective jurors individually and outside the presence of the other prospective jurors regarding their qualifications to serve as jurors. Each party shall be afforded a fair opportunity to question a prospective juror as to any unexplored matter affecting his or her qualifications, including without limitation the possibility of racial bias on the part of the prospective juror, but the court shall not permit questioning that is repetitious or irrelevant, or questions as to a prospective juror's knowledge of rules of law. If necessary to prevent improper questioning as to any matter, the court shall personally examine the prospective jurors as to that matter. The scope of such examination shall be within the discretion of the court. After the parties have concluded their examinations of a prospective juror, the court may ask such further questions as it deems proper regarding the qualifications of the prospective juror.

2. The proceedings provided for in this section shall be conducted on the record; provided, however, that upon motion of either party, and for good cause shown, the court may direct that all or a portion of the record of such proceedings be sealed.

§ 270.20. Trial jury; challenge for cause of an individual juror

1. A challenge for cause is an objection to a prospective juror and may be made only on the ground that:

(a) He does not have the qualifications required by the judiciary law; or

(b) He has a state of mind that is likely to preclude him from rendering an impartial verdict based upon the evidence adduced at the trial; or

(c) He is related within the sixth degree by consanguinity or affinity to the defendant, or to the person allegedly injured by the crime charged, or to a prospective witness at the trial, or to counsel for the people or for the defendant; or that he is or was a party adverse to any such person in a civil action; or that he has complained against or been accused by any such person in a criminal action; or that he bears some other relationship to any such person of such nature that it is likely to preclude him from rendering an impartial verdict; or

(d) He was a witness at the preliminary examination or before the grand jury or is to be a witness at the trial; or

(e) He served on the grand jury which found the indictment in issue or served on a trial jury in a prior civil or criminal action involving the same incident charged in such indictment; or

(f) The crime charged may be punishable by death and the prospective juror entertains such conscientious opinions either against or in favor of such punishment as to preclude such juror from rendering an impartial verdict or from properly exercising the discretion conferred upon such juror by law in the determination of a sentence pursuant to section 400.27.

2. All issues of fact or law arising on the challenge must be tried and determined by the court. If the challenge is allowed, the court must exclude the person challenged from service. An erroneous ruling by the court allowing a challenge for cause by the people does not constitute reversible error unless the people have exhausted their peremptory challenges at the time or exhaust them before the selection of the jury is complete. An erroneous ruling by the court denying a challenge for cause by the defendant does not constitute reversible error unless the defendant has exhausted his peremptory challenges at the time or, if he has not, he peremptorily challenges such prospective juror and his peremptory challenges are exhausted before the selection of the jury is complete.

§ 270.25. Trial jury; peremptory challenge of an individual juror

1. A peremptory challenge is an objection to a prospective juror for which no reason need be assigned. Upon any peremptory challenge, the court must exclude the person challenged from service.

2. Each party must be allowed the following number of peremptory challenges:

(a) Twenty for the regular jurors if the highest crime charged is a class A felony, and two for each alternate juror to be selected.

(b) Fifteen for the regular jurors if the highest crime charged is a class B or class C felony, and two for each alternate juror to be selected.

(c) Ten for the regular jurors in all other cases, and two for each alternate juror to be selected.

3. When two or more defendants are tried jointly, the number of peremptory challenges prescribed in subdivision two is not multiplied by the number of defendants, but such defendants are to be treated as a single party. In any such case, a peremptory

challenge by one or more defendants must be allowed if a majority of the defendants join in such challenge. Otherwise, it must be disallowed.

§ 270.30. Trial jury; alternate jurors

1. Immediately after the last trial juror is sworn, the court may in its discretion direct the selection of one or more, but not more than six additional jurors to be known as "alternate jurors", except that, in a prosecution under section 125.27 of the penal law, the court may, in its discretion, direct the selection of as many alternate jurors as the court determines to be appropriate. Alternate jurors must be drawn in the same manner, must have the same qualifications, must be subject to the same examination and challenges for cause and must take the same oath as the regular jurors. After the jury has retired to deliberate, the court must either (1) with the consent of the defendant and the people, discharge the alternate jurors or (2) direct the alternate jurors not to discuss the case and must further direct that they be kept separate and apart from the regular jurors.

2. In any prosecution in which the people seek a sentence of death, the court shall not discharge the alternate jurors when the jury retires to deliberate upon its verdict and the alternate jurors, in the discretion of the court, may be continuously kept together under the supervision of an appropriate public servant or servants until such time as the jury returns its verdict. If the jury returns a verdict of guilty to a charge for which the death penalty may be imposed, the alternate jurors shall not be discharged and shall remain available for service during any separate sentencing proceeding which may be conducted pursuant to section 400.27.

§ 270.35. Trial jury; discharge of juror; replacement by alternate juror

1. If at any time after the trial jury has been sworn and before the rendition of its verdict, a juror is unable to continue serving by reason of illness or other incapacity, or for any other reason is unavailable for continued service, or the court finds, from facts unknown at the time of the selection of the jury, that a juror is grossly unqualified to serve in the case or has engaged in misconduct of a substantial nature, but not warranting the declaration of a mistrial, the court must discharge such juror. If an alternate juror or jurors are available for service, the court must order that the discharged juror be replaced by the alternate juror whose name was first drawn and called, provided, however, that if the trial jury has begun its deliberations, the defendant must consent to such replacement. Such consent must be in writing and must be signed by the defendant in person in open court in the presence of the court. If the discharged juror was the foreperson, the court shall designate as the new foreperson the juror whose name was second drawn and called. If no alternate juror is available, the court must declare a mistrial pursuant to subdivision three of section 280.10.

2.

(a) In determining pursuant to this section whether a juror is unable to continue serving by reason of illness or other incapacity, or is for any other reason unavailable for continued service, the court shall make a reasonably thorough inquiry concerning such illness, incapacity or unavailability, and shall attempt to ascertain when such juror will be appearing in court. If such juror fails to appear, or if the court determines that there is no reasonable likelihood such juror will be appearing, in court within two hours of the time set by the court for the trial to resume, the court may presume such juror is unavailable for continued service and may discharge such juror. Nothing contained in this paragraph shall affect the court's discretion, under this or any other provision of law, to discharge a juror who repeatedly fails to appear in court in a timely fashion.

(b) The court shall afford the parties an opportunity to be heard before discharging a juror. If the court discharges a juror pursuant to this subdivision, it shall place on the record the facts and reasons for its determination that such juror is ill, incapacitated or unavailable for continued service.

(c) Nothing contained in this subdivision shall affect the requirements of subdivision one of this section pertaining to the discharge of a juror where the trial jury has begun its deliberations.

§ 270.40. Trial jury; preliminary instructions by court

After the jury has been sworn and before the people's opening address, the court must instruct the jury generally concerning its basic functions, duties and conduct. Such instructions must include, among other matters, admonitions that the jurors may not converse among themselves or with anyone else upon any subject connected with the trial; that they may not read or listen to any accounts or discussions of the case reported by newspapers or other news media; that they may not visit or view the premises or place where the offense or offenses charged were allegedly committed or any other premises or place involved in the case; that prior to discharge, they may not request, accept, agree to accept, or discuss with any person receiving or accepting, any payment or benefit in consideration for supplying any information concerning the trial; and that they must promptly report to the court any incident within their knowledge involving an attempt by any person improperly to influence any member of the jury.

§ 270.45. Trial jury; when separation permitted

During the period extending from the time the jurors are sworn to the time they retire to deliberate upon their verdict, the court may in its discretion either permit them to separate during recesses and adjournments or direct that they be continuously kept together during such periods under the supervision of an appropriate public servant or servants. In the latter case, such public servant or servants may not speak to or communicate with any juror concerning any subject connected with the trial nor permit any other person to do so, and must return the jury to the court room at the next designated trial session.

§ 270.50. Trial jury; viewing of premises

1. When the court is of the opinion that a viewing or observation by the jury of the premises or place where an offense on trial was allegedly committed, or of any other premises or place involved in the case, will be helpful to the jury in determining any material factual issue, it may in its discretion, at any time before the commencement of the summations, order that the jury be conducted to such premises or place for such purpose in accordance with the provisions of this section.

2. In such case, the jury must be kept together throughout under the supervision of an appropriate public servant or servants appointed by the court, and the court itself must be present throughout. The prosecutor, the defendant and counsel for the defendant may as a matter of right be present throughout, but such right may be waived.

3. The purpose of such an inspection is solely to permit visual observation by the jury of the premises or place in question, and neither the court, the parties, counsel nor the jurors may engage in discussion or argumentation concerning the significance or implications of anything under observation or concerning any issue in the case.

§ 270.55. Sentencing jury in capital cases

During the period extending from when a jury returns a verdict of guilty upon a count of an indictment charging murder in the first degree as defined by section 125.27 of the penal law until a jury retires to deliberate on the sentence pursuant to section 400.27, the court may in its discretion either permit the jurors to separate during recesses and adjournments or direct that they be continuously kept together during such periods under the supervision of an appropriate public servant or servants. In the latter case, such public servant or servants may not speak to or communicate with any juror concerning any subject connected with the sentencing proceeding nor permit any other person to do so, and must return the jury to the court room at the next designated session. Unless otherwise provided for in section 400.27, the provisions of sections 270.35, 270.40 and 270.50 shall govern the sentencing proceeding provided for in section 400.27.

Article 280 Jury Trial—Motion for a Mistrial

§ 280.10. Motion for mistrial

At any time during the trial, the court must declare a mistrial and order a new trial of the indictment under the following circumstances:

1. Upon motion of the defendant, when there occurs during the trial an error or legal defect in the proceedings, or conduct inside or outside the courtroom, which is prejudicial to the defendant and deprives him of a fair trial. When such an error, defect or conduct occurs during a joint trial of two or more defendants and a mistrial motion is made by one or more but not by all, the court must declare a mistrial only as to the defendant or defendants making or joining in the motion, and the trial of the other defendant or defendants must proceed;

2. Upon motion of the people, when there occurs during the trial, either inside or outside the courtroom, gross misconduct by the defendant or some person acting on his behalf, or by a juror, resulting in substantial and irreparable prejudice to the people's case. When such misconduct occurs during a joint trial of two or more defendants, and when the court is satisfied that it did not result in substantial prejudice to the people's case as against a particular defendant and that such defendant was in no way responsible for the misconduct, it may not declare a mistrial with respect to such defendant but must proceed with the trial as to him;

3. Upon motion of either party or upon the court's own motion, when it is physically impossible to proceed with the trial in conformity with law.

§ 280.20. Motion for mistrial; status of indictment upon new trial

Upon a new trial resulting from an order declaring a mistrial, the indictment is deemed to contain all the counts which it contained at the time the previous trial was commenced, regardless of whether any count was thereafter dismissed by the court prior to the mistrial order.

§ 290.10. Trial order of dismissal

1. At the conclusion of the people's case or at the conclusion of all the evidence, the court may, except as provided in subdivision two, upon motion of the defendant, (a) issue a "trial order of dismissal," dismissing any count of an indictment upon the ground that the trial evidence is not legally sufficient to establish the offense charged therein or any lesser included offense, or (b) reserve decision on the motion until after the verdict has been rendered and accepted by the court. Where the court has reserved decision and the jury thereafter renders a verdict of guilty, the court shall proceed to determine the motion upon such evidence as it would have been authorized to consider upon the motion had the court not reserved decision. If the court determines that such motion should have been granted upon the ground specified in paragraph (a) herein, it shall enter an order both setting aside the verdict and dismissing any count of the indictment upon such ground. If the jury is discharged before rendition of a verdict the court shall proceed to determine the motion as set forth in this paragraph.

2. Despite the lack of legally sufficient trial evidence in support of a count of an indictment as described in subdivision one, issuance of a trial order of dismissal is not authorized and constitutes error when the trial evidence would have been legally sufficient had the court not erroneously excluded admissible evidence offered by the people.

3. When the court excludes trial evidence offered by the people under such circumstances that the substance or content thereof does not appear in the record, the people may, in anticipation of a possible subsequent trial order of dismissal emanating from the allegedly improper exclusion and erroneously issued in violation of subdivision two, and in anticipation of a possible appeal therefrom pursuant to subdivision two of section 450.20, place upon the record, out of the presence of the jury, an "offer of proof" summarizing the substance or content of such excluded evidence. Upon the subsequent issuance of a trial order of dismissal and an appeal therefrom, such offer of proof constitutes a part of the record on appeal and has the effect and significance prescribed in subdivision two of section 450.40. In the absence of such an order and an appeal therefrom, such offer of proof is not deemed a part of the record and does not constitute such for purposes of an ensuing appeal by the defendant from a judgment of conviction.

4. Upon issuing a trial order of dismissal which dismisses the entire indictment, the court must immediately discharge the defendant from custody if he is in custody of the sheriff, or, if he is at liberty on bail, it must exonerate the bail.

§ 300.10. Court's charge; in general

1. At the conclusion of the summations, the court must deliver a charge to the jury.

2. In its charge, the court must state the fundamental legal principles applicable to criminal cases in general. Such principles include, but are not limited to, the presumption of the defendant's innocence, the requirement that guilt be proved beyond a reasonable doubt and that the jury may not, in determining the issue of guilt or innocence, consider or speculate concerning matters relating to sentence or

punishment. Upon request of a defendant who did not testify in his own behalf, but not otherwise, the court must state that the fact that he did not testify is not a factor from which any inference unfavorable to the defendant may be drawn. The court must also state the material legal principles applicable to the particular case, and, so far as practicable, explain the application of the law to the facts, but it need not marshal or refer to the evidence to any greater extent than is necessary for such explanation.

3. Where a defendant has raised the affirmative defense of lack of criminal responsibility by reason of mental disease or defect, as defined in section 40.15 of the penal law, the court must, without elaboration, instruct the jury as follows: "A jury during its deliberations must never consider or speculate concerning matters relating to the consequences of its verdict. However, because of the lack of common knowledge regarding the consequences of a verdict of not responsible by reason of mental disease or defect, I charge you that if this verdict is rendered by you there will be hearings as to the defendant's present mental condition and, where appropriate, involuntary commitment proceedings."

4. The court must specifically designate and submit, in accordance with the provisions of sections 300.30 and 300.40, those counts and offenses contained and charged in the indictment which the jury are to consider. Such determination must be made, and the parties informed thereof, prior to the summations. In its charge, the court must define each offense so submitted and, except as otherwise expressly provided, it must instruct the jury to render a verdict separately and specifically upon each count submitted to it, and with respect to each defendant if there be more than one, and must require that the verdict upon each such count be one of the following:

(a) "Guilty" of the offense submitted, if there be but one; or

(b) Where appropriate, "guilty" of a specified one of two or more offenses submitted under the same count in the alternative pursuant to section 300.40; or

(c) "Not guilty"; or

(d) Where appropriate, "not responsible by reason of mental disease or defect."

5. Both before and after the court's charge, the parties may submit requests to charge, either orally or in writing, and the court must rule promptly upon each request. A failure to rule upon a request is deemed a denial thereof.

6. In a prosecution involving a charge of enterprise corruption, as defined in article four hundred sixty of the penal law, the court must specifically designate and separately submit for jury consideration those criminal acts which are contained and charged in the indictment and which are supported by legally sufficient trial evidence. Every criminal act which is not so supported shall be dismissed and stricken from the indictment. If legally sufficient trial evidence exists to support a lesser included offense which is also a criminal act within the meaning of subdivision one of section 460.10 of the penal law, such lesser offense shall be substituted. Such determination must be made and the parties informed thereof, prior to the summations. In its charge, the court must define each criminal act so submitted and, as when it may or must do so pursuant to sections 300.40 and 300.50 of this article, any lesser included offense that is also a criminal act within the meaning of subdivision one of section 460.10 of the penal law. It must instruct the jury to render a verdict separately and specifically upon each criminal act (and

where necessary, any submitted lesser included offense) submitted to it with respect to each defendant. It must further explain to the jury that they may not consider a charge of enterprise corruption against any defendant until they have separately and unanimously agreed that the defendant has committed each of at least three criminal acts alleged as part of the pattern of criminal activity, including any submitted lesser included offenses.

§ 300.30. Court's charge; submission of indictment to jury; definitions of terms

The following definitions are applicable to this article:

1. "Submission of a count" of an indictment means submission of the offense charged therein, or of a lesser included offense, or submission in the alternative of both the offense charged and a lesser included offense or offenses. When the court "submits a count," it must, at the least, submit the offense charged therein if such is supported by legally sufficient trial evidence, or if it is not, the greatest lesser included offense which is supported by legally sufficient trial evidence.

2. "Consecutive counts" means two or more counts of an indictment upon which consecutive sentences may be imposed in case of conviction thereon.

3. "Concurrent counts" means two or more counts of an indictment upon which concurrent sentences only may be imposed in case of conviction thereon.

4. "Inclusory concurrent counts." Concurrent counts are "inclusory" when the offense charged in one is greater than any of those charged in the others and when the latter are all lesser offenses included within the greater. All other kinds of concurrent counts are "non-inclusory."

5. "Inconsistent counts." Two counts are "inconsistent" when guilt of the offense charged in one necessarily negates guilt of the offense charged in the other.

§ 300.40. Court's charge; submission of indictment to jury; counts to be submitted

The court may submit to the jury only those counts of an indictment remaining therein at the time of its charge which are supported by legally sufficient trial evidence, and every count not so supported should be dismissed by a trial order of dismissal. The court's determination as to which of the sufficient counts are to be submitted must be in accordance with the following rules:

1. If the indictment contains but one count, the court must submit such count.

2. If a multiple count indictment contains consecutive counts only, the court must submit every count thereof.

3. If a multiple count indictment contains concurrent counts of murder in the first degree, the court must submit every such count. In any other case, if a multiple count indictment contains concurrent counts only, the court must submit at least one such count, and may submit more than one as follows:

(a) With respect to non-inclusory concurrent counts, the court may in its discretion submit one or more or all thereof;

(b) With respect to inclusory concurrent counts, the court must submit the greatest or inclusive count and may or must, under circumstances prescribed in section 300.50, also submit, but in the alternative only, one or more of the lesser included counts. A verdict of guilty upon the greatest count submitted is deemed a dismissal of every lesser count submitted, but not an acquittal thereon. A verdict of guilty upon a lesser count is deemed an acquittal upon every greater count submitted.

4. If a multiple count indictment contains two or more groups of counts, with the counts within each group being concurrent as to each other but consecutive as to those of the other group or groups, the court must submit at least one count of each group, in the manner prescribed in subdivision three. If an indictment contains one or more of such groups of concurrent counts, and also one or more other counts each of which is consecutive as to every other count of the indictment, the court must submit each individual consecutive count and at least one count of each group of concurrent counts.

5. If an indictment contains two inconsistent counts, the court must submit at least one thereof. If a verdict of guilty upon either would be supported by legally sufficient trial evidence, the court may submit both counts in the alternative and authorize the jury to convict upon one or the other depending upon its findings of fact. In such case, the court must direct the jury that if it renders a verdict of guilty upon one such count it must render a verdict of not guilty upon the other. If the court is satisfied that a conviction upon one such count, though supported by legally sufficient trial evidence, would be against the weight of the evidence while a conviction upon the other would not, it may in its discretion submit the latter count only.

6. Notwithstanding any other provision of this section, the court is not required to submit any particular count to the jury when:

(a) The people consent that it not be submitted; except that nothing contained in this paragraph limits the right accorded a defendant by section 300.50 to the submission, in certain situations, of counts charging lesser included offenses; or

(b) The number of counts or the complexity of the indictment requires selectivity of counts by the court in order to avoid placing an unduly heavy burden upon the jury in its consideration of the case. In such case, the court may submit to the jury a portion of the counts which are representative of the people's case.

7. Every count not submitted to the jury is deemed to have been dismissed by the court. Where the court, over objection of the people, refuses to submit a count which is consecutive as to every count actually submitted, such count is deemed to have been dismissed by a trial order of dismissal even though no such order was expressly made by the court.

§ 300.50. Court's charge; submission of lesser included offenses

1. In submitting a count of an indictment to the jury, the court in its discretion may, in addition to submitting the greatest offense which it is required to submit, submit in the alternative any lesser included offense if there is a reasonable view of the evidence which would support a finding that the defendant committed such lesser offense but did not commit the greater. If there is no reasonable view of the evidence which would support such a finding, the court may not submit such lesser offense. Any error respecting such submission, however, is waived by the defendant unless he objects thereto before the jury retires to deliberate.

2. If the court is authorized by subdivision one to submit a lesser included offense and is requested by either party to do so, it must do so. In the absence of such a request, the court's failure to submit such offense does not constitute error.

3. The principles prescribed in subdivisions one and two apply equally where the lesser included offense is specifically charged in another count of the indictment.

4. Whenever the court submits two or more offenses in the alternative pursuant to this section, it must instruct the jury that it may render a verdict of guilty with respect to any one of such offenses, depending upon its findings of fact, but that it may not render a verdict of guilty with respect to more than one. A verdict of guilty of any such offense is not deemed an acquittal of any lesser offense submitted, but is deemed an acquittal of every greater offense submitted.

5. Where the indictment charges a crime committed by the defendant while he was under the age of sixteen but a lesser included offense would be one for which the defendant is not criminally responsible by reason of infancy, such lessor included offense may nevertheless be submitted to the jury in the same manner as an offense for which the defendant would be criminally responsible notwithstanding the fact that a verdict of guilty would not result in a criminal conviction.

6. For purposes of this section, the offenses of rape in the third degree as defined in subdivision three of section 130.25 of the penal law and criminal sexual act in the third degree as defined in subdivision three of section 130.40 of the penal law, are not lesser included offenses of rape in the first degree, criminal sexual act in the first degree or any other offense. Notwithstanding the foregoing, either such offense may be submitted as a lesser included offense of the applicable first degree offense when (i) there is a reasonable view of the evidence which would support a finding that the defendant committed such lesser offense but did not commit the greater offense, and (ii) both parties consent to its submission.

Article 310 Jury Trial—Deliberation and Verdict of Jury

§ 310.10. Jury deliberation; requirement of; where conducted

1. Following the court's charge, except as otherwise provided by subdivision two of this section, the jury must retire to deliberate upon its verdict in a place outside the courtroom. It must be provided with suitable accommodations therefor and must, except as otherwise provided in subdivision two of this section, be continuously kept together under the supervision of a court officer or court officers. In the event such court officer or court officers are not available, the jury shall be under the supervision of an appropriate public servant or public servants. Except when so authorized by the court or when performing administerial duties with respect to the jurors, such court officers or public servants, as the case may be, may not speak to or communicate with them or permit any other person to do so.

2. At any time after the jury has been charged or commenced its deliberations, and after notice to the parties and affording such parties an opportunity to be heard on the record outside of the presence of the jury, the court may declare the deliberations to be in recess and may thereupon direct the jury to suspend its deliberations and to separate for a reasonable period of time to be specified by the court, not to exceed twenty-four hours, except that in the case of a Saturday, Sunday or holiday, such separation may extend beyond such twenty-four hour period. Before each recess, the court must admonish the jury as provided in section 270.40 of this chapter and direct it not to

resume its deliberations until all twelve jurors have reassembled in the designated place at the termination of the declared recess.

3. [Repealed]

§ 310.20. Jury deliberation; use of exhibits and other material

Upon retiring to deliberate, the jurors may take with them:

1. Any exhibits received in evidence at the trial which the court, after according the parties an opportunity to be heard upon the matter, in its discretion permits them to take;

2. A written list prepared by the court containing the offenses submitted to the jury by the court in its charge and the possible verdicts thereon. Whenever the court submits two or more counts charging offenses set forth in the same article of the law, the court may set forth the dates, names of complainants or specific statutory language, without defining the terms, by which the counts may be distinguished; provided, however, that the court shall instruct the jury in its charge that the sole purpose of the notations is to distinguish between the counts; and

3. A written list prepared by the court containing the names of every witness whose testimony has been presented during the trial, if the jury requests such a list and the court, in its discretion, determines that such a list will assist the jury.

§ 310.30. Jury deliberation; request for information

At any time during its deliberation, the jury may request the court for further instruction or information with respect to the law, with respect to the content or substance of any trial evidence, or with respect to any other matter pertinent to the jury's consideration of the case. Upon such a request, the court must direct that the jury be returned to the courtroom and, after notice to both the people and counsel for the defendant, and in the presence of the defendant, must give such requested information or instruction as the court deems proper. With the consent of the parties and upon the request of the jury for further instruction with respect to a statute, the court may also give to the jury copies of the text of any statute which, in its discretion, the court deems proper.

§ 310.40. Verdict; rendition thereof

1. The verdict must be rendered and announced by the foreperson of the jury in the courtroom in the presence of the court, a prosecutor, the defendant's counsel and the defendant; provided, however, that where the foreperson refuses or is unable to render and announce the verdict, the court may designate another member of the jury to do so.

2. Before rendering and announcing the verdict, the foreperson of the jury, or such other member of the jury as may be designated by the court pursuant to subdivision one, must be asked whether the jury has agreed upon a verdict and must answer in the affirmative.

§ 310.50. Verdict; form; reconsideration of defective verdict

1. The form of the verdict must be in accordance with the court's instructions, as prescribed in article three hundred.

2. If the jury renders a verdict which in form is not in accordance with the court's instructions or which is otherwise legally defective, the court must explain the defect or error and must direct the jury to reconsider such verdict, to resume its deliberation for such purpose, and to render a proper verdict. If the jury persists in rendering a defective

or improper verdict, the court may in its discretion either order that the verdict in its entirety as to any defendant be recorded as an acquittal, or discharge the jury and authorize the people to retry the indictment or a specified count or counts thereof as to such defendant; provided that if it is clear that the jury intended to find a defendant not guilty upon any particular count, the court must order that the verdict be recorded as an acquittal of such defendant upon such count.

3. If the court accepts a verdict which is defective or incomplete by reason of the jury's failure to render a verdict upon every count upon which it was instructed to do so, such verdict is deemed to constitute an acquittal upon every such count improperly ignored in the verdict.

4. In a prosecution involving a charge of enterprise corruption in violation of article four hundred sixty of the penal law, the jury must separately and specifically render a special verdict with regard to each criminal act and any lesser included offense submitted for its consideration as a part of a pattern of criminal activity in addition to its verdict on the charge of enterprise corruption. In the absence of a unanimous special verdict of guilty with regard to each of at least three criminal acts and/or lesser included offenses submitted for its consideration and legally sufficient to constitute a person's participation in a pattern of criminal activity within the meaning of subdivision four of section 460.10 of the penal law, the court must order that the verdict on the count charging enterprise corruption be recorded as an acquittal.

§ 310.60. Discharge of jury before rendition of verdict and effect thereof

1. A deliberating jury may be discharged by the court without having rendered a verdict only when:

(a) The jury has deliberated for an extensive period of time without agreeing upon a verdict with respect to any of the charges submitted and the court is satisfied that any such agreement is unlikely within a reasonable time; or

(b) The court, the defendant and the people all consent to such discharge; or

(c) A mistrial is declared pursuant to section 280.10.

2. When the jury is so discharged, the defendant or defendants may be retried upon the indictment. Upon such retrial, the indictment is deemed to contain all counts which it contained, except those which were dismissed or were deemed to have resulted in an acquittal pursuant to subdivision one of section 290.10.

§ 310.70. Rendition of partial verdict and effect thereof

1. If a deliberating jury declares that it has reached a verdict with respect to one or more but not all of the offenses submitted to it, or with respect to one or more but not all of the defendants, the court must proceed as follows:

(a) If the possibility of ultimate agreement with respect to the other submitted offenses or defendants is so small and the circumstances are such that if they were the only matters under consideration the court would be authorized to discharge the jury pursuant to paragraph (a) of subdivision one of section 310.60, the court must terminate the deliberation and order the jury to render a partial verdict with respect to those offenses and defendants upon which or with respect to whom it has reached a verdict;

(b) If the court is satisfied that there is a reasonable possibility of ultimate agreement upon any of the unresolved offenses with respect to any defendant, it may either:

(i) Order the jury to render its verdict with respect to those offenses and defendants upon which or with respect to whom it has reached agreement and resume its deliberation upon the remainder; or

(ii) Refuse to accept a partial verdict at the time and order the jury to resume its deliberation upon the entire case.

2. Following the rendition of a partial verdict pursuant to subdivision one, a defendant may be retried for any submitted offense upon which the jury was unable to agree unless:

(a) A verdict of conviction thereon would have been inconsistent with a verdict, of either conviction or acquittal, actually rendered with respect to some other offense, or

(b) The submitted offense which was the subject of the disagreement, and some other submitted offense of higher or equal grade which was the subject of a verdict of conviction, were so related that consecutive sentences thereon could not have been imposed upon a defendant convicted of both such offenses.

3. As used in this section, a "submitted offense" means any offense submitted by the court to the jury, whether it be one which was expressly charged in a count of the indictment or a lesser included offense thereof submitted pursuant to section 300.50.

§ 310.80. Recording and checking of verdict and polling of jury

After a verdict has been rendered, it must be recorded on the minutes and read to the jury, and the jurors must be collectively asked whether such is their verdict. Even though no juror makes any declaration in the negative, the jury must, if either party makes such an application, be polled and each juror separately asked whether the verdict announced by the foreman is in all respects his verdict. If upon either the collective or the separate inquiry any juror answers in the negative, the court must refuse to accept the verdict and must direct the jury to resume its deliberation. If no disagreement is expressed, the jury must be discharged from the case, except as otherwise provided in section 400.27.

§ 310.85. Verdict of guilty where defendant not criminally responsible

1. Where a verdict of guilty is rendered with respect to a crime, but the defendant is not criminally responsible for such crime by reason of infancy, the court shall proceed as provided in this section.

2. If a verdict of guilty also is rendered with respect to a crime for which the defendant is criminally responsible, or if the defendant is awaiting sentence upon another criminal conviction or is under a sentence of imprisonment on another criminal conviction, the verdict rendered with respect to a crime for which he is not criminally responsible must be set aside and shall be deemed a nullity.

3. In any case where the verdict is not set aside pursuant to subdivision two of this section, the court must order that the verdict be deemed vacated and replaced by a juvenile delinquency fact determination. Upon so ordering, the court must direct that the action be removed to the family court in accordance with the provisions of article seven hundred twenty-five of this chapter.

§ 320.10. Non-jury trial; when authorized

1. Except where the indictment charges the crime of murder in the first degree, the defendant, subject to the provisions of subdivision two, may at any time before trial waive a jury trial and consent to a trial without a jury in the superior court in which the indictment is pending.

2. Such waiver must be in writing and must be signed by the defendant in person in open court in the presence of the court, and with the approval of the court. The court must approve the execution and submission of such waiver unless it determines that it is tendered as a stratagem to procure an otherwise impermissible procedural advantage or that the defendant is not fully aware of the consequences of the choice he is making. If the court disapproves the waiver, it must state upon the record its reasons for such disapproval.

§ 320.20. Non-jury trial; nature and conduct thereof

1. A non-jury trial of an indictment must be conducted by one judge of the superior court in which the indictment is pending.

2. The court, in addition to determining all questions of law, is the execlusive [exclusive]* trier of all issues of fact and must render a verdict.

3. The order of the trial must be as follows:

(a) The court must permit the parties to deliver opening addresses in the order provided for a trial by jury pursuant to section 260.30.

(b) The order in which evidence must or may be offered by the respective parties is the same as that applicable to a jury trial of an indictment as prescribed in subdivisions five, six and seven of section 260.30.

(c) The court must permit the parties to deliver summations in the order provided for a trial by jury pursuant to section 260.30.

(d) The court must then consider the case and render a verdict.

4. The provisions governing motion practice and general procedure with respect to a jury trial are, wherever appropriate, applicable to a non-jury trial.

5. Before considering a multiple count indictment for the purpose of rendering a verdict thereon, and before the summations if there be any, the court must designate and state upon the record the counts upon which it will render a verdict and the particular defendant or defendants, if there be more than one, with respect to whom it will render a verdict upon any particular count. In determining what counts, offenses and defendants must be considered by it and covered by its verdict, and the form of the verdict in general, the court must be governed, so far as appropriate and practicable, by the provisions of article three hundred governing the court's submission of counts and offenses to a jury upon a jury trial.

Article 330 Proceedings from Verdict to Sentence

§ 330.10. Disposition of defendant after verdict of acquittal

1. Upon a verdict of complete acquittal, the court must immediately discharge the defendant if he is in the custody of the sheriff, or, if he is at liberty on bail, it must exonerate the bail.

2. Upon a verdict of not responsible by reason of mental disease or defect, the provisions of section 330.20 of this chapter shall govern all subsequent proceedings against the defendant.

§ 330.20. Procedure following verdict or plea of not responsible by reason of mental disease or defect

1. Definition of terms. As used in this section, the following terms shall have the following meanings:

(a) "Commissioner" means the state commissioner of mental health or the state commissioner of mental retardation and developmental disability.

(b) "Secure facility" means a facility within the state office of mental health or the state office of mental retardation and developmental disabilities which is staffed with personnel adequately trained in security methods and is so equipped as to minimize the risk or danger of escapes, and which has been so specifically designated by the commissioner.

(c) "Dangerous mental disorder" means: (i) that a defendant currently suffers from a "mental illness" as that term is defined in subdivision twenty of section 1.03 of the mental hygiene law, and (ii) that because of such condition he currently constitutes a physical danger to himself or others.

(d) "Mentally ill" means that a defendant currently suffers from a mental illness for which care and treatment as a patient, in the in-patient services of a psychiatric center under the jurisdiction of the state office of mental health, is essential to such defendant's welfare and that his judgment is so impaired that he is unable to understand the need for such care and treatment; and, where a defendant is mentally retarded, the term "mentally ill" shall also mean, for purposes of this section, that the defendant is in need of care and treatment as a resident in the in-patient services of a developmental center or other residential facility for the mentally retarded and developmentally disabled under the jurisdiction of the state office of mental retardation and developmental disabilities.

(e) "Examination order" means an order directed to the commissioner requiring that a defendant submit to a psychiatric examination to determine whether the defendant has a dangerous mental disorder, or if he does not have dangerous mental disorder, whether he is mentally ill.

(f) "Commitment order" or "recommitment order" means an order committing a defendant to the custody of the commissioner for confinement in a secure facility for care and treatment for six months from the date of the order.

(g) "First retention order" means an order which is effective at the expiration of the period prescribed in a commitment order for a recommitment order, authorizing continued custody of a defendant by the commissioner for a period not to exceed one year.

(h) "Second retention order" means an order which is effective at the expiration of the period prescribed in a first retention order, authorizing continued custody of a defendant by the commissioner for a period not to exceed two years.

(i) "Subsequent retention order" means an order which is effective at the expiration of the period prescribed in a second retention order or a prior subsequent retention order authorizing continued custody of a defendant by the commissioner for a period not to exceed two years.

(j) "Retention order" means a first retention order, a second retention order or a subsequent retention order.

(k) "Furlough order" means an order directing the commissioner to allow a defendant in confinement pursuant to a commitment order, recommitment order or retention order to temporarily leave the facility for a period not exceeding fourteen days, either with or without the constant supervision of one or more employees of the facility.

(l) "Transfer order" means an order directing the commissioner to transfer a defendant from a secure facility to a non-secure facility under the jurisdiction of the commissioner or to any non-secure facility designated by the commissioner.

(m) "Release order" means an order directing the commissioner to terminate a defendant's in-patient status without terminating the commissioner's responsibility for the defendant.

(n) "Discharge order" means an order terminating an order of conditions or unconditionally discharging a defendant from supervision under the provisions of this section.

(o) "Order of conditions" means an order directing a defendant to comply with this prescribed treatment plan, or any other condition which the court determines to be reasonably necessary or appropriate, and, in addition, where a defendant is in custody of the commissioner, not to leave the facility without authorization. In addition to such conditions, when determined to be reasonably necessary or appropriate, an order of conditions may be accompanied by a special order of conditions set forth in a separate document requiring that the defendant: (i) stay away from the home, school, business or place of employment of the victim or victims, or of any witness designated by the court, of such offense; or (ii) refrain from harassing, intimidating, threatening or otherwise interfering with the victim or victims of the offense and such members of the family or household of such victim or victims as shall be specifically named by the court in such special order. An order of conditions or special order of conditions shall be valid for five years from the date of its issuance, except that, for good cause shown, the court may extend the period for an additional five years.

(p) "District attorney" means the office which prosecuted the criminal action resulting in the verdict or plea of not responsible by reason of mental disease or defect.

(q) "Qualified psychiatrist" means a physician who (i) is a diplomate of the American board of psychiatry and neurology or is eligible to be certified by that board; or (ii) is certified by the American osteopathic board of neurology and psychiatry or is eligible to be certified by that board.

(r) "Licensed psychologist" means a person who is registered as a psychologist under article one hundred fifty-three of the education law.

(s) "Psychiatric examiner" means a qualified psychiatrist or a licensed psychologist who has been designated by the commissioner to examine a defendant pursuant to this section, and such designee need not be an employee of the department of mental hygiene.

2. Examination order; psychiatric examiners. Upon entry of a verdict of not responsible by reason of mental disease or defect, or upon the acceptance of a plea of not responsible by reason of mental disease or defect, the court must immediately issue an examination order. Upon receipt of such order, the commissioner must designate two qualified psychiatric examiners to conduct the examination to examine the defendant. In conducting their examination, the psychiatric examiners may employ any method which is accepted by the medical profession for the examination of persons alleged to be suffering from a dangerous mental disorder or to be mentally ill or retarded. The court may authorize a psychiatrist or psychologist retained by a defendant to be present at such examination. The clerk of the court must promptly forward a copy of the examination order to the mental hygiene legal service and such service may thereafter participate in all subsequent proceedings under this section.

In all subsequent proceedings under this section, prior to the issuance of a special order of conditions, the court shall consider whether any order of protection had been issued prior to a verdict of not responsible by reason of mental disease or defect in the case, or prior to the acceptance of a plea of not responsible by reason of mental disease or defect in the case.

2-a. Firearm, rifle or shotgun surrender order. Upon entry of a verdict of not responsible by reason of mental disease or defect, or upon the acceptance of a plea of not responsible by reason of mental disease or defect, or upon a finding that the defendant is an incapacitated person pursuant to article seven hundred thirty of this chapter, the court shall revoke the defendant's firearm license, if any, inquire of the defendant as to the existence and location of any firearm, rifle or shotgun owned or possessed by such defendant and direct the surrender of such firearm, rifle or shotgun pursuant to subparagraph (f) of paragraph one of subdivision a of section 265.20 and subdivision six of section 400.05 of the penal law.

3. Examination order; place of examination. Upon issuing an examination order, the court must, except as otherwise provided in this subdivision, direct that the defendant be committed to a secure facility designated by the commissioner as the place for such psychiatric examination. The sheriff must hold the defendant in custody pending such designation by the commissioner, and when notified of the designation, the sheriff must promptly deliver the defendant to such secure facility. When the defendant is not in custody at the time of such verdict or plea, because he was previously released on bail or on his own recognizance, the court, in its discretion, may direct that such examination be conducted on an out-patient basis, and at such time and place as the commissioner shall designate. If, however, the commissioner informs the court that confinement of the defendant is necessary for an effective examination, the court must direct that the defendant be confined in a facility designated by the commissioner until the examination is completed.

4. Examination order, duration. Confinement in a secure facility pursuant to an examination order shall be for a period not exceeding thirty days, except that, upon application of the commissioner, the court may authorize confinement for an additional period not exceeding thirty days when a longer period is necessary to complete the examination. If the initial hearing required by subdivision six of this section has not

commenced prior to the termination of such examination period, the commissioner shall retain custody of the defendant in such secure facility until custody is transferred to the sheriff in the manner prescribed in subdivision six of this section. During the period of such confinement, the physician in charge of the facility may administer or cause to be administered to the defendant such emergency psychiatric, medical or other therapeutic treatment as in his judgment should be administered. If the court has directed that the examination be conducted on an out-patient basis, the examination shall be completed within thirty days after the defendant has first reported to the place designated by the commissioner, except that, upon application of the commissioner, the court may extend such period for a reasonable time if a longer period is necessary to complete the examination.

5. Examination order; reports. After he has completed his examination of the defendant, each psychiatric examiner must promptly prepare a report of his findings and evaluation concerning the defendant's mental condition, and submit such report to the commissioner. If the psychiatric examiners differ in their opinion as to whether the defendant is mentally ill or is suffering from a dangerous mental disorder, the commissioner must designate another psychiatric examiner to examine the defendant. Upon receipt of the examination reports, the commissioner must submit them to the court that issued the examination order. If the court is not satisfied with the findings of these psychiatric examiners, the court may designate one or more additional psychiatric examiners pursuant to subdivision fifteen of this section. The court must furnish a copy of the reports to the district attorney, counsel for the defendant and the mental hygiene legal service.

6. Initial hearing; commitment order. After the examination reports are submitted, the court must, within ten days of the receipt of such reports, conduct an initial hearing to determine the defendant's present mental condition. If the defendant is in the custody of the commissioner pursuant to an examination order, the court must direct the sheriff to obtain custody of the defendant from the commissioner and to confine the defendant pending further order of the court, except that the court may direct the sheriff to confine the defendant in an institution located near the place where the court sits if that institution has been designated by the commissioner as suitable for the temporary and secure detention of mentally disabled persons. At such initial hearing, the district attorney must establish to the satisfaction of the court that the defendant has a dangerous mental disorder or is mentally ill. If the court finds that the defendant has a dangerous mental disorder, it must issue a commitment order. If the court finds that the defendant does not have a dangerous mental disorder but is mentally ill, the provisions of subdivision seven of this section shall apply.

7. Initial hearing civil commitment and order of conditions. If, at the conclusion of the initial hearing conducted pursuant to subdivision six of this section, the court finds that the defendant is mentally ill but does not have a dangerous mental disorder, the provisions of articles nine or fifteen of the mental hygiene law shall apply at that stage of the proceedings and at all subsequent proceedings. Having found that the defendant is mentally ill, the court must issue an order of conditions and an order committing the defendant to the custody of the commissioner. The latter order shall be deemed an

order made pursuant to the mental hygiene law and not pursuant to this section, and further retention, conditional release or discharge of such defendant shall be in accordance with the provisions of the mental hygiene law. If, at the conclusion of the initial hearing, the court finds that the defendant does not have a dangerous mental disorder and is not mentally ill, the court must discharge the defendant either unconditionally or subject to an order of conditions.

7-a. Whenever the court issues a special order of conditions pursuant to this section, the commissioner shall make reasonable efforts to notify the victim or victims or the designated witness or witnesses that a special order of conditions containing such provisions has been issued, unless such victim or witness has requested that such notice should not be provided.

8. First retention order. When a defendant is in the custody of the commissioner pursuant to a commitment order, the commissioner must, at least thirty days prior to the expiration of the period prescribed in the order, apply to the court that issued the order, or to a superior court in the county where the secure facility is located, for a first retention order or a release order. The commissioner must give written notice of the application to the district attorney, the defendant, counsel for the defendant, and the mental hygiene legal service. Upon receipt of such application, the court may, on its own motion, conduct a hearing to determine whether the defendant has a dangerous mental disorder, and it must conduct such hearing if a demand therefor is made by the district attorney, the defendant, counsel for the defendant, or the mental hygiene legal service within ten days from the date that notice of the application was given to them. If such a hearing is held on an application for retention, the commissioner must establish to the satisfaction of the court that the defendant has a dangerous mental disorder or is mentally ill. The district attorney shall be entitled to appear and present evidence at such hearing. If such a hearing is held on an application for release, the district attorney must establish to the satisfaction of the court that the defendant has a dangerous mental disorder or is mentally ill. If the court finds that the defendant has a dangerous mental disorder it must issue a first retention order. If the court finds that the defendant is mentally ill but does not have a dangerous mental disorder, it must issue a first retention order and, pursuant to subdivision eleven of this section, a transfer order and an order of conditions. If the court finds that the defendant does not have a dangerous mental disorder and is not mentally ill, it must issue a release order and an order of conditions pursuant to subdivision twelve of this section.

9. Second and subsequent retention orders. When a defendant is in the custody of the commissioner pursuant to a first retention order, the commissioner must, at least thirty days prior to the expiration of the period prescribed in the order, apply to the court that issued the order, or to a superior court in the county where the facility is located, for a second retention order or a release order. The commissioner must give written notice of the application to the district attorney, the defendant, counsel for the defendant, and the mental hygiene legal service. Upon receipt of such application, the court may, on its own motion, conduct a hearing to determine whether the defendant has a dangerous mental disorder, and it must conduct such hearing if a demand therefor is made by the district attorney, the defendant, counsel for the defendant, or the mental hygiene legal

service within ten days from the date that notice of the application was given to them. If such a hearing is held on an application for retention, the commissioner must establish to the satisfaction of the court that the defendant has a dangerous mental disorder or is mentally ill. The district attorney shall be entitled to appear and present evidence at such hearing. If such a hearing is held on an application for release, the district attorney must establish to the satisfaction of the court that the defendant has a dangerous mental disorder or is mentally ill. If the court finds that the defendant has a dangerous mental disorder it must issue a second retention order. If the court finds that the defendant is mentally ill but does not have a dangerous mental disorder, it must issue a second retention order and, pursuant to subdivision eleven of this section, a transfer order and an order of conditions. If the court finds that the defendant does not have a dangerous mental disorder and is not mentally ill, it must issue a release order and an order of conditions pursuant to subdivision twelve of this section. When a defendant is in the custody of the commissioner prior to the expiration of the period prescribed in a second retention order, the procedures set forth in this subdivision for the issuance of a second retention order shall govern the application for and the issuance of any subsequent retention order.

10. Furlough order. The commissioner may apply for a furlough order, pursuant to this subdivision, when a defendant is in his custody pursuant to a commitment order, recommitment order, or retention order and the commissioner is of the view that, consistent with the public safety and welfare of the community and the defendant, the clinical condition of the defendant warrants a granting of the privileges authorized by a furlough order. The application for a furlough order may be made to the court that issued the commitment order, or to a superior court in the county where the secure facility is located. The commissioner must give ten days written notice to the district attorney, the defendant, counsel for the defendant, and the mental hygiene legal service. Upon receipt of such application, the court may, on its own motion, conduct a hearing to determine whether the application should be granted, and must conduct such hearing if a demand therefor is made by the district attorney. If the court finds that the issuance of a furlough order is consistent with the public safety and welfare of the community and the defendant, and that the clinical condition of the defendant warrants a granting of the privileges authorized by a furlough order, the court must grant the application and issue a furlough order containing any terms and conditions that the court deems necessary or appropriate. If the defendant fails to return to the secure facility at the time specified in the furlough order, then, for purposes of subdivision nineteen of this section, he shall be deemed to have escaped.

11. Transfer order and order of conditions. The commissioner may apply for a transfer order, pursuant to this subdivision, when a defendant is in his custody pursuant to a retention order or a recommitment order, and the commissioner is of the view that the defendant does not have a dangerous mental disorder or that, consistent with the public safety and welfare of the community and the defendant, the clinical condition of the defendant warrants his transfer from a secure facility to a non-secure facility under the jurisdiction of the commissioner or to any non-secure facility designated by the commissioner. The application for a transfer order may be made to the court that issued

the order under which the defendant is then in custody, or to a superior court in the county where the secure facility is located. The commissioner must give ten days written notice to the district attorney, the defendant, counsel for the defendant, and the mental hygiene legal service. Upon receipt of such application, the court may, on its own motion, conduct a hearing to determine whether the application should be granted, and must conduct such hearing if the demand therefor is made by the district attorney. At such hearing, the district attorney must establish to the satisfaction of the court that the defendant has a dangerous mental disorder or that the issuance of a transfer order is inconsistent with the public safety and welfare of the community. The court must grant the application and issue a transfer order if the court finds that the defendant does not have a dangerous mental disorder, or if the court finds that the issuance of a transfer order is consistent with the public safety and welfare of the community and the defendant and that the clinical condition of the defendant, warrants his transfer from a secure facility to a non-secure facility. A court must also issue a transfer order when, in connection with an application for a first retention order pursuant to subdivision eight of this section or a second or subsequent retention order pursuant to subdivision nine of this section, it finds that a defendant is mentally ill but does not have a dangerous mental disorder. Whenever a court issues a transfer order it must also issue an order of conditions.

12. Release order and order of conditions. The commissioner may apply for a release order, pursuant to this subdivision, when a defendant is in his custody pursuant to a retention order or recommitment order, and the commissioner is of the view that the defendant no longer has a dangerous mental disorder and is no longer mentally ill. The application for a release order may be made to the court that issued the order under which the defendant is then in custody, or to a superior court in the county where the facility is located. The application must contain a description of the defendant's current mental condition, the past course of treatment, a history of the defendant's conduct subsequent to his commitment, a written service plan for continued treatment which shall include the information specified in subdivision (g) of section 29.15 of the mental hygiene law, and a detailed statement of the extent to which supervision of the defendant after release is proposed. The commissioner must give ten days written notice to the district attorney, the defendant, counsel for the defendant, and the mental hygiene legal service. Upon receipt of such application, the court must promptly conduct a hearing to determine the defendant's present mental condition. At such hearing, the district attorney must establish to the satisfaction of the court that the defendant has a dangerous mental disorder or is mentally ill. If the court finds that the defendant has a dangerous mental disorder, it must deny the application for a release order. If the court finds that the defendant does not have a dangerous mental disorder but is mentally ill, it must issue a transfer order pursuant to subdivision eleven of this section if the defendant is then confined in a secure facility. If the court finds that the defendant does not have a dangerous mental disorder and is not mentally ill, it must grant the application and issue a release order. A court must also issue a release order when, in connection with an application for a first retention order pursuant to subdivision eight of this section or a second or subsequent retention order pursuant to subdivision nine of

this section, it finds that the defendant does not have a dangerous mental disorder and is not mentally ill. Whenever a court issues a release order it must also issue an order of conditions. If the court has previously issued a transfer order and an order of conditions, it must issue a new order of conditions upon issuing a release order. The order of conditions issued in conjunction with a release order shall incorporate a written service plan prepared by a psychiatrist familiar with the defendant's case history and approved by the court, and shall contain any conditions that the court determines to be reasonably necessary or appropriate. It shall be the responsibility of the commissioner to determine that such defendant is receiving the services specified in the written service plan and is complying with any conditions specified in such plan and the order of conditions.

13. Discharge order. The commissioner may apply for a discharge order, pursuant to this subdivision, when a defendant has been continuously on an out-patient status for three years or more pursuant to a release order, and the commissioner is of the view that the defendant no longer has a dangerous mental disorder and is no longer mentally ill and that the issuance of a discharge order is consistent with the public safety and welfare of the community and the defendant. The application for a discharge order may be made to the court that issued the release order, or to a superior court in the county where the defendant is then residing. The commissioner must give ten days written notice to the district attorney, the defendant, counsel for the defendant, and the mental hygiene legal service. Upon receipt of such application, the court may, on its own motion, conduct a hearing to determine whether the application should be granted, and must conduct such hearing if a demand therefor is made by the district attorney. The court must grant the application and issue a discharge order if the court finds that the defendant has been continuously on an out-patient status for three years or more, that he does not have a dangerous mental disorder and is not mentally ill, and that the issuance of the discharge order is consistent with the public safety and welfare of the community and the defendant.

14. Recommitment order. At any time during the period covered by an order of conditions an application may be made by the commissioner or the district attorney to the court that issued such order, or to a superior court in the county where the defendant is then residing, for a recommitment order when the applicant is of the view that the defendant has a dangerous mental disorder. The applicant must give written notice of the application to the defendant, counsel for the defendant, and the mental hygiene legal service, and if the applicant is the commissioner he must give such notice to the district attorney or if the applicant is the district attorney he must give such notice to the commissioner. Upon receipt of such application the court must order the defendant to appear before it for a hearing to determine if the defendant has a dangerous mental disorder. Such order may be in the form of a written notice, specifying the time and place of appearance, served personally upon the defendant, or mailed to his last known address, as the court may direct. If the defendant fails to appear in court as directed, the court may issue a warrant to an appropriate peace officer directing him to take the defendant into custody and bring him before the court. In such circumstance, the court may direct that the defendant be confined in an appropriate institution located near the place where the court sits. The court must

conduct a hearing to determine whether the defendant has a dangerous mental disorder. At such hearing, the applicant, whether he be the commissioner or the district attorney must establish to the satisfaction of the court that the defendant has a dangerous mental disorder. If the applicant is the commissioner, the district attorney shall be entitled to appear and present evidence at such hearing; if the applicant is the district attorney, the commissioner shall be entitled to appear and present evidence at such hearing. If the court finds that the defendant has a dangerous mental disorder, it must issue a recommitment order. When a defendant is in the custody of the commissioner pursuant to a recommitment order, the procedures set forth in subdivisions eight and nine of this section for the issuance of retention orders shall govern the application for and the issuance of a first retention order, a second retention order, and subsequent retention orders.

15. Designation of psychiatric examiners. If, at any hearing conducted under this section to determine the defendant's present mental condition, the court is not satisfied with the findings of the psychiatric examiners, the court may direct the commissioner to designate one or more additional psychiatric examiners to conduct an examination of the defendant and submit a report of their findings. In addition, the court may on its own motion, or upon request of a party, may designate one or more psychiatric examiners to examine the defendant and submit a report of their findings. The district attorney may apply to the court for an order directing that the defendant submit to an examination by a psychiatric examiner designated by the district attorney, and such psychiatric examiner may testify at the hearing.

16. Rehearing and review. Any defendant who is in the custody of the commissioner pursuant to a commitment order, a retention order, or a recommitment order, if dissatisfied with such order, may, within thirty days after the making of such order, obtain a rehearing and review of the proceedings and of such order in accordance with the provisions of section 9.35 or 15.35 of the mental hygiene law.

17. Rights of defendants. Subject to the limitations and provisions of this section, a defendant committed to the custody of the commissioner pursuant to this section shall have the rights granted to patients under the mental hygiene law.

18. Notwithstanding any other provision of law, no person confined by reason of a commitment order, recommitment order or retention order to a secure facility may be discharged or released unless the commissioner shall deliver written notice, at least four days excluding Saturdays, Sundays and holidays, in advance of such discharge or release to all of the following:

(a) the district attorney.

(b) the police department having jurisdiction of the area to which the defendant is to be discharged or released.

(c) any other person the court may designate.

The notices required by this subdivision shall be given by the facility staff physician who was treating the defendant or, if unavailable, by the defendant's treatment team leader, but if neither is immediately available, notice must be given by some other member of the clinical staff of the facility. Such notice must be given by any means reasonably calculated to give prompt actual notice.

240

19. Escape from custody; notice requirements. If a defendant is in the custody of the commissioner pursuant to an order issued under this section, and such defendant escapes from custody, immediate notice of such escape shall be given by the department facility staff to: (a) the district attorney, (b) the superintendent of state police, (c) the sheriff of the county where the escape occurred, (d) the police department having jurisdiction of the area where the escape occurred, (e) any person the facility staff believes to be in danger, and (f) any law enforcement agency and any person the facility staff believes would be able to apprise such endangered person that the defendant has escaped from the facility. Such notice shall be given as soon as the facility staff know that the defendant has escaped from the facility and shall include such information as will adequately identify the defendant and the person or persons believed to be in danger and the nature of the danger. The notices required by this subdivision shall be given by the facility staff physician who was treating the defendant or, if unavailable, by the defendant's treatment team leader, but if neither is immediately available, notice must be given by some other member of the clinical staff of the facility. Such notice must be given by any means reasonably calculated to give prompt actual notice. The defendant may be apprehended, restrained, transported to, and returned to the facility from which he escaped by any peace officer, and it shall be the duty of the officer to assist any representative of the commissioner to take the defendant into custody upon the request of such representative.

20. Required affidavit. No application may be made by the commissioner under this section without an accompanying affidavit from at least one psychiatric examiner supportive of relief requested in the application, which affidavit shall be served on all parties entitled to receive the notice of application. Such affidavit shall set forth the defendant's clinical diagnosis, a detailed analysis of his or her mental condition which caused the psychiatric examiner to formulate an opinion, and the opinion of the psychiatric examiner with respect to the defendant. Any application submitted without the required affidavit shall be dismissed by the court.

21. Appeals.

(a) A party to proceedings conducted in accordance with the provisions of this section may take an appeal to an intermediate appellate court by permission of the intermediate appellate court as follows:

(i) the commissioner may appeal from any release order, retention order, transfer order, discharge order, order of conditions, or recommitment order, for which he has not applied;

(ii) a defendant, or the mental hygiene legal service on his or her behalf, may appeal from any commitment order, retention order, recommitment order, or, if the defendant has obtained a rehearing and review of any such order pursuant to subdivision sixteen of this section, from an order, not otherwise appealable as of right, issued in accordance with the provisions of section 9.35 or 15.35 of the mental hygiene law authorizing continued retention under the original order, provided, however, that a defendant who takes an appeal from a commitment order, retention order, or recommitment order may not subsequently obtain a rehearing and review of such order pursuant to subdivision sixteen of this section;

(iii) the district attorney may appeal from any release order, transfer order, discharge order, order of conditions, furlough order, or order denying an application for a recommitment order which he opposed.

(b) An aggrieved party may appeal from a final order of the intermediate appellate court to the court of appeals by permission of the intermediate appellate court granted before application to the court of appeals, or by permission of the court of appeals upon refusal by the intermediate appellate court or upon direct application.

(c) An appeal taken under this subdivision shall be deemed civil in nature, and shall be governed by the laws and rules applicable to civil appeals; provided, however, that a stay of the order appealed from must be obtained in accordance with the provisions of paragraph (d) hereof.

(d) The court from or to which an appeal is taken may stay all proceedings to enforce the order appealed from pending an appeal or determination on a motion for permission to appeal, or may grant a limited stay, except that only the court to which an appeal is taken may vacate, limit, or modify a stay previously granted. If the order appealed from is affirmed or modified, the stay shall continue for five days after service upon the appellant of the order of affirmance or modification with notice of its entry in the court to which the appeal was taken. If a motion is made for permission to appeal from such an order, before the expiration of the five days, the stay, or any other stay granted pending determination of the motion for permission to appeal, shall:

(i) if the motion is granted, continue until five days after the appeal is determined; or

(ii) if the motion is denied, continue until five days after the movant is served with the order of denial with notice of its entry.

22. Any special order of conditions issued pursuant to subparagraph (i) or (ii) of paragraph (o) of subdivision one of this section shall bear in a conspicuous manner the term "special order of conditions" and a copy shall be filed by the clerk of the court with the sheriff's office in the county in which anyone intended to be protected by such special order resides, or, if anyone intended to be protected by such special order resides within a city, with the police department of such city. The absence of language specifying that the order is a "special order of conditions" shall not affect the validity of such order. A copy of such special order of conditions may from time to time be filed by the clerk of the court with any other police department or sheriff's office having jurisdiction of the residence, work place, or school of anyone intended to be protected by such special order. A copy of such special order may also be filed by anyone intended to be protected by such provisions at the appropriate police department or sheriff's office having jurisdiction. Any subsequent amendment or revocation of such special order may be filed in the same manner as provided in this subdivision. Such special order of conditions shall plainly state the date that the order expires.

§ 330.25. Removal after verdict

1. Where a defendant is a juvenile offender or an adolescent offender who does not stand convicted of murder in the second degree, upon motion and with the consent of the district attorney, the action may be removed to the family court in the interests of justice pursuant to article seven hundred twenty-five of this chapter notwithstanding the verdict.

2. If the district attorney consents to the motion for removal pursuant to this section, he shall file a subscribed memorandum with the court setting forth (1) a recommendation that the interests of justice would best be served by removal of the action to the family court; and (2) if the conviction is of an offense set forth in paragraph (b) of subdivision one of section 722.22 of this chapter, specific factors, one or more of which reasonably support the recommendation, showing, (i) mitigating circumstances that bear directly upon the manner in which the crime was committed, or (ii) where the defendant was not the sole participant in the crime, that the defendant's participation was relatively minor although not so minor as to constitute a defense to prosecution, or (iii) where the juvenile offender has no previous adjudications of having committed a designated felony act, as defined in subdivision eight of section 301.2 of the family court act, regardless of the age of the offender at the time of commission of the act, that the criminal act was not part of a pattern of criminal behavior and, in view of the history of the offender, is not likely to be repeated.

3. If the court is of the opinion, based upon the specific factors set forth in the district attorney's memorandum, that the interests of justice would best be served by removal of the action to the family court, the verdict shall be set aside and a plea of guilty of a crime or act for which the defendant is not criminally responsible may be entered pursuant to subdivision three or four of section 220.10 of this chapter. Upon accepting any such plea, the court must specify upon the record the portion or portions of the district attorney's statement the court is relying upon as the basis of its opinion and that it believes the interests of justice would best be served by removal of the proceeding to the family court. Such plea shall then be deemed to be a juvenile delinquency fact determination and the court upon entry thereof must direct that the action be removed to the family court in accordance with the provisions of article seven hundred twenty-five of this chapter.

§ 330.30. Motion to set aside verdict; grounds for

At any time after rendition of a verdict of guilty and before sentence, the court may, upon motion of the defendant, set aside or modify the verdict or any part thereof upon the following grounds:

1. Any ground appearing in the record which, if raised upon an appeal from a prospective judgment of conviction, would require a reversal or modification of the judgment as a matter of law by an appellate court.

2. That during the trial there occurred, out of the presence of the court, improper conduct by a juror, or improper conduct by another person in relation to a juror, which may have affected a substantial right of the defendant and which was not known to the defendant prior to the rendition of the verdict; or

3. That new evidence has been discovered since the trial which could not have been produced by the defendant at the trial even with due diligence on his part and which is of such character as to create a probability that had such evidence been received at the trial the verdict would have been more favorable to the defendant.

§ 330.40. Motion to set aside verdict; procedure

1. A motion to set aside a verdict based upon a ground specified in subdivision one of section 330.30 need not be in writing, but the people must be given reasonable notice thereof and an opportunity to appear in opposition thereto.

2. A motion to set aside a verdict based upon a ground specified in subdivisions two and three of section 330.30 must be made and determined as follows:

(a) The motion must be in writing and upon reasonable notice to the people. The moving papers must contain sworn allegations, whether by the defendant or by another person or persons, of the occurrence or existence of all facts essential to support the motion. Such sworn allegations may be based upon personal knowledge of the affiant or upon information and belief, provided that in the latter event the affiant must state the sources of such information and the grounds of such belief;

(b) The people may file with the court, and in such case must serve a copy thereof upon the defendant or his counsel, an answer denying or admitting any or all of the allegations of the moving papers;

(c) After all papers of both parties have been filed, the court must consider the same and, if the motion is determinable pursuant to paragraphs (d) or (e), must or may, as therein provided, determine the motion without holding a hearing to resolve questions of fact;

(d) The court must grant the motion if:

(i) The moving papers allege a ground constituting legal basis for the motion; and

(ii) Such papers contain sworn allegations of all facts essential to support such ground; and

(iii) All the essential facts are conceded by the people to be true.

(e) The court may deny the motion if:

(i) The moving papers do not allege any ground constituting legal basis for the motion; or

(ii) The moving papers do not contain sworn allegations of all facts essential to support the motion.

(f) If the court does not determine the motion pursuant to paragraphs (d) or (e), it must conduct a hearing and make findings of fact essential to the determination thereof;

(g) Upon such a hearing, the defendant has the burden of proving by a preponderance of the evidence every fact essential to support the motion.

§ 330.50. Motion to set aside verdict; order granting motion

1. Upon setting aside or modifying a verdict or a part thereof upon a ground specified in subdivision one of section 330.30, the court must take the same action as the appropriate appellate court would be required to take upon reversing or modifying a judgment upon the particular ground in issue.

2. Upon setting aside a verdict upon a ground specified in subdivision two of section 330.30, the court must order a new trial.

3. Upon setting aside a verdict upon a ground specified in subdivision three of section 330.30, the court must, except as otherwise provided in this subdivision, order a new trial. If a verdict is set aside upon the ground that had the newly discovered evidence in question been received at the trial the verdict probably would have been more favorable

to the defendant in that the conviction probably would have been for a lesser offense than the one contained in the verdict, the court may either (a) set aside such verdict or (b) with the consent of the people modify such verdict by reducing it to one of conviction of such lesser offense.

4. Upon a new trial resulting from an order setting aside a verdict, the indictment is deemed to contain all the counts and to charge all the offenses which it contained and charged at the time the previous trial was commenced, regardless of whether any count was dismissed by the court in the course of such trial, except those upon or of which the defendant was acquitted or is deemed to have been acquitted.

Title K Prosecution of Informations in Local Criminal Courts—Plea to Sentence

Article 340 Pre-Trial Proceedings

§ 340.10. Definition of terms

The following definitions are applicable to this title:

1. "Information," in addition to its meaning as defined in subdivision one of section 100.10, includes (a) a simplified information and (b) a prosecutor's information and (c) a misdemeanor complaint upon which the defendant, by a waiver executed pursuant to subdivision three of section 170.65, has consented to be prosecuted.

2. "Single judge trial" means a trial in a local criminal court conducted by one judge sitting without a jury.

3. "Jury trial" means a trial in a local criminal court conducted by one judge sitting with a jury.

§ 340.20. The plea

1. Except as provided in subdivisions two and three, the provisions of article two hundred twenty, governing the kinds of pleas to indictments which may be entered and related matters, are, to the extent that they can be so applied, applicable to pleas to informations, and changes of pleas thereto, in local criminal courts.

2. A plea to an information, other than one against a corporation, must be entered in the following manner:

(a) Subject to the provisions of paragraph (b), a plea to an information must be entered orally by the defendant in person unless the court permits entry thereof by counsel upon the filing by him of a written and subscribed statement by the defendant declaring that he waives his right to plead to the information in person and authorizing his attorney to enter a plea on his behalf as set forth in the authorization.

(b) If the only offense or offenses charged are traffic infractions, the procedure provided in sections eighteen hundred five, eighteen hundred six and eighteen hundred seven of the vehicle and traffic law, relating to pleas in such cases, is, when appropriate, applicable and controlling.

3. A plea to an information against a corporation must be entered by counsel.

4. When a sentence is agreed upon by the prosecutor and a defendant as a predicate to entry of a plea of guilty, the court or the prosecutor must orally on the record, or in writing filed with the court, state the sentence agreed upon as a condition of such plea.

§ 340.30. Pre-trial discovery and notices of defenses

The provisions of article two hundred forty, concerning pre-trial discovery by a defendant under indictment in a superior court, and article two hundred fifty, concerning pre-trial notice to the people by a defendant under indictment in a superior court who intends to advance a trial defense of mental disease or defect or of alibi, apply to a prosecution of an information in a local criminal court.

§ 340.40. Modes of trial

1. Except as otherwise provided in this section, a trial of an information in a local criminal court must be a single judge trial.

2. In any local criminal court a defendant who has entered a plea of not guilty to an information which charges a misdemeanor must be accorded a jury trial, conducted pursuant to article three hundred sixty, except that in the New York city criminal court the trial of an information which charges a misdemeanor for which the authorized term of imprisonment is not more than six months must be a single judge trial. The defendant may at any time before trial waive a jury trial in the manner prescribed in subdivision two of section 320.10, and consent to a single judge trial.

3. A defendant entitled to a jury trial pursuant to subdivision two, shall be so entitled even though the information also charges an offense for which he is otherwise not entitled to a jury trial. In such case, the defendant is not entitled both to a jury trial and a separate single judge trial and the court may not order separate trials.

4. [Renumbered]

5, 6. [Deleted]

7. Notwithstanding any other provision of law, in any local criminal court the trial of a person who is an eligible youth within the meaning of the youthful offender procedure set forth in article seven hundred twenty and who has not prior to commencement of the trial been convicted of a crime or adjudicated a youthful offender must be a single judge trial.

§ 340.50. Defendant's presence at trial

1. Except as provided in subdivision two or three, a defendant must be personally present during the trial.

2. On motion of a defendant represented by counsel, the court may, in the absence of an objection by the people, issue an order dispensing with the requirement that the defendant be personally present at trial. Such an order may be made only upon the filing of a written and subscribed statement by the defendant declaring that he waives his right to be personally present at the trial and authorizing his attorney to conduct his defense.

3. A defendant who conducts himself in so disorderly and disruptive a manner that his trial cannot be carried on with him in the courtroom may be removed from the courtroom if, after he has been warned by the court that he will be removed if he continues such conduct, he continues to engage in such conduct.

Article 350 Non-Jury Trials

§ 350.10. Conduct of single judge trial

1. A single judge trial of an information in a local criminal court must be conducted pursuant to this section.

2. The court, in addition to determining all questions of law, is the exclusive trier of all issues of fact and must render a verdict.

3. The order of the trial must be as follows:

(a) The court may in its discretion permit the parties to deliver opening addresses. If the court grants such permission to one party, it must grant it to the other also. If both parties deliver opening addresses, the people's address must be delivered first.

(b) The order in which evidence must or may be offered by the respective parties is the same as that applicable to a jury trial of an indictment as prescribed in subdivisions five, six and seven of section 260.30.

(c) The court may in its discretion permit the parties to deliver summations. If the court grants such permission to one party, it must grant permission to the other also. If both parties deliver summations, the defendant's summation must be delivered first.

(d) The court must then consider the case and render a verdict.

4. The provisions governing motion practice and general procedure with respect to a jury trial of an indictment are, wherever appropriate, applicable to a non-jury trial of an information.

5. If the information contains more than one count, the court must render a verdict upon each count not previously dismissed or must otherwise state upon the record its disposition of each such count. A verdict which does not so dispose of each count constitutes a verdict of not guilty with respect to each undisposed of count.

6. In rendering a verdict of guilty upon a count charging a misdemeanor, the court may find the defendant guilty of such misdemeanor if it is established by legally sufficient trial evidence, or guilty of any lesser included offense which is established by legally sufficient trial evidence.

§ 350.20. Trial by judicial hearing officer

1. Notwithstanding any provision of section 350.10 of this article, in any case where a single judge trial of an information in a local criminal court is authorized or required, the court may, upon agreement of the parties, assign a judicial hearing officer to conduct the trial. Where such assignment is made, the judicial hearing officer shall entertain the case in the same manner as a court and shall:

(a) determine all questions of law;

(b) act as the exclusive trier of all issues of fact; and

(c) render a verdict.

2. In the discharge of this responsibility, the judicial hearing officer shall have the same powers as a judge of the court in which the proceeding is pending. The rules of evidence shall be applicable at a trial conducted by a judicial hearing officer.

3. Any action taken by a judicial hearing officer in the conduct of a trial shall be deemed the action of the court in which the proceeding is pending.

4. This section shall not apply where the single judge trial is of an information at least one count of which charges a class A misdemeanor.

5. Notwithstanding the provisions of subdivision one of this section, for all proceedings before the district court of Nassau county the administrative judge of Nassau county may, and for all proceedings before the district court of Suffolk county, the administrative judge of Suffolk county may, without the consent of the parties, assign matters involving traffic and parking infractions except those described in paragraphs (a), (b), (c), (d), (e) and (f) of subdivision two of section three hundred seventy-one of the general municipal law to a judicial hearing officer in accordance with the provisions

of section sixteen hundred ninety of the vehicle and traffic law and for all proceedings before the Buffalo city court the administrative judge of the eighth judicial district may, without the consent of the parties, assign matters involving traffic infractions except those described in paragraphs (a), (b), (c), (d), (e), (f) and (g) of subdivision two-a of section three hundred seventy-one of the general municipal law to a judicial hearing officer in accordance with the provisions of section sixteen hundred ninety of the vehicle and traffic law and for all proceedings before the Rochester city court the administrative judge of the seventh judicial district may, without the consent of the parties, assign matters involving traffic infractions except those described in paragraphs (a), (b), (c), (d), (e), (f) and (g) of subdivision two-b of section three hundred seventy-one of the general municipal law to a judicial hearing officer in accordance with the provisions of section sixteen hundred ninety of the vehicle and traffic law.

Article 360 Jury Trial

§ 360.05. Jury trial; order of trial

The provisions of section 260.30, governing the order of proceedings of a jury trial of an indictment in a superior court, are applicable to a jury trial of an information in a local criminal court.

§ 360.10. Trial jury; formation in general

1. A trial jury consists of six jurors, but "alternate jurors" may be selected and sworn pursuant to section 360.35.

2. The panel from which the jury is drawn is formed and selected as prescribed in the uniform district court act, uniform city court act, and uniform justice court act. In the New York city criminal court the panel from which the jury is drawn is formed and selected in the same manner as is prescribed for the formation and selection of a panel in the supreme court in counties within cities having a population of one million or more.

§ 360.15. Trial jury; challenge to the panel

1. A challenge to the panel is an objection made to the entire panel of prospective trial jurors returned for the trial of the action and may be taken to such panel or to any additional panel that may be ordered by the court. Such a challenge may be made only by the defendant and only on the ground that there has been such a departure from the requirements of the appropriate law in the drawing or return of the panel as to result in substantial prejudice to the defendant.

2. A challenge to the panel must be made before the selection of the jury commences, and, if it is not, such challenge is deemed to have been waived. Such challenge must be made in writing setting forth the facts constituting the ground of challenge. If such facts are denied by the people, witnesses may be called and examined by either party. All issues of fact and questions of law arising on the challenge must be tried and determined by the court. If a challenge to the panel is allowed, the court must discharge that panel and order the return of another panel of prospective trial jurors.

§ 360.20. Trial jury; examination of prospective jurors; challenges generally

If no challenge to the panel is made as prescribed by section 360.15, or if such challenge is made and disallowed, the court must direct that the names of not less than six members of the panel be drawn and called. Such persons must take their places in the jury box and must be immediately sworn to answer truthfully questions asked them relative to their qualifications to serve as jurors in the action. The procedural rules prescribed in section 270.15 with respect to the examination of the prospective jurors and to challenges are also applicable to the selection of a trial jury in a local criminal court.

§ 360.25. Trial jury; challenge for cause of an individual juror

1. A challenge for cause is an objection to a prospective member of the jury and may be made only on the ground that:

(a) He does not have the qualifications required by the judiciary law; or

(b) He has a state of mind that is likely to preclude him from rendering an impartial verdict based upon the evidence adduced at the trial; or

(c) He is related within the sixth degree by consanguinity or affinity to the defendant, or to the person allegedly injured by the crime charged, or to a prospective witness at the trial, or to counsel for the people or for the defendant; or that he is or was a party adverse to any such person in a civil action; or that he has complained against or been accused by any such person in a criminal action; or that he bears some other relationship to any such person of such nature that it is likely to preclude him from rendering an impartial verdict; or

(d) He is to be a witness at the trial; or where a prosecutor's information was filed at the direction of a grand jury, he was a witness before the grand jury or at the preliminary hearing; or

(e) He or she served on a trial jury in a prior civil or criminal action involving the same incident charged; or where a prosecutor's information was filed at the direction of a grand jury, he or she served on the grand jury which directed such filing.

2. All issues of fact or questions of law arising on the challenge must be tried and determined by the court. The provisions of subdivision two of section 270.20 with respect to challenges are also applicable to the selection of a trial jury in a local criminal court.

§ 360.30. Trial jury; peremptory challenge of an individaul [individual]* juror

1. A peremptory challenge is an objection to a prospective juror for which no reason need be assigned. Upon any peremptory challenge, the court must exclude the person challenged from service.

2. Each party must be allowed three peremptory challenges. When two or more defendants are tried jointly, such challenges are not multiplied by the number of defendants, but such defendants are to be treated as a single party. In any such case, a peremptory challenge by one or more defendants must be allowed if a majority of the defendants join in such challenge. Otherwise, it must be disallowed.

§ 360.35. Trial jury; alternate juror

1. Immediately after the last trial juror is sworn, the court may in its discretion direct the selection of either one or two additional jurors to be known as "alternate jurors." The alternate jurors must be drawn in the same manner, must have the same qualifications, must be subject to the same examination and challenges for cause and must take the same oath as the regular jurors. Whether or not a party has used its peremptory challenge in the selection of the trial jury, one peremptory challenge is authorized in the selection of the alternate jurors.

2. The provisions of section 270.35 with respect to alternate jurors are also applicable to a trial jury in a local criminal court.

§ 360.40. Trial jury; conduct of jury trial in general

A jury trial of an information must be conducted generally in the same manner as a jury trial of an indictment, and the rules governing preliminary instructions by the court, supervision of the jury, motion practice and other procedural matters involved in the conduct of a jury trial of an indictment are, where appropriate, applicable to the conduct of a jury trial of an information.

§ 360.45. Court's charge and instructions; in general

The general principles, prescribed in section 300.10, governing the court's charge to the jury and requests to charge upon a trial of an indictment, are applicable to a jury trial of an information in a local criminal court.

§ 360.50. Court's submission of information to jury; counts and offenses to be submitted

1. The term definitions contained in section 300.30 are applicable to this section, except that the word "information" is to be substituted for the word "indictment" wherever the latter appears in said section 300.30.

2. The court may submit to the jury only those counts of an information remaining therein at the time of its charge which are supported by legally sufficient trial evidence, and every count not so supported should be dismissed by a trial order of dismissal. If the trial evidence is not legally sufficient to establish a misdemeanor charged in a particular count which the court would otherwise be required to submit pursuant to this section, but is legally sufficient to establish a lesser included offense, the court may submit such lesser included offense and, upon the people's request, must do so. In submitting a count charging a misdemeanor established by legally sufficient trial evidence, the court in its discretion may, in addition to submitting such misdemeanor, submit in the alternative any lesser included offense if there is a reasonable view of the evidence which would support a finding that the defendant committed such lesser offense but did not commit the misdemeanor charged.

3. If the information contains but one count, the court must submit such count.

4. If a multiple count information contains consecutive counts only, the court must submit every count thereof.

5. In any case where the information may be more complex by reason of concurrent counts or inconsistent counts or other factors indicated in subdivisions three, four and five of section 300.40, relating to multiple count indictments, the court, in its submission of such information to the jury, should, so far as practicable, be guided by the provisions of the said subdivisions of said section 300.40.

6. Notwithstanding any other provision of this section, the court is not required to submit to the jury any particular count of a multiple count information if the people consent that it not be submitted.

7. Every count not submitted to the jury is deemed to have been dismissed by the court. Where the court, over objection of the people, refuses to submit a count which is consecutive as to every count actually submitted, such count is deemed to have been dismissed by a trial order of dismissal even though no such order was expressly made by the court.

§ 360.55. Deliberation and verdict of jury

The provisions of article three hundred ten, governing the deliberation and verdict of a jury upon a jury trial of an indictment in a superior court, are applicable to a jury trial of an information in a local criminal court.

Article 370 Proceedings from Verdict to Sentence

§ 370.10. Proceedings from verdict to sentence

The provisions of article three hundred thirty, governing the proceedings from verdict to sentence in an action prosecuted by indictment in a superior court, are applicable to a prosecution by information in a local criminal court; provided, however, where a judicial hearing officer has conducted the trial pursuant to section 350.20 of this chapter, all references to a court therein shall be deemed references to such judicial hearing officer.

§ 370.15. Procedure for determining whether certain misdemeanor crimes are serious offenses under the penal law

1. When a defendant has been charged with assault in the third degree, menacing in the third degree, menacing in the second degree, criminal obstruction of breathing or blood circulation, unlawful imprisonment in the second degree, coercion in the third degree, criminal tampering in the third degree, criminal contempt in the second degree, harassment in the first degree, aggravated harassment in the second degree, criminal trespass in the third degree, criminal trespass in the second degree, arson in the fifth degree, or attempt to commit any of the above-listed offenses, the people may, at arraignment or no later than forty-five days after arraignment, serve on the defendant and file with the court a notice alleging that the defendant and the person alleged to be the victim of such crime were members of the same family or household as defined in subdivision one of section 530.11 of this chapter.

2. Such notice shall include the name of the person alleged to be the victim of such crime and shall specify the nature of the alleged relationship as set forth in subdivision one of section 530.11 of this chapter. Upon conviction of such offense, the court shall advise the defendant that he or she is entitled to a hearing solely on the allegation contained in the notice and, if necessary, an adjournment of the sentencing proceeding in order to prepare for such hearing, and that if such allegation is sustained, that determination and conviction will be reported to the division of criminal justice services.

3. After having been advised by the court as provided in subdivision two of this section, the defendant may stipulate or admit, orally on the record or in writing, that he or she is related or situated to the victim of such crime in the manner described in subdivision one of this section. In such case, such relationship shall be deemed established. If the defendant denies that he or she is related or situated to the victim of the crime as alleged in the notice served by the people, or stands mute with respect to such allegation, then the people shall bear the burden to prove beyond a reasonable doubt that the defendant is related or situated to the victim in the manner alleged in the notice. The court may consider reliable hearsay evidence submitted by either party provided that it is relevant to the determination of the allegation. Facts previously proven at trial or elicited at the time of entry of a plea of guilty shall be deemed established beyond a reasonable doubt and shall not be relitigated. At the conclusion of the hearing, or upon

such a stipulation or admission, as applicable, the court shall make a specific written determination with respect to such allegation.

§ 370.25. Procedure for the surrender of firearms, rifles and shotguns upon judgment of conviction for a felony or a serious offense.

1. Upon judgment of conviction for a felony or a serious offense, the court shall inquire of the defendant as to the existence of all firearms, rifles and shotguns he or she owns or possesses. The court shall order the immediate surrender, pursuant to subparagraph (f) of paragraph one of subdivision a of section 265.20 of the penal law and subdivision six of section 400.05 of the penal law, of any or all firearms, rifles and shotguns owned or possessed by the defendant.

2. The court ordering the surrender of any firearms, rifles or shotguns as provided in this section shall immediately notify the duly constituted police authorities of the locality of such action and the division of state police at its office in the city of Albany. The court shall direct the authority receiving such surrendered firearms, rifles and shotguns to immediately notify the court of such surrender.

3. The disposition of any firearms, rifles or shotguns surrendered pursuant to this section shall be in accordance with the provisions of subdivision six of section 400.05 of the penal law.

4. The provisions of this section shall not be deemed to limit, restrict or otherwise impair the authority of the court to order and direct the surrender of any or all firearms, rifles and shotguns owned or possessed by a defendant pursuant to any other provision of law.

Title L Sentence

Article 380 Sentencing in General

§ 380.10. Applicability

1. In general. The procedure prescribed by this title applies to sentencing for every offense, whether defined within or outside of the penal law; provided, however, where a judicial hearing officer has conducted the trial pursuant to section 350.20 of this chapter, all references to a court herein shall be deemed references to such judicial hearing officer.

2. Exception. Whenever a different or inconsistent procedure is provided by any other law in relation to sentencing for a non-criminal offense defined therein, such different or inconsistent procedure applies thereto.

§ 380.20. Sentence required

The court must pronounce sentence in every case where a conviction is entered. If an accusatory instrument contains multiple counts and a conviction is entered on more than one count the court must pronounce sentence on each count.

§ 380.30. Time for pronouncing sentence

1. In general. Sentence must be pronounced without unreasonable delay.

2. Court to fix time. Upon entering a conviction the court must:

(a) Fix a date for pronouncing sentence; or

(b) Fix a date for one of the pre-sentence proceedings specified in article four hundred; or

(c) Pronounce sentence on the date the conviction is entered in accordance with the provisions of subdivision three.

2. [Expired March 31, 1994 (see 1992 note below)] Court to fix time. Upon entering a conviction the court must:

(a) Fix a date for pronouncing sentence; or

(b) Fix a date for one of the pre-sentence proceedings specified in article four hundred; or

(c) Issue an order deferring sentencing in accordance with the provisions of subdivision three of this section; or

(d) Pronounce sentence on the date the conviction is entered in accordance with the provisions of subdivision three.

3. Sentence on date of conviction. The court may sentence the defendant at the time the conviction is entered if:

(a) A pre-sentence report or a fingerprint report is not required; or

(b) Where any such report is required, the report has been received.

Provided, however, that the court may not pronounce sentence at such time without inquiring as to whether an adjournment is desired by the defendant. Where an adjournment is requested, the defendant must state the purpose thereof and the court may, in its discretion, allow a reasonable time.

3. [Expired March 31, 1994 (see 1992 note below)] Deferral of sentencing. The court may defer sentencing of any offender convicted of a class C, D, or E felony offense under articles two hundred twenty and two hundred twenty-one of the penal law or any class D or E felony offense under articles one hundred fifteen, one hundred forty, one hundred forty-five, one hundred fifty-five, one hundred sixty-five, one hundred seventy and one hundred ninety of the penal law, to a specified date no later than twelve months from the entering of a conviction if:

(a) The defendant stands convicted of his or her first felony offense; and

(b) Pursuant to a plea agreement or the recommendation contained in the pre-sentence report the judge is inclined to impose an indeterminate term of imprisonment; and

(c) The court believes that prompt institutional confinement is not necessary to preserve the safety and security of society, that the individual may benefit from the rehabilitative opportunities presented by the deferral of sentencing, that absent such a rehabilitative opportunity there is a likelihood that the court would impose an indeterminate sentence of imprisonment, and that upon satisfactory completion of the period of deferral the court would be more likely to impose a sentence other than an indeterminate sentence of imprisonment under article seventy of the penal law.

In conjunction with a deferral of sentencing the court may require that the defendant observe specified conditions of conduct and participate in such rehabilitative programs as the court deems appropriate. Upon application of the people made at any time during the period of sentence deferral, or where the court believes that the defendant may have violated the terms or conditions of the deferral order, and the court determines that such a violation occurred, the court may terminate the deferral order and set a date for sentencing.

Nothing contained in this subdivision shall limit the sentencing options which were available to the court prior to the issuance of an order pursuant to paragraph (c) of subdivision two of this section.

4. Time for pre-sentence proceedings. The court may conduct one or more of the pre-sentence proceedings specified in article four hundred at any time before sentence is pronounced. Notice of any such proceeding issued after the date for pronouncing sentence has been fixed automatically adjourns the date for pronouncing sentence. In such case the court must fix a date for pronouncing sentence at the conclusion of such proceeding.

§ 380.40. Defendant's presence at sentencing

1. In general. The defendant must be personally present at the time sentence is pronounced.

2. Exception. Where sentence is to be pronounced for a misdemeanor or for a petty offense, the court may, on motion of the defendant, dispense with the requirement that the defendant be personally present. Any such motion must be accompanied by a waiver, signed and acknowledged by the defendant, reciting the maximum sentence that may be imposed for the offense and stating that the defendant waives the right to be personally present at the time sentence is pronounced.

3. Corporations. Sentence may be pronounced against a corporation in the absence of counsel if counsel fails to appear on the date of sentence after reasonable notice thereof.

§ 380.50. Statements at time of sentence

1. At the time of pronouncing sentence, the court must accord the prosecutor an opportunity to make a statement with respect to any matter relevant to the question of sentence. The court must then accord counsel for the defendant an opportunity to speak on behalf of the defendant. The defendant also has the right to make a statement personally in his or her own behalf, and before pronouncing sentence the court must ask the defendant whether he or she wishes to make such a statement.

2.

(a) For purposes of this section "victim" shall mean:

(1) the victim as indicated in the accusatory instrument; or

(2) if such victim is unable or unwilling to express himself or herself before the court or a person so mentally or physically disabled as to make it impracticable to appear in court in person or the victim is deceased, a member of the family of such victim, or the legal guardian or representative of the legal guardian of the victim where such guardian or representative has personal knowledge of and a relationship with the victim, unless the court finds that it would be inappropriate for such person to make a statement on behalf of the victim.

(b) If the defendant is being sentenced for a felony the court, if requested at least ten days prior to the sentencing date, shall accord the victim the right to make a statement with regard to any matter relevant to the question of sentence. The court shall notify the defendant no less than seven days prior to sentencing of the victim's intent to make a statement at sentencing. If the defendant does not receive timely notice pursuant to this subdivision, the defendant may request a reasonable adjournment.

(c) Any statement by the victim must precede any statement by counsel to the defendant or the defendant made pursuant to subdivision one of this section. The defendant shall have the right to rebut any statement made by the victim.

(d) Where the people and the defendant have agreed to a disposition which includes a sentence acceptable to the court, and the court intends to impose such sentence, any rebuttal by the defendant shall be limited to an oral presentation made at the time of sentencing.

(e) Where (1) the defendant has been found guilty after trial or there is no agreement between the people and the defendant as to a proposed sentence or the court, after the statement by the victim, chooses not to impose the proposed sentence agreed to by the parties; (2) the statement by the victim includes allegations about the crime that were not fully explored during the proceedings or that materially vary from or contradict the evidence at trial; and (3) the court determines that the allegations are relevant to the issue of sentencing, then the court shall afford the defendant the following rights:

(A) a reasonable adjournment of the sentencing to allow the defendant to present information to rebut the allegations by the victim; and

(B) allow the defendant to present written questions to the court that the defendant desires the court to put to the victim. The court may, in its discretion, decline to put any or all of the questions to the victim. Where the court declines to put any or all of the questions to the victim it shall state its reasons therefor on the record.

(f) If the victim does not appear to make a statement at the time of sentencing, the right to make a statement is waived. The failure of the victim to make a statement shall not be cause for delaying the proceedings against the defendant nor shall it affect the validity of a conviction, judgment or order.

3. The court may, either before or after receiving such statements, summarize the factors it considers relevant for the purpose of sentence and afford an opportunity to the defendant or his or her counsel to comment thereon.

4. Regardless of whether the victim requests to make a statement with regard to the defendant's sentence, where the defendant is committed to the custody of the department of corrections and community supervision upon a sentence of imprisonment for conviction of a violent felony offense as defined in section 70.02 of the penal law or a felony defined in article one hundred twenty-five of such law, or a sex offense as defined in subdivision (p) of section 10.03 of the mental hygiene law, within sixty days of the imposition of sentence the prosecutor shall provide the victim with a form, prepared and distributed by the commissioner of the department of corrections and community supervision, on which the victim may indicate a demand to be informed of the escape, absconding, discharge, parole, conditional release, release to post-release supervision, transfer to the custody of the office of mental health pursuant to article ten of the mental hygiene law, or release from confinement under article ten of the mental hygiene law of the person so imprisoned. If the victim submits a completed form to the prosecutor, it shall be the duty of the prosecutor to mail promptly such form to the department of corrections and community supervision.

5. Following the receipt of such form from the prosecutor, it shall be the duty of the department of corrections and community supervision or, where the person is

committed to the custody of the office of mental health, at the time such person is discharged, paroled, conditionally released, released to post-release supervision, or released from confinement under article ten of the mental hygiene law, to notify the victim of such occurrence by certified mail directed to the address provided by the victim. In the event such person escapes or absconds from a facility under the jurisdiction of the department of corrections and community supervision, it shall be the duty of such department to notify immediately the victim of such occurrence at the most current address or telephone number provided by the victim in the most reasonable and expedient possible manner. In the event such escapee or absconder is subsequently taken into custody by the department of corrections and community supervision, it shall be the duty of such department to notify the victim of such occurrence by certified mail directed to the address provided by the victim within forty-eight hours of regaining such custody. In the case of a person who escapes or absconds from confinement under article ten of the mental hygiene law, the office of mental health shall notify the victim or victims in accordance with the procedures set forth in subdivision (g) of section 10.10 of the mental hygiene law. In no case shall the state be held liable for failure to provide any notice required by this subdivision.

6. Regardless of whether the victim requests to make a statement with regard to the defendant's sentence, where the defendant is sentenced for a violent felony offense as defined in section 70.02 of the penal law or a felony defined in article one hundred twenty-five of such law or any of the following provisions of such law sections 130.25, 130.30, 130.40, 130.45, 255.25, 255.26, 255.27, article two hundred sixty-three, 135.10, 135.25, 230.05, 230.06, 230.11, 230.12, 230.13, subdivision two of section 230.30 or 230.32, the prosecutor shall, within sixty days of the imposition of sentence, provide the victim with a form, prepared and distributed by the commissioner of the division of criminal justice services, in consultation with the director of the office of victim services, on which the victim may indicate a demand to be informed of any petition to change the name of such defendant. Such forms shall be maintained by such prosecutor. Upon receipt of a notice of a petition to change the name of any such defendant, pursuant to subdivision two of section sixty-two of the civil rights law, the prosecutor shall promptly notify the victim at the most current address or telephone number provided by such victim in the most reasonable and expedient possible manner of the time and place such petition will be presented to the court.

§ 380.55. Application for poor person relief on appeal

Where counsel has been assigned to represent a defendant at trial on the ground that the defendant is financially unable to retain counsel, the court may in its discretion at the time of sentencing entertain an application to grant the defendant poor person relief on appeal. As part of an application for such relief, assigned counsel must represent that the defendant continues to be eligible for assignment of counsel and that granting the application will expedite the appeal. If the court grants the application, it shall file a written order and shall provide a copy of the order to the appropriate appellate court. The denial of an application shall not preclude the defendant from making a de novo application for poor person relief to the appropriate appellate court.

§ 380.60. Authority for the execution of sentence

Except where a sentence of death is pronounced, a sentence and commitment or certificate of conviction showing the sentence pronounced by the court, or a certified copy thereof, constitutes the authority for execution of the sentence and serves as the order of commitment, and no other warrant, order of commitment or authority is necessary to justify or to require execution of the sentence.

§ 380.65. Sentence and commitment and order of protection to accompany defendant sentenced to imprisonment

A sentence and commitment or certificate of conviction, specifying the section, and to the extent applicable, the subdivision, paragraph and subparagraph of the penal law or other statute under which the defendant was convicted, or a certified copy thereof, and a copy of any order of protection or temporary order of protection issued against the defendant at the time of sentencing, must be delivered to the person in charge of the correctional facility or office of children and family services facility to which the defendant is committed at the time the defendant is delivered thereto. A sentence and commitment or certificate of conviction is not defective by reason of a failure to comply with the provisions of this section.

§ 380.70. Minutes of sentence

[Eff until Sept 1, 2019] In any case where a person receives an indeterminate or determinate sentence of imprisonment, a certified copy of the stenographic minutes of the sentencing proceeding must be delivered by the court to the person in charge of the institution to which the defendant has been delivered within thirty days from the date such sentence was imposed.

[Eff Sept 1, 2019] In any case where a person receives an indeterminate sentence of imprisonment or a reformatory or alternative local reformatory sentence of imprisonment, a certified copy of the stenographic minutes of the sentencing proceeding must be delivered by the court to the person in charge of the institution to which the defendant has been delivered within thirty days from the date such sentence was imposed.

§ 380.80. Reporting sentence to social services

Whenever a person receives a sentence of imprisonment, the court that has sentenced such person shall deliver the certificate of conviction and provide notification of the sentence imposed to the commissioner of social services who, in turn, shall deliver the certificate of conviction and provide notification of the sentence imposed to the appropriate local commissioner of social services.

§ 380.85. Reporting sentences to office of professional medical conduct; licensed physician, physician assistant, or specialist assistant

Whenever a person who is a licensed physician, physician assistant, or specialist assistant or a physician who is practicing under a limited permit or as a medical resident is sentenced for a crime, the court that has sentenced such person shall deliver a copy of the certificate of conviction and provide notification of the conviction and sentence to the office of professional medical conduct.

§ 380.90. Reporting sentences to schools

1. "Designated educational official" shall mean (a) an employee or representative of a school district who is designated by the school district or (b) an employee or representative of a charter school or private elementary or secondary school who is designated by such school to receive records pursuant to this section and to coordinate the student's participation in programs which may exist in the school district or community, including: non-violent conflict resolution programs, peer mediation programs and youth courts, extended day programs and other school violence prevention and intervention programs.

2. Whenever a person under the age of nineteen who is enrolled as a student in a public or private elementary or secondary school is sentenced for a crime, the court that has sentenced such person shall provide notification of the conviction and sentence to the designated educational official of the school in which such person is enrolled as a student. Such notification shall be used by the designated educational official only for purposes related to the execution of the student's educational plan, where applicable, successful school adjustment and reentry into the community. Such notification shall be kept separate and apart from such student's school records and shall be accessible only by the designated educational official. Such notification shall not be part of such student's permanent school record and shall not be appended to or included in any documentation regarding such student and shall be destroyed at such time as such student is no longer enrolled in the school district. At no time shall such notification be used for any purpose other than those specified in this subdivision.

§ 380.95. [There are two sections 380.95] Reporting convictions of certain school employees

Upon conviction of a teacher, as defined in subparagraph three of paragraph b of subdivision seven-a of section three hundred five of the education law, of a sex offense or sex offenses defined in subparagraph two of paragraph b of subdivision seven-a of section three hundred five of the education law, the district attorney or other prosecuting authority who obtained such conviction shall provide notice of such conviction to the commissioner of education identifying the sex offense or sex offenses of which the teacher has been convicted, the name and address of such offender and other identifying information prescribed by the commissioner of education, including the offender's date of birth and social security number, to the extent consistent with federal and state laws governing personal privacy and confidentiality of information. Such district attorney or other prosecuting authority shall include in such notice the name and business address of the offender's counsel of record in the criminal proceeding.

§ 380.95. [There are two sections 380.95] Reporting convictions of certain school employees

Upon conviction of a school administrator or supervisor, as defined in subparagraph three of paragraph b of subdivision seven-b of section three hundred five of the education law, of an offense defined in subparagraph two of paragraph b of subdivision seven-b of section three hundred five of the education law, the district attorney or other prosecuting authority who obtained such conviction shall provide notice of such conviction to the commissioner of education identifying the offense of which the school administrator or supervisor has been convicted, the name and address of such offender and other identifying information prescribed by the commissioner of education, including the offender's date of birth and social security number, to the extent consistent with federal and state laws governing personal privacy and confidentiality of information. Such district attorney or other prosecuting authority shall include in such notice the name and business address of the offender's counsel of record in the criminal proceeding.

§ 380.96. Obligation of sentencing court pursuant to article four hundred of the penal law
Upon judgment of conviction of any offense which would require the seizure of firearms, shotguns or rifles from an individual so convicted, and the revocation of any license or registration issued pursuant to article four hundred of the penal law, the judge pronouncing sentence shall demand surrender of any such license or registration and all firearms, shotguns and rifles. The failure to so demand surrender shall not effect the validity of any revocation pursuant to article four hundred of the penal law.

§ 380.97. Notification to division of criminal justice services of certain misdemeanor convictions
Upon judgment of conviction of assault in the third degree, menacing in the third degree, menacing in the second degree, criminal obstruction of breathing or blood circulation, unlawful imprisonment in the second degree, coercion in the third degree, criminal tampering in the third degree, criminal contempt in the second degree, harassment in the first degree, or aggravated harassment in the second degree, criminal trespass in the third degree, criminal trespass in the second degree, arson in the fifth degree, or attempt to commit any of the above-listed offenses, when the defendant and victim have been determined, pursuant to section 370.15 of this part, to be members of the same family or household as defined in subdivision one of section 530.11 of this chapter, the clerk of the court shall include notification and a copy of the written determination in a report of such conviction to the division of criminal justice services to enable the division to report such determination to the Federal Bureau of Investigation and assist the bureau in identifying persons prohibited from purchasing and possessing a firearm or other weapon due to conviction of an offense specified in paragraph c of subdivision seventeen of section 265.00 of the penal law.

Article 390 Pre-Sentence Reports

§ 390.10. Requirement of fingerprint report
In any case where the defendant is convicted of an offense specified in subdivision one of section 160.10, the court may not pronounce sentence until it has received a fingerprint report from the division of criminal justice services or a police department report with respect to the defendant's prior arrest record. For such purpose, the court may use the original fingerprint report obtained after the arrest or arraignment of the defendant, or it may direct that a new report be prepared and transmitted to it.

§ 390.15. Requirement of HIV related testing in certain cases
1.
(a) In any case where the defendant is convicted of a felony offense enumerated in any section of article one hundred thirty of the penal law, or any subdivision of section 130.20 of such law, where an act of "sexual intercourse", "oral sexual conduct" or "anal sexual conduct," as those terms are defined in section 130.00 of the penal law, is required as an essential element for the commission thereof, the court must, upon a request of the victim, order that the defendant submit to human immunodeficiency (HIV)

related testing. The testing is to be conducted by a state, county, or local public health officer designated by the order. Test results, which shall not be disclosed to the court, shall be communicated to the defendant and the victim named in the order in accordance with the provisions of section twenty-seven hundred eighty-five-a of the public health law, but such results and disclosure need not be completed prior to the imposition of sentence.

(b) For the purposes of this section, the terms "defendant", "conviction" and "sentence" mean and include, respectively, an "eligible youth," a "youthful offender finding" and a "youthful offender sentence" as those terms are defined in section 720.10 of this chapter. The term "victim" means the person with whom the defendant engaged in an act of "sexual intercourse", "oral sexual conduct" or "anal sexual conduct", as those terms are defined in section 130.00 of the penal law, where such conduct with such victim was the basis for the defendant's conviction of an offense specified in paragraph (a) of this subdivision.

2. Any request made by the victim pursuant to this section must be in writing, filed with the court and provided by the court to the defendant or his or her counsel. The request must be filed with the court prior to or within ten days after entry of the defendant's conviction; provided that, for good cause shown, the court may permit such request to be filed at any time before sentence is imposed.

3. Any requests, related papers and orders made or filed pursuant to this section, together with any papers or proceedings related thereto, shall be sealed by the court and not made available for any purpose, except as may be necessary for the conduct of judicial proceedings directly related to the provisions of this section. All proceedings on such requests shall be held in camera.

4. The application for an order to compel a convicted person to undergo an HIV related test may be made by the victim but, if the victim is an infant or incompetent person, the application may also be made by a representative as defined in section twelve hundred one of the civil practice law and rules. The application must state that (a) the applicant was the victim of the offense enumerated in paragraph (a) of subdivision one of this section of which the defendant stands convicted; and (b) the applicant has been offered counseling by a public health officer and been advised of (i) the limitations on the information to be obtained through an HIV test on the proposed subject; (ii) current scientific assessments of the risk of transmission of HIV from the exposure he or she may have experienced, and (iii) the need for the applicant to undergo HIV related testing to definitively determine his or her HIV status.

5. The court shall conduct a hearing only if necessary to determine if the applicant is the victim of the offense of which the defendant was convicted. The court ordered test must be performed within fifteen days of the date on which the court ordered the test, provided, however, that whenever the defendant is not tested within the period prescribed by the court, the court must again order that the defendant undergo an HIV related test.

6.

(a) Test results shall be disclosed subject to the following limitations, which shall be specified in any order issued pursuant to this section:

(i) disclosure of confidential HIV related information shall be limited to that information which is necessary to fulfill the purpose for which the order is granted;

(ii) disclosure of confidential HIV related information shall be limited to the person making the application; redisclosure shall be permitted only to the victim, the victim's immediate family, guardian, physicians, attorneys, medical or mental health providers and to his or her past and future contacts to whom there was or is a reasonable risk of HIV transmission and shall not be permitted to any other person or the court.

(b) Unless inconsistent with this section, the court's order shall direct compliance with and conform to the provisions of article twenty-seven-F of the public health law. Such order shall include measures to protect against disclosure to others of the identity and HIV status of the applicant and of the person tested and may include such other measures as the court deems necessary to protect confidential information.

7. Any failure to comply with the provisions of this section or section twenty-seven hundred eighty-five-a of the public health law shall not impair or affect the validity of any sentence imposed by the court.

8. No information obtained as a result of a consent, hearing or court order for testing issued pursuant to this section nor any information derived therefrom may be used as evidence in any criminal or civil proceeding against the defendant which relates to events that were the basis for the defendant's conviction, provided however that nothing herein shall prevent prosecution of a witness testifying in any court hearing held pursuant to this section for perjury pursuant to article two hundred ten of the penal law.

§ 390.20. Requirement of pre-sentence report

1. Requirement for felonies. In any case where a person is convicted of a felony, the court must order a pre-sentence investigation of the defendant and it may not pronounce sentence until it has received a written report of such investigation.

2. Requirement for misdemeanors. Where a person is convicted of a misdemeanor a pre-sentence report is not required, but the court may not pronounce any of the following sentences unless it has ordered a pre-sentence investigation of the defendant and has received a written report thereof:

(a) A sentence of probation except where the provisions of subparagraph (ii) of paragraph (a) of subdivision four of this section apply;

(b) A sentence of imprisonment for a term in excess of one hundred eighty days;

(c) Consecutive sentences of imprisonment with terms aggregating more than ninety days.

3. Permissible in any case. For purposes of sentence, the court may, in its discretion, order a pre-sentence investigation and report in any case, irrespective of whether such investigation and report is required by subdivision one or two.

4. Waiver.

(a) Notwithstanding the provisions of subdivision one or two of this section, a pre-sentence investigation of the defendant and a written report thereon may be waived by the mutual consent of the parties and with consent of the judge, stated on the record or in writing, whenever:

(i) A sentence of imprisonment has been agreed upon by the parties and will be satisfied by the time served, or

(ii) A sentence of probation or conditional discharge has been agreed upon by the parties and will be imposed, or

(iii) A report has been prepared in the preceding twelve months, or

(iv) A sentence of probation is revoked.

[Eff until Sept 1, 2019] Provided, however, a pre-sentence investigation of the defendant and a written report thereon shall not be waived if an indeterminate or determinate sentence of imprisonment is to be imposed.

[Eff Sept 1, 2019] Provided, however, a pre-sentence investigation of the defendant and a written report thereon shall not be waived if an indeterminate sentence of imprisonment is to be imposed.

(b) Whenever a pre-sentence investigation and report has been waived pursuant to subparagraph (i), (ii) or (iii) of paragraph (a) of this subdivision and the court determines that such information would be relevant to the court disposition, a victim impact statement shall be provided in accordance with this section.

5. Negotiated sentence of imprisonment. In any city having a population of one million or more and notwithstanding the provisions of subdivision one or two of this section, a pre-sentence investigation and written report thereon shall not be required where a negotiated sentence of imprisonment for a term of three hundred sixty-five days or less has been mutually agreed upon by the parties with consent of the judge, as a result of a conviction or revocation of a sentence of probation.

§ 390.30. Scope of pre-sentence investigation and report

1. The investigation. The pre-sentence investigation consists of the gathering of information with respect to the circumstances attending the commission of the offense, the defendant's history of delinquency or criminality, and the defendant's social history, employment history, family situation, economic status, education, and personal habits. Such investigation may also include any other matter which the agency conducting the investigation deems relevant to the question of sentence, and must include any matter the court directs to be included.

2. Physical and mental examinations. Whenever information is available with respect to the defendant's physical and mental condition, the pre-sentence investigation must include the gathering of such information. In the case of a felony or a class A misdemeanor, or in any case where a person under the age of twenty-one is convicted of a crime, the court may order that the defendant undergo a thorough physical or mental examination in a designated facility and may further order that the defendant remain in such facility for such purpose for a period not exceeding thirty days.

3. The report and victim impact statement.

(a) The report of the pre-sentence investigation must contain an analysis of as much of the information gathered in the investigation as the agency that conducted the investigation deems relevant to the question of sentence. The report must also include any other imformation [information]* that the court directs to be included and the material required by paragraph (b) of this subdivision which shall be considered part of the report.

(b) The report shall also contain a victim impact statement, unless it appears that such information would be of no relevance to the recommendation or court disposition, which shall include an analysis of the victim's version of the offense, the extent of injury or economic loss and the actual out-of-pocket loss to the victim and the views of the victim relating to disposition including the amount of restitution and reparation sought by the victim after the victim has been informed of the right to seek restitution and reparation, subject to the availability of such information. In the case of a homicide or where the victim is unable to assist in the preparation of the victim impact statement, the information may be acquired from the victim's family. The victim impact statement shall be made available to the victim by the prosecutor pursuant to subdivision two of section 390.50 of this article. Nothing contained in this section shall be interpreted to require that a victim supply information for the preparation of this report.

4. Abbreviated investigation and short form report. In lieu of the procedure set forth in subdivisions one, two and three of this section, where the conviction is of a misdemeanor the scope of the pre-sentence investigation may be abbreviated and a short form report may be made. The use of abbreviated investigations and short form reports, the matters to be covered therein and the form of the reports shall be in accordance with the general rules regulating methods and procedures in the administration of probation as adopted from time to time by the commissioner of the division of criminal justice services pursuant to the provisions of article twelve of the executive law. No such rule, however, shall be construed so as to relieve the agency conducting the investigation of the duty of investigating and reporting upon:

(a) the extent of the injury or economic loss and the actual out-of-pocket loss to the victim including the amount of restitution and reparation sought by the victim, after the victim has been informed of the right to seek restitution and reparation, or

(b) any matter relevant to the question of sentence that the court directs to be included in particular cases.

5. [As amended by L 2010, ch 56, § 50 (Part A)] [Repealed]

5. [As amended by L 2010, ch 56, § 29 (Part A-1)] Information to be forwarded to the state office of probation and correctional alternatives. Investigating agencies under this article shall be responsible for the collection, and transmission to the state office of probation and correctional alternatives, of data on the number of victim impact statements prepared. Such information shall be transmitted annually to the office of victim services and included in the office's biennial report pursuant to subdivision twenty-one of section six hundred twenty-three of the executive law.

6. [As amended L 2009, ch 56, § 1 (Part O) and § 5 (Part AAA)] Interim probation supervision.

(a) In any case where the court determines that a defendant is eligible for a sentence of probation, the court, after consultation with the prosecutor and upon the consent of the defendant, may adjourn the sentencing to a specified date and order that the defendant be placed on interim probation supervision. In no event may the sentencing be adjourned for a period exceeding one year from the date the conviction is entered, except that upon good cause shown, the court may, upon the defendant's consent, extend the period for an additional one year where the defendant has agreed to and is still participating in a substance abuse treatment program in connection with a court designated a drug court by the chief administrator of the courts. When ordering that the defendant be placed on interim probation supervision, the court shall impose all of the conditions relating to supervision specified in subdivision three of section 65.10 of the penal law and the court may impose any or all of the conditions relating to conduct and rehabilitation specified in subdivisions two, four, five and five-a of section 65.10 of such law. The defendant must receive a written copy of any such conditions at the time he or she is placed on interim probation supervision. The defendant's record of compliance with such conditions, as well as any other relevant information, shall be included in the presentence report, or updated presentence report, prepared pursuant to this section, and the court must consider such record and information when pronouncing sentence. If a defendant satisfactorily completes a term of interim probation supervision, he or she shall receive credit for the time served under the period of interim probation supervision toward any probation sentence that is subsequently imposed in that case.

(b) In its discretion, the supervising probation department may utilize the provisions of sections 410.20, 410.30, 410.40, 410.50, 410.60 and 410.92 of this title, where applicable.

§ 390.40. Defendant's or prosecutor's pre-sentence memorandum

1. Either the defendant or prosecutor may, at any time prior to the pronouncement of sentence, file with the court a written memorandum setting forth any information he may deem pertinent to the question of sentence. Such memorandum may include information with respect to any of the matters described in section 390.30. The defendant may annex written statements by others in support of facts alleged in the memorandum.

2. The memorandum of the prosecutor shall be served on the defendant's attorney at least ten days prior to the date fixed for sentence.

3. The act of seeking health care for someone who is experiencing a drug or alcohol overdose or other life threatening medical emergency shall be considered by the court when presented as a mitigating factor in any criminal prosecution for a controlled substance, marihuana, drug paraphernalia, or alcohol related offense.

§ 390.50. Confidentiality of pre-sentence reports and memoranda

1. In general. Any pre-sentence report or memorandum submitted to the court pursuant to this article and any medical, psychiatric or social agency report or other information gathered for the court by a probation department, or submitted directly to the court, in connection with the question of sentence is confidential and may not be made available to any person or public or private agency except where specifically required or permitted by statute or upon specific authorization of the court. For purposes of this section, any report, memorandum or other information forwarded to a probation department within this state from a probation agency outside this state is governed by the same rules of confidentiality. Any person, public or private agency receiving such material must retain it under the same conditions of confidentiality as apply to the probation department that made it available.

2. Pre-sentence report; disclosure, victim access to impact statements; general principles.

(a) Not less than one court day prior to sentencing, unless such time requirement is waived by the parties, the pre-sentence report or memorandum shall be made available by the court for examination and for copying by the defendant's attorney, the defendant himself, if he has no attorney, and the prosecutor. In its discretion, the court may except from disclosure a part or parts of the report or memoranda which are not relevant to a proper sentence, or a diagnostic opinion which might seriously disrupt a program of rehabilitation, or sources of information which have been obtained on a promise of confidentiality, or any other portion thereof, disclosure of which would not be in the interest of justice. In all cases where a part or parts of the report or memoranda are not disclosed, the court shall state for the record that a part or parts of the report or memoranda have been excepted and the reasons for its action. The action of the court excepting information from disclosure shall be subject to appellate review. The pre-sentence report shall be made available by the court for examination and copying in connection with any appeal in the case, including an appeal under this subdivision. Upon written request, the court shall make a copy of the presentence report, other than a part or parts of the report redacted by the court pursuant to this paragraph, available to the defendant for use before the parole board for release consideration or an appeal of a parole board determination. In his or her written request to the court the defendant shall affirm that he or she anticipates an appearance before the parole board or intends to file an administrative appeal of a parole board determination. The court shall respond to the defendant's written request within twenty days from receipt of the defendant's written request.

(b) The victim impact statement prepared pursuant to subdivision three of section 390.30 of this article shall be made available by the prosecutor prior to sentencing to the victim or victim's family in accordance with his responsibilities under subdivision one of section 60.27 of the penal law and sections six hundred forty-one and six hundred forty-two of the executive law. The district attorney shall also give at least twenty-one days notice to the victim or victim's family of the date of sentencing and of the rights of the victim pursuant to subdivision two of section 380.50 of this chapter, including the victim or victim's family's obligation to inform the court of its intention, at least ten days prior to the sentencing date, to make a statement at sentencing. If the victim has not received timely notice pursuant to this paragraph, the court may proceed with sentencing if it determines that the victim and the defendant have received reasonable notice or may adjourn sentencing for no more than seven days in order to afford such reasonable notice. Failure to give notice shall not affect the validity of any sentence imposed.

3. Public agencies within this state. A probation department must make available a copy of its pre-sentence report and any medical, psychiatric or social agency report submitted to it in connection with its pre-sentence investigation or its supervision of a defendant, to any court, or to the probation department of any court, within this state that subsequently has jurisdiction over such defendant for the purpose of pronouncing or reviewing sentence and to any state agency to which the defendant is subsequently committed or certified or under whose care and custody or jurisdiction the defendant subsequently is placed upon the official request of such court or agency therefor. In any such case, the court or agency receiving such material must retain it under the same conditions of confidentiality as apply to the probation department that made it available, except that an agency with jurisdiction as that term is defined in subdivision (a) of section 10.03 of the mental hygiene law shall make such material available to the

commissioner of mental health, attorney general, case review panel, or psychiatric examiners described in article ten of the mental hygiene law when such persons or entities request such material in the exercise of their statutory functions, powers, and duties under article ten of the mental hygiene law.

4. Public agencies outside this state. Upon official request of any probation, parole or public institutional agency outside this state, a probation department may make any information in its files available to such agency. Any such release of information shall be conditioned upon the agreement of the receiving agency to retain it under the same conditions of confidentiality as apply to the probation department that made it available.

5. Division of criminal justice services. Nothing contained in this section may be construed to prevent the voluntary submission by a probation department of data in its files to the division of criminal justice services.

6. Professional licensing agencies. Probation departments shall provide a copy of presentence reports prepared in the case of individuals who are known to be licensed pursuant to title eight of the education law to the state department of health if the licensee is a physician, a specialist's assistant or a physician's assistant, and to the state education department with respect to all other such licensees. Such reports shall be accumulated and forwarded every three months, shall be in writing, may be submitted in a hard copy or electronically, and shall contain the following information:

(a) the name of the licensee and the profession in which licensure is held,

(b) the date of the conviction and the nature thereof,

(c) the index or other identifying file number.

In any such case, the state department receiving such material must retain it under the same conditions of confidentiality as apply to the probation department that made it available.

§ 390.60. Copy of reports to accompany defendant sentenced to imprisonment

1. Cases where copy of report is required. Whenever a person is sentenced to a term of imprisonment, a copy of any pre-sentence report prepared, a copy of any pre-sentence memorandum filed by the defendant and a copy of any medical, psychiatric or social agency report submitted to the court or to the probation department in connection with the question of sentence must be delivered to the person in charge of the correctional or division for youth facility to which the defendant is committed at the time the defendant is delivered thereto. When a person is committed to any hospital operated by the office of mental health or referred to any program established pursuant to section four hundred one of the correction law, from a correctional facility or division for youth facility, the person in charge of the correctional facility or division for youth facility shall ensure that a copy of any pre-sentence report concerning such person, a copy of any pre-sentence memorandum filed by such person, and a copy of any medical, psychiatric or social agency report submitted to the court or to the probation department in connection with the question of sentence is provided to such hospital or program.

2. Effect of failure to deliver required report. A commitment is not void by reason of failure to comply with the provisions of subdivision one, but the person in charge of the correctional facility to which the defendant has been delivered in execution of the

sentence is authorized to refuse to accept custody of such person until the required report is delivered.

Article 400 Pre-Sentence Proceedings

§ 400.10. Pre-sentence conference

1. Authorization and purpose. Before pronouncing sentence, the court, in its discretion, may hold one or more pre-sentence conferences in open court or in chambers in order to (a) resolve any discrepancies between the pre-sentence report, or other information the court has received, and the defendant's or prosecutor's pre-sentence memorandum submitted pursuant to section 390.40, or (b) assist the court in its consideration of any matter relevant to the sentence to be pronounced.

2. Attendance. Such conference may be held with the prosecutor and defense counsel in the absence of the defendant, or the court may direct that the defendant attend. The court may also direct that any person who has furnished or who can furnish information to the court concerning sentence attend. Reasonable notice of the conference must be given to the prosecutor and the defense counsel, who must be afforded an opportunity to participate therein.

3. Procedure at conference. The court may advise the persons present at the conference of the factual contents of any report or memorandum it has received and afford any of the participants an opportunity to controvert or to comment upon any fact. The court may also conduct a summary hearing at the conference on any matter relevant to sentence and may take testimony under oath. In the discretion of the court, all or any part of the proceedings at the conference may be recorded by a court stenographer and the transcript made part of the pre-sentence report.

4. Pre-sentence conditions. After conviction and prior to sentencing the court may adjourn sentencing to a subsequent date and order the defendant to comply with any of the conditions contained in paragraphs (a) through (f) and paragraph (1) of subdivision two of section 65.10 of the penal law. In imposing sentence, the court shall take into consideration the defendant's record of compliance with pre-sentence conditions ordered by the court.

§ 400.14. [Expired]

§ 400.15. Procedure for determining whether defendant is a second violent felony offender

1. Applicability. The provisions of this section govern the procedure that must be followed in any case where it appears that a defendant who stands convicted of a violent felony offense as defined in subdivision one of section 70.02 of the penal law has previously been subjected to a predicate violent felony conviction as defined in paragraph (b) of subdivision one of section 70.04 of the penal law and may be a second violent felony offender.

2. Statement to be filed. When information available to the court or to the people prior to sentencing for a violent felony offense indicates that the defendant may have previously been subjected to a predicate violent felony conviction, a statement must be filed by the prosecutor before sentence is imposed setting forth the date and place of each alleged predicate violent felony conviction. Where the provisions of subparagraph (v) of paragraph (c) of subdivision one of section 70.04 of the penal law apply, such statement also shall set forth the date of commencement and the date of termination as

well as the place of imprisonment for each period of incarceration to be used for tolling of the ten year limitation set forth in subparagraph (iv) of paragraph (b) of such subdivision.

3. Preliminary examination. The defendant must be given a copy of such statement and the court must ask him whether he wishes to controvert any allegation made therein. If the defendant wishes to controvert any allegation in the statement, he must specify the particular allegation or allegations he wishes to controvert. Uncontroverted allegations in the statement shall be deemed to have been admitted by the defendant.

4. Cases where further hearing is not required. Where the uncontroverted allegations in the statement are sufficient to support a finding that the defendant has been subjected to a predicate violent felony conviction the court must enter such finding and when imposing sentence must sentence the defendant in accordance with the provisions of section 70.04 of the penal law.

5. Cases where further hearing is required. Where the defendant controverts an allegation in the statement and the uncontroverted allegations in such statement are not sufficient to support a finding that the defendant has been subjected to a predicate violent felony conviction the court must proceed to hold a hearing.

6. Time for hearing. In any case where a copy of the statement was not received by the defendant at least two days prior to the preliminary examination, the court must upon request of the defendant grant an adjournment of at least two days before proceeding with the hearing.

7. Manner of conducting hearing.

(a) A hearing pursuant to this section must be before the court without jury. The burden of proof is upon the people and a finding that the defendant has been subjected to a predicate violent felony conviction must be based upon proof beyond a reasonable doubt by evidence admissible under the rules applicable to a trial of the issue of guilt.

(b) A previous conviction in this or any other jurisdiction which was obtained in violation of the rights of the defendant under the applicable provisions of the constitution of the United States must not be counted in determining whether the defendant has been subjected to a predicate violent felony conviction. The defendant may, at any time during the course of the hearing hereunder controvert an allegation with respect to such conviction in the statement on the grounds that the conviction was unconstitutionally obtained. Failure to challenge the previous conviction in the manner provided herein constitutes a waiver on the part of the defendant of any allegation of unconstitutionality unless good cause be shown for such failure to make timely challenge.

(c) At the conclusion of the hearing the court must make a finding as to whether or not the defendant has been subjected to a predicate violent felony conviction.

8. Subsequent use of predicate violent felony conviction finding. Where a finding has been entered pursuant to this section, such finding shall be binding upon that defendant in any future proceeding in which the issue may arise.

§ 400.16. Procedure for determining whether defendant is a persistent violent felony offender

1. Applicability. The provisions of this section govern the procedure that must be followed in any case where it appears that a defendant who stands convicted of a violent felony offense as defined in subdivision one of section 70.02 of the penal law

has previously been subjected to two or more predicate violent felony convictions as defined in paragraph (b) of subdivision one of section 70.04, and may be a persistent violent felony offender as defined in section 70.08 of the penal law.

2. Statement; preliminary examination; hearing; subsequent use of predicate violent felony conviction finding. The requirements set forth in subdivisions two, three, four, five, six, seven and eight of section 400.15 with respect to the statement to be filed, preliminary examination, hearing and subsequent use of a predicate violent felony conviction finding in the case of a second violent felony offender, shall also apply to a determination of whether a defendant has been subjected to two or more violent predicate felony convictions and is a persistent violent felony offender.

§ 400.19. Procedure for determining whether defendant is a second child sexual assault felony offender

1. Applicability. The provisions of this section govern the procedure that must be followed in any case where it appears that a defendant who stands convicted of a felony offense for a sexual assault upon a child as defined in section 70.07 of the penal law has previously been convicted of a predicate felony for a sexual assault upon a child.

2. Statement to be filed. When information available to the people prior to the trial of a felony offense for a sexual assault against a child indicates that the defendant may have previously been subjected to a predicate felony conviction for a sexual assault against a child, a statement may be filed by the prosecutor at any time before trial commences setting forth the date and place of each alleged predicate felony conviction for a sexual assault against a child and a statement whether the defendant was eighteen years of age or older at the time of the commission of the predicate felony. Where the provisions of subparagraph (v) of paragraph (b) of subdivision one of section 70.06 of the penal law apply, such statement also shall set forth the date of commencement and the date of termination as well as the place of imprisonment for each period of incarceration to be used for tolling of the ten year limitation set forth in subparagraph (iv) of paragraph (b) of such subdivision.

3. Preliminary examination. The defendant must be given a copy of such statement and the court must ask him whether he wishes to controvert any allegation made therein. If the defendant wishes to controvert any allegation in the statement, he must specify the particular allegation or allegations he wishes to controvert. Uncontroverted allegations in the statement shall be deemed to have been admitted by the defendant.

4. Cases where further hearing is not required. Where the uncontroverted allegations in the statement are sufficient to support a finding that the defendant has been subjected to a predicate felony conviction for a sexual assault upon a child and that the defendant was 18 years of age or older at the time of the commission of the predicate felony, the court must enter such finding and when imposing sentence must sentence the defendant in accordance with the provisions of section 70.07 of the penal law.

5. Cases where further hearing is required. Where the defendant controverts an allegation in the statement, the court must proceed to hold a hearing.

6. Manner of conducting hearing.

(a) A hearing pursuant to this section must be before the court without jury. The burden of proof is upon the people and a finding that the defendant has been subjected to a predicate felony conviction for a sexual assault against a child as defined in subdivision two of section 70.07 of the penal law and that the defendant was 18 years of age or older at the time of the commission of the predicate felony must be based upon proof beyond a reasonable doubt by evidence admissible under the rules applicable to a trial of the issue of guilt.

(b) Regardless of whether the age of the victim is an element of the alleged predicate felony offense, where the defendant controverts an allegation that the victim of an alleged sexual assault upon a child was less than fifteen years old, the people may prove that the child was less than fifteen years old by any evidence admissible under the rules applicable to a trial of the issue of guilt. For purposes of determining whether a child was less than fifteen years old, the people shall not be required to prove that the defendant knew the child was less than fifteen years old at the time of the alleged sexual assault.

(c) A previous conviction in this or any other jurisdiction which was obtained in violation of the rights of the defendant under the applicable provisions of the constitution of the United States must not be counted in determining whether the defendant has been subjected to a predicate felony conviction for a sexual assault upon a child. The defendant may, at any time during the course of the hearing hereunder, controvert an allegation with respect to such conviction in the statement on the grounds that the conviction was unconstitutionally obtained. Failure to challenge the previous conviction in the manner provided herein constitutes a waiver on the part of the defendant of any allegation of unconstitutionality unless good cause be shown for such failure to make timely challenge.

(d) At the conclusion of the hearing the court must make a finding as to whether or not the defendant has been subjected to a predicate felony conviction for a sexual assault against a child as defined in subdivision two of section 70.07 of the penal law and whether the defendant was 18 years of age or older at the time of the commission of the predicate felony.

7. Subsequent use of predicate felony conviction finding. Where a finding has been entered pursuant to this section, such finding shall be binding in any future proceeding in which the issue may arise.

§ 400.20. Procedure for determining whether defendant should be sentenced as a persistent felony offender

1. Applicability. The provisions of this section govern the procedure that must be followed in order to impose the persistent felony offender sentence authorized by subdivision two of section 70.10 of the penal law. Such sentence may not be imposed unless, based upon evidence in the record of a hearing held pursuant to this section, the court (a) has found that the defendant is a persistent felony offender as defined in subdivision one of section 70.10 of the penal law, and (b) is of the opinion that the history and character of the defendant and the nature and circumstances of his criminal conduct are such that extended incarceration and lifetime supervision of the defendant are warranted to best serve the public interest.

2. Authorization for hearing. When information available to the court prior to sentencing indicates that the defendant is a persistent felony offender, and when, in the opinion of

the court, the available information shows that a persistent felony offender sentence may be warranted, the court may order a hearing to determine (a) whether the defendant is in fact a persistent felony offender, and (b) if so, whether a persistent felony offender sentence should be imposed.

3. Order directing a hearing. An order directing a hearing to determine whether the defendant should be sentenced as a persistent felony offender must be filed with the clerk of the court and must specify a date for the hearing not less than twenty days from the date the order is filed. The court must annex to and file with the order a statement setting forth the following:

(a) The dates and places of the previous convictions which render the defendant a persistent felony offender as defined in subdivision one of section 70.10 of the penal law; and

(b) The factors in the defendant's background and prior criminal conduct which the court deems relevant for the purpose of sentencing the defendant as a persistent felony offender.

4. Notice of hearing. Upon receipt of the order and statement of the court, the clerk of the court must send a notice of hearing to the defendant, his counsel and the district attorney. Such notice must specify the time and place of the hearing and the fact that the purpose of the hearing is to determine whether or not the defendant should be sentenced as a persistent felony offender. Each notice required to be sent hereunder must be accompanied by a copy of the statement of the court.

5. Burden and standard of proof; evidence. Upon any hearing held pursuant to this section the burden of proof is upon the people. A finding that the defendant is a persistent felony offender, as defined in subdivision one of section 70.10 of the penal law, must be based upon proof beyond a reasonable doubt by evidence admissible under the rules applicable to the trial of the issue of guilt. Matters pertaining to the defendant's history and character and the nature and circumstances of his criminal conduct may be established by any relevant evidence, not legally privileged, regardless of admissibility under the exclusionary rules of evidence, and the standard of proof with respect to such matters shall be a preponderance of the evidence.

6. Constitutionality of prior convictions. A previous conviction in this or any other jurisdiction which was obtained in violation of the rights of the defendant under the applicable provisions of the Constitution of the United States may not be counted in determining whether the defendant is a persistent felony offender. The defendant may, at any time during the course of the hearing hereunder controvert an allegation with respect to such conviction in the statement of the court on the grounds that the conviction was unconstitutionally obtained. Failure to challenge the previous conviction in the manner provided herein constitutes a waiver on the part of the defendant of any allegation of unconstitutionality unless good cause be shown for such failure to make timely challenge.

7. Preliminary examination. When the defendant appears for the hearing the court must ask him whether he wishes to controvert any allegation made in the statement prepared by the court, and whether he wishes to present evidence on the issue of whether he is a persistent felony offender or on the question of his background and criminal conduct. If

the defendant wishes to controvert any allegation in the statement of the court, he must specify the particular allegation or allegations he wishes to controvert. If he wishes to present evidence in his own behalf, he must specify the nature of such evidence. Uncontroverted allegations in the statement of the court are deemed evidence in the record.

8. Cases where further hearing is not required. Where the uncontroverted allegations in the statement of the court are sufficient to support a finding that the defendant is a persistent felony offender and the court is satisfied that (a) the uncontroverted allegations with respect to the defendant's background and the nature of his prior criminal conduct warrant sentencing the defendant as a persistent felony offender, and (b) the defendant either has no relevant evidence to present or the facts which could be established through the evidence offered by the defendant would not affect the court's decision, the court may enter a finding that the defendant is a persistent felony offender and sentence him in accordance with the provisions of subdivision two of section 70.10 of the penal law.

9. Cases where further hearing is required. Where the defendant controverts an allegation in the statement of the court and the uncontroverted allegations in such statement are not sufficient to support a finding that the defendant is a persistent felony offender as defined in subdivision one of section 70.10 of the penal law, or where the uncontroverted allegations with respect to the defendant's history and the nature of his prior criminal conduct do not warrant sentencing him as a persistent felony offender, or where the defendant has offered to present evidence to establish facts that would affect the court's decision on the question of whether a persistent felony offender sentence is warranted, the court may fix a date for a further hearing. Such hearing shall be before the court without a jury and either party may introduce evidence with respect to the controverted allegations or any other matter relevant to the issue of whether or not the defendant should be sentenced as a persistent felony offender. At the conclusion of the hearing the court must make a finding as to whether or not the defendant is a persistent felony offender and, upon a finding that he is such, must then make such findings of fact as it deems relevant to the question of whether a persistent felony offender sentence is warranted. If the court both finds that the defendant is a persistent felony offender and is of the opinion that a persistent felony offender sentence is warranted, it may sentence the defendant in accordance with the provisions of subdivision two of section 70.10 of the penal law.

10. Termination of hearing. At any time during the pendency of a hearing pursuant to this section, the court may, in its discretion, terminate the hearing without making any finding. In such case, unless the court recommences the proceedings and makes the necessary findings, the defendant may not be sentenced as a persistent felony offender.

§ 400.21. Procedure for determining whether defendant is a second felony offender or a second felony drug offender

1. Applicability. The provisions of this section govern the procedure that must be followed in any case where it appears that a defendant who stands convicted of a felony has previously been convicted of a predicate felony and may be a second felony

offender as defined in section 70.06 of the penal law or a second felony drug offender as defined in either paragraph (b) of subdivision one of section 70.70 of the penal law, or paragraph (b) of subdivision one of section 70.71 of the penal law.

2. Statement to be filed. When information available to the court or to the people prior to sentencing for a felony indicates that the defendant may have previously been subjected to a predicate felony conviction, a statement must be filed by the prosecutor before sentence is imposed setting forth the date and place of each alleged predicate felony conviction and whether the predicate felony conviction was a violent felony as that term is defined in subdivision one of section 70.02 of the penal law, or in any other jurisdiction of an offense which includes all of the essential elements of any such felony for which a sentence to a term of imprisonment in excess of one year or death was authorized and is authorized in this state regardless of whether such sentence was imposed. Where the provisions of subparagraph (v) of paragraph (b) of subdivision one of section 70.06 of the penal law apply, such statement also shall set forth the date of commencement and the date of termination as well as the state or local incarcerating agency for each period of incarceration to be used for tolling of the ten year limitation set forth in subparagraph (iv) of paragraph (b) of such subdivision.

3. Preliminary examination. The defendant must be given a copy of such statement and the court must ask him or her whether he or she wishes to controvert any allegation made therein. If the defendant wishes to controvert any allegation in the statement, he must specify the particular allegation or allegations he wishes to controvert. Uncontroverted allegations in the statement shall be deemed to have been admitted by the defendant.

4. Cases where further hearing is not required. Where the uncontroverted allegations in the statement are sufficient to support a finding that the defendant has been subjected to a predicate felony conviction the court must enter such finding, including a finding that the predicate felony conviction was of a violent felony as that term is defined in subdivision one of section 70.02 of the penal law, or in any other jurisdiction of an offense which includes all of the essential elements of any such felony for which a sentence to a term of imprisonment in excess of one year or death was authorized and is authorized in this state regardless of whether such sentence was imposed, and when imposing sentence must sentence the defendant in accordance with the applicable provisions of section 70.06, 70.70 or 70.71 of the penal law.

5. Cases where further hearing is required. Where the defendant controverts an allegation in the statement and the uncontroverted allegations in such statement are not sufficient to support a finding that the defendant has been subjected to such a predicate felony conviction the court must proceed to hold a hearing.

6. Time for hearing. In any case where a copy of the statement was not received by the defendant at least two days prior to the preliminary examination, the court must upon request of the defendant grant an adjournment of at least two days before proceeding with the hearing.

7. Manner of conducting hearing.

(a) A hearing pursuant to this section must be before the court without jury. The burden of proof is upon the people and a finding that the defendant has been subjected to such a predicate felony conviction must be based upon proof beyond a reasonable doubt by evidence admissible under the rules applicable to a trial of the issue of guilt.

(b) A previous conviction in this or any other jurisdiction which was obtained in violation of the rights of the defendant under the applicable provisions of the constitution of the United States must not be counted in determining whether the defendant has been subjected to such a predicate felony conviction. The defendant may, at any time during the course of the hearing hereunder controvert an allegation with respect to such conviction in the statement on the grounds that the conviction was unconstitutionally obtained. Failure to challenge the previous conviction in the manner provided herein constitutes a waiver on the part of the defendant of any allegation of unconstitutionality unless good cause be shown for such failure to make timely challenge.

(c) At the conclusion of the hearing the court must make a finding as to whether or not the defendant has been subjected to a predicate felony conviction, including a finding as to whether or not the predicate felony conviction was of a violent felony as that term is defined in subdivision one of section 70.02 of the penal law, or in any other jurisdiction of an offense which includes all of the essential elements of any such felony for which a sentence to a term of imprisonment in excess of one year or death was authorized and is authorized in this state regardless of whether such sentence was imposed.

8. Subsequent use of predicate felony conviction finding. Where a finding has been entered pursuant to this section, such finding shall be binding upon that defendant in any future proceeding in which the issue may arise.

§ 400.22. Evidence of imprisonment

The certificate of the commissioner of correction or of the warden or other chief officer of any prison, or of the superintendent or other chief officer of any penitentiary under the seal of his office containing name of person, a statement of the court in which conviction was had, the date and term of sentence, length of time imprisoned, and date of discharge from prison or penitentiary, shall be prima facie evidence of the imprisonment and discharge of any person under the conviction stated and set forth in such certificate for the purposes of any proceeding under section 400.20.

§ 400.27. Procedure for determining sentence upon conviction for the offense of murder in the first degree

1. Upon the conviction of a defendant for the offense of murder in the first degree as defined by section 125.27 of the penal law, the court shall promptly conduct a separate sentencing proceeding to determine whether the defendant shall be sentenced to death or to life imprisonment without parole pursuant to subdivision five of section 70.00 of the penal law. Nothing in this section shall be deemed to preclude the people at any time from determining that the death penalty shall not be sought in a particular case, in which case the separate sentencing proceeding shall not be conducted and the court may sentence such defendant to life imprisonment without parole or to a sentence of imprisonment for the class A-I felony of murder in the first degree other than a sentence of life imprisonment without parole.

2. The separate sentencing proceeding provided for by this section shall be conducted before the court sitting with the jury that found the defendant guilty. The court may discharge the jury and impanel another jury only in extraordinary circumstances and

upon a showing of good cause, which may include, but is not limited to, a finding of prejudice to either party. If a new jury is impaneled, it shall be formed in accordance with the procedures in article two hundred seventy of this chapter. Before proceeding with the jury that found the defendant guilty, the court shall determine whether any juror has a state of mind that is likely to preclude the juror from rendering an impartial decision based upon the evidence adduced during the proceeding. In making such determination the court shall personally examine each juror individually outside the presence of the other jurors. The scope of the examination shall be within the discretion of the court and may include questions supplied by the parties as the court deems proper. The proceedings provided for in this subdivision shall be conducted on the record; provided, however, that upon motion of either party, and for good cause shown, the court may direct that all or a portion of the record of such proceedings be sealed. In the event the court determines that a juror has such a state of mind, the court shall discharge the juror and replace the juror with the alternate juror whose name was first drawn and called. If no alternate juror is available, the court must discharge the jury and impanel another jury in accordance with article two hundred seventy of this chapter.

3. For the purposes of a proceeding under this section each subparagraph of paragraph (a) of subdivision one of section 125.27 of the penal law shall be deemed to define an aggravating factor. Except as provided in subdivision seven of this section, at a sentencing proceeding pursuant to this section the only aggravating factors that the jury may consider are those proven beyond a reasonable doubt at trial, and no other aggravating factors may be considered. Whether a sentencing proceeding is conducted before the jury that found the defendant guilty or before another jury, the aggravating factor or factors proved at trial shall be deemed established beyond a reasonable doubt at the separate sentencing proceeding and shall not be relitigated. Where the jury is to determine sentences for concurrent counts of murder in the first degree, the aggravating factor included in each count shall be deemed to be an aggravating factor for the purpose of the jury's consideration in determining the sentence to be imposed on each such count.

4. The court on its own motion or on motion of either party, in the interest of justice or to avoid prejudice to either party, may delay the commencement of the separate sentencing proceeding.

5. Notwithstanding the provisions of article three hundred ninety of this chapter, where a defendant is found guilty of murder in the first degree, no presentence investigation shall be conducted; provided, however, that where the court is to impose a sentence of imprisonment, a presentence investigation shall be conducted and a presentence report shall be prepared in accordance with the provisions of such article.

6. At the sentencing proceeding the people shall not relitigate the existence of aggravating factors proved at the trial or otherwise present evidence, except, subject to the rules governing admission of evidence in the trial of a criminal action, in rebuttal of the defendant's evidence. However, when the sentencing proceeding is conducted before a newly impaneled jury, the people may present evidence to the extent reasonably necessary to inform the jury of the nature and circumstances of the count or counts of murder in the first degree for which the defendant was convicted in sufficient

detail to permit the jury to determine the weight to be accorded the aggravating factor or factors established at trial. Whenever the people present such evidence, the court must instruct the jury in its charge that any facts elicited by the people that are not essential to the verdict of guilty on such count or counts shall not be deemed established beyond a reasonable doubt. Subject to the rules governing the admission of evidence in the trial of a criminal action, the defendant may present any evidence relevant to any mitigating factor set forth in subdivision nine of this section; provided, however, the defendant shall not be precluded from the admission of reliable hearsay evidence. The burden of establishing any of the mitigating factors set forth in subdivision nine of this section shall be on the defendant, and must be proven by a preponderance of the evidence. The people shall not offer evidence or argument relating to any mitigating factor except in rebuttal of evidence offered by the defendant.

7.

(a) The people may present evidence at the sentencing proceeding to prove that in the ten year period prior to the commission of the crime of murder in the first degree for which the defendant was convicted, the defendant has previously been convicted of two or more offenses committed on different occasions; provided, that each such offense shall be either (i) a class A felony offense other than one defined in article two hundred twenty of the penal law, a class B violent felony offense specified in paragraph (a) of subdivision one of section 70.02 of the penal law, or a felony offense under the penal law a necessary element of which involves either the use or attempted use or threatened use of a deadly weapon or the intentional infliction of or the attempted intentional infliction of serious physical injury or death, or (ii) an offense under the laws of another state or of the United States punishable by a term of imprisonment of more than one year a necessary element of which involves either the use or attempted use or threatened use of a deadly weapon or the intentional infliction of or the attempted intentional infliction of serious physical injury or death. For the purpose of this paragraph, the term "deadly weapon" shall have the meaning set forth in subdivision twelve of section 10.00 of the penal law. In calculating the ten year period under this paragraph, any period of time during which the defendant was incarcerated for any reason between the time of commission of any of the prior felony offenses and the time of commission of the crime of murder in the first degree shall be excluded and such ten year period shall be extended by a period or periods equal to the time served under such incarceration. The defendant's conviction of two or more such offenses shall, if proven at the sentencing proceeding, constitute an aggravating factor.

(b) In order to be deemed established, an aggravating factor set forth in this subdivision must be proven by the people beyond a reasonable doubt and the jury must unanimously find such factor to have been so proven. The defendant may present evidence relating to an aggravating factor defined in this subdivision and either party may offer evidence in rebuttal. Any evidence presented by either party relating to such factor shall be subject to the rules governing admission of evidence in the trial of a criminal action.

(c) Whenever the people intend to offer evidence of an aggravating factor set forth in this subdivision, the people must within a reasonable time prior to trial file with the court and serve upon the defendant a notice of intention to offer such evidence. Whenever the people intend to offer evidence of the aggravating factor set forth in paragraph (a) of this subdivision, the people shall file with the notice of intention to offer such evidence a statement setting forth the date and place of each of the alleged offenses in paragraph (a) of this subdivision. The provisions of section 400.15 of this chapter, except for subdivisions one and two thereof, shall be followed.

8. Consistent with the provisions of this section, the people and the defendant shall be given fair opportunity to rebut any evidence received at the separate sentencing proceeding.

9. Mitigating factors shall include the following:

(a) The defendant has no significant history of prior criminal convictions involving the use of violence against another person;

(b) The defendant was mentally retarded at the time of the crime, or the defendant's mental capacity was impaired or his ability to conform his conduct to the requirements of law was impaired but not so impaired in either case as to constitute a defense to prosecution;

(c) The defendant was under duress or under the domination of another person, although not such duress or domination as to constitute a defense to prosecution;

(d) The defendant was criminally liable for the present offense of murder committed by another, but his participation in the offense was relatively minor although not so minor as to constitute a defense to prosecution;

(e) The murder was committed while the defendant was mentally or emotionally disturbed or under the influence of alcohol or any drug, although not to such an extent as to constitute a defense to prosecution; or

(f) Any other circumstance concerning the crime, the defendant's state of mind or condition at the time of the crime, or the defendant's character, background or record that would be relevant to mitigation or punishment for the crime.

10. At the conclusion of all the evidence, the people and the defendant may present argument in summation for or against the sentence sought by the people. The people may deliver the first summation and the defendant may then deliver the last summation. Thereafter, the court shall deliver a charge to the jury on any matters appropriate in the circumstances. In its charge, the court must instruct the jury that with respect to each count of murder in the first degree the jury should consider whether or not a sentence of death should be imposed and whether or not a sentence of life imprisonment without parole should be imposed, and that the jury must be unanimous with respect to either sentence. The court must also instruct the jury that in the event the jury fails to reach unanimous agreement with respect to the sentence, the court will sentence the defendant to a term of imprisonment with a minimum term of between twenty and twenty-five years and a maximum term of life. Following the court's charge, the jury shall retire to consider the sentence to be imposed. Unless inconsistent with the provisions of this section, the provisions of sections 310.10, 310.20 and 310.30 shall govern the deliberations of the jury.

11.

(a) The jury may not direct imposition of a sentence of death unless it unanimously finds beyond a reasonable doubt that the aggravating factor or factors substantially outweigh the mitigating factor or factors established, if any, and unanimously determines that the penalty of death should be imposed. Any member or members of the jury who find a mitigating factor to have been proven by the defendant by a preponderance of the evidence may consider such factor established regardless of the number of jurors who concur that the factor has been established.

(b) If the jury directs imposition of either a sentence of death or life imprisonment without parole, it shall specify on the record those mitigating and aggravating factors considered and those mitigating factors established by the defendant, if any.

(c) With respect to a count or concurrent counts of murder in the first degree, the court may direct the jury to cease deliberation with respect to the sentence or sentences to be imposed if the jury has deliberated for an extensive period of time without reaching unanimous agreement on the sentence or sentences to be imposed and the court is satisfied that any such agreement is unlikely within a reasonable time. The provisions of this paragraph shall apply with respect to consecutive counts of murder in the first degree. In the event the jury is unable to reach unanimous agreement, the court must sentence the defendant in accordance with subdivisions one through three of section 70.00 of the penal law with respect to any count or counts of murder in the first degree upon which the jury failed to reach unanimous agreement as to the sentence to be imposed.

(d) If the jury unanimously determines that a sentence of death should be imposed, the court must thereupon impose a sentence of death. Thereafter, however, the court may, upon written motion of the defendant, set aside the sentence of death upon any of the grounds set forth in section 330.30. The procedures set forth in sections 330.40 and 330.50, as applied to separate sentencing proceedings under this section, shall govern the motion and the court upon granting the motion shall, except as may otherwise be required by subdivision one of section 330.50, direct a new sentencing proceeding pursuant to this section. Upon granting the motion upon any of the grounds set forth in section 330.30 and setting aside the sentence, the court must afford the people a reasonable period of time, which shall not be less than ten days, to determine whether to take an appeal from the order setting aside the sentence of death. The taking of an appeal by the people stays the effectiveness of that portion of the court's order that directs a new sentencing proceeding.

(e) If the jury unanimously determines that a sentence of life imprisonment without parole should be imposed the court must thereupon impose a sentence of life imprisonment without parole.

(f) Where a sentence has been unanimously determined by the jury it must be recorded on the minutes and read to the jury, and the jurors must be collectively asked whether such is their sentence. Even though no juror makes any declaration in the negative, the jury must, if either party makes such an application, be polled and each juror separately asked whether the sentence announced by the foreman is in all respects his or her sentence. If, upon either the collective or the separate inquiry, any juror answers in the negative, the court must refuse to accept the sentence and must direct the jury to resume its deliberation. If no disagreement is expressed, the jury must be discharged from the case.

12.

(a) Upon the conviction of a defendant for the offense of murder in the first degree as defined in section 125.27 of the penal law, the court shall, upon oral or written motion of the defendant based upon a showing that there is reasonable cause to believe that the defendant is mentally retarded, promptly conduct a hearing without a jury to determine whether the defendant is mentally retarded. Upon the consent of both parties, such a hearing, or a portion thereof, may be conducted by the court contemporaneously with the separate sentencing proceeding in the presence of the sentencing jury, which in no event shall be the trier of fact with respect to the hearing. At such hearing the defendant has the burden of proof by a preponderance of the evidence that he or she is mentally retarded. The court shall defer rendering any finding pursuant to this subdivision as to whether the defendant is mentally retarded until a sentence is imposed pursuant to this section.

(b) In the event the defendant is sentenced pursuant to this section to life imprisonment without parole or to a term of imprisonment for the class A-I felony of murder in the first degree other than a sentence of life imprisonment without parole, the court shall not render a finding with respect to whether the defendant is mentally retarded.

(c) In the event the defendant is sentenced pursuant to this section to death, the court shall thereupon render a finding with respect to whether the defendant is mentally retarded. If the court finds the defendant is mentally retarded, the court shall set aside the sentence of death and sentence the defendant either to life imprisonment without parole or to a term of imprisonment for the class A-I felony of murder in the first degree other than a sentence of life imprisonment without parole. If the court finds the defendant is not mentally retarded, then such sentence of death shall not be set aside pursuant to this subdivision.

(d) In the event that a defendant is convicted of murder in the first degree pursuant to subparagraph (iii) of paragraph (a) of subdivision one of section 125.27 of the penal law, and the killing occurred while the defendant was confined or under custody in a state correctional facility or local correctional institution, and a sentence of death is imposed, such sentence may not be set aside pursuant to this subdivision upon the ground that the defendant is mentally retarded. Nothing in this paragraph or paragraph (a) of this subdivision shall preclude a defendant from presenting mitigating evidence of mental retardation at the separate sentencing proceeding.

(e) The foregoing provisions of this subdivision notwithstanding, at a reasonable time prior to the commencement of trial the defendant may, upon a written motion alleging reasonable cause to believe the defendant is mentally retarded, apply for an order directing that a mental retardation hearing be conducted prior to trial. If, upon review of the defendant's motion and any response thereto, the court finds reasonable cause to believe the defendant is mentally retarded, it shall promptly conduct a hearing without a jury to determine whether the defendant is mentally retarded. In the event the court finds after the hearing that the defendant is not mentally retarded, the court must, prior to commencement of trial, enter an order so stating, but nothing in this paragraph shall preclude a defendant from presenting mitigating evidence of mental retardation at a separate sentencing proceeding. In the event the court finds after the hearing that the defendant, based upon a preponderance of the evidence, is mentally retarded, the court must, prior to commencement of trial, enter an order so stating. Unless the order is reversed on an appeal by the people or unless the provisions of paragraph (d) of this subdivision apply, a separate sentencing proceeding under this section shall not be conducted if the defendant is thereafter convicted of murder in the first degree. In the event a separate sentencing proceeding is not conducted, the court, upon conviction of a defendant for the crime of murder in the first degree, shall sentence the defendant to life imprisonment without parole or to a sentence of imprisonment for the class A-I felony of murder in the first degree other than a sentence of life imprisonment without parole. Whenever a mental retardation hearing is held and a finding is rendered pursuant to this paragraph, the court may not conduct a hearing pursuant to paragraph (a) of this subdivision. For purposes of this subdivision and paragraph (b) of subdivision nine of this section, "mental retardation" means significantly subaverage general intellectual functioning existing concurrently with deficits in adaptive behavior which were manifested before the age of eighteen.

(f) In the event the court enters an order pursuant to paragraph (e) of this subdivision finding that the defendant is mentally retarded, the people may appeal as of right from the order pursuant to subdivision ten of section 450.20 of this chapter. Upon entering such an order the court must afford the people a reasonable period of time, which shall not be less than ten days, to determine whether to take an appeal from the order finding that the defendant is mentally retarded. The taking of an appeal by the people stays the effectiveness of the court's order and any order fixing a date for trial. Within six months of the effective date of this subdivision, the court of appeals shall adopt rules to ensure that appeals pursuant to this paragraph are expeditiously perfected, reviewed and determined so that pretrial delays are minimized. Prior to adoption of the rules, the court of appeals shall issue proposed rules and receive written comments thereon from interested parties.

13.

(a) As used in this subdivision, the term "psychiatric evidence" means evidence of mental disease, defect or condition in connection with either a mitigating factor defined in this section or a mental retardation hearing pursuant to this section to be offered by a psychiatrist, psychologist or other person who has received training, or education, or has experience relating to the identification, diagnosis, treatment or evaluation of mental disease, mental defect or mental condition.

(b) When either party intends to offer psychiatric evidence, the party must, within a reasonable time prior to trial, serve upon the other party and file with the court a written notice of intention to present psychiatric evidence. The notice shall include a brief but detailed statement specifying the witness, nature and type of psychiatric evidence sought to be introduced. If either party fails to serve and file written notice, no psychiatric evidence is admissible unless the party failing to file thereafter serves and files such notice and the court affords the other party an adjournment for a reasonable period. If a party fails to give timely notice, the court in its discretion may impose upon offending counsel a reasonable monetary sanction for an intentional failure but may not in any event preclude the psychiatric evidence. In the event a monetary sanction is imposed, the offending counsel shall be personally liable therefor, and shall not receive reimbursement of any kind from any source in order to pay the cost of such monetary sanction. Nothing contained herein shall preclude the court from entering an order directing a party to provide timely notice.

(c) When a defendant serves notice pursuant to this subdivision, the district attorney may make application, upon notice to the defendant, for an order directing that the defendant submit to an examination by a psychiatrist, licensed psychologist, or licensed clinical social worker designated by the district attorney, for the purpose of rebutting evidence offered by the defendant with respect to a mental disease, defect, or condition in connection with either a mitigating factor defined in this section, including whether the defendant was acting under duress, was mentally or emotionally disturbed or mentally retarded, or was under the influence of alcohol or any drug. If the application is granted, the district attorney shall schedule a time and place for the examination, which shall be recorded. Counsel for the people and the defendant shall have the right to be present at the examination. A transcript of the examination shall be made available to the defendant and the district attorney promptly after its conclusion. The district attorney shall promptly serve on the defendant a written copy of the findings and evaluation of the examiner. If the court finds that the defendant has wilfully refused to cooperate fully in an examination pursuant to this paragraph, it shall, upon request of the district attorney, instruct the jury that the defendant did not submit to or cooperate fully in such psychiatric examination. When a defendant is subjected to an examination pursuant to an order issued in accordance with this subdivision, any statement made by the defendant for the purpose of the examination shall be inadmissible in evidence against him in any criminal action or proceeding on any issue other than that of whether a mitigating factor has been established or whether the defendant is mentally retarded, but such statement is admissible upon such an issue whether or not it would otherwise be deemed a privileged communication.

14.

(a) At a reasonable time prior to the sentencing proceeding or a mental retardation hearing:

(i) the prosecutor shall, unless previously disclosed and subject to a protective order, make available to the defendant the statements and information specified in subdivision one of section 240.45 and make available for inspection, photographing, copying or testing the property specified in subdivision one of section 240.20; and

(ii) the defendant shall, unless previously disclosed and subject to a protective order, make available to the prosecution the statements and information specified in subdivision two of section 240.45 and make available for inspection, photographing, copying or testing, subject to constitutional limitations, the reports, documents and other property specified in subdivision one of section 240.30.

(b) Where a party refuses to make disclosure pursuant to this section, the provisions of section 240.35, subdivision one of section 240.40 and section 240.50 shall apply.

(c) If, after complying with the provisions of this section or an order pursuant thereto, a party finds either before or during a sentencing proceeding or mental retardation hearing, additional material subject to discovery or covered by court order, the party shall promptly make disclosure or apply for a protective order.

(d) If the court finds that a party has failed to comply with any of the provisions of this section, the court may enter any of the orders specified in subdivision one of section 240.70.

15. The court of appeals shall formulate and adopt rules for the development of forms for use by the jury in recording its findings and determinations of sentence.

§ 400.30. Procedure for determining the amount of a fine based upon the defendant's gain from the offense

1. Order directing a hearing. In any case where the court is of the opinion that the sentence should consist of or include a fine and that, pursuant to article eighty of the penal law, the amount of the fine should be based upon the defendant's gain from the commission of the offense, the court may order a hearing to determine the amount of such gain. The order must be filed with the clerk of the court and must specify a date for the hearing not less than ten days after the filing of the order.

2. Notice of hearing. Upon receipt of the order, the clerk of the court must send a notice of the hearing to the defendant, his counsel and the district attorney. Such notice must specify the time and place of the hearing and the fact that the purpose thereof is to determine the amount of the defendant's gain from the commission of the offense so that an appropriate fine can be imposed.

3. Hearing. When the defendant appears for the hearing the court must ask him whether he wishes to make any statement with respect to the amount of his gain from the commission of the offense. If the defendant does make a statement, the court may accept such statement and base its finding thereon. Where the defendant does not make a statement, or where the court does not accept the defendant's statement, it may proceed with the hearing.

4. Burden and standard of proof; evidence. At any hearing held pursuant to this section the burden of proof rests upon the people. A finding as to the amount of the defendant's gain from the commission of the offense must be based upon a preponderance of the evidence. Any relevant evidence, not legally privileged, may be received regardless of its admissibility under the exclusionary rules of evidence.

5. Termination of hearing. At any time during the pendency of a hearing pursuant to this section the court may, in its discretion, terminate the hearing without making any finding.

§ 400.40. Procedure for determining prior convictions for the purpose of sentence in certain cases

1. Applicability. Where a conviction is entered for an unclassified misdemeanor or for a traffic infraction and the authorized sentence depends upon whether the defendant has a previous judgment of conviction for an offense, or where a conviction is entered for a violation defined outside the penal law and the amount of the fine authorized by the law defining such violation depends upon whether the defendant has a previous judgment of conviction for an offense, such issue is determined as provided in this section.

2. Statement to be filed. If it appears that the defendant has a previous judgment of conviction and if the court is required, or in its discretion desires, to impose a sentence that would not be authorized in the absence of such previous judgment, a statement must be filed after conviction and before sentence setting forth the date and place of the previous judgment or judgments and the court must conduct a hearing to determine whether the defendant is the same person mentioned in the record of such judgment or judgments. In any case where an increased sentence is mandatory, the statement may be filed by the court or by the prosecutor. In any case where an increased sentence is discretionary, the statement may be filed only by the court.

3. Preliminary examination. The defendant must be given a copy of such statement and the court must ask him whether he admits or denies such prior judgment or judgments. If the defendant denies the same or remains mute, the court may proceed with the hearing and, where the increased sentence is mandatory, it must impose such.

4. Time for hearing. In any case where a copy of the statement was not received by the defendant at least two days prior to the preliminary examination, the court must upon request of the defendant grant an adjournment of at least two days before proceeding with the hearing.

5. Manner of conducting hearing. A hearing pursuant to this section must be before the court without a jury. The burden of proof is upon the people and a finding that the defendant has been convicted of any offense alleged in the statement must be based upon proof beyond a reasonable doubt by evidence admissible under the rules applicable to trial of the issue of guilt.

Article 410 [Eff until Sept 1, 2019] Sentences of Probation, Conditional Discharge and Parole Supervision

[Eff Sept 1, 2019] Sentences of Probation and of Conditional Discharge

§ 410.10. Specification of conditions of the sentence

1. When the court pronounces a sentence of probation or of conditional discharge it must specify as part of the sentence the conditions to be complied with. Where the sentence is one of probation, the defendant must be given a written copy of the conditions at the time sentence is imposed. In any case where the defendant is given a written copy of the conditions, a copy thereof must be filed with and become part of the record of the case, and it is not necessary to specify the conditions orally.

2. Commission of an additional offense, other than a traffic infraction, after imposition of a sentence of probation or of conditional discharge, and prior to expiration or termination of the period of the sentence, constitutes a ground for revocation of such sentence irrespective of whether such fact is specified as a condition of the sentence.

3. When the court pronounces a sentence of probation or conditional discharge for a specified crime defined in paragraph (e) of subdivision one of section six hundred thirty-two-a of the executive law, in addition to specifying the conditions of the sentence, the court shall provide written notice to such defendant concerning any requirement to report to the office of victim services funds of a convicted person as defined in section six hundred thirty-two-a of the executive law, the procedures for such reporting and any potential penalty for a failure to comply.

§ 410.11. [Repealed]

§ 410.20. Modification or enlargement of conditions

1. The court may modify or enlarge the conditions of a sentence of probation or of conditional discharge at any time prior to the expiration or termination of the period of the sentence. Such action may not, however, be taken unless the defendant is personally present, except that the defendant need not be present if the modification consists solely of the elimination or relaxation of one or more conditions. Whenever the defendant has not been present, the court shall notify the defendant in writing within twenty days of such modification specifying the nature of the elimination or relaxation of such condition or conditions and the effective date thereof. In any such case the modification or enlargement may be specified in the same manner as the conditions originally imposed and becomes part of the sentence.

2. The procedure set forth in this section applies to the imposition of an additional period of conditional discharge as authorized by subdivision three of section 65.05 of the penal law.

§ 410.30. Declaration of delinquency

If at any time during the period of a sentence of probation or of conditional discharge the court has reasonable cause to believe that the defendant has violated a condition of the sentence, it may declare the defendant delinquent and file a written declaration of delinquency. When the court receives a request for a declaration of delinquency by a probation officer, it shall make a decision on such request within seventy-two hours of its receipt of the request. Upon filing a written declaration of delinquency, the court must promptly take reasonable and appropriate action to cause the defendant to appear before it for the purpose of enabling the court to make a final determination with respect to the alleged delinquency in accordance with section 410.70 of this article.

§ 410.40. Notice to appear, warrant

1. Notice to appear. The court may at any time order that a person who is under a sentence of probation or of conditional discharge appear before it. Such order may be in the form of a written notice, specifying the time and place of appearance, mailed to or served personally upon the defendant as the court may direct. In the absence of a warrant issued pursuant to subdivision two of this section, where a probation officer has submitted a violation petition and report, the court shall promptly consider such petition and, where the court issues a notice to appear, the court shall direct that the defendant appear within ten business days of the court's order. When the order is in the form of such a notice, failure to appear as ordered without reasonable cause therefor constitutes a violation of the conditions of the sentence irrespective of whether such requirement is specified as a condition thereof.

2. Warrant. (a) Where the probation officer has requested that a probation warrant be issued, the court shall, within seventy-two hours of its receipt of the request, issue or deny the warrant or take any other lawful action including issuance of a notice to appear pursuant to subdivision one of this section. If at any time during the period of a sentence of probation or of conditional discharge the court has reasonable grounds to believe that the defendant has violated a condition of the sentence, the court may issue a warrant to a police officer or to an appropriate peace officer directing him or her to take the

defendant into custody and bring the defendant before the court without unnecessary delay; provided, however, if the court in which the warrant is returnable is a superior court, and such court is not available, and the warrant is addressed to a police officer or appropriate probation officer certified as a peace officer, such executing officer may unless otherwise specified under paragraph (b) of this subdivision, bring the defendant to the local correctional facility of the county in which such court sits, to be detained there until not later than the commencement of the next session of such court occurring on the next business day; or if the court in which the warrant is returnable is a local criminal court, and such court is not available, and the warrant is addressed to a police officer or appropriate probation officer certified as a peace officer, such executing officer must without unnecessary delay bring the defendant before an alternate local criminal court, as provided in subdivision five of section 120.90 of this chapter. A court which issues such a warrant may attach thereto a summary of the basis for the warrant. In any case where a defendant arrested upon the warrant is brought before a local criminal court other than the court in which the warrant is returnable, such local criminal court shall consider such summary before issuing a securing order with respect to the defendant.

(b) If the court in which the warrant is returnable is a superior court, and such court is not available, and the warrant is addressed to a police officer or appropriate probation officer certified as a peace officer, such executing officer shall, where a defendant is sixteen years of age or younger who allegedly commits an offense or a violation of his or her probation or conditional discharge imposed for an offense on or after October first, two thousand eighteen, or where a defendant is seventeen years of age or younger who allegedly commits an offense or a violation of his or her probation or conditional discharge imposed for an offense on or after October first, two thousand nineteen, bring the defendant without unnecessary delay before the youth part, provided, however that if the youth part is not in session, the defendant shall be brought before the most accessible magistrate designated by the appellate division.

§ 410.50. Custody and supervision of probationers

1. Custody. A person who is under a sentence of probation is in the legal custody of the court that imposed it pending expiration or termination of the period of the sentence.

2. Supervision. The probation department serving the court that imposed a sentence of probation has the duty of supervising the defendant during the period of such legal custody.

3. Search order. If at any time during the period of probation the court has reasonable cause to believe that the defendant has violated a condition of the sentence, it may issue a search order. Such order must be directed to a probation officer and may authorize such officer to search the person of the defendant and/or any premises in which he resides or any real or personal property which he owns or which is in his possession.

4. Taking custody without warrant. When a probation officer has reasonable cause to believe that a person under his supervision pursuant to a sentence of probation has violated a condition of the sentence, such officer may, without a warrant, take the probationer into custody and search his person.

5. Assistance by police officer. In executing a search order, or in taking a person into custody, pursuant to this section, a probation officer may be assisted by a police officer.

§ 410.60. Appearance before court

A person who has been taken into custody pursuant to section 410.40 or section 410.50 of this article for violation of a condition of a sentence of probation or a sentence of conditional discharge must forthwith be brought before the court that imposed the sentence. Where a violation of probation petition and report has been filed and the person has not been taken into custody nor has a warrant been issued, an initial court appearance shall occur within ten business days of the court's issuance of a notice to appear. If the court has reasonable cause to believe that such person has violated a condition of the sentence, it may commit him to the custody of the sheriff or fix bail or release such person on his own recognizance for future appearance at a hearing to be held in accordance with section 410.70 of this article. If the court does not have reasonable cause to believe that such person has violated a condition of the sentence, it must direct that he be released.

§ 410.70. Hearing on violation

1. In general. The court may not revoke a sentence of probation or a sentence of conditional discharge, or extend a period of probation, unless (a) the court has found that the defendant has violated a condition of the sentence and (b) the defendant has had an opportunity to be heard pursuant to this section. The defendant is entitled to a hearing in accordance with this section promptly after the court has filed a declaration of delinquency or has committed him or has fixed bail pursuant to this article.

2. Statement; preliminary examination. The court must file or cause to be filed with the clerk of the court a statement setting forth the condition or conditions of the sentence violated and a reasonable description of the time, place and manner in which the violation occurred. The defendant must appear before the court within ten business days of the court's issuance of the notice to appear and the court must advise him of the contents of the statement and furnish him with a copy thereof. At the time of such appearance the court must ask the defendant whether he wishes to make any statement with respect to the violation. If the defendant makes a statement, the court may accept it and base its decision thereon. If the court does not accept it, or if the defendant does not make a statement, the court must proceed with the hearing. Provided, however, that upon request, the court must grant a reasonable adjournment to the defendant to enable him to prepare for the hearing.

3. Manner of conducting hearing. The hearing must be a summary one by the court without a jury and the court may receive any relevant evidence not legally privileged. The defendant may cross-examine witnesses and may present evidence on his own behalf. A finding that the defendant has violated a condition of his sentence must be based upon a preponderance of the evidence.

4. Counsel. The defendant is entitled to counsel at all stages of any proceeding under this section and the court must advise him of such right at the outset of the proceeding.

5. Revocation; modification; continuation. At the conclusion of the hearing the court may revoke, continue or modify the sentence of probation or conditional discharge. Where the court revokes the sentence, it must impose sentence as specified in

subdivisions three and four of section 60.01 of the penal law. Where the court continues or modifies the sentence, it must vacate the declaration of delinquency and direct that the defendant be released. If the alleged violation is sustained and the court continues or modifies the sentence, it may extend the sentence up to the period of interruption specified in subdivision two of section 65.15 of the penal law, but any time spent in custody in any correctional institution pursuant to section 410.60 of this article shall be credited against the term of the sentence. Provided further, where the alleged violation is sustained and the court continues or modifies the sentence, the court may also extend the remaining period of probation up to the maximum term authorized by section 65.00 of the penal law. Provided, however, a defendant shall receive credit for the time during which he or she was supervised under the original probation sentence prior to any declaration of delinquency and for any time spent in custody pursuant to this article for an alleged violation of probation.

§ 410.80. Transfer of supervision of probationers

1. Authority to transfer supervision. Where a probationer at the time of sentencing or an interim probationer at the time of the imposition of the period of interim probation supervision resides in another jurisdiction within the state, the sentencing court shall transfer supervision to the appropriate probation department in such other jurisdiction. Where, after a probation sentence or interim probation supervision is pronounced, a probationer or interim probationer desires to reside in another jurisdiction within the state that is not served by the sentencing court, such court, in its discretion, may approve a change in residency and, upon approval, shall transfer supervision to the appropriate probation department serving the county of the probationer's proposed new residence. Any transfer under this subdivision must be in accordance with rules adopted by the commissioner of the division of criminal justice services.

2. Transfer of powers.

(a) Upon completion of transfer of probation as authorized pursuant to subdivision one, the probation department in the receiving jurisdiction shall assume all powers and duties of the probation department in the jurisdiction of the sentencing court. Upon completion of transfer, the appropriate court within the jurisdiction of the receiving probation department shall assume all powers and duties of the sentencing court and shall have sole jurisdiction in the case including jurisdiction over matters specified in article twenty-three of the correction law. Further, the sentencing court shall immediately forward its entire case record to the receiving court.

(i) In transfers involving a defendant sentenced to probation upon conviction of a felony, the receiving court served by the probation department to which supervision is transferred shall be the superior court within the jurisdiction of the probation department.

(ii) In transfers involving a defendant sentenced to probation upon conviction of a misdemeanor, the receiving court served by the probation department to which supervision is transferred shall be the appropriate criminal court within the jurisdiction of the probation department. The sending probation department shall consult with the probation department to which supervision will be transferred to determine the appropriate criminal court to receive the case.

(b) Where a transfer is authorized for a defendant on interim probation supervision pursuant to subdivision one of this section, the sentencing court shall retain jurisdiction during the period of interim probation. The probation department in the receiving jurisdiction shall assume all powers and duties of the original probation department in the jurisdiction of the sentencing court.

3. Interstate compact. Nothing contained in this section affects or limits the provisions of section two hundred fifty-nine-mm of the executive law relating to out-of-state probation supervision.

4. Federal transfer of custody and supervision. Notwithstanding the provisions of any other law, the court served by the probation department may consent to the transfer of custody and supervision of a probationer to the United States Department of Justice pursuant to the Witness Security Act of nineteen hundred eighty-four.

§ 410.90. Termination of sentence

1. The court may at any time terminate either a period of probation, other than a period of lifetime probation, for conviction to a crime or a period of conditional discharge for an offense.

2. The court may terminate a period of probation for a person who is subject to lifetime probation and who has been on unrevoked probation for at least five consecutive years.

3.

(a) The court shall grant a request for termination of a sentence of probation under this section when, having regard to the conduct and condition of the probationer, the court is of the opinion that:

(i) the probationer is no longer in need of such guidance, training or other assistance which would otherwise be administered through probation supervision;

(ii) the probationer has diligently complied with the terms and conditions of the sentence of probation; and

(iii) the termination of the sentence of probation is not adverse to the protection of the public.

No such termination shall be granted unless the court is satisfied that the probationer, who is otherwise financially able to comply with an order of restitution or reparation, has made a good faith effort to comply therewith.

(b) The court shall grant a request for termination of a sentence of conditional discharge under this section when, having regard to the conduct and condition of the defendant, the court is of the opinion that:

(i) the defendant has diligently complied with the terms and conditions of the sentence of conditional discharge; and

(ii) termination of the sentence of conditional discharge is not adverse to protection of the public.

§ 410.90-a. Superior court; youth part

Notwithstanding any other provisions of this article, all proceedings relating to a juvenile offender or adolescent offender shall be heard in the youth part of the superior court having jurisdiction and any intrastate transfers under this article shall be between courts designated as a youth part pursuant to article seven hundred twenty-two of this chapter.

§ 410.91. [Repealed Sept 1, 2019] Sentence of parole supervision

1. A sentence of parole supervision is an indeterminate sentence of imprisonment, or a determinate sentence of imprisonment imposed pursuant to paragraphs (b) and (d) of subdivision three of section 70.70 of the penal law, which may be imposed upon an eligible defendant, as defined in subdivision two of this section. If an indeterminate sentence, such sentence shall have a minimum term and a maximum term within the ranges specified by subdivisions three and four of section 70.06 of the penal law. If a determinate sentence, such sentence shall have a term within the ranges specified by subparagraphs (iii) and (iv) of paragraph (b) of subdivision three of section 70.70 of the penal law. Provided, however, if the court directs that the sentence be executed as a sentence of parole supervision, it shall remand the defendant for immediate delivery to a reception center operated by the state department of corrections and community supervision, in accordance with section 430.20 of this chapter and section six hundred one of the correction law, for a period not to exceed ten days. An individual who receives such a sentence shall be placed under the immediate supervision of the department of corrections and community supervision and must comply with the conditions of parole, which shall include an initial placement in a drug treatment campus for a period of ninety days at which time the defendant shall be released therefrom.

2. A defendant is an "eligible defendant" for purposes of a sentence of parole supervision when such defendant is a felony offender convicted of a specified offense or offenses as defined in subdivision five of this section, who stands convicted of no other felony offense, who has not previously been convicted of either a violent felony offense as defined in section 70.02 of the penal law, a class A felony offense or a class B felony offense other than a class B felony offense defined in article two hundred twenty of the penal law, and is not subject to an undischarged term of imprisonment.

3. When an indeterminate or determinate sentence of imprisonment is imposed upon an eligible defendant for a specified offense, as defined in subdivision five of this section, the court may direct that such sentence be executed as a sentence of parole supervision if the court finds (i) that the defendant has a history of controlled substance dependence that is a significant contributing factor to such defendant's criminal conduct; (ii) that such defendant's controlled substance dependence could be appropriately addressed by a sentence of parole supervision; and (iii) that imposition of such a sentence would not have an adverse effect on public safety or public confidence in the integrity of the criminal justice system.

4. [Repealed]

5. [Eff until July 5, 2021] For the purposes of this section, a "specified offense" is an offense defined by any of the following provisions of the penal law: burglary in the third degree as defined in section 140.20, criminal mischief in the third degree as defined in section 145.05, criminal mischief in the second degree as defined in section 145.10, grand larceny in the fourth degree as defined in subdivision one, two, three, four, five, six, eight, nine or ten of section 155.30, grand larceny in the third degree as defined in section 155.35 (except where the property consists of one or more firearms, rifles or shotguns), unauthorized use of a vehicle in the second degree as defined in section 165.06, criminal possession of stolen property in the fourth degree as defined in

subdivision one, two, three, five or six of section 165.45, criminal possession of stolen property in the third degree as defined in section 165.50 (except where the property consists of one or more firearms, rifles or shotguns), forgery in the second degree as defined in section 170.10, criminal possession of a forged instrument in the second degree as defined in section 170.25, unlawfully using slugs in the first degree as defined in section 170.60, criminal diversion of medical marihuana in the first degree as defined in section 179.10 or an attempt to commit any of the aforementioned offenses if such attempt constitutes a felony offense; or a class B felony offense defined in article two hundred twenty where a sentence is imposed pursuant to paragraph (a) of subdivision two of section 70.70 of the penal law; or any class C, class D or class E controlled substance or marihuana felony offense as defined in article two hundred twenty or two hundred twenty-one.

5. [Eff July 5, 2021] For the purposes of this section, a "specified offense" is an offense defined by any of the following provisions of the penal law: burglary in the third degree as defined in section 140.20, criminal mischief in the third degree as defined in section 145.05, criminal mischief in the second degree as defined in section 145.10, grand larceny in the fourth degree as defined in subdivision one, two, three, four, five, six, eight, nine or ten of section 155.30, grand larceny in the third degree as defined in section 155.35 (except where the property consists of one or more firearms, rifles or shotguns), unauthorized use of a vehicle in the second degree as defined in section 165.06, criminal possession of stolen property in the fourth degree as defined in subdivision one, two, three, five or six of section 165.45, criminal possession of stolen property in the third degree as defined in section 165.50 (except where the property consists of one or more firearms, rifles or shotguns), forgery in the second degree as defined in section 170.10, criminal possession of a forged instrument in the second degree as defined in section 170.25, unlawfully using slugs in the first degree as defined in section 170.60, or an attempt to commit any of the aforementioned offenses if such attempt constitutes a felony offense; or a class B felony offense defined in article two hundred twenty where a sentence is imposed pursuant to paragraph (a) of subdivision two of section 70.70 of the penal law; or any class C, class D or class E controlled substance or marihuana felony offense as defined in article two hundred twenty or two hundred twenty-one.

6. Upon delivery of the defendant to the reception center, he or she shall be given a copy of the conditions of parole by a representative of the department of corrections and community supervision and shall acknowledge receipt of a copy of the conditions in writing. The conditions shall be established in accordance with article twelve-B of the executive law and the rules and regulations of the board of parole. Thereafter and while the parolee is participating in the intensive drug treatment program provided at the drug treatment campus, the department of corrections and community supervision shall assess the parolee's special needs and shall develop an intensive program of parole supervision that will address the parolee's substance abuse history and which shall include periodic urinalysis testing. Unless inappropriate, such program shall include the provision of treatment services by a community-based substance abuse service

provider which has a contract with the department of corrections and community supervision.

7. Upon completion of the drug treatment program at the drug treatment campus, a parolee will be furnished with money, clothing and transportation in a manner consistent with section one hundred twenty-five of the correction law to permit the parolee's travel from the drug treatment campus to the county in which the parolee's supervision will continue.

8. If the parole officer having charge of a person sentenced to parole supervision pursuant to this section has reasonable cause to believe that such person has violated the conditions of his or her parole, the procedures of subdivision three of section two hundred fifty-nine-i of the executive law shall apply to the issuance of a warrant and the conduct of further proceedings; provided, however, that a parole violation warrant issued for a violation committed while the parolee is being supervised at a drug treatment campus shall constitute authority for the immediate placement of the parolee into a correctional facility operated by the department of corrections and community supervision, which to the extent practicable shall be reasonably proximate to the place at which the violation occurred, to hold in temporary detention pending completion of the procedures required by subdivision three of section two hundred fifty-nine-i of the executive law.

§ 410.92. [Repealed]

Article 420 Fines, Restitution and Reparation

§ 420.05. Payment of fines, mandatory surcharges and fees by credit card.

When the court imposes a fine, mandatory surcharge or fee upon an individual who stands convicted of any offense, such individual may pay such fine, mandatory surcharge or fee by credit card or similar device. In such event, notwithstanding any other provision of law, he or she also may be required to pay a reasonable administrative fee. The amount of such administrative fee and the time and manner of its payment shall be in accordance with the system established by the chief administrator of the courts pursuant to paragraph (j) of subdivision two of section two hundred twelve of the judiciary law.

§ 420.10. Collection of fines, restitution or reparation

1. Alternative methods of payment. When the court imposes a fine upon an individual, it shall designate the official other than the district attorney to whom payment is to be remitted. When the court imposes restitution or reparation and requires that the defendant pay a designated surcharge thereon pursuant to the provisions of subdivision eight of section 60.27 of the penal law, it shall designate the official or organization other than the district attorney, selected pursuant to subdivision eight of this section, to whom payment is to be remitted.

(a) The court may direct:

(i) That the defendant pay the entire amount at the time sentence is pronounced;

(ii) That the defendant pay the entire amount at some later date; or

(iii) That the defendant pay a specified portion at designated periodic intervals.

(b) When the court imposes both (i) a fine and (ii) restitution or reparation and such designated surcharge upon an individual and imposes a schedule of payments, the court shall also direct that payment of restitution or reparation and such designated surcharge take priority over the payment of the fine.

(c) Where the defendant is sentenced to a period of probation as well as a fine, restitution or reparation and such designated surcharge, the court may direct that payment of the fine, restitution or reparation and such designated surcharge be a condition of the sentence.

(d) When a court requires that restitution or reparation and such designated surcharge be made it must direct that notice be given to a person or persons to whom it is to be paid of the conditions under which it is to be remitted; the name and address of the public official or organization to whom it is to be remitted for payment and the amount thereof; and the availability of civil proceedings for collection under subdivision six of this section. An official or organization designated to receive payment under this subdivision must report to the court any failure to comply with the order and shall cooperate with the district attorney pursuant to his responsibilities under subdivision six of this section.

(e) Where cash bail has been posted by the defendant as the principal and is not forfeited or assigned, the court at its discretion may order that bail be applied toward payment of any order of restitution or reparation or fine. If the court so orders, the bail proceeds shall be applied to payment first of the restitution or reparation and then of the fine.

2. Death of victim. In the event that the individual to whom restitution or reparation is to be made dies prior to completion of said restitution or reparation, the remaining payments shall be made to the estate of the deceased.

3. Imprisonment for failure to pay. Where the court imposes a fine, restitution or reparation, the sentence may provide that if the defendant fails to pay the fine, restitution or reparation in accordance with the direction of the court, the defendant must be imprisoned until the fine, restitution or reparation is satisfied. Such provision may be added at the time sentence is pronounced or at any later date while the fine, restitution or reparation or any part thereof remains unpaid; provided, however, that if the provision is added at a time subsequent to the pronouncement of sentence the defendant must be personally present when it is added. In any case where the defendant fails to pay a fine, restitution or reparation as directed the court may issue a warrant directing a peace officer, acting pursuant to his special duties, or a police officer, to take him into custody and bring him before the court; provided, however, if the court in which the warrant is returnable is a city, town or village court, and such court is not available, and the warrant is addressed to a police officer, such executing police officer must without unnecessary delay bring the defendant before an alternate local criminal court, as provided in subdivision five of section 120.90 of this chapter; or if the court in which the warrant is returnable is a superior court, and such court is not available, and the warrant is addressed to a police officer, such executing police officer may bring the defendant to the local correctional facility of the county in which such court sits, to be detained there until not later than the commencement of the next session of such court occurring on the next business day. Such warrant may also be delegated in the same manner as a warrant pursuant to section 530.70 of this chapter. Where a sentence provides that the

defendant be imprisoned for failure to pay a fine, the court shall advise the defendant that if he is unable to pay such fine, he has a right, at any time, to apply to the court to be resentenced as provided in subdivision five of this section.

4. Period of imprisonment. When the court directs that the defendant be imprisoned until the fine, restitution or reparation be satisfied, it must specify a maximum period of imprisonment subject to the following limits:

(a) Where the fine, restitution or reparation is imposed for a felony, the period may not exceed one year;

(b) Where the fine, restitution or reparation is imposed for a misdemeanor, the period may not exceed one-third of the maximum authorized term of imprisonment;

(c) Where the fine, restitution or reparation is imposed for a petty offense, the period may not exceed fifteen days; and

(d) Where a sentence of imprisonment as well as a fine, restitution or reparation is imposed, the aggregate of the period and the term of the sentence may not exceed the maximum authorized term of imprisonment.

(e) Jail time and good behavior time shall be credited against the full period of imprisonment, if served, as provided in section 70.30 of the penal law for definite sentences.

5. Application for resentence. In any case where the defendant is unable to pay a fine, restitution or reparation imposed by the court, he may at any time apply to the court for resentence. In such case, if the court is satisfied that the defendant is unable to pay the fine, restitution or reparation it must:

(a) Adjust the terms of payment; or

(b) Lower the amount of the fine, restitution or reparation; or

(c) Where the sentence consists of probation or imprisonment and a fine, restitution or reparation, revoke the portion of the sentence imposing the fine, restitution or reparation; or

(d) Revoke the entire sentence imposed and resentence the defendant. Upon such resentence the court may impose any sentence it originally could have imposed, except that the amount of any fine, restitution or reparation imposed may not be in excess of the amount the defendant is able to pay.

In any case where the defendant applies for resentencing with respect to any condition of the sentence relating to restitution or reparation the court must order that notice of such application and a reasonable opportunity to be heard be given to the person or persons given notice pursuant to subdivision one of this section. If the court grants the defendant's application by changing the original order for restitution or reparation in any manner, the court must place the reasons therefor on the record.

For the purposes of this subdivision, the court shall not determine that the defendant is unable to pay the fine, restitution or reparation ordered solely because of such defendant's incarceration but shall consider all the defendant's sources of income including, but not limited to, moneys in the possession of an inmate at the time of his admission into such facility, funds earned by him in a work release program as defined in subdivision four of section one hundred fifty of the correction law, funds earned by him as provided for in section one hundred eighty-seven of the correction law and any other funds received by him or on his behalf and deposited with the superintendent or the municipal official of the facility where the person is confined.

6. Civil proceeding for collection.

(a) A fine, restitution or reparation imposed or directed by the court shall be imposed or directed by a written order of the court containing the amount thereof required to be paid by the defendant. The court's order also shall direct the district attorney to file a certified copy of such order with the county clerk of the county in which the court is situate except where the court which issues such order is the supreme court in which case the order itself shall be filed by the clerk of the court acting in his or her capacity as the county clerk of the county in which the court is situate. Such order shall be entered by the county clerk in the same manner as a judgment in a civil action in accordance with subdivision (a) of rule five thousand sixteen of the civil practice law and rules. Even if the defendant was imprisoned for failure to pay such fine, restitution or reparation, or has served the period of imprisonment imposed, such order after entry thereof pursuant to this subdivision may be collected in the same manner as a judgment in a civil action by the victim, as defined in paragraph (b) of subdivision four of section 60.27 of the penal law, to whom restitution or reparation was ordered to be paid, the estate of such person or the district attorney. The entered order shall be deemed to constitute a judgment-roll as defined in section five thousand seventeen of the civil practice law and rules and immediately after entry of the order, the county clerk shall docket the entered order as a money judgment pursuant to section five thousand eighteen of such law and rules. Wherever appropriate, the district attorney shall file a transcript of the docket of the judgment with the clerk of any other county of the state. Such a restitution or reparation order, when docketed shall be a first lien upon all real property in which the defendant thereafter acquires an interest, having preference over all other liens, security interests, and encumbrances whatsoever, except:

(i) a lien or interest running to the benefit of the government of the United States or the state of New York, or any political subdivision or public benefit corporation thereof; or

(ii) a purchase money interest in any property.

(b) The district attorney may, in his or her discretion, and must, upon order of the court, institute proceedings to collect such fine, restitution or reparation.

7. Undisbursed restitution payments. Where a court requires that restitution or reparation be made by a defendant, the official or organization to whom payments are to be remitted pursuant to subdivision one of this section may place such payments in an interest-bearing account. The interest accrued and any undisbursed payments shall be designated for the payment of restitution orders that have remained unsatisfied for the longest period of time. For the purposes of this subdivision, the term "undisbursed restitution payments" shall mean those payments which have been remitted by a defendant but not disbursed to the intended beneficiary and such payment has gone unclaimed for a period of one year and the location of the intended beneficiary cannot be ascertained by such official or organization after using reasonable efforts.

8. Designation of restitution agency.

(a) The chief elected official in each county, and in the city of New York the mayor, shall designate an official or organization other than the district attorney to be responsible for the collection and administration of restitution and reparation payments under provisions of the penal law and this chapter. This official or organization shall be eligible for the designated surcharge provided for by subdivision eight of section 60.27 of the penal law.

(b) The restitution agency, as designated by paragraph (a) of this subdivision, shall be responsible for the collection of data on a monthly basis regarding the numbers of restitution and reparation orders issued, the numbers of satisfied restitution and reparation orders and information concerning the types of crimes for which such orders were required. A probation department designated as the restitution agency shall then forward such information to the office of probation and correctional alternatives within the first ten days following the end of each month. In all other cases the restitution agency shall report to the division of criminal justice services directly. The division of criminal justice services shall compile and review all such information and make recommendations to promote the use of restitution and encourage its enforcement.

§ 420.20. Collection of fines, restitution or reparation imposed upon corporations

Where a corporation is sentenced to pay a fine, restitution or reparation, the fine, restitution or reparation must be paid at the time sentence is imposed. If the fine, restitution or reparation is not so paid, it may be collected in the same manner as a judgment in a civil action, and if execution issued upon such judgment be returned unsatisfied an action may be brought in the name of the people of the state of New York to procure a judgment sequestering the property of the corporation, as provided by the business corporation law. It is the duty of the attorney general in all criminal proceedings prosecuted by him, and, in all other proceedings, the county attorney for counties outside the city of New York, and, in the city of New York the corporation counsel of the city of New York, to institute proceedings to collect such fine, restitution or reparation.

§ 420.30. Remission of fines, restitution or reparation

1. Applicability. The procedure specified in this section governs remission of fines, restitution or reparation in all cases not covered by subdivision four of section 420.10.

2. Procedure.

(a) Any superior court which has imposed a fine, restitution or reparation for any offense may, in its discretion, on five days notice to the district attorney of the county in which such fine, restitution or reparation was imposed and to each person otherwise required to be given notice of restitution or reparation pursuant to subdivision one of section 420.10, remit such fine, restitution or reparation or any portion thereof. In case of a fine, restitution or reparation imposed by a local criminal court for any offense, a superior court holding a term in the county in which the fine, restitution or reparation was imposed may, upon like notice, remit such fine, restitution or reparation or any portion thereof.

(b) The court shall give each person given notice a reasonable opportunity to be heard on the question of remitting an order of restitution or reparation. If the court remits such restitution or reparation, or any part thereof, the reasons therefor shall be placed upon the record.

3. Restrictions. In no event shall a mandatory surcharge, sex offender registration fee, DNA databank fee or crime victim assistance fee be remitted provided, however, that a court may waive the crime victim assistance fee if such defendant is an eligible youth as defined in subdivision two of section 720.10 of this chapter, and the imposition of such fee would work an unreasonable hardship on the defendant, his or her immediate family, or any other person who is dependent on such defendant for financial support.

§ 420.35. Mandatory surcharge and crime victim assistance fee; applicability to sentences mandating payment of fines

1. The provisions of section 420.10 of this article governing the collection of fines and the provisions of section 420.40 of this article governing deferral of mandatory surcharges, sex offender registration fees, DNA databank fees and financial hardship hearings and the provisions of section 430.20 of this chapter governing the commitment of a defendant for failure to pay a fine shall be applicable to a mandatory surcharge, sex offender registration fee, DNA databank fee and a crime victim assistance fee imposed pursuant to subdivision one of section 60.35 of the penal law, subdivision twenty-a of section three hundred eighty-five of the vehicle and traffic law, subdivision nineteen-a of section four hundred one of the vehicle and traffic law, or a mandatory surcharge imposed pursuant to section eighteen hundred nine of the vehicle and traffic law or section 27.12 of the parks, recreation and historic preservation law. When the court directs that the defendant be imprisoned until the mandatory surcharge, sex offender registration fee or DNA databank fee is satisfied, it must specify a maximum period of imprisonment not to exceed fifteen days; provided, however, a court may not direct that a defendant be imprisoned until the mandatory surcharge, sex offender registration fee, or DNA databank fee is satisfied or otherwise for failure to pay the mandatory surcharge, sex offender registration fee or DNA databank fee unless the court makes a contemporaneous finding on the record, after according defendant notice and an opportunity to be heard, that the payment of the mandatory surcharge, sex offender registration fee or DNA databank fee upon defendant will not work an unreasonable hardship upon him or her or his or her immediate family.

2. Under no circumstances shall the mandatory surcharge, sex offender registration fee, DNA databank fee or the crime victim assistance fee be waived provided, however, that a court may waive the crime victim assistance fee if such defendant is an eligible youth as defined in subdivision two of section 720.10 of this chapter, and the imposition of such fee would work an unreasonable hardship on the defendant, his or her immediate family, or any other person who is dependent on such defendant for financial support. A court shall waive any mandatory surcharge, DNA databank fee and crime victim assistance fee when: (i) the defendant is convicted of loitering for the purpose of engaging in prostitution under section 240.37 of the penal law (provided that the defendant was not convicted of loitering for the purpose of patronizing a person for prostitution); (ii) the defendant is convicted of prostitution under section 230.00 of the penal law; (iii) the defendant is convicted of a violation in the event such conviction is in lieu of a plea to or conviction for loitering for the purpose of engaging in prostitution under section 240.37 of the penal law (provided that the defendant was not alleged to be loitering for the purpose of patronizing a person for prostitution) or prostitution under

section 230.00 of the penal law; or (iv) the court finds that a defendant is a victim of sex trafficking under section 230.34 of the penal law or a victim of trafficking in persons under the trafficking victims protection act (United States Code, Title 22, Chapter 78); or (v) the court finds that the defendant is a victim of sex trafficking of a child under section 230.34-a of the penal law.

3. It shall be the duty of a court of record or administrative tribunal to report to the division of criminal justice services on the disposition and collection of mandatory surcharges, sex offender registration fees or DNA databank fees and crime victim assistance fees. Such report shall include, for all cases, whether the surcharge, sex offender registration fee, DNA databank fee or crime victim assistance fee levied pursuant to subdivision one of section 60.35 of the penal law or section eighteen hundred nine of the vehicle and traffic law has been imposed pursuant to law, collected, or is to be collected by probation or corrections or other officials. The form, manner and frequency of such reports shall be determined by the commissioner of the division of criminal justice services after consultation with the chief administrator of the courts and the commissioner of the department of motor vehicles.

§ 420.40. Deferral of a mandatory surcharge; financial hardship hearings

1. Applicability. The procedure specified in this section governs the deferral of the obligation to pay all or part of a mandatory surcharge, sex offender registration fee or DNA databank fee imposed pursuant to subdivision one of section 60.35 of the penal law and financial hardship hearings relating to mandatory surcharges.

2. On an appearance date set forth in a summons issued pursuant to subdivision three of section 60.35 of the penal law, section eighteen hundred nine of the vehicle and traffic law or section 27.12 of the parks, recreation and historic preservation law, a person upon whom a mandatory surcharge, sex offender registration fee or DNA databank fee was levied shall have an opportunity to present on the record credible and verifiable information establishing that the mandatory surcharge, sex offender registration fee or DNA databank fee should be deferred, in whole or in part, because, due to the indigence of such person the payment of said surcharge, sex offender registration fee or DNA databank fee would work an unreasonable hardship on the person or his or her immediate family.

3. In assessing such information the superior court shall be mindful of the mandatory nature of the surcharge, sex offender registration fee and DNA databank fee, and the important criminal justice and victim services sustained by such fees.

4. Where a court determines that it will defer part or all of a mandatory surcharge, sex offender registration fee or DNA databank fee imposed pursuant to subdivision one of section 60.35 of the penal law, a statement of such finding and of the facts upon which it is based shall be made part of the record.

5. A court which defers a person's obligation to pay a mandatory surcharge, sex offender registration fee or DNA databank fee imposed pursuant to subdivision one of section 60.35 of the penal law shall do so in a written order. Such order shall not excuse the person from the obligation to pay the surcharge, sex offender registration fee or DNA databank fee. Rather, the court's order shall direct the filing of a certified copy of the order with the county clerk of the county in which the court is situate except where

the court which issues such order is the supreme court in which case the order itself shall be filed by the clerk of the court acting in his or her capacity as the county clerk of the county in which the court is situate. Such order shall be entered by the county clerk in the same manner as a judgment in a civil action in accordance with subdivision (a) of rule five thousand sixteen of the civil practice law and rules. The order shall direct that any unpaid balance of the mandatory surcharge, sex offender registration fee or DNA databank fee may be collected in the same manner as a civil judgment. The entered order shall be deemed to constitute a judgment-roll as defined in section five thousand seventeen of the civil practice law and rules and immediately after entry of the order, the county clerk shall docket the entered order as a money judgment pursuant to section five thousand eighteen of such law and rules.

Article 430 Sentences of Imprisonment

§ 430.10. Sentence of imprisonment not to be changed after commencement

Except as otherwise specifically authorized by law, when the court has imposed a sentence of imprisonment and such sentence is in accordance with law, such sentence may not be changed, suspended or interrupted once the term or period of the sentence has commenced.

§ 430.20. Commitment of defendant

1. In general. When a sentence of imprisonment is pronounced, or when th [the]* sentence consists of a fine and the court has directed that the defendant be imprisoned until it is satisfied, the defendant must forthwith be committed to the custody of the appropriate public servant and detained until the sentence is complied with.

2. [Eff until Sept 1, 2019] Indeterminate and determinate sentences. In the case of an indeterminate or determinate sentence of imprisonment, commitment must be to the custody of the state department of corrections and community supervision as provided in subdivision one of section 70.20 of the penal law. The order of commitment must direct that the defendant be delivered to an institution designated by the commissioner of corrections and community supervision in accordance with the provisions of the correction law.

2. [Eff Sept 1, 2019] Indeterminate sentences. In the case of an indeterminate sentence of imprisonment, commitment must be to the custody of the state department of corrections and community supervision as provided in subdivision one of section 70.20 of the penal law. The order of commitment must direct that the defendant be delivered to an institution designated by the commissioner of corrections and community supervision in accordance with the provisions of the correction law.

3. Definite and intermittent sentences. In the case of a definite or intermittent sentence of imprisonment, commitment must be as follows:

(a) In counties contained within New York City or in any county that has a county department of correction, commitment must be to the custody of the department of correction of such city or county;

(b) In any other case, commitment must be to the county jail, workhouse or penitentiary, or to a penitentiary outside the county and the order of commitment must specify the institution to which the defendant is to be delivered.

4. [Eff until Sept 1, 2019] Certain resentences. When a sentence of imprisonment that has been imposed on a defendant is vacated and a new sentence is imposed on such defendant for the same offense, or for an offense based upon the same act, if the term of the new definite or determinate sentence or the maximum term of the new indeterminate sentence so imposed is less than or equal to that of the vacated sentence:

(a) where the time served by the defendant on the vacated sentence is equal to or greater than the term or maximum term of the new sentence, the new sentence shall be deemed to be served in its entirety and the defendant shall not be committed to a correctional facility pursuant to said sentence; and

(b) where the defendant was under the supervision of a local conditional release commission or the department of corrections and community supervision at the time the sentence was vacated, then the commitment shall direct that said conditional release or parole be recommenced, and the defendant shall not be committed to a correctional facility pursuant to said sentence, except as a result of revocation of parole or of conditional release; and

(c) where the defendant was not under the supervision of the department of corrections and community supervision at the time the indeterminate or determinate sentence was vacated, but would immediately be eligible for conditional release from the new indeterminate or determinate sentence, the court shall ascertain from the department of corrections and community supervision whether the defendant has earned a sufficient amount of good time under the vacated sentence so as to require the conditional release of the defendant under the new sentence; in the event the defendant has earned a sufficient amount of good time, the court shall stay execution of sentence until the defendant surrenders at a correctional facility pursuant to the direction of the department of corrections and community supervision, which shall occur no later than sixty days after imposition of sentence; upon said stay of execution, the court clerk shall immediately mail to the commissioner of corrections and community supervision a certified copy of the commitment reflecting said stay of execution and the name, mailing address and telephone number of the defendant's legal representative; in the event the defendant fails to surrender as directed by the department of corrections and community supervision, the department shall notify the court which shall thereafter remand the defendant to custody pursuant to section 430.30 of this article; and

(d) upon the resentence of a defendant as described in this subdivision, the court clerk shall immediately mail a certified copy of the commitment to the commissioner of corrections and community supervision if the vacated sentence or the new sentence is an indeterminate or determinate sentence and no mailing is required by paragraph (c) of this subdivision; additionally, the court clerk shall immediately mail a certified copy of the new commitment to the head of the appropriate local correctional facility if the vacated sentence or the new sentence is a definite sentence.

4. [Eff Sept 1, 2019] Certain resentences. When a sentence of imprisonment that has been imposed on a defendant is vacated and a new sentence is imposed on such defendant for the same offense, or for an offense based upon the same act, if the term

of the new definite sentence or the maximum term of the new indeterminate sentence so imposed is less than or equal to that of the vacated sentence:

(a) where the time served by the defendant on the vacated sentence is equal to or greater than the term or maximum term of the new sentence, the new sentence shall be deemed to be served in its entirety and the defendant shall not be committed to a correctional facility pursuant to said sentence; and

(b) where the defendant was under the supervision of a local conditional release commission or the department of corrections and community supervision at the time the sentence was vacated, then the commitment shall direct that said conditional release or parole be recommenced, and the defendant shall not be committed to a correctional facility pursuant to said sentence, except as a result of revocation of parole or of conditional release; and

(c) where the defendant was not under the supervision of the department of corrections and community supervision at the time the indeterminate sentence was vacated, but would immediately be eligible for conditional release from the new indeterminate sentence, the court shall ascertain from the department of corrections and community supervision whether the defendant has earned a sufficient amount of good time under the vacated sentence so as to require the conditional release of the defendant under the new sentence; in the event the defendant has earned a sufficient amount of good time, the court shall stay execution of sentence until the defendant surrenders at a correctional facility pursuant to the direction of the department of corrections and community supervision, which shall occur no later than sixty days after imposition of sentence; upon said stay of execution, the court clerk shall immediately mail to the commissioner of corrections and community supervision a certified copy of the commitment reflecting said stay of execution and the name, mailing address and telephone number of the defendant's legal representative; in the event the defendant fails to surrender as directed by the department of corrections and community supervision, the department shall notify the court which shall thereafter remand the defendant to custody pursuant to section 430.30 of this article; and

(d) upon the resentence of a defendant as described in this subdivision, the court clerk shall immediately mail a certified copy of the commitment to the commissioner of corrections and community supervision if the vacated sentence or the new sentence is an indeterminate sentence and no mailing is required by paragraph (c) of this subdivision; additionally, the court clerk shall immediately mail a certified copy of the new commitment to the head of the appropriate local correctional facility if the vacated sentence or the new sentence is a definite sentence.

5. Commitment for failure to pay fine. Where the sentence consists of a fine and the court has directed that the defendant be imprisoned until it is satisfied, commitment must be as follows:

(a) If the sentence also includes a term of imprisonment, commitment must be to the same institution as is designated for service of the term of imprisonment, and the period of commitment commences (i) when the term of imprisonment is satisfied, or (ii) with the approval of the state board of parole, when the defendant becomes eligible for parole, or (iii) when the defendant becomes eligible for conditional release, whichever occurs first; provided, however, that the court may direct that the period of imprisonment for the fine run concurrently with the term of imprisonment; and

(b) In any other case, commitment must be to the agency or institution that would be designated in the case of a definite sentence.

§ 430.30. Duty to deliver defendant

In counties contained within New York City and in counties that have a commissioner of correction who is responsible for detention of defendants in criminal actions, it is the duty of the commissioner of correction of such city or county to deliver the defendant forthwith to the proper institution in accordance with the commitment. In all other counties it is the duty of the sheriff to deliver the defendant forthwith to the proper institution in accordance with the commitment.

Title M Proceedings After Judgment

Article 440 Post-Judgment Motions

§ 440.10. Motion to vacate judgment

1. At any time after the entry of a judgment, the court in which it was entered may, upon motion of the defendant, vacate such judgment upon the ground that:

(a) The court did not have jurisdiction of the action or of the person of the defendant; or

(b) The judgment was procured by duress, misrepresentation or fraud on the part of the court or a prosecutor or a person acting for or in behalf of a court or a prosecutor; or

(c) Material evidence adduced at a trial resulting in the judgment was false and was, prior to the entry of the judgment, known by the prosecutor or by the court to be false; or

(d) Material evidence adduced by the people at a trial resulting in the judgment was procured in violation of the defendant's rights under the constitution of this state or of the United States; or

(e) During the proceedings resulting in the judgment, the defendant, by reason of mental disease or defect, was incapable of understanding or participating in such proceedings; or

(f) Improper and prejudicial conduct not appearing in the record occurred during a trial resulting in the judgment which conduct, if it had appeared in the record, would have required a reversal of the judgment upon an appeal therefrom; or

(g) New evidence has been discovered since the entry of a judgment based upon a verdict of guilty after trial, which could not have been produced by the defendant at the trial even with due diligence on his part and which is of such character as to create a probability that had such evidence been received at the trial the verdict would have been more favorable to the defendant; provided that a motion based upon such ground must be made with due diligence after the discovery of such alleged new evidence; or

(g-1)Forensic DNA testing of evidence performed since the entry of a judgment, (1) in the case of a defendant convicted after a guilty plea, the court has determined that the defendant has demonstrated a substantial probability that the defendant was actually innocent of the offense of which he or she was convicted, or (2) in the case of a defendant convicted after a trial, the court has determined that there exists a reasonable probability that the verdict would have been more favorable to the defendant.

(h) The judgment was obtained in violation of a right of the defendant under the constitution of this state or of the United States; or

(i) The judgment is a conviction where the arresting charge was under section 240.37 (loitering for the purpose of engaging in a prostitution offense, provided that the defendant was not alleged to be loitering for the purpose of patronizing a person for prostitution or promoting prostitution) or 230.00 (prostitution) or 230.03 (prostitution in a school zone) of the penal law, and the defendant's participation in the offense was a result of having been a victim of sex trafficking under section 230.34 of the penal law, sex trafficking of a child under section 230.34-a of the penal law, labor trafficking under section 135.35 of the penal law, aggravated labor trafficking under section 135.37 of the penal law, compelling prostitution under section 230.33 of the penal law, or trafficking in persons under the Trafficking Victims Protection Act (United States Code, title 22, chapter 78); provided that

(i) a motion under this paragraph shall be made with due diligence, after the defendant has ceased to be a victim of such trafficking or compelling prostitution crime or has sought services for victims of such trafficking or compelling prostitution crime, subject to reasonable concerns for the safety of the defendant, family members of the defendant, or other victims of such trafficking or compelling prostitution crime that may be jeopardized by the bringing of such motion, or for other reasons consistent with the purpose of this paragraph; and

(ii) official documentation of the defendant's status as a victim of trafficking, compelling prostitution or trafficking in persons at the time of the offense from a federal, state or local government agency shall create a presumption that the defendant's participation in the offense was a result of having been a victim of sex trafficking, compelling prostitution or trafficking in persons, but shall not be required for granting a motion under this paragraph.

2. Notwithstanding the provisions of subdivision one, the court must deny a motion to vacate a judgment when:

(a) The ground or issue raised upon the motion was previously determined on the merits upon an appeal from the judgment, unless since the time of such appellate determination there has been a retroactively effective change in the law controlling such issue; or

(b) The judgment is, at the time of the motion, appealable or pending on appeal, and sufficient facts appear on the record with respect to the ground or issue raised upon the motion to permit adequate review thereof upon such an appeal. This paragraph shall not apply to a motion under paragraph (i) of subdivision one of this section; or

(c) Although sufficient facts appear on the record of the proceedings underlying the judgment to have permitted, upon appeal from such judgment, adequate review of the ground or issue raised upon the motion, no such appellate review or determination occurred owing to the defendant's unjustifiable failure to take or perfect an appeal during the prescribed period or to his unjustifiable failure to raise such ground or issue upon an appeal actually perfected by him; or

(d) The ground or issue raised relates solely to the validity of the sentence and not to the validity of the conviction.

3. Notwithstanding the provisions of subdivision one, the court may deny a motion to vacate a judgment when:

(a) Although facts in support of the ground or issue raised upon the motion could with due diligence by the defendant have readily been made to appear on the record in a manner providing adequate basis for review of such ground or issue upon an appeal from the judgment, the defendant unjustifiably failed to adduce such matter prior to sentence and the ground or issue in question was not subsequently determined upon appeal. This paragraph does not apply to a motion based upon deprivation of the right to counsel at the trial or upon failure of the trial court to advise the defendant of such right, or to a motion under paragraph (i) of subdivision one of this section; or

(b) The ground or issue raised upon the motion was previously determined on the merits upon a prior motion or proceeding in a court of this state, other than an appeal from the judgment, or upon a motion or proceeding in a federal court; unless since the time of such determination there has been a retroactively effective change in the law controlling such issue; or

(c) Upon a previous motion made pursuant to this section, the defendant was in a position adequately to raise the ground or issue underlying the present motion but did not do so.

Although the court may deny the motion under any of the circumstances specified in this subdivision, in the interest of justice and for good cause shown it may in its discretion grant the motion if it is otherwise meritorious and vacate the judgment.

4. If the court grants the motion, it must, except as provided in subdivision five or six of this section, vacate the judgment, and must dismiss the accusatory instrument, or order a new trial, or take such other action as is appropriate in the circumstances.

5. Upon granting the motion upon the ground, as prescribed in paragraph (g) of subdivision one, that newly discovered evidence creates a probability that had such evidence been received at the trial the verdict would have been more favorable to the defendant in that the conviction would have been for a lesser offense than the one contained in the verdict, the court may either:

(a) Vacate the judgment and order a new trial; or

(b) With the consent of the people, modify the judgment by reducing it to one of conviction for such lesser offense. In such case, the court must re-sentence the defendant accordingly.

6. If the court grants a motion under paragraph (i) of subdivision one of this section, it must vacate the judgment and dismiss the accusatory instrument, and may take such additional action as is appropriate in the circumstances.

7. Upon a new trial resulting from an order vacating a judgment pursuant to this section, the indictment is deemed to contain all the counts and to charge all the offenses which it contained and charged at the time the previous trial was commenced, regardless of whether any count was dismissed by the court in the course of such trial, except (a) those upon or of which the defendant was acquitted or deemed to have been acquitted, and (b) those dismissed by the order vacating the judgment, and (c) those previously dismissed by an appellate court upon an appeal from the judgment, or by any court upon a previous post-judgment motion.

8. Upon an order which vacates a judgment based upon a plea of guilty to an accusatory instrument or a part thereof, but which does not dismiss the entire

accusatory instrument, the criminal action is, in the absence of an express direction to the contrary, restored to its prepleading status and the accusatory instrument is deemed to contain all the counts and to charge all the offenses which it contained and charged at the time of the entry of the plea, except those subsequently dismissed under circumstances specified in paragraphs (b) and (c) of subdivision six. Where the plea of guilty was entered and accepted, pursuant to subdivision three of section 220.30, upon the condition that it constituted a complete disposition not only of the accusatory instrument underlying the judgment vacated but also of one or more other accusatory instruments against the defendant then pending in the same court, the order of vacation completely restores such other accusatory instruments; and such is the case even though such order dismisses the main accusatory instrument underlying the judgment.

§ 440.20. Motion to set aside sentence; by defendant

1. At any time after the entry of a judgment, the court in which the judgment was entered may, upon motion of the defendant, set aside the sentence upon the ground that it was unauthorized, illegally imposed or otherwise invalid as a matter of law. Where the judgment includes a sentence of death, the court may also set aside the sentence upon any of the grounds set forth in paragraph (b), (c), (f), (g) or (h) of subdivision one of section 440.10 as applied to a separate sentencing proceeding under section 400.27, provided, however, that to the extent the ground or grounds asserted include one or more of the aforesaid paragraphs of subdivision one of section 440.10, the court must also apply subdivisions two and three of section 440.10, other than paragraph (d) of subdivision two of such section, in determining the motion. In the event the court enters an order granting a motion to set aside a sentence of death under this section, the court must either direct a new sentencing proceeding in accordance with section 400.27 or, to the extent that the defendant cannot be resentenced to death consistent with the laws of this state or the constitution of this state or of the United States, resentence the defendant to life imprisonment without parole or to a sentence of imprisonment for the class A-I felony of murder in the first degree other than a sentence of life imprisonment without parole. Upon granting the motion upon any of the grounds set forth in the aforesaid paragraphs of subdivision one of section 440.10 and setting aside the sentence, the court must afford the people a reasonable period of time, which shall not be less than ten days, to determine whether to take an appeal from the order setting aside the sentence of death. The taking of an appeal by the people stays the effectiveness of that portion of the court's order that directs a new sentencing proceeding.

2. Notwithstanding the provisions of subdivision one, the court must deny such a motion when the ground or issue raised thereupon was previously determined on the merits upon an appeal from the judgment or sentence, unless since the time of such appellate determination there has been a retroactively effective change in the law controlling such issue.

3. Notwithstanding the provisions of subdivision one, the court may deny such a motion when the ground or issue raised thereupon was previously determined on the merits upon a prior motion or proceeding in a court of this state, other than an appeal from the judgment, or upon a prior motion or proceeding in a federal court, unless since the time

of such determination there has been a retroactively effective change in the law controlling such issue. Despite such determination, however, the court in the interest of justice and for good cause shown, may in its discretion grant the motion if it is otherwise meritorious.

4. An order setting aside a sentence pursuant to this section does not affect the validity or status of the underlying conviction, and after entering such an order the court must resentence the defendant in accordance with the law.

§ 440.30. Motion to vacate judgment and to set aside sentence; procedure

1.

(a) A motion to vacate a judgment pursuant to section 440.10 of this article and a motion to set aside a sentence pursuant to section 440.20 of this article must be made in writing and upon reasonable notice to the people. Upon the motion, a defendant who is in a position adequately to raise more than one ground should raise every such ground upon which he or she intends to challenge the judgment or sentence. If the motion is based upon the existence or occurrence of facts, the motion papers must contain sworn allegations thereof, whether by the defendant or by another person or persons. Such sworn allegations may be based upon personal knowledge of the affiant or upon information and belief, provided that in the latter event the affiant must state the sources of such information and the grounds of such belief. The defendant may further submit documentary evidence or information supporting or tending to support the allegations of the moving papers. The people may file with the court, and in such case must serve a copy thereof upon the defendant or his or her counsel, if any, an answer denying or admitting any or all of the allegations of the motion papers, and may further submit documentary evidence or information refuting or tending to refute such allegations. After all papers of both parties have been filed, and after all documentary evidence or information, if any, has been submitted, the court must consider the same for the purpose of ascertaining whether the motion is determinable without a hearing to resolve questions of fact.

(b) In conjunction with the filing or consideration of a motion to vacate a judgment pursuant to section 440.10 of this article by a defendant convicted after a trial, in cases where the court has ordered an evidentiary hearing upon such motion, the court may order that the people produce or make available for inspection property, as defined in subdivision three of section 240.10 of this part, in its possession, custody, or control that was secured in connection with the investigation or prosecution of the defendant upon credible allegations by the defendant and a finding by the court that such property, if obtained, would be probative to the determination of defendant's actual innocence, and that the request is reasonable. The court shall deny or limit such a request upon a finding that such a request, if granted, would threaten the integrity or chain of custody of property or the integrity of the processes or functions of a laboratory conducting DNA testing, pose a risk of harm, intimidation, embarrassment, reprisal, or other substantially negative consequences to any person, undermine the proper functions of law enforcement including the confidentiality of informants, or on the basis of any other factor identified by the court in the interests of justice or public safety. The court shall further ensure that any property produced pursuant to this paragraph is subject to a protective order, where appropriate. The court shall deny any request made pursuant to this paragraph where:

(i)

(1) the defendant's motion pursuant to section 440.10 of this article does not seek to demonstrate his or her actual innocence of the offense or offenses of which he or she was convicted that are the subject of the motion, or (2) the defendant has not presented credible allegations and the court has not found that such property, if obtained, would be probative to the determination of the defendant's actual innocence and that the request is reasonable;

(ii) the defendant has made his or her motion after five years from the date of the judgment of conviction; provided, however, that this limitation period shall be tolled for five years if the defendant is in custody in connection with the conviction that is the subject of his or her motion, and provided further that, notwithstanding such limitation periods, the court may consider the motion if the defendant has shown: (A) that he or she has been pursuing his or her rights diligently and that some extraordinary circumstance prevented the timely filing of the motion; (B) that the facts upon which the motion is predicated were unknown to the defendant or his or her attorney and could not have been ascertained by the exercise of due diligence prior to the expiration of the statute of limitations; or (C) considering all circumstances of the case including but not limited to evidence of the defendant's guilt, the impact of granting or denying such motion upon public confidence in the criminal justice system, or upon the safety or welfare of the community, and the defendant's diligence in seeking to obtain the requested property or related relief, the interests of justice would be served by considering the motion;

(iii) the defendant is challenging a judgment convicting him or her of an offense that is not a felony defined in section 10.00 of the penal law; or

(iv) upon a finding by the court that the property requested in this motion would be available through other means through reasonable efforts by the defendant to obtain such property.

1-a.

(a)

(1) Where the defendant's motion requests the performance of a forensic DNA test on specified evidence, and upon the court's determination that any evidence containing deoxyribonucleic acid ("DNA") was secured in connection with the trial resulting in the judgment, the court shall grant the application for forensic DNA testing of such evidence upon its determination that if a DNA test had been conducted on such evidence, and if the results had been admitted in the trial resulting in the judgment, there exists a reasonable probability that the verdict would have been more favorable to the defendant.

(2) Where the defendant's motion for forensic DNA testing of specified evidence is made following a plea of guilty and entry of judgment thereon convicting him or her of:

(A) a homicide offense defined in article one hundred twenty-five of the penal law, any felony sex offense defined in article one hundred thirty of the penal law, a violent felony offense as defined in paragraph (a) of subdivision one of section 70.02 of the penal law, or (B) any other felony offense to which he or she pled guilty after being charged in an indictment or information in superior court with one or more of the offenses listed in clause (A) of this subparagraph, then the court shall grant such a motion upon its determination that evidence containing DNA was secured in connection with the investigation or prosecution of the defendant, and if a DNA test had been conducted on such evidence and the results had been known to the parties prior to the entry of the defendant's plea and judgment thereon, there exists a substantial probability that the evidence would have established the defendant's actual innocence of the offense or offenses that are the subject of the defendant's motion; provided, however, that:

(i) the court shall consider whether the defendant had the opportunity to request such testing prior to entering a guilty plea, and, where it finds that the defendant had such opportunity and unjustifiably failed to do so, the court may deny such motion; and

(ii) a court shall deny the defendant's motion for forensic DNA testing where the defendant has made his or her motion more than five years after entry of the judgment of conviction; except that the limitation period may be tolled if the defendant has shown: (A) that he or she has been pursuing his or her rights diligently and that some extraordinary circumstance prevented the timely filing of the motion for forensic DNA testing; (B) that the facts upon which the motion is predicated were unknown to the defendant or his or her attorney and could not have been ascertained by the exercise of due diligence prior to the expiration of this statute of limitations; or (C) considering all circumstances of the case including but not limited to evidence of the defendant's guilt, the impact of granting or denying such motion upon public confidence in the criminal justice system, or upon the safety or welfare of the community, and the defendant's diligence in seeking to obtain the requested property or related relief, the interests of justice would be served by tolling such limitation period.

(b) In conjunction with the filing of a motion under this subdivision, the court may direct the people to provide the defendant with information in the possession of the people concerning the current physical location of the specified evidence and if the specified evidence no longer exists or the physical location of the specified evidence is unknown, a representation to that effect and information and documentary evidence in the possession of the people concerning the last known physical location of such specified evidence. If there is a finding by the court that the specified evidence no longer exists or the physical location of such specified evidence is unknown, such information in and of itself shall not be a factor from which any inference unfavorable to the people may be drawn by the court in deciding a motion under this section. The court, on motion of the defendant, may also issue a subpoena duces tecum directing a public or private hospital, laboratory or other entity to produce such specified evidence in its possession and/or information and documentary evidence in its possession concerning the location and status of such specified evidence.

(c) In response to a motion under this paragraph, upon notice to the parties and to the entity required to perform the search the court may order an entity that has access to the combined DNA index system ("CODIS") or its successor system to compare a DNA profile obtained from probative biological material gathered in connection with the investigation or prosecution of the defendant against DNA databanks by keyboard searches, or a similar method that does not involve uploading, upon a court's determination that (1) such profile complies with federal bureau of investigation or state requirements, whichever are applicable and as such requirements are applied to law enforcement agencies seeking such a comparison, and that the data meet state DNA index system and/or national DNA index system criteria as such criteria are applied to law enforcement agencies seeking such a comparison and (2) if such comparison had been conducted, and if the results had been admitted in the trial resulting in the judgment, a reasonable probability exists that the verdict would have been more favorable to the defendant, or in a case involving a plea of guilty, if the results had been available to the defendant prior to the plea, a reasonable probability exists that the conviction would not have resulted. For purposes of this subdivision, a "keyboard search" shall mean a search of a DNA profile against the databank in which the profile that is searched is not uploaded to or maintained in the databank.

2. If it appears by conceded or uncontradicted allegations of the moving papers or of the answer, or by unquestionable documentary proof, that there are circumstances which require denial thereof pursuant to subdivision two of section 440.10 or subdivision two of section 440.20, the court must summarily deny the motion. If it appears that there are circumstances authorizing, though not requiring, denial thereof pursuant to subdivision three of section 440.10 or subdivision three of section 440.20, the court may in its discretion either (a) summarily deny the motion, or (b) proceed to consider the merits thereof.

3. Upon considering the merits of the motion, the court must grant it without conducting a hearing and vacate the judgment or set aside the sentence, as the case may be, if:

(a) The moving papers allege a ground constituting legal basis for the motion; and

(b) Such ground, if based upon the existence or occurrence of facts, is supported by sworn allegations thereof; and

(c) The sworn allegations of fact essential to support the motion are either conceded by the people to be true or are conclusively substantiated by unquestionable documentary proof.

4. Upon considering the merits of the motion, the court may deny it without conducting a hearing if:

(a) The moving papers do not allege any ground constituting legal basis for the motion; or

(b) The motion is based upon the existence or occurrence of facts and the moving papers do not contain sworn allegations substantiating or tending to substantiate all the essential facts, as required by subdivision one; or

(c) An allegation of fact essential to support the motion is conclusively refuted by unquestionable documentary proof; or

(d) An allegation of fact essential to support the motion (i) is contradicted by a court record or other official document, or is made solely by the defendant and is unsupported by any other affidavit or evidence, and (ii) under these and all the other circumstances attending the case, there is no reasonable possibility that such allegation is true.

5. If the court does not determine the motion pursuant to subdivisions two, three or four, it must conduct a hearing and make findings of fact essential to the determination

thereof. The defendant has a right to be present at such hearing but may waive such right in writing. If he does not so waive it and if he is confined in a prison or other institution of this state, the court must cause him to be produced at such hearing.

6. At such a hearing, the defendant has the burden of proving by a preponderance of the evidence every fact essential to support the motion.

7. Regardless of whether a hearing was conducted, the court, upon determining the motion, must set forth on the record its findings of fact, its conclusions of law and the reasons for its determination.

§ 440.40. Motion to set aside sentence; by people

1. At any time not more than one year after the entry of a judgment, the court in which it was entered may, upon motion of the people, set aside the sentence upon the ground that it was invalid as a matter of law.

2. Notwithstanding the provisions of subdivision one, the court must summarily deny the motion when the ground or issue raised thereupon was previously determined on the merits upon an appeal from the judgment or sentence, unless since the time of such appellate determination there has been a retroactively effective change in the law controlling such issue.

3. Notwithstanding the provisions of subdivision one, the court may summarily deny such a motion when the ground or issue raised thereupon was previously determined on the merits upon a prior motion or proceeding in a court of this state, other than an appeal from the judgment or sentence, unless since the time of such determination there has been a retroactively effective change in the law controlling such issue. Despite such circumstance, however, the court, in the interests of justice and for good cause shown, may in its discretion grant the motion if it is otherwise meritorious.

4. The motion must be made upon reasonable notice to the defendant and to the attorney if any who appeared for him in the last proceeding which occurred in connection with the judgment or sentence, and the defendant must be given adequate opportunity to appear in opposition to the motion. The defendant has a right to be present at such proceeding but may waive such right in writing. If he does not so waive it and if he is confined in a prison or other institution of this state, the court must cause him to be produced at the proceeding upon the motion.

5. An order setting aside a sentence pursuant to this section does not affect the validity or status of the underlying conviction, and after entering such an order the court must resentence the defendant in accordance with the law.

6. Upon a resentence imposed pursuant to subdivision five, the terms of which are more severe than those of the original sentence, the defendant's time for taking an appeal from the judgment is automatically extended in the manner prescribed in subdivision four of section 450.30.

§ 440.46. Motion for resentence; certain controlled substance offenders

1. Any person in the custody of the department of corrections and community supervision convicted of a class B felony offense defined in article two hundred twenty of the penal law which was committed prior to January thirteenth, two thousand five, who is serving an indeterminate sentence with a maximum term of more than three years, may, except as provided in subdivision five of this section, upon notice to the

appropriate district attorney, apply to be resentenced to a determinate sentence in accordance with sections 60.04 and 70.70 of the penal law in the court which imposed the sentence.

2. As part of any such application, the defendant may also move to be resentenced to a determinate sentence in accordance with section 70.70 of the penal law for any one or more class C, D, or E felony offenses defined in article two hundred twenty or two hundred twenty-one of the penal law, the sentence or sentences for which were imposed by the sentencing court at the same time or were included in the same order of commitment as such class B felony.

3. The provisions of section twenty-three of chapter seven hundred thirty-eight of the laws of two thousand four shall govern the proceedings on and determination of a motion brought pursuant to this section; provided, however that the court's consideration of the institutional record of confinement of such person shall include but not be limited to such person's participation in or willingness to participate in treatment or other programming while incarcerated and such person's disciplinary history. The fact that a person may have been unable to participate in treatment or other programming while incarcerated despite such person's willingness to do so shall not be considered a negative factor in determining a motion pursuant to this section.

4. Subdivision one of section seven hundred seventeen and subdivision four of section seven hundred twenty-two of the county law, and the related provisions of article eighteen-A of such law, shall apply to the preparation of and proceedings on motions pursuant to this section, including any appeals.

5. The provisions of this section shall not apply to any person who is serving a sentence on a conviction for or has a predicate felony conviction for an exclusion offense. For purposes of this subdivision, an "exclusion offense" is:

(a) a crime for which the person was previously convicted within the preceding ten years, excluding any time during which the offender was incarcerated for any reason between the time of commission of the previous felony and the time of commission of the present felony, which was: (i) a violent felony offense as defined in section 70.02 of the penal law; or (ii) any other offense for which a merit time allowance is not available pursuant to subparagraph (ii) of paragraph (d) of subdivision one of section eight hundred three of the correction law; or

(b) a second violent felony offense pursuant to section 70.04 of the penal law or a persistent violent felony offense pursuant to section 70.08 of the penal law for which the person has previously been adjudicated.

§ 440.50. Notice to crime victims of case disposition

1. Upon the request of a victim of a crime, or in any event in all cases in which the final disposition includes a conviction of a violent felony offense as defined in section 70.02 of the penal law, a felony defined in article one hundred twenty-five of such law, or a felony defined in article one hundred thirty of such law, the district attorney shall, within sixty days of the final disposition of the case, inform the victim by letter of such final disposition. If such final disposition results in the commitment of the defendant to the custody of the department of corrections and community supervision for an indeterminate sentence, the notice provided to the crime victim shall also inform the

victim of his or her right to submit a written, audiotaped, or videotaped victim impact statement to the department of corrections and community supervision or to meet personally with a member of the state board of parole at a time and place separate from the personal interview between a member or members of the board and the inmate and make such a statement, subject to procedures and limitations contained in rules of the board, both pursuant to subdivision two of section two hundred fifty-nine-i of the executive law. A copy of such letter shall be provided to the board of parole. The right of the victim under this subdivision to submit a written victim impact statement or to meet personally with a member of the state board of parole applies to each personal interview between a member or members of the board and the inmate.

2. As used in this section, "victim" means any person alleged or found, upon the record, to have sustained physical or financial injury to person or property as a direct result of the crime charged or a person alleged or found to have sustained, upon the record, an offense under article one hundred thirty of the penal law, or in the case of a homicide or minor child, the victim's family.

3. As used in this section, "final disposition" means an ultimate termination of the case at the trial level including, but not limited to, dismissal, acquittal, or imposition of sentence by the court, or a decision by the district attorney, for whatever reason, to not file the case.

§ 440.55. Notice to education department where a licensed professional has been convicted of a felony

The district attorney shall give written notification to the department of education upon the conviction of a felony of any person holding a license pursuant to title eight of the education law. In addition, the district attorney shall give written notification to the department upon the vacatur or reversal of any felony conviction of any such person.

§ 440.60. Notification of invalid sentences of probation

Whenever it shall appear to the satisfaction of the appropriate director of the probation department that a person sentenced pursuant to article sixty of the penal law has received a sentence which is invalid as a matter of law, it shall become his duty to notify the district attorney of the county in which such person was convicted. Upon such notification, the district attorney shall immediately investigate the matter and if such sentence of probation is in fact invalid as a matter of law, the district attorney shall immediately move to set aside such sentence pursuant to section 440.40 of this chapter.

§ 440.65. Notice to child protective agency of conviction for certain crimes against a child

Upon conviction of any person for a crime under article one hundred twenty, article one hundred twenty-five, article one hundred thirty, article two hundred sixty or article two hundred sixty-three of the penal law committed against a child under the age of eighteen by a person legally responsible for such child, as defined in subdivision three of section four hundred twelve of the social services law, the district attorney serving the jurisdiction in which such conviction is entered shall notify the local child protective services agency of such conviction including the name of the defendant, the name of the child, the court case number and the name of the prosecutor who appeared for the people.

§ 440.70. Notice to the secretary of state when false financing statement filed

Upon conviction of any person for a crime where the defendant intentionally filed or caused to be filed a financing statement pursuant to article nine of the uniform commercial code on form UCC1 that falsely claims that a person is indebted or obligated to such defendant, the court wherein such conviction is entered, or the clerk thereof, shall issue and cause to be filed a certificate with the New York secretary of state: (a) certifying that a judgment of conviction has been entered in such court against the defendant who was listed as the secured party in such form; and (b) specifying the date and location of the filing, any filing or indexing number assigned to such filing, the debtor named in such statement, and a description of the collateral encumbered by the instrument.

Article 450 Appeals—In What Cases Authorized and to What Courts Taken

§ 450.10. Appeal by defendant to intermediate appellate court; in what cases authorized as of right

An appeal to an intermediate appellate court may be taken as of right by the defendant from the following judgment, sentence and order of a criminal court:

1. A judgment other than one including a sentence of death, unless the appeal is based solely upon the ground that a sentence was harsh or excessive when such sentence was predicated upon entry of a plea of guilty and the sentence imposed did not exceed that which was agreed to by the defendant as a condition of the plea and set forth on the record or filed with the court as required by subdivision five of section 220.50 or subdivision four of section 340.20;

2. A sentence other than one of death, as prescribed in subdivision one of section 450.30, unless the appeal is based solely upon the ground that a sentence was harsh or excessive when such sentence was predicated upon entry of a plea of guilty and the sentence imposed did not exceed that which was agreed to by the defendant as a condition of the plea and set forth in the record or filed with the court as required by subdivision five of section 220.50 or subdivision four of section 340.20;

3. A sentence including an order of criminal forfeiture entered pursuant to section 460.30 of the penal law with respect to such forfeiture order.

4. An order, entered pursuant to section 440.40, setting aside a sentence other than one of death, upon motion of the People.

5. An order denying a motion, made pursuant to subdivision one-a of section 440.30, for forensic DNA testing of evidence.

§ 450.15. Appeal by defendant to intermediate appellate court; in what cases authorized by permission

If an appeal by defendant is not authorized as of right pursuant to section 450.10, the defendant may appeal from the following orders of a criminal court, provided that a certificate granting leave to appeal is issued pursuant to section 460.15:

1. An order denying a motion, made pursuant to section 440.10, to vacate a judgment other than one including a sentence of death;

2. An order denying a motion by the defendant made pursuant to section 440.20, to set aside a sentence other than one of death;

3. A sentence which is not otherwise appealable as of right pursuant to subdivision one or two of section 450.10.

§ 450.20. Appeal by people to intermediate appellate court; in what cases authorized

An appeal to an intermediate appellate court may be taken as of right by the people from the following sentence and orders of a criminal court:

1. An order dismissing an accusatory instrument or a count thereof, entered pursuant to section 170.30, 170.50 or 210.20, or an order terminating a prosecution pursuant to subdivision four of section 180.85;

1-a. An order reducing a count or counts of an indictment or dismissing an indictment and directing the filing of a prosecutor's information, entered pursuant to subdivision one-a of section 210.20;

2. An order setting aside a verdict and dismissing an accusatory instrument or a count thereof, entered pursuant to paragraph (b) of subdivision one of section 290.10 or 360.40;

3. An order setting aside a verdict, entered pursuant to section 330.30 or 370.10;

4. A sentence other than one of death, as prescribed in subdivisions two and three of section 450.30;

5. An order, entered pursuant to section 440.10, vacating a judgment other than one including a sentence of death;

6. An order, entered pursuant to section 440.20, setting aside a sentence other than one of death;

7. An order denying a motion by the people, made pursuant to section 440.40, to set aside a sentence other than one of death;

8. An order suppressing evidence, entered before trial pursuant to section 710.20; provided that the people file a statement in the appellate court pursuant to section 450.50.

9. An order entered pursuant to section 460.30 of the penal law setting aside or modifying a verdict of forfeiture.

10. An order, entered pursuant to paragraph (e) of subdivision twelve of section 400.27, finding that the defendant is mentally retarded.

11. An order granting a motion, made pursuant to subdivision one-a of section 440.30, for forensic DNA testing of evidence.

§ 450.30. Appeal from sentence

1. An appeal by the defendant from a sentence, as authorized by subdivision two of section 450.10, may be based upon the ground that such sentence either was (a) invalid as a matter of law, or (b) harsh or excessive. A sentence is invalid as a matter of law not only when the terms thereof are unauthorized but also when it is based upon an erroneous determination that the defendant had a previous valid conviction for an offense or, in the case of a resentence following a revocation of a sentence of probation or conditional discharge, upon an improper revocation of such original sentence. An appeal by the defendant from a sentence, as authorized by subdivision three of section 450.15, may be based upon the ground that such sentence was harsh or excessive.

2. An appeal by the people from a sentence, as authorized by subdivision four of section 450.20, may be based only upon the ground that such sentence was invalid as a matter of law.

3. An appeal from a sentence, within the meaning of this section and sections 450.10 and 450.20, means an appeal from either the sentence originally imposed or from a resentence following an order vacating the original sentence. For purposes of appeal, the judgment consists of the conviction and the original sentence only, and when a resentence occurs more than thirty days after the original sentence, a defendant who has not previously filed a notice of appeal from the judgment may not appeal from the judgment, but only from the resentence.

4. When as a result of a successful appeal by the people from a sentence, the defendant receives a resentence the terms of which are more severe than those of the original or reversed sentence, the defendant, if he has not taken an appeal from the judgment, may, even though the period for doing so as prescribed in section 460.10 has expired, take such an appeal by filing and serving a notice of appeal, or an affidavit of errors as the case may be, within thirty days after imposition of the resentence. Upon such an appeal, only the conviction is reviewable; and any appellate challenge to the resentence must be made upon a separate appeal therefrom.

§ 450.40. Appeal by people from trial order of dismissal

1. An appeal by the people from a trial order of dismissal, as authorized by subdivision two of section 450.20, may, as indicated by section 290.10, be based either (a) upon the ground that the evidence adduced at the trial was legally sufficient to support the count or counts of the accusatory instrument dismissed by the order, or (b) upon the ground that, though not legally sufficient, such evidence would have been legally sufficient had the court not erroneously excluded admissible evidence offered by the people.

2. If the appeal is based upon the ground specified in paragraph (b) of subdivision one, and if the appellate court determines that the evidence unsuccessfully offered by the people was improperly excluded, and if at the trial the people made on [an]* offer of proof with respect thereto pursuant to subdivision three of section 290.10, the appellate court, in making its determination whether the people's evidence would have been legally sufficient had it not been for the improper exclusion, must treat the excluded evidentiary matter as it is summarized in the offer of proof as evidence constituting a part of the people's case.

§ 450.50. Appeal by people from order suppressing evidence; filing of statement in appellate court

1. In taking an appeal, pursuant to subdivision eight of section 450.20, to an intermediate appellate court from an order of a criminal court suppressing evidence, the people must file, in addition to a notice of appeal or, as the case may be, an affidavit of errors, a statement asserting that the deprivation of the use of the evidence ordered suppressed has rendered the sum of the proof available to the people with respect to a criminal charge which has been filed in the court either (a) insufficient as a matter of law, or (b) so weak in its entirety that any reasonable possibility of prosecuting such charge to a conviction has been effectively destroyed.

2. The taking of an appeal by the people, pursuant to subdivision eight of section 450.20, from an order suppressing evidence constitutes a bar to the prosecution of the accusatory instrument involving the evidence ordered suppressed, unless and until such suppression order is reversed upon appeal and vacated.

§ 450.55. Appeal by people from order reducing a count of an indictment or directing the filing of a prosecutor's information

In taking an appeal to an intermediate appellate court pursuant to subdivision one-a of section 450.20, the people shall file a notice of appeal. Upon request of either party, the hearing and determination of such appeal shall be conducted in an expeditious manner. The chief administrator of the courts, with the advice and consent of the administrative board of the courts, shall adopt rules for the expeditious briefing, hearing and determination of such appeals.

§ 450.60. Appeal to intermediate appellate court; to what court taken

The particular intermediate appellate courts to which appeals authorized by sections 450.10 and 450.20 must be taken are as follows:

1. An appeal from a judgment, sentence or order of the supreme court must be taken to the appellate division of the department in which such judgment, sentence or order was entered.

2. An appeal from a judgment, sentence or order of a county court must be taken to the appellate division of the department in which such judgment, sentence or order was entered.

3. An appeal from a judgment, sentence or order of a local criminal court located outside of New York City must, except as otherwise provided in this subdivision, be taken to the county court of the county in which such judgment, sentence or order was entered.

If the appellate division of the second, third or fourth department has established an appellate term of the supreme court for its department, it may direct that appeals from such judgments, sentences and orders of such local criminal courts, or of particular classifications of such local criminal courts, be taken to such appellate term of the supreme court instead of to the county court; and in such case such an appeal must be so taken.

4. An appeal from a judgment, sentence or order of the New York City criminal court must be taken, if such judgment, sentence or order was entered at a term of such court held in New York or Bronx county, to the appellate division of the first department, and, if entered at a term of such court held in Kings, Queens or Richmond county, to the appellate division of the second department; except that if the appellate division of either such department has established an appellate term of the supreme court for its department, it may direct that all such appeals be taken thereto; and in such case such an appeal must be so taken.

§ 450.70. Appeal by defendant directly to court of appeals; in what cases authorized

An appeal directly to the court of appeals may be taken as of right by the defendant from the following judgment and orders of a superior court:

1. A judgment including a sentence of death;

2. An order denying a motion, made pursuant to section 440.10, to vacate a judgment including a sentence of death;

3. An order denying a motion, made pursuant to section 440.20, to set aside a sentence of death;

4. An order denying a motion, made pursuant to paragraph (d) of subdivision eleven of section 400.27, to set aside a sentence of death.

§ 450.80. Appeal by people directly to court of appeals; in what cases authorized

An appeal directly to the court of appeals may be taken as of right by the people from the following orders of a superior court:

1. An order, entered pursuant to section 440.10, vacating a judgment including a sentence of death;

2. An order, entered pursuant to section 440.20, setting aside a sentence of death

3. An order, entered pursuant to paragraph (d) of subdivision eleven of section 400.27, setting aside a sentence of death;

4. An order, entered pursuant to subdivision twelve of section 400.27, setting aside a sentence of death.

§ 450.90. Appeal to court of appeals from order of intermediate appellate court; in what cases authorized

1. Provided that a certificate granting leave to appeal is issued pursuant to section 460.20, an appeal may, except as provided in subdivision two, be taken to the court of appeals by either the defendant or the people from any adverse or partially adverse order of an intermediate appellate court entered upon an appeal taken to such intermediate appellate court pursuant to section 450.10, 450.15, or 450.20, or from an order granting or denying a motion to set aside an order of an intermediate appellate court on the ground of ineffective assistance or wrongful deprivation of appellate counsel, or by either the defendant or the people from any adverse or partially adverse order of an intermediate appellate court entered upon an appeal taken to such intermediate appellate court from an order entered pursuant to section 440.46 of this chapter. An order of an intermediate appellate court is adverse to the party who was the appellant in such court when it affirms the judgment, sentence or order appealed from, and is adverse to the party who was the respondent in such court when it reverses the judgment, sentence or order appealed from. An appellate court order which modifies a judgment or order appealed from is partially adverse to each party.

2. An appeal to the court of appeals from an order of an intermediate appellate court reversing or modifying a judgment, sentence or order of a criminal court may be taken only if:

(a) The court of appeals determines that the intermediate appellate court's determination of reversal or modification was on the law alone or upon the law and such facts which, but for the determination of law, would not have led to reversal or modification; or

(b) The appeal is based upon a contention that corrective action, as that term is defined in section 470.10, taken or directed by the intermediate appellate court was illegal.

§ 460.10. Appeal; how taken

1. Except as provided in subdivisions two and three, an appeal taken as of right to an intermediate appellate court or directly to the court of appeals from a judgment, sentence or order of a criminal court is taken as follows:

(a) A party seeking to appeal from a judgment or a sentence or an order and sentence included within such judgment, or from a resentence, or from an order of a criminal court not included in a judgment, must, within thirty days after imposition of the sentence or, as the case may be, within thirty days after service upon such party of a copy of an order not included in a judgment, file with the clerk of the criminal court in which such sentence was imposed or in which such order was entered a written notice of appeal, in duplicate, stating that such party appeals therefrom to a designated appellate court.

(b) If the defendant is the appellant, he must, within such thirty day period, serve a copy of such notice of appeal upon the district attorney of the county embracing the criminal court in which the judgment or order being appealed was entered. If the appeal is directly to the court of appeals, the district attorney, following such service upon him, must immediately give written notice thereof to the public servant having custody of the defendant.

(c) If the people are the appellant, they must, within such thirty day period, serve a copy of such notice of appeal upon the defendant or upon the attorney who last appeared for him in the court in which the order being appealed was entered.

(d) Upon filing and service of the notice of appeal as prescribed in paragraphs (a), (b) and (c), the appeal is deemed to have been taken.

(e) Following the filing with him of the notice of appeal in duplicate, the clerk of the court in which the judgment, sentence or order being appealed was entered or imposed, must endorse upon such instruments the filing date and must transmit the duplicate notice of appeal to the clerk of the court to which the appeal is being taken.

2. An appeal taken as of right to a county court or to an appellate term of the supreme court from a judgment, sentence or order of a local criminal court in a case in which the underlying proceedings were recorded by a court stenographer is taken in the manner provided in subdivision one; except that where no clerk is employed by such local criminal court the appellant must file the notice of appeal with the judge of such court, and must further file a copy thereof with the clerk of the appellate court to which the appeal is being taken.

3. An appeal taken as of right to a county court or to an appellate term of the supreme court from a judgment, sentence or order of a local criminal court in a case in which the underlying proceedings were not recorded by a court stenographer is taken as follows:

(a) Within thirty days after entry or imposition in such local criminal court of the judgment, sentence or order being appealed, the appellant must file with such court either (i) an affidavit of errors, setting forth alleged errors or defects in the proceedings which are the subjects of the appeal, or (ii) a notice of appeal. Where a notice of appeal is filed, the appellant must serve a copy thereof upon the respondent in the manner provided in paragraphs (b) and (c) of subdivision one, and, within sixty days after the appellant receives a transcript of the electronically recorded proceedings, must file with such court an affidavit of errors.

(b) Not more than three days after the filing of the affidavit of errors, the appellant must serve a copy thereof upon the respondent or the respondent's counsel or authorized representative. If the defendant is the appellant, such service must be upon the district attorney of the county in which the local criminal court is located. If the people are the appellant, such service must be upon the defendant or upon the attorney who appeared for him in the proceedings in the local criminal court.

(c) Upon filing and service of the affidavit of errors as prescribed in paragraphs (a) and (b), the appeal is deemed to have been taken.

(d) Within ten days after the appellant's filing of the affidavit of errors with the local criminal court, such court must file with the clerk of the appellate court to which the appeal has been taken both the affidavit of errors and the court's return, and must deliver a copy of such return to each party or a representative thereof as indicated in paragraph (b). The court's return must set forth or summarize evidence, facts or occurrences in or adduced at the proceedings resulting in the judgment, sentence or order, which constitute the factual foundation for the contentions alleged in the affidavit of errors.

(e) If the local criminal court does not file such return within the prescribed period, or if it files a defective return, the appellate court, upon application of the appellant, must order such local criminal court to file a return or an amended return, as the case may be, within a designated time which such appellate court deems reasonable.

4. An appeal by a defendant to an intermediate appellate court by permission, pursuant to section 450.15, is taken as follows:

(a) Within thirty days after service upon the defendant of a copy of the order sought to be appealed, the defendant must make application, pursuant to section 460.15, for a certificate granting leave to appeal to the intermediate appellate court.

(b) If such application is granted and such certificate is issued, the defendant, within fifteen days after issuance thereof, must file with the criminal court in which the order sought to be appealed was rendered the certificate granting leave to appeal together with a written notice of appeal, or if the appeal is from a local criminal court in a case in which the underlying proceedings were not recorded by a court stenographer, either (i) an affidavit of errors, or (ii) a notice of appeal. In all other respects the appeal shall be taken as provided in subdivisions one, two and three.

5. An appeal to the court of appeals from an order of an intermediate appellate court is taken as follows:

(a) Within thirty days after service upon the appellant of a copy of the order sought to be appealed, the appellant must make application, pursuant to section 460.20, for a certificate granting leave to appeal to the court of appeals. The appellate division of each judicial department shall adopt rules governing the procedures for service of a copy of such order.

(b) If such application is granted, the issuance of the certificate granting leave to appeal shall constitute the taking of the appeal.

6. Where a notice of appeal, an affidavit of errors, an application for leave to appeal to an intermediate appellate court, or an application for leave to appeal to the court of appeals is premature or contains an inaccurate description of the judgment, sentence or order being or sought to be appealed, the appellate court, in its discretion, may, in the interest of justice, treat such instrument as valid. Where an appellant files a notice of appeal within the prescribed period but, through mistake, inadvertence or excusable neglect, omits to serve a copy thereof upon the respondent within the prescribed period, the appellate court to which the appeal is sought to be taken may, in its discretion and for good cause shown, permit such service to be made within a designated period of time, and upon such service the appeal is deemed to be taken.

§ 460.15. Certificate granting leave to appeal to intermediate appellate court

1. A certificate granting leave to appeal to an intermediate appellate court is an order of one judge or justice of the intermediate appellate court to which the appeal is sought to be taken granting such permission and certifying that the case involves questions of law or fact which ought to be reviewed by the intermediate appellate court.

2. An application for such a certificate must be made in a manner determined by the rules of the appellate division of the department in which such intermediate appellate court is located. Not more than one application may be made for such a certificate.

§ 460.20. Certificate granting leave to appeal to court of appeals

1. A certificate granting leave to appeal to the court of appeals from an order of an intermediate appellate court is an order of a judge granting such permission and certifying that the case involves a question of law which ought to be reviewed by the court of appeals.

2. Such certificate may be issued by the following judges in the indicated situations:

(a) Where the appeal sought is from an order of the appellate division, the certificate may be issued by (i) a judge of the court of appeals or (ii) a justice of the appellate division of the department which entered the order sought to be appealed.

(b) Where the appeal sought is from an order of an intermediate appellate court other than the appellate division, the certificate may be issued only by a judge of the court of appeals.

3. An application for such a certificate must be made in the following manner:

(a) An application to a justice of the appellate division must be made upon reasonable notice to the respondent;

(b) An application seeking such a certificate from a judge of the court of appeals must be made to the chief judge of such court by submission thereof, either in writing or first orally and then in writing, to the clerk of the court of appeals. The chief judge must then designate a judge of such court to determine the application. The clerk must then notify the respondent of the application and must inform both parties of such designation.

4. A justice of the appellate division to whom such an application has been made, or a judge of the court of appeals designated to determine such an application, may in his discretion determine it upon such papers as he may request the parties to submit, or upon oral argument, or upon both.

5. Every judge or justice acting pursuant to this section shall file with the clerk of the court of appeals, immediately upon issuance, a copy of every certificate granting or denying leave to appeal.

§ 460.30. Extension of time for taking appeal

1. Upon motion to an intermediate appellate court of a defendant who desires to take an appeal to such court from a judgment, sentence or order of a criminal court but has failed to file a notice of appeal, an application for leave to appeal, or, as the case may be, an affidavit of errors, with such criminal court within the prescribed period, or upon motion to the court of appeals of a defendant who desires to take an appeal to such court from an order of a superior court or of an intermediate appellate court, but has failed to make an application for a certificate granting leave to appeal to the court of appeals, or has failed to file a notice of appeal with the intermediate appellate court, within the prescribed period, such intermediate appellate court or the court of appeals, as the case may be, may order that the time for the taking of such appeal or applying for leave to appeal be extended to a date not more than thirty days subsequent to the determination of such motion, upon the ground that the failure to so file or make application in timely fashion resulted from (a) improper conduct of a public servant or improper conduct, death or disability of the defendant's attorney, or (b) inability of the defendant and his attorney to have communicated, in person or by mail, concerning whether an appeal should be taken, prior to the expiration of the time within which to take an appeal due to defendant's incarceration in an institution and through no lack of due diligence or fault of the attorney or defendant. Such motion must be made with due diligence after the time for the taking of such appeal has expired, and in any case not more than one year thereafter.

2. The motion must be in writing and upon reasonable notice to the people and with opportunity to be heard. The motion papers must contain sworn allegations of facts claimed to establish the improper conduct, inability to communicate, or other facts essential to support the motion, and the people may file papers in opposition thereto. After all papers have been filed, the court must consider the same for the purpose of ascertaining whether the motion is determinable without a hearing to resolve issues of fact.

3. If the motion papers allege facts constituting a legal basis for the motion, and if the essential allegations are either conclusively substantiated by unquestionable documentary proof or are conceded by the people to be true, the court must grant the motion.

4. If the motion papers do not allege facts constituting a legal basis for the motion, or if an essential allegation is conclusively refuted by unquestionable documentary proof, the court may deny the motion.

5. If the court does not determine the motion pursuant to subdivision three or four, it must order the criminal court which entered or imposed the judgment, sentence or order sought to be appealed to conduct a hearing and to make and report findings of fact essential to the determination of such motion. Upon receipt of such report, the intermediate appellate court or the court of appeals, as the case may be, must determine the motion.

6. An order of an intermediate appellate court granting or denying a motion made pursuant to this section is appealable to the court of appeals if (a) such order states that the determination was made upon the law alone, and (b) a judge of the court of appeals, pursuant to procedure provided in section 460.20, of this chapter, issues a certificate granting leave to the appellant to appeal to the court of appeals.

§ 460.40. Effect of taking of appeal upon judgment or order of courts below; when stayed

1. The taking of an appeal by the defendant directly to the court of appeals, pursuant to subdivision one of section 450.70, from a superior court judgment including a sentence of death stays the execution of such sentence. Except as provided in subdivision two of this section, in no other case does the taking of an appeal, by either party, in and of itself stay the execution of any judgment, sentence or order of either a criminal court or an intermediate appellate court.

2. The taking of an appeal by the people to an intermediate appellate court pursuant to subdivision one-a of section 450.20, from an order reducing a count or counts of an indictment or dismissing an indictment and directing the filing of a prosecutor's information, stays the effect of such order. In addition, the taking of an appeal by the people to an intermediate appellate court pursuant to subdivision one of section 450.20, from an order dismissing a count or counts of an indictment charging murder in the first degree, stays the effect of such order.

3. Within six months of the effective date of this subdivision, the court of appeals shall adopt rules to ensure that a defendant is granted a stay of the execution of any death warrant issued pursuant to article twenty-two-B of the correction law to allow the defendant an opportunity to prepare and timely file an initial motion pursuant to section 440.10 or 440.20 seeking to set aside a sentence of death or vacate a judgment including a sentence of death and to allow the motion and any appeal from the denial thereof to be timely determined. The rules shall provide that in the event a defendant seeks to file any subsequent motion with respect to the judgment or sentence following a final determination of the defendant's initial motion pursuant to section 440.10 or 440.20, a motion for a stay of the execution of the death warrant may only be granted for good cause shown. The people and the defendant shall have a right to appeal to the court of appeals from orders granting or denying such stay motions and any rules adopted pursuant to this subdivision shall provide that the court of appeals may affirm such orders, reverse them or modify them upon such terms as the court deems appropriate and shall provide for the expeditious perfection and determination of such appeals. Prior to adoption of the rules, the court of appeals shall issue proposed rules and receive written comments thereon from interested parties.

§ 460.50. Stay of judgment pending appeal to intermediate appellate court

1. Upon application of a defendant who has taken an appeal to an intermediate appellate court from a judgment or from a sentence of a criminal court, a judge designated in subdivision two may issue an order both (a) staying or suspending the execution of the judgment pending the determination of the appeal, and (b) either releasing the defendant on his own recognizance or fixing bail pursuant to the provisions of article five hundred thirty. That phase of the order staying or suspending

execution of the judgment does not become effective unless and until the defendant is released, either on his own recognizance or upon the posting of bail.

2. An order as prescribed in subdivision one may be issued by the following judges in the indicated situations:

(a) If the appeal is to the appellate division from a judgment or a sentence of either the supreme court or the New York City criminal court, such order may be issued by (i) a justice of the appellate division of the department in which the judgment was entered, or (ii) a justice of the supreme court of the judicial district embracing the county in which the judgment was entered;

(b) If the appeal is to the appellate division from a judgment or a sentence of a county court, such order may be issued by (i) a justice of such appellate division, or (ii) a justice of the supreme court of the judicial district embracing the county in which the judgment was entered, or (iii) a judge of such county court;

(c) If the appeal is to an appellate term of the supreme court from a judgment or sentence of the New York City criminal court, such order may be issued by a justice of the supreme court of the judicial district embracing the county in which the judgment was entered;

(d) With respect to appeals to county courts from judgments or sentences of local criminal courts, and with respect to appeals to appellate terms of the supreme court from judgments or sentences of any criminal courts located outside of New York City, the judges who may issue such orders in any particular situation are determined by rules of the appellate division of the department embracing the appellate court to which the appeal has been taken.

3. An application for an order specified in this section must be made upon reasonable notice to the people, and the people must be accorded adequate opportunity to appear in opposition thereto. Not more than one application may be made pursuant to this section.

4. Notwithstanding the provisions of subdivision one, if within one hundred twenty days after the issuance of such an order the appeal has not been brought to argument in or submitted to the intermediate appellate court, the operation of such order terminates and the defendant must surrender himself to the criminal court in which the judgment was entered in order that execution of the judgment be commenced or resumed; except that this subdivision does not apply where the intermediate appellate court has (a) extended the time for argument or submission of the appeal to a date beyond the specified period of one hundred twenty days, and (b) upon application of the defendant, expressly ordered that the operation of the order continue until the date of the determination of the appeal or some other designated future date or occurrence.

5. Where the defendant is at liberty during the pendency of an appeal as a result of an order issued pursuant to this section, the intermediate appellate court, upon affirmance of the judgment, must by appropriate certificate remit the case to the criminal court in which such judgment was entered. The criminal court must, upon at least two days notice to the defendant, his surety and his attorney, promptly direct the defendant to surrender himself to the criminal court in order that execution of the judgment be

commenced or resumed, and if necessary the criminal court may issue a bench warrant to secure his appearance.

6. Upon application of a defendant who has been granted a certificate granting leave to appeal pursuant to section 460.15 of this chapter, and in accordance with the procedures set forth in subdivisions three, four and five of this section, the intermediate appellate court may issue an order both (a) staying or suspending the execution of the judgment pending the determination of the appeal, and (b) either releasing the defendant on his own recognizance or fixing bail pursuant to the provisions of article five hundred thirty. That phase of the order staying or suspending execution of the judgment does not become effective unless and until the defendant is released, either on his own recognizance or upon the posting of bail.

§ 460.60. Stay of judgment pending appeal to court of appeals from intermediate appellate court

1.

(a) A judge who, pursuant to section 460.20 of this chapter, has received an application for a certificate granting a defendant leave to appeal to the court of appeals from an order of an intermediate appellate court affirming or modifying a judgment including a sentence of imprisonment, a sentence of imprisonment, or an order appealed pursuant to section 450.15 of this chapter, of a criminal court, may, upon application of such defendant-appellant issue an order both (i) staying or suspending the execution of the judgment pending the determination of the application for leave to appeal, and, if that application is granted, staying or suspending the execution of the judgment pending the determination of the appeal, and (ii) either releasing the defendant on his own recognizance or continuing bail as previously determined or fixing bail pursuant to the provisions of article five hundred thirty. Such an order is effective immediately and that phase of the order staying or suspending execution of the judgment does not become effective unless and until the defendant is released, either on his own recognizance or upon the posting of bail.

(b) If the application for leave to appeal is denied, the stay or suspension pending the application automatically terminates upon the signing of the certificate denying leave. Upon such termination, the certificate denying leave must be sent to the criminal court in which the original judgment was entered, and the latter must proceed in the manner provided in subdivision five of section 460.50 of this chapter.

2. An application pursuant to subdivision one must be made upon reasonable notice to the people, and the people must be accorded adequate opportunity to appear in opposition thereto. Such an application may be made immediately after the entry of the order sought to be appealed or at any subsequent time during the pendency of the appeal. Not more than one application may be made pursuant to this section.

3. Notwithstanding the provisions of subdivision one, if within one hundred twenty days after the issuance of a certificate granting leave to appeal, the appeal or prospective appeal has not been brought to argument in or submitted to the court of appeals, the operation of an order issued pursuant to subdivision one of this section terminates and the defendant must surrender himself to the criminal court in which the original judgment was entered in order that execution of such judgment be commenced or

resumed; except that this subdivision does not apply where the court of appeals has (a) extended the time for argument or submission of the appeal to a date beyond the specified period of one hundred twenty days and (b) upon application of the defendant expressly ordered that the operation of such order continue until the date of the determination of the appeal or some other designated future date or occurrence.

4. Where the defendant is at liberty during the pendency of an appeal as a result of an order issued pursuant to this section, the court of appeals upon affirmance of the judgment or order, must, by appropriate certificate, remit the case to the criminal court in which the judgment was entered, and the latter must proceed in the manner provided in subdivision five of section 460.50 of this chapter.

§ 460.70. Appeal; how perfected

1. Except as provided in subdivision two, the mode of and time for perfecting an appeal which has been taken to an intermediate appellate court from a judgment, sentence or order of a criminal court are determined by rules of the appellate division of the department in which such appellate court is located. Among the matters to be determined by such court rules are the times when the appeal must be noticed for and brought to argument, the content and form of the records and briefs to be served and filed, and the time when such records and briefs must be served and filed.

When an appeal is taken by a defendant pursuant to section 450.10, a transcript shall be prepared and settled and shall be filed with the criminal court by the court reporter. Electronically recorded proceedings that were not recorded by a stenographer shall be transcribed and filed with the court as directed by the chief administrator of the courts. The expense for such transcript and any reproduced copies of such transcript shall be paid by the defendant. Where the defendant is granted permission to proceed as a poor person by the appellate court, the court reporter shall promptly make and file with the criminal court a transcript of the stenographic minutes of such proceedings as the appellate court shall direct. The expense of transcripts and any reproduced copies of transcripts prepared for poor persons under this section shall be a state charge payable out of funds appropriated to the office of court administration for that purpose. The appellate court shall where such is necessary for perfection of the appeal, order that the criminal court furnish a reproduced copy of such transcript to the defendant or his counsel.

2. An appeal which has been taken to a county court or to an appellate term of the supreme court from a judgment, sentence or order of a local criminal court pursuant to subdivision three of section 460.10 is perfected as follows:

(a) After the local criminal court has, pursuant to paragraph (d) of subdivision three of section 460.10, filed its return with the clerk of the appellate court and delivered a copy thereof to the appellant, the appellant must file with such clerk, and serve a copy thereof upon the respondent, a notice of argument, noticing the appeal for argument at the term of such appellate court immediately following the term being held at the time of the appellant's receipt of the return. Upon motion of the appellant, however, such appellate court may for good cause shown enlarge the time to a subsequent term, in which case the appellant must notice the appeal for argument at such subsequent term;

(b) The appellant must further comply with all court rules applicable to the mode of perfecting such appeals;

(c) If the appellant does not file a notice of argument as provided in paragraph (a) or does not comply with all applicable court rules as provided in paragraph (b), the appellate court may, either upon motion of the respondent or upon its own motion, dismiss the appeal.

3. The mode of and time for perfecting any appeal which has been taken to the court of appeals are determined by the rules of the court of appeals. Among the matters to be determined by such court rules are the times when the appeal must be noticed for and brought to argument, the content, form and number of the records and briefs and copies thereof to be served and filed, and the times when such records and briefs must be served and filed.

When an appeal is taken by a defendant pursuant to section 450.70, the defendant shall cause to be prepared and printed or otherwise duplicated pursuant to rules of the court of appeals the record on appeal and the required number of copies thereof. If the defendant is granted permission to appeal as a poor person, the expense thereof shall be a state charge payable out of funds appropriated to the office of court administration for that purpose.

§ 460.80. Appeal; argument and submission thereof

The mode of and procedure for arguing or otherwise litigating appeals in criminal cases are determined by rules of the individual appellate courts. Among the matters to be determined by such court rules are the circumstances in which oral argument is required and those in which the case may be submitted by either or both parties without oral argument; the consequences or effect of failure to present oral argument when such is required; the amount of time for oral argument allowed to each party; and the number of counsel entitled to be heard.

§ 460.90. [Expires and repealed Sept 1, 2019] Filing of papers on appeal to the appellate division by electronic means.

Notwithstanding any other provision of law, the appellate division in each judicial department may promulgate rules authorizing a program in the use of electronic means for the taking and perfection of appeals in accordance with the provisions of section twenty-one hundred twelve of the civil practice law and rules. Provided however, such rules shall not require an unrepresented party or any attorney who furnishes a certification specified in subparagraph (i) or (ii) of paragraph (c) of subdivision two of section 10.40 of this chapter to take or perfect an appeal by electronic means. Provided further, however, before promulgating any such rules, the appellate division in each judicial department shall consult with the chief administrator of the courts and shall provide an opportunity for review and comment by all those who are or would be affected including district attorneys; representatives of the office of indigent legal services; not-for-profit legal service providers; public defenders; statewide and local specialty bar associations whose membership devotes a significant portion of their practice to assigned criminal cases pursuant to subparagraph (i) of paragraph (a) of subdivision three of section seven hundred twenty-two of the county law; institutional providers of criminal defense services and other members of the criminal defense bar;

representatives of victims' rights organizations; unaffiliated attorneys who regularly appear in proceedings that are or would be affected by such electronic filing program; interested members of the criminal justice community; and any other persons in whose county a program has been implemented in any of the courts therein as deemed to be appropriate by any appellate division. To the extent practicable, rules promulgated by the appellate division in each judicial department pursuant to this section shall be uniform. For purposes of this section, "electronic means" shall be as defined in subdivision (f) of rule twenty-one hundred three of such law and rules.

Article 470 Appeals—Determination Thereof

§ 470.05. Determination of appeals; general criteria

1. An appellate court must determine an appeal without regard to technical errors or defects which do not affect the substantial rights of the parties.

2. For purposes of appeal, a question of law with respect to a ruling or instruction of a criminal court during a trial or proceeding is presented when a protest thereto was registered, by the party claiming error, at the time of such ruling or instruction or at any subsequent time when the court had an opportunity of effectively changing the same. Such protest need not be in the form of an "exception" but is sufficient if the party made his position with respect to the ruling or instruction known to the court, or if in reponse [response]* to a protest by a party, the court expressly decided the question raised on appeal. In addition, a party who without success has either expressly or impliedly sought or requested a particular ruling or instruction, is deemed to have thereby protested the court's ultimate disposition of the matter or failure to rule or instruct accordingly sufficiently to raise a question of law with respect to such disposition or failure regardless of whether any actual protest thereto was registered.

§ 470.10. Determination of appeals; definitions of terms

The following definitions are applicable to this article:

1. "Reversal" by an appellate court of a judgment, sentence or order of another court means the vacating of such judgment, sentence or order.

2. "Modification" by an appellate court of a judgment or order of another court means the vacating of a part thereof and affirmance of the remainder.

3. "Corrective action" means affirmative action taken or directed by an appellate court upon reversing or modifying a judgment, sentence or order of another court, which disposes of or continues the case in a manner consonant with the determinations and principles underlying the reversal or modification.

§ 470.15. Determination of appeals by intermediate appellate courts; scope of review

1. Upon an appeal to an intermediate appellate court from a judgment, sentence or order of a criminal court, such intermediate appellate court may consider and determine any question of law or issue of fact involving error or defect in the criminal court proceedings which may have adversely affected the appellant.

2. Upon such an appeal, the intermediate appellate court must either affirm or reverse or modify the criminal court judgment, sentence or order. The ways in which it may modify a judgment include, but are not limited to, the following:

(a) Upon a determination that the trial evidence adduced in support of a verdict is not legally sufficient to establish the defendant's guilt of an offense of which he was convicted but is legally sufficient to establish his guilt of a lesser included offense, the court may modify the judgment by changing it to one of conviction for the lesser offense:

(b) Upon a determination that the trial evidence is not legally sufficient to establish the defendant's guilt of all the offenses of which he was convicted but is legally sufficient to establish his guilt of one or more of such offenses, the court may modify the judgment by reversing it with respect to the unsupported counts and otherwise affirming it;

(c) Upon a determination that a sentence imposed upon a valid conviction is illegal or unduly harsh or severe, the court may modify the judgment by reversing it with respect to the sentence and by otherwise affirming it.

3. A reversal or a modification of a judgment, sentence or order must be based upon a determination made:

(a) Upon the law; or

(b) Upon the facts; or

(c) As a matter of discretion in the interest of justice; or

(d) Upon any two or all three of the bases specified in paragraphs (a), (b) and (c).

4. The kinds of determinations of reversal or modification deemed to be upon the law include, but are not limited to, the following:

(a) That a ruling or instruction of the court, duly protested by the defendant, as prescribed in subdivision two of section 470.05, at a trial resulting in a judgment, deprived the defendant of a fair trial;

(b) That evidence adduced at a trial resulting in a judgment was not legally sufficient to establish the defendant's guilt of an offense of which he was convicted;

(c) That a sentence was unauthorized, illegally imposed or otherwise invalid as a matter of law.

5. The kinds of determinations of reversal or modification deemed to be on the facts include, but are not limited to, a determination that a verdict of conviction resulting in a judgment was, in whole or in part, against the weight of the evidence.

6. The kinds of determinations of reversal or modification deemed to be made as a matter of discretion in the interest of justice include, but are not limited to, the following:

(a) That an error or defect occurring at a trial resulting in a judgment, which error or defect was not duly protested at trial as prescribed in subdivision two of section 470.05 so as to present a question of law, deprived the defendant of a fair trial;

(b) That a sentence, though legal, was unduly harsh or severe.

§ 470.20. Determination of appeals by intermediate appellate courts; corrective action upon reversal or modification

Upon reversing or modifying a judgment, sentence or order of a criminal court, an intermediate appellate court must take or direct such corrective action as is necessary and appropriate both to rectify any injustice to the appellant resulting from the error or defect which is the subject of the reversal or modification and to protect the rights of the respondent. The particular corrective action to be taken or directed is governed in part by the following rules:

1. Upon a reversal of a judgment after trial for error or defect which resulted in prejudice to the defendant or deprived him of a fair trial, the court must, whether such reversal be on the law or as a matter of discretion in the interest of justice, order a new

trial of the accusatory instrument and remit the case to the criminal court for such action.

2. Upon a reversal of a judgment after trial for legal insufficiency of trial evidence, the court must dismiss the accusatory instrument.

3. Upon a modification of a judgment after trial for legal insufficiency of trial evidence with respect to one or more but not all of the offenses of which the defendant was convicted, the court must dismiss the count or counts of the accusatory instrument determined to be legally unsupported and must otherwise affirm the judgment. In such case, it must either reduce the total sentence to that imposed by the criminal court upon the counts with respect to which the judgment is affirmed or remit the case to the criminal court for re-sentence upon such counts; provided that nothing contained in this paragraph precludes further sentence reduction in the exercise of the appellate court's discretion pursuant to subdivision six.

4. Upon a modification of a judgment after trial which reduces a conviction of a crime to one for a lesser included offense, the court must remit the case to the criminal court with a direction that the latter sentence the defendant accordingly.

5. Upon a reversal or modification of a judgment after trial upon the ground that the verdict, either in its entirety or with respect to a particular count or counts, is against the weight of the trial evidence, the court must dismiss the accusatory instrument or any reversed count.

6. Upon modifying a judgment or reversing a sentence as a matter of discretion in the interest of justice upon the ground that the sentence is unduly harsh or severe, the court must itself impose some legally authorized lesser sentence.

§ 470.25. Determination of appeals by intermediate appellate courts; form and content of order

1. An order of an intermediate appellate court which affirms a judgment, sentence or order of a criminal court need only state such affirmance.

2. An order of an intermediate appellate court which reverses or modifies a judgment, sentence or order of a criminal court must contain the following:

(a) A statement of whether the determination was upon the law or upon the facts or as a matter of discretion in the interest of justice, or upon any specified two or all three of such bases; and

(b) If the decision is rendered without opinion, a brief statement of the specific grounds of the reversal or modification; and

(c) A statement of the corrective action taken or directed by the court; and

(d) If the determination is exclusively upon the law, a statement of whether or not the facts upon which the criminal court's judgment, sentence or order is based have been considered and determined to have been established. In the absence of such a statement, it is presumed that the intermediate appellate court did not consider or make any determination with respect to such facts.

§ 470.30. Determination by court of appeals of appeals taken directly thereto from judgments and orders of criminal courts

1. Wherever appropriate, the rules set forth in sections 470.15 and 470.20, governing the consideration and determination by intermediate appellate courts of appeals thereto from judgments and orders of criminal courts, and prescribing their scope of review and

the corrective action to be taken by them upon reversal or modification, apply equally to the consideration and determination by the court of appeals of appeals taken directly thereto, pursuant to sections 450.70 and 450.80, from judgments and orders of superior criminal courts.

2. Whenever a sentence of death is imposed, the judgment and sentence shall be reviewed on the record by the court of appeals. Review by the court of appeals pursuant to subdivision one of section 450.70 may not be waived.

3. With regard to the sentence, the court shall, in addition to exercising the powers and scope of review granted under subdivision one of this section, determine:

(a) whether the sentence of death was imposed under the influence of passion, prejudice, or any other arbitrary or legally impermissible factor including whether the imposition of the verdict or sentence was based upon the race of the defendant or a victim of the crime for which the defendant was convicted;

(b) whether the sentence of death is excessive or disproportionate to the penalty imposed in similar cases considering both the crime and the defendant. In conducting such review the court, upon request of the defendant, in addition to any other determination, shall review whether the sentence of death is excessive or disproportionate to the penalty imposed in similar cases by virtue of the race of the defendant or a victim of the crime for which the defendant was convicted; and

(c) whether the decision to impose the sentence of death was against the weight of the evidence.

4. The court shall include in its decision: (a) the aggravating and mitigating factors established in the record on appeal; and (b) those similar cases it took into consideration.

5. In addition to exercising any other corrective action pursuant to subdivision one of this section, the court, with regard to review of a sentence of death, shall be authorized to:

(a) affirm the sentence of death; or

(b) set the sentence aside and remand the case for resentencing pursuant to the procedures set forth in section 400.27 for a determination as to whether the defendant shall be sentenced to death, life imprisonment without parole or to a term of imprisonment for the class A-I felony of murder in the first degree other than a sentence of life imprisonment without parole; or

(c) set the sentence aside and remand the case for resentencing by the court for a determination as to whether the defendant shall be sentenced to life imprisonment without parole or to a term of imprisonment for the class A-I felony of murder in the first degree other than a sentence of life imprisonment without parole.

§ 470.35. Determination by court of appeals of appeals from orders of intermediate appellate courts; scope of review

1. Upon an appeal to the court of appeals from an order of an intermediate appellate court affirming a judgment, sentence or order of a criminal court, the court of appeals may consider and determine not only questions of law which were raised or considered upon the appeal to the intermediate appellate court, but also any question of law involving alleged error or defect in the criminal court proceedings resulting in the original

criminal court judgment, sentence or order, regardless of whether such question was raised, considered or determined upon the appeal to the intermediate appellate court.

2. Upon an appeal to the court of appeals from an order of an intermediate appellate court reversing or modifying a judgment, sentence or order of a criminal court, the court of appeals may consider and determine:

(a) Any question of law which was determined by the intermediate appellate court and which, as so determined, constituted a basis for such court's order of reversal or modification; and

(b) Any other question of law involving alleged or possible error or defect in the criminal court proceedings resulting in the original judgment, sentence or order which may have adversely affected the party who was appellant in the intermediate appellate court and who is respondent in the court of appeals. The court of appeals is not precluded from considering and determining such a question by the circumstance that it was not considered or determined by the intermediate appellate court, or that it did not constitute a basis for such court's reversal or modification, or that the party who may have been adversely affected thereby is the respondent rather than the appellant in the court of appeals; and the court of appeals, even though rejecting the intermediate appellate court's reasons for its order of reversal or modification, may affirm or modify such order upon the basis of such other questions; and

(c) Any question concerning the legality of the corrective action taken by the intermediate appellate court.

3. Upon such an appeal, the court must affirm, reverse or modify the intermediate appellate court order.

§ 470.40. Determination by court of appeals of appeals from intermediate appellate courts; corrective action upon reversal or modification

1. Upon reversing or modifying an order of an intermediate appellate court affirming a criminal court judgment, sentence or order, the court of appeals must take or direct such corrective action as the intermediate appellate court would, pursuant to section 470.20, have been required or authorized to take or direct had it reversed or modified the criminal court judgment, sentence or order upon the same ground or grounds.

2. Upon reversing an order of an intermediate appellate court reversing or modifying a criminal court judgment, sentence or order upon the ground that questions of law were erroneously determined by the intermediate appellate court in favor of the party appellant therein, the court of appeals must take or direct corrective action as follows:

(a) If the facts underlying the original criminal court judgment, sentence or order were considered and determined to have been established by the intermediate appellate court, the court of appeals must reinstate and affirm the original criminal court judgment, sentence or order and remit the case to such criminal court for whatever further proceedings may be necessary to complete the action or proceedings therein; provided, however, that where such facts were applied to an erroneous determination of law, the court of appeals may remit the case to the intermediate appellate court for a further determination of the facts;

(b) If the facts underlying the original criminal court judgment, sentence or order were not, or are presumed not to have been, considered and determined by the intermediate appellate court, the court of appeals must remit the case to such intermediate appellate court for determination of the facts.

3. Upon modifying an intermediate appellate court order reversing or modifying a criminal court judgment or order, upon the ground that corrective action taken or directed by the intermediate appellate court was illegal, the court of appeals must either (a) itself take or direct the appropriate corrective action or (b) remit the case to the intermediate appellate court for appropriate corrective action by the latter.

§ 470.45. Remission of case by appellate court to criminal court upon reversal or modification of judgment; action by criminal court

Upon reversing or modifying a judgment and directing corrective action, an appellate court must remit the case to the criminal court in which the judgment was entered. Such criminal court must execute the direction of the appellate court and must, depending upon the nature of such direction, either discharge the defendant from custody, exonerate his bail or issue a securing order.

§ 470.50. Reargument of appeal; motion and criteria for

1. After its determination of an appeal taken pursuant to article four hundred fifty, an appellate court, in the interest of justice and for good cause shown, may in its discretion, upon motion of a party adversely affected by its determination, or upon its own motion, order a reargument or reconsideration of the appeal. Upon such an order the court may either direct further oral argument by the parties or confine its reconsideration to re-examination of the issues as previously argued or submitted upon the appeal proper. Upon ordering a reargument or reconsideration of an appeal, the court must again determine the appeal pursuant to the provisions of this article.

2. The court of appeals may promulgate rules limiting the time within which a motion for reargument of appeals determined by such court may be made, and the appellate division of each department may similarly promulgate such rules with respect to appeals determined by such appellate division and appeals determined by the other intermediate appellate courts located within such department. In the absence of any such rule of limitation, a motion for reargument may be made at any time.

§ 470.55. Status of accusatory instrument upon order of new trial or restoration of action to pre-pleading status

1. Upon a new trial of an accusatory instrument resulting from an appellate court order reversing a judgment and ordering such new trial, such accusatory instrument is deemed to contain all the counts and to charge all the offenses which it contained and charged at the time the previous trial was commenced, regardless of whether any count was dismissed by the court in the course of such trial, except (a) those upon or of which the defendant was acquitted or deemed to have been acquitted, and (b) those dismissed upon appeal or upon some other post-judgment order.

2. Upon an appellate court order which reverses a judgment based upon a plea of guilty to an accusatory instrument or a part thereof, but which does not dismiss the entire accusatory instrument, the criminal action is, in the absence of express appellate court direction to the contrary, restored to its pre-pleading status and the accusatory instrument is deemed to contain all the counts and to charge all the offenses which it contained and charged at the time of the entry of the plea, except those dismissed upon

appeal or upon some other post-judgment order. Where the plea of guilty was entered and accepted, pursuant to subdivision three of section 220.30, upon the condition that it constituted a complete disposition and dismissal not only of the accusatory instrument underlying the judgment reversed but also of one or more other accusatory instruments against the defendant then pending in the same court, the appellate court order of reversal completely restores such other accusatory instruments; and such is the case even where the order of reversal dismisses the entire accusatory instrument underlying the judgment reversed.

§ 470.60. Dismissal of appeal

1. At any time after an appeal has been taken and before determination thereof, the appellate court in which such appeal is pending may, upon motion of the respondent or upon its own motion, dismiss such appeal upon the ground of mootness, lack of jurisdiction to determine it, failure of timely prosecution or perfection thereof, or other substantial defect, irregularity or failure of action by the appellant with respect to the prosecution or perfection of such appeal.

2. Such motion must be made upon reasonable notice to the appellant and with opportunity to be heard. If the people are the appellant, such notice must be served upon the appropriate district attorney either personally or by ordinary mail. If the appellant is a defendant, such notice must be served upon him by ordinary mail at his last known place of residence or, if he is imprisoned, at the institution in which he is confined, and similar notice must be served upon the attorney, if any, who last appeared for him. Upon determination of the motion, a copy of the order entered thereon must similarly be served.

3. Provided that a certificate granting leave to appeal is issued pursuant to this subdivision, an appeal may be taken, in the manner prescribed in subdivision four of section 460.10, to the court of appeals from an order of an intermediate appellate court dismissing an appeal thereto. Such appeal may be based either upon the ground that the dismissal was invalid as a matter of law or upon the ground that it constituted an abuse of discretion. A certificate granting leave to appeal from such an order of dismissal may be issued only by a judge of the court of appeals upon an application made in the manner prescribed in paragraph (b) of subdivision three of section 460.20. Upon such an appeal, the court of appeals must either affirm or reverse the intermediate appellate court order.

Part THREE Special Proceedings and Miscellaneous Procedures

Title P Procedures for Securing Attendance at Criminal Actions and Proceedings of Defendants and Witnesses Under Control of Court—Recognizance, Bail and Commitment

Article 500 Recognizance, Bail and Commitment—Definition of Terms

§ 500.10. Recognizance, bail and commitment; definitions of terms

As used in this title, and in this chapter generally, the following terms have the following meanings:

1. "Principal" means a defendant in a criminal action or proceeding, or a person adjudged a material witness therein, or any other person so involved therein that he

may by law be compelled to appear before a court for the purpose of having such court exercise control over his person to secure his future attendance at the action or proceeding when required, and who in fact either is before the court for such purpose or has been before it and been subjected to such control.

2. "Release on own recognizance." A court releases a principal on his own recognizance when, having acquired control over his person, it permits him to be at liberty during the pendency of the criminal action or proceeding involved upon condition that he will appear thereat whenever his attendance may be required and will at all times render himself amenable to the orders and processes of the court.

3. "Fix bail." A court fixes bail when, having acquired control over the person of a principal, it designates a sum of money and stipulates that, if bail in such amount is posted on behalf of the principal and approved, it will permit him to be at liberty during the pendency of the criminal action or proceeding involved.

4. "Commit to the custody of the sheriff." A court commits a principal to the custody of the sheriff when, having acquired control over his person, it orders that he be confined in the custody of the sheriff during the pendency of the criminal action or proceeding involved.

5. "Securing order" means an order of a court committing a principal to the custody of the sheriff, or fixing bail, or releasing him on his own recognizance.

6. "Order of recognizance or bail" means a securing order releasing a principal on his own recognizance or fixing bail.

7. "Application for recognizance or bail" means an application by a principal that the court, instead of committing him to or retaining him in the custody of the sheriff, either release him on his own recognizance or fix bail.

8. "Post bail" means to deposit bail in the amount and form fixed by the court, with the court or with some other authorized public servant or agency.

9. "Bail" means cash bail or a bail bond.

10. "Cash bail" means a sum of money, in the amount designated in an order fixing bail, posted by a principal or by another person on his behalf with a court or other authorized public servant or agency, upon the condition that such money will become forfeit to the people of the state of New York if the principal does not comply with the directions of a court requiring his attendance at the criminal action or proceeding involved or does not otherwise render himself amenable to the orders and processes of the court.

11. "Obligor" means a person who executes a bail bond on behalf of a principal and thereby assumes the undertaking described therein. The principal himself may be an obligor.

12. "Surety" means an obligor who is not a principal.

13. "Bail bond" means a written undertaking, executed by one or more obligors, that the principal designated in such instrument will, while at liberty as a result of an order fixing bail and of the posting of the bail bond in satisfaction thereof, appear in a designated criminal action or proceeding when his attendance is required and otherwise render himself amenable to the orders and processes of the court, and that in the event that he

fails to do so the obligor or obligors will pay to the people of the state of New York a specified sum of money, in the amount designated in the order fixing bail.

14. "Appearance bond" means a bail bond in which the only obligor is the principal.

15. "Surety bond" means a bail bond in which the obligor or obligors consist of one or more sureties or of one or more sureties and the principal.

16. "Insurance company bail bond" means a surety bond, executed in the form prescribed by the superintendent of financial services, in which the surety-obligor is a corporation licensed by the superintendent of financial services to engage in the business of executing bail bonds.

17. "Secured bail bond" means a bail bond secured by either:

(a) Personal property which is not exempt from execution and which, over and above all liabilities and encumbrances, has a value equal to or greater than the total amount of the undertaking; or

(b) Real property having a value of at least twice the total amount of the undertaking. For purposes of this paragraph, value of real property is determined by either:

(i) dividing the last assessed value of such property by the last given equalization rate or in a special assessing unit, as defined in article eighteen of the real property tax law, the appropriate class ratio established pursuant to section twelve hundred two of such law of the assessing municipality wherein the property is situated and by deducting from the resulting figure the total amount of any liens or other encumbrances upon such property; or

(ii) the value of the property as indicated in a certified appraisal report submitted by a state certified general real estate appraiser duly licensed by the department of state as provided in section one hundred sixty-j of the executive law, and by deducting from the appraised value the total amount of any liens or other encumbrances upon such property. A lien report issued by a title insurance company licensed under article sixty-four of the insurance law, that guarantees the correctness of a lien search conducted by it, shall be presumptive proof of liens upon the property.

18. "Partially secured bail bond" means a bail bond secured only by a deposit of a sum of money not exceeding ten percent of the total amount of the undertaking.

19. "Unsecured bail bond" means a bail bond, other than an insurance company bail bond, not secured by any deposit of or lien upon property.

20. "Court" includes, where appropriate, a judge authorized to act as described in a particular statute, though not as a court.

Article 520 Bail and Bail Bonds

§ 520.10. Bail and bail bonds; fixing of bail and authorized forms thereof

1. The only authorized forms of bail are the following:

(a) Cash bail.

(b) An insurance company bail bond.

(c) A secured surety bond.

(d) A secured appearance bond.

(e) A partially secured surety bond.

(f) A partially secured appearance bond.

(g) An unsecured surety bond.

(h) An unsecured appearance bond.

(i) Credit card or similar device; provided, however, that notwithstanding any other provision of law, any person posting bail by credit card or similar device also may be required to pay a reasonable administrative fee. The amount of such administrative fee and the time and manner of its payment shall be in accordance with the system established pursuant to subdivision four of section 150.30 of this chapter or paragraph (j) of subdivision two of section two hundred twelve of the judiciary law, as appropriate.

2. The methods of fixing bail are as follows:

(a) A court may designate the amount of the bail without designating the form or forms in which it may be posted. In such case, the bail may be posted in either of the forms specified in paragraphs (g) and (h) of subdivision one;

(b) The court may direct that the bail be posted in any one of two or more of the forms specified in subdivision one, designated in the alternative, and may designate different amounts varying with the forms;[.]*

§ 520.15. Bail and bail bonds; posting of cash bail

1. Where a court has fixed bail pursuant to subdivision two of section 520.10, at any time after the principal has been committed to the custody of the sheriff pending the posting thereof, cash bail in the amount designated in the order fixing bail may be posted even though such bail was not specified in such order. Cash bail may be deposited with (a) the county treasurer of the county in which the criminal action or proceeding is pending or, in the city of New York with the commissioner of finance, or (b) the court which issued such order, or (c) the sheriff in whose custody the principal has been committed. Upon proof of the deposit of the designated amount the principal must be forthwith released from custody.

2. The person posting cash bail must complete and sign a form which states (a) the name, residential address and occupation of each person posting cash bail; and (b) the title of the criminal action or proceeding involved; and (c) the offense or offenses which are the subjects of the action or proceeding involved, and the status of such action or proceeding; and (d) the name of the principal and the nature of his involvement in or connection with such action or proceeding; and (e) that the person or persons posting cash bail undertake that the principal will appear in such action or proceeding whenever required and will at all times render himself amendable to the orders and processes of the court; and (f) the date of the principal's next appearance in court; and (g) an acknowledgment that the cash bail will be forfeited if the principal does not comply with any requirement or order of process to appear in court; and (h) the amount of money posted as cash bail.

3. Money posted as cash bail is and shall remain the property of the person posting it unless forfeited to the court.

§ 520.20. Bail and bail bonds; posting of bail bond and justifying affidavits; form and contents thereof

1.

(a) Except as provided in paragraph (b) when a bail bond is to be posted in satisfaction of bail, the obligor or obligors must submit to the court a bail bond in the amount fixed, executed in the form prescribed in subdivision two, accompanied by a justifying affidavit of each obligor, executed in the form prescribed in subdivision four.

(b) When a bail bond is to be posted in satisfaction of bail fixed for a defendant charged by information or simplified information or prosecutor's information with one or more traffic infractions and no other offense, the defendant may submit to the court, with the consent of the court, an insurance company bail bond covering the amount fixed, executed in a form prescribed by the superintendent of financial services.

2. Except as provided in paragraph (b) of subdivision one, a bail bond must be subscribed and sworn to by each obligor and must state:

(a) The name, residential address and occupation of each obligor; and

(b) The title of the criminal action or proceeding involved; and

(c) The offense or offenses which are the subjects of the action or proceeding involved, and the status of such action or proceeding; and

(d) The name of the principal and the nature of his involvement in or connection with such action or proceeding; and

(e) That the obligor, or the obligors jointly and severally, undertake that the principal will appear in such action or proceeding whenever required and will at all times render himself amenable to the orders and processes of the court; and

(f) That in the event that the principal does not comply with any such requirement, order or process, such obligor or obligors will pay to the people of the state of New York a designated sum of money fixed by the court.

3. A bail bond posted in the course of a criminal action is effective and binding upon the obligor or obligors until the imposition of sentence or other termination of the action, regardless of whether the action is dismissed in the local criminal court after an indictment on the same charge or charges by a superior court, and regardless of whether such action is partially conducted or prosecuted in a court or courts other than the one in which the action was pending when such bond was posted, unless prior to such termination such order of bail is vacated or revoked or the principal is surrendered, or unless the terms of such bond expressly limit its effectiveness to a lesser period; provided, however, the effectiveness of such bond may only be limited to a lesser period if the obligor or obligors submit notice of the limitation to the court and the district attorney not less than fourteen days before effectiveness ends.

4. A justifying affidavit must be subscribed and sworn to by the obligor-affiant and must state his name, residential address and occupation. Depending upon the kind of bail bond which it justifies, such affidavit must contain further statements as follows:

(a) An affidavit justifying an insurance company bail bond must state:

(i) The amount of the premium paid to the obligor; and

(ii) All security and all promises of indemnity received by the surety-obligor in connection with its execution of the bond, and the name, occupation and residential and business addresses of every person who has given any such indemnifying security or promise.

An action by the surety-obligor against an indemnitor, seeking retention of security deposited by the latter with the former or enforcement of any indemnity agreement of a kind described in this sub-paragraph, will not lie except with respect to agreements and security specified in the justifying affidavit.

(b) An affidavit justifying a secured bail bond must state every item of personal property deposited and of real property pledged as security, the value of each such item, and the nature and amount of every lien or encumbrance thereon.

(c) An affidavit justifying a partially secured bail bond or an unsecured bail bond must state the place and nature of the obligor-affiant's business or employment, the length of time he has been engaged therein, his income during the past year, and his average income over the past five years.

§ 520.30. Bail and bail bonds; examination as to sufficiency

1. Following the posting of a bail bond and the justifying affidavit or affidavits or the posting of cash bail, the court may conduct an inquiry for the purpose of determining the reliability of the obligors or person posting cash bail, the value and sufficiency of any security offered, and whether any feature of the undertaking contravenes public policy; provided that before undertaking an inquiry, of a person posting cash bail the court, after application of the district attorney, must have had reasonable cause to believe that the person posting cash bail is not in rightful possession of money posted as cash bail or that such money constitutes the fruits of criminal or unlawful conduct. The court may inquire into any matter stated or required to be stated in the justifying affidavits, and may also inquire into other matters appropriate to the determination, which include but are not limited to the following:

(a) The background, character and reputation of any obligor, and, in the case of an insurance company bail bond, the qualifications of the surety-obligor and its executing agent; and

(b) The source of any money or property deposited by any obligor as security, and whether any such money or property constitutes the fruits of criminal or unlawful conduct; and

(c) The source of any money or property delivered or agreed to be delivered to any obligor as indemnification on the bond, and whether any such money or property constitutes the fruits of criminal or unlawful conduct; and

(d) The background, character and reputation of any person who has indemnified or agreed to indemnify an obligor upon the bond; and whether any such indemnitor, not being licensed by the superintendent of financial services in accordance with the insurance law, has within a period of one month prior to such indemnity transaction given indemnification or security for like purpose in more than two cases not arising out of the same transaction; and

(e) The source of any money posted as cash bail, and whether any such money constitutes the fruits of criminal or unlawful conduct; and

(f) The background, character and reputation of the person posting cash bail.

2. Upon such inquiry, the court may examine, under oath or otherwise, the obligors and any other persons who may possess material information. The district attorney has a right to attend such inquiry, to call witnesses and to examine any witness in the proceeding. The court may, upon application of the district attorney, adjourn the proceeding for a reasonable period to allow him to investigate the matter.

3. At the conclusion of the inquiry, the court must issue an order either approving or disapproving the bail.

§ 520.40. Transfer of cash bail from local criminal court to superior court

When a local criminal court acquires control over the person of an accused and such court designates the amount of bail that the accused may post and such bail is posted in cash and subsequently the accused is arraigned in superior court where bail is fixed by such court, the accused may request that the cash bail posted in the local criminal court be transferred to the superior court. Notice of such request must be given to the person who posted cash bail. Upon such a request the superior court shall make an order directing the local criminal court to transfer the cash bail that it holds to the superior court for use in the superior court. If there is an overage, the superior court shall order it be paid over to the person who posted the cash bail in the local criminal court. If there is a deficiency, the accused shall post additional bail as directed by the superior court.

Article 540 Forfeiture of Bail and Remission Thereof

§ 540.10. Forfeiture of bail; generally

1. If, without sufficient excuse, a principal does not appear when required or does not render himself amenable to the orders and processes of the criminal court wherein bail has been posted, the court must enter such facts upon its minutes and the bail bond or the cash bail, as the case may be, is thereupon forfeited.

2. If the principal appears at any time before the final adjournment of the court, and satisfactorily excuses his neglect, the court may direct the forfeiture to be discharged upon such terms as are just. If the forfeiture is not so discharged and the forfeited bail consisted of a bail bond, the district attorney, within one hundred twenty days after the adjournment of the court at which such bond was directed to be forfeited, must proceed against the obligor or obligors who executed such bond, in the manner prescribed in subdivision three. If the forfeited bail consisted of cash bail, the county treasurer with whom it is deposited shall give written notice of the forfeiture to the person who posted cash bail for the defendant may [and]* at any time after the final adjournment of the court or forty-five days after notice of forfeiture required herein has been given, whichever comes later, apply the money deposited to the use of the county.

3. A bail bond or cash bail, upon being forfeited, together with a certified copy of the order of the court forfeiting the same, must be filed by the district attorney in the office of the clerk of the county wherein such order was issued. Such clerk must docket the same in the book kept by him for docketing of judgments and enter therein a judgment against the obligor or obligors who executed such bail bond for the amount of the penalty of said bond or against the person who posted the cash bail for the amount of the cash bail, and the bond and the certified copy of the order of the court forfeiting the bond or the cash bail constitutes the judgment roll. Such judgment constitutes a lien on the real estate of the obligor or obligors who executed such bail bond from the time of the entry of the judgment. An execution may be issued to collect the amount of said bail bond in the same form and with the same effect as upon a judgment recovered in an action in said county upon a debt in favor of the people of the state of New York against such obligor or obligors.

338

§ 540.20. Forfeiture of bail; certain local criminal courts

Nowithstanding the provisions of section 540.10, when bail has been posted in a city court, town court or village court in connection with a local criminal court accusatory instrument, other than a felony complaint, and thereafter such bail is forfeited, the following rules are applicable:

1. If such bail consists of a bail bond, the financial officer of such city, town or village must promptly commence an action for the recovery of the sum of money specified in such bond, and upon collection thereof shall pay the same over to the treasurer or financial officer of the city, the supervisor of the town or the treasurer of the village. Any amount recovered in such action, unless otherwise provided by law, shall be the property of the city, town or village in which the offense charged is alleged to have been committed.

2. If such bail consists of cash bail, the local criminal court must:

(a) If it is a city court, pay the forfeited bail to the treasurer or other financial officer of the city. Such forfeited bail, unless otherwise provided by law, is the property of such city.

(b) If it is a town court or a village court, pay the forfeited bail to the state comptroller on or before the tenth day of the month next succeeding such forfeiture. Such forfeited bail, unless otherwise provided by law, is the property of the town or village in which the offense charged is alleged to have been committed; provided, however, that when (i) a single amount of bail is posted for more than a single offense charged, and (ii) the town or village justice court does not attribute a specific amount of bail to each offense, and (iii) forfeited bail for at least two of the offenses would be the property of different governmental entities, the entire amount of forfeited bail shall be the property of the town or village in which the offenses charged are alleged to have been committed, except that, when forfeited bail for at least one of the offenses would be the property of the state, the entire amount of forfeited bail shall be the property of the state.

§ 540.30. Remission of forfeiture

1. After the forfeiture of a bail bond or cash bail, as provided in section 540.10, an application for remission of such forfeiture may be made to a court as follows:

(a) If the forfeiture has been ordered by a superior court, the application must be made in such court;

(b) If the forfeiture has been ordered by a local criminal court, the application must be made to a superior court in the county, except that if the local criminal court which ordered the forfeiture was a district court, the application may alternatively be made to that district court.

2. The application must be made within one year after the forfeiture of the bail is declared upon at least five days notice to the district attorney and service of copies of the affidavits and papers upon which the application is founded. The court may grant the application and remit the forfeiture or any part thereof, upon such terms as are just. The application may be granted only upon payment of the costs and expenses incurred in the proceedings for the enforcement of the forfeiture.

Article 550 Securing Attendance of Defendants—In General

§ 550.10. Securing attendance of defendants; in general

Depending upon the status of a criminal action pending against a defendant, the geographical location of the defendant at the time and other factors, his attendance thereat for purposes of arraignment or prosecution may be secured by the following methods:

1. If the defendant has never been arraigned in the action, and if he is at liberty within the state, his attendance may, under given circumstances, be secured by a warrant of arrest, as prescribed in article one hundred twenty, a superior court warrant of arrest, as prescribed in subdivision three of section 210.10, or a summons, as prescribed in article one hundred thirty.

2. If the defendant has been arraigned in the action and, by virtue of a securing order, is either in the custody of the sheriff or at liberty within the state on his own recognizance or on bail, his attendance may be secured as follows:

(a) If the defendant is confined in the custody of the sheriff, the court may direct the sheriff to produce him;

(b) If the defendant is at liberty within the state as a result of an order releasing him on his own recognizance or on bail, the court may secure his attendance by notification or by the issuance of a bench warrant.

3. If the defendant's attendance cannot be secured by methods described in subdivisions one and two, either because he is outside the state or because he is confined in an institution within the state as a result of an order issued in some other action, proceeding or matter, his attendance may, under indicated circumstances, be secured by procedures prescribed in the ensuing articles of this title.

Article 560 Securing Attendance of Defendants Confined in Institutions Within the State

§ 560.10. Securing attendance of defendants confined in institutions within the state

1. When a criminal action is pending against a defendant who is confined in an institution within the state pursuant to a court order issued in a different action, proceeding or matter, the following courts and judges may, under the indicated circumstances, order that the defendant be produced in the court in which the criminal action is pending for purposes of arraignment or prosecution therein:

(a) If the action is pending in a superior court or with a superior court judge sitting as a local criminal court, or in a district court or the New York City criminal court, such court may, upon application of the district attorney, order the production therein of a defendant confined in any institution within the state.

(b) If the action is pending in a city court or a town court or a village court, such court may, upon application of the district attorney, order production therein of a defendant confined in a county jail of such county. Production therein of a defendant confined in any other institution within the state may, upon application of the district attorney, be ordered by a judge of a superior court holding a term thereof in the county in which the action is pending.

2. An application by a district attorney, pursuant to subdivision one, for production of a defendant confined in an institution located in another county in connection with a criminal action or proceeding pending in such other county, must be made upon reasonable notice to the district attorney of such other county and to the attorney representing such defendant in or in connection with the action or proceeding pending therein, and the court or judge must accord them reasonable opportunity to be heard in the matter. If such court or judge determines that production of the defendant would result in an unreasonable interference with the conduct of the action in such other county, it must deny the application. If an order of production is issued, a justice of the appellate division, of either the department embracing the county of issuance thereof or of the department embracing the county of the defendant's confinement, upon application of the district attorney of the county of confinement or of the attorney representing the defendant in or in connection with the action pending therein, may for good cause shown vacate such order of production.

Article 590 Securing Attendance of Defendants Who Are Outside the United States

§ 590.10. Securing attendance of defendants who are outside the United States

1. When a criminal action for an offense committed in this state is pending in a criminal court of this state against a defendant who is in a foreign country with which the United States has an extradition treaty, and when the accusatory instrument charges an offense which is declared in such treaty to be an extraditable one, the district attorney of the county in which such offense was allegedly committed may make an application to the Governor, requesting him to make an application to the President of the United States to institute extradition proceedings for the return of the defendant to this country and state for the purpose of prosecution of such action. The district attorney's application must comply with rules, regulations and guidelines established by the Governor for such applications and must be accompanied by all the accusatory instruments, affidavits and other documents required by such rules, regulations and guidelines.

2. Upon receipt of the district attorney's application, the Governor, if satisfied that the defendant is in the foreign country in question, that the offense charged is an extraditable one pursuant to the treaty in question, and that there are no factors or impediments which in law preclude such an extradition, may in his discretion make an application, addressed to the secretary of state of the United States, requesting that the President of the United States institute extradition proceedings for the return of the defendant from such foreign country. The Governor's application must comply with rules, regulations and guidelines established by the secretary of state for such applications and must be accompanied by all the accusatory instruments, affidavits and other documents required by such rules, regulations and guidelines.

3. If the Governor's application is granted and the extradition is achieved or attempted, all expenses incurred therein must be borne by the county from which the application emanated.

4. The provisions of this section apply equally to extradition or attempted extradition of a person who is a fugitive following the entry of a judgment of conviction against him in a criminal court of this state.

§ 600.10. Corporate defendants; securing attendance

1. The court attendance of a corporation for purposes of commencing or prosecuting a criminal action against it may be accomplished by the issuance and service of a summons or an appearance ticket if such action has been or is about to be commenced in a local criminal court, and by a corporate summons if such action has been commenced in a superior court. Such process must be served upon the corporation by delivery thereof to an officer, director, managing or general agent, or cashier or assistant cashier of such corporation or to any other agent of such corporation authorized by appointment or by law to receive service of process.

2. A "corporate summons" is a process issued by a superior court directing a corporate defendant designated in an indictment to appear before it at a designated future time in connection with such indictment. A corporate summons must be generally in the form of a summons as prescribed in subdivision two of section 130.10. A corporate summons may be served by a public servant designated by the issuing court, and may be served anywhere in the state.

§ 600.20. Corporate defendants; prosecution thereof

At all stages of a criminal action, from the commencement thereof through sentence, a corporate defendant must appear by counsel. Upon failure of appearance at the time such defendant is required to enter a plea to the accusatory instrument, the court may enter a plea of guilty and impose sentence.

Title R Procedures for Securing Attendance of Witnesses in Criminal Actions

Article 610 Securing Attendance of Witnesses by Subpoena

§ 610.10. Securing attendance of witnesses by subpoena; in general

1. Under circumstances prescribed in this article, a person at liberty within the state may be required to attend a criminal court action or proceeding as a witness by the issuance and service upon him of a subpoena.

2. A "subpoena" is a process of a court directing the person to whom it is addressed to attend and appear as a witness in a designated action or proceeding in such court, on a designated date and any recessed or adjourned date of the action or proceeding. If the witness is given reasonable notice of such recess or adjournment, no further process is required to compel his attendance on the adjourned date.

3. As used in this article, "subpoena" includes a "subpoena duces tecum." A subpoena duces tecum is a subpoena requiring the witness to bring with him and produce specified physical evidence.

§ 610.20. Securing attendance of witnesses by subpoena; when and by whom subpoena may be issued

1. Any criminal court may issue a subpoena for the attendance of a witness in any criminal action or proceeding in such court.

2. A district attorney, or other prosecutor where appropriate, as an officer of a criminal court in which he is conducting the prosecution of a criminal action or proceeding, may issue a subpoena of such court, subscribed by himself, for the attendance in such court

or a grand jury thereof of any witness whom the people are entitled to call in such action or proceeding.

3. An attorney for a defendant in a criminal action or proceeding, as an officer of a criminal court, may issue a subpoena of such court, subscribed by himself, for the attendance in such court of any witness whom the defendant is entitled to call in such action or proceeding. An attorney for a defendant may not issue a subpoena duces tecum of the court directed to any department, bureau or agency of the state or of a political subdivision thereof, or to any officer or representative thereof. Such a subpoena duces tecum may be issued in behalf of a defendant upon order of a court pursuant to the rules applicable to civil cases as provided in section twenty-three hundred seven of the civil practice law and rules.

§ 610.25. Securing attendance of witness by subpoena; possession of physical evidence

1. Where a subpoena duces tecum is issued on reasonable notice to the person subpoenaed, the court or grand jury shall have the right to possession of the subpoenaed evidence. Such evidence may be retained by the court, grand jury or district attorney on behalf of the grand jury.

2. The possession shall be for a period of time, and on terms and conditions, as may reasonably be required for the action or proceeding. The reasonableness of such possession, time, terms, and conditions shall be determined with consideration for, among other things, (a) the good cause shown by the party issuing the subpoena or in whose behalf the subpoena is issued, (b) the rights and legitimate needs of the person subpoenaed and (c) the feasibility and appropriateness of making copies of the evidence. The cost of reproduction and transportation incident thereto shall be borne by the person or party issuing the subpoena unless the court determines otherwise in the interest of justice. Nothing in this article shall be deemed to prohibit the designation of a return date for a subpoena duces tecum prior to trial. Where physical evidence specified to be produced will be sought to be retained in custody, notice of such fact shall be given the subpoenaed party. In any case where the court receives or retains evidence prior to trial, it may, as may otherwise be authorized by law, grant the issuing party a reasonable opportunity to inspect such evidence.

§ 610.30. Securing attendance of witnesses by subpoena; where subpoena may be served

1. A subpoena of any criminal court, issued pursuant to section 610.20, may be served anywhere in the county of issuance or anywhere in an adjoining county.

2. A subpoena of a superior court or of a superior court judge sitting as a local criminal court, issued pursuant to section 610.20, may be served anywhere in the state.

3. A subpoena of a district court or of the New York City criminal court, issued pursuant to section 610.20, may be served anywhere in the state; provided that, if such subpoena is issued by a prosecutor or by an attorney for a defendant, it may be served in a county other than the county of issuance or an adjoining county only if such court, upon application of such prosecutor or attorney, endorses upon such subpoena an order for the attendance of the witness.

4. A subpoena of a city court or a town court or a village court, issued pursuant to section 610.20, may be served in a county other than the one of issuance or an adjoining county if a judge of a superior court, upon application of the issuing court or

the district attorney or an attorney for the defendant, endorses upon such subpoena an order for the attendance of the witness.

§ 610.40. Securing attendance of witnesses by subpoena; how and by whom subpoena may be served

A subpoena may be served by any person more than eighteen years old. Service must be made in the manner provided by the civil practice law and rules for the service of subpoenas in civil cases.

§ 610.50. Securing attendance of witness by subpoena; fees

1. A witness subpoenaed by the people in a criminal action is entitled to the same fees and mileage as a witness in a civil action, payable by the treasurer of the county upon the certificate of the court or the clerk thereof, stating the number of days the witness actually attended and the number of miles traveled by him in order to attend. In any such action, the court may, by order, direct the county treasurer to pay to such witness a further reasonable sum for expenses, to be specified in the order, and the county treasurer, upon the production of the order or a certified copy thereof, must pay the witness the sum specified therein out of the county treasury. Such certificates shall only be issued by the court or the clerk thereof, upon the production of the affidavit of the witness, stating that he attended as such either on subpoena or request of the district attorney, the number of miles necessarily traveled and the duration of attendance. An officer in any state department who attends as a witness under this section in his official capacity, or in consequence of any official action taken by him, and who receives a fixed sum in lieu of expenses, or who is entitled to receive the actual expenses incurred by him in the discharge of his official duties, is not entitled to the compensation herein provided.

2. A witness subpoenaed by the defendant in a criminal action is not entitled as of right to witness and mileage fees, but the court may in its discretion, by order, direct the county treasurer to pay to such a witness a reasonable sum for expenses, to be specified in the order. Upon the production of the order or a certified copy thereof, the county treasurer must pay the witness the sum specified therein, out of the county treasury.

Article 620 Securing Attendance of Witnesses by Material Witness Order

§ 620.10. Material witness order; defined

A material witness order is a court order (a) adjudging a person a material witness in a pending criminal action and (b) fixing bail to secure his future attendance thereat.

§ 620.20. Material witness order; when authorized; by what courts issuable; duration thereof

1. A material witness order may be issued upon the ground that there is reasonable cause to believe that a person whom the people or the defendant desire to call as a witness in a pending criminal action:

(a) Possesses information material to the determination of such action; and

(b) Will not be amenable or responsive to a subpoena at a time when his attendance will be sought.

2. A material witness order may be issued only when:

(a) An indictment has been filed in a superior court and is currently pending therein; or

(b) A grand jury proceeding has been commenced and is currently pending; or

(c) A felony complaint has been filed with a local criminal court and is currently pending therein.

3. The following courts may issue material witness orders under the indicated circumstances:

(a) When an indictment has been filed, or a grand jury proceeding has been commenced, or a defendant has been held by a local criminal court for the action of a grand jury, a material witness order may be issued only by the superior court in which such indictment is pending or by which such grand jury has been or is to be impaneled;

(b) When a felony complaint is currently pending in a district court or in the New York City criminal court or before a superior court judge sitting as a local criminal court, a material witness order may be issued either by such court or by the superior court which would have jurisdiction of the case upon a holding of the defendant for the action of the grand jury;

(c) When a felony complaint is currently pending in a city court or a town court or a village court, a material witness order may be issued only by the superior court which would have jurisdiction of the case upon a holding of the defendant for the action of the grand jury.

4. Unless vacated pursuant to section 620.60, a material witness order remains in effect during the following periods of time under the indicated circumstances:

(a) An order issued by a superior court under the circumstances prescribed in paragraph (a) of subdivision three remains in effect during the pendency of the criminal action in such superior court;

(b) An order issued by a district court or the New York City criminal court or a superior court judge sitting as a local criminal court, under circumstances prescribed in paragraph (b) of subdivision three, remains in effect (i) until the disposition of the felony complaint pending in such court, and (ii) if the defendant is held for the action of a grand jury, during the pendency of the grand jury proceeding, and (iii) if an indictment results, for a period of ten days following the filing of such indictment, and (iv) if within such ten day period such order is indorsed by the superior court in which the indictment is pending, during the pendency of the action in such superior court. Upon such indorsement, the order is deemed to be that of the superior court.

(c) An order issued by a superior court under circumstances prescribed in paragraph (c) of subdivision three remains in effect (i) until the disposition of the felony complaint pending in the city, town or village court, and (ii) if the defendant is held for the action of the grand jury, during the pendency of the action in the superior court.

§ 620.30. Material witness order; commencement of proceeding by application; procurement of appearance of prospective witness

1. A proceeding to adjudge a person a material witness must be commenced by application to the appropriate court, made in writing and subscribed and sworn to by the applicant, demonstrating reasonable cause to believe the existence of facts, as specified in subdivision one of section 620.20, warranting the adjudication of such person as a material witness.

2. If the court is satisfied that the application is well founded, the prospective witness may be compelled to appear in response thereto as follows:

(a) The court may issue an order directing him to appear therein at a designated time in order that a determination may be made whether he should be adjudged a material witness, and, upon personal service of such order or a copy thereof within the state, he must so appear.

(b) If in addition to the allegations specified in subdivision one, the application contains further allegations demonstrating to the satisfaction of the court reasonable cause to believe that (i) the witness would be unlikely to respond to such an order, or (ii) after previously having been served with such an order, he did not respond thereto, the court may issue a warrant addressed to a police officer, directing such officer to take such prospective witness into custody within the state and to bring him before the court forthwith in order that a proceeding may be conducted to determine whether he is to be adjudged a material witness.

§ 620.40. Material witness order; arraignment

1. When the prospective witness appears before the court, the court must inform him of the nature and purpose of the proceeding, and that he is entitled to a prompt hearing upon the issue of whether he should be adjudged a material witness. The prospective witness possesses all the rights, and is entitled to all the court instructions, with respect to right to counsel, opportunity to obtain counsel and assignment of counsel in case of financial inability to retain such, which, pursuant to subdivisions three through five of section 180.10, accrue to a defendant arraigned upon a felony complaint in a local criminal court.

2. If the proceeding is adjourned at the prospective witness' instance, for the purpose of obtaining counsel or otherwise, the court must order him to appear upon the adjourned date. The court may further fix bail to secure his appearance upon such date or until the proceeding is completed and, upon default thereof, may commit him to the custody of the sheriff for such period.

§ 620.50. Material witness order; hearing, determination and execution of order

1. The hearing upon the application must be conducted as follows:

(a) The applicant has the burden of proving by a preponderance of the evidence all facts essential to support a material witness order, and any testimony so adduced must be given under oath;

(b) The prospective witness may testify under oath or may make an unsworn statement;

(c) The prospective witness may call witnesses in his behalf, and the court must cause process to be issued for any such witness whom he reasonably wishes to call, and any testimony so adduced must be given under oath;

(d) Upon the hearing, evidence tending to demonstrate that the prospective witness does or does not possess information material to the criminal action in issue, or that he will or will not be amenable or respond to a subpoena at the time his attendance will be sought, is admissible even though it consists of hearsay.

2. If the court is satisfied after such hearing that there is reasonable cause to believe that the prospective witness (a) possesses information material to the pending action or proceeding, and (b) will not be amenable or respond to a subpoena at a time when his

attendance will be sought, it may issue a material witness order, adjudging him a material witness and fixing bail to secure his future attendance.

3. A material witness order must be executed as follows:

(a) If the bail is posted and approved by the court, the witness must, as provided in subdivision three of section 510.40, be released and be permitted to remain at liberty; provided that, where the bail is posted by a person other than the witness himself, he may not be so released except upon his signed written consent thereto;

(b) If the bail is not posted, or if though posted it is not approved by the court, the witness must, as provided in subdivision three of section 510.40, be committed to the custody of the sheriff.

§ 620.60. Material witness order; vacation, modification and amendment thereof

1. At any time after a material witness order has been issued the court must, upon application of such witness, with notice to the party upon whose application the order was issued, and with opportunity to be heard, make inquiry whether by reason of new or changed facts or circumstances the material witness order is no longer necessary or warranted, or, if it is, whether the original bail currently appears excessive. Upon making any such determination, the court must vacate the order. If its determination is that the order is no longer necessary or warranted, it must, as the situation requires, either discharge the witness from custody or exonerate the bail. If its determination is that the bail is excessive, it must issue a new order fixing bail in a lesser amount or on less burdensome terms.

2. At any time when a witness is at liberty upon bail pursuant to a material witness order, the court may, upon application of the party upon whose application the order was issued, with notice to the witness if possible and to his attorney if any and opportunity to be heard, make inquiry whether, by reason of new or changed facts or circumstances, the original bail is no longer sufficient to secure the future attendance of the witness at the pending action. Upon making such a determination, the court must vacate the order and issue a new order fixing bail in a greater amount or on terms more likely to secure the future attendance of the witness.

§ 620.70. Material witness order; compelling attendance of witness who fails to appear

If a witness at liberty on bail pursuant to a material witness order cannot be found or notified at the time his appearance as a witness is required, or if after notification he fails to appear in such action or proceeding as required, the court may issue a warrant, addressed to a police officer, directing such officer to take such witness into custody anywhere within the state and to bring him to the court forthwith.

§ 620.80. Material witness order; witness fee

A witness held in the custody of the sheriff as a result of a material witness order must be paid the sum of three dollars per day for each day of confinement in such custody. Such compensation is a county charge and is payable upon release of such material witness from custody or, in the discretion of the court, at any designated times or intervals during the confinement as the court may deem appropriate.

§ 630.10. Securing attendance of witnesses confined in institutions within the state; in general

Under the circumstances prescribed in this article, a person confined in an institution within this state pursuant to a court order may, upon application of a party to a criminal action or proceeding, demonstrating reasonable cause to believe that such person possesses information material thereto, be produced by court order and compelled to attend such action or proceeding as a witness.

§ 630.20. Securing attendance of witnesses confined in institutions within the state; when and by what courts order may be issued

The following courts and judges may, under the indicated circumstances, order production as witnesses of persons confined by court order in institutions within the state.

1. If the criminal action or proceeding is one pending in a superior court or with a superior court judge sitting as a local criminal court, such court may, except as provided in subdivision four, order the production as a witness therein of a person confined in any institution in the state.

2. If the criminal action or proceeding is one pending in a district court or the New York City criminal court, such court may order the production as a witness therein of a person confined in any institution within the state other than a state prison. Production therein of a prospective witness confined in a state prison may, except as provided in subdivision four, be ordered, upon application of the party desiring to call him, by a judge of a superior court holding a term thereof in the county in which the action or proceeding is pending.

3. If the criminal action or proceeding is one pending in a city court or a town court or a village court, such court may order the production as a witness therein of a person confined in a county jail of such county. Production therein of a prospective witness confined in any other institution within the state may, except as provided in subdivision four, be ordered, upon application of the party desiring to call him, by a judge of a superior court holding a term thereof in the county in which the action or proceeding is pending.

4. Regardless of the court in which the criminal action or proceeding is pending, production as a witness therein of a prisoner who has been sentenced to death may be ordered, upon application of the party desiring to call him, only by a justice of the appellate division of the department in which the action or proceeding is pending. The application for such order, if made by the defendant, must be upon notice to the district attorney of the county in which the action or proceeding is pending, and an application made by either party must be based upon a showing that the prisoner's attendance is clearly necessary in the interests of justice. Upon issuing such an order, the appellate division justice may fix and include therein any terms or conditions which he deems appropriate for execution thereof.

§ 650.10. Securing attendance of prisoner in this state as witness in proceeding without the state

If a judge of a court of record in any other state, which by its laws has made provision for commanding a prisoner within that state to attend and testify in this state, certifies under the seal of that court that there is a criminal prosecution pending in such court or that a grand jury investigation has commenced, and that a person confined in a New York state correctional institution or prison within the department of corrections and community supervision, other than a person confined as criminally mentally ill, or as a defective delinquent, or confined in the death house awaiting execution, is a material witness in such prosecution or investigation and that his or her presence is required for a specified number of days, upon presentment of such certificate to a judge of a superior court in the county where the person is confined, upon notice to the attorney general, such judge, shall fix a time and place for a hearing and shall make an order directed to the person having custody of the prisoner requiring that such prisoner be produced at the hearing.

If at such hearing the judge determines that the prisoner is a material and necessary witness in the requesting state, the judge shall issue an order directing that the prisoner attend in the court where the prosecution or investigation is pending, upon such terms and conditions as the judge prescribes, including among other things, provision for the return of the prisoner at the conclusion of his or her testimony, proper safeguards on his or her custody, and proper financial reimbursement or other payment by the demanding jurisdiction for all expenses incurred in the production and return of the prisoner.

The attorney general is authorized as agent for the state of New York, when in his or her judgment it is necessary, to enter into such agreements with the appropriate authorities of the demanding jurisdiction as he or she determines necessary to ensure proper compliance with the order of the court.

§ 650.20. Securing attendance of prisoner outside the state as witness in criminal action in the state

1. When (a) a criminal action is pending in a court of record of this state, or a grand jury proceeding has been commenced, and (b) there is reasonable cause to believe that a person confined in a correctional institution or prison of another state, other than a person awaiting execution of a sentence of death or one confined as mentally ill or as a defective delinquent, possesses information material to such criminal action or proceeding, and (c) the attendance of such person as a witness in such action or proceeding is desired by a party thereto, and (d) the state in which such person is confined possesses a statute equivalent to section 650.10, the court in which such action or proceeding is pending may issue a certificate under the seal of such court, certifying all such facts and that the attendance of such person as a witness in such court is required for a specified number of days.

2. Such certificate may be issued upon application, of either the people or a defendant, demonstrating all the facts specified in subdivision one.

3. Upon issuing such a certificate, the court may deliver it, or cause or authorize it to be delivered, to a judge or a court of such other state who or which, pursuant to the laws thereof, is authorized to initiate or undertake legal action for the delivery of such prisoners to this state as witnesses.

§ 650.30. Securing attendance of prisoner in federal institution as witness in criminal action in the state

1. When (a) a criminal action is pending in a court of record of this state by reason of the filing therewith of an accusatory instrument, or a grand jury proceeding has been commenced, and (b) there is reasonable cause to believe that a person confined in a federal prison or other federal custody, either within or outside this state, possesses information material to such criminal action or proceeding, and (c) the attendance of such person as a witness in such action or proceeding is desired by a party thereto, a superior court, at a term held in the county in which such action or proceeding is pending, may issue a certificate, known as a writ of habeas corpus ad testificandum, addressed to the attorney general of the United States, certifying all such facts and requesting the attorney general of the United States to cause the attendance of such person as a witness in such court for a specified number of days under custody of a federal public servant.

2. Such a certificate may be issued upon application of either the people or a defendant, demonstrating all the facts specified in subdivision one.

3. Upon issuing such certificate, the court may deliver it, or cause or authorize it to be delivered, to the attorney general of the United States or to his representative authorized to entertain the request.

Title S Procedures for Securing Testimony for Future Use, and For Using Testimony Given in a Prior Proceeding

Article 660 Securing Testimony for Use in a Subsequent Proceeding—Examination of Witnesses Conditionally

§ 660.10. Examination of witnesses conditionally; in general

After a defendant has been arraigned upon an accusatory instrument, and under circumstances prescribed in this article, a criminal court may, upon application of either the people or a defendant, order that a witness or prospective witness in the action be examined conditionally under oath in order that such testimony may be received into evidence at subsequent proceedings in or related to the action.

§ 660.20. Examination of witnesses conditionally; grounds for order

An order directing examination of a witness conditionally must be based upon the ground that there is reasonable cause to believe that such witness:

1. Possesses information material to the criminal action or proceeding in issue; and

2. Will not be amenable or responsive to legal process or available as a witness at a time when his testimony will be sought, either because he is:

(a) About to leave the state and not return for a substantial period of time; or

(b) Physically ill or incapacited [incapacitated]*.

§ 660.30. Examination of witnesses conditionally; when and to what courts application may be made

1. An application to examine a witness conditionally may be made at any time after the defendant has been arraigned upon an accusatory instrument and before termination of the action, or of a proceeding therein or related thereto, in which the witness's testimony is sought.

2. Such application must be made to and determined by the following courts under the indicated circumstances:

(a) If the action is pending in a local criminal court as a result of an accusatory instrument filed therewith, the application must be made to and determined by such local criminal court;

(b) If the defendant has been held by a local criminal court for the action of a grand jury on the basis of a felony complaint, or if an indictment has been filed against him, the application must be made to and determined by the superior court by which the grand jury was or is to be impaneled or in which the indictment is pending. If the superior court by which the grand jury is to be impaneled is the supreme court, the motion may, in the alternative, be made in the county court of the county in which the action is pending.

§ 660.40. Examination of witnesses conditionally; application and notice

1. An application to examine a witness conditionally must be made in writing, must be subscribed and sworn to, and must contain:

(a) The title of the action, the offense or offenses charged, the nature and status of the action, and the name and residential address of the witness sought to be examined; and

(b) A statement that there is reasonable cause to believe that grounds for such an examination, as specified in section 660.20, exist, together with allegations of fact supporting such statement. Such allegations of fact may be those of the applicant, or those of another person in an accompanying deposition, or of both. They may be based either upon personal knowledge of the deponent or upon information and belief, provided that in the latter event the sources of such information and the grounds of such belief are stated.

2. The application may also contain a request that the examination, in addition to its being recorded in the same manner as would be required were the witness testifying at trial, also be recorded by videotape or other photographic method approved by and subject to standards and administrative policies promulgated pursuant to section twenty-eight of article six of the constitution.

3. A copy of the application, with reasonable notice and opportunity to be heard, must be served upon the other party to the action. If the defendant is the applicant, such service must be upon the district attorney. If the people are the applicant, such service must be upon the defendant and upon his attorney if any. The respondent party may file and serve a sworn written answer to the application.

§ 660.50. Examination of witnesses conditionally; determination of application

1. Before ruling upon the application, the court may, in addition to examining the papers and hearing oral argument, make any inquiry it deems appropriate for the purpose of making findings of fact essential to the determination. For such purpose, it may examine

351

witnesses, under oath or otherwise, subpoena or call witnesses and authorize the attorneys for the parties to do so.

2. If the court is satisfied that grounds for the application exist, it must order an examination of the witness conditionally at a designated time and place. Such examination must be conducted by the same court; except that, if it is to be held in another county, it may be conducted by a designated superior court of such other county.

3. The court must order that the examination be recorded in the same manner as would be required were the witness testifying at trial, and the court may, in addition, order that the examination also be recorded by videotape or other photographic method approved by and subject to standards and administrative policies promulgated pursuant to section twenty-eight of article six of the constitution.

4. Upon ordering the examination, the court must direct the party securing the order of examination to serve a copy of the order upon the respondent party and, if a defendant be such, upon his attorney also, and must either issue a subpoena for the witness' attendance thereat or authorize the applicant party's attorney to do so.

§ 660.60. Examination of witnesses conditionally; the examination proceeding

1. The examination proceeding must be conducted in the same manner as would be required were the witness testifying at a trial, and must be recorded in such fashion as the court has directed pursuant to subdivision three of section 660.50 of this chapter. The witness must testify under oath. The applicant party must first examine the witness and the respondent party may then cross-examine him, with each party entitled to register objections and to receive rulings of the court thereon.

2. Upon conclusion of the examination, a transcript and any videotape or photographic recording thereof must be certified and filed with the court which ordered the examination.

Article 670 Use in a Criminal Proceeding of Testimony Given in a Previous Proceeding

§ 670.10. Use in a criminal proceeding of testimony given in a previous proceeding; when authorized

1. Under circumstances prescribed in this article, testimony given by a witness at (a) a trial of an accusatory instrument, or (b) a hearing upon a felony complaint conducted pursuant to section 180.60, or (c) an examination of such witness conditionally, conducted pursuant to article six hundred sixty, may, where otherwise admissible, be received into evidence at a subsequent proceeding in or relating to the action involved when at the time of such subsequent proceeding the witness is unable to attend the same by reason of death, illness or incapacity, or cannot with due diligence be found, or is outside the state or in federal custody and cannot with due diligence be brought before the court. Upon being received into evidence, such testimony may be read and any videotape or photographic recording thereof played. Where any recording is received into evidence, the stenographic transcript of that examination shall also be received.

2. The subsequent proceedings at which such testimony may be received in evidence consist of:

(a) Any proceeding constituting a part of a criminal action based upon the charge or charges which were pending against the defendant at the time of the witness's testimony and to which such testimony related; and

(b) Any post-judgment proceeding in which a judgment of conviction upon a charge specified in paragraph (a) is challenged.

§ 670.20. Use in a criminal proceeding of testimony given in a previous proceeding; procedure

1. In any criminal action or proceeding other than a grand jury proceeding, a party thereto who desires to offer in evidence testimony of a witness given in a previous action or proceeding as provided in section 670.10, must so move, either in writing or orally in open court, and must submit to the court, and serve a copy thereof upon the adverse party, an authenticated transcript of the testimony and any videotape or photographic recording thereof sought to be introduced. Such moving party must further state facts showing that personal attendance of the witness in question is precluded by some factor specified in subdivision one of section 670.10. In determining the motion, the court, with opportunity for both parties to be heard, must make inquiry and conduct a hearing to determine whether personal attendance of the witness is so precluded. If the court determines that such is the case and grants the motion, the moving party may introduce the transcript in evidence and read into evidence the testimony contained therein. In such case, the adverse party may register any objection or protest thereto that he would be entitled to register were the witness testifying in person, and the court must rule thereon.

2. Without obtaining any court order or authorization, a district attorney may introduce in evidence in a grand jury proceeding testimony of a witness given in a previous action or proceeding specified in subdivision one of section 670.10, provided that a foundation for such evidence is laid by other evidence demonstrating that personal attendance of such witness is precluded by some factor specified in subdivision one of section 670.10.

Article 680 Securing Testimony Outside the State for Use in Proceeding Within the State—Examination of Witnesses on Commission

§ 680.10. Examination of witnesses on commission; in general

1. Under circumstances prescribed in this article, testimony material to a trial or pending trial of an accusatory instrument which charges a crime, may be taken by "examination on a commission" outside the state and received in evidence at such trial.

2. A "commission" is a process issued by a superior court designating one or more persons as commissioners and authorizing them to conduct a recorded examination of a witness or witnesses under oath, primarily on the basis of interrogatories annexed to the commission, and to remit to the issuing court the transcript of such examination.

§ 680.20. Examination of witnesses on commission; when commission issuable; form and content of application

1. Upon a pre-trial application of a defendant who has pleaded not guilty to an indictment or other accusatory instrument which charges a crime, the superior court in which such indictment is pending, or a superior court in the county in which such other accusatory instrument is pending, may issue a commission for examination of a designated person as a witness in the action, at a designated place outside this state, if

it is satisfied that (a) such person possesses information material to the action which in the interest of justice should be disclosed at the trial, and (b) resides outside the state.

2. The application and moving papers must be in writing and must be subscribed and sworn to by the defendant or his attorney. A copy thereof must be served on the district attorney, with reasonable notice and opportunity to be heard. The moving papers must allege:

(a) The offense or offenses charged; and

(b) The status of the action; and

(c) The name of the prospective witness; and

(d) A statement that such prospective witness resides outside the state, and his address in the jurisdiction in which the examination sought is to occur; and

(e) A statement that he possesses information material to the action which in the interest of justice should be disclosed at the trial, together with a brief summary of the facts supporting such statement.

3. An application for issuance of a commission may request examination pursuant thereto of more than one person residing in the particular jurisdiction. In such case, it must contain allegations specified in subdivision two with respect to each such person, and the court must make separate rulings as to each.

§ 680.30. Examination of witnesses on commission; application by people for examination of witnesses

1. Upon granting the defendant's application for issuance of a commission, the court may, upon application of the people, determine that the commission shall also authorize examination of a person or persons designated by the people, who reside in the jurisdiction in which the examination proceeding is to occur, if it is satisfied that such person or persons possess material information, reside outside the state and otherwise meet the standards for examination of witnesses on a commission as prescribed in subdivision one of section 680.20.

2. Such application and the moving papers must be in writing, must be subscribed and sworn to by the district attorney, and copies thereof must be served upon the defendant and his attorney, with reasonable notice and opportunity to be heard. The moving papers must contain all of the allegations required upon a defendant's application, as specified in subdivision two of section 680.20.

§ 680.40. Examination of witnesses on commission; when commission issuable upon application of people

When a commission has been issued upon application of a defendant pursuant to section 680.20, the court may, upon application of the people, issue another commission for examination, either in the same or another jurisdiction, of a person designated by the people, under the same conditions as prescribed in said section 680.20. In such case, the court may, upon application of the defendant, determine, in the manner provided in section 680.30, that such commission shall also authorize examination of a person or persons designated by the defendant.

§ 680.50. Examination of witnesses on commission; interrogatories

1. Following an order for the issuance of a commission and the court's designation of the witnesses to be examined thereon, each party must prepare interrogatories or

questions to be asked of each witness who is to be examined upon his or its request, and must submit the same to the court and serve a copy thereof upon the other party. Following such submission and service, such other party may in the same manner submit and serve cross-interrogatories or questions, to be asked of the witness following his examination upon the direct inquiry.

2. After all such interrogatories and cross-interrogatories have been submitted and served, the court may examine them and, with opportunity for counsel to be heard, exclude and strike any question which it considers irrelevant, incompetent or otherwise improper or violative of the rules of evidence which prevail at a criminal trial.

§ 680.60. Examination of witnesses on commission; form and content of the commission

1. The commission must be subscribed by the court and must contain:

(a) The name and address of each witness to be examined; and

(b) The name, or a descriptive title, of a commissioner or commissioners who, pursuant to subdivision two, are authorized to conduct the examination; and

(c) A statement authorizing such commissioner or commissioners to administer the oath to witnesses; and

(d) A direction that, upon completion of such examination, such commissioner or commissioners cause it to be transcribed and remit to the court the transcript, the commission, the interrogatories and all other pertinent instruments and documents.

2. The following persons may be designated commissioners:

(a) If the examination is to occur within the United States or any territory thereof, any attorney authorized to practice law in the specified jurisdiction or any person authorized to administer oaths therein;

(b) If the examination is to occur in a foreign country, any diplomatic or consular agent or representative of the United States employed in such capacity in such country, or any commissioned officer of the armed forces.

3. The court must cause the commission to be delivered to a commissioner designated therein, together with a copy of this article.

§ 680.70. Examination of witnesses on commission; the examination

The examination on the commission must be conducted as follows:

1. Each witness must testify under oath, and the examination must be recorded and transcribed.

2. Each witness must first be asked all the questions contained in the interrogatories submitted by the party requesting his examination. He must then be asked all the questions contained in the cross-interrogatories, if any, submitted by the other party.

3. The defendant has a right to be represented by counsel at the examination, and the district attorney also has a right to be present, but both such rights may be waived. Upon the conclusion of the questioning of a witness upon the written interrogatories, he may be further examined by the attorney or representative of the party who requested his examination, and may then be cross-examined by the attorney or representative of the adverse party. Each such attorney or representative may register objections to the authority or qualifications of the commissioner, to the manner in which the examination is conducted, and to the admissibility of evidence, and all such objections must be recorded and transcribed.

4. Documentary or other physical evidence may be produced and submitted by a witness. Such evidence must be subscribed or otherwise identified by the witness, and certified by a commissioner and annexed to the transcript of the examination as a part of the record.

5. After the examination is transcribed, the commissioner or commissioners must subscribe and certify the transcript as an accurate record of the proceedings, and must then remit such transcript and all other pertinent instruments, documents and evidence to the court which issued the commission, in accordance with the directions thereof.

§ 680.80. Examination of witnesses on commission; use at trial of transcript of examination

1. When the transcript and record of the examination on commission are received by the superior court which issued the commission, they must be filed therewith if such court be the trial court, and, if not, transmitted to the trial court. A copy of the transcript must be delivered by the trial court to each party.

2. Upon the trial of the action, either party may, subject to the provisions of subdivision three, introduce and read into evidence the transcript or that portion thereof containing the testimony of a witness examined on the commission.

3. At any time prior to the introduction of such evidence, the trial court may examine the transcript and, upon according both parties opportunity to be heard and to register objections, may exclude and strike therefrom irrelevant, incompetent or otherwise inadmissible testimony. While the transcript or any portion thereof is being read into evidence at the trial by a party, the other party may register any objection or protest thereto that he would be entitled to register were the witness testifying in person, regardless of whether such protest has previously been raised and passed upon by the court, and the court must rule thereon.

Title T Procedures for Securing Evidence by Means of Court Order and for Suppressing Evidence Unlawfully or Improperly Obtained

Article 690 Search Warrants

§ 690.05. Search warrants; in general; definition

1. Under circumstances prescribed in this article, a local criminal court may, upon application of a police officer, a district attorney or other public servant acting in the course of his official duties, issue a search warrant.

2. A search warrant is a court order and process directing a police officer to conduct:

(a) a search of designated premises, or of a designated vehicle, or of a designated person, for the purpose of seizing designated property or kinds of property, and to deliver any property so obtained to the court which issued the warrant; or

(b) a search of a designated premises for the purpose of searching for and arresting a person who is the subject of:

(i) a warrant of arrest issued pursuant to this chapter, a superior court warrant of arrest issued pursuant to this chapter, or a bench warrant for a felony issued pursuant to this chapter, where the designated premises is the dwelling of a third party who is not the subject of the arrest warrant; or

(ii) a warrant of arrest issued by any other state or federal court for an offense which would constitute a felony under the laws of this state, where the designated premises is the dwelling of a third party who is not the subject of the arrest warrant.

§ 690.10. Search warrants; property subject to seizure thereunder

Personal property is subject to seizure pursuant to a search warrant if there is reasonable cause to believe that it:

1. Is stolen; or

2. Is unlawfully possessed; or

3. Has been used, or is possessed for the purpose of being used, to commit or conceal the commission of an offense against the laws of this state or another state, provided however, that if such offense was against the laws of another state, the court shall only issue a warrant if the conduct comprising such offense would, if occurring in this state, constitute a felony against the laws of this state; or

4. Constitutes evidence or tends to demonstrate that an offense was committed in this state or another state, or that a particular person participated in the commission of an offense in this state or another state, provided however, that if such offense was against the laws of another state, the court shall only issue a warrant if the conduct comprising such offense would, if occurring in this state, constitute a felony against the laws of this state.

§ 690.15. Search warrants; what and who are subject to search thereunder

1. A search warrant must direct a search of one or more of the following:

(a) A designated or described place or premises;

(b) A designated or described vehicle, as that term is defined in section 10.00 of the penal law;

(c) A designated or described person.

2. A search warrant which directs a search of a designated or described place, premises or vehicle, may also direct a search of any person present threat or therein.

§ 690.20. Search warrants; where executable

1. A search warrant issued by a district court, the New York City criminal court or a superior court judge sitting as a local criminal court may be executed pursuant to its terms anywhere in the state.

2. A search warrant issued by a city court, a town court or a village court may be executed pursuant to its terms only in the county of issuance or an adjoining county.

§ 690.25. Search warrants; to whom addressable and by whom executable

1. A search warrant must be addressed to a police officer whose geographical area of employment embraces or is embraced or partially embraced by the county of issuance. The warrant need not be addressed to a specific police officer but may be addressed to any police officer of a designated classification, or to any police officer of any classification employed or having general jurisdiction to act as a police officer in the county.

2. A police officer to whom a search warrant is addressed, as provided in subdivision one, may execute it pursuant to its terms anywhere in the county of issuance or an adjoining county, and he may execute it pursuant to its terms in any other county of the state in which it is executable if (a) his geographical area of employment embraces the entire county of issuance or (b) he is a member of the police department or force of a city located in such county of issuance.

3. [Repealed]

§ 690.30. Search warrants; when executable

1. A search warrant must be executed not more than ten days after the date of issuance and it must thereafter be returned to the court without unnecessary delay.

2. A search warrant may be executed on any day of the week. It may be executed only between the hours of 6:00 A.M. and 9:00 P.M., unless the warrant expressly authorizes execution thereof at any time of the day or night, as provided in subdivision five of section 690.45.

§ 690.35. Search warrants; the application

1. An application for a search warrant may be in writing or oral. If in writing, it must be made, subscribed and sworn to by a public servant specified in subdivision one of section 690.05. If oral, it must be made by such a public servant and sworn to and recorded in the manner provided in section 690.36.

2. The application shall be made to:

(a) A local criminal court, as defined in section 10.10 of this chapter, having preliminary jurisdiction over the underlying offense, or geographical jurisdiction over the location to be searched when the search is to be made for personal property of a kind or character described in section 690.10 of this article except that:

(i) if a town court has such jurisdiction but is not available to issue the search warrant, the warrant may be issued by the local criminal court of any village within such town or, any adjoining town, village embraced in whole or in part by such adjoining town, or city of the same county;

(ii) if a village court has such jurisdiction but is not available to issue the search warrant, the warrant may be issued by the town court of the town embracing such village or any other village court within such town, or, if such town or village court is not available either, before the local criminal court of any adjoining town, village embraced in whole or in part by such adjoining town, or city of the same county; and

(iii) if a city court has such jurisdiction but is not available to issue the search warrant, the warrant may be issued by the local criminal court of any adjoining town or village, or village court embraced by an adjoining town, within the same county as such city.

(b) A local criminal court, as defined in section 10.10 of this chapter, with geographical jurisdiction over the location where the premises to be searched is located, or which issued the underlying arrest warrant, when the search warrant is sought pursuant to paragraph (b) of subdivision two of section 690.05 of this article, for the purpose of arresting a wanted person.

Any search warrant issued pursuant to this section shall be subject to the territorial limitations provided by section 690.20 of this article.

3. The application must contain:

(a) The name of the court and the name and title of the applicant; and

(b) A statement that there is reasonable cause to believe that property of a kind or character described in section 690.10 may be found in or upon a designated or described place, vehicle or person, or, in the case of an application for a search warrant as defined in paragraph (b) of subdivision two of section 690.05, a statement that there is reasonable cause to believe that the person who is the subject of the warrant of arrest may be found in the designated premises; and

(c) Allegations of fact supporting such statement. Such allegations of fact may be based upon personal knowledge of the applicant or upon information and belief, provided that in the latter event the sources of such information and the grounds of such belief are stated. The applicant may also submit depositions of other persons containing allegations of fact supporting or tending to support those contained in the application; and

(d) A request that the court issue a search warrant directing a search for and seizure of the property or person in question; and

(e) In the case of an application for a search warrant as defined in paragraph (b) of subdivision two of section 690.05, a copy of the warrant of arrest and the underlying accusatory instrument.

4. The application may also contain:

(a) A request that the search warrant be made executable at any time of the day or night, upon the ground that there is reasonable cause to believe that (i) it cannot be executed between the hours of 6:00 A.M. and 9:00 P.M., or (ii) the property sought will be removed or destroyed if not seized forthwith, or (iii) in the case of an application for a search warrant as defined in paragraph (b) of subdivision two of section 690.05, the person sought is likely to flee or commit another crime, or may endanger the safety of the executing police officers or another person if not seized forthwith or between the hours of 9:00 P.M. and 6:00 A.M.; and

(b) A request that the search warrant authorize the executing police officer to enter premises to be searched without giving notice of his authority and purpose, upon the ground that there is reasonable cause to believe that (i) the property sought may be easily and quickly destroyed or disposed of, or (ii) the giving of such notice may endanger the life or safety of the executing officer or another person, or (iii) in the case of an application for a search warrant as defined in paragraph (b) of subdivision two of section 690.05 for the purpose of searching for and arresting a person who is the subject of a warrant for a felony, the person sought is likely to commit another felony, or may endanger the life or safety of the executing officer or another person.

Any request made pursuant to this subdivision must be accompanied and supported by allegations of fact of a kind prescribed in paragraph (c) of subdivision two.

§ 690.36. Search warrants; special provisions governing oral applications therefor

1. An oral application for a search warrant may be communicated to a judge by telephone, radio or other means of electronic communication.

2. Where an oral application for a search warrant is made, the applicant therefor must identify himself and the purpose of his communication. After being sworn as provided in subdivision three of this section, the applicant must also make the statement required by paragraph (b) of subdivision two of section 690.35 and provide the same allegations of fact required by paragraph (c) of such subdivision; provided, however, persons, properly identified, other than the applicant may also provide some or all of such allegations of fact directly to the court. Where appropriate, the applicant may also make a request specified in subdivision three of section 690.35.

3. Upon being advised that an oral application for a search warrant is being made, a judge shall place under oath the applicant and any other person providing information in

support of the application. Such oath or oaths and all of the remaining communication must be recorded, either by means of a voice recording device or verbatim stenographic or verbatim longhand notes. If a voice recording device is used or a stenographic record made, the judge must have the record transcribed, certify to the accuracy of the transcription and file the original record and transcription with the court within twenty-four hours of the issuance of a warrant. If longhand notes are taken, the judge shall subscribe a copy and file it with the court within twenty-four hours of the issuance of a warrant.

§ 690.40. Search warrants; determination of application

1. In determining an application for a search warrant the court may examine, under oath, any person whom it believes may possess pertinent information. Any such examination must be either recorded or summarized on the record by the court.

2. If the court is satisfied that there is reasonable cause to believe that property of a kind or character referred to in section 690.10, and described in the application, may be found in or upon the place, premises, vehicle or person designated or described in the application, or, in the case of an application for a search warrant as defined in paragraph (b) of subdivision two of section 690.05, that there is reasonable cause to believe that the person who is the subject of a warrant of arrest, a superior court warrant of arrest, or a bench warrant for a felony may be found at the premises designated in the application, it may grant the application and issue a search warrant directing a search of the said place, premises, vehicle or person and a seizure of the described property or the described person. If the court is further satisfied that grounds, described in subdivision four of section 690.35, exist for authorizing the search to be made at any hour of the day or night, or without giving notice of the police officer's authority and purpose, it may make the search warrant executable accordingly.

3. When a judge determines to issue a search warrant based upon an oral application, the applicant therefor shall prepare the warrant in accordance with section 690.45 and shall read it, verbatim, to the judge.

§ 690.45. Search warrants; form and content

A search warrant must contain:

1. The name of the issuing court and, except where the search warrant has been obtained on an oral application, the subscription of the issuing judge; and

2. Where the search warrant has been obtained on an oral application, it shall so indicate and shall state the name of the issuing judge and the time and date on which such judge directed its issuance.

3. The name, department or classification of the police officer to whom it is addressed; and

4. A description of the property which is the subject of the search, or, in the case of a search warrant as defined in paragraph (b) of subdivision two of section 690.05, a description of the person to be searched for; and

5. A designation or description of the place, premises or person to be searched, by means of address, ownership, name or any other means essential to identification with certainty; and

6. A direction that the warrant be executed between the hours of 6:00 A.M. and 9:00 P.M., or, where the court has specially so determined, an authorization for execution thereof at any time of the day or night; and

7. An authorization, where the court has specially so determined, that the executing police officer enter the premises to be searched without giving notice of his authority and purpose; and

8. A direction that the warrant and any property seized pursuant thereto be returned and delivered to the court without unnecessary delay; and

9. In the case of a search warrant as defined in paragraph (b) of subdivision two of section 690.05, a copy of the warrant of arrest and the underlying accusatory instrument.

§ 690.50. Search warrants; execution thereof

1. In executing a search warrant directing a search of premises or a vehicle, a police officer must, except as provided in subdivision two, give, or make reasonable effort to give, notice of his authority and purpose to an occupant thereof before entry and show him the warrant or a copy thereof upon request. If he is not thereafter admitted, he may forcibly enter such premises or vehicle and may use against any person resisting his entry or search thereof as much physical force, other than deadly physical force, as is necessary to execute the warrant; and he may use deadly physical force if he reasonably believes such to be necessary to defend himself or a third person from what he reasonably believes to be the use or imminent use of deadly physical force.

2. In executing a search warrant directing a search of premises or a vehicle, a police officer need not give notice to anyone of his authority and purpose, as prescribed in subdivision one, but may promptly enter the same if:

(a) Such premises or vehicle are at the time unoccupied or reasonably believed by the officer to be unoccupied; or

(b) The search warrant expressly authorizes entry without notice.

3. In executing a search warrant directing or authorizing a search of a person, a police officer must give, or make reasonable effort to give, such person notice of his authority and purpose and show him the warrant or a copy thereof upon request. If such person, or another, thereafter resists or refuses to permit the search, the officer may use as much physical force, other than deadly physical force, as is necessary to execute the warrant; and he may use deadly physical force if he reasonably believes such to be necessary to defend himself or a third person from what he reasonably believes to be the use or imminent use of deadly physical force.

4. Upon seizing property pursuant to a search warrant, a police officer must write and subscribe a receipt itemizing the property taken and containing the name of the court by which the warrant was issued. If property is taken from a person, such receipt must be given to such person. If property is taken from premises or a vehicle, such receipt must be given to the owner, tenant or other person in possession thereof if he is present; or if he is not, the officer must leave such a receipt in the premises or vehicle from which the property was taken.

5. Upon seizing property pursuant to a search warrant, a police officer must without unnecessary delay return to the court the warrant and the property, and must file therewith a written inventory of such property, subscribed and sworn to by such officer.

6. Upon arresting a person during a search for him or her pursuant to a search warrant as defined in paragraph (b) of subdivision two of section 690.05, a police officer shall comply with the terms of the warrant of arrest, superior court warrant of arrest, or bench warrant for a felony, and shall proceed in the manner directed by this chapter. Upon arresting such person, the police officer shall also, without unnecessary delay, file a written statement with the court which issued the search warrant, subscribed and sworn to by such officer, setting forth that the person has been arrested and duly brought before the appropriate court, return to the court the warrant and the property seized in the course of its execution, and file therewith a written inventory of any such property, subscribed and sworn to by such officer.

§ 690.55. Search warrants; disposition of seized property

1. Upon receiving property seized pursuant to a search warrant, the court must either:

(a) Retain it in the custody of the court pending further disposition thereof pursuant to subdivision two or some other provision of law; or

(b) Direct that it be held in the custody of the person who applied for the warrant, or of the police officer who executed it, or of the governmental or official agency or department by which either such public servant is employed, upon condition that upon order of such court such property be returned thereto or delivered to another court.

2. A local criminal court which retains custody of such property must, upon request of another criminal court in which a criminal action involving or relating to such property is pending, cause it to be delivered thereto.

Article 700 Eavesdropping and Video Surveillance Warrants

§ 700.05. Eavesdropping and video surveillance warrants; definitions of terms

As used in this article, the following terms have the following meanings:

1. "Eavesdropping" means "wiretapping", "mechanical overhearing of conversation," or the "intercepting or accessing of an electronic communication", as those terms are defined in section 250.00 of the penal law, but does not include the use of a pen register or trap and trace device when authorized pursuant to article 705 of this chapter.

2. "Eavesdropping warrant" means an order of a justice authorizing or approving eavesdropping.

3. "Intercepted communication" means (a) a telephonic or telegraphic communication which was intentionally overheard or recorded by a person other than the sender or receiver thereof, without the consent of the sender or receiver, by means of any instrument, device or equipment, or (b) a conversation or discussion which was intentionally overheard or recorded, without the consent of at least one party thereto, by a person not present thereat, by means of any instrument, device or equipment; or (c) an electronic communication which was intentionally intercepted or accessed, as that term is defined in section 250.00 of the penal law. The term "contents," when used with respect to a communication, includes any information concerning the identity of the parties to such communications, and the existence, substance, purport, or meaning of that communication. The term "communication" includes conversation and discussion.

3-a. "Telephonic communication", "electronic communication", and "intentionally intercepted or accessed" have the meanings given to those terms by subdivisions three, five, and six respectively, of section 250.00 of the penal law.

4. "Justice," except as otherwise provided herein, means any justice of an appellate division of the judicial department in which the eavesdropping warrant is to be executed, or any justice of the supreme court of the judicial district in which the eavesdropping warrant is to be executed, or any county court judge of the county in which the eavesdropping warrant is to be executed. When the eavesdropping warrant is to authorize the interception of oral communications occurring in a vehicle or wire communications occurring over a telephone located in a vehicle, "justice" means any justice of the supreme court of the judicial department or any county court judge of the county in which the eavesdropping device is to be installed or connected or of any judicial department or county in which communications are expected to be intercepted. When such a justice issues such an eavesdropping warrant, such warrant may be executed and such oral or wire communications may be intercepted anywhere in the state.

5. "Applicant" means a district attorney or the attorney general or if authorized by the attorney general, the deputy attorney general in charge of the organized crime task force. If a district attorney or the attorney general is actually absent or disabled, the term "applicant" includes that person designated to act for him and perform his official function in and during his actual absence or disability.

6. "Law enforcement officer" means any public servant who is empowered by law to conduct an investigation of or to make an arrest for a designated offense, and any attorney authorized by law to prosecute or participate in the prosecution of a designated offense.

7. "Exigent circumstances" means conditions requiring the preservation of secrecy, and whereby there is a reasonable likelihood that a continuing investigation would be thwarted by alerting any of the persons subject to surveillance to the fact that such surveillance had occurred.

8. "Designated offense" means any one or more of the following crimes:

(a) A conspiracy to commit any offense enumerated in the following paragraphs of this subdivision, or an attempt to commit any felony enumerated in the following paragraphs of this subdivision which attempt would itself constitute a felony;

(b) Any of the following felonies: assault in the second degree as defined in section 120.05 of the penal law, assault in the first degree as defined in section 120.10 of the penal law, reckless endangerment in the first degree as defined in section 120.25 of the penal law, promoting a suicide attempt as defined in section 120.30 of the penal law, strangulation in the second degree as defined in section 121.12 of the penal law, strangulation in the first degree as defined in section 121.13 of the penal law, criminally negligent homicide as defined in section 125.10 of the penal law, manslaughter in the second degree as defined in section 125.15 of the penal law, manslaughter in the first degree as defined in section 125.20 of the penal law, murder in the second degree as defined in section 125.25 of the penal law, murder in the first degree as defined in section 125.27 of the penal law, rape in the third degree as defined in section 130.25 of the penal law, rape in the second degree as defined in section 130.30 of the penal law, rape in the first degree as defined in section 130.35 of the penal law, criminal sexual act in the third degree as defined in section 130.40 of the penal law, criminal sexual act in the second degree as defined in section 130.45 of the penal law, criminal sexual act in the first degree as defined in section 130.50 of the penal law, sexual abuse in the first degree as defined in section 130.65 of the penal law, unlawful imprisonment in the first degree as defined in section 135.10 of the penal law, kidnapping in the second degree as defined in section 135.20 of the penal law, kidnapping in the first degree as defined in section 135.25 of the penal law, labor trafficking as defined in section 135.35 of the penal law, aggravated labor trafficking as defined in section 135.37 of the penal law, custodial interference in the first degree as defined in section 135.50 of the penal law, coercion in the first degree as defined in section 135.65 of the penal law, criminal trespass in the first degree as defined in section 140.17 of the penal law, burglary in the third degree as defined in section 140.20 of the penal law, burglary in the second degree as defined in section 140.25 of the penal law, burglary in the first degree as defined in section 140.30 of the penal law, criminal mischief in the third degree as defined in section 145.05 of the penal law, criminal mischief in the second degree as defined in section 145.10 of the penal law, criminal mischief in the first degree as defined in section 145.12 of the penal law, criminal tampering in the first degree as defined in section 145.20 of the penal law, arson in the fourth degree as defined in section 150.05 of the penal law, arson in the third degree as defined in section 150.10 of the penal law, arson in the second degree as defined in section 150.15 of the penal law, arson in the first degree as defined in section 150.20 of the penal law, grand larceny in the fourth degree as defined in section 155.30 of the penal law, grand larceny in the third degree as defined in section 155.35 of the penal law, grand larceny in the second degree as defined in section 155.40 of the penal law, grand larceny in the first degree as defined in section 155.42 of the penal law, health care fraud in the fourth degree as defined in section 177.10 of the penal law, health care fraud in the third degree as defined in section 177.15 of the penal law, health care fraud in the second degree as defined in section 177.20 of the penal law, health care fraud in the first degree as defined in section 177.25 of the penal law, robbery in the third degree as defined in section 160.05 of the penal law, robbery in the second degree as defined in section 160.10 of the penal law, robbery in the first degree as defined in section 160.15 of the penal law, unlawful use of secret scientific material as defined in section 165.07 of the penal law, criminal possession of stolen property in the fourth degree as defined in section 165.45 of the penal law, criminal possession of stolen property in the third degree as defined in section 165.50 of the penal law, criminal possession of stolen property in the second degree as defined by section 165.52 of the penal law, criminal possession of stolen property in the first degree as defined by section 165.54 of the penal law, trademark counterfeiting in the second degree as defined in section 165.72 of the penal law, trademark counterfeiting in the first degree as defined in section 165.73 of the penal law, forgery in the second degree as defined in section 170.10 of the penal law, forgery in the first degree as defined in section 170.15 of the penal law, criminal possession of a forged instrument in the second degree as defined in section

170.25 of the penal law, criminal possession of a forged instrument in the first degree as defined in section 170.30 of the penal law, criminal possession of forgery devices as defined in section 170.40 of the penal law, falsifying business records in the first degree as defined in section 175.10 of the penal law, tampering with public records in the first degree as defined in section 175.25 of the penal law, offering a false instrument for filing in the first degree as defined in section 175.35 of the penal law, issuing a false certificate as defined in section 175.40 of the penal law, criminal diversion of prescription medications and prescriptions in the second degree as defined in section 178.20 of the penal law, criminal diversion of prescription medications and prescriptions in the first degree as defined in section 178.25 of the penal law, residential mortgage fraud in the fourth degree as defined in section 187.10 of the penal law, residential mortgage fraud in the third degree as defined in section 187.15 of the penal law, residential mortgage fraud in the second degree as defined in section 187.20 of the penal law, residential mortgage fraud in the first degree as defined in section 187.25 of the penal law, escape in the second degree as defined in section 205.10 of the penal law, escape in the first degree as defined in section 205.15 of the penal law, absconding from temporary release in the first degree as defined in section 205.17 of the penal law, promoting prison contraband in the first degree as defined in section 205.25 of the penal law, hindering prosecution in the second degree as defined in section 205.60 of the penal law, hindering prosecution in the first degree as defined in section 205.65 of the penal law, sex trafficking as defined in section 230.34 of the penal law, sex trafficking of a child as defined in section 230.34-a of the penal law, criminal possession of a weapon in the third degree as defined in subdivisions two, three and five of section 265.02 of the penal law, criminal possession of a weapon in the second degree as defined in section 265.03 of the penal law, criminal possession of a weapon in the first degree as defined in section 265.04 of the penal law, manufacture, transport, disposition and defacement of weapons and dangerous instruments and appliances defined as felonies in subdivisions one, two, and three of section 265.10 of the penal law, sections 265.11, 265.12 and 265.13 of the penal law, or prohibited use of weapons as defined in subdivision two of section 265.35 of the penal law, relating to firearms and other dangerous weapons, or failure to disclose the origin of a recording in the first degree as defined in section 275.40 of the penal law;

(c) Criminal possession of a controlled substance in the seventh degree as defined in section 220.03 of the penal law, criminal possession of a controlled substance in the fifth degree as defined in section 220.06 of the penal law, criminal possession of a controlled substance in the fourth degree as defined in section 220.09 of the penal law, criminal possession of a controlled substance in the third degree as defined in section 220.16 of the penal law, criminal possession of a controlled substance in the second degree as defined in section 220.18 of the penal law, criminal possession of a controlled substance in the first degree as defined in section 220.21 of the penal law, criminal sale of a controlled substance in the fifth degree as defined in section 220.31 of the penal law, criminal sale of a controlled substance in the fourth degree as defined in section 220.34 of the penal law, criminal sale of a controlled substance in the third degree as defined in section 220.39 of the penal law, criminal sale of a controlled substance in the second degree as defined in section 220.41 of the penal law, criminal sale of a controlled substance in the first degree as defined in section 220.43 of the penal law, criminally possessing a hypodermic instrument as defined in section 220.45 of the penal law, criminal sale of a prescription for a controlled substance or a controlled substance by a practitioner or pharmacist as defined in section 220.65 of the penal law, criminal possession of methamphetamine manufacturing material in the second degree as defined in section 220.70 of the penal law, criminal possession of methamphetamine manufacturing material in the first degree as defined in section 220.71 of the penal law, criminal possession of precursors of methamphetamine as defined in section 220.72 of the penal law, unlawful manufacture of methamphetamine in the third degree as defined in section 220.73 of the penal law, unlawful manufacture of methamphetamine in the second degree as defined in section 220.74 of the penal law, unlawful manufacture of methamphetamine in the first degree as defined in section 220.75 of the penal law, unlawful disposal of methamphetamine laboratory material as defined in section 220.76 of the penal law, operating as a major trafficker as defined in section 220.77 of the penal law, criminal possession of marihuana in the first degree as defined in section 221.30 of the penal law, criminal sale of marihuana in the first degree as defined in section 221.55 of the penal law, promoting gambling in the second degree as defined in section 225.05 of the penal law, promoting gambling in the first degree as defined in section 225.10 of the penal law, possession of gambling records in the second degree as defined in section 225.15 of the penal law, possession of gambling records in the first degree as defined in section 225.20 of the penal law, and possession of a gambling device as defined in section 225.30 of the penal law;

(d) Commercial bribing, commercial bribe receiving, bribing a labor official, bribe receiving by a labor official, sports bribing and sports bribe receiving, as defined in article one hundred eighty of the penal law;

(e) Criminal usury, as defined in article one hundred ninety of the penal law;

(f) Bribery in the third degree, bribery in the second degree, bribery in the first degree, bribe receiving in the third degree, bribe receiving in the second degree, bribe receiving in the first degree, bribe giving for public office, bribe receiving for public office and corrupt use of position or authority, as defined in article two hundred of the penal law;

(g) Bribing a witness, bribe receiving by a witness, bribing a juror and bribe receiving by a juror, as defined in article two hundred fifteen of the penal law;

(h) Promoting prostitution in the first degree, as defined in section 230.32 of the penal law, promoting prostitution in the second degree, as defined by subdivision one of section 230.30 of the penal law, promoting prostitution in the third degree, as defined in section 230.25 of the penal law;

(i) Riot in the first degree and criminal anarchy, as defined in article two hundred forty of the penal law;

(j) Eavesdropping, as defined in article two hundred fifty of the penal law;

(k) Any of the acts designated as felonies in subdivisions two and four of section four hundred eighty-one of the tax law, which section relates to penalties under the tax on cigarettes imposed by article twenty of such law, and any of the acts designated as felonies in subdivision c of section 11-1317 of the administrative code of the city of New

York, which section relates to penalties under the cigarette tax imposed by chapter thirteen of title eleven of such code.

(l) Scheme to defraud in the first degree as defined in article one hundred ninety of the penal law.

(m) Any of the acts designated as felonies in section three hundred fifty-two-c of the general business law.

(n) Any of the acts designated as felonies in title twenty-seven of article seventy-one of the environmental conservation law.

(o) Money laundering in the first degree, as defined in section 470.20 of the penal law, money laundering in the second degree as defined in section 470.15 of the penal law, money laundering in the third degree as defined in section 470.10 of such law, and money laundering in the fourth degree as defined in section 470.05 of such law, where the property involved represents or is represented to be the proceeds of specified criminal conduct which itself constitutes a designated offense within the meaning of this subdivision.

(p) Stalking in the second degree as defined in section 120.55 of the penal law, and stalking in the first degree as defined in section 120.60 of the penal law.

(q) Soliciting or providing support for an act of terrorism in the second degree as defined in section 490.10 of the penal law, soliciting or providing support for an act of terrorism in the first degree as defined in section 490.15 of the penal law, making a terroristic threat as defined in section 490.20 of the penal law, crime of terrorism as defined in section 490.25 of the penal law, hindering prosecution of terrorism in the second degree as defined in section 490.30 of the penal law, hindering prosecution of terrorism in the first degree as defined in section 490.35 of the penal law, criminal possession of a chemical weapon or biological weapon in the third degree as defined in section 490.37 of the penal law, criminal possession of a chemical weapon or biological weapon in the second degree as defined in section 490.40 of the penal law, criminal possession of a chemical weapon or biological weapon in the first degree as defined in section 490.45 of the penal law, criminal use of a chemical weapon or biological weapon in the third degree as defined in section 490.47 of the penal law, criminal use of a chemical weapon or biological weapon in the second degree as defined in section 490.50 of the penal law, and criminal use of a chemical weapon or biological weapon in the first degree as defined in section 490.55 of the penal law.

(r) Falsely reporting an incident in the second degree as defined in section 240.55 of the penal law, falsely reporting an incident in the first degree as defined in section 240.60 of the penal law, placing a false bomb in the second degree as defined in section 240.61 of the penal law, placing a false bomb in the first degree as defined in section 240.62 of the penal law, and placing a false bomb in a sports stadium or arena, mass transportation facility or enclosed shopping mall as defined in section 240.63 of the penal law.

(s) Identity theft in the second degree, as defined in section 190.79 of the penal law, identity theft in the first degree, as defined in section 190.80 of the penal law, unlawful possession of personal identification information in the second degree, as defined in section 190.82 of the penal law, and unlawful possession of personal identification information in the first degree, as defined in section 190.83 of the penal law.

(t) Menacing a police officer or peace officer as defined in section 120.18 of the penal law; aggravated criminally negligent homicide as defined in section 125.11 of the penal law; aggravated manslaughter in the second degree as defined in section 125.21 of the penal law; aggravated manslaughter in the first degree as defined in section 125.22 of the penal law; aggravated murder as defined in section 125.26 of the penal law.

(u) Any felony defined in article four hundred ninety-six of the penal law.

(v) Any of the acts designated as felonies in section three hundred fifty-one of the agriculture and markets law.

9. "Video surveillance" means the intentional visual observation by law enforcement of a person by means of a television camera or other electronic device that is part of a television transmitting apparatus, whether or not such observation is recorded on film or video tape, without the consent of that person or another person thereat and under circumstances in which such observation in the absence of a video surveillance warrant infringes upon such person's reasonable expectation of privacy under the constitution of this state or of the United States.

10. "Video surveillance warrant" means an order of a justice authorizing or approving video surveillance.

§ 700.10. Eavesdropping and video surveillance warrants; in general

1. Under circumstances prescribed in this article, a justice may issue an eavesdropping warrant or a video surveillance warrant upon ex parte application of an applicant who is authorized by law to investigate, prosecute or participate in the prosecution of the particular designated offense which is the subject of the application.

2. No eavesdropping or video surveillance warrant may authorize or approve the interception of any communication or the conducting of any video surveillance for any period longer than is necessary to achieve the objective of the authorization, or in any event longer than thirty days. Such thirty day period shall begin on the date designated in the warrant as the effective date, which date may be no later than ten days after the warrant is issued.

§ 700.15. Eavesdropping and video surveillance warrants; when issuable

An eavesdropping or video surveillance warrant may issue only:

1. Upon an appropriate application made in conformity with this article; and

2. Upon probable cause to believe that a particularly described person is committing, has committed, or is about to commit a particular designated offense; and

3. Upon probable cause to believe that particular communications concerning such offense will be obtained through eavesdropping, or upon probable cause to believe that particular observations concerning such offense will be obtained through video surveillance; and

4. Upon a showing that normal investigative procedures have been tried and have failed, or reasonably appear to be unlikely to succeed if tried, or to be too dangerous to employ; and

5. Upon probable cause to believe that the facilities from which, or the place where, the communications are to be intercepted or the video surveillance is to be conducted, are

being used, or are about to be used, in connection with the commission of such offense, or are leased to, listed in the name of, or commonly used by such person.

§ 700.20. Eavesdropping and video surveillance warrants; application

1. An ex parte application for an eavesdropping or video surveillance warrant must be made to a justice in writing, except as provided in section 700.21 of this article, and must be subscribed and sworn to by an applicant.

2. The application must contain:

(a) The identity of the applicant and a statement of the applicant's authority to make such application; and

(b) A full and complete statement of the facts and circumstances relied upon by the applicant, to justify his belief that an eavesdropping or video surveillance warrant should be issued, including (i) a statement of facts establishing probable cause to believe that a particular designated offense has been, is being, or is about to be committed, (ii) a particular description of the nature and location of the facilities from which or the place where the communication is to be intercepted or the video surveillance is to be conducted, (iii) a particular description of the type of the communications sought to be intercepted or of the observations sought to be made, and (iv) the identity of the person, if known, committing such designated offense and whose communications are to be intercepted or who is to be the subject of the video surveillance; and

(c) A statement that such communications or observations are not otherwise legally privileged; and

(d) A full and complete statement of facts establishing that normal investigative procedures have been tried and have failed or reasonably appear to be unlikely to succeed if tried or to be too dangerous to employ, to obtain the evidence sought; and

(e) A statement of the period of time for which the eavesdropping or video surveillance is required to be maintained. If the nature of the investigation is such that the authorization for eavesdropping or video surveillance should not automatically terminate when the described type of communication has been first obtained or when the described type of observation has been first made, a particular description of facts establishing probable cause to believe that additional communications or observations of the same type will occur thereafter; and

(f) A full and complete statement of the facts concerning all previous applications, known to the applicant, for an eavesdropping or video surveillance warrant involving any of the same persons, facilities or places specified in the application, and the action taken by the justice on each such application.

3. Allegations of fact in the application may be based either upon the personal knowledge of the applicant or upon information and belief. If the applicant personally knows the facts alleged, it must be so stated. If the facts stated in the application are derived in whole or part from the statements of persons other than the applicant, the sources of such facts must be either disclosed or described, and the application must contain facts establishing the existence and reliability of the informants or the reliability of the information supplied by them. The application must also state, so far as possible, the basis of the informant's knowledge or belief. Affidavits of persons other than the applicant may be submitted in conjunction with the application if they tend to support

any fact or conclusion alleged therein. Such accompanying affidavits may be based either on personal knowledge of the affiant, or information and belief with the source thereof and the reason therefor specified.

§ 700.21. Temporary authorization for eavesdropping or video surveillance in emergency situations

1. In an emergency situation where imminent danger of death or serious physical injury exists and, under the circumstances, it is impractical for the applicant to prepare a written application without risk of such death or injury occurring, an application for an eavesdropping or video surveillance warrant need not be in writing but may be communicated to a justice by telephone, radio or other means of electronic communication.

2. Where an oral application for an eavesdropping or video surveillance warrant is made, the applicant therefor must identify himself and the purpose of his communication or observation, after being sworn as provided in subdivision three of this section. The application must meet the requirements of section 700.20 of this article and provide the same allegations of fact required by that section.

3. Upon being advised that an oral application for an eavesdropping or video surveillance warrant is being made, a justice shall place under oath the applicant and any other person providing information in support of the application. Such oath or oaths and all of the remaining communication must be recorded, either by means of a voice recording device or verbatim stenographic or verbatim longhand notes. If a voice recording device is used or a stenographic record made, the justice must have the record transcribed, certify to the accuracy of the transcription and file the original record and transcription with the court within twenty-four hours of the issuance of a warrant. If longhand notes are taken, the justice shall subscribe a copy and file it with the court within twenty-four hours of the issuance of a warrant.

4. Upon oral application, the court may, where it finds that an emergency situation exists and that the requirements of section 700.15 of this article have been satisfied, issue a temporary eavesdropping or video surveillance warrant authorizing eavesdropping or video surveillance for a period not to exceed twenty-four hours. Such eavesdropping or video surveillance warrant shall be executed in the manner prescribed by this article. The twenty-four hour period may not be extended nor may a temporary warrant be renewed except by written application in conformity with the requirements of this article.

§ 700.25. Eavesdropping warrants; determination of application

1. If the application conforms to section 700.20, the justice may require the applicant to furnish additional testimony or documentary evidence in support of the application. He may examine, under oath, any person for the purpose of determining whether grounds exist for the issuance of the warrant pursuant to section 700.15. Any such examination must be either recorded or summarized in writing.

2. If the justice determines on the basis of the facts submitted by the applicant that grounds exist for the issuance of an eavesdropping warrant pursuant to section 700.15, the justice may grant the application and issue an eavesdropping warrant, in accordance with section 700.30.

3. If the application does not conform to section 700.20, or if the justice is not satisfied that grounds exist for the issuance of an eavesdropping warrant, the application must be denied.

§ 700.30. Eavesdropping and video surveillance warrants; form and content

An eavesdropping or video surveillance warrant must contain:

1. The name of the applicant, date of issuance, and the subscription and title of the issuing justice; and

2. The identity of the person, if known, whose communications are to be intercepted or who is to be the subject of video surveillance; and

3. The nature and location of the communications facilities as to which, or the place where, authority to intercept or conduct video surveillance is granted; and

4. A particular description of the type of communications sought to be intercepted or of the type of observations to be made, and a statement of the particular designated offense to which it relates; and

5. The identity of the law enforcement agency authorized to intercept the communications or conduct the video surveillance; and

6. The period of time during which such interception or observation is authorized, including a statement as to whether or not the interception or video surveillance shall automatically terminate when the described communication has been first obtained or the described observation has been first made; and

7. A provision that the authorization to intercept or conduct video surveillance shall be executed as soon as practicable, shall be conducted in such a way as to minimize the interception of communications or the making of observations not otherwise subject to eavesdropping or video surveillance under this article, and must terminate upon attainment of the authorized objective, or in any event in thirty days; and

8. An express authorization to make secret entry upon a private place or premises to install an eavesdropping or video surveillance device, if such entry is necessary to execute the warrant; and

9. An order authorizing eavesdropping or video surveillance may direct that providers of wire or electronic communication services furnish the applicant information, facilities, or technical assistance necessary to accomplish the interception unobtrusively and with a minimum of interference with the services that the service provider accords the party whose communications are to be intercepted. The order shall not direct the service providers to perform the intercept or use the premises of the service provider for such activity.

§ 700.35. Eavesdropping and video surveillance warrants; manner and time of execution

1. An eavesdropping or video surveillance warrant must be executed according to its terms by a law enforcement officer who is a member of the law enforcement agency authorized in the warrant to intercept the communications or conduct the video surveillance.

2. Upon termination of the authorization in the warrant, eavesdropping or video surveillance must cease and as soon as practicable thereafter any device installed for such purpose either must be removed or must be permanently inactivated as soon as practicable by any means approved by the issuing justice. Entry upon a private place or

premise for the removal or permanent inactivation of such device is deemed to be authorized by the warrant.

3. The contents of any communication intercepted or of any observation made by any means authorized by this article must, if possible, be recorded on tape or wire or other comparable device. The recording of the contents of any such communication or observation must be done in such way as will protect the recording from editing or other alterations.

4. In the event an intercepted communication is in a code or foreign language, and the services of an expert in that foreign language or code cannot reasonably be obtained during the interception period, where the warrant so authorizes and in a manner specified therein, the minimization required by subdivision seven of section 700.30 of this article may be accomplished as soon as practicable after such interception.

5. A good faith reliance by a provider of a wire or electronic communication service upon the validity of a court order issued pursuant to this article is a complete defense against any civil cause of action or criminal action based solely on a failure to comply with this article.

§ 700.40. Eavesdropping and video surveillance warrants; order of extension

At any time prior to the expiration of an eavesdropping or video surveillance warrant, the applicant may apply to the issuing justice, or, if he is unavailable, to another justice, for an order of extension. The period of extension shall be no longer than the justice deems necessary to achieve the purposes for which it was granted and in no event longer than thirty days. The application for an order of extension must conform in all respects to the provisions of section 700.20 and, in addition, must contain a statement setting forth the results thus far obtained from the interception, or a reasonable explanation of the failure to obtain such results. The provisions of sections 700.15 and 700.25 are applicable in the determination of such application. The order of extension must conform in all respects to the provisions of section 700.30. In the execution of such order of extension the provisions of section 700.35 are applicable.

§ 700.50. Eavesdropping and video surveillance warrants; progress reports and notice

1. An eavesdropping or video surveillance warrant may require reports to be made to the issuing justice showing what progress has been made toward achievement of the authorized objective and the need for continued eavesdropping or video surveillance. Such reports shall be made at such intervals as the justice may require.

2. Immediately upon the expiration of the period of an eavesdropping or video surveillance warrant, the recordings of communications or observations made pursuant to subdivision three of section 700.35 must be made available to the issuing justice and sealed under his directions.

3. Within a reasonable time, but in no case later than ninety days after termination of an eavesdropping or video surveillance warrant, or expiration of an extension order, except as otherwise provided in subdivision four, written notice of the fact and date of the issuance of the eavesdropping or video surveillance warrant, and of the period of authorized eavesdropping or video surveillance, and of the fact that during such period communications were or were not intercepted or observation were or were not made, must be served upon the person named in the warrant and such other parties to the

intercepted communications or subjects of the video surveillance as the justice may determine in his discretion is in the interest of justice. Service reasonably calculated to give affected parties the notice required by this subdivision shall be effected within the time limits provided for herein and in a manner prescribed by the justice. The justice, upon the filing of a motion by any person served with such notice, may in his discretion make available to such person or his counsel for inspection such portions of the intercepted communications or video surveillance, applications and warrants as the justice determines to be in the interest of justice.

4. On a showing of exigent circumstances to the issuing justice, the service of the notice required by subdivision three may be postponed by order of the justice for a reasonable period of time. Renewals of an order of postponement may be obtained on a new showing of exigent circumstances.

§ 700.55. Eavesdropping and video surveillance warrants; custody of warrants, applications and recordings

1. Applications made and warrants issued under this article shall be sealed by the justice. Any eavesdropping or video surveillance warrant, together with a copy of papers upon which the application is based, shall be delivered to and retained by the applicant as authority for the eavesdropping or video surveillance authorized therein. A copy of such eavesdropping or video surveillance warrant, together with all the original papers upon which the application was based, must be retained by the justice issuing the same, and, in the event of the denial of an application for such an eavesdropping or video surveillance warrant, a copy of the papers upon which the application was based must be retained by the justice denying the same. Such applications and warrants may be disclosed only upon a showing of good cause before a court and may not be destroyed except on order of the issuing or denying justice, and in any event must be kept for ten years.

2. Custody of the recordings made pursuant to subdivision three of section 700.35 may be wherever the justice orders. They may not be destroyed except upon an order of the justice who issued the warrant and in any event must be kept for ten years. Duplicate recordings may be made for use or disclosure pursuant to the provisions of subdivisions one and two of section 700.65 for investigations.

§ 700.60. Eavesdropping warrants; reports to the administrative office of the United States courts

1. Within thirty days after the termination of an eavesdropping warrant or the expiration of an extension order, the issuing or denying justice must submit such report to the administrative office of the United States courts as is required by federal law.

2. In January of each year, the attorney general and each district attorney must submit such report to the administrative office of the United States courts as is required by federal law.

§ 700.65. Eavesdropping and video surveillance warrants; disclosure and use of information; order of amendment

1. Any law enforcement officer who, by any means authorized by this article, has obtained knowledge of the contents of any intercepted communication or video surveillance, or evidence derived therefrom, may disclose such contents to another law

enforcement officer to the extent that such disclosure is appropriate to the proper performance of the official duties of the officer making or receiving the disclosure.

2. Any law enforcement officer who, by any means authorized by this article, has obtained knowledge of the contents of any intercepted communication or video surveillance, or evidence derived therefrom, may use such contents to the extent such use is appropriate to the proper performance of his official duties.

3. Any person who has received, by any means authorized by this article, any information concerning a communication or video surveillance, or evidence derived therefrom, intercepted or conducted in accordance with the provisions of this article, may disclose the contents of that communication or video surveillance, or such derivative evidence, while giving testimony under oath in any criminal proceeding in any court, in any grand jury proceeding or in any action commenced pursuant to article thirteen-A or thirteen-B of the civil practice law and rules; provided, however, that the presence of the seal provided for by subdivision two of section 700.50, or a satisfactory explanation of the absence thereof, shall be a prerequisite for the use or disclosure of the contents of any communication or video surveillance, or evidence derived therefrom; and provided further, however, that where a criminal court of competent jurisdiction has ordered exclusion or suppression of the contents of an intercepted communication or video surveillance, or evidence derived therefrom, such determination shall be binding in an action commenced pursuant to article thirteen-A or thirteen-B of the civil practice law and rules.

4. When a law enforcement officer, while engaged in intercepting communications or conducting video surveillance in the manner authorized by this article, intercepts a communication or makes an observation which was not otherwise sought and which constitutes evidence of any crime that has been, is being or is about to be committed, the contents of such communications or observation, and evidence derived therefrom, may be disclosed or used as provided in subdivisions one and two. Such contents and any evidence derived therefrom may be used under subdivision three when a justice amends the eavesdropping or video surveillance warrant to include such contents. The application for such amendment must be made by the applicant as soon as practicable by giving notice to the court of the interception of the communication or the making of the observation and of the contents of such interception or observation; provided that during the period in which the eavesdropping or video surveillance is continuing, such notice must be given within ten days after probable cause exists to believe that a crime not named in the warrant has been, is being, or is about to be committed, or at the time an application for an order of extension is made pursuant to section 700.40 of this article, if such probable cause then exists, whichever is earlier. If the justice finds that such contents were otherwise intercepted in accordance with the provisions of this article, he may grant the application.

§ 700.70. Eavesdropping warrants; notice before use of evidence

The contents of any intercepted communication, or evidence derived therefrom, may not be received in evidence or otherwise disclosed upon a trial of a defendant unless the people, within fifteen days after arraignment and before the commencement of the trial, furnish the defendant with a copy of the eavesdropping warrant, and accompanying application, under which interception was authorized or approved. This fifteen day period may be extended by the trial court upon good cause shown if it finds that the defendant will not be prejudiced by the delay in receiving such papers.

Article 705 Pen Registers and Trap and Trace Devices

§ 705.00. Definitions

As used in this article, the following terms have the following meanings:

1. "Pen register" means a device which records or decodes electronic or other impulses which identify the numbers dialed or otherwise transmitted on the telephone line to which such device is attached, but such term does not include any device used by a provider or customer of a wire or electronic communication service for billing, or recording as an incident to billing, for communications services provided by such provider or any device used by a provider or customer of a wire communication service for cost accounting or other like purposes in the ordinary course of its business.

2. "Trap and trace device" means a device which captures the incoming electronic or other impulses which identify the originating number of an instrument or device from which a wire or electronic communication was transmitted.

3. "Applicant" means a district attorney, an assistant district attorney, and when empowered by law to conduct an investigation of or to prosecute or participate in the prosecution of a designated crime, the attorney general, an assistant attorney general, the deputy attorney general in charge of the statewide organized crime task force, or an assistant deputy attorney general of such task force.

4. "Law enforcement agency" means any agency which is empowered by law to conduct an investigation or to make an arrest for a felony, and any agency which is authorized by law to prosecute or participate in the prosecution of a felony.

5. "Designated crime" means any crime included within the definition of a "designated offense" in subdivision eight of section 700.05 of this chapter, any criminal act as defined in subdivision one of section 460.10 of the penal law, bail jumping in the first and second degree as defined in sections 215.57 and 215.56 of such law, or aggravated harassment as defined in subdivisions one and two of section 240.30 of such law.

6. "Justice" means justice as defined in subdivision four of section 700.05 of this chapter.

§ 705.05. Pen register and trap and trace authorizations; in general

Under circumstances prescribed in this article, a justice may issue an order authorizing the use of a pen register or a trap and trace device upon ex parte application of an applicant who is authorized by law to investigate, prosecute or participate in the prosecution of the designated crimes which are the subject of the application.

§ 705.10. Orders authorizing the use of a pen register or a trap and trace device; when issuable

An order authorizing the use of a pen register or a trap and trace device may issue only:

1. Upon an appropriate application made in conformity with this article; and

2. Upon a determination that an application sets forth specific, articulable facts, warranting the applicant's reasonable suspicion that a designated crime has been, is being, or is about to be committed and demonstrating that the information likely to be

obtained by use of a pen register or trap and trace device is or will be relevant to an ongoing criminal investigation of such designated crime.

§ 705.15. Application for an order authorizing the use of a pen register or a trap and trace device

1. An ex parte application for an order or an extension of an order authorizing the use of a pen register or a trap and trace device must be made to a justice in writing, and must be subscribed and sworn to by the applicant.

2. The application must contain:

(a) The identity of the applicant and the identity of the law enforcement agency conducting the investigation; and

(b) A statement of facts and circumstances sufficient to justify the applicant's belief that an order authorizing the use of a pen register or a trap and trace device should be issued, including (i) a statement of the specific facts on the basis of which the applicant reasonably suspects that the designated crime has been, is being, or is about to be committed and demonstrating that the information likely to be obtained by use of a pen register or a trap and trace device is or will be relevant to an ongoing criminal investigation of such designated offense, (ii) the identity, if known, of the person to whom is leased or in whose name is listed the telephone line to which the pen register or trap and trace device is to be attached, (iii) the identity, if known, of the person who is the subject of the criminal investigation, (iv) the number and, if known, the physical location of the telephone line to which the pen register or trap and trace device is to be attached and, in the case of a trap and trace device, the geographic limits of the trap and trace order, and (v) a statement of the designated crime or crimes to which the information likely to be obtained by the use of the pen register or trap and trace device relates; and

(c) A statement of the period of time for which the authorization for the use of a pen register or a trap and trace device is required; and

(d) A statement of the facts concerning all previous applications, known to the applicant, for an order authorizing the use of a pen register or a trap and trace device involving any of the same persons or facilities specified in the application, and the action taken by the justice on each such application.

3. Allegations of fact in the application may be based either upon the personal knowledge of the applicant or upon information and belief. If the applicant personally knows the facts alleged, it must be so stated. If the facts stated in the application are derived in whole or in part from the statements of persons other than the applicant, the sources of such facts must be either disclosed or described.

§ 705.20. Orders authorizing the use of a pen register or a trap and trace device; determination of application

1. If the justice determines on the basis of the facts submitted by the applicant that grounds exist for the issue of an order authorizing the use of a pen register or a trap and trace device pursuant to section 705.10 of this article, the justice shall grant the application and issue an order authorizing the use of a pen register or a trap and trace device, in accordance with subdivision three of this section.

2. If the application does not conform to section 705.15 of this article, or if the justice is not satisfied that grounds exist for the issuance of an order authorizing the use of a pen register or a trap and trace device, the application must be denied.

3. An order issued under this section must contain:

(a) the name of the applicant, date of issuance, and the subscription and title of the issuing justice; and

(b) the identity, if known, of the person to whom is leased or in whose name is listed the telephone line to which the pen register or trap and trace device is to be attached; and

(c) the identity, if known, of the person who is the subject of the criminal investigation; and

(d) the number and, if known, the physical location of the telephone line to which the pen register or trap and trace device is to be attached and, in the case of a trap and trace device, the geographic limits of the trap and trace order; and

(e) a statement of the designated crime or crimes to which the information likely to be obtained by the pen register or trap and trace device relates.

4. An order issued under this section shall direct, upon the request of the applicant, the furnishing of information, facilities, and technical assistance necessary to accomplish the installation of the pen register or trap and trace device under section 705.25 of this article.

§ 705.25. Pen register or trap and trace device orders; time period and extensions

1. An order issued under this section shall authorize the installation and use of a pen register or a trap and trace device for a period not to exceed sixty days.

2. Extensions of such an order may be granted, but only upon an application for an order under section 705.05 of this article and upon the judicial finding required by subdivision one of section 705.10 of this article. The period of extension shall be for a period not to exceed sixty days.

§ 705.30. Nondisclosure of existence of pen register or a trap and trace device

An order authorizing or approving the installation and use of a pen register or a trap and trace device shall direct that:

1. the order be sealed until otherwise ordered by the court; and

2. the person owning or leasing the line to which the pen register or a trap and trace device is attached, or who has been ordered by the court to provide assistance to the applicant, not disclose the existence of the pen register or trap and trace device or the existence of the investigation to the listed subscriber, or to any other person, unless or until otherwise ordered by the court.

§ 705.35. Assistance in installation and use of a pen register or a trap and trace device

1. Upon the request of an applicant authorized to use a pen register under this article, a provider of a wire or electronic communication service, landlord, custodian, or other person shall furnish such applicant, or his agent, forthwith all information, facilities and technical assistance necessary to accomplish the installation of the pen register unobtrusively and with a minimum of interference with the services that the person so ordered by the court accords the party with respect to whom the installation and use is to take place, if such assistance is directed by a court order as provided in section 705.10 of this article.

2. Upon the request of an applicant authorized to receive the results of a trap and trace device under this article, a provider of a wire or electronic communication service, landlord, custodian, or other person shall install such device forthwith on the appropriate line and shall furnish such applicant forthwith all information, facilities and technical assistance including installation and operation of the device unobtrusively and with a minimum of interference with the services that the person so ordered by the court accords the party with respect to whom the installation and use is to take place, if such installation and assistance is directed by the court order as provided in section 705.10 of this article. Unless otherwise ordered by the court, the results of the trap and trace device shall be furnished to the applicant, or his agent, at reasonable intervals during regular business hours for the duration of the order.

3. A provider of a wire or electronic communication service, landlord, custodian, or other person who furnishes facilities or technical assistance pursuant to this section shall be reasonably compensated for such reasonable expenses incurred in providing such facilities and assistance.

4. No cause of action shall lie in any court against any provider of a wire or electronic communication service, its officers, employees, agents or other specified persons for providing information, facilities or assistance in accordance with the terms of a court order under this article. A good faith reliance by a provider of a wire or electronic communication service upon the validity of a court order issued pursuant to this article is a complete defense against any civil cause of action or criminal action based entirely on a failure to comply with this article.

Article 710 Motion to Suppress Evidence

§ 710.10. Motion to suppress evidence; definitions of terms

As used in this article, the following terms have the following meanings:

1. "Defendant" means a person who has been charged by an accusatory instrument with the commission of an offense.

2. "Evidence," when referring to matter in the possession of or available to a prosecutor, means any tangible property or potential testimony which may be offered in evidence in a criminal action.

3. "Potential testimony" means information or factual knowledge of a person who is or may be available as a witness.

4. "Eavesdropping" means "wiretapping", "mechanical overhearing of a conversation," or "intercepting or accessing of an electronic communication", as those terms are defined in section 250.00 of the penal law.

5. "Aggrieved." An "aggrieved person" includes, but is in no wise limited to, an "aggrieved person" as defined in subdivision two of section forty-five hundred six of the civil practice law and rules.

6. "Video surveillance" has the meaning given to that term by section 700.05 of this chapter.

7. "Pen register" and "trap and trace device" have the meanings given to those terms by subdivisions one and two respectively of section 705.00 of this chapter.

§ 710.20. Motion to suppress evidence; in general; grounds for

Upon motion of a defendant who (a) is aggrieved by unlawful or improper acquisition of evidence and has reasonable cause to believe that such may be offered against him in a criminal action, or (b) claims that improper identification testimony may be offered against him in a criminal action, a court may, under circumstances prescribed in this article, order that such evidence be suppressed or excluded upon the ground that it:

1. Consists of tangible property obtained by means of an unlawful search and seizure under circumstances precluding admissibility thereof in a criminal action against such defendant; or

2. Consists of a record or potential testimony reciting or describing declarations, conversations, or other communications overheard, intercepted, accessed, or recorded by means of eavesdropping, or observations made by means of video surveillance, obtained under circumstances precluding admissibility thereof in a criminal action against such defendant; or

3. Consists of a record or potential testimony reciting or describing a statement of such defendant involuntarily made, within the meaning of section 60.45; or

4. Was obtained as a result of other evidence obtained in a manner described in subdivisions one, two and three; or

5. Consists of a chemical test of the defendant's blood administered in violation of the provisions of subdivision three of section eleven hundred ninety-four of the vehicle and traffic law, subdivision eight of section forty-nine-a of the navigation law, subdivision seven of section 25.24 of the parks, recreation and historic preservation law, or any other applicable law; or

6. Consists of potential testimony regarding an observation of the defendant either at the time or place of the commission of the offense or upon some other occasion relevant to the case, which potential testimony would not be admissible upon the prospective trial of such charge owing to an improperly made previous identification of the defendant or of a pictorial, photographic, electronic, filmed or video recorded reproduction of the defendant by the prospective witness. A claim that the previous identification of the defendant or of a pictorial, photographic, electronic, filmed or video recorded reproduction of the defendant by a prospective witness did not comply with paragraph (c) of subdivision one of section 60.25 of this chapter or with the protocol promulgated in accordance with subdivision twenty-one of section eight hundred thirty-seven of the executive law shall not constitute a legal basis to suppress evidence pursuant to this subdivision. A claim that a public servant failed to comply with paragraph (c) of subdivision one of section 60.25 of this chapter or of subdivision twenty-one of section eight hundred thirty-seven of the executive law shall neither expand nor limit the rights an accused person may derive under the constitution of this state or of the United States.

7. Consists of information obtained by means of a pen register or trap and trace device installed or used in violation of the provisions of article seven hundred five of this chapter.

§ 710.30. Motion to suppress evidence; notice to defendant of intention to offer evidence

1. Whenever the people intend to offer at a trial (a) evidence of a statement made by a defendant to a public servant, which statement if involuntarily made would render the evidence thereof suppressible upon motion pursuant to subdivision three of section 710.20, or (b) testimony regarding an observation of the defendant either at the time or place of the commission of the offense or upon some other occasion relevant to the case, to be given by a witness who has previously identified him or her or a pictorial, photographic, electronic, filmed or video recorded reproduction of him or her as such, they must serve upon the defendant a notice of such intention, specifying the evidence intended to be offered.

2. Such notice must be served within fifteen days after arraignment and before trial, and upon such service the defendant must be accorded reasonable opportunity to move before trial, pursuant to subdivision one of section 710.40, to suppress the specified evidence. For good cause shown, however, the court may permit the people to serve such notice, thereafter and in such case it must accord the defendant reasonable opportunity thereafter to make a suppression motion.

3. In the absence of service of notice upon a defendant as prescribed in this section, no evidence of a kind specified in subdivision one may be received against him upon trial unless he has, despite the lack of such notice, moved to suppress such evidence and such motion has been denied and the evidence thereby rendered admissible as prescribed in subdivision two of section 710.70.

§ 710.40. Motion to suppress evidence; when made and determined

1. A motion to suppress evidence must be made after the commencement of the criminal action in which such evidence is allegedly about to be offered, and, except as otherwise provided in section 710.30 and in subdivision two of this section, it must be made within the period provided in subdivision one of section 255.20.

2. The motion may be made for the first time when, owing to unawareness of facts constituting the basis thereof or to other factors, the defendant did not have reasonable opportunity to make the motion previously, or when the evidence which he seeks to suppress is of a kind specified in section 710.30 and he was not served by the people, as provided in said section 710.30, with a pre-trial notice of intention to offer such evidence at the trial.

3. When the motion is made before trial, the trial may not be commenced until determination of the motion.

4. If after a pre-trial determination and denial of the motion the court is satisfied, upon a showing by the defendant, that additional pertinent facts have been discovered by the defendant which he could not have discovered with reasonable diligence before the determination of the motion, it may permit him to renew the motion before trial or, if such was not possible owing to the time of the discovery of the alleged new facts, during trial.

§ 710.50. Motion to suppress evidence; in what courts made

1. The particular courts in which motions to suppress evidence must be made are as follows:

(a) If an indictment is pending in a superior court, or if the defendant has been held by a local criminal court for the action of a grand jury, the motion must be made in the superior court in which such indictment is pending or which impaneled or will impanel such grand jury. If the superior court which will impanel such grand jury is the supreme court, the motion may, in the alternative, be made in the county court of the county in which the action is pending;

(b) If a currently undetermined felony complaint is pending in a local criminal court, the motion must be made in the superior court which would have trial jurisdiction of the offense or offenses charged were an indictment therefor to result;

(c) If an information, a simplified information, a prosecutor's information or a misdemeanor complaint is pending in a local criminal court, the motion must be made in such court.

2. If after a motion has been made in and determined by a superior court a local criminal court acquires trial jurisdiction of the action by reason of an information, a prosecutor's information or a misdemeanor complaint filed therewith, such superior court's determination is binding upon such local criminal court. If, however, the motion has been made in but not yet determined by the superior court at the time of the filing of such information, prosecutor's information or misdemeanor complaint, the superior court may not determine the motion but must refer it to the local criminal court of trial jurisdiction.

§ 710.60. Motion to suppress evidence; procedure

1. A motion to suppress evidence made before trial must be in writing and upon reasonable notice to the people and with opportunity to be heard. The motion papers must state the ground or grounds of the motion and must contain sworn allegations of fact, whether of the defendant or of another person or persons, supporting such grounds. Such allegations may be based upon personal knowledge of the deponent or upon information and belief, provided that in the latter event the sources of such information and the grounds of such belief are stated. The people may file with the court, and in such case must serve a copy thereof upon the defendant or his counsel, an answer denying or admitting any or all of the allegations of the moving papers.

2. The court must summarily grant the motion if:

(a) The motion papers comply with the requirements of subdivision one and the people concede the truth of allegations of fact therein which support the motion; or

(b) The people stipulate that the evidence sought to be suppressed will not be offered in evidence in any criminal action or proceeding against the defendant.

3. The court may summarily deny the motion if:

(a) The motion papers do not allege a ground constituting legal basis for the motion; or

(b) The sworn allegations of fact do not as a matter of law support the ground alleged; except that this paragraph does not apply where the motion is based upon the ground specified in subdivision three or six of section 710.20.

4. If the court does not determine the motion pursuant to subdivisions [subdivision]* two or three, it must conduct a hearing and make findings of fact essential to the determination thereof. All persons giving factual information at such hearing must testify under oath, except that unsworn evidence pursuant to subdivision two of section 60.20 of this chapter may also be received. Upon such hearing, hearsay evidence is admissible to establish any material fact.

5. A motion to suppress evidence made during trial may be in writing and may be litigated and determined on the basis of motion papers as provided in subdivisions one through four, or it may, instead, be made orally in open court. In the latter event, the court must, where necessary, also conduct a hearing as provided in subdivision four, out of the presence of the jury if any, and make findings of fact essential to the determination of the motion.

6. Regardless of whether a hearing was conducted, the court, upon determining the motion, must set forth on the record its findings of fact, its conclusions of law and the reasons for its determination.

§ 710.70. Motion to suppress evidence; orders of suppression; effects of orders and of failure to make motion

1. Upon granting a motion to suppress evidence, the court must order that the evidence in question be excluded in the criminal action pending against the defendant. When the order is based upon the ground specified in subdivision one of section 710.20 and excludes tangible property unlawfully taken from the defendant's possession, and when such property is not otherwise subject to lawful retention, the court may, upon request of the defendant, further order that such property be restored to him.

2. An order finally denying a motion to suppress evidence may be reviewed upon an appeal from an ensuing judgment of conviction notwithstanding the fact that such judgment is entered upon a plea of guilty.

3. A motion to suppress evidence made pursuant to this article is the exclusive method of challenging the admissibility of evidence upon the grounds specified in section 710.20, and a defendant who does not make such a motion before or in the course of a criminal action waives his right to judicial determination of any such contention. Nothing contained in this article, however, precludes a defendant from attempting to establish at a trial that evidence introduced by the people of a pre-trial statement made by him should be disregarded by the jury or other trier of the facts on the ground that such statement was involuntarily made within the meaning of section 60.45. Even though the issue of the admissibility of such evidence was not submitted to the court, or was determined adversely to the defendant upon motion, the defendant may adduce trial evidence and otherwise contend that the statement was involuntarily made. In the case of a jury trial, the court must submit such issue to the jury under instructions to disregard such evidence upon a finding that the statement was involuntarily made.

Article 715 Destruction of Dangerous Drugs

§ 715.05. Dangerous drugs; definition

"Dangerous drugs" means any substance listed in schedule I, II, III, IV or V of section thirty-three hundred six of the public health law.

§ 715.10. Pretrial motion to destroy dangerous drugs

1. Subject to the limitations in paragraph (b) of subdivision two hereof a district attorney may move in a superior court for an order of destruction of the dangerous drugs in felony cases involving the possession or sale of such drugs.

2. A motion for an order of destruction of dangerous drugs shall be in writing, have attached thereto a copy of the report of analysis and shall be made in the following manner:

(a) Ex parte; where no defendants have been arrested in connection with the seizure of such drugs and a showing is made upon affidavit that the likelihood of any future arrest in connection therewith is nonexistent; or

(b) Upon notice, when a defendant has been arraigned in a superior court upon an indictment charging him with a felony involving the possession or sale of a dangerous drug and the dangerous drugs sought to be destroyed are material to the prosecution of said indictment.

3. When such motion is ex parte, the court may order the destruction of all or part of the subject drugs.

4. When such motion is upon notice, further proceedings shall be had as provided in section 715.20 hereof.

§ 715.20. Proceedings on motion upon notice

1. When such motion is on notice, a hearing thereon shall be held by the court before which it is returnable not later than thirty days after the return date and the defendant shall be present at such hearing.

2. A hearing held pursuant to this section shall be conducted and recorded in the same manner as would be required were the witnesses testifying at trial. The district attorney shall establish by competent evidence the nature and quantity of the dangerous drugs which are the subject of the motion. Each party shall have the right to call and cross examine witnesses and to register objections and to receive rulings of the court thereon.

3. If the court finds upon the conclusion of the hearing that neither the prosecution nor the defendant will be prejudiced thereby it may grant the motion and may make such order as it may deem appropriate for the destruction of part or all of such drugs.

4. A defendant may waive such hearing and consent to the granting of the motion and entry of an order of destruction either by sworn affidavit or by personal appearance in court and declaration on the record of such waiver and consent.

§ 715.30. Orders of the court

1. In any proceeding brought pursuant to this article, the court may grant or deny any motion made hereunder or the relief requested therein in whole or in part and issue any order thereon as it may deem proper and as the interests of justice may require in order to effectuate the provisions of this article.

2. An order of destruction of a dangerous drug issued by the court pursuant to this article shall state the time within which the provisions of such order are to be complied with. It shall direct the person having custody of the drug to make provision for the destruction thereof in the presence of at least two witnesses, at least one of whom shall be a police officer.

§ 715.40. Affidavit of destruction

An affidavit attesting to the date, time, place and manner of destruction of a dangerous drug pursuant to an order therefor and identifying the same by reference to the report of analysis or by other identifying number or system and the order of the court issued thereon, shall be filed with the court by the person who destroyed the drugs and by each of the witnesses required to be present by subdivision two of section 715.30 of this article.

§ 715.50. Analysis of dangerous drugs

1. On and after September first, nineteen hundred seventy-three, in every felony case involving the possession or sale of a dangerous drug, the head of the agency charged with custody of such drugs, or his designee, shall within forty-five days after receipt thereof perform or cause to be performed an analysis of such drugs, such analysis to include qualitative identification; weight and quantity where appropriate.

2. Within ten days after the report of such analysis is received by such agency, the head thereof or his designee shall forward a copy thereof to the appropriate district attorney and inform him of the location where the subject drugs are being held.

3. The failure to have an analysis made or to forward a copy thereof within the time specified in subdivisions one and two of this section shall not be deemed or construed to bar the making or granting of a motion pursuant to this article or to the prosecution of a case involving such drugs.

Title U Special Proceedings Which Replace, Suspend or Abate Criminal Actions

Article 720 Youthful Offender Procedure

§ 720.05. [Repealed]

§ 720.10. Youthful offender procedure; definition of terms

As used in this article, the following terms have the following meanings:

1. "Youth" means a person charged with a crime alleged to have been committed when he was at least sixteen years old and less than nineteen years old or a person charged with being a juvenile offender as defined in subdivision forty-two of section 1.20 of this chapter.

2. "Eligible youth" means a youth who is eligible to be found a youthful offender. Every youth is so eligible unless:

(a) the conviction to be replaced by a youthful offender finding is for (i) a class A-I or class A-II felony, or (ii) an armed felony as defined in subdivision forty-one of section 1.20, except as provided in subdivision three, or (iii) rape in the first degree, criminal sexual act in the first degree, or aggravated sexual abuse, except as provided in subdivision three, or

(b) such youth has previously been convicted and sentenced for a felony, or

(c) such youth has previously been adjudicated a youthful offender following conviction of a felony or has been adjudicated on or after September first, nineteen hundred seventy-eight a juvenile delinquent who committed a designated felony act as defined in the family court act.

3. Notwithstanding the provisions of subdivision two, a youth who has been convicted of an armed felony offense or of rape in the first degree, criminal sexual act in the first degree, or aggravated sexual abuse is an eligible youth if the court determines that one or more of the following factors exist: (i) mitigating circumstances that bear directly upon the manner in which the crime was committed; or (ii) where the defendant was not the sole participant in the crime, the defendant's participation was relatively minor although not so minor as to constitute a defense to the prosecution. Where the court determines that the eligible youth is a youthful offender, the court shall make a statement on the record of the reasons for its determination, a transcript of which shall be forwarded to the state division of criminal justice services, to be kept in accordance with the

provisions of subdivision three of section eight hundred thirty-seven-a of the executive law.

4. "Youthful offender finding" means a finding, substituted for the conviction of an eligible youth, pursuant to a determination that the eligible youth is a youthful offender.

5. "Youthful offender sentence" means the sentence imposed upon a youthful offender finding.

6. "Youthful offender adjudication". A youthful offender adjudication is comprised of a youthful offender finding and the youthful offender sentence imposed thereon and is completed by imposition and entry of the youthful offender sentence.

§ 720.15. Youthful offender procedure; sealing of accusatory instrument; privacy of proceedings; preliminary instructions to jury

1. When an accusatory instrument against an apparently eligible youth is filed with a court, it shall be filed as a sealed instrument, though only with respect to the public.

2. When a youth is initially arraigned upon an accusatory instrument, such arraignment and all proceedings in the action thereafter may, in the discretion of the court and with the defendant's consent, be conducted in private.

3. The provisions of subdivisions one and two of this section requiring or authorizing the accusatory instrument filed against a youth to be sealed, and the arraignment and all proceedings in the action to be conducted in private shall not apply in connection with a pending charge of committing any felony offense as defined in the penal law. The provisions of subdivision one requiring the accusatory instrument filed against a youth to be sealed shall not apply where such youth has previously been adjudicated a youthful offender or convicted of a crime.

4. Notwithstanding any provision in this article, a person charged with prostitution as defined in section 230.00 of the penal law or loitering for the purposes of prostitution as defined in subdivision two of section 240.37 of the penal law, provided that the person does not stand charged with loitering for the purpose of patronizing a prostitute, and such person is aged sixteen or seventeen when such offense occurred, regardless of whether such person (i) had prior to commencement of trial or entry of a plea of guilty been convicted of a crime or found a youthful offender, or (ii) subsequent to such conviction for prostitution or loitering for prostitution is convicted of a crime or found a youthful offender, the provisions of subdivisions one and two of this section requiring or authorizing the accusatory instrument filed against a youth to be sealed, and the arraignment and all proceedings in the action to be conducted in private shall apply.

§ 720.20. Youthful offender determination; when and how made; procedure thereupon

1. Upon conviction of an eligible youth, the court must order a pre-sentence investigation of the defendant. After receipt of a written report of the investigation and at the time of pronouncing sentence the court must determine whether or not the eligible youth is a youthful offender. Such determination shall be in accordance with the following criteria:

(a) If in the opinion of the court the interest of justice would be served by relieving the eligible youth from the onus of a criminal record and by not imposing an indeterminate term of imprisonment of more than four years, the court may, in its discretion, find the eligible youth is a youthful offender; and

(b) Where the conviction is had in a local criminal court and the eligible youth had not prior to commencement of trial or entry of a plea of guilty been convicted of a crime or found a youthful offender, the court must find he is a youthful offender.

2. Where an eligible youth is convicted of two or more crimes set forth in separate counts of an accusatory instrument or set forth in two or more accusatory instruments consolidated for trial purposes, the court must not find him a youthful offender with respect to any such conviction pursuant to subdivision one of this section unless it finds him a youthful offender with respect to all such convictions.

3. Upon determining that an eligible youth is a youthful offender, the court must direct that the conviction be deemed vacated and replaced by a youthful offender finding; and the court must sentence the defendant pursuant to section 60.02 of the penal law.

4. Upon determining that an eligible youth is not a youthful offender, the court must order the accusatory instrument unsealed and continue the action to judgment pursuant to the ordinary rules governing criminal prosecutions.

§ 720.25. [Repealed]

§ 720.25. Youthful offender adjudication; certain exemptions

Notwithstanding any inconsistent provisions of law:

1. where the court is required to find that a person is a youthful offender pursuant to section 170.80 of this chapter, the fact that such person has previously been convicted of a crime or adjudicated a youthful offender shall not prevent such person from being adjudicated a youthful offender as required by such section; and

2. a youthful offender adjudication pursuant to section 170.80 of this chapter shall not be considered in determining whether a person is an eligible youth, or in determining whether to find a person a youthful offender, in any subsequent youthful offender adjudication.

§ 720.30. Youthful offender adjudication; post-judgment motions and appeal

The provisions of this chapter, governing the making and determination of post-judgment motions and the taking and determination of appeals in criminal cases, apply to post-judgment motions and appeals with respect to youthful offender adjudications wherever such provisions can reasonably be so applied.

§ 720.35. Youthful offender adjudication; effect thereof; records

1. A youthful offender adjudication is not a judgment of conviction for a crime or any other offense, and does not operate as a disqualification of any person so adjudged to hold public office or public employment or to receive any license granted by public authority but shall be deemed a conviction only for the purposes of transfer of supervision and custody pursuant to section two hundred fifty-nine-m of the executive law. A defendant for whom a youthful offender adjudication was substituted, who was originally charged with prostitution as defined in section 230.00 of the penal law or loitering for the purposes of prostitution as defined in subdivision two of section 240.37 of the penal law provided that the person does not stand charged with loitering for the purpose of patronizing a prostitute, for an offense allegedly committed when he or she was sixteen or seventeen years of age, shall be deemed a "sexually exploited child" as defined in subdivision one of section four hundred forty-seven-a of the social services

law and therefore shall not be considered an adult for purposes related to the charges in the youthful offender proceeding or a proceeding under section 170.80 of this chapter.

2. Except where specifically required or permitted by statute or upon specific authorization of the court, all official records and papers, whether on file with the court, a police agency or the division of criminal justice services, relating to a case involving a youth who has been adjudicated a youthful offender, are confidential and may not be made available to any person or public or private agency, other than the designated educational official of the public or private elementary or secondary school in which the youth is enrolled as a student provided that such local educational official shall only have made available a notice of such adjudication and shall not have access to any other official records and papers, such youth or such youth's designated agent (but only where the official records and papers sought are on file with a court and request therefor is made to that court or to a clerk thereof), an institution to which such youth has been committed, the department of corrections and community supervision and a probation department of this state that requires such official records and papers for the purpose of carrying out duties specifically authorized by law; provided, however, that information regarding an order of protection or temporary order of protection issued pursuant to section 530.12 of this chapter or a warrant issued in connection therewith may be maintained on the statewide automated order of protection and warrant registry established pursuant to section two hundred twenty-one-a of the executive law during the period that such order of protection or temporary order of protection is in full force and effect or during which such warrant may be executed. Such confidential information may be made available pursuant to law only for purposes of adjudicating or enforcing such order of protection or temporary order of protection and, where provided to a designated educational official, as defined in section 380.90 of this chapter, for purposes related to the execution of the student's educational plan, where applicable, successful school adjustment and reentry into the community. Such notification shall be kept separate and apart from such student's school records and shall be accessible only by the designated educational official. Such notification shall not be part of such student's permanent school record and shall not be appended to or included in any documentation regarding such student and shall be destroyed at such time as such student is no longer enrolled in the school district. At no time shall such notification be used for any purpose other than those specified in this subdivision.

3. If a youth who has been adjudicated a youthful offender is enrolled as a student in a public or private elementary or secondary school the court that has adjudicated the youth as a youthful offender shall provide notification of such adjudication to the designated educational official of the school in which such youth is enrolled as a student. Such notification shall be used by the designated educational official only for purposes related to the execution of the student's educational plan, where applicable, successful school adjustment and reentry into the community. Such notification shall be kept separate and apart from such student's school records and shall be accessible only by the designated educational official. Such notification shall not be part of such student's permanent school record and shall not be appended to or included in any documentation regarding such student and shall be destroyed at such time as such

student is no longer enrolled in the school district. At no time shall such notification be used for any purpose other than those specified in this subdivision.

4. Notwithstanding subdivision two of this section, whenever a person is adjudicated a youthful offender and the conviction that was vacated and replaced by the youthful offender finding was for a sex offense as that term is defined in article ten of the mental hygiene law, all records pertaining to the youthful offender adjudication shall be included in those records and reports that may be obtained by the commissioner of mental health or the commissioner of developmental disabilities, as appropriate; the case review panel; and the attorney general pursuant to section 10.05 of the mental hygiene law.

§§ 720.40–720.70. [Repealed]

Article 722 Proceedings Against Juvenile Offenders and Adolescent Offenders; Establishment of Youth Part and Related Procedures

§ 722.00. Probation case plans

1. All juvenile offenders and adolescent offenders shall be notified of the availability of services through the local probation department. Such services shall include the ability of the probation department to conduct a risk and needs assessment, utilizing a validated risk assessment tool, in order to help determine suitable and individualized programming and referrals. Participation in such risk and needs assessment shall be voluntary and the adolescent offender or juvenile offender may be accompanied by counsel during any such assessment. Based upon the assessment findings, the probation department shall refer the adolescent offender or juvenile offender to available and appropriate services.

2. Nothing shall preclude the probation department and the adolescent offender or juvenile offender from entering into a voluntary service plan which may include alcohol, substance use and mental health treatment and services. To the extent practicable, such services shall continue through the pendency of the action and shall further continue where such action is removed in accordance with this article.

3. When preparing a pre-sentence investigation report of any such adolescent offender or juvenile offender, the probation department shall incorporate a summary of any assessment findings, referrals and progress with respect to mitigating risk and addressing any identified needs.

4. The probation service shall not transmit or otherwise communicate to the district attorney or the youth part any statement made by the juvenile or adolescent offender to a probation officer. However, the probation service may make a recommendation regarding the completion of his or her case plan to the youth part and provide such information as it shall deem relevant.

5. No statement made to the probation service may be admitted into evidence at a fact-finding hearing at any time prior to a conviction.

§ 722.10. Youth part of the superior court established

1. The chief administrator of the courts is hereby directed to establish, in a superior court in each county of the state, a part of the court to be known as the youth part of the superior court for the county in which such court presides. Judges presiding in the youth part shall be family court judges, as described in article six, section one of the constitution. To aid in their work, such judges shall receive training in specialized areas,

including, but not limited to, juvenile justice, adolescent development, custody and care of youths and effective treatment methods for reducing unlawful conduct by youths, and shall be authorized to make appropriate determinations within the power of such superior court with respect to the cases of youths assigned to such part. The youth part shall have exclusive jurisdiction in all proceedings in relation to juvenile offenders and adolescent offenders, except as provided in this article or article seven hundred twenty-five of this chapter.

2. The chief administrator of the courts shall also direct the presiding justice of the appellate division, in each judicial department of the state, to designate judges authorized by law to exercise criminal jurisdiction to serve as accessible magistrates, for the purpose of acting in place of the youth part for certain first appearance proceedings involving youths, as provided by law. When designating such magistrates, the presiding justice shall ensure that all areas of a county are within a reasonable distance of a designated magistrate. A judge authorized to preside as such a magistrate shall have received training in specialized areas, including, but not limited to, juvenile justice, adolescent development, custody and care of youths and effective treatment methods for reducing unlawful conduct by youths.

§ 722.20. Proceedings upon felony complaint; juvenile offender

1. When a juvenile offender is arraigned before a youth part, the provisions of this section shall apply. If the youth part is not in session, the defendant shall be brought before the most accessible magistrate designated by the appellate division of the supreme court to act as a youth part for the purpose of making a determination whether such juvenile shall be detained. If the defendant is ordered to be detained, he or she shall be brought before the next session of the youth part. If the defendant is not detained, he or she shall be ordered to appear at the next session of the youth part.

2. If the defendant waives a hearing upon the felony complaint, the court must order that the defendant be held for the action of the grand jury with respect to the charge or charges contained in the felony complaint.

3. If there be a hearing, then at the conclusion of the hearing, the youth part court must dispose of the felony complaint as follows:

(a) If there is reasonable cause to believe that the defendant committed a crime for which a person under the age of sixteen is criminally responsible, the court must order that the defendant be held for the action of a grand jury; or

(b) If there is not reasonable cause to believe that the defendant committed a crime for which a person under the age of sixteen is criminally responsible but there is reasonable cause to believe that the defendant is a "juvenile delinquent" as defined in subdivision one of section 301.2 of the family court act, the court must specify the act or acts it found reasonable cause to believe the defendant did and direct that the action be removed to the family court in accordance with the provisions of article seven hundred twenty-five of this title; or

(c) If there is not reasonable cause to believe that the defendant committed any criminal act, the court must dismiss the felony complaint and discharge the defendant from custody if he is in custody, or if he is at liberty on bail, it must exonerate the bail.

4. Notwithstanding the provisions of subdivisions two and three of this section, the court shall, at the request of the district attorney, order removal of an action against a juvenile offender to the family court pursuant to the provisions of article seven hundred twenty-five of this title if, upon consideration of the criteria specified in subdivision two of section 722.22 of this article, it is determined that to do so would be in the interests of justice. Where, however, the felony complaint charges the juvenile offender with murder in the second degree as defined in section 125.25 of the penal law, rape in the first degree as defined in subdivision one of section 130.35 of the penal law, criminal sexual act in the first degree as defined in subdivision one of section 130.50 of the penal law, or an armed felony as defined in paragraph (a) of subdivision forty-one of section 1.20 of this chapter, a determination that such action be removed to the family court shall, in addition, be based upon a finding of one or more of the following factors: (i) mitigating circumstances that bear directly upon the manner in which the crime was committed; or (ii) where the defendant was not the sole participant in the crime, the defendant's participation was relatively minor although not so minor as to constitute a defense to the prosecution; or (iii) possible deficiencies in proof of the crime.

5. Notwithstanding the provisions of subdivision two, three, or four of this section, if a currently undetermined felony complaint against a juvenile offender is pending, and the defendant has not waived a hearing pursuant to subdivision two of this section and a hearing pursuant to subdivision three of this section has not commenced, the defendant may move to remove the action to family court pursuant to 722.22 of this article. The procedural rules of subdivisions one and two of section 210.45 of this chapter are applicable to a motion pursuant to this subdivision. Upon such motion, the court shall proceed and determine the motion as provided in section 722.22 of this article; provided, however, that the exception provisions of paragraph (b) of subdivision one of section 722.22 of this article shall not apply when there is not reasonable cause to believe that the juvenile offender committed one or more of the crimes enumerated therein, and in such event the provisions of paragraph (a) thereof shall apply.

6.

(a) If the court orders removal of the action to family court, it shall state on the record the factor or factors upon which its determination is based, and the court shall give its reasons for removal in detail and not in conclusory terms.

(b) The district attorney shall state upon the record the reasons for his consent to removal of the action to the family court where such consent is required. The reasons shall be stated in detail and not in conclusory terms.

(c) For the purpose of making a determination pursuant to subdivision four or five of this section, the court may make such inquiry as it deems necessary. Any evidence which is not legally privileged may be introduced. If the defendant testifies, his testimony may not be introduced against him in any future proceeding, except to impeach his testimony at such future proceeding as inconsistent prior testimony.

(d) Where a motion for removal by the defendant pursuant to subdivision five of this section has been denied, no further motion pursuant to this section or section 722.22 of this article may be made by the juvenile offender with respect to the same offense or offenses.

(e) Except as provided by paragraph (f) of this subdivision, this section shall not be construed to limit the powers of the grand jury.

(f) Where a motion by the defendant pursuant to subdivision five of this section has been granted, there shall be no further proceedings against the juvenile offender in any local or superior criminal court including the youth part of the superior court for the offense or offenses which were the subject of the removal order.

§ 722.21. Proceedings upon felony complaint; adolescent offender

1. When an adolescent offender is arraigned before a youth part, the provisions of this section shall apply. If the youth part is not in session, the defendant shall be brought before the most accessible magistrate designated by the appellate division of the supreme court to act as a youth part for the purpose of making a determination whether such adolescent offender shall be detained. If the defendant is ordered to be detained, he or she shall be brought before the next session of the youth part. If the defendant is not detained, he or she shall be ordered to appear at the next session of the youth part.

2. If the defendant waives a hearing upon the felony complaint, the court must order that the defendant be held for the action of the grand jury with respect to the charge or charges contained in the felony complaint.

3. If there be a hearing, then at the conclusion of the hearing, the youth part court must dispose of the felony complaint as follows:

(a) If there is reasonable cause to believe that the defendant committed a felony, the court must order that the defendant be held for the action of a grand jury; or

(b) If there is not reasonable cause to believe that the defendant committed a felony but there is reasonable cause to believe that the defendant is a "juvenile delinquent" as defined in subdivision one of section 301.2 of the family court act, the court must specify the act or acts it found reasonable cause to believe the defendant did and direct that the action be transferred to the family court in accordance with the provisions of article seven hundred twenty-five of this title, provided, however, notwithstanding any other provision of law, section 308.1 of the family court act shall apply to actions transferred pursuant to this subdivision and such actions shall not be considered removals subject to subdivision thirteen of such section 308.1; or

(c) If there is not reasonable cause to believe that the defendant committed any criminal act, the court must dismiss the felony complaint and discharge the defendant from custody if he is in custody, or if he is at liberty on bail, it must exonerate the bail.

4. Notwithstanding the provisions of subdivisions two and three of this section, where the defendant is charged with a felony, other than a class A felony defined outside article two hundred twenty of the penal law, a violent felony defined in section 70.02 of the penal law or a felony listed in paragraph one or two of subdivision forty-two of section 1.20 of this chapter, except as provided in paragraph (c) of subdivision two of section 722.23 of this article, the court shall, upon notice from the district attorney that he or she will not file a motion to prevent removal pursuant to section 722.23 of this article, order transfer of an action against an adolescent offender to the family court pursuant to the provisions of article seven hundred twenty-five of this title, provided, however, notwithstanding any other provision of law, section 308.1 of the family court

act shall apply to actions transferred pursuant to this subdivision and such actions shall not be considered removals subject to subdivision thirteen of such section 308.1.

5. Notwithstanding subdivisions two and three of this section, at the request of the district attorney, the court shall order removal of an action against an adolescent offender charged with an offense listed in paragraph (a) of subdivision two of section 722.23 of this article, to the family court pursuant to the provisions of article seven hundred twenty-five of this title and upon consideration of the criteria specified in subdivision two of section 722.22 of this article, it is determined that to do so would be in the interests of justice. Where, however, the felony complaint charges the adolescent offender with murder in the second degree as defined in section 125.25 of the penal law, rape in the first degree as defined in subdivision one of section 130.35 of the penal law, criminal sexual act in the first degree as defined in subdivision one of section 130.50 of the penal law, or an armed felony as defined in paragraph (a) of subdivision forty-one of section 1.20 of this chapter, a determination that such action be removed to the family court shall, in addition, be based upon a finding of one or more of the following factors: (i) mitigating circumstances that bear directly upon the manner in which the crime was committed; or (ii) where the defendant was not the sole participant in the crime, the defendant's participation was relatively minor although not so minor as to constitute a defense to the prosecution; or (iii) possible deficiencies in proof of the crime.

6.

(a) If the court orders removal of the action to family court pursuant to subdivision five of this section, it shall state on the record the factor or factors upon which its determination is based, and the court shall give its reasons for removal in detail and not in conclusory terms.

(b) The district attorney shall state upon the record the reasons for his consent to removal of the action to the family court where such consent is required. The reasons shall be stated in detail and not in conclusory terms.

(c) For the purpose of making a determination pursuant to subdivision five the court may make such inquiry as it deems necessary. Any evidence which is not legally privileged may be introduced. If the defendant testifies, his testimony may not be introduced against him in any future proceeding, except to impeach his testimony at such future proceeding as inconsistent prior testimony.

(d) Except as provided by paragraph (e), this section shall not be construed to limit the powers of the grand jury.

(e) Where an action against a defendant has been removed to the family court pursuant to this section, there shall be no further proceedings against the adolescent offender in any local or superior criminal court including the youth part of the superior court for the offense or offenses which were the subject of the removal order.

§ 722.22. Motion to remove juvenile offender to family court

1. After a motion by a juvenile offender, pursuant to subdivision five of section 722.20 of this article, or after arraignment of a juvenile offender upon an indictment, the court may, on motion of any party or on its own motion:

(a) except as otherwise provided by paragraph (b) of this subdivision, order removal of the action to the family court pursuant to the provisions of article seven hundred twenty-five of this title, if, after consideration of the factors set forth in subdivision two of this section, the court determines that to do so would be in the interests of justice; or

(b) with the consent of the district attorney, order removal of an action involving an indictment charging a juvenile offender with murder in the second degree as defined in section 125.25 of the penal law; rape in the first degree, as defined in subdivision one of section 130.35 of the penal law; criminal sexual act in the first degree, as defined in subdivision one of section 130.50 of the penal law; or an armed felony as defined in paragraph (a) of subdivision forty-one of section 1.20 of this chapter, to the family court pursuant to the provisions of article seven hundred twenty-five of this title if the court finds one or more of the following factors: (i) mitigating circumstances that bear directly upon the manner in which the crime was committed; (ii) where the defendant was not the sole participant in the crime, the defendant's participation was relatively minor although not so minor as to constitute a defense to the prosecution; or (iii) possible deficiencies in the proof of the crime, and, after consideration of the factors set forth in subdivision two of this section, the court determined that removal of the action to the family court would be in the interests of justice.

2. In making its determination pursuant to subdivision one of this section the court shall, to the extent applicable, examine individually and collectively, the following:

(a) the seriousness and circumstances of the offense;

(b) the extent of harm caused by the offense;

(c) the evidence of guilt, whether admissible or inadmissible at trial;

(d) the history, character and condition of the defendant;

(e) the purpose and effect of imposing upon the defendant a sentence authorized for the offense;

(f) the impact of a removal of the case to the family court on the safety or welfare of the community;

(g) the impact of a removal of the case to the family court upon the confidence of the public in the criminal justice system;

(h) where the court deems it appropriate, the attitude of the complainant or victim with respect to the motion; and

(i) any other relevant fact indicating that a judgment of conviction in the criminal court would serve no useful purpose.

3. The procedure for bringing on a motion pursuant to subdivision one of this section, shall accord with the procedure prescribed in subdivisions one and two of section 210.45 of this chapter. After all papers of both parties have been filed and after all documentary evidence, if any, has been submitted, the court must consider the same for the purpose of determining whether the motion is determinable on the motion papers submitted and, if not, may make such inquiry as it deems necessary for the purpose of making a determination.

4. For the purpose of making a determination pursuant to this section, any evidence which is not legally privileged may be introduced. If the defendant testifies, his testimony

may not be introduced against him in any future proceeding, except to impeach his testimony at such future proceeding as inconsistent prior testimony.

5.

a. If the court orders removal of the action to family court, it shall state on the record the factor or factors upon which its determination is based, and, the court shall give its reasons for removal in detail and not in conclusory terms.

b. The district attorney shall state upon the record the reasons for his consent to removal of the action to the family court. The reasons shall be stated in detail and not in conclusory terms.

§ 722.23. Removal of adolescent offenders to family court

1.

(a) Following the arraignment of a defendant charged with a crime committed when he or she was sixteen, or commencing October first, two thousand nineteen, seventeen years of age, other than any class A felony except for those defined in article two hundred twenty of the penal law, a violent felony defined in section 70.02 of the penal law or a felony listed in paragraph one or two of subdivision forty-two of section 1.20 of this chapter, or an offense set forth in the vehicle and traffic law, the court shall order the removal of the action to the family court in accordance with the applicable provisions of article seven hundred twenty-five of this title unless, within thirty calendar days of such arraignment, the district attorney makes a motion to prevent removal of the action pursuant to this subdivision. If the defendant fails to report to the probation department as directed, the thirty day time period shall be tolled until such time as he or she reports to the probation department.

(b) A motion to prevent removal of an action in youth part shall be made in writing and upon prompt notice to the defendant. The motion shall contain allegations of sworn fact based upon personal knowledge of the affiant, and shall indicate if the district attorney is requesting a hearing. The motion shall be noticed to be heard promptly.

(c) The defendant shall be given an opportunity to reply. The defendant shall be granted any reasonable request for a delay. Either party may request a hearing on the facts alleged in the motion to prevent removal of the action. The hearing shall be held expeditiously.

(d) The court shall deny the motion to prevent removal of the action in youth part unless the court makes a determination upon such motion by the district attorney that extraordinary circumstances exist that should prevent the transfer of the action to family court.

(e) The court shall make a determination in writing or on the record within five days of the conclusion of the hearing or submission by the defense, whichever is later. Such determination shall include findings of fact and to the extent practicable conclusions of law.

(f) For the purposes of this section, there shall be a presumption against custody and case planning services shall be made available to the defendant.

(g) Notwithstanding any other provision of law, section 308.1 of the family court act shall apply to all actions transferred pursuant to this section provided, however, such cases shall not be considered removals subject to subdivision thirteen of such section 308.1.

(h) Nothing in this subdivision shall preclude, and a court may order, the removal of an action to family court where all parties agree or pursuant to this chapter.

2.

(a) Upon the arraignment of a defendant charged with a crime committed when he or she was sixteen or, commencing October first, two thousand nineteen, seventeen years of age on a class A felony, other than those defined in article 220 of the penal law, or a violent felony defined in section 70.02 of the penal law, the court shall schedule an appearance no later than six calendar days from such arraignment for the purpose of reviewing the accusatory instrument pursuant to this subdivision. The court shall notify the district attorney and defendant regarding the purpose of such appearance.

(b) Upon such appearance, the court shall review the accusatory instrument and any other relevant facts for the purpose of making a determination pursuant to paragraph (c) of this subdivision. Both parties may be heard and submit information relevant to the determination.

(c) The court shall order the action to proceed in accordance with subdivision one of this section unless, after reviewing the papers and hearing from the parties, the court determines in writing that the district attorney proved by a preponderance of the evidence one or more of the following as set forth in the accusatory instrument:

(i) the defendant caused significant physical injury to a person other than a participant in the offense; or

(ii) the defendant displayed a firearm, shotgun, rifle or deadly weapon as defined in the penal law in furtherance of such offense; or

(iii) the defendant unlawfully engaged in sexual intercourse, oral sexual conduct, anal sexual conduct or sexual contact as defined in section 130.00 of the penal law.

(d) Where the court makes a determination that the action shall not proceed in accordance with subdivision one of this section, such determination shall be made in writing or on the record and shall include findings of fact and to the extent practicable conclusions of law.

(e) Nothing in this subdivision shall preclude, and the court may order, the removal of an action to family court where all parties agree or pursuant to this chapter.

3. Notwithstanding the provisions of any other law, if at any time one or more charges in the accusatory instrument are reduced, such that the elements of the highest remaining charge would be removable pursuant to subdivisions one or two of this section, then the court, sua sponte or in response to a motion pursuant to subdivisions one or two of this section by the defendant, shall promptly notify the parties and direct that the matter proceed in accordance with subdivision one of this section, provided, however, that in such instance, the district attorney must file any motion to prevent removal within thirty days of effecting or receiving notice of such reduction.

4. A defendant may waive review of the accusatory instrument by the court and the opportunity for removal in accordance with this section, provided that such waiver is made by the defendant knowingly, voluntarily and in open court, in the presence of and

with the approval of his or her counsel and the court. An earlier waiver shall not constitute a waiver of review and the opportunity for removal under this section.

§ 722.24. Applicability of chapter to actions and matters involving juvenile offenders or adolescent offenders

Except where inconsistent with this article, all provisions of this chapter shall apply to all criminal actions and proceedings, and all appeals and post-judgment motions relating or attached thereto, involving a juvenile offender or adolescent offender.

Article 725 Removal of Proceeding Against Juvenile Offender to Family Court

§ 725.00. Applicability

The provisions of this article apply in any case where a court directs that an action or charge is to be removed to the family court under section 180.75, 190.71, 210.43, 220.10, 310.85 or 330.25 of this chapter.

§ 725.05. Order of removal

When a youth part directs that an action or charge is to be removed to the family court the youth part must issue an order of removal in accordance with this section. Such order must be as follows:

1. It must provide that the action or charge is to be removed to the family court of the county in which such action or charge was pending, and it must specify the section pursuant to which the removal is authorized.

2. Where the direction is authorized pursuant to paragraph (b) of subdivision three of sections 722.20 or 722.21 of this title, it must specify the act or acts it found reasonable cause to believe the defendant did.

3. Where the direction is authorized pursuant to subdivision four of section 722.20 or section 722.21 of this title, it must specify the act or acts it found reasonable cause to allege.

4. Where the direction is authorized pursuant to section 190.71 of this chapter, the court shall annex to the order as part thereof a certified copy of the grand jury request.

4-a. Where the direction is authorized pursuant to subdivision seven of section 210.30 of this chapter, it must specify the act or acts for which there was sufficient evidence to believe that defendant did.

5. Where the direction is authorized pursuant to section 220.10, 310.85 or 330.25 of this chapter, it must specify the act or acts for which a plea or verdict of guilty was rendered or accepted and entered.

6. Where a securing order has not been made, the order of removal must provide that the police officer or peace officer who made the arrest or some other proper officer forthwith and with all reasonable speed take the juvenile to the designated family court or, where that cannot be done, it must provide for release or detention in the same manner as provided for a family court proceeding pursuant to section 320.5 of the family court act.

7. Whether or not a securing order has been made, the order of removal must specify a date certain within ten days from the date of the order of removal for the defendant's appearance in the family court and where the defendant is in detention or in the custody of the sheriff that date must be not later than the next day the family court is in session.

8. The order of removal must direct that all of the pleadings and proceedings in the action, or a certified copy of same be transferred to the designated family court and be delivered to and filed with the clerk of that court. For the purposes of this subdivision the term "pleadings and proceedings" includes the minutes of any hearing inquiry or trial held in the action, the minutes of any grand jury proceeding and the minutes of any plea accepted and entered.

9. The order of removal must be signed by a judge or justice of the court that directed the removal.

§ 725.10. Removal of action

1. When an order of removal is filed with the family court a proceeding pursuant to article three of the family court act must be originated. The family court thereupon must assume jurisdiction and proceed to render such judgment as the circumstances require, in the manner and to the extent provided by law.

2. Upon the filing of an order of removal in a criminal court the criminal action upon which the order is based shall be terminated, and there shall be no further criminal proceedings in any criminal court as defined in section 10.10 of this chapter with respect to the offense or offenses charged in the accusatory instrument which was the subject of removal. All further proceedings including motions and appeals shall be in accordance with laws appertaining to the family court and for this purpose all findings, determinations, verdicts and orders other than the order of removal, shall be deemed to have been made by the family court.

§ 725.15. Sealing of records

Except where specifically required or permitted by statute or upon specific authorization of the court that directed removal of an action to the family court all official records and papers of the action up to and including the order of removal, whether on file with the court, a police agency or the division of criminal justice services, are confidential and must not be made available to any person or public or private agency, provided however that availability of copies of any such records and papers on file with the family court shall be governed by provisions that apply to family court records, and further provided that all official records and papers of the action shall be included in those records and reports that may be obtained upon request by the commissioner of mental health or commissioner of mental retardation and developmental disabilities, as appropriate; the case review panel; and the attorney general pursuant to section 10.05 of the mental hygiene law.

§ 725.20. Record of certain actions removed

1. The provisions of this section shall apply in any case where an order of removal to the family court is entered pursuant to a direction authorized by article 722 of this title, or subparagraph (iii) of paragraph (g) of subdivision five of section 220.10 of this chapter, or section 330.25 of this chapter.

2. When such an action is removed the court that directed the removal must cause the following additional records to be filed with the clerk of the county court or in the city of New York with the clerk of the supreme court of the county wherein the action was pending and with the division of criminal justice services:

(a) A certified copy of the order of removal;

(b) Where the direction is one authorized by subparagraph (iii) of paragraph (g) of subdivision five of section 220.10 or section 330.25 of this chapter, a copy of the minutes of the plea of guilty, including the minutes of the memorandum submitted by the district attorney and the court; and

(c) In addition to the records specified in this subdivision, such further statement or submission of additional information pertaining to the proceeding in criminal court in accordance with standards established by the commissioner of the division of criminal justice services, subject to the provisions of subdivision three of this section.

3. It shall be the duty of said clerk to maintain a separate file for copies of orders and minutes filed pursuant to this section. Upon receipt of such orders and minutes the clerk must promptly delete such portions as would identify the defendant, but the clerk shall nevertheless maintain a separate confidential system to enable correlation of the documents so filed with identification of the defendant. After making such deletions the orders and minutes shall be placed within the file and must be available for public inspection. Information permitting correlation of any such record with the identity of any defendant shall not be divulged to any person except upon order of a justice of the supreme court based upon a finding that the public interest or the interests of justice warrant disclosure in a particular cause for a particular case or for a particular purpose or use.

Article 730 Mental Disease or Defect Excluding Fitness to Proceed

§ 730.10. Fitness to proceed; definitions

As used in this article, the following terms have the following meanings:

1. "Incapacitated person" means a defendant who as a result of mental disease or defect lacks capacity to understand the proceedings against him or to assist in his own defense.

2. "Order of examination" means an order issued to an appropriate director by a criminal court wherein a criminal action is pending against a defendant or by a court evaluating the capacity of an alleged violator in a parole revocation proceeding pursuant to subparagraph (xii) of paragraph (f) of subdivision three of section two hundred fifty-nine-i of the executive law, or by a family court pursuant to section 322.1 of the family court act wherein a juvenile delinquency proceeding is pending against a juvenile, directing that such person be examined for the purpose of determining if he is an incapacitated person.

3. "Commissioner" means the state commissioner of mental health or the state commissioner of mental retardation and developmental disabilities.

4. "Director" means (a) the director of a state hospital operated by the office of mental health or the director of a developmental center operated by the office of mental retardation and developmental disabilities, or (b) the director of a hospital operated by any local government of the state that has been certified by the commissioner as having adequate facilities to examine a defendant to determine if he is an incapacitated person, or (c) the director of community mental health services.

5. "Qualified psychiatrist" means a physician who:

(a) is a diplomate of the American board of psychiatry and neurology or is eligible to be certified by that board; or,

(b) is certified by the American osteopathic board of neurology and psychiatry or is eligible to be certified by that board.

6. "Certified psychologist" means a person who is registered as a certified psychologist under article one hundred fifty-three of the education law.

7. "Psychiatric examiner" means a qualified psychiatrist or a certified psychologist who has been designated by a director to examine a defendant pursuant to an order of examination.

8. "Examination report" means a report made by a psychiatric examiner wherein he sets forth his opinion as to whether the defendant is or is not an incapacitated person, the nature and extent of his examination and, if he finds that the defendant is an incapacitated person, his diagnosis and prognosis and a detailed statement of the reasons for his opinion by making particular reference to those aspects of the proceedings wherein the defendant lacks capacity to understand or to assist in his own defense. The state administrator and the commissioner must jointly adopt the form of the examination report; and the state administrator shall prescribe the number of copies thereof that must be submitted to the court by the director.

9. "Appropriate institution" means: (a) a hospital operated by the office of mental health or a developmental center operated by the office for people with developmental disabilities; or (b) a hospital licensed by the department of health which operates a psychiatric unit licensed by the office of mental health, as determined by the commissioner provided, however, that any such hospital that is not operated by the state shall qualify as an "appropriate institution" only pursuant to the terms of an agreement between the commissioner and the hospital. Nothing in this article shall be construed as requiring a hospital to consent to providing care and treatment to an incapacitated person at such hospital.

§ 730.20. Fitness to proceed; generally

1. The appropriate director to whom a criminal court issues an order of examination must be determined in accordance with rules jointly adopted by the judicial conference and the commissioner. Upon receipt of an examination order, the director must designate two qualified psychiatric examiners, of whom he may be one, to examine the defendant to determine if he is an incapacitated person. In conducting their examination, the psychiatric examiners may employ any method which is accepted by the medical profession for the examination of persons alleged to be mentally ill or mentally defective. The court may authorize a psychiatrist or psychologist retained by the defendant to be present at such examination.

2. When the defendant is not in custody at the time a court issues an order of examination, because he was theretofore released on bail or on his own recognizance, the court may direct that the examination be conducted on an out-patient basis, and at such time and place as the director shall designate. If, however, the director informs the court that hospital confinement of the defendant is necessary for an effective examination, the court may direct that the defendant be confined in a hospital designated by the director until the examination is completed.

3. When the defendant is in custody at the time a court issues an order of examination, the examination must be conducted at the place where the defendant is being held in

custody. If, however, the director determines that hospital confinement of the defendant is necessary for an effective examination, the sheriff must deliver the defendant to a hospital designated by the director and hold him in custody therein, under sufficient guard, until the examination is completed.

4. Hospital confinement under subdivisions two and three shall be for a period not exceeding thirty days, except that, upon application of the director, the court may authorize confinement for an additional period not exceeding thirty days if it is satisfied that a longer period is necessary to complete the examination. During the period of hospital confinement, the physician in charge of the hospital may administer or cause to be administered to the defendant such emergency psychiatric, medical or other therapeutic treatment as in his judgment should be administered.

5. Each psychiatric examiner, after he has completed his examination of the defendant, must promptly prepare an examination report and submit it to the director. If the psychiatric examiners are not unanimous in their opinion as to whether the defendant is or is not an incapacitated person, the director must designate another qualified psychiatric examiner to examine the defendant to determine if he is an incapacitated person. Upon receipt of the examination reports, the director must submit them to the court that issued the order of examination. The court must furnish a copy of the reports to counsel for the defendant and to the district attorney.

6. When a defendant is subjected to examination pursuant to an order issued by a criminal court in accordance with this article, any statement made by him for the purpose of the examination or treatment shall be inadmissible in evidence against him in any criminal action on any issue other than that of his mental condition, but such statement is admissible upon that issue whether or not it would otherwise be deemed a privileged communication.

7. A psychiatric examiner is entitled to his reasonable traveling expenses, a fee of fifty dollars for each examination of a defendant and a fee of fifty dollars for each appearance at a court hearing or trial but not exceeding two hundred dollars in fees for examination and testimony in any one case; except that if such psychiatric examiner be an employee of the state of New York he shall be entitled only to reasonable traveling expenses, unless such psychiatric examiner makes the examination or appears at a court hearing or trial outside his hours of state employment in a county in which the director of community mental health services certifies to the fiscal officer thereof that there is a shortage of qualified psychiatrists available to conduct examinations under the criminal procedure law in such county, in which event he shall be entitled to the foregoing fees and reasonable traveling expenses. Such fees and traveling expenses and the costs of sending a defendant to another place of detention or to a hospital for examination, of his maintenance therein and of returning him shall, when approved by the court, be a charge of the county in which the defendant is being tried.

§ 730.30. Fitness to proceed; order of examination

1. At any time after a defendant is arraigned upon an accusatory instrument other than a felony complaint and before the imposition of sentence, or at any time after a defendant is arraigned upon a felony complaint and before he is held for the action of the grand jury, the court wherein the criminal action is pending must issue an order of

examination when it is of the opinion that the defendant may be an incapacitated person.

2. When the examination reports submitted to the court show that each psychiatric examiner is of the opinion that the defendant is not an incapacitated person, the court may, on its own motion, conduct a hearing to determine the issue of capacity, and it must conduct a hearing upon motion therefor by the defendant or by the district attorney. If no motion for a hearing is made, the criminal action against the defendant must proceed. If, following a hearing, the court is satisfied that the defendant is not an incapacitated person, the criminal action against him must proceed; if the court is not so satisfied, it must issue a further order of examination directing that the defendant be examined by different psychiatric examiners designated by the director.

3. When the examination reports submitted to the court show that each psychiatric examiner is of the opinion that the defendant is an incapacitated person, the court may, on its own motion, conduct a hearing to determine the issue of capacity and it must conduct such hearing upon motion therefor by the defendant or by the district attorney.

4. When the examination reports submitted to the court show that the psychiatric examiners are not unanimous in their opinion as to whether the defendant is or is not an incapacitated person, or when the examination reports submitted to the superior court show that the psychiatric examiners are not unanimous in their opinion as to whether the defendant is or is not a dangerous incapacitated person, the court must conduct a hearing to determine the issue of capacity or dangerousness.

§ 730.40. Fitness to proceed; local criminal court accusatory instrument

1. When a local criminal court, following a hearing conducted pursuant to subdivision three or four of section 730.30 of this article, is satisfied that the defendant is not an incapacitated person, the criminal action against him or her must proceed. If it is satisfied that the defendant is an incapacitated person, or if no motion for such a hearing is made, such court must issue a final or temporary order of observation committing him or her to the custody of the commissioner for care and treatment in an appropriate institution for a period not to exceed ninety days from the date of the order, provided, however, that the commissioner may designate an appropriate hospital for placement of a defendant for whom a final order of observation has been issued, where such hospital is licensed by the office of mental health and has agreed to accept, upon referral by the commissioner, defendants subject to final orders of observation issued under this subdivision. When a local criminal court accusatory instrument other than a felony complaint has been filed against the defendant, such court must issue a final order of observation. When a felony complaint has been filed against the defendant, such court must issue a temporary order of observation committing him or her to the custody of the commissioner for care and treatment in an appropriate institution or, upon the consent of the district attorney, committing him or her to the custody of the commissioner for care and treatment on an out-patient basis, for a period not to exceed ninety days from the date of such order, except that, with the consent of the district attorney, it may issue a final order of observation. Upon the issuance of a final order of observation, the district attorney shall immediately transmit to the commissioner, in a manner intended to protect the confidentiality of the information, a list of names and

contact information of persons who may reasonably be expected to be the victim of any assault or any violent felony offense, as defined in the penal law, or any offense listed in section 530.11 of this chapter which would be carried out by the committed person; provided that the person who reasonably may be expected to be a victim does not need to be a member of the same family or household as the committed person.

2. When a local criminal court has issued a final order of observation, it must dismiss the accusatory instrument filed in such court against the defendant and such dismissal constitutes a bar to any further prosecution of the charge or charges contained in such accusatory instrument. When the defendant is in the custody of the commissioner pursuant to a final order of observation, the commissioner or his or her designee, which may include the director of an appropriate institution, immediately upon the discharge of the defendant, must certify to such court that he or she has complied with the notice provisions set forth in paragraph (a) of subdivision six of section 730.60 of this article. When the defendant is in the custody of the commissioner at the expiration of the period prescribed in a temporary order of observation, the proceedings in the local criminal court that issued such order shall terminate for all purposes and the commissioner must promptly certify to such court and to the appropriate district attorney that the defendant was in his or her custody on such expiration date. Upon receipt of such certification, the court must dismiss the felony complaint filed against the defendant.

3. When a local criminal court has issued an order of examination or a temporary order of observation, and when the charge or charges contained in the accusatory instrument are subsequently presented to a grand jury, such grand jury need not hear the defendant pursuant to section 190.50 unless, upon application by defendant to the superior court that impaneled such grand jury, the superior court determines that the defendant is not an incapacitated person.

4. When an indictment is filed against a defendant after a local criminal court has issued an order of examination and before it has issued a final or temporary order of observation, the defendant must be promptly arraigned upon the indictment, and the proceedings in the local criminal court shall thereupon terminate for all purposes. The district attorney must notify the local criminal court of such arraignment, and such court must thereupon dismiss the accusatory instrument filed in such court against the defendant. If the director has submitted the examination reports to the local criminal court, such court must forward them to the superior court in which the indictment was filed. If the director has not submitted such reports to the local criminal court, he must submit them to the superior court in which the indictment was filed.

5. When an indictment is timely filed against the defendant after the issuance of a temporary order of observation or after the expiration of the period prescribed in such order, the superior court in which such indictment is filed must direct the sheriff to take custody of the defendant at the institution in which he is confined and bring him before the court for arraignment upon the indictment. After the defendant is arraigned upon the indictment, such temporary order of observation or any order issued pursuant to the mental hygiene law after the expiration of the period prescribed in the temporary order of observation shall be deemed nullified. Notwithstanding any other provision of law, an indictment filed in a superior court against a defendant for a crime charged in the felony

complaint is not timely for the purpose of this subdivision if it is filed more than six months after the expiration of the period prescribed in a temporary order of observation issued by a local criminal court wherein such felony complaint was pending. An untimely indictment must be dismissed by the superior court unless such court is satisfied that there was good cause for the delay in filing such indictment.

§ 730.50. Fitness to proceed; indictment

1. When a superior court, following a hearing conducted pursuant to subdivision three or four of section 730.30 of this article, is satisfied that the defendant is not an incapacitated person, the criminal action against him or her must proceed. If it is satisfied that the defendant is an incapacitated person, or if no motion for such a hearing is made, it must adjudicate him or her an incapacitated person, and must issue a final order of observation or an order of commitment. When the indictment does not charge a felony or when the defendant has been convicted of an offense other than a felony, such court (a) must issue a final order of observation committing the defendant to the custody of the commissioner for care and treatment in an appropriate institution for a period not to exceed ninety days from the date of such order, provided, however, that the commissioner may designate an appropriate hospital for placement of a defendant for whom a final order of observation has been issued, where such hospital is licensed by the office of mental health and has agreed to accept, upon referral by the commissioner, defendants subject to final orders of observation issued under this subdivision, and (b) must dismiss the indictment filed in such court against the defendant, and such dismissal constitutes a bar to any further prosecution of the charge or charges contained in such indictment. Upon the issuance of a final order of observation, the district attorney shall immediately transmit to the commissioner, in a manner intended to protect the confidentiality of the information, a list of names and contact information of persons who may reasonably be expected to be the victim of any assault or any violent felony offense, as defined in the penal law, or any offense listed in section 530.11 of this chapter which would be carried out by the committed person; provided that the person who reasonably may be expected to be a victim does not need to be a member of the same family or household as the committed person. When the indictment charges a felony or when the defendant has been convicted of a felony, it must issue an order of commitment committing the defendant to the custody of the commissioner for care and treatment in an appropriate institution or, upon the consent of the district attorney, committing him or her to the custody of the commissioner for care and treatment on an out-patient basis, for a period not to exceed one year from the date of such order. Upon the issuance of an order of commitment, the court must exonerate the defendant's bail if he or she was previously at liberty on bail; provided, however, that exoneration of bail is not required when a defendant is committed to the custody of the commissioner for care and treatment on an out-patient basis. When the defendant is in the custody of the commissioner pursuant to a final order of observation, the commissioner or his or her designee, which may include the director of an appropriate institution, immediately upon the discharge of the defendant, must certify to such court that he or she has complied with the notice provisions set forth in paragraph (a) of subdivision six of section 730.60 of this article.

2. When a defendant is in the custody of the commissioner immediately prior to the expiration of the period prescribed in a temporary order of commitment and the superintendent of the institution wherein the defendant is confined is of the opinion that the defendant continues to be an incapacitated person, such superintendent must apply to the court that issued such order for an order of retention. Such application must be made within sixty days prior to the expiration of such period on forms that have been jointly adopted by the judicial conference and the commissioner. The superintendent must give written notice of the application to the defendant and to the mental hygiene legal service. Upon receipt of such application, the court may, on its own motion, conduct a hearing to determine the issue of capacity, and it must conduct such hearing if a demand therefor is made by the defendant or the mental hygiene legal service within ten days from the date that notice of the application was given them. If, at the conclusion of a hearing conducted pursuant to this subdivision, the court is satisfied that the defendant is no longer an incapacitated person, the criminal action against him must proceed. If it is satisfied that the defendant continues to be an incapacitated person, or if no demand for a hearing is made, the court must adjudicate him an incapacitated person and must issue an order of retention which shall authorize continued custody of the defendant by the commissioner for a period not to exceed one year.

3. When a defendant is in the custody of the commissioner immediately prior to the expiration of the period prescribed in the first order of retention, the procedure set forth in subdivision two shall govern the application for and the issuance of any subsequent order of retention, except that any subsequent orders of retention must be for periods not to exceed two years each; provided, however, that the aggregate of the periods prescribed in the temporary order of commitment, the first order of retention and all subsequent orders of retention must not exceed two-thirds of the authorized maximum term of imprisonment for the highest class felony charged in the indictment or for the highest class felony of which he was convicted.

4. When a defendant is in the custody of the commissioner at the expiration of the authorized period prescribed in the last order of retention, the criminal action pending against him in the superior court that issued such order shall terminate for all purposes, and the commissioner must promptly certify to such court and to the appropriate district attorney that the defendant was in his custody on such expiration date. Upon receipt of such certification, the court must dismiss the indictment, and such dismissal constitutes a bar to any further prosecution of the charge or charges contained in such indictment.

5. When, on the effective date of this subdivision, any defendant remains in the custody of the commissioner pursuant to an order issued under former code of criminal procedure section six hundred sixty-two-b, the superintendent or director of the institution where such defendant is confined shall, if he believes that the defendant continues to be an incapacitated person, apply forthwith to a court of record in the county where the institution is located for an order of retention. The procedures for obtaining any order pursuant to this subdivision shall be in accordance with the provisions of subdivisions two, three and four of this section, except that the period of retention pursuant to the first order obtained under this subdivision shall be for not more than one year and any subsequent orders of retention must be for periods not to exceed

two years each; provided, however, that the aggregate of the time spent in the custody of the commissioner pursuant to any order issued in accordance with the provisions of former code of criminal procedure section six hundred sixty-two-b and the periods prescribed by the first order obtained under this subdivision and all subsequent orders of retention must not exceed two-thirds of the authorized maximum term of imprisonment for the highest class felony charged in the indictment or the highest class felony of which he was convicted.

§ 730.60. Fitness to proceed; procedure following custody by commissioner

1. When a local criminal court issues a final or temporary order of observation or an order of commitment, it must forward such order and a copy of the examination reports and the accusatory instrument to the commissioner, and, if available, a copy of the pre-sentence report. Upon receipt thereof, the commissioner must designate an appropriate institution operated by the department of mental hygiene in which the defendant is to be placed, provided, however, that the commissioner may designate an appropriate hospital for placement of a defendant for whom a final order of observation has been issued, where such hospital is licensed by the office of mental health and has agreed to accept, upon referral by the commissioner, defendants subject to final orders of observation issued under this subdivision. The sheriff must hold the defendant in custody pending such designation by the commissioner, and when notified of the designation, the sheriff must deliver the defendant to the superintendent of such institution. The superintendent must promptly inform the appropriate director of the mental hygiene legal service of the defendant's admission to such institution. If a defendant escapes from the custody of the commissioner, the escape shall interrupt the period prescribed in any order of observation, commitment or retention, and such interruption shall continue until the defendant is returned to the custody of the commissioner.

2. Except as otherwise provided in subdivisions four and five, when a defendant is in the custody of the commissioner pursuant to a temporary order of observation or an order of commitment or an order of retention, the criminal action pending against the defendant in the court that issued such order is suspended until the superintendent of the institution in which the defendant is confined determines that he is no longer an incapacitated person. In that event, the court that issued such order and the appropriate district attorney must be notified, in writing, by the superintendent of his determination. The court must thereupon proceed in accordance with the provisions of subdivision two of section 730.30 of this chapter; provided, however, if the court is satisfied that the defendant remains an incapacitated person, and upon consent of all parties, the court may order the return of the defendant to the institution in which he had been confined for such period of time as was authorized by the prior order of commitment or order of retention. Upon such return, the defendant shall have all rights and privileges accorded by the provisions of this article.

3. When a defendant is in the custody of the commissioner pursuant to an order issued in accordance with this article, the commissioner may transfer him to any appropriate institution operated by the department of mental hygiene, provided, however, that the commissioner may designate an appropriate hospital for placement of a defendant for

whom a final order of observation has been issued, where such hospital is licensed by the office of mental health and has agreed to accept, upon referral by the commissioner, defendants subject to final orders of observation issued under this section. The commissioner may discharge a defendant in his custody under a final order of observation at any time prior to the expiration date of such order, or otherwise treat or transfer such defendant in the same manner as if he were a patient not in confinement under a criminal court order.

4. When a defendant is in the custody of the commissioner pursuant to an order of commitment or an order of retention, he may make any motion authorized by this chapter which is susceptible of fair determination without his personal participation. If the court denies any such motion it must be without prejudice to a renewal thereof after the criminal action against the defendant has been ordered to proceed. If the court enters an order dismissing the indictment and does not direct that the charge or charges be resubmitted to a grand jury, the court must direct that such order of dismissal be served upon the commissioner.

5. When a defendant is in the custody of the commissioner pursuant to an order of commitment or an order of retention, the superior court that issued such order may, upon motion of the defendant, and with the consent of the district attorney, dismiss the indictment when the court is satisfied that (a) the defendant is a resident or citizen of another state or country and that he will be removed thereto upon dismissal of the indictment, or (b) the defendant has been continuously confined in the custody of the commissioner for a period of more than two years. Before granting a motion under this subdivision, the court must be further satisfied that dismissal of the indictment is consistent with the ends of justice and that custody of the defendant by the commissioner pursuant to an order of commitment or an order of retention is not necessary for the protection of the public and that care and treatment can be effectively administered to the defendant without the necessity of such order. If the court enters an order of dismissal under this subdivision, it must set forth in the record the reasons for such action, and must direct that such order of dismissal be served upon the commissioner. The dismissal of an indictment pursuant to this subdivision constitutes a bar to any further prosecution of the charge or charges contained in such indictment.

6.

(a) Notwithstanding any other provision of law, no person committed to the custody of the commissioner pursuant to this article, or continuously thereafter retained in such custody, shall be discharged, released on condition or placed in any less secure facility or on any less restrictive status, including, but not limited to vacations, furloughs and temporary passes, unless the commissioner or his or her designee, which may include the director of an appropriate institution, shall deliver written notice, at least four days, excluding Saturdays, Sundays and holidays, in advance of the change of such committed person's facility or status, or in the case of a person committed pursuant to a final order of observation written notice upon discharge of such committed person, to all of the following:

(1) The district attorney of the county from which such person was committed;

(2) The superintendent of state police;

(3) The sheriff of the county where the facility is located;

(4) The police department having jurisdiction of the area where the facility is located;

(5) Any person who may reasonably be expected to be the victim of any assault or any violent felony offense, as defined in the penal law, or any offense listed in section 530.11 of this part which would be carried out by the committed person; provided that the person who reasonably may be expected to be a victim does not need to be a member of the same family or household as the committed person; and

(6) Any other person the court may designate.

Said notice may be given by any means reasonably calculated to give prompt actual notice.

(b) The notice required by this subdivision shall also be given immediately upon the departure of such committed person from the actual custody of the commissioner or an appropriate institution, without proper authorization. Nothing in this subdivision shall be construed to impair any other right or duty regarding any notice or hearing contained in any other provision of law.

(c) Whenever a district attorney has received the notice described in this subdivision, and the defendant is in the custody of the commissioner pursuant to a final order of observation or an order of commitment, he may apply within three days of receipt of such notice to a superior court, for an order directing a hearing to be held to determine whether such committed person is a danger to himself or others. Such hearing shall be held within ten days following the issuance of such order. Such order may provide that there shall be no further change in the committed person's facility or status until the hearing. Upon a finding that the committed person is a danger to himself or others, the court shall issue an order to the commissioner authorizing retention of the committed person in the status existing at the time notice was given hereunder, for a specified period, not to exceed six months. The district attorney and the committed person's attorney shall be entitled to the committed person's clinical records in the commissioner's custody, upon the issuance of an order directing a hearing to be held.

(d) Nothing in this subdivision shall be construed to impair any other right or duty regarding any notice or hearing contained in any other provision of law.

§ 730.70. Fitness to proceed; procedure following termination of custody by commissioner

When a defendant is in the custody of the commissioner on the expiration date of a final or temporary order of observation or an order of commitment, or on the expiration date of the last order of retention, or on the date an order dismissing an indictment is served upon the commissioner, the superintendent of the institution in which the defendant is confined may retain him for care and treatment for a period of thirty days from such date. If the superintendent determines that the defendant is so mentally ill or mentally defective as to require continued care and treatment in an institution, he may, before the expiration of such thirty day period, apply for an order of certification in the manner prescribed in section 31.33 of the mental hygiene law*.

Made in the USA
Columbia, SC
26 January 2021